The Russian Revo

SUKHANOV
(Nikolai Nikolayevich Himmer)

The Russian Revolution 1917

★

A PERSONAL RECORD BY

N. N. SUKHANOV

Edited, abridged and translated by

JOEL CARMICHAEL

from *Zapiski O Revolutsii*

With new Addendum

by the editor

PRINCETON UNIVERSITY PRESS
PRINCETON, NEW JERSEY

Published by Princeton University Press,
41 William Street, Princeton, New Jersey 08540
In the United Kingdom:
Princeton University Press, Guildford, Surrey

First Princeton Paperback printing, 1983

LCC 83-43102

ISBN 0-691-05406-1
ISBN 0-691-00799-3 (pbk.)
First Oxford University Press edition, 1955
First Harper Torchbook edition, 1962

The map of St. Petersburg is reprinted here courtesy of
Harper & Row Publishers, Inc.

Printed in the United States of America by
Princeton University Press,
Princeton, New Jersey

PREFACE

THIS BOOK is an abridgement of a seven-volume memoir of the Russian Revolution of 1917, written by Nikolai Nikolayevich Himmer, better known as Sukhanov. It is, as he assures us repeatedly, by no means a history, but merely his own personal reminiscences, written down shortly after the events it describes.

His claim on our attention is unique. A well-known political and economic journalist and authority on agrarian questions, he was the only theoretician of importance actually present in St. Petersburg when the revolution broke out, and was a key figure in the formation of the first revolutionary Government.

Though not a member of any political party at the time, his widespread connexions throughout the Socialist movement, as an editor of Maxim Gorky's paper and a friend of Kerensky's, made him an intimate spectator of the life of the revolutionary capital, and his passionate concern with politics, combined with his freedom from any party discipline, make him in many ways an ideal witness for posterity. His work, in fact, constitutes the sole full-length eye-witness account of the entire revolutionary period.

His memoir must be one of the most completely forgotten books in contemporary history. When published in the Soviet Union in 1922 it created a great stir; it was required reading for party circles and considered an indispensable source-book for the study of the revolution. By the end of the twenties, however, Soviet public life was already taking such a turn towards the stereotype that Sukhanov's memoirs, representing a highly personal viewpoint which was not only hostile to the Bolshevik Party as such but was, more particularly, wildly out of harmony with the official theories of the revolution then being elaborated by Stalin's faction, swiftly achieved oblivion, and Sukhanov's name was not to be found in any Soviet encyclopaedia.

Sukhanov began his political career at the age of twenty-one as a Socialist-Revolutionary, a member of a non-Marxist Socialist party that believed in 'going to the people': in 1904 he was imprisoned in Moscow for his part in running an underground Socialist-Revolutionary printing-shop. He was released in the amnesty that followed the abortive revolution of 1905, and in 1906 left the Socialist-Revolutionaries, to remain outside all parties until the middle of 1917, when he joined the Social-Democratic Party.

Between the two revolutions of 1905 and 1917 he specialized in research into economic and agrarian affairs, on which he became an authority, and was at the same time very active as a political journalist.

One of the entertaining oddities of this period, with its characteristic Tsarist combination of oppression, mildness, and inefficiency, is illustrated by his employment during the First World War in the Tsarist Government itself, in a section dealing with the irrigation of Turkestan, while at the same time he was being looked for by the police because of his subversive activities.

His superior knew quite well who Sukhanov was, but in accordance with the Witte tradition of employing political suspects because of their ability he willingly protected him. The desire to eliminate suspect elements emanated chiefly from the Ministry of the Interior, and because of the classical interdepartmental rivalry common to all governments it gave other departments special pleasure to conceal those wanted by the police.

Thus, while Sukhanov was signing his own articles 'Sukhanov' in Gorky's paper *Letopis*, he was dodging the police at home and reporting for work regularly to the irrigation department under his real name of Himmer.

Upon the outbreak of the revolution in February Sukhanov automatically found himself at the centre of events, in so far as they were given political expression. He was, indeed, the principal Soviet figure in the negotiations with 'bourgeois elements' that led to the formation of the Provisional Government, and as soon as the unbridled turbulence of the movement in the streets of St. Petersburg had subsided into relatively conventional forms —his lack of organizational contact with the masses had made him feel helpless—Sukhanov, with what Kerensky has called his

Dostoyevskyan quality of circumspection against a background of violent upheaval, had found his medium.

. . .

An oblique example of Sukhanov's detachment may be seen in the fact that he had his memoir printed at all. Published in 1922–23—i.e., when Lenin and Trotsky were paramount figures and Stalin was in course of absorbing the party apparatus—it calls Lenin a dictator and anarchist, sneers at Trotsky's highhandedness, and refers to Stalin as a 'sort of grey blur, dimly looming up now and then and not leaving any trace. There is really nothing more to be said about him.' This in 1922!

Nevertheless history owes a great deal to Sukhanov's honesty, cantankerousness, and power of detached analysis. Quite apart from its indispensability for the historian, his book is one of the few things written about this most dramatic and momentous event, in the shadow of which we are all living today, which actually has the smell of life, and gives us a feeling for the personalities, the emotions, and the play of ideas of the whole revolutionary period.

It is a revelation of the interchange between character, ideas, and the intellectual abstraction that constitutes the stuff of political life. It is a sort of political manual precisely because of Sukhanov's intermediate position between thought and action. There is, after all, a conceptual difficulty inherent in the nature of political activity, or at least in the nature of political theoreticians: How can theory encompass adequately the indescribable, protean, and elusive substance of collective behaviour? The inarticulate man of action and the secluded theoretician would seem to be antithetical—in Sukhanov this paralysing antithesis is made flesh. His mélange of ratiocination and wilfulness, of analysis and self-justification, articulates for us the intimate interaction of theory and life.

For he was, after all, an intellectual, a member of the intelligentsia—the very word for which Russia has given to the world. But he was an intellectual whose overriding passion was politics. Now this is an abstraction which differs from other abstractions doted on by the intelligentsia chiefly in that it deals, at least potentially, with the interests and passions of real people—real people moreover, who are unified in moments of crisis by the irrational occasions of collective impulse. And we must not forget that it was in Russia that armed intellectuals burst to the surface of public life for the first time in history, and with brutal, nervous hands snatched the mantle of authority from the fumbling, inarticulate masses.

But not all the intellectuals were armed; in the event only the Bolsheviks had the audacity to embark on this unprecedented enterprise, and by virtue of their characteristic will-power and organizational ruthlessness constituted themselves the heirs of the revolutionary upsurge after it had spent itself.

Sukhanov, hostile to the Bolshevik project, found himself left by the wayside, and it may be that it is just this detachment of his that makes all the more penetrating the insight into politics provided by his memoir. It is a very honest book, and Sukhanov's honesty enables us to discern, through the screen of his rationalizations and complaints, the impalpable functioning of this elusive abstraction of politics, reflected in the behaviour of the actors, all so articulate, so dogmatic, yet nevertheless undone in varying ways, some through failure, some through success, and all of them because of a perhaps inevitable inability to constrain the elemental flux of life within their own Olympian schemata.

Sukhanov's attitude towards the Bolsheviks illuminates the ambivalence that hamstrung so many of their opponents. As a Socialist, Sukhanov grew more and more indignant with the Bolsheviks as their intention of taking power became increasingly manifest. But his anger was rendered ineffectual because of his allegiance to principles which the Bolsheviks also accepted in theory, while disregarding them in practice.

It was not, after all, doctrine that made the Bolsheviks a magnet for the masses, but their conforming to the primordial desires of the Russian peasants and workers by their promises of bread, peace, and land. And actually, as Sukhanov points out with bitterness, their whole positive programme for the new society—the ultimate goal of Sukhanov as of all Socialists—was no more than a hasty improvisation. But, incensed though he was with Leninism, which he thought demagogic, irresponsible, violent, and dictatorial, Sukhanov was nevertheless compelled by his own belief in the ideals common to the whole Socialist movement to think of the Bolsheviks, regardless of their tactics, as 'champions of democracy', in contrast to their opponents. Sukhanov was far *more* angry with the adversaries of the Bolsheviks, precisely for allowing the Bolsheviks to pass themselves off as spokesmen of the people. Sukhanov felt himself paralysed by what he thought was an inescapably realistic estimate of the situation: in *fact* the Bolsheviks had secured a genuine mass following as a result of the suicidal blunders of their rivals, and thus were capable of outflanking them. Truly an insoluble problem. How, indeed, could Sukhanov reconcile his fidelity to the masses with his opinion that their actual goal under Bolshevik leadership was a fateful adventure implemented by unscrupulous means? How right he was to feel neglected by history!

Thus, describing a highly emotional speech made by Trotsky to a stirred and mesmerized mass-meeting, in one of the concluding episodes of the Bolshevik assumption of power, Sukhanov, with characteristically torn feelings, remarks: "With an unusual feeling of oppression I looked on at this really magnificent scene."

Sukhanov was headstrong by nature; although his principal interest was politics, he ran 'wild' most of his life. In the revolution, however, he swallowed his congenital unruliness for a short time and joined a group led by Martov, the man he had most respect and affection for. Martov, who was looked up to by everyone who knew him, including Lenin and Trotsky, was one of the most massive figures in the Russian Social-Democracy, but character and fate did not allow him to live up to his abilities, and his fraction spent itself in pathetic impotence. After assuring us repeatedly of Martov's magnificent intellect, Sukhanov sadly points out that he lacked revolutionary will-power. When the Russian *émigrés* were stewing in exile the implications of this lack of will were not specially noticeable, any more than Lenin's single-minded identification of himself with his theories made him unique in the Social-Democratic movement. Sukhanov gives an angry description of Martov during one of the continual crises of the revolution: Martov had made a brilliant speech—as usual; he had dazzled his audience—as usual; but he had failed to tell them what to *do*—as usual. Sukhanov, enthralled like the others by Martov's brilliance, bitterly complains that at a crucial moment he had failed to find the words of action they were desperately in need of. He was a victim, as

Sukhanov says, of Menshevik indecisiveness. The words might sum up Sukhanov himself and his entire fraction.

Sukhanov provides us with a curious symbol of this fateful incapacity, in his melancholy account of how the Bolshevik insurrection, which he thought to be against Marx, nature, and common sense, was decided on and planned—in his own flat. Sukhanov—naturally—knew nothing about it: his wife, already propagandized, as he puts it, by the Bolsheviks, had known of his having to go somewhere at the other end of town, and sweetly advised him not to bother returning that night. An engaging twist to the tradition of the philandering husband staying late at the office!

Sukhanov heard about the conspiratorial decision only later, but at Lenin's sensational reappearance from the underground after the successful Bolshevik *coup* he saw its fruition. And he gives us his feelings at the triumphal scene—feelings that found many an echo then and later:

'The entire Praesidium, headed by Lenin, were standing up singing, with excited, exalted faces and blazing eyes. . . The mass of delegates were permeated by the faith that all would go well in future too. They were persuaded of the imminence of peace, land, and bread.

'Applause, hurrahs, caps flung up in the air. . .

'But I didn't believe in the success, in the rightfulness, or in the historic mission of a Bolshevik régime. Sitting in the back seats I watched this celebration with a heavy heart. How I longed to join in and merge with this mass and with its leaders in a single feeling! But I couldn't. . .'

. . .

Sukhanov's differences with the Bolsheviks, though profound, were not such as to make it impossible for him to reconcile himself to a Bolshevik régime, as long as he thought that the Bolshevik leaders, though they had made a terrible mistake by taking power in the absence of an alliance with other 'democratic' groups, were nevertheless authentic representatives of the Russian working class. Indeed, he may have thought it his duty to do his best to mitigate this historic blunder.

He left the Martov group at the end of 1920, resuming the 'wild' status he felt more at home in, and during the twenties, when optimism about the Soviet 'experiment' was fashionable all over the world, he worked as a Soviet functionary, without ever becoming a Communist. Throughout this period, though violently hostile to the political régime, he felt that in the sphere of planned economy something constructive might still be accomplished. In 1924–25, while on a Soviet Trade Mission in Berlin and Paris, he edited a journal for foreigners, published in German and French, devoted to explaining the work of Socialist construction then thought to be taking place in the Soviet Union. He had not merely been reconciled to the purely *economic* aspects of Soviet policy, but become an ardent supporter.

At least—that is what he said when tried for treason in 1931.

For the fact is that it was during the twenties that economics and politics had become inextricably intertwined, and Sukhanov's personality did not help him survive the Stalin strait-jacket.

In 1931 the so-called Trial of the Mensheviks was presented to the world, a precursor of the bloody and far more notorious Purge Trials of the Old Bolsheviks in 1936–37.

This Menshevik trial, which was largely ignored by the world press, has a certain interest nowadays because it is a replica in miniature of the later trials, a sort of dress rehearsal *pianissimo*. The charges were not so horrendous, the confessions not so absurd, and the sentences—from the point of view of a later and more experienced epoch—relatively mild. A decade or so in a concentration camp—practically nothing.

Sukhanov and the other defendants (almost none of them, oddly enough, real Mensheviks) were accused of having set up, in collaboration with the chiefs of 'World Menshevism', a so-called Allied Bureau in order to promote military intervention, the destruction of the Soviet State and the restoration of capitalism.

At this late date it would doubtless be pointless to attempt an analysis of the evidence at this trial: it is interesting primarily for the exactitude with which it foreshadows the later trials. Sukhanov distinguished himself by a sort of inverted honesty: he gave a perfectly persuasive description of his views on a variety of political themes, and then, having perhaps enjoyed his favourite pastime of political exposition and analysis, he simply leaped over the hurdle between theory and action, and ended by blandly saying, more or less, that since he had had such and such opinions in the past about, for instance, the pernicious absurdities of 'War Communism', and had once been sympathetic to Menshevism, *therefore* he began actively plotting to promote armed intervention on the part of the 'bourgeois democracies', etc.

The 1931 trial differed from the later Purge Trials chiefly in that the accused were not Bolsheviks, and that the historical and theoretical foundations of the evidence are distortions and exaggerations less grotesque than the act of creation *en bloc* that underlay the trials of 1936–37.

Sukhanov had doubtless made a bargain with the Soviet authorities, but it availed him little: his career ends, as far as we know, on a characteristically poignant note.

In the late spring of 1931, a few months after the trial, Sukhanov and the other defendants finally arrived at a concentration camp in Verkhne-Uralsk, a GPU 'isolator'. The Yugoslav A. Ciliga, who reports this, and who was himself one of the thousands and tens of thousands of ex-Communists, Oppositionists, etc., who were beginning to fill the gaols and concentration camps of the Soviet Union at this time, asked one of them how their statements at the trial had been made. 'We ourselves don't understand it,' was the reply. 'It was all like a horrible nightmare.'

But Sukhanov was the child of a more humane epoch than that which the thirties were to bring to light; the full implications of this nightmare had not yet been grasped. He wrote an indignant appeal to the Soviet Government—now run by the 'grey blur'—and circulated a copy of it through the gaol.

Insisting on his bargain with the GPU, he demanded that they keep their promise 'to release those willing to make untrue confessions'.

From our generation, inured to the bestialities of the past twenty years, his very indignation evokes a nostalgic sigh.

It is the last we hear of him.

1954 J. C.

EDITORIAL NOTE

In the Russian original Sukhanov's *Zapiski o Revolutsii* (Notes on the Revolution) contain some 2,700 pages, and the abridged

English text represents a full translation of roughly half, the remainder having been bridged over by means of transitional sequences in Sukhanov's own words. The headings of the chapters and parts are, except for a few in brackets, Sukhanov's, though they may include material taken from other sections. The few headings in brackets are conflations of two or more of Sukhanov's headings.

The criterion of omission and inclusion, generally speaking, grew out of an attempt to arrive at the lowest common denominator of Sukhanov's narrative and the actual sequence of the more important historical events. It proved possible to extract from Sukhanov's avowedly personal reminiscences an account which, perforce omitting digressions and an inevitable preoccupation with relatively outdated material, nevertheless constitutes a connected narrative of the major events of the revolution, entirely in Sukhanov's words and without burdensome indication of omissions. In no case has his style or thought been distorted.

Sukhanov himself, to be sure, is naturally often compelled to refer to events on the basis of hearsay, rumour, etc., in order to make his own behaviour comprehensible, but since he does not do this in the manner of a historian the purely historical gaps in his narrative have *a fortiori* been widened in the abridgement, without altering its general balance.

The skeleton of Sukhanov's account, in short, has been retained intact, more or less abundantly articulated at the points of major interest.

The occasional three dots (. . .) are Sukhanov's own pauses, and the asterisks between passages are uniformly his, although a series of asterisks used by him as a break of a certain magnitude may have been retained for an editorial omission of greater magnitude, again while seldom disturbing the sequence of events.

The proportion of material omitted varies from part to part of the abridgement. In Part I, for instance, almost three-quarters of Volume I of the Russian original has been reproduced, whereas most of the Russian Volumes V and VI, dealing with the background of the abortive Kornilov putsch and the disintegration of the democratic Government before the Bolshevik assumption of power, has been omitted.

The footnotes have been inserted merely by way of supplementing Sukhanov's own discussions of personalities, for the purpose of making the actual narrative easily understandable. An attempt has been made to keep a balance between the necessity of providing a minimum of elementary information in an exotic field, and reluctance to burden the reader with inappropriate dilation on personages since become famous. Lenin, Trotsky, and Stalin, for instance, have not been given footnotes, while on the other hand some far less well-known though important personalities have, simply because Sukhanov says little about them.

Since most of the outstanding events of the Russian Revolution became known in history according to the Julian calendar in force during the revolution itself, it has been considered appropriate to retain the old dates throughout the book. Dates mentioned are, accordingly, thirteen days behind the present international calendar, which was adopted by the Soviet Union after the revolution.

. . .

Sukhanov's *Notes* have never before been translated, and have appeared in only one Russian edition, printed in Germany, in 1922 and 1923.

NOTE OF ACKNOWLEDGEMENT

It gives me pleasure to make the following acknowledgements.

The help given me by Lydia Ossipovna Dan, whose knowledge of the Russian revolutionary movement and its principal figures is profound, has been invaluable for the sketch of Sukhanov in the Preface and for the balance of the abridgement as a whole.

The authoritative judgement of Mr. D. M. Davin with respect to the prose style of the manuscript has been of the greatest assistance.

In particular I must record the quite exceptional value of Mrs. Jessie Coulson's contribution to the preparation of the text: her intelligence and zeal have been irreplaceable, with respect both to the accuracy of the translation itself and to the technical organization of the abridgement.

I am also indebted to Mr. A. F. Kerensky for a lengthy interview devoted in the main to a discussion of Sukhanov as a person.

CONTENTS

PART IV

THE TRIUMPH OF THE REACTION, MAY 6TH–JULY 8TH

PART V

COUNTER-REVOLUTION AND THE DISSOLUTION OF THE DEMOCRACY, JULY 8TH–OCTOBER 20TH

PART VI

THE OCTOBER INSURRECTION, OCTOBER 3RD–NOVEMBER 1ST

ILLUSTRATIONS

INTRODUCTION

By The Editor

The consequences of the Russian Revolution have altered the velocity of history so pervasively that the revolution itself, together with the men who made it, has been muffled by a collective amnesia. Sukhanov's memoir, disinterred now from the archives, comes to us a lone voice from a world that has completely vanished, engulfed by the titanic upheaval it helped to bring about. The Russian intelligentsia of which Sukhanov was an offshoot has been swallowed up by its revolutionary by-product, the bureaucracy of the Soviet state. The intellectual atmosphere and the political life revealed by Sukhanov's book have gone the way of the dodo.

It is difficult to recall the volatile, bickering, and unflaggingly garrulous Russian political exiles who contrived the web of ideas that lay in wait to ensnare the turbulent events of 1917. The endless polemical subtleties that were the stuff of life to the Russian Left wing now seem so dryly cerebral by contrast with the primordial explosion on the Russian land that as a medium of expression for it they must remain a source of astonishment.

From the point of view of the relationship between the intentions of its protagonists and their accomplishments, the revolution acquires the look of a vast comedy of errors. The forensic intricacies that formed the actual medium of contention cast into high relief, not the acumen of the disputants, but the naked qualities of passion and character that emerge as the moving force of political achievement.

The irony is inescapable that the Russian revolution, doubtless one of the most theorized about, talked about, and argued about events in history, frustrated the analysis of the innumerable intellectuals whose lives revolved around politics. Few details of this elemental outburst were foreseen. The fact itself, indeed, came as a complete surprise to every one of the old parties and leaders, both on the spot and abroad. As Sukhanov says, 'not one party was preparing for the great overturn'. And the actual development of the revolution, from the collapse of

Tsarism in February, which paved the way for Kerensky's 'bourgeois democratic' régime, to the Bolshevik seizure of power the following October, radically modified the theories of the Bolshevik victors themselves.

This irony to be sure is heightened by one of the qualities of Marxist debate in general, which is the tendency to erect timeless 'inevitable' generalizations on the basis of data more or less arbitrarily arranged so as to justify, naturally, the generalizations. It is this specious form of 'logical' rigour that ran aground on the facts of history.

But theory is only one component of political action. It is so plastic in its nature, so flexible when applied to specific tactics, that in many ways it was precisely this all-embracing quality of Marxist discourse that enabled Lenin to make the supple improvizations that put his party in power. For while Marxism does not provide a guide to *specific* conduct any more than any other system of general ideas, neither does it preclude any *ad hoc* contrivances to attain the goal of power. Perhaps Lenin's chief distinction lay in his ability to combine dynamic tactical improvizations with long-range strategical goals in a form that was both an effective debating technique and a magnet for the masses.

The unexpected collapse of Tsarism in February 1917 was of course the result of a crisis deep within the organism of the Russian State. It was caused by three factors: the radical incapacity of the Tsarist economy to deal with a modern industrial war, the organization of the mass army drawn from the peasantry and working class, and a growing hatred of the war amongst those who bore the brunt of it.

These general processes culminated in the contrast between the paralysis of the ruling class and the high temper, discipline, and intelligence of the industrial workers of St. Petersburg, steeped in revolutionary agitation for a generation and trained by the revolution of 1905.

The ruling class was just as much taken by surprise as the Left-wing parties. There is general agreement with Sukhanov that the revolution began in February with disorders of exactly the same kind as had become commonplace during the preceding months. No alarm was felt. It was thought the disorders would subside again more or less of their own accord, or through the exercise of routine administrative and police pressure. There was little political tension. Indeed, since the 1905 revolution dissident movements of all kinds had been relatively quiescent. The political groups which were to leap into prominence during the revolution itself (Bolsheviks, Mensheviks, Socialist-Revolutionaries) had spent the preceding decade and a half in venomous squabbling which to outsiders looked like the activity of psychopaths. Anyone acquainted with the discussions that were common fare amongst the Bolsheviks and Mensheviks must be amazed at the fantastic energy displayed in the interminable procedural, textual, and metaphysical wrangling that governed the lives of these fanatical partisans of an identical world outlook and an identical political programme. In any case the Bolsheviks and Mensheviks seemed still becalmed in the trough of the 1905 wave, and were thought a more or less negligible factor.

Yet in the space of three days the Tsarist régime was totally extinguished, and in another eight months the Bolshevik fraction, negligible in March, had become the Russian State.

It should perhaps be recalled that Tsarist 'stagnancy' and 'oppression' have been widely exaggerated. The oppression in any case would seem child's play to us nowadays. Russian prerevolutionary development was immensely active, the play of ideas was extraordinarily free (as compared with the later postrevolutionary period), and the youthful industrial proletariat had congregated in enterprises that were larger than anywhere else in the world. It was Russian socio-economic backwardness as a *whole* that subjected the entire society to an unprecedented strain, aggravated by the war, and gave the schismatic movement its opportunity.

With the collapse of Tsarism, so unexpected and so complete, all political groups were catapulted into a scramble for power.

For the Marxist parties, however, this was fraught with difficulties, theoretical and practical. For them the struggle for power was far from the simple proposition it sounds. On top of their not having foreseen the revolution as occurring at this particular time, it was theoretically *impossible* for the Marxist parties to take power. Sukhanov gives a lengthy analysis of the 'ideology' (which he shared) according to which the Left wing *could* not snatch up the power left hanging in the air by the more or less uncontrolled movement of the workers into the streets. It provides a penetrating insight into political prejudice.

The sovereignty formerly embodied in the Russian monarchy and its quasi-parliamentary *aide-de-camp*, the State Duma, remained dissolved while the capital was plunged in the anarchy caused by the undirected mass movement; when sovereignty finally coagulated again its locus was the Soviet of Workers' and Soldiers' Deputies, with the 'constitutional' power officially incarnate in the Provisional Government.

But the genesis of the Soviet as the source of authority for the masses of Petersburg workers, together with the hordes of soldiers, i.e., peasants in uniform, took place in spite of all the rationalizing of the Left-wing parties. What made itself felt was the practical or administrative effect of the *de facto* authority of the Soviet, long before the 'recognition' of that authority, which did not, indeed, take place until the eve of the Bolshevik insurrection in October. The trains would not move, municipal institutions would not function, the police were paralysed, and the most routine and indispensable functions of administration were suspended, until authorized, sanctioned, or specifically enjoined by the 'illegitimate' Soviet, which according to 'official' theory remained a private body until October. And the Provisional Government itself, despite its constitutional 'theory', was living by the grace of the 'private' Soviet, which in its turn also refused to recognize its own authority theoretically while nevertheless in *de facto* control of all administration.

Thus on the one hand the Left-wing parties (viz. the Socialist-Revolutionaries, the Mensheviks, and the Bolsheviks until Lenin's appearance in April), willy-nilly representing the soldiers and factory workers who had actually brought about the dissolution of the Tsarist régime, theoretically 'declined' to wield the power, and on the other hand the bourgeois groups, propped up in power by the unrecognized Soviet authority, were in fact incapable of wielding the power they were still formally in possession of.

This paradoxical situation was known as the dual power, and in one way or another it constituted the framework of political life until the Bolsheviks liquidated the paradox in October.

This reluctance to assume power was not, of course, a mere caprice, but the product of decades of Marxist cogitation.

There was no substantial theoretical disagreement between Bolsheviks and Mensheviks on this: they both thought Russia was too backward for a Socialist revolution headed by the industrial proletariat, and consequently would have to have a 'bourgeois' revolution first. That is, it was thought the Russian bourgeoisie would have to eliminate the feudal heritage of Tsarism and lay the foundation for a capitalist economy in which the productive forces of the country as a whole would be multiplied, while the proletariat would develop concomitantly to the point of being able to carry out later its own revolution for the construction of Socialism.

The method, timing, and details of all this provided, of course, material for endless debate.

Trotsky, who had no stable organizational attachments until the middle of 1917, had developed a theory of his own (suggested by Parvus, a cosmopolitan Marxist) to the effect that the Russian bourgeoisie was too feeble to vanquish Tsarism and realize the whole series of needed capitalist reforms *before* the Russian industrial working class grew strong enough to push it out, and hence that it would be necessary for the working class to take power in order to accomplish the bourgeois revolution that was beyond the capacities of the Russian bourgeoisie and thus create a situation in which—again later on—it could construct a Socialist society.

It was in the realm of organization that Lenin made his most characteristic and most specialized contribution. He formulated the celebrated idea of limiting the membership of the revolutionary party to professional revolutionaries who would devote their entire lives to party work. The dictatorship of the proletariat was to be spearheaded by a small, tightly welded political caucus, which would present a closed front to the outside world regardless of how freely policy might be discussed within.

This distinction, which was the source of the 1903 split into Bolsheviks and Mensheviks, was founded on such a delicate shading of emphasis that it was difficult even for those involved in the argument to understand why it generated so much heat or why Lenin fought for it so tigerishly. With the benefit of hindsight and a greater understanding of the vital importance of technique in contemporary politics, we can see what consequences these differing conceptions of organization were pregnant with.

In any case it was largely this view of organization that constituted the great divide between Lenin and his opponents, who on this question included Trotsky—before 1917.

In many ways this discussion of organization was a specific illustration of a more general discussion of the rhythm and modality of guided upheaval that went by the exotic name of 'tail-endism'. This was one of the principal axes of discussion in the Social-Democracy, and the philosophical background of the organizational distinction between Mensheviks and Bolsheviks.

By and large the Marxist school represented in Russia by the Mensheviks took the view that Socialism could not be established until the working class had matured organically through the development of capitalist society: had acquired, that is, the requisite culture, technical competence, and specific social weight which alone guaranteed the industrialization of backward agrarian Russia and so made Socialism feasible. Since Socialism was always conceived of as an economy of abundance predicated on industrial technology, it was considered necessary for Russia to have a working class large and well-developed enough to institute such an abundance while simultaneously overcoming the clashes of interest inevitable in a society afflicted by scarcity. The process of developing such a working class was thought to be rather a long-range one, and hence required the establishment of a 'bourgeois democratic' society first.

The Bolsheviks agreed with this in theory, but nevertheless conceived of the Social-Democracy as a guiding factor in these long-range subterranean processes. They regarded the Social-Democracy as the leaven in the social ferment and the sole channel for the revolutionary education of the proletarian masses.

Other Social-Democrats assumed that the necessary evolution of bourgeois society would make the working class assume power more or less automatically (they all considered it inevitable): it was thought that after a sufficient stage of culture plus technical competence had been reached, and class relations had ripened, the actual change of régime would become a mere, though possibly insurrectionary, formality.

The Mensheviks, consequently, were said to be following

along at the 'tail end' of events, whereas the attitude of the Bolsheviks amounted to the contention that they represented that element of the 'event' that actively promoted its crystallization.

The ambiguity at the root of all this is obvious. Since events are brought about by people, both attitudes towards this focal question of 'tail-endism' are perfectly defensible, or indeed 'inevitable'—in theory. In practice the decisive rôle must be played by temperament, the only arbiter between contending interpretations of theory. In the same way that the word *kismet*, often vulgarly thought to explain the inertness of Muslim society, was presumably also the slogan of Islam during its dynamic expansion, so the resolution of this question of inevitability must be and historically always has been a function of character.

The ambiguity itself is not accidental: it has its roots deep in Marxism, in the concept of the 'dialectical' interaction between 'acting' and 'knowing', or in the inconceivability of knowledge except as a function of action. Since the time of Marx himself Marxism has combined a passion for the scientific demonstration of the 'inevitability' of its prognosis with a dynamic will to action, a combination which in essence constitutes an injunction to will the inevitable.

An amusing thing in Sukhanov's book is this vision of the Left-wing parties thrust into power by the spontaneous movement of the industrial proletariat they had spent their lives predicting and analysing, and refusing to accept this power because it conflicted with their assumption of the unripeness of Russia for a Socialist revolution. Both the Socialist-Revolutionaries and the Mensheviks, who had *de facto* power after the Tsarist collapse, seem to have wilfully blinded themselves to the temper of their own followers, and stubbornly (in the event suicidally) refused to accept political power. This mystical devotion to a dogma is all the more astonishing when one considers that it was just this that brought about not only their liquidation as a party but the collapse of their personal fortunes. They immolated themselves on the altar of a manifestly irrelevant, inadequate, or outmoded theory.

This in itself naturally explains little: nothing could have been simpler for these adroit casuists than to change the theory while simultaneously maintaining that—properly understood—the new theory was the same as the old one, applied to a different situation. The source of their failure to do this must evidently be explained by character structure.

A graphic reminder of the decisiveness of temperament is the fact that both Bolsheviks and Mensheviks, despite their incessant factional wrangling, accepted the same programme (as members of the Russian Social-Democratic Party) until a couple of years *after* the revolution. It turned out under fire that their concise summation of principles was either ambiguous or noncommittal on the point which actual events were to make the crux of decision, i.e., the assumption of power.

On this question of following or preceding the 'event', it is entertaining to reflect that in the actual revolution the rôles of the Bolsheviks and Mensheviks were apparently reversed. For here the 'event' was the more or less spontaneous dissolution of Tsarist society, accompanied by an uncontrollable upheaval of the youthful, lively Russian proletariat and furthered by the despair of the peasants in uniform at the prolongation of the war.

From this point of view what the Bolshevik Party actually did was to surrender to the event, and allow itself to be swung along on the coat-tails of a powerful upsurge of the industrial proletariat alienated from the traditional order. It is true, of course, that after Lenin's arrival the Bolsheviks manipulated this upsurge positively in the direction of taking power, but basically they merely provided an administrative expression for the primitive slogans that had rallied the masses sufficiently to their support. Lenin claimed repeatedly, and effectively, that the masses were always a hundred times more Left than the Bolsheviks.

It was the Mensheviks whose congenital passivity made them disregard the manifest facts of life through clinging to their outlived and suicidal exegesis of Marx. They were really more 'fanatical' from this point of view than the Bolsheviks, for the essential quality of fanaticism as rigidity of character surely emerges with greater clarity when it encompasses the undoing of the fanatics.

The Bolsheviks' preoccupation with compactness of organization, coupled with Lenin's will to power, merely enabled them to take advantage of the real situation. They constituted the crest of the tidal wave that bore them into power. Their opponents stubbornly remained blind to the actual correlation of social forces as determined by the real and imagined interests of the masses of the population, who exerted a constant, unflagging, and immediate pressure on all political groups; and this blindness made them quite incapable of grasping the reasons for first the gradual and then the impetuous shifting of the masses into the Bolshevik fold.

It should be remembered that the Bolsheviks themselves, while more 'intransigent' than the Mensheviks, in fact shared the same attitudes on all essential matters, and did so until Lenin arrived on the scene and confounded his lieutenants by his brusque abandonment of what they had all thought to be the ABC of Marxist doctrine. Lenin's remark about the masses being a hundred times more Left than the Bolsheviks was directed at his own party comrades, who, while their tactics (i.e., the *independent* organization of the masses under the banner of a combative party) were 'objectively' aimed at a radical upset, were still enthralled by the common Social-Democratic view that Russia had to go through its bourgeois revolution before it could go on—an unforeseeable length of time later—to a Socialist one.

Sukhanov has a striking description of the consternation Lenin caused by the very first speech he made on Russian soil, the day he arrived. Sukhanov complains indignantly that Lenin not only spoke out of the 'context' of the Russian revolution as it had hitherto proceeded, i.e., against the general assumptions shared by the whole Left wing, but also flabbergasted his own Bolsheviks by his anarchist intransigence.

What Lenin did in effect was to embrace the Trotsky–Parvus theory of 'Permanent Revolution', that is, the necessity for the proletariat to take power in order to accomplish even the bourgeois revolution the Russian bourgeoisie was too feeble to carry out.

Lenin's espousal of an immediate conquest of power by the industrial working class (regardless of the objective possibilities of constructing Socialism) stunned his whole party. Sukhanov records his own pious siding with the Bolshevik editors of *Pravda*, including Stalin, in their dismay at Lenin's April Theses, which amplified the intransigent speech Lenin had made on his arrival. Sukhanov says that as against Lenin's 'anarchist abstractions' the Marxist foundations of *Pravda* were firm!

Sukhanov, a passionate debater, merely thought Lenin's intransigence an aberration due to remoteness from practical politics. He records a brief dialogue between himself, a Menshevik, and Miliukov, the chief bourgeois leader, in which they comfortably agree that Lenin would no doubt settle down soon enough and acclimatize himself to Russian conditions—presumably, that is, become a parliamentarian like themselves. Sukhanov sighs in recalling that neither of them ever thought that Lenin, while clinging to his 'anarchism', would conquer not only the revolution, or the masses, or the Soviet, but even his own Bolshevik Party. They were, as Sukhanov says, 'cruelly mistaken'.

They were indeed. They had assumed that Lenin's characteristic intransigence was only a matter of style, and not the expression of the man. They assumed that the universalizing, exclusive tendency of Marxist statement was a mere intellectual mannerism, whereas in fact Lenin's unique feature would now seem to have been his will-power allied to his administrative preoccupation.

In the crucible of events Lenin accepted Trotsky's theory of 'Permanent Revolution', and Trotsky accepted Lenin's characteristic view of the revolutionary party as a centralized organization of dedicated professionals. It was the union of these two concepts, of the renovated party ideology and the traditional party technique, that gave practical expression to the audacity of the Bolsheviks in making themselves the State.

This is the context that illuminates the implications of Lenin's habitual machine-mindedness. Since up to 1917 he had shared the general Social-Democratic assumption that Russia would first have to pass through a bourgeois democratic phase of society, he could never have regarded the disciplined centralization of the party, which he thought indispensable for agitation, as a necessary condition for taking *power*. The streamlined authoritarianism seems to have stemmed from his unconscious identification of himself with his political ideals. He was always intensely preoccupied with the desire to forge a party apparatus in which his own fraction would be identical with the party. This had been his characteristic political trait since the 1903 congress that engendered the Bolshevik and Menshevik fractions. The importance of this personal quality of Lenin's is emphasized by the fact that in all crises Lenin generally stood completely isolated not only as against the Mensheviks but as against his own Bolsheviks. In the absence of any broad 'programmatic' differences this question of will-power and method acquired decisive importance.

But of course Lenin's act of will in plumping for the seizure of power in 1917 was not performed in the void. It too had its 'ideology', drawn from the common storehouse of Marxism.

It was generally held that, quite apart from the question of whether or not the Russian proletariat could conquer power in a backward country like Russia, *Socialism itself* would be out of the question in such a country. Hence the only thing the Russian proletariat could do would be to cling to power while waiting for a Socialist proletarian revolution in Western Europe to come to its rescue, and provide it with a sufficiently developed industrial base and with populations sufficiently trained technically and administratively to go ahead with the Socialist reconstruction of society as a whole. In the long run it was this that was considered the justification for the proletarian vanguard, i.e., Lenin's party, in seizing power at all.

That desire for ecclesiastical uniformity, for prescience and omniscience, characteristic of so many Marxists and embalmed in official Soviet myth, would naturally have it now that Lenin's decision to take power could only be justified objectively by the actual process of Socialist construction now supposed to be taking place in the Soviet Union. The aim of contemporary Soviet propaganda is clear: if Socialism in Russia can only be secured by a revolution in Europe, and that has not taken place, *ergo*, either Lenin was wrong or there is no Socialism in Russia. The repugnancy of both alternatives to Soviet myth thus provides the emotional basis for a retroactive exegesis.

Without venturing into this question—doubtless a thorny one—it must be clear that while Lenin had a wholehearted faith in the *general* inevitability of a European and for that matter a worldwide revolution, his actual seizure of power was essentially an act of boldness performed out of sheer high spirits. For there can be no doubt that even though under the pressure of events (learning from life, as he liked to say) he changed his mind about the possibility of *power* for the Bolshevik Party (since this in fact happened we can now see it to have been simple realism) he never thought Socialism could possibly be realized in isolated, primitive Russia. Nor for that matter did anyone else. And as to what was going to happen if the European revolution were delayed (as indeed it was) or frustrated (as indeed it was) no prophecies were possible, since the question had never before arisen in history.

The title of Lenin's last work, published in January 1923, when he was already dying, was one of Napoleon's remarks he was fond of: '*On s'engage, et puis—on voit.*' You commit yourself, and then—you see. Fundamentally that is what Lenin did: he committed himself, and his party, and his country, and perhaps the world, and then—but he died before seeing.

He had written this work in a final attempt to answer the classic Menshevik reproach that he had seized power in a country unripe for Socialism and in the name of a class insufficiently developed to exercise it—that the Bolshevik seizure of power was, in short, a tremendous and irresponsible adventure. On looking back it would seem that the reproach of the Mensheviks was no more than the acid complaint of a theoretical economist whose colleague has made a fortune on the Stock Exchange. What Lenin had done in effect was to transform the traditional Marxist formula that in the last analysis economics determines politics into the Leninist view that political power may succeed in determining economics. The element of will embedded in the core of Marxism had become paramount. Although as a theoretician Lenin accepted these general Marxist formulae, as a man of action in a situation that demanded action he was bound to commit himself, and—see.

Reports have it that he actually had begun to see, but when it was far too late to do anything about it. As he lay on his death-bed half-paralysed he is supposed to have muttered his forebodings: 'The machine has got out of control', doubtless meaning his own control, or, since he always identified himself unconsciously with the forces of history, out of the control of the idea that had given it life. There are also reports that when death intervened he had been preparing to circumvent Stalin, the machine incarnate. He had doubtless begun to see.

In any case it was too late. And the really astonishing thing is that all these voluble Marxists, so self-confident, so ready with intrepretations, analyses, and forecasts, actually disregarded just what would really happen in a backward, peasant, war-torn country if the Bolsheviks were isolated by the collapse of the revolution in Europe. This disregard of the eventual fate of the Bolshevik Party itself is all the more astonishing since it disregards not only the rudiments of Marxism as a doctrine but also elementary common sense.

It is a Marxist commonplace that the material situation of a society is what determines its spiritual superstructure. Put so broadly the statement indeed seems unexceptionable. What, then, would happen to the Bolshevik Party, claiming to represent the vanguard of the industrial Russian proletariat, if it embarked on this risky Socialist experiment in a backward peasant country and were left to cope alone with the gargantuan tasks of administration?

The oddity is that no one foresaw not only that a radical degeneration in the Bolshevik cadres themselves was possible, but that it was inevitable. What was going to guarantee the continuing spiritual superiority of the vanguard itself? If the material underpinnings of society determine its politics, what was bound to happen to a party committed by its nature to accomplish something its own theories said was impossible? If Marxism is correct in maintaining that thought itself is determined 'in the last analysis' by the economic process in the broadest sense, it must have seemed obvious—one would think—to the leaders of the revolution that as soon as the Bolshevik Party, however tempered by discipline and self-sacrificing devotion, had been saddled with the burden, by definition unbearable, of propelling a peasant country into an economy of Socialist abundance, it would be corrupted *at once* and *inevitably*.

Concretely, that is to say, it would be corrupted through the progressive ossification of the party apparatus, the progressive elevation of the former Bolshevik cadres above the masses, and the progressive re-stratification of society in terms of the national income (wage differentiation, concealed or not), fortified by the progressive magnification of the police—to keep the country yoked to a project all previous Marxist theory had thought unrealizable, i.e., the creation of abundance on an inadequate technical foundation.

Inevitably a comprehensive process took place which resulted in the transformation of the political intelligentsia into a corps of administrators. This process had two aspects: one was the actual replacement of the personnel of the Party, the other was the institutionalization of the party as myth.

In 1917 the Bolsheviks were no more than a party of armed intellectuals, a generally uprooted and declassed élite. They were blood-brothers of all the other Russian political exiles, and Lenin himself was considered simply as one more gifted member of a movement that contained many gifted, devoted, and self-sacrificing people.

It was only in upheaval that Lenin revealed himself as a man of action *par excellence*; his traditional idiosyncrasy as a specialist in machine politics, which had aroused merely polemical vituperation, was not seen in its true dimensions until his party had become the State. Trotsky himself, after having predicted (in 1904) that 'the organization of the Party would take the place of the Party itself, the Central Committee would take the place of the organization, and finally the Dictator would take the place of the Central Committee', under the pressure of circumstance came to the view in 1917 that it was just such a streamlined organizational structure that could ensure the conquest and retention of power by the Bolshevik Party. It was this acceptance by Lenin of Trotsky's theoretical justification of the possibility, and indeed of the necessity, of the proletarian assumption of power, and Trotsky's acceptance of Lenin's organization, that constituted a tacit compromise between them in 1917 and served as the springboard for joint action.

But with the cares of state the party of armed intellectuals dwindled away, not only through physical losses, but in the deeper sense of the Party's becoming an élite welded together not by the free play of polemics within a rigorously defined though non-hierarchical party system, but by the concrete function of administration.

It is this administrative function that has inevitably 'in the last analysis!' determined the character of the régime that emerged victorious from the crumbling of the old Party, for when the Bolsheviks were a disaffected splinter faction, as yet outside the manifest course of history and with only their reasoning and agitational powers to secure them a foothold in society, they were at once more enchained by theory and 'representative' of a social interest as a matter of will rather than as an actual component of the body politic.

This administrative metamorphosis of the intelligentsia was paralleled, doubtless also inevitably, by the ikonization that placed the Bolshevik Party as such beyond rational criticism very soon after it took power. The assumption of statehood enveloped the Bolshevik Party in the entire mystic cult of statehood, in an absolute form. There is a world of difference between the sustained contentiousness of the Russian exiles, in which it would never have occurred to anyone *not* to disagree with Lenin or with anyone else, and the rigidity of the pious ritual that succeeded it after the Bolsheviks became the apex of an actual society and a dehydrated Lenin had become the senior Father of the Church.

This ikonization of the Bolshevik Party, which has borne such strange fruits, was rooted at its inception in the extraordinary glamour that attended the emergence of the first Socialist party to become a world power. None of the Opposition elements was capable of waging a genuine struggle for the control of the Party: they were all paralysed by a profound inhibition due to the extraordinary success of the Party machine, pieced together by Stalin, in identifying itself with the Party as cult—with the Party as the voice of the 'inalienable class interests' of the proletariat.

Even Trotsky, the most formidable internal critic of the régime, though he might attack every single Bolshevik leader with all the virulence of his brilliant, acid-dipped pen, behaved as though the Party itself were sacrosanct. Individual Bolsheviks were mere men, weak, fallible, and prone to bafflement by the Dialectic, but the Party—the Party that in October had soared aloft out of the morass of its mortal elements into the stratosphere of the Absolute—the Party was inviolate in the bosom of History.

All Stalin's opponents were fundamentally in this insoluble psychological dilemma: within the Party they had already lost control of the machine that with bewildering rapidity was coming to dominate theoretical discussion, and consequently they would have had to step outside the Party in order to carry on a struggle against him. But stepping outside the Party was unthinkable; according to its own myth the Party was ritually unique as the locus of dogma and brute force combined. The lynchpin of this inhibition was of course a tidy piece of Marxist reasoning: if parties represent class interests, and the Bolshevik Party represents the proletariat, stepping outside the Party would automatically place the schismatic at the service of some other class, and in the event this could only be a counter-revolutionary class. *Ergo*, the factional dispute had to be confined within the Party.

But within the Party Stalin's grip on the administrative apparatus was rapidly narrowing down the area in which manœuvring was still possible, and this psychological dilemma, however cogent Marxists found the reasoning behind it, could only be baffling. In fact it enabled Stalin to disarm one oppositional group after another by exploiting their common acceptance of the moral and material supremacy of the Party. He did this, moreover, without their grasping—until too late—either the source of his power or the personal qualities which, allied with his strategic position, made him a formidable opponent. The inevitably expanded rôle of administration, after the conquest of the State, and the attendant magnification of the administrators, seem to have been ignored even by the most astute theorists in the movement.

The question of the Bolshevik Party's incorruptibility became a matter of basic principle precisely because the revolutionary act of seizing power with no allies wrenched the Party out of the organic process of social evolution. Lenin himself had been perfectly aware of the dangers inherent in launching a Socialist experiment without political democracy. As a consistent democrat—in theory—he had foreseen the risk in a characteristic statement made in 1905: 'Whoever wants to approach Socialism by any path except that of political democracy will inevitably arrive at the most absurd and reactionary conclusions, political and economic.' And once he had decided to commit himself—and see, it was obvious that the clamping of the Party strait-jacket on the Russian economy excluded the possibility of a democratic régime.

It was this that made the personal quality of the Bolsheviks of vital importance, since the only thing that presumably could mitigate the suppression of the democratic process—devotion to which had not been a mere foible but a matter of hard-headed politics—was the existence of a pure and high-minded Bolshevik Party, tempered in political struggle and holding the credentials of a lifetime of service to the cause. This was the only assurance, such as it was, of a *tour de force* that could avoid the ominous consequences foreseen by Lenin.

The Bolshevik Party thus assigned itself the rôle of moulding history in defiance of its conventional processes, and it was doubtless the crucial importance this gave it that explains the curious blind spot of even uncompromising critics of the later régime like Trotsky with respect to the degeneration of a Socialist party in a primitive country. Too much was at stake for professional revolutionists to view with an unbiased eye the incalculable consequences of the failure of the European revolution to correct and safeguard the Bolshevik adventure.

The ikonization of the Party led not merely to the replacement of the Party's ideology by the Party's interests, but eventually to the decapitation of the Party by the physical extirpation of the original élite, together with their 'credentials'. Since the physical extirpation ran parallel with the deification of the former political caucus, the 'Old Bolsheviks', after a period of incubation during which Stalin's faction triumphantly consolidated its rule, were stripped naked of all honour when they were flung into the mangling-machine of the mass purges of 1936–38. While the mystic cult of the Party grew in sanctity, the flesh-and-blood members of the historic Party itself lost not only their lives but their political reputations. In this case death and dishonour were complementary.

. . .

A strange sense of fatality must move us as we discern in Sukhanov's account of the revolution the germ of a régime that has come to exercise a direct control over the lives of almost half the human race and a compelling influence on the entire world. For this is where it all began: ideas dreamed of for decades achieved their embodiment in the travail of 1917, and from the vantage-point of a generation we cannot but wonder at the passionate involvement of those who, all unsuspecting the Gargantua it would grow into, brought forth the infant organism.

Lenin's party, which was a dense compound of administrative and programmatic attributes, has branched out into two distinct phenomena. Its organizational preoccupation has achieved fruition in the vast executive apparatus of the Soviet Government, propped up on a ramified police power and elevated beyond anything but administrative contact with the masses. Its programmatic aspect, on the other hand, or 'ideology', has become the fountainhead of authority for *bona fide* mass movements throughout the world, largely through the prestige attaching to the Soviet Government as heir of the two revolutions of 1917.

There is a widespread reluctance to accept the authentic quality of these mass movements: it is based on a shallow misconception. Properly understood, it is precisely their authenticity that accentuates the egocentrism of the Soviet régime. For with respect to *programme* the Communist Parties no longer preach a radical upset in *social* relations; they stand everywhere for demands which from the point of view of programme alone are rather diffident—such Socialist and for that matter liberal commonplaces as land-reform, equitable taxation, 'peace', etc. The *characteristic* political element in all these minimal social demands is that they be realized by the Communist Parties, i.e., that they can be accomplished, specifically and exclusively, *only* by the Soviet Union and its instruments.

These two characteristic aspects of the régime—programme and apparatus—are now distinct, in the sense that whereas the original Bolshevik Party was a unitary organism in which apparatus and programme were inextricably intertwined, the Soviet Government now has an external, engineering relationship to the mass movements under its control. It is not itself an element in agitation, but administers it, manipulating the national mass movements in its own state interests. It must, however, be remembered that the effectiveness of these mass movements lies precisely in the degree to which they reflect—'representatively'—the spontaneous hurly-burly of society. If this were not the source of the magnetism of Communism the problem facing the adversaries of the Soviet Government would be exclusively technical, that is, military or bureaucratic.

It is this union of organization and idea, whose potency in our era derives ultimately from the fabulous growth of technology and the consequent shrinking of the world, that now holds our generation transfixed. And 1917 in Russia gave this union body, shape, and direction.

As we open Sukhanov's book the personages of that primordial drama, all of whom, in the wake of a single turbulent generation, have become shadowy memories or lifeless mummies, awaken to the urge of life, and twitch and tumble once again. This is where it all began. The stage is set, and Sukhanov carries us, dreamlike, to the original act of creation.

J. C.

New York, 1954

ADDENDUM (1984)

THIRTY years ago, when I wrote the Introduction to the first edition of Sukhanov's Personal Record, a situation that had baffled Sukhanov himself was still unclear. It had to do with the paramount conundrum of the Bolshevik coup d'état: How could Trotsky have replaced Lenin as its stage-manager?

Trotsky was a new recruit to the Bolshevik Party; for a decade beforehand he had been the target of venomous diatribes by Lenin and his entourage and had, of course, responded in kind. Yet in the event Trotsky not only stage-managed the putsch but formulated its political justification.

The very existence of this conundrum has been camouflaged by the spate of propaganda emanating from the Soviet government and from Trotsky himself, who a few years after the putsch became the most celebrated enemy of the parvenu regime and in 1940 its outstanding victim.

The circumstances that obliged Lenin to flee the scene in July 1917 are well-known: the anti-Bolshevik press campaign launched during the "July Days" revolved around the charge that Lenin, thought to be preparing a putsch, had been subsidized by the German Imperial Government. Lenin fled Petrograd, in fact, to save his life: Trotsky, immune as a new Bolshevik to this particular charge, was the only figure capable, as President of the Soviet, of conducting the putsch on behalf of the Bolshevik Party.

Sukhanov believed Lenin to be innocent: to his mind, therefore, Lenin's flight was wholly inexplicable. Yet it was precisely this charge that was to explain the emergence of Trotsky as a state figure.

The German Imperial Government had been distributing vast sums of money, as far afield as South America. Its programme for Russia had been inspired by Alexander Israel Helphand, a Marxist, one of the most gifted—and least remembered—personages of the Russian revolutionary movement.

A few years before the war broke out Helphand had moved to the Balkans, where he amassed a fortune in business; no doubt he was the only Marxist multi-millionaire in history. In January 1915 he proposed to the German Ambassador in Constantinople a scheme to undermine the Tsarist Government by utilizing Russian dissidents and the agitation for independence on the part of various ethnic minorities. Distracted by a two-front war, allured by the prospect of immobilizing the eastern front, the German Imperial Government had accepted his proposal at once; it began funneling substantial sums to dissident groups in Russia.

After the Tsarist short-circuit in February, the only group still determined to sabotage the front, despite the transformation of Russia under its Socialist leadership, was the Bolshevik Party: shortly before Lenin's arrival in Petrograd in April, the Bolshevik Party began receiving the German subsidy, camouflaged by Helphand's international trading network, based in Scandinavia, which was carrying on a brisk trade between Germany and Russia at the height of the war.

The German subsidy was enormous (the equivalent today of $800 million). It sustained a gigantic press (some 41 periodicals) as well as the Party's agitation and other activities far beyond the Bolsheviks' meagre resources. The subsidy was continued until the summer of 1917, more than half a year *after* the putsch, i.e., until the very eve of the German collapse in 1918.

In 1921, two articles by Eduard Bernstein, the celebrated Marxist theoretician and one of the key figures in the German Social-Democratic government that succeeded the Kaiser, appeared in the *Vorwärts*, the official organ of the German Social-Democratic Party and hence of the German Government, mentioning the actual sum of money given to the Bolsheviks. The theme was dropped, and for decades there was no detailed documentation.

But with the publication in 1958 of German Foreign Office

memoranda and with a life of Helphand that appeared in 1965, the story of this subterranean alliance—for compelling reasons never admitted by either side—has been substantiated beyond doubt.*

In 1917, though it was obvious that Bolshevik revenues (membership dues, gifts from supporters, etc.) could not explain the Party's vast press, nothing was done about it before July: despite differences with rivals in the revolutionary movement, Lenin had the backing of all left wing, and for that matter, liberal groups: there could be "no enemy on the Left."

In July 1917, accordingly, when Lenin fled the country, he had good reason to—high treason in wartime. The "leak" of the German subsidy was based on puerilely forged documents, but it would have been out of the question for Lenin to be subjected to an official enquiry. Trotsky, on the other hand, immune to the charge, could present his talents to the Bolsheviks on the basis of a common "view"—that under certain conditions a Marxist party could take power in a backward peasant country.

Moreover, with his authority as chairman of the Soviet, which he was elected to shortly before the putsch, Trotsky could formulate it (in sharp opposition to Lenin's own conception of it as a purely Bolshevik operation) as an enterprise of the more or less democratically elected Soviet. This imposture, remarkably successful, won over the bulk of non-Bolshevik left wing and liberal opinion both at the time and during the subsequent Civil War. It has, indeed, survived in the very name of the Soviet Union.

This basic paradox in the genesis of the Soviet regime has been systematically glossed over by all apologists, notably Isaac Deutscher, whose million-word trilogy on Trotsky's life slides past the whole question, like all other questions distasteful to doctrinaires, with an anodyne phrase or two.

Sukhanov himself, while devoting in his chapter on the "July Days" an intriguing description to the furore concerning the (imperfect) disclosure of Lenin's connection with the German Imperial Government, seems to have been in the dark about the true situation.

* See my *Trotsky*, London and New York, 1975, and Z.A.B. Zeman and W. B. Scharlau, *The Merchant of Revolution: The Life of Alexander Israel Helphand (Parvus)*, London and New York, 1965.

Strongly opposed to Lenin's dictatorial intransigence, Sukhanov, for just that reason, believed in his sincerity. He thought it outrageous for Lenin to be accused of being in the pay of the German General Staff—"a monstrous slander . . . vile and shameful from every point of view" (p. 472) and hence found Lenin's flight wholly baffling, another proof of the complexity of his character; Sukhanov seemed unaware of the commonsense reasons for it. Yet by showing that—despite later Bolshevik explanations of Lenin's flight as due to the possibility of a lynching in the overheated atmosphere of the times—Lenin could have been in no danger whatever—if he had been innocent—he confirms in his own way the compelling reasons for the flight.

On the other hand, to be sure, Sukhanov, writing under the Soviet regime, might have been guided by mere prudence: no Soviet citizen, then or now, could have dared to air any speculation as to whether Lenin had collaborated with the German General Staff for any reason whatsoever! Or, in other words, question the legitimacy of the Bolshevik regime.

In retrospect, of course, it would seem obvious that this murderous alliance between the Bolsheviks and the German General Staff, in which each side was gambling on the destruction of the other, was simply won, historically, by the Bolsheviks. They were saved by the German debacle.

J. C.

New York, 1984

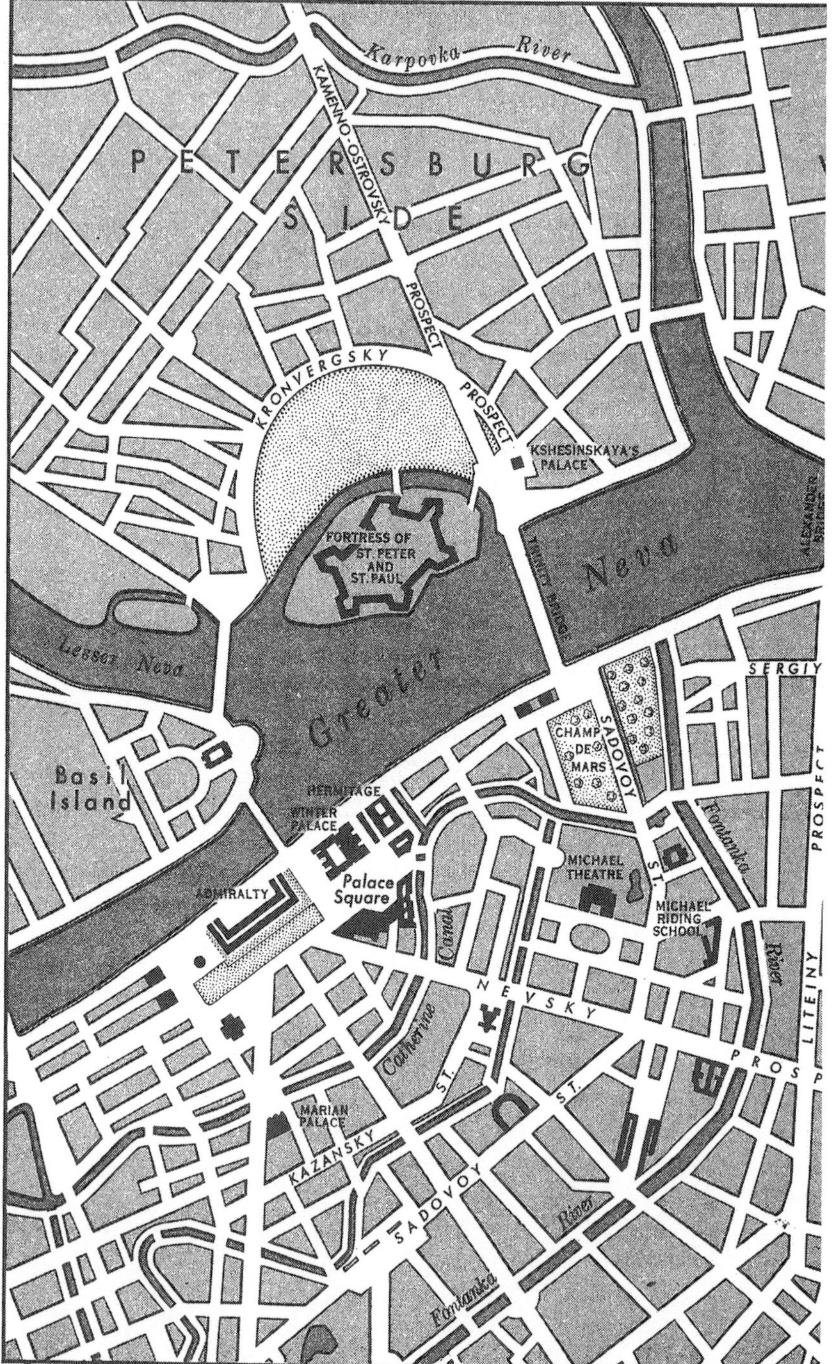
Karpovka River
KAMENNO-OSTROVSKY PROSPECT
PETERSBURG SIDE
KRONVERGSKY PROSPECT
KSHESINSKAYA'S PALACE
ALEXANDER BRIDGE
FORTRESS OF ST. PETER AND ST. PAUL
TRINITY BRIDGE
Neva
Lesser Neva
Greater
SERGIY
CHAMP DE MARS
SADOVOY ST.
Basil Island
HERMITAGE
WINTER PALACE
Fontanka
PROSPECT
MICHAEL THEATRE
Palace Square
ADMIRALTY
Canal
MICHAEL RIDING SCHOOL
River
NEVSKY PROSPECT
LITEINY
Catherine
MARIAN PALACE
KAZANSKY ST.
SADOVOY ST.
River
Fontanka

City Map of St. Petersburg

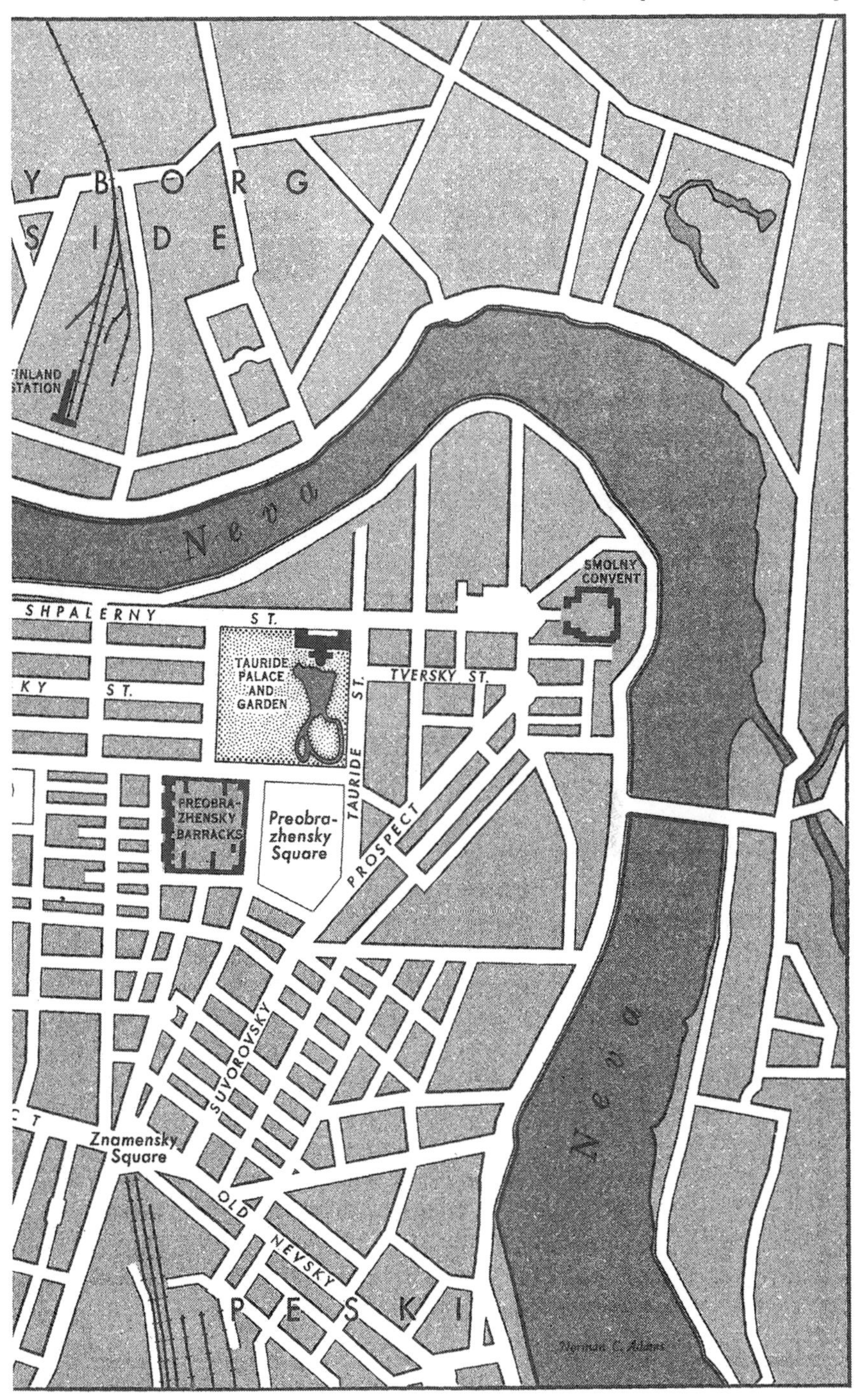

Part I

THE COLLAPSE OF THE TSARIST RÉGIME AND THE FORMATION OF THE FIRST REVOLUTIONARY GOVERNMENT

February 23rd–March 2nd, 1917

CHAPTER 1

PROLOGUE

February 21st–24th, 1917

I HAD been banished from St. Petersburg by May 10, 1914. At that time I was editor of the non-party but Left-wing *Sovremennik* (Contemporary), which took an internationalist line during the war, to the great dissatisfaction of its 'defensist' Petersburg contributors but the equal satisfaction of its *émigré* contributors, most of whom had rallied to the banner of Zimmerwald.[1] Though under sentence of banishment, I spent most of my time, up to the revolution itself, living underground in the capital—sometimes on a false passport, sometimes sleeping in a different place every night, sometimes slipping past the night-porter in the shadows as a 'frequent visitor'[2] to my own flat, where my family was living.

From November 1916 on I was on the staff of Maxim Gorky's *Letopis* (Chronicle), and practically its principal contributor, keeping the entire magazine going under the Damocles' sword of police repression. Moreover, my illegal position did not stop me from working as an economist, under my own name, in a government department, the Ministry of Agriculture, in a section that dealt with the irrigation of Turkestan.

Such were my official position, rank, and titles when the revolution of 1917 overtook me.

* * *

Tuesday, February 21st. I was sitting in my office in the Turkestan section. Behind a partition two typists were gossiping about food difficulties, rows in the shopping queues, unrest among the women, an attempt to smash into some warehouse.

'D'you know,' suddenly declared one of these young ladies, 'if you ask me, it's the beginning of the revolution!'

These girls didn't understand what a revolution was. Nor did

[1] A symbol of Socialist internationalism during the war, from the programme of the Conference of international Socialists opposed to the war that was held in Zimmerwald, Switzerland, in 1915. (Ed.)

[2] i.e., not on the list of tenants all porters were obliged to keep for the police. (Ed.)

I believe them for a second. But in those days, sitting over my irrigation systems and aqueducts, over my articles and pamphlets, my *Letopis* manuscripts and proofs, I kept thinking and brooding about the inevitable revolution that was whirling down on us at full speed.

In this period of the agony of Tsarism, the attention of Russian, or at any rate of Petersburg 'society', and of political circles in the capital revolved primarily around the State Duma[1] convened on February 14th. By some people—the more conservative Left (Socialist) elements—the workers' street demonstrations under the slogans of 'Bread!' and 'Down with the Autocracy!' were linked to this date. Elements further to the Left, including myself, spoke out at various party meetings *against* tying up the workers' movement with the Duma. For bourgeois Duma circles had given proof enough, not only of their inability to join the proletariat even against Rasputin, but also of their mortal fear even of utilizing the strength of the proletariat in the struggle for a constitutional régime or for 'carrying on the war to total victory'.

This fear was completely justified. It was possible, of course, to summon up a spirit, but to force it into one's own service—never. And the Progressive Bloc[2] of the Duma, which embodied the attitude of the entire propertied bourgeoisie,[3] was in favour only of sharpening its weapons for use against the proletarian movement. Miliukov,[4] its leader, had declared not long before

[1] This was the Fourth Duma (Parliament), elected in 1912. The State Duma, created by the October Manifesto of 1905, was the lower house of the legislature and (except for the representatives of five large cities) was indirectly elected. The Ministers, who were appointed by the Tsar, were not responsible to the Duma, and its powers and influence, limited enough in theory, were in practice almost non-existent. (Ed.)

[2] A patriotic oppositional majority, including all the Duma fractions as well as national groups (Poles, Lithuanians, Jews, Muslims, etc.). On the Left the Social-Democrats and the Trudoviks (see note, p. 17) were out, on the Right the Black *Hundred* (see note, p. 47). (Ed.)

[3] i.e., the bourgeoisie whose right to vote was based on a rather high property qualification (Russian *tsenz, tsenzovoy*). (Ed.)

[4] Miliukov, Pavel Nikolayevich (1859–1943): leader and one of the founders (in 1905) of the 'Cadets', a colloquial name for the Constitutional Democrats (taken from the Russian initials), later also called 'Party of the People's Freedom'. This was a large liberal party that favoured a constitutional monarchy, or even, eventually, a republic. It was roughly the party of progressive landowners, the middle class, and middle-class intellectuals. Miliukov was a member of the Third and Fourth Dumas. (Ed.)

that he was ready to renounce even his 'total victory', even the Dardanelles, even the service of the gallant Allies, if all these were attainable only at the price of a revolution. And now, in view of the rumours about the forthcoming workers' demonstration, this same Miliukov published his memorable address to the workers, in which every wartime movement of theirs against the Government was declared to have been fomented by the Secret Police and by *provocateurs*.

Finally, the burning question for the Petersburg politicians was the transfer to the Town Council of the task of provisioning the capital. For the Petersburg liberal and democratic[1] circles this was the catchword of the moment.

Not one party was preparing for the great upheaval. Everyone was dreaming, ruminating, full of foreboding, feeling his way . . .

These philistine girls whose tongues and typewriters were rattling away behind the partition didn't know what a revolution was. I believed neither them, nor the inflexible facts, nor my own judgement. Revolution—highly improbable! Revolution!—everyone knew this was only a dream—a dream of generations and of long laborious decades. Without believing the girls, I repeated after them mechanically:

'Yes, the beginning of the revolution.'

* * *

On Wednesday and Thursday—February 22nd and 23rd—the movement in the streets became clearly defined, going beyond the limits of the usual factory meetings. At the same time the feebleness of the authorities was exposed. They were plainly not succeeding—with all the machinery they had been building up for decades—in suppressing the movement at its source. The city was filled with rumours and a feeling of 'disorders'.

As far as scale went, similar disorders had taken place scores of times in our day. And if there was anything distinctive here it was just this irresolution of the authorities, who were obviously neglecting to deal with the movement. But these were 'disorders'—there was still no revolution. A favourable outcome was not only not discernible as yet, but not one of the parties was even

[1] Sukhanov uses the words 'democracy', 'democratic', etc., essentially in contrast to the old Tsarist régime, and not *necessarily* to the bourgeoisie, though sometimes he narrows them to refer to the peasantry and working class together. (Ed.)

steering towards it; they merely strove to exploit the movement for agitational purposes.

On Friday the 24th the movement swept over Petersburg like a great flood. The Nevsky and many squares in the centre were crowded with workers. Fugitive meetings were held in the main streets and were dispersed by Cossacks and mounted police—but without any energy or zeal and after lengthy delays. The Petersburg military commander, General Khabalov, got out a proclamation, which essentially only served to reveal the impotence of the authorities, pointing out that repeated warnings had been without effect and promising to take the sternest measures—in the future. Naturally this had no result, but it was another sign of helplessness.

The movement was plainly out of hand. A new situation, distinct from the previous disorders, was apparent to every attentive observer. On Friday I began categorically maintaining that we were dealing with a revolution, as an accomplished fact. However, I was waved aside as an optimist.

It seemed to me the evidence was already sufficient, and my thoughts were already turning in another direction, towards the *political problem.*

We had to aim at a radical political overturn. That was clear. But what was to be its programme? Who was to be the successor of the Tsarist autocracy? This was the point on which my attention was focused that day.

I won't say this enormous problem presented many difficulties to me at the time. Later I pondered over it much more and felt some doubt as to whether its solution at the time had been correct. During the shilly-shallyings of the Coalition and the smothering of the revolution by the Kerensky–Tereshchenko–Tsereteli policies in August–September 1917,[1] and also after the Bolshevik insurrection, it often seemed to me that the solution of this problem in the February days could have, and for that matter should have, been different. But at the time I decided this problem of 'high policy' almost without any hesitation.

The Government that was to take the place of Tsarism must be exclusively bourgeois. Trepov[2] and Rasputin could and

[1] see Parts V and VI. (Ed.)

[2] A non-political, personal friend of the Tsar's, who had been called upon, and failed, to save the situation. He was the son of D. F. Trepov, a founder of the Black Hundred (see p. 47) and former Governor-General of St. Petersburg. (Ed.)

should be replaced only by the bosses of the Progressive Bloc. This was the solution to be aimed at. Otherwise the overturn would fail and the revolution perish.

My starting-point was the complete disintegration of democratic Russia under the autocracy. At that time the democratic movement had control of no strong organization, whether political, trade-union, or municipal. And in its state of disintegration the proletariat, isolated as it was from other classes, could create only fighting organizations which, while representing a real force in the class struggle, were not a genuine element of State power.

This disintegrated democratic movement, moreover, if it were to make an attempt to govern, would have had to accomplish the impossible: the technique of State administration in the given conditions of war and destruction was far beyond the capacity of the democratic movement in isolation. The destruction of the State and its economic organism was already immense. Industry, transport, and supply had been enfeebled by the autocracy. The capital was starving. Not only could the State machine not stand idle for a single moment, but it had to find new energy and increased resources, without loss of time, for a colossal technical task. And if the Government were one which was incapable of setting in motion all the cogs of the State mechanism, the revolution would not hold out.

The entire available state machinery, the army of bureaucrats, the *Zemstvos*[1] and municipalities, which had had the co-operation of all the forces of the democracy, could obey Miliukov, but not Chkheidze.[2] There was, however, and could be, no other machinery.

But all this was, so to speak, *technique*. The other aspect of the matter was *political*. Setting up a democratic Government and by-passing the Progressive Bloc not only meant not utilizing at

[1] *Zemstvos*: established in 1864 as one of Alexander II's Great Reforms. An autonomous elected institution with a high property qualification. The *Zemstvos* were important culturally and economically; they established throughout Russia schools, hospitals, etc., and created cadres of *Zemstvo* intellectuals—statisticians, physicians, teachers—who constituted the so-called Third Estate, and played a very important rôle in the Russian revolutionary movement. They were dissolved after the October Revolution. (Ed.)

[2] Chkheidze, Nikolai Semyonovich (1864–1926): a Georgian, leader of the Menshevik fraction of the Social-Democratic Party in the Third and Fourth Dumas. (Ed.)

the critical moment the only state apparatus available, it also meant rallying the whole of propertied Russia against the democratic movement and the revolution. The whole of the bourgeoisie as one man would have thrown all the strength it had in the scales on the side of Tsarism and formed with it a strong and united front—against the revolution. It would have roused up against the revolution the entire middle class and the press at a time when hunger and disorganization were threatening to smash the revolution at any moment and Nicholas II was still at liberty and calling himself Tsar of all the Russias. In these circumstances a Socialist seizure of power would mean the inevitable and immediate failure of the revolution. At that moment, in February, the first revolutionary Government could only be a bourgeois one.

There was also another argument, of narrower scope but to me equally convincing. During the war I was one of the two or three writers who managed to advocate the anti-defensist Zimmerwald position in the legal press. And in particular, during the first days of the war, when patriotic enthusiasm seemed universal and people with a correct estimate of the meaning of the war and Tsarist Russia's place in it were absolutely impossible to find even amongst the Socialists then in Russia (Gorky was an exception), I resolutely spurned all 'patriotic' notions. On the contrary, at that time I was guilty of something else—namely, a simplification of the proletarian class position (later taken at Zimmerwald), debasing it somewhat in the direction of that primitive 'defeatism' that characterized broad strata of Russian society during the Japanese war of 1905. In any case from the beginning of the war and up to the revolution every public action of mine was as far as possible a *struggle against the war*, a struggle for its liquidation.

And now, at the first thunder-clap of the revolutionary tempest, I was pulled up short before the practical impossibility of creating a purely democratic Government, for the reason—among others—that this would have meant the *immediate liquidation of the war* by the Russian democracy. For of course I considered it impossible for a democratic Government to continue the war, since the contradiction between participation in an imperialist war and victory for the democratic revolution seemed to me fundamental. But I thought it out of the question to add an immediate radical change in foreign policy, with all its unforeseeable consequences, to all the difficulties of a revolution. Moreover, any peace policy worthy of the 'dictatorship of the proletariat' must involve all the colossal tasks of demobilization and the transfer of industry to a peace-time basis, with the consequent large-scale shutting down of factories and mass unemployment at a moment when the national economy was completely disorganized.

It seemed to me absolutely indispensable to lay the problems of foreign policy temporarily on the shoulders of the bourgeoisie, in order to create the possibility of a struggle for the most rapid and painless liquidation of the war under a bourgeois Government that was carrying on the military policy of the autocracy. The *creation of the conditions* for the liquidation of the war, and not the liquidation itself—that was the fundamental problem of the overturn. And for this a bourgeois, not a democratic, Government was essential.

In general the solution of the problem of power seemed to me self-evident. And during the first revolutionary upsurge, February 24th–25th, my attention was taken up not by the programmatic aspect, so to speak, of this political problem, but by its other, *tactical* side.

Power must go to the bourgeoisie. But was there any chance that they would take it? What was the position of the propertied elements on this question? Could they and would they march in step with the popular movement? Would they, after calculating all the difficulties of their position, especially in foreign policy, accept power from the hands of the revolution? Or would they prefer to dissociate themselves from the revolution which had already begun and destroy the movement in alliance with the Tsarist faction? Or would they, finally, decide to destroy the movement by their 'neutrality'—by abandoning it to its own devices and to mass impulses that would lead to anarchy?

This again was just one aspect of the matter. The other was: what was the position in this question of the Socialist parties, which ought to assume control of the movement that had now begun? Would all the Socialist groups unite in the solution of the problem of power, or might the unleashed elemental forces be exploited by a few of them for some insanely infantile attempt to establish the dictatorship of the proletariat and divide up at once the spoils that were still unwon?

And naturally, having put these questions, one must go further. If the correct solution of the problem of power could be wrecked from either side, was it not possible to take an active part now in the suitable manipulation of social forces, if only by seeking an appropriate compromise?

So on Friday the 24th, as the street movement swept in an ever-broadening flood through Petersburg, and when the revolution had become an objective fact and only its outcome was obscure, I scarcely listened to the uninterrupted accounts of street incidents. All my attention was directed at what was going on in the Socialist centres on the one hand and in the bourgeois circles, especially amongst the Duma fractions, on the other.

I knew a great many people in the most varied strata of the capital, but since there was almost no public opinion in Petersburg at that time and because of my illegal situation and my responsible literary work, I could not consider myself familiar with the moods of the various groups, who had been confronted with completely new problems during these days. I felt myself to be out of contact with the basic channel or channels where events now seemed to be forming. This sensation of isolation and helplessness, a longing to be near some sort of crucible of events, an unsatisfied desire to fling myself into the matrix of the revolution in order to do what I could, were my dominant feelings in those days.

* * *

The first thing to do was to collect information about this 'high policy'. It was necessary to visit those centres of both camps where one could get trustworthy intelligence. On Friday evening I 'phoned a well-known Petersburg political lawyer, traditionally considered a Bolshevik but more closely connected with the Petersburg radical groups—the ubiquitous and omniscient N. D. Sokolov, one of the principal personalities of the first period of the revolution. We arranged to convoke the representatives of different groups on the following day, Saturday, at 3 o'clock, in his apartment in the Sergiyevsky, to discuss the situation. At this conference I hoped to clear up for myself the position of the propertied as well as of the leading demo-

WORKERS LEAVING THE PUTILOV FACTORY AFTER THE PROCLAMATION OF A GENERAL STRIKE
February 1917

KSHESINSKAYA'S PALACE
Seat of the Central Committee of the Bolshevik Party

THE WINTER PALACE, FROM THE NEVA
Seat of the Kerensky Government after July

cratic elements. At the same time, as a representative of the Socialist Left I hoped to speak forcefully, if need arose, in support of a purely bourgeois revolutionary Government, and also to demand a compromise as indispensable in the interests of forming such a Government.

The character and limits of this compromise were clear. The mass street movement in the February days revealed no sort of purposefulness, nor was it possible to discern in it any kind of proper leadership. In general, as is always the case, the organized Socialist centres were not controlling the popular movement or leading it to any definite political goal. Of course our traditional, one might say ancient, national slogan, 'Down with the Autocracy', was on the lips of all the many street orators from the Socialist parties. But this was not yet a political programme; it was a negative idea that was taken for granted. The problem of *government* had not yet been put before the masses. And in particular the slogan of a 'Constituent Assembly', not being on the order of the day, but merely part of the general programme of all the Socialist parties, was left completely in the shadow during those days.

On the other hand, the street agitators developed at great length another slogan, with extremely grave and far-reaching implications. This was 'Down with the War', which dominated all the meetings of the February days.

The development of this slogan was quite inevitable. Russian Socialism, and the thinking Russian proletariat, unlike the Socialists of the Western European warring countries (with the exception of Italy), were for the most part resolutely against supporting the imperialist war. In the course of the war years our proletariat had been educated, as far as conditions allowed, in the spirit of Zimmerwald and the war against war. The defensist groups who had made themselves a niche in both capitals and here and there in the provinces had no authority whatever amongst the masses. There was nothing surprising or unexpected in the fact that a revolution against Tsarism should, at least amongst the proletariat of the capital, coincide with a movement in favour of peace. On the contrary, nothing else could have been expected of the street movement during the February days.

But at the same time it was quite clear that precisely this

character of the movement must determine the attitude of the entire bourgeoisie towards it and the whole revolution. If these elements could accept the idea of liquidating Tsarism at all they could do so primarily to win the war. And this was precisely what the struggle against Tsarism of all our liberal groups had degenerated into in the course of the war. The liquidation of the Rasputin régime had come to be conceived of by the entire bourgeoisie merely as a means of strengthening our military power.

Hence it was evident that the bourgeoisie could have nothing in common with a movement that undermined the idea of 'war to complete victory'. It saw, or at least spoke of, any such movement as simply the result of German provocation. All propertied circles must have decisively dissociated themselves from it, and not merely left it to its own devices but felt obliged to hand it over to be destroyed by the forces of Tsarist reaction, and themselves take what share they could in that destruction.

It was clear then *a priori* that if a bourgeois Government and the adherence of the bourgeoisie to the revolution were to be counted on, it was temporarily necessary to *shelve the slogans against the war*, and furl for a time the banner of Zimmerwald, which had become the banner of the Russian, and especially of the Petersburg, proletariat. This was self-evident to me—a Zimmerwaldite.

At the same time, if the creation of a propertied Government was plainly impossible without such a compromise, it was still quite unclear whether this compromise would suffice to attain its objective. *Without it* the bourgeoisie together with Tsarism would crush the movement, but would it by itself ensure a different outcome for the revolution? Would it at least secure the formation of a bourgeois Government?

Information concerning this was indispensable. What were the plans of the Miliukov–Guchkov[1] camp? It was also necessary

[1] Guchkov, Alexander Ivanovich (1862–1936): a wealthy Moscow capitalist, monarchist, and leader of the Octobrist Party, named for its support of the Imperial Manifesto of October 1905 that established the Duma. The Octobrist Party was the party of substantial commercial, industrial, and landowning interests. Though the party was monarchist, Guchkov was opposed to the dynasty during the First World War on patriotic grounds. He was an organizer of the palace revolution against the Tsar which the February Revolution prevented from maturing. He emigrated after the October Revolution. (Ed.)

to know just what the opposite camp thought about all this; it was impossible to conceal from oneself that the advanced Socialists were being burdened with an extraordinarily heavy task, and perhaps one beyond their capacity, which demanded not only a deep understanding of events, but also a restraint and submission to circumstances which to the outsider's eye might look like a betrayal of their basic principles and be misunderstood by the masses they were leading.

First of all a careful reconnaissance of the moods of both camps had to be made. The reports which came to me from both sides equally were extremely vague. In Duma circles, the question of a revolutionary Government had not even been raised. I could not see the slightest sign of any awareness among the parties or their leaders that the movement might end with a radical overturn. I could see only fear of the 'provocative' movement and the intention of coming to the aid of Tsarism and liquidating the 'disorders' with the 'full authority' of the Duma. I could see also an attempt by the bourgeois groups to use the movement as a counter in coming to terms with Tsarism for a joint struggle—at the cost of any concessions in politics and the organization of the Government.

The bourgeoisie was frightened by the movement and was not with it; therefore it was against it. But it could not afford to ignore it and make no use of it. *During these days the political slogan of the bourgeoisie, to which the entire radical intelligentsia also subscribed, was 'a Ministry responsible to the Duma'.*

At the same time attempts were made at a niggling solution of various urgent problems, attempts quite independent of the movement of the proletarian masses and, in the general situation, merely obscuring the issues with which our 'society' was confronted. Thus on Saturday a meeting of the Town Council with various public organizations and workers' representatives proposed, in an almost revolutionary manner, to take the business of supplying Petersburg into their own hands.

In sum, looked at from the bourgeois side, hardly anything was clear on Friday the 24th, and what was clear was rather inauspicious. A session of the Duma Steering Committee, to which great significance was ascribed, was called for the next day. I counted on hearing a report of the results at Sokolov's.

In the other camp representatives of the Bolsheviks and the

Socialist-Revolutionaries[1] of the Zimmerwald complexion had to be interviewed. Conversations with them gave me the same unfavourable impression. First of all the complete shapelessness of the movement and the absence of any strong, really authoritative centres were confirmed. Then I found complete indifference to the problems that were preoccupying me. Attention was wholly concentrated on immediate agitation based on general slogans and the immediate furtherance of the movement. Finally, my attempts to direct the thoughts of my interlocutors towards a concrete programme, and even more my propaganda for the creation of a revolutionary Government—even by way of a radical compromise—were received in a very sceptical and unfriendly spirit.

And yet, if these underground organizations could count on exercising any influence at all, it was just the Zimmerwaldite centres which could principally influence the movement. Thus the information obtainable both from this side and from the democratic camp was neither very specific nor very encouraging.

* * *

The movement of the Petersburg proletariat during those days and hours was not, however, confined to party agitation, factory meetings, and street demonstrations. There were attempts to create inter-party centres, there were joint conferences of active members of the various branches of the workers' movement—Duma deputies and representatives of the parties and of various trades and co-operatives. Meetings of this kind were held on Thursday and Friday. I was not present, but people who were told me afterwards that the discussions were chiefly devoted to the food question, or at any rate began with it. Afterwards, of course, they went on to the general situation, bringing to light only the bewilderment and confusion of the organizations.

[1] The Socialist-Revolutionaries (SRs): a party that arose in the beginning of the 20th century as a development of earlier Populist parties (see note, p. 16); it regarded terrorism as the most effective method of struggle against the autocracy, but also engaged in propaganda amongst the workers and peasants. It boycotted the elections to the First Duma, although a number of sympathisers took part in them and in the First Duma formed the fairly substantial Trudovik group, controlled largely by Populists and SRs. They took a negative stand on the October Revolution, with the exception of the so-called Left SRs, who split from the party. The party was finally dissolved after the SR trial of 1920. (Ed.)

Reliable reporters said that Chkheidze, who was present, was indecision personified, and could only urge them to keep in step with the Duma. He represented the Right wing of the meetings and was disinclined to believe in the wide range of the movement. The Left, on the contrary, hailed the revolution with delight, and held that it was vital and urgently necessary to create fighting organizations of workers in the capital. F. A. Cherevanin, the old liquidator[1] and defensist, who was one of those who represented this Left view, also originated, so I was told, the idea of holding immediate elections in the Petersburg factories for a *Soviet of Workers' Deputies*.

In any case instructions for the elections were issued by this meeting. These instructions were instantly taken up by the party organizations and, as is known, successfully carried out in the factories of the capital.

But I know that the *political* problem was never officially raised or resolved at these meetings. They have great historical merit for having prepared the *technique and organization* of the revolutionary forces, but no more. As for the political position of their participants, there was a preponderance of Menshevik defensists, and there could be no doubt that when they put the problem to themselves the majority of them would decide in favour of a bourgeois Government. The only trouble was that they had no serious influence on the masses.

Meanwhile the movement kept growing. The impotence of the police machinery became more evident with every hour. Meetings were already taking place almost with permission, and the military units, in the person of their commanding officers, were failing to take active steps against the growing crowds that filled the main streets. Unexpectedly the Cossack units displayed special sympathy with the revolution at various points, when in direct conversations they emphasized their neutrality and sometimes showed a clear tendency to fraternize. And on Friday evening they were saying in the city that elections were being held in the factories for the Soviet of Workers' Deputies.

[1] i.e., one of those who after the dissolution of the Second Duma (1907) had held that the conspiratorial and revolutionary activities of the Social-Democrats should be abandoned and the legal workers' organisations be built up until they were strong enough to defend their economic and social interests. Lenin bitterly attacked those who took this view as 'Liquidators'. (Ed.)

CHAPTER 2

THE LAST THROW

February 25th–26th

On Saturday the 25th Petersburg seethed in an atmosphere of extraordinary events from the morning on. The streets, even where there was no concentration of people, were a picture of extreme excitement. I was reminded of the 1905 Moscow insurrection. The entire civil population felt itself to be in one camp united against the enemy—the police and the military. Strangers passing by conversed with each other, asking questions and talking about the news, about clashes with and the diversionary movements of the enemy.

But something else was noticeable that hadn't existed in the Moscow insurrection: the wall between the two camps—the people and the authorities—was not so impenetrable; a certain diffusion could be felt between them. This increased the excitement and filled the masses with something like enthusiasm.

Khabalov's proclamations were quite openly torn down from the walls. Policemen suddenly vanished from their posts.

Factories were at a standstill. No trams were running. I don't remember whether any newspapers appeared that day, but in any case events had far outstripped anything the half-stifled press of the day could have conveyed to the people.

That morning I proceeded as usual to my Turkestan office at the end of the Kamenno-ostrovsky Prospect, but naturally not for any reason connected with the irrigation of Turkestan. I rang up A. V. Peshekhonov,[1] inviting him to come to the Sergiyevsky, to N. D. Sokolov's, at 3 o'clock. In accordance with the conspiratorial habits well known to every Russian intellectual, he

[1] Peshekhonov, Alexei Vasilyevich (1867–1934): a prominent Populist journalist, later to become Supply Minister in the Provisional Government. The Populists were revolutionists with Socialist ideals who were, however, indifferent or hostile to Marxist theory. They thought the peasants rather than the working class should lead in the overthrow of Tsarism and the transformation of Russia. The word refers both to the terrorists who hoped to destroy Tsarism and rouse the peasants by the 'propaganda of the deed', and to the gentlest and most idealistic Socialists who hoped to transform Russia by 'going to the people'. (*Narodnik* in Russian.) (Ed.)

asked for no details—neither why, nor who else would be there; he promised to come himself or send one of his associates.

Before 2 o'clock, after having invited by telephone still another representative of a Left-wing organization, I went along to the Sergiyevsky, to an apartment as well known to all radical and democratic Petersburg as to the whole of the police force...

On the way, I dropped in at the editorial offices of the *Letopis* in the Monetny. No one, either on the editorial staff or in the office, was doing any work. They were all full of the events and the news. I was told which districts of the city were cordoned off by police and troops, and which was the best way to get through to the Tauride Gardens. But these accounts turned out to be false—for the reason that the actions of the authorities showed no trace of determination and still less of planning. Districts were cordoned off and released without any system or sense. In general the movement swept through the streets quite freely, and even the most thorough-going pessimists began to be persuaded of the impotence of the Khabalovs and Trepovs.

Near the entrance to the *Letopis* offices, at the gates of the neighbouring factory, I met a small group of civilians, workers by the look of them.

'What do they want?' said one grim-looking fellow. 'They want bread, peace with the Germans, and equality for the Yids.'

'Right in the bull's eye,' I thought, delighted with this brilliant formulation of the programme of the great revolution.

A disappointment awaited me at N. D. Sokolov's. The meeting bore no resemblance to a representative gathering of organized groups or democratic fractions. It had a quite haphazard and at the same time uniform character. Most of those who came were representatives of the radical Populist intelligentsia. In this sort of meeting even a theoretical examination of the questions which interested me didn't have much point.

Sokolov was expecting some authorized representatives of the Bolsheviks, but not one of them turned up. In their place Kerensky[1] appeared; he had come straight from a session of the

[1] Kerensky, Alexander Fyodorovich (1881–1970): at this time leader of the Trudoviks (Labourites) in the Duma, later to become Premier. The Trudoviks were a group of Populist intellectuals who defended the peasants as against the landowners. They were not, however, much more radical than the Cadets (see note p. 4). (Ed.)

Steering Committee of the Duma, and naturally could be a unique source of information about the mood and plans of the leading political circles of the bourgeoisie.

Kerensky, as always excitable, emotional, and somewhat theatrical, spoke for the most part of the panic and confusion of the mass of the bourgeois deputies. As far as the leading circles were concerned, all their thoughts and efforts boiled down, not to shaping the revolution, or joining it and trying to make themselves the crest of the wave, but exclusively to avoiding it. Attempts were being made at deals with Tsarism; the political game was in full swing. All this was not only independent of the popular movement but at its expense and obviously aimed at its destruction.

At this moment the position of the bourgeoisie was quite clear: it was a position on the one hand of keeping their distance from the revolution and betraying it to Tsarism, and on the other of exploiting it for their own manœuvres. But this was far from a position of *alliance* with it, even in the form of patronizing it.

Since Kerensky's account had given me no information on those aspects of the matter that specially interested me, I made a few hopeless efforts to clear up the problem for myself by direct and indirect questioning. Kerensky himself, of course, might have some relevant information, through his uninterrupted contact with various Duma circles. But these efforts of mine elicited nothing except a bewilderment which showed that for Kerensky, as well as for some of his supporters who were present, my way of formulating the problems of the future Government seemed futile and, in any case, ill-timed and irrelevant. I came up against the same mood in these people that I had encountered the day before amongst the Left (Zimmerwald) groups and that I also encountered later on, up to the very moment of the formation of the first revolutionary Government.

Kerensky assumed the polemical tone usual in his conversations with me and soon began to lose his temper; I preferred to cut short a conversation which had not aroused enough interest in those present.

* * *

New people kept coming to Sokolov's flat bringing with them reports, all agreeing, of the unprecedented scale of the movement in the streets. The central districts looked like a continuous mass-meeting, and the populace seemed specially drawn to Znamensky Square. There, from the plinth of the statue of Alexander III, speakers of the Left parties spoke uninterruptedly and without any interference. The basic slogan was, as before, 'Down with the War', which together with the autocracy was interpreted as the source of all misfortunes and especially of the breakdown in supplies.

The reports spoke also of the growing demoralization of the police and troops. Mounted and unmounted police and Cossack units in great numbers were patrolling the streets, slowly pushing their way through the crowds. But they took no action, and this immensely cheered the demonstrators. The police and troops limited themselves to removing red banners wherever this was technically convenient and could be done without a scuffle.

At this time there was the first report about a symptomatic 'excess' in some Cossack unit. A police inspector, on horseback at the head of a police detachment, attacked some flag-bearer or orator with his sabre, whereupon a Cossack nearby flew at the inspector and slashed off his hand. The inspector was carried off, but the incident had no sequel in the street.

Our conference finally took on the character of a haphazard private conversation. I remember Sokolov telling me in particular something I appreciated only later on. As a defensist he indicated the danger of the anti-war slogans around which the popular movement was revolving and on which the party orators were chiefly concentrating the attention of the masses; however, he did not emphasize the aspect of the question that occupied me all this time—the inevitable refusal of the bourgeoisie to join the revolution in such circumstances—but referred to the inevitability of a split on this ground within the democratic movement itself and even within the proletariat. At that time I ascribed no importance to this point, merely because I had too strong a belief (perhaps exaggerated) in the exclusive rule over the masses of those parties and groups represented by the Socialist minority in Germany or France. Moreover the character of the approaching revolution was completely obscure; in particular no one could foresee the rôle in it of the army, made up as it was of officers and peasants. But a split within the most active revolutionary proletarian army cadres rapidly proved to be really a most important factor, in the light of which the entire 'military' policy of the revolutionary democracy had to be guided. At that time, however, I had no interest in this aspect of the matter, devoting most of my attention to the attitude of the *haute* bourgeoisie and their relations with the revolution.

As it happened, though, in our practical conclusions Sokolov and I were in complete agreement. As a man who had come out against the war more than others and more definitely, and as a writer who had a fairly solid reputation as a defeatist, an internationalist, and a hater of patriotism, I was urged by Sokolov to speak out now as decisively as possible against the anti-war slogans and to collaborate in seeing to it that the movement did not proceed under the cry of 'Down with the War'. He said that the appropriate arguments, coming from me, would be devoid of any counter-revolutionary character and be more convincing to the leaders of the movement. For if it began as a movement against the war, the revolution would quickly be undone by internal dissensions.

Whatever my attitude towards this argument, I was in wholehearted sympathy with its final conclusions and promised my full co-operation with the defensists and radical groups against consistent internationalist class principles—in fact against my own principles.

However, I felt myself completely cut off from the centres of the revolution and completely powerless to do anything. I did not claim for myself the slightest influence on the controlling centres of the movement. I must recall here that from 1906 or 1907 on I had no formal connexion with any party or organization. My 'wild' position naturally excluded the possibility of any direct activity in practical Socialism, to say nothing of leadership. I was primarily a writer. But nevertheless my literary work was closely tied up with the movement, and during the war, owing to accidental circumstances, my writings enjoyed wide popularity amongst active Socialists and served as material for their practical work. At the same time, without having any formal ties I was in fact, by virtue of personal acquaintance and professional connexions, linked to many, one might say all, the Socialist parties and organizations of Petersburg.

It is of no interest to describe my position among the parties and explain its causes. I shall simply say that from the time when I was editor of the *Sovremennik*—which I unquestionably succeeded in making a non-party literary centre for prominent Socialists of all shades—I had maintained rather close contacts with all the Socialist groups. Party centres knew me quite well and often made use of me. And in particular as an editor of the *Letopis* I kept up the closest relations with the literary Socialist *émigrés* of various tendencies. During the war people were always trying to attract me into various illegal literary enterprises of an internationalist complexion. Moreover, probably not one attempt of the inter-party blocs at unification or coalition during those last years was made without my participation. This was my situation during the revolution also.

At the time of the revolution this undoubtedly had some advantages from the point of view of ease of personal relationship and of mobility between those points which had the greatest importance and interest, but it deprived me of the advantages of being a party man and leader, for everybody still considered me 'wild' and an outsider.

Nevertheless it is essential to emphasize at this point the great difference between the Petersburg party centres at that time and those that sprang up during the revolution. This was that *there were no authoritative leaders on the spot* in any of the parties, almost without exception. They were in exile, in prison, or abroad. In the positions of the responsible heads of the great movement, at its most important moments, there were absolutely second-rate people, who may have been clever organizers but nevertheless were routine party hacks of the days of the autocracy. It was impossible to expect of them, in the great majority of cases, a proper political perspective in the new situation or any real political guidance of events. Placed beside such leaders of the movement I felt competent and useful. But I was cut off from the work they were doing; and at the time of my conversation with Sokolov there was nothing in my mind but a consciousness of my inability to influence events in any way.

* * *

The gathering began to disperse, some going off into the streets, some into other rooms, some home. Kerensky rushed off, saying he was returning to the Duma, which was crowded with deputies from morning to night, and invited Zenzinov[1] and me to visit him in roughly an hour's time to hear the latest news. After talking about various topics for another half-hour at Sokolov's, Zenzinov and I quietly proceeded to Kerensky's. We were remembering Moscow in 1905, and going over scenes from the December uprising, in which both of us had taken part. But the district round the Sergiyevsky and the Tversky, and the Tauride Gardens, were quiet and empty. There is some interest in recording this. The people *were not gravitating toward the Duma*, had no interest in it, and did not think of making it the centre of the movement either politically or technically. Our liberal politicians later spent all their energies representing the Duma as the banner, and its fate as the cause, of the movement. But these attempts were all completely implausible.

We did not, however, find Kerensky at home. In the hall his two little boys, who knew what was going on, ran out to us and told us that 'Papa had just rung up from the Duma'. He had said there was shooting along the Nevsky, and a great many casualties.

At this point Kerensky's wife, Olga Lvovna, came back from her work. She was employed in some social institute or other, located around the centre of Nevsky Prospect near Kazansky Square. She had just seen from her windows a big demonstration making for Kazansky Square; it had been fired on, the shooting had gone on for a few minutes, and there had been a fight. But just which army unit had done the firing, and what the casualties were, it had been impossible either to see in the dusk or to find out.

Things were coming to a head. It was no longer thinkable for the authorities not to make some effort to suppress the disorders. That would mean the irrevocable laying down of their arms and the being confronted by an accomplished fact—the defeat of the 'existing order'. The authorities, without losing a single hour, *had to* find a suitable army or police unit and push it into action. Vacillation or procrastination was obviously and literally

[1] Zenzinov, Vladimir Mikhailovich (1881–1953): an SR from 1903; adherent of the terrorist wing of the party. Member of the Ex. Com. in 1917 and ardent partisan of Kerensky's. He was elected to the Constituent Assembly in 1918, and after its dissolution took up arms against the Bolsheviks. An *émigré* since 1921, first in France, then in the United States. He died in New York. (Ed.)

equivalent to death. The moment was decisive for the fate of age-old Tsarism. . . Just which unit fired on the Nevsky demonstration that evening of February 25th, I don't know to this day. But one way or another the authorities had gone over to the offensive. This was the turning point of events, which had entered a new phase.

If there had been adequate forces for an offensive, if it had been possible to terrorize the unarmed and still scattered populace and drive them home, then the movement might have been liquidated (though not for long) as 'disorders' had been liquidated dozens of times before. It was important to pass beyond the dead point, and with one stunning blow simultaneously destroy the morale of the masses and check any tendency to disintegration within the army. A risky, desperate, and perhaps final attempt had to be made without delay. It was made—and it proved to be the last.

When Zenzinov and I left Kerensky's it was already almost completely dark. After walking the length of the Tversky from Smolny,[1] past the dimly lit Tauride Palace and its silent square, we went along the Shpalerny. I made my way home to the Petersburg Side.

No shooting could be heard. Nearer the Liteiny, where we separated, we met a few small groups of workers who passed on rumours of the beginning of the offensive: bloody, though small, fights had begun somewhere in the working-class suburbs. A few of the biggest factories had been occupied, others were besieged by troops. Here and there the attackers had met with resistance—some pistol-shots from young workers, but mostly stones thrown by youths.

On the Vyborg Side, passers-by said, barricades were being constructed of tram-cars and telegraph poles.

* * *

After cutting across the ice on the empty Neva, from the Liteiny to Trinity Bridge, I called on Gorky in the Kronvergsky. I found a small group there, including the other editors

[1] The Smolny Institute, a building designed by Quarenghi. From 1808 to the middle of 1917 an exclusive college for the education of the young daughters of the nobility. The Petersburg Soviet and the Central Ex. Com. of the Soviet of Workers' and Soldiers' Deputies moved there on August 4th, 1917. (Ed.)

of the *Letopis*—Bazarov and Tikhonov, with whom, in discussing what was happening, I quickly got into a violent argument. Like the others I had spoken to, they refused to agree with me in placing the problem of the organization of the revolutionary Government in the forefront and were chiefly interested in the actual course of events, which they judged far more pessimistically than I; and they teased me for seeing mirages.

One after another people both known and unknown, to Gorky himself as well as to me, kept coming in. They came in for consultation, to share their impressions, to make inquiries, and to find out what was going on in various circles. Gorky naturally had connexions throughout Petersburg, from top to bottom. We began to talk, and we, the editors of the *Letopis*, soon set up a united front against representatives of the Left, the internationalist representatives of our own views, heedless of the charges of betrayal of our old watchwords at the decisive moment.

Meanwhile some fairly responsible Bolshevik leaders came along. And their flatfootedness or, more properly, their incapacity to think their way into the political problem and formulate it, had a depressing effect on us. But it must be said that our own arguments were not without some influence on these people, who had appeared straight from the turbulent excitement of workers' centres or party committees. In those days they were completely absorbed in a different kind of work, serving the technical needs of the movement, forcing a decisive set-to with Tsarism, and organizing propaganda and the illegal press. And our arguments compelled them to think about what was new in the vast problems which they now consciously confronted for the first time.

In these conversations Gorky took the most active part. Apart from the Bolsheviks, with whom Gorky traditionally had closer ties than with the other Socialist organizations, others came in too; a few of these in two more days were to be my colleagues on the Executive Committee. Gorky's flat had begun to be the natural centre, if not of any organization, at least of information, which attracted various elements involved in one way or another in the movement. We arranged to meet there the following day about noon.

Towards the time when house-gates in Petersburg were

usually locked, I left Gorky's house to go home, to give myself as usual time to slip past the house-porter and into my apartment unnoticed, by the back way. The streets were quiet. As before consciousness of my helplessness never left me; I felt a longing for more immediate activity.

* * *

The next day, Sunday, February 26th, I went over to Gorky's again. The streets were hung with General Khabalov's new proclamations, and others, torn down and crumpled, littered the ground. Publicly admitting in them his own helplessness and implying that his previous warnings had been of no avail, he was once again threatening decisive measures and a resort to arms against disorders and mobs.

And Sunday really was given over to decisive measures and a resort to arms. The last desperate throw was being made. What was at stake was the age-old régime, embodying not merely the bric-à-brac of old privileges but also the hopes of the bourgeoisie, who scented a more dangerous enemy. The day was passed in the last grapple, amid the sound of firing and the smoke of powder. Nightfall showed that the game was lost: by evening the card had been trumped.

The siege of factories and working-class districts continued and was intensified. Great numbers of infantry units were moved out into the streets: they cordoned off bridges, isolated various districts, and set about a thorough-going clearance of the streets.

Around 1 o'clock the infantry trained rifle-fire of great intensity on the Nevsky. The Prospect, strewn with corpses of innocent passers-by, was cleared. Rumours of this flew swiftly about the city. The inhabitants were terrorized, and in the central parts of the city the movement in the streets was quelled.

Towards 5 o'clock it might well have seemed that Tsarism had again won the throw and that the movement was going to be suppressed.

However, even in these critical hours the atmosphere in the streets was completely different from what must very often have been observed during the crushing of 'disorders'. And in spite of the panic of the urban population and the inevitable psychological reaction of the conscious democratic groups, this atmosphere continued to give every reason for the most legitimate optimism.

The difference from the previous 'disorders' consisted in the composition and the whole outward aspect of the troops, Cossacks, and even police, who were suppressing the movement. One of these units, perhaps of army cadets, was ordered to fire, and so terrorized the unarmed, scattered crowd. Others obediently formed dense cordons around a few points. Still others, also obeying orders, went around the city in groups as patrols. But all this had a rather casual, unserious, and unreal character. Both the cordons and the patrols looked as though they were hoping for organized attacks on themselves and seeking an occasion to surrender. Single policemen had long since completely vanished. The patrols, who were not marching but strolling around the city, were as a matter of fact disarmed in many places without offering serious resistance. Into every crowd and group an enormous number of soldiers' grey greatcoats had been 'organically assimilated'.

Around 2 or 3 o'clock a small group of us from Gorky's went out into the streets to see for ourselves.

From the Petersburg Side we tried to make our way to the Nevsky. As we went toward Trinity Bridge the crowd got denser and denser. Blocking the squares, the Kamenno-ostrovsky Prospect, and the gardens at the end of Trinity Bridge, it was breaking up into a multitude of groups, clustering round people who had returned to the Petersburg Side from the city.

Independently of sex, age, or condition, they were excitedly discussing the shooting of the casual, unorganized, and non-demonstrating crowd in the main streets of the centre. All the eye-witnesses agreed in their impression of the bewildered and terrified state of mind of the units involved who, a great distance away from the 'enemy', had opened up a disorderly fire down the length of the streets. They spoke of an enormous number of casualties, although of course their figures varied from a few dozen to many thousands.

We made our way to the bridge. There was a lively bustle on the wall of the Peter-Paul Fortress and armed detachments of infantry could be seen around the guns. The crowd expected some aggressive action from there and watched with curiosity, but it did not disperse.

On the bridge, shoulder to shoulder and barring the way, stood a cordon of Grenadiers. In spite of the presence of an officer, they were standing easy and conversing animatedly with the crowd on political topics. Agitators were haranguing them in quite unambiguous terms. Some soldiers were chuckling, others were listening in attentive silence. They refused to let anyone pass through the line on to the bridge, but a few individuals filtered through without being turned back. There was no direct insubordination, but they were obviously unsuitable material for any active operations, and there was clearly nothing for the officers to do but turn a blind eye on this scene of 'corruption'.

For this detachment to take aim and open fire on the people it had been conversing with was unthinkable, and no one in the crowd believed for a moment that it was possible. On the contrary, the soldiers obviously would not have objected if their front were broken through, and many of them would probably have shared their arms with the crowd. But the crowd had no such intentions.

We went back to Gorky's; he was talking on the 'phone to various representatives of the bourgeois and bureaucratic world. His basic impression was of the same perplexity and bafflement prevailing among them. Strangely enough the rifle-fire had a great effect on the entire situation; it made an extremely strong impression not only on the man in the street, but also on political circles, where voices were heard demanding 'the most energetic steps'. The firing had obviously produced a Leftward reaction among the whole crowd of bourgeois politicians.

I telephoned a great many Left writers and deputies at home, but for the most part without success. At Kerensky's I caught Sokolov, who was sitting with Olga Lvovna expecting some information from the Duma, but he could not tell me anything important.

In general, however, 'high policy' in these hours proceeded as before—not under the banner of revolution and the overthrow of Tsarism, but on the basis of an accord with it founded on minor concessions. Some telephone reports said that various districts of the city had been isolated and that it was impossible to get to the centre; others denied this. But there was no definite goal to warrant an excursion anywhere. None of the deputies left the Duma, which was impossible to get into. People kept coming to Gorky's as before and information kept accumulating, and however little this could alleviate the strain and my longing to be in the crucible of events I had to stay there.

The time passed in interrogation, fruitless speculations, and arguments which had become tedious and nerve-wracking. There were reports that in the working-class districts street demonstrations and meetings were continuing. From Vyborg, the most militant, later a Bolshevik district, came reports of serious action by workers against police and troops. From time to time distant rifle-fire was heard.

Between 7 and 8 o'clock Gorky 'phoned Chaliapine,[1] among others, to find out what was known in his circle. Chaliapine had a strange story to tell. He had just been rung up by Leonid Andreyev,[2] whose flat was on the Champ de Mars on the same side as the Pavlovsky barracks. From the window Andreyev had personally seen an infantry unit systematically firing for a long time from the Champ de Mars at the Pavlovsky barracks. Andreyev could report nothing further, and as for the meaning of it all, Chaliapine said, they were both completely at a loss. It seemed impossible to doubt the reliability of these reports, but there really was no way of making sense of them.

I intensified my 'phoning. Luckily I quickly got in touch with Kerensky, who had come home from the Duma for a short time. Kerensky told me, in the most categorical terms, that the *Pavlovsky Regiment had mutinied.* Most of them had come out into the street and begun skirmishing with the minority who had stayed behind in the barracks. It was this skirmish that Andreyev had seen from his window.

Events had all at once taken a new turn, which presaged victory. The revolt of a regiment, in the general framework of the last few days, meant almost to a certainty that the Tsarist card was trumped. But Kerensky was exaggerating.

It became clear later that what had happened was this: A small detachment of mounted police had orders to disperse a crowd that had collected along the Catherine Canal; for safety's

[1] Chaliapine, Fyodor Ivanovich (1873–1938): the celebrated *basso.* (Ed.)

[2] Andreyev, Leonid Nikolayevich (1874–1919): belletristic writer, playwright, and journalist. (Ed.)

sake the police began to fire on it from the opposite bank, across the canal. Just then a detachment of Pavlovskys was passing along the bank that was occupied by the crowd. It was then that an historic incident took place that marked an abrupt break in the course of events and opened up new perspectives for the movement: seeing this shooting at unarmed people and the wounded falling around them, and finding themselves in the zone of fire, the Pavlovskys opened fire at the police across the canal.

This was the first instance of a massive open clash between armed detachments. It was described to us in detail by a friend who came to Gorky's later on; he had been walking along the Catherine Canal at the time and had personally seen the wounded policemen and their bloodstained horses. Then the Pavlovskys, now 'mutineers' who had burnt their boats, returned to their barracks and appealed to their comrades to join them. This was when the firing took place between the loyal and the rebel parts of the regiment. How far all this was deliberate on the part of the Pavlovskys and how far it was the result of momentary instinct, nervous impulse, and simple self-defence, it is impossible to say. But the objective importance of this affair at the Catherine Canal was enormous and quite unmistakable. In any case, to the Pavlovsky Regiment belongs the honour of having performed the first revolutionary act of the military against the armed forces of Tsarism.

It was obvious that there could be no talk of a conclusive victory for the revolution without a victory over the army and the transference of the greater part of it to the side of the revolutionary populace. And the Pavlovsky Regiment had made a beginning on the evening of February 26th.

This was a terrible breach in the stronghold of Tsarism. Now, after a period of depression, we were all seized anew by a spirit of optimism, even enthusiasm, and our thoughts turned again to the political problems of the revolution. For events had again shifted our course towards revolution, making us disdain all attempts to liquidate the movement by a rotten compromise with the Rasputin régime. . .

Kerensky as before failed to sum up the political situation in any practical way. The Progressive Bloc of the Duma was growing hourly more Leftist—that was all Kerensky had to report. The people at his place were already dispersing, nor for that matter did they promise anything substantial in the way of information. There was no sense in going over there at the risk of getting held up by some police barrier.

Before 11 o'clock I rang up the Duma, intending to speak to the first Left deputy who could be found. Skobelev[1] came to the telephone and told me the Tauride Palace was already empty. Everyone had gone away confused, shaken, and worn out. A session had been called for the following day, but rumours, quasi-reliable, were going around that the next morning a ukase dissolving the Duma would be published. Skobelev had nothing more to tell.

We sat around Gorky's conversing deep into the night. Events were clearly developing favourably. There was news of the defection of other military units.

I made my way home without troubling to choose my time, boldly woke the porter by ringing the bell, and went in by the front door.

The streets were quiet.

A Word about Kerensky

By way of a footnote to the above it may be in place to say something here about Kerensky, simply as a commentary to this exposition, which in my opinion would otherwise lose a great deal of its lucidity.

I had known Kerensky for quite a long time, since my return from exile in Archangel at the very beginning of 1913. From that time on my relations with him, social, professional, and personal, constituted if not a very close sequence at least an uninterrupted one. I had seen him in every possible guise, from his advocate's frock-coat in court, his morning coat in the Duma, and his lounge suit at meetings large and small, to the dazzlingly striped Turkestani dressing-gown he had brought from his own part of the country.

I had seen him on dozens of minor and major occasions—as an orator in the Duma, as a political *rapporteur*, in conversation with friends, as one of an intimate group of not more than half a

[1] Skobelev, Matvei Ivanovich (1885–1939): Menshevik member of Fourth Duma. Joined the Bolsheviks in 1922, holding many posts in planning institutions. (Ed.)

dozen people, and finally as a paterfamilias, with his wife and two boys.

During the time I was underground I had spent many, many nights at his flat, and often after he had made up a bed for me in his study the two of us would fall into a real, long-drawn-out Russian conversation lasting into the small hours. More than once he turned up at the *Sovremennik* to see me, usually bursting into the ante-chamber like a tornado, leaving his ubiquitous pair of 'shadows' keeping watch at the entrance and making me redouble my precautionary measures afterwards.[1]

Our conversations always started out with information or stories from Kerensky, who as a deputy had been at the very heart of things, the fountain-head of the news and the poverty-stricken public opinion of the time. But these stories always developed quickly into the most venomous disputes and desperate wrangling. Though these quarrels had no effect on our personal relations, no intimacy could for a moment blot out the awareness that we did not agree on anything, that we approached any party (or rather inter-party) or socio-political question from opposite poles, and thought about it on different planes, and that consequently we were in opposite camps politically, and temperamentally inhabited different worlds. . .

* * *

It was a heavy load that history laid upon feeble shoulders. I used to say that Kerensky had golden hands, meaning his supernatural energy, amazing capacity for work, and inexhaustible temperament. But he lacked the head for statesmanship and had no real political schooling. Without these elementary and indispensable attributes, the irreplaceable Kerensky of expiring Tsarism, the ubiquitous Kerensky of the February–March days could not but stumble headlong and flounder into his July–September situation, and then plunge

[1] Kerensky's nickname among the Secret Police was 'Speedy'. He did, in fact, rush headlong through the streets, and leap in and out of moving trams. The police spies couldn't keep up with him: in addition to two of them on foot, Kerensky was always followed by another in a droshky. Keeping the future Premier under observation cost the Government quite a lot. From the windows of the *Sovremennik*, after putting out the lights, we would watch the 'shadows', having caught sight of Kerensky running out of the entrance, hurriedly climb into the droshky and start out after him. . .

into his October nothingness, taking with him, alas! an enormous part of what we had achieved in the February–March revolution.

But it was clear to me that it was precisely Kerensky with his 'golden hands', with his views and inclinations, and with his situation as a deputy and his exceptional popularity who, by the will of fate, had been summoned to be the central figure of the revolution, or at least of its beginnings.

Not very long before the February days I remember visiting him on a holiday, during his illness. He was sitting alone in his study in a thick grey sweater, trying to warm himself in the cold room. He had the latest issue of *Letopis* in his hands, and lost no time in coming down on me with some polemical sarcasms. But then the conversation unexpectedly took a peaceful, speculative turn about approaching events and revolutionary perspectives. And I recall that I gently reproached him for his pernicious views, and seriously and without heat exposed what appeared to me to be his weak points. My starting-point in all this was that in the near future he would have to become the head of the State. Kerensky did not interrupt; he listened in silence. Perhaps at this time he was only *dreaming* about a Kerensky ministry; but he may also have been seriously preparing for it. . . Alas! it was indeed a heavy load that history laid upon feeble shoulders!

Now, when Kerensky is a political corpse and there is almost no hope of his resurrection (for his importance in all spheres has completely dwindled away), nothing is easier than to throw one more stone on this political tomb and soothe oneself with the consciousness of having been correct in this historical evaluation. But I am not particularly tempted by such laurels. I was a convinced political opponent of Kerensky's from the day of our first meeting and throughout the time of his greatest power, and to this day I have not changed my opinions, unlike thousands of his champions who later lost no time in selling their worthless swords.

But now that his political reputation is ruined this gives me all the greater right to emphasize his brighter side, with all the greater satisfaction and hope of being believed. This is only just.

And above all, in the face of Bolshevism now triumphant and reviling Kerensky, in the face of his incontestable alliance with the forces of bourgeois reaction against democracy, despite the Kerensky–Kornilov[1] affair, in spite of the fact that he really did do his best to strangle the revolution and did, more than anyone else, lead it to Brest-Litovsk, I maintain that he was a sincere democrat and fighter for revolutionary victory—as he understood it. I know he was incapable of realizing his good intentions, but you cannot wring blood from a stone. That is a matter of his inadequate objective resources as a statesman, not his subjective characteristics as a man. I reaffirm: Kerensky was really persuaded that he was a Socialist and a democrat. He never suspected that by conviction, taste, and temperament he was the most consummate middle-class radical.

But he believed in his providential mission to such an extent that he could not separate his own career from the fate of the contemporary democratic movement in Russia. This was why Kerensky saw himself not only as a Socialist but also as a little bit of a Bonaparte.

His tempestuous Turkestan temperament made him grow dizzy almost immediately, simply from the grandiose events of the revolution and his own rôle in them. And his indubitable innate inclination to pomposity, preciosity, and theatricality completed the process before he became Premier.

'Kerensky the Little Braggart'—this epithet of Lenin's is, of course, by no means an exhaustive description of Kerensky's character, but it does hit the mark and schematize the picture by simplifying it. All this is incontestable. But none of it shakes in any way my conviction that Kerensky was a sincere democrat. For if he naïvely failed to distinguish between his personality and the revolution, he could never have *consciously* sacrificed the interests of democracy to himself and his place in history.

He sincerely believed in the correctness of his line and equally sincerely hoped that his course would bring the country to the triumph of democracy. He was cruelly mistaken. And I personally, even at the time, did all I could to expose him and his cruel errors publicly. But Kerensky, feeble politician as he was, without the schooling or wisdom of a statesman, was sincere in his delusions and plunged in all good faith into his anti-democratic policies, and so, as far as his influence was effective, interred the revolution, together with himself.

[1] See Part V. (Ed.)

CHAPTER 3

THE FIRST DAY OF THE REVOLUTION

February 27th

THE unforgettable 27th of February came. By conspiratorial habit, I did not telephone from my own flat, but hurried over to my Turkestan office between 9 and 10 o'clock to collect information by 'phone and from the people around.

Even on the short walk from the Karpovka to the end of the Kamenno-ostrovsky Prospect one could see that the doubts of the troops were nearing their final resolution, and that the breakdown of discipline was reaching extreme limits.

There were no officers visible at all with the patrols and detachments. And these demonstrated their complete demoralization as Tsarist fighting forces: they were disorderly groups of grey greatcoats, mingling and fraternizing openly with the working-class crowd and casual passers-by. Large numbers of soldiers had left their units and were strolling about singly and in pairs, with or without arms. Passers-by were saying they were willingly giving up their rifles, and great quantities of arms were already being collected in the workers' centres.

The employees at the Turkestan office, many of whom came from a long way off, described more or less the same picture, a breaking down of the organized 'defence' of Petersburg.

I stayed glued to the 'phone and tried to get about ten numbers. The hour of decision, for which generations had laboured, had clearly arrived. Gripping events were at hand.

My impatience turned into frenzy whenever it encountered the indifferent 'busy' of the languid operator. I very soon, however, learned the principal item of political news belonging to the morning hours of that unforgettable day. The decree dissolving the Duma had been published, and the Duma had answered with a refusal to disperse, and elected a Provisional Committee from the representatives of all fractions except the Right.

Here a fact must be mentioned that is well known in all the advanced political strata of Russia but may have failed to impress those who had no direct contact with Petersburg events. The idea of taking the place of the Government was completely alien to the Provisional Committee of the Duma elected on the morning of February 27th. This Duma Committee, headed by Rodzianko,[1] was formed with a specific goal which it proclaimed officially—'to restore order in the capital and establish contact with public organizations and institutions'.

There is no doubt that this act of the Provisional Committee of the Duma was a *revolutionary act* of the Progressive Bloc. It ran counter to the law-abiding traditions as well as the elementary obligations of the Duma. But did it mean the adherence of the Duma to the revolution? Did it prove even a shadow of solidarity of the Progressive Bloc with the masses, who were storming the stronghold of Tsarism?

The most categorical 'no' must be the answer; the revolutionary act of the bourgeoisie as represented by the Progressive Bloc and the Duma majority was intended to save the dynasty and the plutocratic dictatorship from the democratic revolution—by the help of trivial rectifications of the old order devoid of any principled significance. In those hours hopes for the salvation of the Romanov régime had far from vanished; the defection of the Petersburg garrison was not yet a fact.

The general line of action of our bourgeois groups up to this culminating point could only be one of struggle against the revolution and the defence of Tsarism against 'anarchy' and the demoralization of the army. But in contradistinction to the wretched Tsarist bureaucrats, the bourgeois leaders clearly perceived that events had gone so far that without a revolutionary act of disobedience it was impossible to rescue the witless and decrepit offspring of Tsarism.

The revolutionary act was accomplished. Among the most distinguished members of the Provisional Committee, besides Rodzianko, were Miliukov, Konovalov, Yefremov, V. N. Lvov, Shulgin, and Adzhemov. The Duma Left was represented by Kerensky and Chkheidze.

[1] Rodzianko, Mikhail Vladimirovich (1859–1923): Tsarist statesman; a great landowner; President of the Third Duma; emigrated to Yugoslavia after the Civil War in Russia. (Ed.)

The Provisional Committee of the Duma, having officially proclaimed its modest technical assignment, immediately busied itself with 'high policy', in the direction just indicated. Rodzianko, after presenting himself most deferentially at Tsarist headquarters, also conferred by direct wire with the chief military commanders on the different fronts, asking them to support the Duma *vis-à-vis* the Tsar. Only concessions by the nationalist-liberal plutocracy could save the dynasty—such was the sense of the proposed joint pressure on the ill-fated autocrat by the top generals and the progressive bloc of landholders and bourgeois.

I also learnt by 'phone of the answers already received from the generals, answers inspired by probity, honesty, and that devotion to the revolution which these gentlemen would vie with each other in demonstrating a few days later.

But fortunately events did not wait for the backstage machinations of these lords of the old order. The popular revolution was going ahead at full steam, making hourly changes in the entire political situation, upsetting the 'combinations' of the liberals, generals, and plutocrats, and dragging along in its wake the Duma as the political centre of the bourgeoisie.

Imparting these reports to the engineers and other fellow-workers who had abandoned all thought of work and squeezed into the director's room, avidly drinking in the dizzying news, I kept up my telephonic quest for information. Soon the well-known story of the mutiny of the Volhynian and Lithuanian Regiments was revealed by various sources.

The affair begun by the Pavlovsky, and then by the Volhynian and Lithuanian Regiments, was continued by the Izmailovskys. Towards 1 o'clock the men of the Petersburg garrison on the people's side already numbered 25,000. The mutinous regiments made their way to the Duma, encountering feeble resistance from one unit on the Liteiny Prospect. But part of the revolutionary troops went off with the people to the Kresty[1] and the Detention Prison to free the political prisoners.

I shall not even try to give a general description of what happened in the insurrection of the garrison on February 27th. Nor can I cast any light—I find this still more distressing—on

[1] A prison built in 1893 for more than 1000 men, modelled after American prisons for solitary confinement. (Ed.)

the *internal* aspect of the passing of these first units, or more precisely individual soldiers, to the side of the revolution. Only one thing is certain: there were great numbers of politically conscious and party elements in all the units of the Petersburg garrison. And not only were they capable of taking up the movement and lending it the inspiration of some political generalization, but their doing so was inevitable.

The Volhynian and Lithuanian Regiments made their way to the Duma. There may have been various reasons for this movement. It may have been a purely spontaneous drift, or a conscious effort on the part of the leaders to make the bourgeois 'patriotic' Duma the political centre of the movement and of future events. It may have been merely a demonstration of solidarity with the 'revolutionary' parliament that had just been dissolved by the Tsar. I don't know.

More than once later I heard from Sokolov that it was he himself who had led the first mutinying regiments to the Duma. This may really have been so. But it casts absolutely no light on the important fact that the Duma, which hitherto had been clearly outside the popular movement, was now given not merely the importance of its territorial, but also the appearance of its political, centre.

The social mountain, in the shape of the Duma, would not come to the revolution. So one way or another the revolution had gone to *it*. (I shall have occasion to return to this fact of principled importance, for it was made good use of by a personality who now became the head of the movement of all bourgeois Russia, a man who henceforth determined its entire attitude and policy—P. N. Miliukov.)

The representatives of the Duma Left—Kerensky, Chkheidze, and Skobelev—met the first soldiers of the revolution with welcoming speeches. The latter answered them with military salutes. The revolution was not merely developing with great breadth, its character was already defined; it contained within itself what had been the main prop of the old order, and had become nation-wide and embraced the whole democracy.

Its outcome was far from settled. Fateful internecine conflicts might explode at any moment and in view of the imminent final liquidation of Tsarism were more than probable. But nevertheless its all-democratic character was already determined. How supremely ignorant were the well-meaning simpletons of democracy, how supremely contemptible the malicious hypocrites of the bourgeoisie, who did not scruple to call the great cause of the entire democracy a military revolt!

What the Tsarist command did in those hours, what 'measures' it conceived of or put into practice for the struggle against the revolution, I neither know nor remember. Who cares anyhow? No one in Petersburg could have doubted any longer that the Tsarist authorities could not influence the course of events in any way. It is likely that in those hours even they understood that there could now be only one method of struggle against the revolution—a compromise with the bourgeoisie without delay.

The leaders of the Progressive Bloc stubbornly continued their refusal, not only to adhere to the revolution, not only to attempt to lead it, but even to acknowledge it as an accomplished fact. This is incontestable. But what 'combinations' the leading circles of the bourgeoisie, the Progressive Bloc, and the Provisional Committee of the Duma attempted to bring about during those hours, I don't know either, nor did I ever have any interest in finding out. That too was now *outside* the course of events, and could not change them in any way at all. These 'combinations' also were merely the result of confusion and blindness. It was too late. . .

A new factor had emerged which had not been present before: a plenipotentiary organization of the entire democracy of revolutionary Petersburg—an organization ready for combat, hallowed by a glorious tradition,[1] and ready to take the cause of the revolution, *its own cause, into its own hands.*

This was the Soviet of Workers' Deputies.

* * *

The mutinous troops, together with crowds of the people, had set free a great many Socialist workers from the Petersburg prisons. In particular they had freed the Workers' Group of the Central War Industries Committee, headed by K. A. Gvozdev.[2]

[1] i.e., that of the Soviet established by the abortive revolution of 1905. (Ed.)

[2] Gvozdev, Kuzma Antonovich (1883– ?): a metal-worker who joined the Social-Democracy in 1903. Minister of Labour in the Provisional Government. Arrested after the October Revolution, but soon freed, and from 1920 on active in the Supreme Council of the National Economy. A witness in the 1931 Trial of the Mensheviks, which sent Sukhanov to a concentration camp. (Ed.)

The leaders of this group immediately made their way from the prison, together with the troops and the crowd, to the Tauride Palace, where large numbers of Petersburg public figures of various views, ranks, calibres, and specialities were already assembling.

Towards 2 o'clock some fairly prominent representatives of the trade-union and co-operative movements appeared. Together with them and the Left deputies, the leaders of this Workers' Group formed 'The Provisional Executive Committee of the Soviet of Workers' Deputies'. Essentially it had only one assignment: as organizing committee it was supposed to convoke the Petersburg Soviet of Workers' Deputies. It performed its task splendidly, with lightning speed getting out and distributing around the capital a proclamation to the workers, fixing the first session of the Soviet for 7 in the evening of that day in the Tauride Palace.

Elections to the Soviet, as I have said, had taken place even before this, but illegally and casually, with no more definite goal than to be prepared for any eventuality. Now the whole of working-class Petersburg had to be mobilized in a few hours and a plenipotentiary body with the duty of taking the fate of the revolution into its hands formed from it.

However, the Provisional Executive Committee of the Soviet of Workers' Deputies did not limit itself to the function of convoking the Soviet. It also took emergency measures to organize supplies for the mutinying, scattered, and homeless military units who had abandoned their barracks. It immediately elected a 'provisional supply commission' (Grohman,[1] Frankorussky, and others) which first of all set up a soldiers' supply base in the Tauride Palace, and secondly appealed directly to the townspeople for assistance in feeding the soldiers.

The Provisional Executive Committee[2] arose, so to speak, from the *technical* needs of the moment. But in essence, through its supply measures, it also solved a most important political

[1] Grohman, Vladimir Gustavovich (1873– ?): Menshevik. A statistician and economist. Chief inspirer of a planned economy. He stayed on in Russia after the October Revolution, holding important posts in topmost Soviet planning bodies. Hostile to the methods of industrialization after 1929, he was dismissed from his posts. He was a defendant, together with Sukhanov, at the 1931 Trial of the Mensheviks and was sentenced to 10 years' imprisonment. (Ed.)

[2] Henceforth 'Ex. Com.' (Ed.)

problem. For the armed, hungry, shelterless, terrorized, and ignorant masses of soldiery now represented no less a danger to the cause of the revolution than the organized forces of Tsarism. Indeed, there might be doubts as to the existence of the latter, but the former were there to be seen.

But of course the Ex. Com. also took all the steps in its power to defend the revolution from destruction by Tsarist troops. It made an immediate effort to set up a military staff for the revolution in the Tauride Palace. But what a staff, what forces, what an organization! It was set up by telephoning a number of officers who were known to be democrats; this handful of officers, sedately seated at a table, worked out dispositions. But the difference from Tolstoy's generals lay in this, that these dispositions were bound to come to nothing owing to the known absence of any executive machinery or of any real powers whatsoever—independently of Tolstoy's fate and his myriad accidents. . .

Afterwards Kerensky united this group of officers of the Ex. Com. with a similar group formed in the Military Committee of the Duma, and so the foundation was laid of a Military Commission, an institution we shall be encountering continually in the following pages. . .

The Ex. Com. was made up of: K. A. Gvozdev, B. O. Bogdanov, N. Y. Kapelinsky, Grinevich, Chkheidze, Skobelev, Frankorussky, and perhaps some others.

* * *

I played no part whatever in all this activity. Until after 6 o'clock that evening I did not even know what was going on amongst the proletariat and the political parties which served as the intellectual and organizational centres and without which, however weak and imperfect they were, no mobilization would have been possible. My own time was passed in a completely senseless and depressing way.

Having left my office between 12 and 1 o'clock, I went out into the streets of the Petersburg Side, to watch the people's revolution being accomplished.

Military detachments were going past, no one knew where to, some with red banners and some without, mingling and fraternizing with the crowd, stopping for conversation, and breaking up into argumentative groups. Faces were burning with excitement. The exhortations of countless street orators to stand with the people and not to go against it to the defence of Tsarist absolutism were received as something self-evident and already assimilated. But the excitement on the soldiers' faces reflected chiefly perplexity and uneasiness: What are we doing and what may come of it?

One must imagine the upheaval in the objective and subjective circumstances of the rank-and-file soldiers to appreciate the fantastic giddiness of the situation that had come about, which hovered between daylight and a dream. It was inevitable that on many faces perplexity and discomfort were becoming intoxication. These were signs which, while not yet disquieting, at any rate demanded immediate consideration from any thinking participant in the movement. Otherwise they threatened the unbridled debauchery of the armed elements.

The soldiers' excitement and uneasiness, which arose from the vagueness of the situation, were based in the first place on the fact that their commanders, including the junior officers, were not with them to serve as rudder, and secondly that in those hours only a minority of the garrison were in the streets with the people. The remainder were maintaining at the very least neutrality and an attitude of watchfulness, and some units were still definitely obedient to their commanders.

There were rumours everywhere of clashes on the Liteiny between Tsarist and revolutionary troops. Of course these were exaggerated. How many loyal troops there were, ready for combat, no one knew. In any case the mutinous soldiers must have felt themselves on the eve of battle.

It was clear to me that I must make my way at once towards the centre, to the Tauride Palace. But what I should find there was not clear at all, nor whom I should join, nor what I should do. My dejection at being in the miserable position of an observer of great events reached its lowest depths. I would do anything at all, so long as it was active, as any sort of cog in these events. . .

I decided that if I couldn't find anybody or anything I would start my own activities and try to conduct an agitation among a detachment of soldiers right there in the street, with their help occupy some printing-plant, and there together with the workers compose and distribute some kind of bulletin explaining what was happening. There was nothing whatever to be found in print. The need and the thirst for it were colossal, and the minds of the inhabitants must have been a chaos for want of it. To make use of myself as a 'literary force', by any means whatever, in the next few hours and if possible minutes, had become the goal of my longings and my efforts to get to the central districts of the city.

Passing by Gorky's I dropped in to invite him to come with me, as well as any colleagues I found there who shared my useless condition. But the sworn defenders of Gorky's personal well-being were reluctant to let him go out into the turbulence of Petersburg on a risky excursion with no fixed purpose.

It was said to be impossible to get into the Tauride Palace district, also that access at a few points was apparently possible only in motor-cars with an official look, but not on foot.

We began ringing up for a car, which was promised by a motor-car unit near by. It had to be caught on its return from somewhere else. I. P. Ladyzhnikov quickly went off to get hold of it, while we waited around gloomy and depressed, in an aimless discussion of events, making up silly plans. There was talk of an armed clash on the Liteiny.

It was somewhere between 3 and 5 o'clock.

I surveyed the panorama of the city which was revealed from the windows of Gorky's flat. Motor-cars filled with armed people were beginning to nose about. Some of them contained both soldiers and workers; they were decked out with red flags and were rapturously welcomed by the crowd. Others had only soldiers, with rifles levelled at the pavements, full of menace—no one knew to whom. Where they were rushing off to, why, on whose orders or initiative, which side they were on—all this was unknown, and the crowd was inclined to keep its distance.

It was said that a few of these cars had been shot at, near Trinity Bridge, from the Peter-Paul Fortress, which was also visible from the window.

Far off, across the river, towards the left, columns of smoke were floating over the city, and the flames of an enormous conflagration could be seen. This was the quite blameless District Court, destroyed and set on fire by the excited crowd to keep the neighbouring Detention Prison company. Archives, countless documents belonging to civil suits, and notarial deeds were burning there. Looking at all this I kept being reminded of the scenes of the Moscow uprising.

Ladyzhnikov came back, naturally without the car, on which an extra hour and a half had been wasted. I proposed stopping the first one that came along, but this was turned down as too risky. It was decided to go on foot.

It was already past 5 o'clock when we left at sunset—myself, Tikhonov, Gorky, and two or three others, I forget who. Before we got to Trinity Bridge we had managed to lose each other in the dense crowd. Gorky fell behind, and going back for him we saw he had been stopped by an acquaintance who was a member of the Bolshevik Central Committee, probably the most prominent representative of the party then in Petersburg, and a future Bolshevik minister—Shlyapnikov, whom I had met casually a number of times before. In former days, though he was not really a writer, he had made a few contributions to the *Sovremennik* from abroad.

A party patriot, you might say fanatic, prepared to appraise the entire revolution from the point of view of the well-being of the Bolshevik Party; an experienced conspirator, a first-rate technical organizer, and a practical trade-unionist, as a politician he was quite incapable of grasping and generalizing the essence of the conjuncture that had been created. If he had any political ideas they were the clichés of ancient party resolutions of a general nature, but this responsible leader of the most influential workers' organization lacked all independence of thought and all ability or desire to appraise the concrete reality of the moment.

We had to go back to Gorky's flat for some reason. At the door we noticed a police 'shadow', a breed whose existence all of us had by now managed to forget; this old acquaintance already looked like an apparition from a forgotten world. We left again, this time three of us, Gorky staying at home. Throughout the walk I conscientiously tried to explain to Shlyapnikov the present conjuncture as I understood it, with the intention of achieving some co-ordination of activity in the direction outlined above. But there was only one result. I merely convinced myself of all the qualities indicated above of this 'central' Bolshevik I was with. But at the same time I was convinced that the most influential workers' organization in Petersburg, that very Left-wing organization which contained the danger of an unbridled explosion and a recklessly extremist solution of the question of power, had no solution of this question at all, that up to that moment its central leadership had not formulated it in any serious way and that it was impossible to expect from it any prepared slogans or any efforts at a systematic struggle in accordance with a prepared plan. I considered this at any rate a favourable factor.

Under these conditions the solution of the political problem was to a significant extent in the hands of the more moderate elements of the democratic movement, in as far as their influence had been spared by the elemental struggle of forces and the accidental combination of circumstances. Below I shall have occasion to show how primitive and badly grounded were the then bosses of the Petersburg Bolsheviks, how they could not see the wood of revolutionary politics for the trees of their party technique; they really must have been the despair of their own party leaders, who did know what was what but were thousands of miles away from Petersburg to the east or west. In the given situation the more moderate elements seemed to me the more trustworthy.

* * *

It was already getting dark as the three of us—Shlyapnikov, Tikhonov, and myself—walked quickly, almost at a run, from the Kronvergsky Prospect to the Tauride Palace. Trinity Bridge was unobstructed, but rather deserted. The crowd densely scattered about the square in front of the bridge was a little afraid of the activity displayed by the Peter-Paul Fortress and the soldiers on its walls near the guns, though as far as I know no attacks took place from there.

We met cars and lorries, in which soldiers, workers, students, and young women, some wearing arm-bands, were sitting or standing. God knows where all these came from, where they were rushing to, or with what purpose! But all these passengers were extremely excited, shouting and waving their arms, scarcely aware of what they were doing. Rifles were at the ready, and panicky shooting would have started on the least excuse.

Near the Fontanka we turned towards the Shpalerny and the Sergiyevsky. Quite often shots were heard, sometimes in series. Who was firing, why and at what—no one knew. But the spirit of the groups of workers, middle-class people, and soldiers we met, both armed and unarmed, standing about and moving in various directions, was extraordinarily raised by this.

Arms were visible in great quantities in the hands of the workers. Single soldiers were straggling about in all directions in search of shelter, food, and safety. Just as in the Moscow uprising, passers-by started talking to each other, asking what was going on over in one place or whether you could get through to some place else.

It was already dark when we came out on the Liteiny, near the bridge where there had been a skirmish a few hours before between Tsarist and revolutionary troops. To the left the District Court was blazing. Guns had been set up at random near the Sergiyevsky. Ammunition boxes were standing behind them, in what looked to me a disorderly fashion. Something like a barricade could be seen there too. But it was crystal clear to every passer-by that neither guns nor barricades would protect anybody or anything from the slightest onslaught.

One might have despaired. But it was impossible to forget the other side of the picture: the arms at the disposal of the revolutionary people were, in their hands, certainly no protection against any organized force; but *Tsarism lacked that force.*

A soldier, evidently imagining himself the commander of a redoubt, shouted something at us and pointed somewhere. But we did not hear what he said, and calmly stepping over the barricade hurried along the Sergiyevsky to the Tauride Palace. The firing continued.

In the Shpalerny, where the Tauride Palace buildings began, things were considerably more lively. A heterogeneous mob was pushing along the roadway and pavements. There was no sign of any mass-meetings or orators. Nearer the entrance to the Palace there was a row of motor-cars of various types. Armed people were getting into them and they were being loaded with some kind of supplies. Some had machine-guns. In practically every one of them you noticed women, who in such numbers seemed superfluous.

It was evident that someone or other was equipping a mission somewhere. There was shouting and confusion. There were obviously too many people wanting to give orders and too few willing to obey.

We made our way inside the Palace by the main entrance, into which a dense and motley crowd was struggling. Near the doors, ordering everybody about, stood a volunteer watchdog in whom I recognized a certain Left-wing journalist. I have no idea what signs he guided himself by in letting people through or barring their way into the Palace. But I, having fallen a little way behind my companions, was allowed by him to penetrate further, through a dense barrier of soldiers, as an editor of the *Letopis* and a representative of the Socialist press.

In the enormous ante-chamber and the adjoining Catherine Hall, which were rather dimly lit, there were more people than one would suppose was usual, but nevertheless compared with the following days it was almost deserted. The limitless spaces of the Palace swallowed up effortlessly and unnoticeably many hundreds of people, scurrying about with a busy look or obviously bored with inactivity. These were the deputies, who 'belonged' here, and looked like masters of the house rather shocked by the roistering of their uninvited guests. Having left their top-coats as usual with the hall porters, they stood out because of their gleaming shirt-fronts, black cassocks, or sedate peasant-tunics. But they were in the minority. The Palace was obviously filling up with an alien population, in fur coats, working-class caps, or army greatcoats. Among these, well-known figures from the intellectual political circles of Petersburg were seen at every step. All the Petersburgers active in political and public life were already gravitating here.

Meanwhile what had been done? And what had to be done? Were the railway stations being held in case troops were moved up from the front and from the provinces against Petersburg? Were the Treasury, the State Bank, the Telegraphs occupied and being guarded? What measures had been taken for the arrest of the Tsarist Government and where was it? What was being done to win over the remaining neutral and perhaps even 'loyal' units of the garrison to the side of the revolution? Had steps been taken to annihilate the police centres of Tsarism—the Police and Secret Police Departments? Were their archives safe against destruction? How did matters stand with the defence of the city and food supplies? What measures had been taken to combat pogroms, Black Hundred[1] provocation, and treacherous police attacks? Was the centre of the revolution—the Tauride Palace, where the Soviet of Workers' Deputies was due to meet in two hours—defended by any real force at all? And had any organization been set up capable in one way or another of performing any of these tasks?

At that time I did not know how to answer any of these questions. But now I know very well: nothing at all had been done, and there were no forces to do anything with. Can this be the inevitable rule of all revolutions? Nothing of the sort. In time I shall describe, on the basis of my personal recollections, the meticulously executed October insurrection. Quite a different picture!

* * *

In the ante-chamber, not far from the entrance and to the left of it, stood a long table over which leaned many people, principally military. In the centre I saw Kerensky, giving some orders or other. Here, evidently, work was being done by some strategic revolutionary organization or at least its embryo. Kerensky was here acting as a member of the Military Commission I mentioned above, which had taken over Room 41 in the first wing of the Palace.

I was told that the railway stations were being held by troop units on the orders of the Military Commission. The occupation of some of the other most important points of the city was talked of vaguely—people saying that dispositions had been taken, detachments dispatched, etc. Judging by the way a number of missions were being equipped near the Tauride Palace their results were doubtful.

No better impression was made by the work of the 'staff' of the revolution which I watched for a while in the ante-chamber. Up to this time there was clearly not the slightest strategic plan nor anyone to execute it. In the *street*, the detachments of soldiers were casual groups, mixed in with a casual crowd. On the *staff*, there were none of their officers but only an equally casual

[1] An extremist monarchist organization with a terrorist character founded in 1905 under the sponsorship of the Police Department itself, with the help of which it organized pogroms against Jews and liberal intellectuals. Most of its members were declassed elements and petty artisans. (Ed.)

group of military and civilians, who had no definite cadres of armed soldiers, or even of workers, at their disposal. For the equally casual operations Kerensky had not appointed anybody specific from among those present, but had called for volunteers. And anyone who stepped forward had no choice but to look around for and collect together a volunteer detachment which would offer to accompany him on the given mission.

I reminded Kerensky of Secret Police headquarters. It appeared that it hadn't been taken, and Kerensky proposed that I myself undertake to seize it and secure all its archives. He spoke as though there were a detachment and some transport for this; but I saw this was not so. In any case, as a deep-dyed civilian I refused this enterprise, since I was more attracted to politics than strategy and wished to take part in the work of the political centre of the revolution—the Soviet, whose members were already beginning to drift into the Tauride Palace.

In short, the revolutionary army—in both the direct and the transferred meaning of the word—was obviously and completely disintegrated. The situation was critical and menacing. It seemed that if it went on this way for another few hours the forces of Tsarism would be able to conquer the revolution with their bare hands. Nevertheless a group with a proper understanding of its tasks and made up of politically authoritative and technically competent persons was already functioning. And as an individual I had no grounds for intruding. The problem was how to strengthen the transmitting mechanism and communicate some real power to the organization. But here the individual was powerless to act—the driving force could only be the Soviet. I waited for it to open and although at the hub of events found myself still without anything to do.

From the city came vague rumours of the beginnings of anarchy, pogroms, and fires. The Palace was filling up. People active in the Socialist movement were glimpsed more and more often. The entire Socialist and radical intelligentsia of Petersburg was assembling.

Quite alone in the Catherine Hall P. N. Miliukov was walking around, the central figure of bourgeois Russia, the leader of the only official organ of power in Petersburg at the moment, and *de facto* head of the first revolutionary Government.

He too found himself inactive. His whole appearance said

plainly that he had nothing to do, that he did not in the least know what to do. Various people went up to him, began to talk to him, asked him questions, gave him information. He replied with evident reluctance and vagueness. They left him, and he started walking around alone again.

Miliukov was stopped by a professor of the Military Academy of Medicine, Yurevich, who was a few hours later to become Civil Governor[1] of Petersburg. Energetically, succinctly, and intelligently he talked to Miliukov about the position of the soldiers of the mutinous units. There were now tens of thousands of such soldiers in the city. Many thousands of them belonged to units and barracks who had not rebelled and gone out into the street as a whole or in full formation; scattered as they were, they would of course never go back to the barracks, where they might expect to be trapped. Lacking both shelter and bread, they would naturally gravitate to the Tauride Palace as the centre of the movement, and it was incumbent on the Provisional Committee of the Duma or, if they wanted, on anyone who could, to care for these soldiers, supply the Tauride Palace with bread for them, and give shelter on its spacious premises to those who needed it. Otherwise it was just these cadres of homeless and hungry soldiers who might prove to be the fountainhead of anarchy and pillage.

On the other hand the Tauride Palace as the centre of the revolution needed reliable defences and a rallying around it of the mass of the soldiery; the requisite detachments could and should be formed precisely of such soldiers as were drifting to the Duma as the centre of the spiritual rally and of physical refuge and safety.

The weightiness of these considerations, which were evidently communicated to Miliukov in his official capacity, was incontestable. Yurevich demanded immediate measures and offered his services. Miliukov listened attentively and apparently with sympathy. But his aspect left no doubt of his being helpless in this, and quite incapable of undertaking anything; and perhaps his plans were quite different. Yurevich hastened to set his ideas in motion through other channels. I don't know whether he knew that the Provisional Ex. Com. of the Soviet was already attending to this and that for some hours a supplies committee

[1] There were no police: the Soviet appointed a civic head to take the place of the old Tsarist Military Governor of the city. (Ed.)

headed by Grohman had already been working on it. Miliukov continued strolling about the Catherine Hall.

The Palace really was being invaded by more and more soldiers. They huddled together in clusters, meandering around the hall like sheep without a shepherd, and filling up the Palace. There were no shepherds for them.

From the city there were rumours not only of excesses seen somewhere or other, on the part of some sinister elements, but also of the adherence of new regiments to the revolution, of gigantic demonstrations, of the enthusiasm that had taken hold of broad strata of the populace. It was said that people were stopping soldiers and inviting them into their houses, chatting with them, asking questions, 'agitating', and treating them very lavishly with whatever came to hand.

* * *

Before the Soviet opened I wanted to get my bearings on the mood of the bourgeois circles and clarify their leaders' attitude towards the problem of power by direct questioning. I left the Catherine Hall and made my way through the crowded ante-chamber into the right, still deserted, wing of the Tauride Palace, looking for any fairly prominent bourgeois-liberal deputy I happened to know.

This right wing, with all its rooms and the corridor running through it, was the seat of the Provisional Committee of the Duma, and in general of the circles and institutions grouped around the Provisional Government, throughout the first period of the revolution. Members of the Duma, formally maintaining their titles (and their salaries) during this period, regarded this right wing of the Palace as their own domain. But as I have said before, in those days it was also the seat (in Room 41) of the Military Commission, that is, the military staff of the revolution. The left wing, on the other hand, at the very beginning fell into the hands of the democratic movement, in the shape of the Soviet and its organs. The future struggle between the democratic movement and the bourgeoisie, between the Soviet and the Government (plus the Provisional Committee of the Duma) in the first period had its territorial counterpart in the struggle between *the right and the left wings* of the Tauride Palace.

Glancing into Rodzianko's office at the beginning of the corridor, I saw V. A. Rzhevsky, one of the leaders of the 'Progressive' Party, whom I knew fairly well. If he wanted to be frank with me he could give me perfectly adequate information, and he, for his part, quickly showed a desire to interview me, as someone from another world. I went in and we sat down in comfortable arm-chairs not far from the door. The huge, dimly lit room was almost empty. Off in the distance two or three moderate deputies were languidly chatting at a table.

Rzhevsky was in the state of mind characteristic of our liberal society. 'We are all very anxious,' he began. 'A few hours ago Rodzianko and some of the Provisional Committee went to see the President of the Council of Ministers, Prince Golitsyn, to discuss the situation. So far Rodzianko hasn't come back and there is no news of him. We're afraid he's been arrested by way of reply to Shcheglovitov's[1] detention.'

I hastened to express my profound conviction that this anxiety was quite unfounded. If the Duma Committee saw any point in conversations with Tsarist officials even after all that had happened, even after the arrest of Shcheglovitov, a Tsarist Minister, in the precincts of the Duma, then in my view it ought to be all the more evident to Golitsyn, Trepov, and their colleagues that there could now be no way out for the *Tsarist Government outside of conversations with the Duma majority*. Not in any circumstances would the Tsarist Ministers decide to reject any conversations intended to save the autocracy or its remnants. Still less would they dare declare open war on the Duma majority, which up to then had been so eager to demonstrate its loyalty.

'Believe me,' I added, 'they have a first-rate appreciation of the position and will seize the sheet-anchor represented by Rodzianko. They will not behave like a drowning man clutching his rescuer by the throat only to go down with him. After all, the Duma Committee is far enough from either supporting anarchy or sympathizing with a Socialist republic.'

I don't know to what extent my irony was clear and convincing to this confused liberal (later to become an SR!) who had no notion of where to direct his thoughts. In any case these thoughts as expressed in further conversation showed the utter vagueness of liberal inclinations.

[1] Shcheglovitov, Ivan Grigoriyevich (1861–1918): Tsarist statesman; sponsor of the Black Hundred (see p. 47); shot after the October Revolution. (Ed.)

The basic problems were still unsolved. As before the attitude towards events showed vacillation—from the *psychological* thirst of the best representatives of our liberal movement for a radical overturn, to the *practical* desire for an agreement with Tsarism as the only way out of the situation. The question of revolutionary power had obviously not yet been worked out or ventilated in the minds of even the advanced representatives of the Duma 'Left'.

As for Shcheglovitov's arrest, I can only report the scene in the words of an eye-witness who told me about it later. Shcheglovitov was arrested in his flat by a student who had asked some armed soldiers he had met in the street to come along with him for this purpose. They escorted Shcheglovitov to the Duma around 3 o'clock; he was taken into the Catherine Hall, where the student who had begun all this asked for Kerensky. An inquisitive crowd assembled at this unprecedented sight. The Tsarist statesman stood there with hanging head, and Kerensky, who had come up, declaimed a sentence he was to repeat more than once in those days.

'Mr. Shcheglovitov,' he said, 'in the name of the people I declare you under arrest!'

Just then the powerful figure of Rodzianko elbowed its way through the crowd.

'Ivan Grigoriyevich,' he said, addressing Shcheglovitov like a beaming host, 'please come into my office!'

The awkwardness was resolved by the student, who declared:

'No, ex-Minister Shcheglovitov will go into custody; he has been arrested in the name of the people.'

Kerensky and Rodzianko looked at each other a few minutes in eloquent silence, then went off in different directions. Shcheglovitov was taken away under guard.

* * *

Dissatisfied and without having received any practical information that might clarify the line to be taken by the democracy in the decisive next few hours, I started to go off to the left half of the Palace, where dense groups of workers' representatives were already assembling and their credentials being checked at full speed. The session was due to open any minute.

I came out of Rodzianko's office and in the next room accidentally came upon the chairman of the Duma, A. I. Konovalov, engaged in a business talk with I. I. Yefremov. These more important figures of the Left bourgeoisie, from the same Progressive Party, were also known to me quite well enough for a private talk. In addition, both of them were members of the Provisional Committee of the Duma (and afterwards both became Ministers).

There was no time to waste, and simply as a personal friend I asked them directly about the plans of the groups they controlled and their attitude to the formation of the revolutionary Government. However, my interlocutors were merely embarrassed; they had simply no idea of how to reply to the question I had put so plainly.

Perhaps they did know but merely didn't want to say? Hardly. At that moment Miliukov came into the room and the two men I was talking to obviously saw in him a way out of their difficulties. Cheered up by his appearance, the leaders of the Progressive Party pointed out to me the leader of another party —the Cadets—and with one accord suggested that I speak to *him* about the subject I was interested in. Not only did this naïvely emphasize their powerlessness, it demonstrated just as naïvely something which I, however, had not doubted even before this: *Miliukov* was at that time the central figure, the spirit and backbone of all bourgeois political circles. It was he who determined the policy of the entire Progressive Bloc, where officially he stood on the extreme Left. Without him all bourgeois and Duma circles would at that moment have constituted a chaotic mass, and without him there would have been no bourgeois policy at all in the first period of the revolution.

This was how his rôle was evaluated by everyone independently of party, and how he himself evaluated it.

With Miliukov, unlike Kerensky, Konovalov, and others, I had up to this time been completely unacquainted. If I were to attempt a more detailed discussion of this figure, as I did with Kerensky, it would go far beyond the bounds of personal reminiscence. But I cannot help remarking now that I always considered this fateful man to be head and shoulders above all his colleagues in the Progressive Bloc, that is, head and shoulders above the flower, the cream, and the pride of our bourgeoisie.

This man of destiny carried out a policy that was fatal not

only to democracy and the revolution but also to the country, his own theories, and himself personally. While making obeisance to the principle of Great Russia, he contrived, with one brutal, violent blow, to smash both the principle and himself. Nevertheless, for me there was no doubt whatever: this fateful man was the only one capable of incarnating, in the eyes of Europe, the new bourgeois Russia that had arisen on the ruins of Rasputin's land-holding society.

In particular I had no doubt whatever that, unlike my previous interlocutors, Miliukov very well knew what was what and that the problem of the government was being weighed by him in the most careful manner in these days—or at least in these hours; that Miliukov would *understand* whatever I wanted from the very first hint. As to what he would *answer*, and how he would *solve* the problem—that was another question.

As a matter of fact, at that moment Miliukov, and in his person the whole of propertied Russia, was confronted by a genuinely tragic problem, which at that time only isolated individuals in the mass of middle-class liberals, even when they were close to the Duma, were capable of grasping in its full scope: as long as Tsarism was not conclusively done for, it was necessary to cling to it, *support* it, and construct any domestic or foreign programme of national liberalism on the *basis* of it. This was understood by every bourgeois element with any experience at all.

But what was to be done when Tsarism had *almost* fallen beneath the blows of the popular movement but its final fate was not known? Obviously, the natural solution was to maintain neutrality until the last minute and not burn one's boats. But in practice it was clear that there had to be definite limits to neutrality, beyond which neutrality itself would burn the boats on one side and perhaps on both. Here one must be specially clear-sighted, supple, and agile.

But the real tragedy began later. What was to be done after the popular revolution had wiped Tsarism off the face of the earth? To take the power out of the hands of Tsarism was natural. To make an alliance with Tsarism to smash the revolution, if it tried to sweep away both the bourgeoisie and Tsarism in the same breath, was even more natural and absolutely inevitable. But what if, on the one hand, Tsarism was hopeless, and on the other the *possibility of standing at the head of the revolution was not excluded? What if some prospect of 'using' it developed?* What was to be done then? Take the power out of the hands of the revolution and the democracy after they had become masters of the situation?

I had no doubt that for Miliukov (and possibly for him alone) all the shoals and hidden sandbanks of the situation were obvious. And it was on him more than on anyone else that the practical resolution of all these accursed questions depended.

How, then, was Miliukov solving these problems, and consequently, how would they be solved in practice in the next few hours? It is obvious why a conversation with Miliukov had an absolutely exceptional interest for me.

But it was completely outside my plans. I couldn't speak to him as a personal friend, and I hadn't the slightest justification for interviewing him as though I were a leader or representative of the democratic camp. It was awkward to ask such an official personage to satisfy my personal, theoretical curiosity. And of course I couldn't have the slightest hope that this interview would be of any practical importance. My position as a man not only without the shadow of any authority but aware of his own isolation from the democratic centres completely tied my hands.

But whether I liked it or not the conversation was already being begun by Yefremov and Konovalov, and I was fated to continue it. I introduced myself to Miliukov, who had come up.

'Your worst enemy'—I added jokingly, having told him my name and wishing to give a completely private tone to our conversation from the outset.

'Very pleased . . .,' Miliukov replied, somewhat too solemnly. Then, having emphasized that the motivating reason for this interview was my personal curiosity, I said roughly the following to him:

'At this moment, a few rooms away, the Soviet of Workers' Deputies is assembling. The success of the popular uprising means that within a few hours all the effective real power in the State or at least in Petersburg, if not the Government itself, will be in its hands. With the capitulation of Tsarism it is the Soviet that will be master of the situation. At the same time popular demands in such circumstances will inevitably be expanded to the most extreme limits. The movement does not have to be driven along by anyone just now—it is already running downhill too fast without that. But confining it within definite bounds would require enormous efforts. Besides, any attempt to keep the popular demands within set limits would be quite risky; it might discredit the controlling groups of the democracy in the eyes of the masses. The movement might turn into an uncontrollable explosion of elemental forces. In any case the extent to which attempts to direct the movement might reasonably be made must be carefully defined. Can the collaboration in the liquidation of Tsarism of the circles you represent be gained at the price of such attempts? . . .

'What is the position of the Progressive Bloc and of the Provisional Committee of the Duma?' I asked. 'Do you propose, now that we are in an atmosphere of revolution, to take state power into your own hands?'

I may have said more than I should to a 'worst enemy'. In any case it was possible to understand from my words that in the democracy and even among the Left democrats[1] there were elements (though without great influence) who were interested in the formation of a bourgeois Government, considering it indispensable for the consolidation of the revolution and even ready to defend one compromise or another for the sake of that consolidation. But all the more curious and characteristic was Miliukov's reply, the precise wording of which I don't guarantee, but whose exact purport—which I vouch for completely—was this:

'In the first place, I belong to a party which is bound by the decisions of a more general group—the Progressive Bloc. Without this it cannot undertake or decide anything, since both together constitute one entity. Secondly, we, as a responsible opposition, were certainly striving for power and moving towards it, but not along the path of revolution. That way was not ours. . .'

I had had enough. In this answer, as in a drop of water, was reflected the whole of our liberalism, its fox's brush and wolf's teeth, its cowardice, flabbiness, and reactionary nature. . . At the decisive hour, in the light of the elementary considerations expressed by me, the autocratic representative of the progressive bourgeoisie could only murmur a few words about the Pro-

[1] Miliukov knew very well I belonged to the Left: afterwards he told me that he had read my books and followed my 'defeatist' articles in the press.

gressive Bloc and his only decision was to act, at the moment of the revolution, as he had been acting *before* the revolution and *without* the revolution!

In any event the situation was clear. To assume that the bourgeoisie, in the form of the Progressive Bloc and the Duma Committee, would take up and support the revolution and unite with it, even provisionally and formally, was impossible. Our point of departure had to be that if the revolution was to be continued, consummated, and fortified the democracy had to be ready to take on *itself alone* the burden of this feat, in opposition to the united forces of Tsarism and all the propertied classes.

Miliukov wanted to go on developing his ideas in the same spirit. But I'd had enough. I thanked him for his kindness and hurried off to the meeting of the Soviet.

* * *

The right corridor of the Palace was already crowded, noisy, and animated. Round the door of Room 41, where the Military Commission was in session, buzzed a crowd of many civilians and even more army people. Whole strings of arrested members of the police and Secret Police were being led along the corridor by soldiers, sailors, and armed workers. In the ante-chamber of the Catherine Hall there was already a crush, which got worse the nearer one came to the left wing, where the Soviet was assembling.

In addition to random idling soldiers one saw the concentrated earnest soldierly faces of the official representatives and delegates of the insurrectionary units; fully armed, with their credentials in their hands, they were asking how and where to 'report' to the Soviet.

At every step one glimpsed well-known faces of personalities from every conceivable party and organization. Everyone you ever came across anywhere, at any time and in any public activity, was there.

I met an old fellow-exile, M. A. Braunstein, a Menshevik. He had just that moment arrived, having crossed an enormous part of the city on foot, and was still shaken by everything he had seen.

'Complete anarchy is beginning in the city,' he said. 'Soldiers are looting and destroying. They're being led by the Black Hundred, the Secret Police and the police. No authority, no organization, no restraint. The police, the military cadets—the entire strength of the old order is being mobilized. They're shooting from garrets and windows, to provoke the crowd. *The first thing the Soviet must do is organize the defence of the city* and suppress anarchy. A workers' militia and energetic Commissars in charge of the city districts are indispensable right away. This question must be first on the agenda, otherwise the movement will be crushed.'

Doctor Vecheslov was hurrying past, an old Menshevik, a Left internationalist in wartime, and a skilful physician who talked about nothing but politics (at least with me) even when listening to your heart or giving you injections of diphtheria serum. 'Troops are moving on Petersburg,' he said, panting, 'from the front or the provinces. We're going to be crushed. Is any defence being organized? What's the Military Commission doing? We must open the meeting at once and raise the question of the defence of the revolution!'

The doctor hurried on. I elbowed my way through the crowd from the Catherine Hall to the rooms occupied by the Soviet.

The hall was filling up. Sokolov was running around giving orders and seating the deputies. In an authoritative way, without, however, any discernible justification, he was explaining to those present what sort of vote they had, whether consulting or deciding,[1] and who had no voice at all. In particular he explained to me that I had a vote—I don't remember now what kind. But of course these judicial decisions of the future senator had not the slightest practical significance.

I ran into Tikhonov, and we took places at the table at a respectful distance from its head, which was occupied by official personages, the deputies Chkheidze and Skobelev, members of the self-appointed Ex. Com., Gvozdev, Kapelinsky of the Co-operative movement,[2] and Grinevich, one of the leaders of the Petersburg Mensheviks.

[1] A 'consulting' vote or voice merely gave one the right to express his opinion without participating in the voting. (Ed.)

[2] A broad democratic movement completely independent of the Government, created to organize the so-called consumers' unions in an attempt to dispense with middlemen in retail commerce, thus substantially lowering prices of consumer commodities. Started in Russia in the sixties of the 19th century, and developed vigorously after 1905. It also had cultural aims, and was strongly supported by workers, peasants, and liberals. Before the First World War it comprised more than two million members. (Ed.)

B. O. Bogdanov, the most active member of the Ex. Com., was missing for some reason; I think he only turned up a day later. Nearby at the table towered the massive figure of Steklov,[1] more reminiscent of a bearded central-Russian smallholder than an Odessa Jew.

Also there at the head of the table, pestering all and sundry with something or other, was Khrustalev-Nosar, the former chairman and leader (together with Trotsky) of the Soviet in 1905. Sokolov was bustling about there too; at 9 o'clock precisely he opened the session of the Soviet with a resolution to elect the Praesidium. . . Kerensky turned up for a short time.

I no longer felt any longing for the centres of the movement; I had no feeling of being cut off from the living process. I was in the very crucible of great events, the laboratory of the revolution.

* * *

At the moment the meeting opened around 250 deputies were there. But new groups kept pouring into the hall, God knows with what mandates or intentions.

What ought to be the agenda for this plenipotentiary assembly of the representatives of the democracy in the decisive hour of the revolution? Under any circumstances it was plainly impossible to make the *political* problem the first item, and force the task of forming the revolutionary Government. What with the general vagueness of the situation and the above-mentioned temper of the right wing of the Tauride Palace, this problem could only be put on the agenda with one object—to decide it out of hand by proclaiming the Soviet the supreme state power. Under these conditions it was up to others to place the question of power on the agenda—to the advocates of an immediate dictatorship of the Soviet, who might have been the Bolsheviks headed by Shlyapnikov, or the SRs led by Alexandrovich.

In any case both these groups were weak and unprepared, without initiative and incapable of taking their bearings in the situation. Neither introduced the question. Meanwhile

[1] Steklov (Nakhamkes), Yurii Mikhailovich (1873–1937): active revolutionary from the beginning of the nineties in Odessa. Outside all fractions for a long time. Joined the Bolsheviks after the October insurrection and for a long time was the editor of the official *Izvestiya* (News). (Ed.)

circumstances themselves introduced some absolutely unpostponable business concerning the technique of revolution itself.

The people I talked to incidentally about the agenda were of course right: the movement would be crushed without emergency *economic* measures—organizing the provisioning of the capital, taking immediate steps to defend the city and stop anarchy, and mobilizing the forces of the local garrison and the working-class population to repel a possible attack on Petersburg—that is, without the strategic defence of the revolution. Whatever the ultimate form of government, only the Soviet could achieve this 'technique' of the revolution.

As for the strategic measures, defensive and offensive, they were being handled by the Military Commission, the kernel and majority of which in those hours was composed of Soviet elements. To carry strategy into the general meeting of the Soviet was absurd. But it was vital to do something else—place under Soviet control the activities of this Military Commission, which was established—topographically—in the right wing of the Palace.

Naturally, the Duma deputies Chkheidze, Kerensky, and Skobelev were nominated to the Praesidium and elected immediately without opposition. Besides the chairman and his two colleagues four secretaries were elected—Gvozdev, Sokolov, Grinevich, and the worker Pankov, a Left Menshevik. If I'm not mistaken Kerensky declaimed a few meaningless phrases that were supposed to be a hymn to the people's revolution, and immediately vanished into the right wing, not to appear again in the Soviet.

I don't remember what happened to the future permanent chairman of the Soviet, Chkheidze. Skobelev was left to take the chair; in the midst of the hurly-burly and the general excitement he had neither a general plan of action nor control of the meeting itself, which proceeded noisily and quite chaotically. But this by no means prevented the Soviet from performing at this very first session its basic task, vital to the revolution—that of concentrating into one centre all the ideological and organizational strength of the Petersburg democracy, with undisputed authority and a capacity for rapid and decisive action.

Immediately after the formation of the Praesidium the customary demands for 'order' rang out from various sides. The chairman, wishing to end formalities, put forward for confirmation the already functioning Credentials Committee, headed by Gvozdev, but it was not in the least surprising that business was interrupted at this point by the soldiers, who demanded the floor to make their reports. The demand was enthusiastically supported, and the scene that followed was worthy of enthusiasm.

Standing on stools, their rifles in their hands, agitated and stuttering, straining all their powers to give a connected account of the messages entrusted to them, with their thoughts concentrated on the narrative itself, in unaccustomed and half-fantastic surroundings, without thinking and perhaps quite unaware of the whole significance of the facts they were reporting, in simple, rugged language that infinitely strengthened the effect of the absence of emphasis—one after another the soldiers' delegates told of what had been happening in their companies. Their stories were artless, and repeated each other almost word for word. The audience listened as children listen to a wonderful, enthralling fairy-tale they know by heart, holding their breaths, with craning necks and unseeing eyes.

'We're from the Volhynian Regiment . . . the Pavlovsky . . . the Lithuanian . . . the Keksholm . . . the Sappers . . . the Chasseurs . . . the Finnish . . . the Grenadiers . . .'

The name of each of the magnificent regiments that had launched the revolution was met with a storm of applause.

'We had a meeting . . .' 'We've been told to say . . .' 'The officers hid . . .' 'To join the Soviet of Workers' Deputies . . .' 'They told us to say that we refuse to serve against the people any more, we're going to join with our brother workers, all united, to defend the people's cause . . . We would lay down our lives for that.' 'Our general meeting told us to greet you . . .' 'Long live the revolution!' the delegate would add in a voice already completely extinguished by the throbbing roar of the meeting.

Dreadful rifles, hateful greatcoats, strange words! Theoretically all this had been known, well known, known since that morning. But in practice no one had understood or digested the events that had turned everything topsy-turvy. . .

It was then and there proposed, and approved with storms of applause, to fuse together the revolutionary army and the proletariat of the capital and create a united organization to be called from then on the 'Soviet of Workers' and Soldiers' Deputies. . .'

But a great many regiments were still not with us. Were they hesitating, consciously neutral, or ready to fight the 'enemy within'?

The situation was still critical. There was the possibility of bloody skirmishes between the organized regiments and their officers. The revolution might still be captured with bare hands.

* * *

Frankorussky, the 'Supply Man', finally got the floor, and having given a short sketch of the supply position in Petersburg and all the possible consequences of hunger amongst the masses, proposed that a Supply Commission be elected, ordered to set to work at once, and given adequate powers. There was of course no debate on this. The Commission was elected at once from the Socialist supply specialists headed by V. G. Grohman. Having waited for this moment, all those elected immediately withdrew in order to work.

Meanwhile M. A. Braunstein, who had apparently been elected to the Supply Commission, came up to me and urged me to take the floor at once with a resolution on the defence of the city. I didn't see the slightest advantage in coming forward and suggested that I merely second his motion. He got the floor and very successfully, with the full attention and sympathy of the meeting, described the state of affairs.

Braunstein proposed that directives be given the city districts through the delegates present for every factory to appoint a militia (100 men out of every thousand), for district committees to be formed, and for plenipotentiary Commissars to be appointed in each district to restore order and direct the struggle against anarchy and pogroms.[1] I spoke in support of his resolution, after informing the meeting of the activities of the Military Commission and warning them of the danger of confusing functions and powers. The resolution was accepted in principle, but there was still no machinery to put it into practice; there were neither boundaries between the districts (were they to be

[1] Braunstein, by the way, was the first of us to use this word Commissar, which was later so needlessly misused.

the future Soviet and municipal wards or the old police divisions?) nor assembly points, nor volunteer Commissars. . .

In connexion with the defence of the city there naturally cropped up a proposal for a proclamation to the populace in the name of the Soviet. In general, supplying the capital, and as far as possible the provinces, with information and elementary directives to the populace was the most pressing task of the moment, even though it was relatively simple and required no special attention from the meeting. One of my neighbours proposed the election of a Literary Commission to be entrusted with the immediate composition of an appeal to be presented to the Soviet later for confirmation.

But this organizational work, which had already taken up about an hour, was interrupted again. A young soldier burst through the flimsy barrier at the doors and rushed to the centre of the hall. Without asking for the floor or waiting for permission to speak he raised his rifle above his head and shook it, choking and gasping as he shouted the joyful news:

'Comrades and brothers, I bring you brotherly greetings from all the lower ranks of the entire Semyonovsky Regiment of Life Guards. All of us to the last man are determined to join the people against the accursed autocracy, and we swear to serve the people's cause to the last drop of our blood!'

In his emotion, bordering on frenzy, the youthful delegate of the mutinous Semyonovskys, who had plainly attended a school of party propaganda, was really, in these banal phrases and stereotyped terminology, pouring out his soul, overflowing with the majestic impressions of the day and consciousness that the longed-for victory had been achieved. In the meeting, disturbed in the midst of current business, there gushed forth once again a torrent of romantic enthusiasm. No one stopped the Semyonovsky from finishing his lengthy speech, accompanied by thunderous applause. The importance of this news was obvious to everyone: the Semyonovsky Regiment had been one of the most trustworthy pillars of Tsarism. There was not a man in the room who was not familiar with the 'glorious' traditions of the 'Semyonovsky boys' and in particular did not remember their Moscow exploits in 1905.[1] All that was over. In a flash the

[1] The Semyonovskys were notorious for their part in the brutal suppression of the Moscow uprising in 1905. (Ed.)

stinking fog was dispersed by the light of this new and blinding sun.

It appeared that there were delegates from the newly insurgent regiments in the hall. They had not ventured to ask for the floor but now came forward after the Semyonovsky had opened the way for them. Once again the assembly heard tales of a whole series of army units—one of the Cossack regiments, I think an armoured division, an electro-technical battalion, a machine-gun regiment—the terrible enemies of the people just a short while before and from now on a firmly united band of friends of the revolution. The revolution was growing and increasing in strength with every moment.

Elections continued for the Literary Commission. Sokolov, Peshekhonov, Steklov, Grinevich, and I were elected. No objections were raised: there were no fractional struggles or party candidates. Moreover, no directives at all were given to the Commission, and it was clear to everyone that the proclamation would be published in the form in which they submitted it. Thus was accomplished the Soviet's first act of any political significance.

* * *

We left the meeting immediately and looked for a place where we could compose the proclamation. Aside from Grinevich all the members of the Commission knew each other quite well, and it was clear that in view of our broad political range, stretching from Right to Left, we might have some fundamental disagreements and have a great deal of work to do.

One after the other we made our way through the dense crowd, even more tightly packed in the Catherine Hall at the doors of Room 11. Tens of thousands of people of all ages and conditions had come to meet the revolution at its very core.

We couldn't find anywhere to work, and we made our way through the crowded ante-chamber over to the right wing, hoping to settle ourselves in one of the offices of the Duma. As before, we were passed by files of police and other 'politicals' of a completely novel and unheard-of kind, all under arrest. Some were picked out and sent into the ministerial pavilion, now turned into a common room for higher Tsarist dignitaries. The small fry, having filled up two or three of the Duma apartments, were placed in the galleries of the big White Hall, where they also stayed during the days that followed.

In the Catherine Hall and the ante-chamber, soldiers, arms in hand, were standing in groups or columns where someone had drawn them up in orderly, but loose, formation. Others had stacked their arms and were sitting on the floor supping on bread, herrings, and tea. Others, finally, were already asleep, stretched out on the floor like third-class passengers huddled together for warmth in railway stations.

Going over to the right corridor, we saw tired soldiers coming out of the street into the ante-chamber and neighbouring rooms, shouting and jostling their way through the crowd, carrying burdens and throwing down part of their load right there at the entrance. Most of it consisted of an enormous number of cases of shells, rifles, revolvers, and also machine-gun belts. The machine-guns themselves, protected by guards, were also visible here and there.

Sacks of meal had been heaped into a pile a step or two from the entrance. Near them stood two obedient guards, just like those posted by Tsarist officers, who didn't show the slightest sign of understanding what was taking place around them. 'Whom are they obeying and just why?' flashed through my mind. . .

'Here it is, finally got here, the best flour!' called out a soldier cheerfully, giving me a vigorous push with his case.

One's feet slid on the floor, where mud and snow were mingled. Chaos was everywhere. There was a merciless draught through the door from the street, and a reek of soldiers' boots and greatcoats.

We pushed on further but could find nowhere to work until we came to the room of the chairman of the Duma, where three hours earlier I had talked to Konovalov and Miliukov. It was empty or nearly empty. We settled ourselves at the desk, on which were a telephone and writing things. Until we were all assembled, I decided to slip into the Military Commission's rooms opposite, to find out what the situation was. The Commission had removed into the next room (to avoid the crowds with no business there), and I was told that work, under the inspiration of Kerensky, was going rapidly ahead. But others, with sceptical smiles or hopeless shrugs, reported differently.

I was more interested in gathering the latest objective reports from the city. There were some, and not unimportant ones. The Peter-Paul Fortress had fallen—this was the first. It is common knowledge that the fall of this age-old citadel of the Tsars was a *peaceful* victory of the revolution: the fortress and its commanding staff had surrendered without a shot. But this news was premature; the fall of the fortress took place only after the Duma Provisional Committee had joined the revolution.

Then a second piece of news: the Tsarist Government had barricaded itself in the Admiralty and was being guarded there by some still-loyal troops with artillery; revolutionary troops, also with artillery, were storming the Admiralty by order of the Military Commission. The report of this assault by storm was false: in fact the 'loyal' troops ran away the following day, and for a short time the Tsarist ministers hid in other refuges. But in any case the report, indicating the presence of active Tsarist troops, was quite alarming.

It was, to be sure, swallowed up by a third report: *all Kronstadt had joined the revolution.* No one had any grounds to doubt this; Kronstadt's reputation was too definite and too well deserved.

But this joyful news paled before another report: troops sent out against the revolutionary capital were moving on Petersburg; the 171st infantry regiment, loyal to the Government, had already arrived; it had occupied Nicholas Station and an engagement was taking place in Znamensky Square between part of it and a detachment of revolutionary troops.

Later we became persuaded that any attempt to dispatch troops for the pacification of Petersburg was fruitless. All the 'loyal' troops preserved their loyalty and obeyed their commanders only as far as the railway stations, then immediately went over to the side of the revolution, and the commanders obeyed them.

Dozens of times later on, in the days of the Kornilov revolt, I was to remind my companions of this, not believing for a second that Kornilov could get as far as Petersburg and 'pacify' it. But in these critical moments everything appeared in a completely different light. The latest report of the exchange of shots in Znamensky Square, in view of the evident disorganization of the revolutionary forces and their obvious technical helplessness against officered troops, was menacing in the highest degree. It was evident to everyone what an enormous gap there was between readiness for a bloody battle for freedom and the ability to win that battle against regular and possibly front-line troops.

'We're finished, finished!' Grinevich, who had been listening to all this, shrieked, clutching his head, when I came across him in the corridor. I drew him into the office of the chairman of the Duma—to compose the Soviet proclamation.

All these reports about current events concerned the technique, the strategy of the revolution. What had happened during this time in the sphere of 'high policy'?

* * *

When I returned to the Duma chairman's office I could only learn that Rodzianko had some time before come back quite safely from his mission, which had been undertaken in order to give some final warnings and form a united front of Tsarism and the bourgeoisie against the people's revolution. But, in any event, Rodzianko was too late.

In the first place the people's revolution would not wait for the mobilization of hostile forces, and had already advanced so far that even a blind man could see the futility of the counter-revolutionary 'combinations' of the Cabinet coterie. Secondly, the last Tsarist 'Cabinet' could not help Rodzianko: they were holding out in the Admiralty and thinking not of 'combinations' but of their own skins. I don't know whom Rodzianko consulted in the name of the Duma and the propertied classes, but in any case it had become clear in those hours that the tactic of vanquishing the revolution through a united front with the forces of Tsarism had perhaps already become rather riskier than the tactic of vanquishing the democratic movement by trying to exploit the revolution and keep it in check by leading it.

Rodzianko's fruitless mission, combined with what was taking place two steps away from his office, in the Soviet, finally moved the mountain to Mohammed and put point blank the question of a switch in tactics. The fateful moment had come when the fox's brush would decisively replace the wolf's teeth on the stage of bourgeois politics—replace them for a long time, for the entire succeeding period of the revolution.

One of the radical deputies, with a mysterious look and

blazing eyes, burst into the office where we were sitting, and told us this political news: Rodzianko after a consultation with the Duma Committee had locked himself in his office (next door to us) and had asked for a few moments for reflection.

We had no time. Our proclamation could not wait, and we were hard at work. People kept coming into the room, shouting, jostling us. We were in alien territory, but we had nowhere else to go. The work was going with considerable difficulty. We had decided to cut out all politics and devote the proclamation to an elementary explanation of what had happened, an announcement of the creation of a centre of revolutionary democracy in the form of the Soviet, and an appeal for organization and the maintenance of order. Only at the end was a Constituent Assembly mentioned, as the incarnation of the democratic society which had been proclaimed as the goal of the revolution.

We worked about fifteen minutes. It was around midnight. The telephone on the table rang; I took it.

'Duma? Could you get hold of one of the members of the Provisional Committee? Could you possibly get Miliukov?'

Doubtless some 'intellectual', with an insistent shrill voice. But how could we get hold of Miliukov or the Duma leaders, when every minute was precious to us? I pointed out my difficulty and asked for his 'phone number.

'In that case please tell him they've rung up from the Preobrazhensky Regiment. The entire regiment is joining the people, is at the disposition of the Duma, and is waiting for orders from the Provisional Committee. . .'

Just then Miliukov came into the room from Rodzianko's office. At the sight of our group he came straight over to our table: he had a triumphant look and a repressed smile on his lips.

'A decision has been reached,' he said; 'we're taking power. . .'

I didn't ask who this 'we' was. I didn't ask anything further. But in all my being, as they say, I sensed the new and favourable position of the revolution, and the new tasks of democracy that were now on the order of the day. I felt that the ship of the revolution, tossed about in those hours by a squall and at the mercy of the elements, had spread its sails, acquired stability and obedience to the helm in the midst of the buffetings of the terrible storm, and had taken a definite course between the shoals and reefs towards a distant point, invisible in the mists but known with certainty. The gear was all in order, the engines were beginning to turn over; the only thing needed was skilful navigation.

The easy and painless liquidation of the old order throughout the limitless expanse of the country was certain. Any attempts to interfere with the overturn on the part of the plutocracy, the front-line generals, or any of the other forces of Tsarism were doomed in advance to failure.

But a new programme had now been presented to the democracy: to prevent the revolution, once accomplished, from becoming the foundation of a bourgeois dictatorship, and ensure that it formed the starting point for a real triumph of the democracy.

I was still holding the 'phone. I passed it to Miliukov. After listening to the Preobrazhensky officer, the leader of the future Government at once answered, swiftly passing into his new rôle:

'Very well, Colonel Engelhardt will be coming to you immediately in the name of the Provisional Committee of the Duma and will take command of the regiment.'

As a matter of fact this Colonel Engelhardt—a Duma deputy and I think an Octobrist—got another assignment: he became the head of the Military Commission, which the Provisional Committee of the Duma hastened to lay hands on officially.

It was essential first of all for the Duma bourgeoisie to demonstrate that the motive power of the Duma was the forces of the revolution and that it was wresting a new social order from Tsarism; secondly for the 'right' half of the Tauride Palace to have *de facto* control of the military machine as a whole.

It was at this point that the knot of the first revolutionary Government's policy was tied and its line of conduct defined in relation to the democracy embodied in the Soviet.

* * *

The room where we were working had grown so busy that we were obliged to look for a new anchorage. We moved on again, down the right corridor, and finished our proclamation in an office full of typewriters. Most of our Commission returned to the Soviet and soon I too hurried off, leaving Grinevich typing out the proclamation in the empty office, with one lamp burning.

From the window we could see the square in front of the Tauride Palace. The crowd had thinned out and the square looked more like a camp. There were camp-fires with soldiers standing in groups around them, and armoured cars hung with red flags sputtered among cannon and machine-guns.

* * *

The general question of the press now arose in the Soviet. The brief fugitive debates concerning it were quite characteristic. I remember two opposing speeches—Steklov's and Sokolov's. The former fought for the shutting-down of the press for the next few days, pointing out the danger to the revolution of Black Hundred press agitation. Sokolov appealed to the principle of liberty, claiming that the immediate restoration of normal conditions of life could only strengthen the revolution.

I was wholeheartedly on the side of this view, and throughout the revolution, at all its most critical moments, fought for the total and unlimited freedom of the press, with responsibility only to the courts: in this I proceeded just as much from principle as from the practical expediency of this arrangement; however, I was not only usually in the minority but often alone. In this case, though, I was quite sure that not one organ would dare come out against the revolution in defence of the old order.

During the night of the 27th–28th of February a compromise decision was reached, to permit newspapers to come out on the editor's responsibility. Whatever doubts may have arisen about this decision itself, what was characteristic was this, that *no one had any doubt that this question should be decided by the Soviet*, which alone had any real power here, especially through its control of the whole army of typographical workers. The Soviet was also interested in the outcome of the revolution independently of the bourgeois attitude on this question; and it did not hesitate to decide it at its own discretion. This was also extremely characteristic of the place of the 'right' and 'left' wings of the Tauride Palace and the interrelationships that took shape between the Soviet and the first revolutionary Government.

* * *

It was now essential to proceed to the election of an Executive Committee, and it was decided to elect eight members. The maximum number of votes went to the non-party candidates—Steklov, Kapelinsky, and myself—and the fewest to the Bolshevik Shlyapnikov and the SR Alexandrovich. It had been resolved to include in the Ex. Com. the members of the Praesidium (the chairman, two vice-chairmen, and four secretaries), and also to co-opt representatives of the central and local organizations of the Socialist parties.

There remained one important piece of business: to define our relations with the Military Commission. It was resolved to demand that all of the elected Ex. Com. should be admitted to the Military Commission, and we received an immediate answer inviting our attendance.

I made my way over to the Military Commission and with other members of the Ex. Com. joined a group round a writing-table, where Colonel Engelhardt was sitting. A map was spread out in front of him—apparently a plan of Petersburg. Leaning on his elbow he was contemplating this map with great thoughtfulness, making an occasional remark and pointing to something. His general air was unmistakable: he had no idea what to do with his map, or what had to be or could be done in general. Officers who had been in the room before and had just broken through the line of watchdogs again were addressing 'emergency' questions, reports, and requests to him. These 'emergency' and 'urgent' questions, these 'extraordinary reports'—a cruel scourge to anyone doing systematic work—were apparently received by the head of the Commission not only without annoyance but even with satisfaction. It was obvious that aside from these improvisations hardly anything was being done, or could be done. Meanwhile the Ex. Com. still had to tackle the urgent task of organizing the defence of the city, in conformity with the decision of the Soviet.

We returned to the Soviet. It was around 4 o'clock. The Soviet session had just been closed; the next one was scheduled for noon the following day. The deputies were scattering, but the hall was still occupied by groups of workers conferring. We detained the representatives of the districts, through whom alone we could act, in the absence of any technical apparatus.

Not only did the Ex. Com. have as yet no executive organization, it also lacked any secluded place to work. At each end of the Catherine Hall, at the time of the Duma, there used to be semi-circular tables with arm-chairs. In the half-dark and practically empty hall tired soldiers and workers were sitting, or half-lying, or sleeping in these chairs. They readily cleared a place for us and we were about to settle down at one of these tables. But a motley crowd hung so close around us that it was impossible to work and we had to leave. Utterly harassed and irritated by these absurd hindrances we thought of trying to settle down in the galleries of the great hall and straggled over there. But the galleries and passage-ways were occupied by prisoners: the sentries wouldn't let us through, and we had to turn back.

Finally we found an anchorage in the Duma Chamber itself. The huge dark room was almost empty. Scarcely visible figures were scattered in ones and twos about the amphitheatre of seats. Some were sleeping, others conversing quietly. We went into the Press Gallery, opposite the Duma 'Left', and it was here that the *first session of the Ex. Com. was held.*

Sombre figures from all over the chamber started drifting quietly over to our gallery. They stood near by and listened. We paid no attention. In about an hour we had worked out instructions for the city districts concerning militia, planned the locations of assembly points, and nominated Commissars. Then we communicated our decisions on to the district representatives, who set off at once.

We limited the agenda of the first Ex. Com. session to this. With the prospect of the work before us we had to think of rest, even if only for two or three hours. The Ex. Com. members living close by began appearing in fur coats and hats. . . We had only to call in again on the Military Commission.

There was a little more room there now. But we found the same general scene, though there were fewer officers scurrying around in field uniform with a martial look and less shouting, giving of orders, hurly-burly, and excitement. There seemed to be a lull. Apparently nothing new had happened. The late night, fatigue, and a feeling of helplessness seemed to have shackled all energy. The Tauride Palace, the brain and heart of the revolution, ringed round by menacing unguarded guns and meagre little groups of soldiers without officers or discipline, awaited the will of God. . .

At the Military Commission three or four of us 'visiting' Ex.

Com. members found a pleasant surprise. In the middle of the room on a garden bench stood an enormous tin bowl, half full of cutlets; the people standing round were devouring the other half. A loaf of bread and a huge rusty penknife lay near the bowl. We asked no questions about who had brought these wonderful things or for whom.

* * *

Those living near by or with a place to stay overnight went back into the city, so as to return the next morning for work. I of course couldn't even dream of my own Petersburg Side. Having squeezed all I could out of the Military Commission, I went off to look for a free sofa, arm-chair, or bench. The halls were half in darkness; there were practically only soldiers left in them. The quiet conversation of the groups sitting on the floor and an occasional loud order given by someone only emphasized the relative silence that now reigned. I made the round of all the accessible rooms, but my search was quite fruitless. The familiar offices of the right wing had been locked by cautious and zealous servants who had grown grey in 'good society' and were shocked by the unprecedented invasion of the *sans-culottes*.

I went back to the Catherine Hall; but sleeping or dozing in the midst of that camp was unthinkable. I went into the White Hall to settle myself in some deputy's arm-chair. I wandered past the rows as far as the gallery of the Council of State in the corner.[1] The seats were very uncomfortable. In a corner of the gallery I saw an empty space, threw my fur coat and cap on the floor, and stretched out on them.

It was long past 5 o'clock. Through the glass roof (which had once fallen in!) the hall was filled with a quiet milky light. Occasionally soldiers wandered through the hall, chatting together, and glanced into my gallery. . . I had to sleep. I turned towards the wall. From the Catherine Hall there came a steady tramping, and occasional loud shouts of command. . . Was the Palace filling up again? Could any organized units be marching about?

I fell asleep, or perhaps dozed heavily.

That was the first day of the revolution.

[1] Members of the Council of State had a gallery in the State Duma simply to observe the sessions of the Duma in comfort, without having the right to intervene in the debates. (Ed.)

CHAPTER 4

THE SECOND DAY

February 28th

I WAS aroused by strange noises. I realized at once where I was, but could not explain these sounds to myself.

I got up and saw two soldiers, their bayonets hooked into the canvas of Repin's portrait of Nicholas II, rhythmically tugging it down from both sides. A minute later, over the chairman's seat in the White Hall of the Duma there was an empty frame, which for many months continued to yawn in this revolutionary hall. . . Strange! It never came into my head to worry about the fate of this portrait. To this day I don't know what happened to it; I was more interested in other things.

A number of soldiers were standing on the upper levels of the chamber, at the height of my gallery. Leaning on their rifles they watched what their comrades were doing, and quietly made their own comments. I went over to them and listened eagerly. . . Twenty-four hours before, these rank-and-file soldiers had been the dumb slaves of the despot who was now thrown down, and at this moment the outcome of the revolution depended on them. What had taken place in their heads during those twenty-four hours? What would they say to the shameful treatment of the portrait of the 'adored monarch' of yesterday? It evidently made no strong impression: there was neither surprise, nor any sign of intense intellectual activity, nor a shadow of that enthusiasm from which even I myself was ready to catch fire. They were making remarks in a tranquil and matter-of-fact way, so down-to-earth they can't be repeated.

The break had been accomplished with a sort of fabulous ease. No better sign was needed of the definitive rottenness of Tsarism and its irremediable ruin.

* * *

The hands of the large clock over the entrance doors of the hall pointed to 7.30. It was time to begin the second day of the revolution.

In the rooms of the Military Commission I found the people and everything else much the same as 'yesterday', that is, two hours earlier. I was told, in answer to my questions, that things were improving. First of all, whether or not regiments had arrived from the provinces or the suburbs there was no report of any fighting. Secondly, in Petersburg the officers were returning to their posts. Mass offers of service were reaching the Commission from them—a thing which had not happened before. In addition, the taking of the Peter-Paul Fortress was already fully confirmed; the whole garrison, led by their commander, had acknowledged the authority of the Duma Committee. As for the Admiralty, it was still held by some detachment which hadn't joined the revolution, but exactly who was holding out there was unknown.

The return of the officers to their regiments and their adherence to the revolution were undoubtedly of enormous importance. In the first place, at this point the revolution lacked any force at all to replace the officers and save the army from immediate and complete disintegration and conversion into a source of universal anarchy or of absolute power for a rabble of leaderless soldiery. Only an effective corps of officers—in the absence of any firm, habitual, authoritative democratic organization—could now serve as the indispensable solder, and for this it must be used.

Then, the neutralization of the officers or their detachment from Tsarism and attraction to the side of the revolution was imperative, since they might be the most active force of the entire bourgeoisie in the event of any immediate counter-revolutionary attempt to suppress the movement. If the liquidation of Tsarism could not be brought about without the bourgeoisie in general, or in opposition to it, it was even more important to swing the strength of the officers' corps over to the side of the revolution.

In addition it should not be forgotten that the corps of officers then in Petersburg was far from being the old 'regular' guardee officerdom: it was full of 'temporary officers', that is, of every kind of representative of the Third Estate,[1] ready to join the

[1] Third Estate (from the French *tiers état*)—used for educated people of no means who worked for their living in public organizations, but were not members of the intelligentsia. They were largely radical-minded. (See note on *Zemstvos*, p. 7.) (Ed.)

revolution not out of fear but through conviction—given physical safety and a possibility of harmonizing their relations one way or another with the mistrustful soldiery. Because of all this the democratic leaders, and in particular the Ex. Com., were striving with all their might to get the officers to return to their units and their duties, and make the soldiers acknowledge their officers again. In this respect the aims of the Ex. Com. of the Soviet completely coincided with those of the Duma Committee, which had officially announced as one of its first tasks 'the restoration of the bonds between the officers and the lower ranks'.

But this was only one small part of the whole task of the bourgeoisie and democracy in relation to the army. It was still merely the *form,* not the *content* of the task.

Taken as a whole, the desires of the leading circles of the bourgeoisie and democracy not only did not coincide here, but were naturally bound to become the mainspring of a profound, stubborn, principled, and, baldly speaking, 'class' struggle between the Soviet democracy and the first Government to emerge from the revolution. This struggle constitutes the basic content of that period of the revolution which culminated in the fall of the Guchkov–Miliukov Government; it will also serve as the basic material for my subsequent notes.

* * *

The Provisional Committee of the Duma, in trying to restore the bonds between the officers and the soldiers, wanted those bonds to be just what they had been under Tsarism. It had every reason for hoping that the officers' corps, in joining the revolution and placing itself at the disposition of the Duma, would be making itself a faithful servant of the bourgeoisie; the Provisional Committee, naturally, wanted the 'other ranks', in the hands of these officers, to be the passive weapons they had been before and the whole army, thus passing over in its old form from the hands of the Tsar into the hands of an autocratic plutocracy, to be the foundation of its dictatorship in general and of its struggle against the democracy in particular.

It was precisely in the cause of such a bond between the officers' corps and the other ranks that the Duma Committee developed extremely active propaganda from the morning of

February 28th on. The watchwords of this propaganda were 'order', 'discipline', 'submission', 'obedience', and every other possible variation on the theme of the officer's mailed fist. In this propaganda the bourgeoisie naturally tried to exploit as broadly as possible the efforts of the democratic leaders to restore order and 'harmonize relationships' between soldiers and officers.

The Soviet Ex. Com., in the midst of the revolutionary tempest and the impossible conditions of work, had to keep in view both the Scylla of the loss of the officers' corps, anarchy, and the destruction of the movement under the direct blows of a counter-revolution, and the Charybdis of the tenacious embrace of the plutocracy, its seizure of all the real power which had come into the hands of the people, and the gradual but rapid swallowing up by the triumphant bourgeoisie, after the pattern of other revolutions, of everything that had been won. Keen eyes were needed to trace out the narrow pathway between the swamp and the deep water; tact was needed to pass along this pathway; authority was needed to compel all those whom there was no time to persuade and enlighten to follow along it.

The Soviet Ex. Com. immediately took steps to restore the link between the different elements of the army, but it could not allow this link to be the former mechanical discipline, the elemental and absolute obedience of the democratic mass of soldiers to their bourgeois officers. New foundations were being laid for our existence as a state; for the democracy they of necessity presupposed certain new relationships within the army, which would exclude any possibility of exploiting the army *against* the people for the consummation of the overturn in the narrow class interests of the plutocracy.

In the face of the tragic lessons of history, guarantees to this effect *had to be held by the democracy at all costs*. For our bourgeoisie, unlike others, betrayed the people not the day after the overturn but even before the overturn took place: it hadn't started a revolution with the intention of turning against the people at an opportune moment, but had been dragged by the hair into the movement when the people's revolution had already developed to its full extent. This bourgeoisie of ours left no room for doubt as to its goals. We had to keep our ears and eyes open if we didn't want to exchange one Duma Protopopov[1] under Tsar Nicholas for another. Hadn't Miliukov, the indispensable and monopolistic leader of the revolutionary Government, just put down the entire Russian working-class movement to provocation?

* * *

Civilians were already thronging into the Palace and mingling with the soldiers, and the rooms were beginning to look as they had the day before. People who had come from the city told us that it was still far from restored to order. Shops, warehouses, and flats had been broken into in various places and the destruction was continuing. The criminals released with the political prisoners on the previous day had joined the Black Hundred and were leading the rioters, pillaging and burning. It was not altogether safe in the streets: police, house-porters, Secret Police, and gendarmes were firing from the attics. They were an incitement to rioting and anarchy. A few fires were burning.

* * *

The members of the Ex. Com. were gradually assembling in the hall where the Soviet held its sittings. It was essential to find a quiet place for us to work in. I appropriated Room 13, the office of the chairman of the Finance Committee, which was divided into two by a curtain. We could hold our meetings behind the curtain, while the other half of the room could be used as an office, with all outsiders strictly forbidden to enter. I wrote out a notice to this effect and hung it on the door into the Soviet hall. As I drove the bystanders out of the room I had requisitioned I saw Gorky in the Soviet Hall, which was still fairly empty. I was delighted to see him, as usual, and pleased that he had come at this time to see for himself everything that was going on in the Tauride Palace.

But Gorky was in a bad mood. He answered questions morosely and monosyllabically. I could not discover the source of his scepticism and pessimism, but it was clear that he found something displeasing in everything that was happening. He

[1] Protopopov, Alexander Dmitriyevich (1866–1918): an Octobrist; member of the Third and Fourth Dumas; Minister of the Interior from 1916 till revolution; a protégé of Rasputin's. After the February Revolution he was arrested and after the October Revolution he was shot. (Ed.)

was about to go into Room 13, but a sentry just stationed there, a young, intelligent-looking grenadier, resolutely stopped him, and Gorky retreated.

'Comrade, do you know who that is?' I asked the sentry, who looked carefully at him and answered: 'No; why?' When I mentioned Gorky's name the effect was stronger than I expected. The soldier looked stunned and thoughtful. . .

Many times afterwards I asked Gorky to come to the meetings of the Soviet organizations, pointing out that his participation might have significance not only for himself. But Gorky remained more than indifferent to my invitations.

* * *

The Ex. Com. session could now be opened. Not only were all the elected members gathered together, but the party representatives who were to be included in the Ex. Com. with a vote had also assembled.

I must now say something about the composition of this first Ex. Com., which laid the foundations of the revolution and held its fate in its hands during the first two months. An idea of its character can be given by its membership, elected at the first session of the Soviet on February 27th, and supplemented later by the representatives of the democratic party organizations.

The Soviet elected to the Ex. Com., first of all the members of the Praesidium, the Duma deputies Kerensky, Skobelev, and Chkheidze, and the secretaries, Gvozdev, Grinevich-Schechter, Pankov, and Sokolov; then the following eight men (in alphabetical order): Alexandrovich-Dimitrevsky, Belenin-Shlyapnikov, Kapelinsky, Pavlovich-Krasikov, Petrov-Zalutsky, Shatrov-Sokolovsky, Steklov-Nakhamkes, and Sukhanov-Himmer.

The first half of each hyphenated name is the pseudonym by which its bearer was known in public or literary work and under which he was elected.

These pseudonyms and anonyms quickly became a favourite excuse for baiting the leaders of the Soviet. The bourgeois press unanimously began to harp on the idea that the democracy and later on practically all Russia was being run by no one knew whom—perhaps highly sinister and in any case quite unknown persons hiding behind the Soviet masses. Not a new method, and one thoroughly tried out by the jackals of the reaction!

Our respectable press in both capitals pointed out how repugnant pseudonyms, concealment of names, and similar 'irresponsible' behaviour were on the part of people who had assumed an immense public responsibility. The aspersion was essentially correct. But there was absolutely no evil intent on the part of the members of the Ex. Com. Party sobriquets and literary pseudonyms under the Tsarist régime were the result of manifest necessity. In the immediate post-revolutionary period they were current for the simple reason that in one way or another they were more or less widely known, whereas the official names on passports were frequently quite unknown. As for any desire to hide behind a pseudonym, perhaps at the very beginning some may have been swayed by a feeling of caution in view of the possible imminent collapse of the revolution. But even here of course the main stimulus was the habit everyone had of calling himself in every public activity by his familiar pseudonym. And then in the following days it simply never came into one's head to bother about such trifles. No one was in the least interested in making a public proclamation of his names or such particulars of himself as were contained in the old police passport.

But I testify that no one ever actively *concealed* his official names. Anyone interested could always find out and publish any name he pleased. At the time when this dirty game of the bourgeois yellow press was attracting attention all our names and pseudonyms were published in the *Izvestiya* by order of the Ex. Com. But the fact is that the Right newspapers of that time, *just for the sake of this game*, were deliberately keeping up this pretence of 'back-stage secrets' in the Soviet organizations: they were, as a matter of fact, quite uninterested in our names.

On the morning I am describing the elected Ex. Com. members already enumerated were joined by the party representatives. These did not all turn up at once: a few took no part in the sessions until the following day, and others a few days later, I don't remember exactly when. But most of them were present on February 28th.

These were the Bolsheviks—Molotov-Scriabin, then Stalin-Dzhugashvili; the Bundists[1]—Ehrlich and Rafes, replaced a few

[1] The Bund—a Jewish working-class organization in Russia and Poland that carried on Socialist propaganda amongst Jewish workmen. It was closely allied

days later by Lieber; the Mensheviks—Bogdanov and Batursky; the Trudoviks—Bramson and Chaikovsky (replaced by Stankevich); the SRs—N. S. Rusanov and V. M. Zenzinov; the Populist Socialists—A. V. Peshekhonov and Chernolussky; the Social-Democratic 'Interdistrictite'[1]—I. Yurenev; and the Lettish Social-Democrats—the inseparable Stuchka and Kozlovsky.

I may have left out someone or added a few, since the representatives of the Populist parties very rarely assembled in full strength, and the Right wing of the Ex. Com. was not so strong as a simple list of names might give the impression of.

* * *

We must say something here about the most important thing —the interrelationships of tendencies within the first Ex. Com. Regardless of the fact that a substantial share cannot be denied to accident in the elections of its members at the first session of the Soviet, nevertheless the elected section of the Ex. Com. was much more Left, and in its overwhelming majority consisted of representatives of the Zimmerwald tendency. The defensist, Right section, on the other hand, rather insignificant at first though later it acquired a decisive importance in the revolution, was made up of party representatives ordered into the Ex. Com. by their headquarters.

As for the Praesidium, which formed part of the Ex. Com., Kerensky very soon abandoned the Soviet, fleeing over to the right wing of the Tauride Palace, and going on from there later to the Marian and Winter Palaces; he appeared in the Ex. Com. only on special occasions (two or three times in all) and did not participate in its work at all. But the members of the Duma

---

with the young Social-Democratic movement in Russia, and helped in the convocation of the first congress that laid the foundations of the Russian Social-Democratic Workers' Party (Minsk, 1898). The Bund left the party in 1903, at the London Congress, because of organizational differences that revolved around its desire to be the sole representative of the Jewish working class, but nevertheless remained in close contact with it, and was especially close to the Mensheviks. In the Ukraine in 1919 the Bund fused with the Communist Party, but in Poland it remained independent, wielding considerable influence. After Hitler's invasion of Poland it was destroyed; its survivors, in France and the United States, still carry on political and literary activities amongst the Jewish working class. (Ed.)

[1] The Interdistrict Committee was an autonomous organization of about 4,000 workers and revolutionists, later to be led by Trotsky, Lunacharsky, Ryazanov, and others, which formally fused with the Bolsheviks in July. (Ed.)

Social-Democratic fraction who were on the Praesidium, Skobelev and Chkheidze, throughout the first period of the revolution stubbornly occupied the position of a typical and impenetrable Swamp;[1] afterwards, when a firm, opportunist SR peasant-soldier majority was formed, they ceased being its *de facto* leaders. We shall speak of this later.

Of the remaining twelve Ex. Com. members elected the night of February 28th, four—Grinevich, Kapelinsky, Pankov (a worker), and Sokolovsky—were members of the Menshevik organization, belonging to the Left (Zimmerwald) wing of which Martov[2] was the leader. All four of them later joined the isolated group of Menshevik-Internationalists.

Sokolov, Steklov, and myself wholeheartedly joined these four, and in all political questions before the Ex. Com. we and they constituted a unified group; at that time we were (organizationally) outside all fractions. Sokolov later joined the controlling 'conciliationist' majority, remaining on its Left wing. Steklov, after lengthy roamings from group to group, between the defensists and the Bolsheviks, finally joined the Bolsheviks after their victory in October. As for myself, I formally entered the group of Menshevik-Internationalists in May, soon after Martov's arrival from abroad.

Consequently the Zimmerwald tendency in the first Ex. Com. should have been sure of a thoroughly stable majority. But on the following day, March 1st, its composition was diluted by nine representatives of the newly formed Soldiers' Section of the Soviet. By far the greater number of these latter had no definite political complexion and during the first steps of the revolution represented a Swamp. When the SR majority took shape most of them joined it, gravitating toward the peasant party. But at the beginning these nine soldiers made the ground beneath the feet of the Left majority unstable, though they didn't shift the centre of gravity of the Ex. Com. or change its complexion.

Another trait of the first Ex. Com. leaps to the eye: it was rather poor in personalities. During the first weeks of the revolution not one of the recognized leaders of the Socialist

[1] From the French Revolution: unstable persons of shifting views. (Ed.)

[2] Martov (Tsederbaum), Julius Ossipovich (1873–1923): Lenin's closest intimate until the Bolshevik–Menshevik split in 1903, then leader of the Mensheviks. (See pp. 350–56 *et passim.*) (Ed.)

parties or the future central figures of the revolution entered it. Some were in exile, others abroad.

However, in a short time the leaders of the Ex. Com. who had begun the revolution were reduced to a minority and had to pass into opposition. The leading rôles were yielded to deserving veteran party leaders. But by then these were representatives of other tendencies who had changed the policy of the Soviet in their own way. It is doubtful whether the revolution gained anything in exchanging its more modest cuckoos for these brilliant hawks.

* * *

It was already about 11 o'clock when the Ex. Com. session opened. I have the impression that during these first days its work went on almost uninterruptedly around the clock. But what work it was! They were not meetings, but a frenzied and exhausting obstacle race.

The agenda had been set up, as pointed out above, in relation to the urgent tasks of the moment. But neither at that session nor in general during the days that followed could there be any question of fulfilling a programme of work.

Every five or ten minutes business was interrupted by 'urgent announcements', or 'emergency reports', 'matters of exceptional importance' which couldn't 'tolerate the slightest delay', and on which the 'fate of the revolution depended', etc. These emergency questions were for the most part raised by the Ex. Com. members themselves, who kept getting some sort of information on the side, or prompted by people who were besieging the Ex. Com. But again and again the petitioners, delegates, and messengers from every possible organization and agency, or simply from the nearby crowds, would themselves burst into the meeting.

In the great majority of cases these emergency matters were not worth a barley-corn. I don't remember what the Ex. Com. did during these hours. I remember only unimaginable hubbub, tension, hunger, and the feeling of irritation at these 'exceptional reports'. There was simply no way of stopping them.

There was no order even in the meeting itself. There was no permanent chairman. Chkheidze, who later performed the chairman's duties almost permanently, didn't do much work in the Ex. Com. during its first days. He was constantly being summoned—either to the Duma Committee or the Soviet sessions or, above all, 'to the people', the constantly-changing crowd standing in front of the Tauride Palace. He spoke practically without stopping both in the Catherine Hall and in the street, sometimes to workers and sometimes to soldiers. He would scarcely have time to return to the meeting of the Ex. Com. and take his things off before some delegate would burst in with a categorical demand for Chkheidze, sometimes even reinforced by threats—that the mob would break in. And the tired and sleepy old Georgian would get his fur coat on again with a resigned look, put on his hat, and disappear from the Ex. Com.

There was still no permanent secretary, nor were any minutes taken. If they had been taken and preserved, they would not report any 'measures' or 'acts of state' during these hours. They would reflect nothing but chaos and 'emergency reports' about every possible danger and excess we lacked the means to combat. There were accounts of pillage, fires, and pogroms; pogromist Black Hundred leaflets were brought in—handwritten, alas, and thoroughly illiterate. We gave orders not expecting them to be carried out and sent out detachments without any hope that they would really be formed or do their duty.

I don't remember who presided at this meeting, nor whether there was any chairman at all. . . On the writing-desk of the chairman of the former Finance Committee there appeared from somewhere or other tin mugs of tea with crusts of black bread and other eatables. Someone was looking after us. But there was not much food, or else there was simply no time to get it. A feeling of hunger remains in my memory. . .

* * *

It began to grow noisy in the neighbouring hall. The Soviet was assembling, and of course every kind of individual who wanted to join the revolution filtered through into Room 12. Neither the Mandates Commission which had settled in Room 11, the sentries, nor the volunteer watchdogs, could do anything with the crowd which had squeezed from the street into the Palace, and everyone from the Catherine Hall thought his place was in the Soviet.

Members of the Ex. Com. were summoned at every minute by every possible delegate from the most unexpected organizations and groups, who had demanded that they should be admitted to the Soviet. They all wanted to participate in the overturn and become part of the core of the revolutionary democracy. Officials from the Posts and Telegraphs came along, teachers, engineers, *Zemstvo* and municipal employees, representatives of the doctors, the lawyers, the 'Socialist officers', the artists—they all thought they belonged in the Soviet.

There is no doubt that the more conscious representatives of the bourgeois intelligentsia were gravitating towards the Right, towards the Duma Committee. These elements undoubtedly felt that the Soviet was the source of 'dual power', perhaps of 'anarchy', and only an 'impediment' to the triumph of the 'free order' which Guchkov and Miliukov had taken it upon themselves to set up.

But the *masses* of the intelligentsia were seized with 'revolutionary democratic' fervour: just as in 1905 all the ordinary middle-class and 'former'[1] people became 'Socialists' in a flash and an irresistible spontaneous drift towards the Soviet took place amongst them.

The popularization of the Soviet was of course aided also by the fact that the virtual authority, or more accurately the real power, was in its hands, in so far as there was any authority at all at that time. And this was obvious to every man in the street.

Formally the power belonged to the Duma Committee, which displayed considerable activity and quickly distributed departments and functions among deputies of the Progressive Bloc and (very characteristically) some Trudoviks. Besides this, in the course of the day and night of the 28th the Duma Committee found time to publish a whole pile of decrees, appointments, orders, and proclamations. But theirs was only a paper, or if you like a 'moral', power; it had authority for all the 'statesmanlike' and 'right-thinking' elements and served as a fairly reliable protection against the Tsarist counter-revolution. But in these crucial hours of convulsion it was absolutely unable to *govern*. In particular it had no real validity for the current 'technical' tasks—the restoration of order and of normal life in the city.

[1] i.e., people who used to be active in politics; sometimes used for 'formed' ruling classes, etc. (Ed.)

If anyone had the means to achieve this it was the Soviet, which was beginning to acquire control over the masses of the workers and soldiers. It was clear to everyone that all effective workers' organizations were at the disposal of the Soviet, and that it was for it to set in motion the immobilized tramways, factories, and newspapers, and even to restore order and safeguard the inhabitants from violence.

There is no doubt that if the 'conscious' bourgeois-intellectual groups were completely in favour of the Duma Committee's having sole power, the *neutral* petty-bourgeois intelligentsia and the entire Third Estate were indiscriminately forcing their way into our meeting-hall.

I personally received on that day a whole series of this kind of delegation and, not having any constitution to guide me, had neither the powers nor any ground for refusing admission to the Soviet of every kind of delegate, burning with the first ardour of revolution. Other members of the Ex. Com. and our Mandates Commission itself acted in the same way. As a result, a few days later the number of members of the Soviet had reached Homeric and absurd figures, barely short of 2000. This caused considerable difficulty and unpleasantness for the Ex. Com., which was supposed to set up a correct organization for the Soviet and correct representation in it.

I must note another characteristic thing: to this day I, a member of the Ex. Com., am completely ignorant of what the Soviet was doing in the course of that day. It never interested me, either then or later, simply because it was self-evident that all the practical, pivotal work had fallen on the shoulders of the Ex. Com. As for the Soviet at that moment, in the given situation, with its given quantitative and qualitative composition, it was clearly incapable of any work even as a Parliament, and performed merely *moral functions*.

The Ex. Com. had to accomplish by itself all the current work as well as bring into being a scheme of government. In the first place, to pass this programme through the Soviet was plainly a formality; secondly this formality was not difficult and no one cared about it. Awareness of this imperceptibly but swiftly penetrated every member of the Ex. Com., and we devoted ourselves to our work almost without paying any attention to what was being done in the neighbouring hall.

'And what's going on in the Soviet?' I remember asking someone who had come in from beyond the curtain. He waved his hand hopelessly: 'A mass-meeting! Anyone who wants to gets up and says whatever he likes. . .'

I had several occasions to pass through the meeting-hall. At first it looked as it had done the night before: deputies were sitting on chairs and benches, at the table and along the walls; among them and in the aisles, and at each end of the hall, people of every description were standing, creating confusion and disorganizing the meeting. Then the crowds of people standing became so dense that it was difficult to get through them, and they filled up all the room to such an extent that those who had chairs also abandoned them, and the entire hall, except for the first rows, was one confused mass of people standing up and craning their necks. A few hours later the chairs had completely vanished from the hall, so that they should not take up space, and people, pouring with sweat, were standing tightly squeezed together. The Praesidium itself stood on the table, while a whole crowd of enterprising people who had climbed up on the table was hovering over the chairman's shoulders, preventing him from running the meeting. Next day or the day after, the tables too had vanished, except for the chairman's, and the assembly finally acquired the look of a mass-meeting in a riding-school.

There was some talk of transferring the Soviet to the Duma meeting-hall. But the galleries there held the arrested Secret Police and the 'pharaohs'.[1] By the fourth or fifth day, when they had been transferred to more suitable quarters or sent home, the Soviet had already grown so large that the White Hall could not contain it in full strength: only the sessions of the Soldiers' and Workers' Sections of the Soviet took place there.

* * *

I looked in on the Military Commission two or three times, though I was scarcely able to make my way through the dense crowd that filled the whole Palace. The officers were going back to their regiments—going back in compact batches. This was a sign of improvement in the situation. In any clash with Tsarist troops the great bulk of these returning regular or temporary officers could be counted on. But the point was that the *regiments*

[1] Nickname for the police. (Ed.)

were not going back to their officers or placing themselves under their orders. The *soldiers* could not be counted on, and in this sense there was no improvement.

But in general the situation was not only improving, it was becoming obvious that the danger of the crushing of the revolution was being dissipated like smoke with every hour. New regiments were arriving in Petersburg on foot and by rail one after another; and those of them who, under the command of their officers, were coming in with aggressive intentions either dispersed or came over to the people at the first slight contact with the red capital. *Here* was salvation, in the absence of any forces at the disposal of Tsarism, which was collapsing like a house of cards. But as before the revolution still lacked any real military power.

There were reports that the soldiers of the Admiralty garrison (where the Tsarist Ministers were holding out), tired of the long-drawn-out uncertainty of the situation and having thought things out sensibly, finally scattered in the interests of safety wherever they could. But one after the other the Ministers (also in the interests of their safety) began to be brought over to the Tauride Palace.

In one of my visits to the right wing, around 4 o'clock, I came across a group of arrested Tsarist dignitaries near Rodzianko's office at the beginning of the right corridor. They were standing against the wall, clustered into a tight little bunch and surrounded by armed men. A crowd of soldiers in a rather aggressive mood pressed round them, flinging out hostile remarks. Kurlov[1] looked very grim. He was pale but seemed in control of himself; he was looking around and listening to the remarks, half interestedly, half challengingly. On the other hand Stürmer,[2] in utter panic and confusion, with a hangdog look and chattering teeth, made an extremely disagreeable impression. I didn't know any of the other former lords of creation by sight and I don't remember who they were.

I hurried past.

* * *

[1] Kurlov, Pavel Grigoriyevich (1860–1923): Minister of the Interior under Protopopov; emigrated after the October Revolution. (Ed.)

[2] Stürmer, Boris Vladimirovich (1848–1917): Premier of Russia during most of 1916; a favourite of Rasputin's and the Tsarina's. (Ed.)

It was imperative to come to the help of one very important branch of the Soviet economy now taking shape—the printing-shops. By the previous evening V. D. Bonch-Bruyevich, with the help of some volunteers, had occupied the *Kopeika* printing-presses on the Ligovka, where the *Izvestiya* was also issued. This was one of the best printing-shops in Petersburg. Bonch set up some sort of a guard there and collected some workers. But there were neither funds, essential for wages, nor supplies, nor safety. The workers scattered, and the Soviet might have found itself at the decisive moment without this cardinal means of influencing the populace.

First Bonch sent a note to the Ex. Com. couched in the most vigorous terms, and then he came himself—with a demand that the printing-shop be provided with funds, supplies, and an armed guard. I was detailed to arrange this matter with Bonch; my activities may give some notion of working conditions in the Ex. Com. in these first hours of the revolution.

There were absolutely no funds whatever; but there *had to be*, and I gave Bonch *carte blanche* with respect to arrangements with the workers. But the printing-shop had to be supplied with provisions for a hundred men of the working personnel and guard, so that the workers could stay on at the printing-shop uninterruptedly. This was indispensable, according to Bonch, who moreover maintained that an armed attack on the *Kopeika* was being prepared by the Black Hundred.

This matter of provisioning had to be referred to the Supply Commission. But whom could we send? And if a volunteer were found, where was the guarantee that he would reach his goal, and that he would be listened to? There were no requisition forms; no one knew just whom to apply to. It was doubtful whether the names of the Ex. Com. members were known, and whether the volunteer's own name would be convincing to those persons appointed by the Supply Commission for the actual execution of the orders. Finally, were there provisions available and means of transporting them? In any case I had to go myself, leaving the session for an indefinite time and elbowing through the impenetrable crowds along the interminable draughty corridors, slippery with swill, to the supply stores set up in the Palace by the Supply Commission.

More than anything else I was embittered by consciousness of this misuse and irrevocable waste of time. But I was comforted by the thought that no other way was possible, nor could have been possible.

After long and weary wanderings I found my way to a room near the kitchen, where some unknown man, besieged by a crowd, was satisfying requests for provisions at his own discretion. After many attempts to attract his attention and after the endless exhortations and pleas assailing the store-keeper from every side in the middle of this babel, I got my orders executed, but—had to find my own transport. I simply got an order, and was told, as Xerxes had been once before by the Athenians —'go and take it'. Faced by the hundredweight or so of my load I clearly risked finding myself in the same position as Xerxes.

Accidentally overhearing a conversation in the crowd on my way I stopped a man, unknown to me but with an agreeable look, who had mentioned having a car. I 'agitated' at him and convinced him of the extreme importance of helping the cause of the press, and he promised to take the provisions over to the printing-shop. We arranged for him to wait for me at a certain spot where I was to bring him the order at some unspecified time. All this was practically hopeless in the atmosphere of crowds, muddle, and the general nervous strain from the mass of grandiose feelings and niggling details. But it was the only possible way.

I don't know whether I wandered about for an hour or more. But strange as it may seem, I nevertheless found this man at the appointed spot and handed him the order. He undertook to perform the task, taking two or three armed men in the car with him for protection. Now the only question was whether he would have enough patience to get hold of what the order called for, whether he would find his car in its place, and whether anything would happen to him on the way.

But strangely enough the provisions were finally brought to the printing-shop. Bonch, however, would not answer for them without a reliable guard of about forty men, with whose help he intended to set up an 'iron dictatorship' in the printing-shop (and he really did terrorize practically the whole quarter later on, even posting sentries with machine-guns).

A detachment had to be sent, or rather a garrison for the printing-shop had to be created. This was complicated.

I started trying to force my way into the Military Commission. At several points the lines of sentries would not let anyone through, sending them to other points where one was required to show some sort of pass, issued by no one knew whom, which had not been distributed to members of the Ex. Com. Together with the crush, hunger, fatigue, and the consciousness of the absurdity of such 'work', all this was maddening.

Having somehow forced my way with great difficulty into the heart of the Military Commission, with equal difficulty I compelled the attention of one of the people in charge, who were being torn to pieces by petty, futile, and impracticable matters. Finally I talked him into realizing the importance of my business for the whole course of the revolution. But he could do nothing. He ordered one of the crowd of officers to take command of the printing-shop garrison and proceed there immediately—then he ordered out a second and a third. Not one obeyed, each using the first excuse that occurred to him: special missions, the lack of men, more important tasks, etc. . .

Clearly, I should have to 'agitate' myself, and I set about it, with a shrug of the shoulders at the military headquarters, this sole staff and only 'real force' of the revolution. After a lengthy search I came across a lieutenant or captain of ripe years and modest appearance, who agreed to be the military commander of the printing-shop. But this 'Captain Timokhin', as I baptized him at once (from *War and Peace*), had, like the other officers, absolutely no one under his command. And it was clear that this honest but inefficient fellow would never find himself a detachment through his own efforts.

In order to assemble one for him, I now had to carry on not individual agitation among the 'thinkers' but a 'mass' agitation among the ignorant and uncomprehending. I considered this business completely hopeless for myself, or at least excessively lengthy. I went off in search of Kerensky, the only man able to settle the matter at one stroke, by a single propaganda speech to the soldiers in the Catherine Hall. But it was necessary first of all to find him, then to pry him loose, and thirdly to talk him into it.

After further tribulations I found him in the apartments of the Duma Committee, in the depths of the right wing. There were really serious obstacles there to be surmounted, and I found Kerensky running around in circles in his eagerness to encompass the entire revolution and in no condition to do anything whatever practical for it, but only something 'moral'. . . Around him thronged a dense crowd from every democratic or bourgeois circle, buttonholing him or grasping his coat-tails and interrupting each other. It was clear that he was completely at the mercy of these petty current tasks, without the slightest possibility of grasping or furthering the motive forces of the strategic and political situation. I evidently not only had to interest him in my printing-shop business but had every right to do so.

Taking hold of him, like the others, by his buttonhole, I explained the matter to him in a tone that precluded any objections, not sparing the most resounding expressions about the 'fate of the revolution'. He listened, agreed at once, and shouldering aside the crowd rushed off into the Catherine Hall, to the soldiers, to give one of his innumerable speeches and make up a garrison for the printing-shop. I barely had time to point out to him 'Captain Timokhin', who hurried after him. But I left them and turned to further tasks of a similar kind that came up, accomplishing them by the same methods.

Later it turned out that a garrison had indeed been organized and I encountered 'Captain Timokhin' for several weeks afterwards in the printing-shop, where he was living in peace and peacefully 'commanding' the garrison, 'holding' the citadel of the revolution, 'almost regularly' receiving provisions and blessing his fate. . .

This was how work had to be done and technical functions performed during the first few days, until—little by little, out of nothing—a huge machine and a more or less adequate organization were created. Even now, in front of the curtain in the Ex. Com. room and in Room 11, where our women and families had gathered, eager to take part and demanding assignments—even now typewriters had turned up from somewhere and begun to clatter away.

* * *

I went back to the Ex. Com. Reports of excesses and requests for immediate assistance of all kinds were still coming in there. But nevertheless it was clear that the defence of revolutionary order was being established by the independent activity of the districts. Somehow or another the organism of the city, left to itself, had produced white corpuscles and, having shaken off the shackles of Tsarism, was itself healing the wounds it had received in the upheaval. Moreover the excesses involved almost exclusively the police and the really hated enemies of the people and the revolution. The hysterical reports about the destruction of churches, palaces, the Academy of Sciences, etc., generally speaking turned out to be false alarms.

The Soviet 'mass-meeting' was still going on, full of fervent talk—I don't know what about. Real mass-meetings, at which appeared Chkheidze, Kerensky, and deputies from the right wing, were going on in every corner of the crowded Palace and around it in the courtyard and square, among puffing or silent motor-cars belonging to no one knew whom, soldiers' camp-fires, and occasional big guns and machine-guns.

That day there was another false alarm. Some time after 4 o'clock one or two shots were heard in the courtyard—a fairly usual and now no longer alarming occurrence. In the tightly-packed Soviet hall a rather shameful panic took place. In a flash the customary 'Cossacks!' resounded through the huge crowd. How they could suddenly have turned up in front of the Palace and why nothing like counter-fire had been heard—no one asked himself. Some deputies flung themselves on the floor, others started running—God knows where. There was the beginning of a riot. Chkheidze saved the situation by leaping on to a table and ferociously bellowing out a few lofty meaningless words that shamed and calmed the crowd.

But I didn't see this. At this time I was in the Military Commission, where Kerensky also was fussing about. The windows of Room 41 opened on to the square, which looked the same as before—irregular masses of soldiers, guns, horses, machine-guns, and all sorts of civilians. When the shots were heard the crowd of officers and other military personnel filling the room did not fling themselves on the floor or start running away, but there were signs of panic and alarm too. No one knew what to do, where his place was, or how to defend the revolution and its citadel, the Tauride Palace.

There could be no doubt: if there had really been Cossacks or any sort of organized unit, however negligible numerically, attacking us, we could not have looked anywhere for salvation and they would have conquered the revolution with their bare hands.

It was interesting to see Kerensky, who could have done absolutely nothing in case of real danger, but whose conduct in this incident would perhaps have been quite correct, if it had not been a little comical. The phraseology of his speech (an earnest of the future!) was characteristic; I give it verbatim, and vouch for it.

As soon as the shots rang out Kerensky rushed to the window, leaped on the sill, and sticking his head out shouted in a hoarse, broken voice:

'Stations everyone! Defend the Duma! Listen to me—I, Kerensky, am speaking to you, Kerensky is speaking to you! Defend your freedom and the revolution, defend the Duma! Stations everyone!'

But in the courtyard there was a panic too; everyone was preoccupied by the shots. Apparently no one heard Kerensky, or only very few. In any case no one went to 'stations'; no one knew where they were. But the enemy didn't appear, no one attacked, and no one frightened anyone except for those who frightened themselves.

At the same time as Kerensky I jumped up on the other window-sill and looked out through the hinged pane to see what could be seen. It was clear that it was a false alarm and that the shots were accidental—most probably from the inexperienced hands of some worker handling a rifle for the first time. It was ridiculous and a little embarrassing. I went over to Kerensky.

'Everything's all right', I said in a low voice, but one quite audible in the silence that had supervened. 'Why create a worse panic than the shots?'

I hadn't reckoned on the result of this remark. Standing in the middle of the room, Kerensky broke into a rage and began bellowing at me, shakily picking his words:

'I demand—that everyone—do his duty and not—interfere—when I—give orders!'

'Absolutely right!' I heard someone remark approvingly.

I smiled to myself and apologized aloud with the straightest of faces. Discipline and organization were as necessary as air. Let him who had ears listen to Kerensky—without laughing.

I had no idea who was shooting or why. Indeed, there was a

feeling that by now there was no longer any danger for the revolution from the armed forces of Tsarism. The acuteness of the general situation was diminishing by the minute. Reports had been received that Moscow had already 'joined up' and that with the help of the garrison the overturn was being consummated there easily and painlessly.

Russia was free—there was no autocracy, there was no Peter-Paul Fortress, there was no Secret Police, there was no underground, there was nothing old left: ahead everything was completely different, unknown, wonderful. This flashed through one's mind in the midst of the current microscopic and 'vulgar' matters which seemed to have no relationship to the magnificent victory of the people. But there were moments when each of us thought that surely all this was an illusion, nonsense, all a dream. Wasn't it time to wake up?

* * *

It was already past 5. The crowd in the halls was rapidly thinning out. The Soviet was scattering, after deciding to meet again the following day. Work was also slackening in the Ex. Com., which was beginning to dwindle away rather rapidly and obviously needed some rest.

Circumstances allowed a breathing-spell, and some friends of mine persuaded me to go off for dinner to I. I. Manukhin's, a doctor who had cured Gorky of tuberculosis on Capri and become friendly with him since. Manukhin lived a step or two away from the Tauride Palace, at the corner of Sergiyevsky and Potyomkin Streets. It was possible to dine there and return very quickly.

A whole crowd of us went off to dine at Manukhin's, where we found Gorky and some other literary friends. Gorky was still out of spirits. The impressions he had received during the day had not lightened but intensified his gloom. For an hour by the clock he snarled and grumbled at the chaos, the disorder, the excesses, at the displays of political ignorance, at the girls driving around the city, God knows where, in God knows whose cars—and forecast that the movement would probably collapse in ruin worthy of our Asiatic savagery. Two or three people present added illustrations of this theme and seconded whatever Gorky said.

Facts were facts, and impressions were true in so far as they were called forth by the facts. But these were the impressions of a man of letters, who did not wish to go beyond what was apparent to his eyes, impressions whose power obscured theoretical insight and warped his objective perspective.

The *political* conclusions drawn from them were not only nonsensical, but simply comical to me. To me it seemed, on the contrary, self-evident that things were going brilliantly, that the development of the revolution couldn't have been better, that victory could now be considered secure, and that the excesses, the man-in-the-street's stupidity, vulgarity, and cowardice, the muddles, the motor-cars, the girls—all this was only what the revolution could not in any circumstances avoid, without which nothing similar had *ever* happened anywhere.

Coming in hungry and tired, in a mood of happy excitement, I attempted to protest only during the first few minutes, before I saw how much my mood was out of harmony with the tone of the conversation that had already begun. Then, ignoring the shafts directed at me, I stubbornly kept quiet. I felt an intolerable boredom and took no pains to conceal it, allowing anyone who pleased to take it for fatigue. Instead of the elation of victory the first meeting of the 'Letopisites' in their own circle took place in gloom, depression, and a mutual lack of understanding.

* * *

At last dinner was over, and I hurried back to the Tauride Palace.

One after the other, self-appointed groups had been coming all day to the members of the Ex. Com. with orders, written by themselves, for the arrest of innocent as well as of really dangerous persons, and they were still doing so now, late in the evening. Withholding our signatures, in such circumstances, meant in effect countenancing the use of unauthorized force and perhaps even excesses against some chosen victim. But signing the order meant, in some instances, sanctioning a perfectly politic action, in others, simply ensuring the personal safety of the man who had come under suspicion. In our atmosphere of passions running high there were more chances of provoking excesses by opposing an arrest than by duly carrying it out. But

I don't remember one case (I can even maintain there weren't any) of an arrest taking place by order of the Ex. Com. or on its initiative.[1]

From the very first the revolution had felt itself to be too powerful to be obliged to resort to such means of self-defence. The methods of autocracy began to be cultivated again only later, during the Coalition, and blossomed with unexampled luxuriance under the Bolsheviks.

Thanks to the activity of these self-appointed groups and the initiative of the new organizations, the population of the Ministerial Pavilion kept growing. By the evening of the 28th this pavilion was densely peopled by several dozen dignitaries of all kinds and high police officials. Some were arresting themselves, appearing in the Tauride Palace and presenting themselves to the first person they met, or else asking by telephone to be arrested and taken to the Palace. This was really the best thing for their safety—even though those days were not darkened by the invocation of lynch-law against a single representative of the civil authorities, and only a few military commanders were sacrificed on the altar of their own ferocity.

Even the especially execrable Sukhomlinov[2] lived through the tempest of the revolution safe and sound. The Minister of Justice Dobrovolsky, among others, was taken to the Tauride Palace at his own request. And at midnight on this same day Protopopov, the last powerful favourite of the musical-comedy Rasputin days, also appeared in the Catherine Hall, and timidly asked the first person he met to arrest him. There was considerable interest in this notorious Minister and more than once questions were asked from the crowd as to where Protopopov was and whether he had been arrested.

* * *

Work was finally slackening. Someone had volunteered to stay in the Ex. Com. until morning and was already settling down on a sofa near the 'phone. About 1 o'clock in the morning

[1] Later, the Ex. Com. ordered the arrest of Nicholas II only when reports had been received that he was escaping to England. This is the only case I know of in this period of the revolution.

[2] Sukhomlinov, Vladimir Alexandrovich (1848–1926): Minister of War, 1909. Suspected of Germanophilia, he was arrested even under the old régime; he was re-arrested after the February Revolution and condemned to life imprisonment. He escaped abroad after the October Revolution. (Ed.)

I started off towards a near-by friend's house to sleep. I felt weighed down by the necessity of telling my friends, who had been longing for news and pining without reliable information, how things stood. But the thought of a bed was extremely tempting. . .

I went out of the Palace alone. The square was now quite empty. I don't remember whether the guns and machine-guns were still there, but there was no longer anyone guarding either them or the Palace of the revolution. It was believed that there was no longer any danger. All the same it was remarkable. The very heart of the revolution was undefended. The organization for its defence had proved inadequate and the handful of volunteers needed had not been found.

* * *

I walked along the deserted streets reflecting. For the first time I was alone and for the first time I was walking through a free city of the new Russia. Now and then my consideration of practical matters was shot through by luminous shafts of acute happiness, triumphant pride, and a sort of wonder before the boundless, radiant, and incomprehensible achievements of those days. Could it be that I should not wake up in my 'illegal' bed, or over the map of Turkestan, or over the galley-proofs of the *Letopis*, drenched in the red ink of the Tsarist censors?

There were occasional shots somewhere. Motor-cars and lorries were hurtling by, God knows where to or where from. Every once in a while there would be groups of soldiers with rifles going past or standing by the camp-fires. Now and then I would meet armed civilian detachments of workers and students, with the soldiers or by themselves. They were the new militia, or rather self-appointed volunteers. It was to them that Petersburg was so greatly indebted for the swift restoration of order and security. The rare passers-by walked confidently and cheerfully, demonstrating that the streets of the troubled city really were safe at night and that it was beyond the power of the Black Hundred *provocateurs* to create an atmosphere of pogrom and panic.

But were all these people I met, all these soldiers I came across singly and in groups, really ours? It was hard to say, but it would be interesting to test it. In the lonely quarter of Peski some soldiers were tinkering with a broken-down car. A patrol was walking towards them.

'Comrades, listen!' I shouted across the street to them.

They all pricked up their ears and looked at me.

'Protopopov has been arrested and is under lock and key in the Tauride Palace with his friends!'

I heard exclamations of approval and pleasure from the crowd.

'Thanks, comrade!' they called after me. 'Thanks for the good news!'

Yes, the victory of the revolution was irrevocable! I remembered the soldiers tearing down the portrait of Nicholas that morning. Nicholas was still free and calling himself Tsar. But where was Tsarism? It was gone. It had crumbled away in an instant. Three centuries to build it up, and three days for it to vanish.

In the house where I was going I found my impatient hosts, tea, supper, and a bed waiting for me. I hastily satisfied their avid curiosity and went to bed. My mind revolved around trivial preoccupations and practical preparations for the morning. But my whole being was celebrating a great holiday. And not only the panorama of the future glimmering faintly through a magic crystal but fragments of the actual scenes I had just witnessed made my heart throb wildly, tickled my throat, and would not let me sleep.

CHAPTER 5

THE THIRD DAY

March 1st

THE next morning I was approaching the Tauride Palace before 10 o'clock. There were the usual queues, but unusual liveliness, in the streets. At street-corners people were clustering around the proclamations of the Ex. Com. and the Provisional Committee of the Duma. There were red flags everywhere.

I went in by the side entrance, from Tauride Street, thus coming straight into the enemy camp in the right corridor, in the Duma Committee's territory. Here things were still comparatively seemly—hall-porters in livery were standing about, spruce and solemn young officers were guarding the entrances from the corridor into the inner rooms of the Committee; men with morning-coats, beaver collars, and handsome liberal faces were darting about. The Palace was already animated and crowded.

The first member of the Ex. Com. I met reported that the Tsar's train, headed for Tsarskoe-Selo, had been detained by revolutionary troops at the station of Dno.

This was enough to put the question of liquidating the Romanovs on the agenda. The news was excellent. But this whole matter seemed to me secondary, in comparison with the question of the formation of a Government, the delimitation of its activities, and the creation of a definite constitution, and definite conditions for political life and the further struggle of the democracy.

I was even rather apprehensive that the dynastic question might squeeze off the agenda the problem of the régime, which was being settled quite independently of the fate of the Romanovs. No one was in any doubt about this last: the Romanovs might be *restored* as a dynasty, or *exploited* as a principle of monarchy—but by now it was absolutely impossible to regard them as a *factor* in the establishment of new political relationships in the country.

*   *   *

I made my way right through the Palace to the Soviet rooms; but there I was told that Kerensky had been looking for me on a matter of urgency. I retraced my steps to find him. Everybody was talking about the Tsar, asking what it had been decided to do with him and saying what *ought* to be done.

I found Kerensky in one of the Duma Committee's rooms, in earnest conversation with Sokolov. Kerensky turned to me, continuing the conversation. The point was that a majority of the Duma Committee were suggesting that he should join the bourgeois Cabinet now being formed. Kerensky wanted to talk to me about it, in order to get an approximate idea of the attitude of Left-wing individuals and groups and of the leaders of the Soviet.

Neither in the Ex. Com. nor in the Soviet had these questions yet been raised and it was premature to talk about them. But I gave Kerensky my personal opinion explicitly and at once. I said that I was definitely opposed both to the Soviet's taking power and to the formation of a coalition Government. I did not think official representation of Socialist democracy in a bourgeois ministry was possible. A Soviet hostage in a bourgeois-imperialist Cabinet would tie the hands of the democracy not only in its efforts to forward the magnificent national revolution but also in the great *international* problems it must face. Kerensky's entry into Miliukov's Government as an individual, on the other hand, I considered to be not unprofitable. As I told him, his peculiar personal position made this quite possible. He had no formal ties with any Socialist party and was the leader only of a labour group which had nothing to do with the International.

Such an answer, of course, could not satisfy Kerensky . . . He obviously wanted to be a *Minister*. But he needed to be the *ambassador of the democracy* and its official representative in the first revolutionary Government. He parted from me more than dissatisfied.

* * *

What were the aims of the bourgeoisie that had taken power? And from another point of view, what social and political conditions were essential for the democracy?

As far as propertied Russia and the imperialist bourgeoisie

were concerned, there could be no doubt—the aims of the Guchkovs and Miliukovs boiled down to the liquidation of the arbitrary Rasputin régime with the help of the popular movement (or better still without it), the reinforcement of the dictatorship of capital and rents on the basis of a semi-free 'liberal' political régime with 'wider political and civil rights for the people', and the establishment of a sovereign parliament secured by a propertied bourgeois majority. Propertied Russia must try to bring the revolution to a halt at this point, after turning the State into an instrument of its class rule and the country into an oligarchy of capitalists—like England and France, the 'great democracies of the West'. If the movement passed *beyond* the dictatorship of capital, propertied Russia, after taking power, was bound to attempt to crush it by all available means.

Our bourgeoisie also had some special tasks of its own—in the service of national imperialism and Russian chauvinism in the war. 'War to the finish' and 'Loyalty to our gallant allies'—for the sake of the Dardanelles, Armenia, and other nonsense—were indispensable slogans for propertied Russia. Since these slogans were of course in flagrant contradiction to the development of the revolution, the revolution had to be curbed and subjugated.

Something else again was the attitude of the Soviet democracy, that of the soldiers, peasants, and workers, the petty bourgeoisie, and the proletariat. Its tasks were far from being so obvious and were extremely controversial. Its understanding of the course the revolution ought to take might be and indeed was completely different.

Its Right wing (or those among them who were thinking Marxists of the camp of Potresov[1] & Co.) was convinced that our *revolution was a bourgeois revolution.* Our Right-wing Marxists did not abandon this idea until their own disappearance from the political stage. As a theoretical proposition it was, generally speaking, possible, and not especially harmful.

But what was extremely harmful was that these groups drew conclusions from the given proposition that were logically not

[1] Potresov (Starover), Alexander Nikolayevich (1869–1934): very prominent in early Russian Marxism, one of the founders and editors of *Iskra* (the Spark; see p. 354). He became a leading Menshevik after the 1903 split between Mensheviks and Bolsheviks; he was violently opposed to the October Revolution, emigrated in 1922 and died in Paris. (Ed.)

inevitable and factually quite incorrect. These conclusions were that under these conditions all the above-mentioned plans and aims of the bourgeoisie were quite legitimate; that the establishment in Russia of a dictatorship of capital (as in 'the great democracies of the West') was the basic task of our epoch and the sole object of the revolution; that the imperialism of the new revolutionary Russia and also, consequently, unity in the war with our gallant Allies were inevitable and lawful phenomena, demanding the support of the democracy in the avoidance of a 'national catastrophe'; that in connexion with this the working class and the peasantry should cut down their demands and their programme, which otherwise would be 'unrealizable', etc. . .

This was the real position of the Right-wing members of the Soviet, and hence one of the possible positions of the *whole* Soviet, personifying the entire revolutionary democracy. In essence this position simply implied an absolutely unconditional surrender of power to Guchkov and Miliukov, for them to realize their liberal imperialist programme and establish a 'rightful' régime on the Western model.

The Left wing of the Soviet, its Bolshevik and SR members, occupied a contrary position; hence it was possible that this contrary position would be adopted by the Soviet as a whole. It was based on a belief that the World War would result in an absolutely inevitable worldwide Socialist revolution and that the national revolt in Russia would lay its foundations, blazing a trail not only towards the liquidation of the Tsarist autocracy, but also towards the *annihilation of the power of capital.* In such circumstances the insurgent people, who had all the real power, must exploit it to the full, take the state power into their own hands and without delay move on to the realization of a maximum programme in general and the liquidation of the war in particular. According to this view there should be no government of the propertied classes at all in the revolution, and in no circumstances could there be any question of handing the power over to it.

It must be said, however, that the representatives of these views were very ineffectual in the Ex. Com., both quantitatively and qualitatively. They merely chattered inaudibly and scribbled a bit—mostly for demagogic reasons and as a sop to their consciences—but they did not even think of engaging in any real struggle for their principles, either in the Ex. Com. or the Soviet, or amongst the masses.

When the question was debated these people were almost unnoticeable; they never came forward with an independent formulation of their position, and when it came to voting they constituted a single majority with the representatives of the third tendency, to which I too belonged.

* * *

This is how I personally saw the question: The epoch of worldwide imperialist war could not but culminate in worldwide Socialist revolution. The historical development of Europe was entering the phase of the liquidation of capitalism and we had to view the course of our own revolution in the light of that fact. For this reason worship of the idea of a bourgeois revolution in Russia, the cult of political and social minimalism, was not only pernicious but shortsighted and utopian.

It is true that even though our revolution had been consummated by the democratic masses it lacked both the material power and the indispensable prerequisites for an immediate Socialist transformation of Russia. We should only construct a Socialist society against the background of a Socialist Europe and with its help. But as for the consolidation of a bourgeois dictatorship in the present revolution—*that was quite out of the question.*

We were bound to count on a development of our revolution in which popular demands could evolve and be satisfied in all fields independently of the limitations imposed on them by contemporary Western plutocratic states. The revolution, not having given Russia immediate Socialism, must lead her straight towards it, and for this it was essential to establish the proper *political premises* at once and to ensure and consolidate the *dictatorship of the democratic classes.*

The Soviet democracy had to entrust the power to the propertied elements, its class enemy, without whose participation it could not now master the technique of administration in the desperate conditions of disintegration, nor deal with the forces of Tsarism and of the bourgeoisie, united against it. But the *conditions* of this transfer of power had to assure the democracy of a complete victory over the class enemy in the near future.

Consequently the gist of the question was whether propertied Russia *would consent* to take power in such conditions, and the task consisted of compelling it to embark on this risky experiment as the least of the evils lying before it.

Pending the working out of the conditions for the transfer of power, we must not, while anticipating an immediate struggle against the bourgeoisie, a struggle to the death, and already starting this struggle (because of the army), deprive them of the hope of winning. We must be wary of confronting them with any demands which might make them consider the experiment not worth while and turn to other methods of consolidating their class rule.

We must make every effort not to 'disrupt the combination', and therefore limit ourselves to a minimal, really indispensable programme.

But just what would create the kind of constitution vital to the revolution and the democracy? That is, on just what concrete conditions should the power be entrusted to Miliukov's Government?

In essence I thought there was just one such condition: the assurance of *complete political freedom in the country, an absolute freedom of organization and agitation.*

At this point—I reasoned—democratic Russia was completely disintegrated and deprived of all inner cohesion; it was not a living organism but a bed of sand. But with the revolution the masses of the people would be sprinkled with the water of life, and in a flash be reborn to organic existence. In the course of the next few weeks democratic Russia would undoubtedly be covered with a firm network of class, party, trade-union, municipal, and Soviet organizations. It would rally as one and become invincible in the face of the united front of capital and imperialism. This was one aspect of the matter: the creation of the *new body* of the revolutionary democracy.

The other task was to breathe into this living body the requisite living soul. If the first task was performed by the *organization* of the masses of the people, then the second would be ensured by complete freedom of *agitation*.

The emancipated masses, shaken up and enlightened by the

great tempest, could not remain blind to their own interests. Led by the proletarian vanguard under the banner of Zimmerwald, they could not surrender to the landowners and plutocrats, and turn the new State into the instrument of the latter's class rule.

I considered freedom of agitation sufficient to prevent the imperialist bourgeoisie from consolidating the dictatorship of capital, prevent the establishment of the forms of a European bourgeois republic in our midst, give scope for the further continuation of the movement and for the widening of the revolution, and lead the country in the near future to the political dictatorship of the worker-peasant majority—with all the attendant consequences.

In this I was reasoning essentially just like the Bolsheviks a few months later. During the formation of one of the 'Coalitions', when the anti-democratic nature of Kerensky's Government had already become completely clear and when at the same time every real force within the 'Coalition' was already oozing away and going over to the side of the Bolsheviks—they shrugged their shoulders at the Government of the Winter Palace and, leaving it to its own devices, demanded for themselves the guarantee of just one thing: freedom of agitation.

This basic condition for the transfer of power to the bourgeoisie seemed to me first of all to be completely obligatory, with no reservations, and secondly, to lay a quite adequate foundation for the fulfilment of the whole necessary future programme of the democracy.

On the other hand, this condition was bound to be accepted by the opposing side. Any other demands, while undoubtedly of less essential importance, might 'disrupt the combination'. In a great many of them Miliukov & Co. could not concur, in view of the situation of their class and themselves personally, but this demand—not to attack the principles of liberty—they could not but accept, if they were prepared to take power at all with the consent of the Soviet democracy. To concur in the given experiment meant to concur in this condition, pick up the gauntlet thrown down by the revolutionary democracy, and attempt to realize their programme and consolidate their dictatorship through single combat in the open arena under conditions of complete political freedom.

Nevertheless it was impossible to limit to this fundamental point the conditions of transferring the power to the propertied elements. First of all—this was self-evident—a full and universal *amnesty* was indispensable. Secondly, the revolution must provide not only a charter of liberties but also a form of constitution capable of embodying the idea of the people's sovereignty, the people's freedom, and the people's rights. It was necessary to sanction and reinforce with a legal framework the work of the provisional catastrophic period and make the new status permanent and capable of organic evolution, wider scope, and development to its logical conclusion. It was necessary to ensure as quickly as possible the convocation of a nation-wide, sovereign *Constituent Assembly* based on the most democratic electoral law.

These three conditions: the proclamation of complete political freedom, an amnesty, and immediate measures for the convocation of a Constituent Assembly, seemed to me to be the absolutely indispensable, but also exhaustive, tasks of the democracy in the transfer of the functions of the Government to the propertied bourgeoisie. Everything else would take care of itself.

This was how I saw things, and more or less what I said on March 1st in the Ex. Com., in the debate on the political problem of the revolution.

The debate began quite amicably and sensibly. The mood of the meeting—against any participation in the Government—very quickly defined itself, and then Chkheidze, getting needlessly excited, and threatening to issue ultimata, suddenly began to rant on the same theme.

Chkheidze was always mortally afraid of accepting any share of power, not only now and not only for the Soviet democracy, but also later, both for himself and for his closest friends.

At this point there was no strong and reasonable defence of coalition on principle. However, its most interesting advocates were not present at this time—Bogdanov, who had been entrusted with the organization of the clerical staff, and Peshekhonov, who was 'playing the commissar' on the Petersburg Side.

In any case, the focus of the debate shifted to the conditions for the transfer of power to the Provisional Government formed by the Duma Committee. As for the actual formation of a propertied régime, that was accepted as something already decided, and as far as I remember not one voice was raised against it on behalf of a democratic régime. Yet there were present at the meeting from the very beginning the official Bolshevik Zalutsky and the unofficial one Krasikov, and a little later Shlyapnikov, who was going about here and there on party business, presented the new Bolshevik representative Molotov to the Ex. Com. I am not of course speaking about 'Bolsheviks' like Steklov: not only at that time but right down to October he had nothing in common with the Bolsheviks; in those days, like myself, he represented the Ex. Com. *Centre.*

As before no minutes were kept.

This debate, however, was fairly short. Probably not more than half an hour later it was interrupted by the rather noisy appearance from behind the curtain of a colonel in field uniform, accompanied by a midshipman with a truculent look and a taut, excited face. We all turned on them with exclamations of annoyance. What was all this?

Instead of a precise reply the Colonel, standing bolt upright, began making a speech to the effect that the Ex. Com. was now a Government with full powers, that it was impossible to do anything without it, that everything depended on it, that all good citizens should and would obey it, and more in the same style. The Colonel's servile tone, usual in relations with his superiors, his ridiculous babbling, and especially his disturbance of our business naturally created a disagreeable impression and made most of us very angry.

There were shouts of 'What's up? Talk sense, and get on with it!' from all sides. Many got to their feet and in a flash the disorder was general. A sense of helplessness swept over us, a feeling of dejection and tedium. . . But the Colonel wouldn't let up, and began talking about his devotion to the revolution, about how even before he was always, etc.

Finally we lost patience. We had to raise our voices and order the Colonel to explain what it was all about or leave. It turned out that this stupid officer was an ambassador from the Duma Committee in Rodzianko's name and all the preceding was a diplomatic flourish he had thought indispensable to the success of his mission.

What had happened was that Rodzianko, having received a

telegram from the Tsar with a request to come to Dno for an interview, was unable to comply, since the railway workers wouldn't give him a train without the Ex. Com.'s permission. This had to be discussed at once, interrupting the business already begun. The Colonel was asked to leave for the time being. He had already managed to start another speech about his devotion to the revolution, fortifying this by references to facts from his biography, but he was interrupted by the excited midshipman.

'I take the liberty,' said the latter, 'of asking in the name of the sailors and their officers what your attitude is towards the war and the defence of the fatherland? Since we obey you and acknowledge your authority, we ought to know.'

But this was too much. Both of them were categorically ordered to leave. On his way out the midshipman continued his declaration.

'I feel bound to say that we all stand for the war, for the continuation of the war. The entire army is with us, both here and at the front. The "Workers' Committee" can count on us only if it too . . .'

The midshipman was interrupted.

'The question of war and peace has not been debated as yet in the Soviet. When a decision is reached you'll hear about it. Now be so good as not to interrupt the proceedings.'

And indeed the question of war and peace had not yet been debated. It had been removed from the agenda, as the first systematic intervention in the spontaneous process of the revolution. The Ex. Com. had not yet had the slightest opportunity of taking up one position or another on this question, but the chief thing was that it was not part of the plan of the controlling majority to force the problem of peace. On the contrary, it was vital to wait as long as possible. For in the Soviet this question had not been broached even by the workers themselves, who instinctively felt that it might turn out to be extremely complicated and teeming with submerged rocks. But it was clear that the problem had to be put on the agenda, if not today, then tomorrow. The midshipman's speech, reminding us both of the acuteness of the problem and of its danger, was extremely symptomatic.

The question of Rodzianko's train was settled in one concerted effort. We discussed it on our feet, as we had been when contending with the Colonel and the midshipman.

I said: 'Rodzianko must not be allowed to see the Tsar. We still don't know the intentions of the leading groups of the bourgeoisie, the Progressive Bloc and the Duma Committee, and no one can vouch for them. So far they have not publicly bound themselves in any way whatever. If the Tsar has any power on his side—which again we don't know—then the "revolutionary" Duma, which "stands for the people", will certainly side with the Tsar against the revolution. There can be no doubt that this is what the Duma and others long to do. The only question is whether it is *possible*. We must not create this possibility of the formation of a counter-revolutionary force disguised as a union of the Tsar and the people in the shape of a 'people's Government'. Their negotiations at headquarters and the Tsar's successes may bring about the greatest confusion in the army—already perplexed, doubtful, and unstable. And what the Tsar would not be strong enough to do alone he will easily be able to do with the help of the Duma and Rodzianko: collect and move up forces to restore order in Petersburg, which is not merely in a state of revolution, but also completely disorganized and undefended. After all, everyone knows what the real attitude of the Duma majority is: it would be enough for the counter-revolution to have one loyal scratch regiment to destroy the whole movement. Who can guarantee that the fate of the revolution does not depend on the decision whether to give Rodzianko a train? We must thank the railway workers for their correct understanding and conscientious performance of their duty towards the revolution, and refuse Rodzianko a train.'

I don't know whether anyone expressed the view that authorizing the train would be useful. Someone may have said it would do no harm. But in any case the discussion was extremely brief and it was decided, if not unanimously at any rate by an overwhelming majority, to refuse Rodzianko a train.

The Colonel was recalled, given our decision, and dismissed. He had plainly not expected this outcome of his mission, but the tone of the statement was so categorical that Rodzianko's courier, with his devotion to the revolution, was obliged to confine himself to saying 'Yes, sir!' and take himself off with a click of his spurs.

We turned to the agenda. I don't remember whether we tried to go on with the debate on the question of the Government, or plunged for a while into 'emergency' and 'extraordinary' business. But, about twenty minutes after the Colonel had left, a request in Rodzianko's name from the Duma wing was conveyed through our secretary to 'Member of the Provisional Committee of the Duma Chkheidze' to report at once to the chairman of the Duma. After some hesitations and grumbling from a good half of these present Chkheidze submissively prepared to go. The purpose of the summons was obvious.

But just then Kerensky, pale and already completely worn out, flew into the room. His face was filled with despair, as though something horrible had happened.

'What have you done? How could you?' he began, in a broken, tragic whisper. 'You wouldn't provide a train! Rodzianko was supposed to go to make Nicholas sign his abdication, and you've ruined everything. . . You've played into the hands of the Monarchy, of the Romanovs. It will be your responsibility!'

Kerensky gasped for breath, and, deathly pale, fell swooning or half-swooning into an arm-chair. People ran for water and loosened his collar. He was stretched out on some chairs, sprinkled with water, and fussed over generally. Everything was done to bring him round. I took no part in all this but sat gloomily in a nearby arm-chair. The scene sickened me.

For Kerensky, who had not slept for several nights and who had expended a superhuman amount of nervous energy during the days of the revolution, to have weakened to the point of banal hysteria—that was still tolerable. His substituting semi-theatrical pathos for common sense and sober judgement in an important matter of business, which demanded a swift practical summing-up—also had nothing specially bad about it. What was worse was that Kerensky on the third day of the revolution had already appeared in the left wing from the right as a direct, if unwitting, mouthpiece of the Miliukovs and Rodziankos. Moreover I was anxious about the fate of the decision concerning the train. Kerensky had of course come to get it cancelled, and his hysterical pressure might influence many people.

And as a matter of fact, after coming round, Kerensky made

a long and senseless speech, not so much about the train and the abdication as about everybody's duty towards the revolution and the necessity of contact between the right and left wings of the Tauride Palace. He spoke in a tiresome and exasperated way, more than once emphasizing that he, Kerensky, was staying in the right wing to defend the interests of democracy, that he was watching out for them, and making them secure, that he was a sufficient guarantee, that in such conditions a lack of confidence in the Duma Committee was a lack of confidence in him, Kerensky, that in such conditions it was out of place, dangerous, criminal, etc. . .

Now, *sub specie aeternitatis*, in the light of everything that happened later, this whole naïve, hysterically egocentric speech seems to me extraordinarily characteristic: it contained the germ of the future helpless hysteric who imagined that he was, not the 'mathematical centre of Russian bonapartism', but a real Bonaparte, called to save the country and the revolution.

Kerensky demanded reconsideration of the decision about Rodzianko's train. The resulting vote was absurd: all those present against three—Zalutsky, Krasikov, and myself—gave in to Kerensky's hysteria, and Rodzianko's train was authorized.

Rodzianko, however, never left. Too much time had passed, and it was impossible to equip a train so quickly. It was already after 1 o'clock. The Tsar did not wait for Rodzianko in Dno but left for Pskov, where he arrived at 8 o'clock in the evening of March 1st.

* * *

A 'note' arrived from the above-mentioned Yurevich, whom the Duma Committee had appointed Civil Governor of Petersburg. He wanted the Ex. Com. to give him an assistant.

Henceforth, obviously, no governors ought to have been appointed. But temporarily, in the process of establishing the new order, there was extremely useful work to be done in the governor's office, if only in the destruction of the old police nest. Both the Soviet's authority and its control in this matter might thus prove very appropriate. But the work demanded, first of all, a great deal of energy and just as much tact, and secondly a special man. Who could be sent? Having accidentally met in the corridors my old friend and co-thinker Nikitsky, the specialist in finance and public law, I sent him off to be Governor without any lengthy discussions.

Later on that evening, before the opening of the famous night session of March 2nd in the Duma Committee apartments, while gulping down a glass of tea, I told Yurevich and Nekrasov[1] about this change of offices in the city governorship, adding that I, an 'illegal', had submitted a request to Nikitsky to give me the right of residence in Petersburg, and that I was hoping for a favourable response.

* * *

Around 10 o'clock, going back behind the curtain of Room 13, where the Ex. Com. had been in session shortly before, I found the following scene: N. D. Sokolov was sitting at a table writing. He was surrounded on all sides by soldiers, standing, sitting, and leaning on the table, half-dictating and half-suggesting to Sokolov what he should write. There flashed through my mind Tolstoy's description of how he used to make up stories together with the children in the school at Yasnaya Polyana.

It appeared that this was a committee elected by the Soviet to compose an 'Order' to the soldiers. There was no agenda and no discussion of any kind, everyone spoke, and all were completely absorbed in the work, formulating their collective opinion without any voting. I stood and listened, extraordinarily interested. When the work was finished they put a heading on the sheet: 'Order No. 1'.[2]

This is the background of the document that earned such resounding fame. Its contents were completely covered by decisions of the Soviet and had nothing terrible in them. It was

[1] Nekrasov, Nikolai Vissarionovich (1879-1940): a Left Cadet and member of the Third and Fourth Dumas; Minister of Communications in the Provisional Government. He left the Cadet Party in the summer of 1917 and remained in Russia after the October Revolution, occupying important Government posts. He was a witness in the 1931 Trial of the Mensheviks. (Ed.)

[2] This order provided for the election throughout all army and fleet units of 'committees' from the lower ranks; for the similar election of representatives to the Soviet; for the orders of the Duma Military Commission to be obeyed only insofar as they were sanctioned by the Soviet; for the retention by committees elected from the lower ranks of all arms, which were in no circumstances to be handed over to officers; for the soldiers to enjoy ordinary citizens' rights, including the abolition of saluting when off duty; for the abolition of honorific forms of address for officers, and the prohibition of any rudeness to soldiers of all ranks, including the use of 'thou'. (Ed.)

called forth by the general conditions of the revolution and especially by the tactless provocative policy of the representatives of the Duma Committee towards the soldiers.

This order was in the full sense a popular creation and by no means a malevolent contrivance of individuals or even of a leading group. The bourgeois press, quickly making this order the occasion of a frenzied campaign of slander, for some reason ascribed its authorship to Steklov, who disavowed it more than once and had not a shred of responsibility for it. But Sokolov cannot be considered its author either. This 'fa-a-ateful man,' as Chkheidze liked to call him, was merely the technical executor of the plans of the masses. On the contrary, this was practically the sole independently-creative political act of the Soviet plenum throughout the revolution.

* * *

It was time to organize a conference with the Duma Committee, with the object of forming a Provisional Government and settling its programme. But the members of the Ex. Com., insufficiently concerned with this matter of 'high policy', had scattered. On my own responsibility I went over to the right wing of the Palace to arrange about the meeting. It was best to work through Kerensky, and I wanted to find him.

The third day of the revolution was swiftly coming to a close; the Palace was growing empty and dark once more. But in different corners of it there were those for whom a working night lay ahead. I considered it necessary to insist on an immediate joint conference and not have it put off till morning. But my head was swimming and I was tormented by hunger; I, and probably the others too, had eaten nothing all day.

I found Kerensky in the former apartments of the Military Commission, where there were crowds of officers and armed soldiers as before, but no longer the same crush. What was going on there I don't know. Kerensky, who had been summoned somewhere, was wearing his fur coat, ready to leave. As always, people were thronging around him. He was whiter than snow, and answered questions loudly, vaguely, and disconnectedly.

I got hold of him and explained what I wanted. But he was inattentive and failed to understand me. Busy with his own thoughts he called me aside and led me off to a solitary corner of the room, and, literally squeezing me against the wall, started a strange, incoherent speech, shouting out individual words, his eyes roving about. He talked about confidence again, or rather about the lack of confidence in him personally on the part of the democratic leaders. He spoke of some campaign of baiting that was supposed to have been organized against him, about some desire to alienate the masses from him, all but using the actual words 'plots', 'machinations', 'intrigues'.

I looked at him, dumbfounded. The only feeling I had was one of astonishment and pity for the man. I saw before me plain signs of a nervous breakdown. I made some attempts, not to protest or explain, but to talk Kerensky round and soothe him.

This was the first time I saw him that way, but later I saw him that way more than once. And later on it became obvious to me that it was not only a question of fatigue and strain, but that there was also another side to the matter—Kerensky's belief from the beginning that he had a *mission*, his instant readiness to defend this mission by Bonapartist methods, and his tremendous irritation with all those who had not yet divined its existence. That evening I saw only the seeds of what I witnessed later.

But I had accomplished nothing at all in the matter of organizing a meeting between the future Government and the representatives of the democracy. Kerensky went off somewhere, promising to return shortly. And I left for the apartments of the Duma Committee.

Breaking through the phalanx of young regular officers I came into a room which plainly had a completely different atmosphere from our own. There were no longer many people around, and those remaining were the spruce dapper young men who served the technical needs of the Duma Committee. Then there were some glossy officers and substantial burghers. Some were strolling about the hall, others sedately chatting and sipping tea, served in a manner unheard-of in the left wing, with glasses, little spoons, almost even with sugar-bowls, etc. . . The Provisional Committee of the Duma was sitting in the other room, which was hedged around with even solider obstacles.

I saw Yurevich, the new Civil Governor, sitting at a table talking to Chkheidze, who looked sleepy and limp. I sat down with them and greedily fell on the tea. Sokolov came up and in passing we had a brief consultation about the situation in the city and the tasks of the new Governor.

But steps had to be taken for an immediate 'constituent' conference. The Ex. Com. members present were agreed on this, and in their name I asked that one of the Duma Committee members be called. Nekrasov came out.

'Just what exactly are you suggesting we talk about?' he asked after hearing my explanations.

From his air of restraint I formed the impression that our decisive meeting was regarded as inevitable by their Committee also. But since they hadn't taken the proper bearings with respect to the temper of the Soviet they obviously preferred an attitude of waiting, allowing events to follow their natural course. It may be that the Duma Committee thought that having taken the *formal* power into their hands unimpeded they would assume control of the *material* power too on their own terms, without any obstacles or interference, and quietly consolidate it by their own efforts in the right wing. They may have thought that no question of general policy would arise between us any more than it had up to that time.

But in any case one thing was indubitable: the Duma Committee wanted to have a 'talk' with the representatives of democracy about 'anarchy' and the 'collapse of the army'. There was no doubt that with this purpose in mind they were preparing to ask for our 'help' in an attempt to use *us* to make the revolutionary army and the proletariat submit to *them*. Consequently, I cannot express how astonished and vexed Nekrasov was when I answered: 'We should and must have a talk about the general situation.' . . .

Nekrasov went off to inform the Provisional Committee of this, then came back and told me the representatives of the Soviet of Workers' Deputies would be expected at 12 o'clock.

* * *

It was not more than half an hour to midnight. Kerensky was expected to come back then and it was up to us—the Ex. Com. —to select our representatives at once. But the Ex. Com. had dispersed and was unable to be present at the meeting as a whole. Nor was there any need for this. What was worse was that we had no formally authorized delegation, and there was no time left to elect one. Some of the members, who were present, had to talk it over privately, and as a result the conduct of the negotiations was entrusted to four persons: Chkheidze, Sokolov, Steklov, and myself.

Just after midnight we assembled in the ante-room of the Duma Committee. Coming from another world, we were surrounded by officers and other people of the 'right wing', who questioned us about the situation and showed an interest in our plans and ideas. Steklov had a sheet of paper in his hands, the one on which he had made notes of the Ex. Com. decisions for his report to the Soviet.

Kerensky came back. We were invited into the Duma Committee's meeting-room, evidently a former office, with a whole row of office-tables and chairs in the usual government-office arrangement; there were also two or three assorted arm-chairs standing about, but no large table where we might have settled down. There was not the same chaos and confusion here as with us, but the room nevertheless gave an impression of disorder: it was smoke-filled and dirty, and cigarette butts, bottles, and dirty glasses were scattered about. There were also innumerable plates, both empty and holding food of all kinds, which made our eyes glitter and our mouths water.

To the left of the door, at the farthest end of the room, Rodzianko was sitting at a table drinking soda-water. At another parallel table Miliukov sat facing him over a pile of papers, notes, and telegrams. Further away Nekrasov was seated at the next table nearer the entrance. Behind him, opposite the entrance, there were four or five unknown and negligible deputies or other people, who were simply spectators. In the middle of the room, between Rodzianko's table and Nekrasov's, the arm-chairs and chairs were occupied by the future Premier G. E. Lvov, Godnev, Shidlovsky, and another Lvov, the future Procurator of the Holy Synod—the same who was to go as Kornilov's courier to Kerensky. Beyond them, usually standing or strolling about, was Shulgin.[1]

[1] Shulgin, Vasilii Vitalyevich (1878–1945): Right-wing Tsarist statesman and writer. Member of the Second, Third, and Fourth Dumas. During the war he joined the Progressive Bloc together with his fraction. Author of memoirs (*Days*) and of an account of a secret trip to Soviet Russia in 1926 (*Three Capitals*). (Ed.)

I don't remember whether anyone else was there, and in any case I don't know their names. During the conference not only any others but most of those already named preserved utter silence. Prince Lvov in particular, the 'head' of the future Government, didn't utter a single word all night.

After the meeting had already begun Kerensky settled himself at one of the tables standing along the other wall, in a line with Miliukov's. Sunk in sullen meditation the whole time, he also took not the slightest part in the talks.

After shaking hands we sat down in a row on the chairs at the far end of the room. I was next to Rodzianko, at some slight distance and not at the table, Sokolov next to me, then Steklov, and Chkheidze almost at the wall opposite Kerensky.

There was no chairman formally elected: Rodzianko was informally asked for the floor. The meeting was not formally constituted, opened, or conducted. The talks began in a rather domestic way; it was some time before they took on a business-like and 'responsible' tone and still longer before they took the bull by the horns.

But that doesn't mean that Messieurs the members of the Duma Committee were wasting their valuable time. They had no accurate idea of just what *we* needed from them, nor consequently of how to deal with us in a 'tactful' way. But they knew very well what *they* needed from us, and in semi-private remarks and short speeches were actively preparing the ground for the 'utilization' of the Soviet for their own goals. They may have hoped that if they used sufficient 'tact' the matter would end there.

The conversation naturally started with the 'reign of anarchy' in the capital. One after the other—Rodzianko, Miliukov, Nekrasov—expressed horror at what had been going on and told boring stories about isolated instances of excesses. They told us things we knew by heart: disorganization in the regiments, violence to officers, pogroms, clashes, etc. . . They were trying to persuade us by 'agitation' to let ourselves be used later to restore 'order'.

But the agitators quickly convinced themselves that they were trying to force an open door. They saw not only that we were not raising objections or even trying to say anything to excuse the 'anarchy'—but were thoroughly in accord with them in our full awareness both of the facts themselves and of their extreme danger for the revolution. Then the Duma leaders shifted to direct proposals concerning 'contact', collaboration, and support.

It seemed plain to me that there had been enough of this desultory conversation and of the obscuring alike of the central question and of the general situation; enough, too, of the obscuring of the mutual relations between the two sides. I spoke for the first time, and pointed out that the basic 'technical' task of the Soviet now consisted of the struggle against anarchy; this struggle was in its own interests no less than in those of the Duma Committee; it was conducting it and would go on conducting it; and in particular, with respect to relations with the officers, we were already printing a special appeal to the soldiers. However, all this was far from covering the main object of this conference. The Provisional Committee of the Duma, which had taken the executive power into its hands, was *still not a Government*, not even a 'provisional' one; the creation of this Government still lay ahead, and the leading groups of the Duma undoubtedly had definite intentions and plans on that score. The Soviet, for its part, would leave the formation of a provisional Government to the bourgeois groups, on the view that this followed from the existing general situation and suited the interests of the revolution. However, as the organizational and ideological centre of the popular movement, as the only organ capable of guiding the movement into one channel or another, and as the only organ now wielding any real power in the capital, it wished to express its relationship to the Government being formed in the right wing, make clear its views on the tasks of that Government, and state the demands which in the name of the entire democracy it was presenting to the Government created by the revolution.

Our interlocutors could have nothing to object to in this 'agenda' and prepared to listen. Steklov, as we had agreed, gave the report, solemnly standing up with his sheet of paper. He spoke for quite a while, giving a logical exposition and detailed justification of each of our demands. In this conference of the most highly-qualified politicians of the whole of bourgeois Russia he was evidently simply repeating the report he had just made to the Soviet mass-meeting, explaining the Socialist minimum programme point by point in the most generally accessible form.

'A popular lecture for a workers' study-circle,' I thought, listening to his flow of words.

But I do not say that a popular lecture was uncalled-for. I am sure a majority of the politicians present lacked a correct understanding of the principles underlying our position, of the democratic programme, and in particular of 'some kind of Constituent Assembly'. They all listened attentively, Kerensky alone being absent-minded, gloomy, and ostentatiously indifferent.

Steklov tried to unify all our demands, arguing, proving their rationality and acceptability, making historical excursions and giving illustrations from the practice of Western Europe. He dwelt especially on 'the conversion of the army to a civilian basis', thinking that this point would inevitably provoke opposition and trying to demonstrate that the demand was thoroughly compatible with keeping the army fighting fit; its strength would not be weakened, but would increase to the extent of the army's union with the revolution and the granting to the mass of the soldiery of all human, political, and civil rights.

A look of uneasiness and perplexity had appeared on the faces of many of the 'propertied' persons present. But as far as I recall Nekrasov remained completely serene, and on Miliukov's face signs of deep satisfaction could even be detected.

This was understandable to anyone who had been attending not so much to the speech as to the listeners and trying to orient himself as accurately as possible in the whole conjuncture: Miliukov, after all, had undoubtedly been expecting some demands concerning foreign affairs; he had been afraid that we would want him to bind himself to a peace policy. This had not happened, and the fact not only made infinitely easier the position of the then leader of propertied Russia, who had already had a taste of power, but gave him a few moments of heartfelt satisfaction and a feeling of triumph at this 'historic' conference.

Steklov concluded by expressing the hope that the Cabinet then being formed would accept our demands and publish them as its programme in the proclamation which announced to the people the creation of the first new Government of the revolution.

Miliukov spoke in reply. He spoke for the entire Duma Committee; everyone considered this a matter of course. It was clear that Miliukov here was not only a leader, but the *boss* of the right wing.

'In general the conditions of the Soviet of Workers' and Soldiers' Deputies are acceptable,' he said, 'and in general they may constitute the groundwork for an agreement with the Committee of the Duma. Nevertheless there are some points the Committee definitely objects to.'

Miliukov asked for the sheet of paper on which our programme had been set out and made his comments as he copied it out. The amnesty was a matter of course. Miliukov didn't think it proper to contest it and rather reluctantly but obediently wrote down: 'for all crimes: agrarian, military, or terrorist'. It was the same with the second point—political liberties, the abolition of religious or class disabilities, etc. These were *demanded* of Miliukov and he *yielded.*

But the third point aroused his resolute opposition. This read: 'The Provisional Government must not take any steps to predetermine the future form of government.' Miliukov defended the Romanov monarchy and dynasty, with Alexis as Tsar and Michael as Regent.

What I personally found rather unexpected was not that Miliukov should fight for the Romanov monarchy, but that he should make this the most contentious point of all our terms. *Now* I understand him very well and think that from his point of view he was absolutely right and extremely perspicacious.

He was calculating that with a Romanov Tsar, and perhaps *only* with him, he would win the forthcoming battle and justify the enormous risk which in his person the entire bourgeoisie as a ruling class was taking.

He thought that, given a Romanov Tsar, all the rest would follow, and was not afraid—not *so* afraid—either of the freedom of the army or of 'some' Constituent Assembly, considering these permissible and surmountable.

His companions-in-arms, most of them ordinary average citizens compared with him, and moreover now consumed by 'revolutionary fervour', on this question showed little sense ('the average man is stupid', I had heard Miliukov say before at various gatherings). The other Duma members, almost up to Rodzianko himself, did not cling to the monarchy and the

Romanovs so much; and Miliukov, from having been a leader of the Opposition, now suddenly found himself on the extreme Right wing. It was a come-down, but he knew what he was doing.

His position, however, was extremely difficult. In front of us, of course, he couldn't develop this argument squarely or even hint at it. And of course his attitude on this was extremely weak, even inarticulate, although this far from lessened his insistence.

He made some 'liberal advances' to us, pointing out that the Romanovs could no longer be dangerous now; and that Nicholas was unacceptable to him too and must be removed. He naïvely tried to convince us of the acceptability to the democracy of his arrangement, saying of his candidates that 'one was a sick child, the other a thoroughly stupid man'.

In Miliukov's position, of course, no theoretical arguments could help him; they could only spoil his case. But the other kind of argument, the practical, was unsuitable, and Miliukov simply insisted, without any arguments, somewhat disconcerting even his colleagues from the Progressive Bloc.

Chkheidze and Sokolov observed that Miliukov's plan was not only unacceptable, but also *utopian,* in view of the general hatred of the monarchy amongst the masses of the people. They said that an attempt to defend the Romanovs, with our sanction, was completely absurd and would lead to nothing. But the bourgeois leader was irreconcilable and, seeing the fruitlessness of wrangling, turned to the succeeding points.

He went through the whole programme to the end, accepting municipal elections, the abolition of the police, and a Constituent Assembly, in the authentic sense. Further, while protesting against the shifting of the army to a civil status when off duty, he did not reject this point in principle and merely spoke of its dangers. Finally he again returned to the third point, indicating that for him this was the only inadmissible one, whereas the others could be discussed.

Rodzianko spoke next. As far as I remember he dwelt primarily on the date for the convocation of the Constituent Assembly and its elections. We were demanding an immediate start on the work of organizing the elections, and the elections themselves as quickly as possible, independent of any circumstances whatsoever. Rodzianko pointed out the impossibility of this, particularly for the army in wartime. However, he spoke far from categorically, but rather by way of expressing doubt. I don't remember whether he supported Miliukov on the question of the monarchy and regency.

Then Shulgin made a speech which shifted the centre of gravity to the point concerning the army disorders. He spoke about the war, victory, patriotism, and the extreme danger of our 'military programme'. But I don't remember any intransigence in his speech either, and with respect to the monarchy he, introducing himself as a monarchist, was milder than Miliukov, merely expressing his own general views on the subject.

Nekrasov can scarcely have been altogether silent, but nothing of his speech, if there was one, remains in my memory.

But I clearly recall the comical, elongated, bald-headed, and moustachioed figure of Lvov, the future Procurator, who made a long, noisy, and naïve speech from the depths of his easy-chair. This personality—an extremely odd type—belonged to some Right-wing party or other in the Duma, the Nationalists or *Zemstvo* Octobrists. In his first words, however, he declared himself a republican and spoke of his horror of a possible return of Tsarism, than which death itself would be better. But a return of Tsarism was possible as the result of a military defeat, and a military defeat might be the result of the policy of the Soviet and especially those transformations of the army on which we were insisting. In general he added nothing substantial to what had been said before.

The next speaker was myself. I very briefly pointed out that the demands which had been presented were in the first place a minimum, and secondly absolutely categorical and final. I observed that among the masses an incomparably broader programme was developing with every day and every hour, and that the masses were supporting it and would go on doing so. The leaders were straining all their energies to direct the movement into a definite channel and keep it within reasonable limits. But if these limits were to be imprudently contracted a spontaneous explosion would sweep them away together with all the contemplated governmental 'combinations'. Either we could stop this explosion or nobody could. The real power therefore was either ours or nobody's. There was only one solution: to agree to our conditions and accept them as the Government programme.

The exchange of opinions on the substance of our demands was concluded. Miliukov took the floor again.

'These were *your* demands,' he said, 'addressed to us. But *we* have our own demands of you. . .'

'We're off!' I thought, sure that then would follow an attempt to pledge the Soviet to the support of the Government.

But strangely enough no such attempt was made, or at least it never took any definite form. Miliukov began talking of something quite different—the immediate action to be taken by the Ex. Com. to restore law and order and, in particular and especially, to establish contact between soldiers and officers.

Miliukov demanded from us a declaration which would point out that *whereas* the Government was being formed by agreement with the Soviet of Workers' Deputies, this Government should be recognized as legitimate by the masses of the people and enjoy their confidence. The main thing he demanded, however, was that the declaration should contain an appeal for confidence in the officers' corps and for recognition by the soldiers of the commanding staff.

Miliukov had taken very accurate bearings. He understood that without an accord with the Soviet no Government could either arise or remain in existence. He understood that it was entirely within the power of the Ex. Com. to give authority to a bourgeois régime or withhold it. He saw where the real strength lay, he saw in whose hands were the means of assuring to the new Government both the indispensable conditions for work and its very existence. Miliukov realized he was accepting power not from the hands of the monarch in Tsarskoe-Selo, as he had counted on doing throughout the preceding decade, but from the hands of the victorious revolutionary people. How well he understood this and what significance he ascribed to it were clear, if only from his insistence that *our proclamations be printed and posted up together, if possible on a single sheet of paper, one under the other.*

All this did not prevent Miliukov later on—the Minister Miliukov, the leader of the opposition from the Right—from frothing and raging against the 'private institutions and groups', in the person of the Soviet, who had laid their hands on the running of the country and were interfering in the life of the State and the affairs of the Government. In March Miliukov, just like his colleagues, was perfectly well aware what these 'private groups and institutions' were. . .

As for the 'minimal' nature of our demands and the general attitude taken by the Zimmerwaldite Ex. Com., Miliukov had not expected such 'moderation' and 'good sense'. He was agreeably surprised by our general attitude towards the question of power and felt the greatest satisfaction at the Zimmerwaldite solution of the problem of war and peace as it affected the formation of the Government. He didn't even think of concealing his satisfaction and pleasant surprise.

In answer to the remark that our demands were an indispensable minimum and our conditions final, Miliukov semi-privately threw out a characteristic phrase: 'Yes, I was thinking as I listened to you how far our working-class movement has advanced since 1905'. This compliment of Miliukov's would not have been especially flattering to us, if it had not been premature.

* * *

At this point Engelhardt came in with an orderly and said that Headquarters was asking to speak to Rodzianko by direct wire. As a matter of fact it was not Headquarters but Pskov, where the Tsar had arrived (via Dno) towards 8 o'clock in the evening. . .

Rodzianko refused to go to the telegraph-office alone. 'Let Messieurs the Workers' and Soldiers' Deputies give me a guard or accompany me,' he said, turning to us, 'or else I shall be arrested there, at the telegraph-office. I don't know whether I shall be able to travel; we must ask Messieurs the Deputies!'

The old man was suddenly very agitated. 'Really! You have the power and the authority,' he continued excitedly. 'You can of course arrest me. Perhaps you will arrest all of us, who knows!'

We calmed the former 'Jupiter of the Duma', whose nerves were beginning to fail under the burden of events. We reassured him that we would not only not touch his person but would guard it most carefully.

Sokolov left to get him a reliable escort, and Rodzianko went off to the telegraph-office for a last conversation with his recent ruler, the musical-comedy 'sovereign' of a sixth of the globe.

It was 3 o'clock. General Ruzsky was waiting at the telephone in Pskov for Rodzianko, who described the state of affairs while under the impact of our discussion. The necessity, or at any rate the inevitability of Nicholas's abdication was stated by Rodzianko in explicit terms. Of course! Now even Miliukov acknowledged this necessity.

* * *

The question of the conditions for forming the Government had been cleared up first. We passed on to the last item, concerning its personal composition, and reported the Ex. Com.'s decision. We were told the proposed Cabinet members, no mention being made, however, of Kerensky. We made some adverse comments on Guchkov, pointing out that he might prove a source of complications. In reply we were told that in view of his organizational talents and extremely widespread army contacts he was completely irreplaceable. Well, let him apply his talents and exploit his contacts: we intended to start up our own.

Tereshchenko's name caused some surprise. Where had this gentleman sprung from and why, and by what stroke of fortune had he popped up among the Ministers of the revolution?

The answer was rather evasive and obscure: it was clear that we were not the only ones at a loss. But we didn't insist on a positive response.

* * *

Our preliminary conference was over. We agreed to meet again in an hour, around 5 o'clock, in the same room. Among the 'property-holders' Miliukov was forcing this business along just as I was in the left wing. According to him every hour might still bring something unexpected, any procrastination might make the people think there were insurmountable differences between the bourgeoisie and the democracy, and so on. The situation had to be defined immediately.

Regardless of the general exhaustion and the obvious desire for rest on the part of most of the 'Duma people', we decided that each side would attend to its own business at once, then meet and settle the Government question as quickly as possible.

* * *

It was around 4 in the morning. I started to write out the Ex. Com. proclamation and sat down with a notebook right there, in the Duma Committee's rooms. But I couldn't do a thing; my head was as empty as my stomach. The room was crowded and noisy—people were arguing loudly and addressing questions to me. I wrote down a few sentences about the struggle against anarchy which made up the second paragraph of this document, and had to stop, completely incapable of finishing it. Sokolov came over and undertook to relieve me, and I started back to the Ex. Com.

Just then Kerensky came out of the room where we had had the conference and told us that he was being offered the portfolio of Minister of Justice. Not only that, but he was being urged and persuaded to accept it. There could be no doubt of the sincerity of those who were seeking to persuade him: in the given conjuncture a hostage in the person of Kerensky was extremely desirable to them.

Kerensky again asked what he should do. But what he *would* do was obvious. He didn't want any *advice*. His object was to learn whether the Soviet, in the person of its leaders, would support him and acknowledge him as its own when he became Minister. He wanted *backing*.

I did not encourage him in this idea, but as before expressed myself negatively. He got angry again; he wanted to be both a 'Soviet man' and a Minister, but—a Minister more.

However, he looked much better and more tranquil than he had a few hours before.

*　　*　　*

The Palace was silent and almost empty. Some inconspicuous groups of soldiers were sleeping on the floor of the ante-chamber and the Catherine Hall. The others had already scattered to their barracks, no longer seeing any sense in staying there overnight.

The whole city, however, was completely filled with soldiers, pouring into the capital from all sides and by every road. . .

Two or three members were working in the Ex. Com. Nothing special had happened. Steklov was telling them about our conversation with the future Government. I hurried over to the 'phone to give *Izvestiya* the latest news. But No. 3 was already in the presses; I was too late, and I passed on the news simply for the editors' benefit.

I inquired in passing whether the proclamation to the soldiers sent out during the day had been printed and how they thought of distributing it. Inquiries were made and the answer came back that *two* proclamations to the soldiers had been sent out, which according to the man I was speaking to (Tikhonov, I think) contradicted each other. One of them, about the soldiers' rights, had been printed: this was 'Order No. 1'. But the other had been read by the type-setters, who didn't agree with it and refused to set it up: this was the appeal against lynch-law and violence to officers, written by me and corrected by Steklov.

The high-handedness of the type-setters made me all the more indignant since it had so little justification, and consequently was a sign of their undesirable attitude towards violence to officers. Formally, too, this situation was unendurable: at such a moment it was, to say the least, unsatisfactory that the conduct of high policy should be entrusted to a random group of type-setters. I made a row over the 'phone and asked one of the Ex. Com. members to back me up, but nothing could be done about it, the type-setters had already left and it was no longer possible to set up the proclamation—and in the Duma apartments Sokolov was already drudging away at another proclamation to be ready next day, which would make the first unnecessary.

Just then one of the Right-wing members of the Ex. Com. burst into the room, waving some printed leaflets and spitting out curses.

The leaflet turned out to be a proclamation published jointly by the Petersburg SR organization led by Alexandrovich, and the Interdistrictites, i.e., the autonomous group of Bolsheviks. In those days these groups were united not only because one and the same printing-shop had agreed to work for them, but also on the basis of their ultra-Left views, which they were incapable of defending (or even expressing) in the Soviet, but which they expounded in their proclamations—with more ardour than skill or common sense. The first, which had fallen into my hands earlier in the day, had demanded the formation of a working-class Government (similar to the Bolshevik Central Committee). But now their second proclamation made things much worse: it was directed specifically against the officers.

As far as I remember there were phrases in it like 'Down with the Romanov lackeys'. In any event it sanctioned violence and called for a complete break with the officers' corps. There could be no doubt that at that moment it was more out of place and dangerous than ever, not only because of its pogromist technique, but also for reasons of 'high policy'.

The Ex. Com. member who had come running in was shouting that this was a direct incitement to general carnage and pogroms and to the destruction of the whole revolution. He said this proclamation was already circulating in the city in large numbers, and that whole stacks of it were piled up ready for the morning in the office used by the Ex. Com. He was in complete despair, almost in tears, and demanded that the proclamation be held back for the time being. Then and there the question was submitted to the Ex. Com. members present.

The problem was not only disagreeable, but also difficult: it was a question of violating the freedom of expression of a Socialist group. On the other hand, both the occasion and the question were extremely critical, perhaps decisive. What with the mistrust, excitement, and alarm prevailing amongst the masses of soldiery crowded into the city, and the innumerable varieties of provocation practised by 'dark forces'—such a document might turn out to be a spark in a powder-magazine, unleashing elemental forces and placing the victorious revolution once again in hazard.

In particular no Government could have been formed in such circumstances; it would be not a Government but an impotent victim of elemental forces. And finally, an important formal question arose here: a group represented in the Soviet and on the Ex. Com. was taking some very important steps without their knowledge *and in direct contradiction to* their decisions. Could this be permitted? And how should the Soviet behave in such a case? This question had to be posed in all its amplitude the very next morning in the Ex. Com.

Kerensky came flying in like a hurricane, completely beside himself and out of breath with rage and despair. Pounding on the table, he not only accused the authors and publishers of this leaflet of provocation, but called it the work of the Tsarist Secret Police. He threatened the culprits with all sorts of punishments. Most of those present tried to restrain the fury of the over-wrought tribune of the people, but on the whole they agreed with him in the objective evaluation of the fact.

It was resolved to suspend the proclamation until the Ex. Com. had reached a decision and to put the question before them in its widest aspect the following morning. I voted for this resolution and even went off to Room 11 to put it into effect.

There really were two or three bales of the proclamation lying there, with Molotov, a Bolshevik member of the Ex. Com., standing near them; we got into a fairly spirited dispute, but nevertheless he gave in and handed over the bales without a real row. It is possible that he simply acknowledged that we were right—in a question these groups had not asked themselves before.

Having spent some time on this petty business I went off again to the right wing.

In the corridor I met Kerensky, who was leaving the Duma Committee rooms for the former apartments of the Military Commission. By now he was not so much frenzied as distraught, confused, and cowed.

'Well, that's what they've been waiting for,' he began; 'the combination is off . . . the agreement is broken. . . In such circumstances they won't agree to form a Government.'

Kerensky turned to Room 41. I was at a loss to understand, and followed. What was the matter? Had something new happened or was it all a trick of the bourgeoisie, a way of applying pressure through Kerensky, a kind of blackmail?

I was on the point of losing my head too and demanded some explanation.

'Just look at what Sokolov has written! What a proclamation!' said Kerensky, with despair and also a kind of spiteful pleasure, seeing in me a suitable object for his dissatisfaction with the 'Leftists'. 'Instead of the declaration he was talking about, he's written a pogromist proclamation against the officers. The others have read it and said it's impossible to form a Government if the Soviet takes that position.'

The thing wouldn't have been so terrible if it had been no more than Kerensky said. But it wasn't only that. Someone told me later that Guchkov, appearing after our conference, had kicked up a row with his colleagues, primarily about the principles of the part of our agreement that concerned the army.

But the chief thing was that he was shaken by the facts of the relation between our forces and by the prospect he saw before him of the future position of the Government. He refused to participate in a Government that could not even issue a simple proclamation.

Guchkov's speech had a very disturbing effect and it is possible that it had really undermined that 'contact' which seemed to have already secured the formation of a Government on the basis we had demanded. It is possible that under Guchkov's influence our agreement really was a bit shaken—though I don't think so.

But Kerensky didn't say a word to me about Guchkov at that point. The proclamation written by Sokolov was a very timely help to Kerensky, allowing him in his conversation with me to blame the 'breaking of the agreement' on the 'Leftists'.

I naturally wanted to go over to the Duma Committee to find out what the trouble was and take the right steps from my point of view. But Kerensky said they were having a conference there and preparing a final decision, which we would have to wait for.

Room 41 was almost empty. Kerensky's wife Olga Lvovna was sitting on a sofa, I think with Zenzinov. Kerensky sat down next to them, crossed his legs, and went on talking angrily. He was directing his shafts at the leaders of the Soviet, although in this matter they were not to blame in the slightest degree. . .

'What else could you expect? How can you come to an agreement when the parties act in concert with *provocateurs*?. . . The whole thing has collapsed. . . No leadership and no government. . . The soldiery are looting everywhere, and there's nothing to stop them with. . . Of course there are going to be pogroms, murders, hunger riots. . . I foresee a fearful end to the whole thing!

'There, it's beginning! D'you hear?' he continued hysterically, getting to his feet and listening to the sound of steps and the tramping of dozens of feet, which had begun again in the neighbouring halls. 'D'you hear? The day is beginning; more crowds will be swarming here, people with no business, and no one knows what they come for! There'll be another idle crowd strolling around the whole day, not working, getting in the way. . . An atmosphere of disintegration. And all this is fostered by—class warfare! . . . Internationalists! Zimmerwald!'

Kerensky had got himself into a hysterical state again. I hurried away, not because he was completely wrong, but because talk on this theme was quite futile.

I went off to the Duma Committee rooms, where two or three adjutants in the almost empty reception-room were speaking in a secretive half-whisper about Guchkov's refusal to enter the Government; they were very upset. I continued on my way.

* * *

It turned out that Sokolov really had written out a draft proclamation and without telling us its contents had read it directly to the Duma Committee, or, more accurately, to the few bourgeois still left.

This draft was really disastrous. The whole thing was devoted to an explanation to the soldiers of the characteristics of the officers' corps. The wording of a number of passages gave grounds for the conclusion that no kind of contact with the officers was conceivable and perhaps that they should be attacked root and branch. It goes without saying that Sokolov intended nothing of the sort; the misunderstanding could only be explained by the extraordinary working conditions.

Of course the result was consternation among this 'fa-a-ateful' man's bourgeois listeners. Some of them, perhaps, were not indeed averse to exploiting this unfortunate literary début for the 'disruption of the combination'. But hardly; at most it could have served only to terrorize Kerensky. In fact there were no repercussions of any kind on our negotiations.

In our conference room almost no one was now left of the former participants and witnesses. The lights were extinguished, morning was already looking in through the windows; the snow-drifts and trees covered with hoar-frost could be seen in the empty Tauride gardens. . . Miliukov and Sokolov were sitting at a table, near the last lighted lamp.

Miliukov was writing, and when I asked I was told everything was all right, that Rodzianko had not yet returned from the telegraph office, that Sokolov's proclamation was no good and was being radically revised. I saw no traces whatever of the incident with Guchkov, or in general of any incident at all that had sent Kerensky into a panic.

It was plain that Miliukov's judgement was more sober than

Guchkov's and that he was counting on either smoothing things over with him or doing without him. I don't know how the bourgeois discussion of our demands had gone, but—'everything was all right', and things were moving forward as though the agreement were already in effect. And the scene before my eyes not only bore witness to this, but was even touching.

Miliukov was finishing the Ex. Com.'s proclamation—in the version I had begun. He added a third (and last) paragraph to the second paragraph that I had written, and fixed his signature below mine.

'This version begins better and is clearer and shorter,' Miliukov explained. But he was already completely worn out, and finally got to his feet, interrupting the work.

'No, I can't go on,' he said, stuffing the papers into his pocket. 'We'll finish to-morrow. Let it be postponed a day.'

We all went our separate ways.

* * *

I decided to rest, even if only for two or three hours, and saying goodbye went off to the left wing for my fur coat. A few people were still there. When I went out, Steklov stayed on with them, and later told me that in my absence there was again some kind of conference with the right-wing people, but who was there, at what time it was, or what they talked about—I don't remember.

I only remember Steklov's telling me that when the conference was over he and Miliukov embraced each other!

* * *

The Palace was rapidly growing animated. The day promised to be like the previous one. The courtyard and the square were empty on that fresh, frosty, winter morning, but it was sunny and cheerful. As before there was not a soul on guard, but now both the guns and machine-guns had vanished from the courtyard in the wake of the defences. This was no longer a fortress, but the peaceful palace of the revolution. . .

The victory was already won. The major steps to consolidate it were already taken, and only bagatelles remained. We had only to make skilful use of the victory! At that time there was no idea that more than one generation of Soviet leaders would break their necks on those bagatelles. At that time, on that frosty, cheerful, sunlit morning I breathed easily and happily—even with my mind completely numb and an aching vacuum in my stomach.

I went over to the Old Nevsky, past the queues and the red flags, to spend the night at 'Governor' Nikitsky's.

'Well, Anna Mikhailovna, I suppose your "general's son" isn't here?' I asked Nikitsky's old nanny, who opened the door for me. She had lived with him for many years, dozens of revolutionaries had known her and benefited by her good offices, and she always took good care of me when I was underground and used to spend the night at Nikitsky's. . . We had revolutionary figures like that too! . . . But she never missed a chance to refer to the generals in Nikitsky's family tree.

'No, no, he's not,' she answered, distressed. 'He went out yesterday and simply didn't come back. And I don't know where he is or what's happened to him.'

'Your Andrey Alexandrovich has been appointed Governor of the City, that's what! Now I've done with running away from the police! Just let even the head porter try to stop me, now I've got a foot in the Governor's! Please wake me in about two hours, towards 10. . .'

'Lord, Lord, Lord!' the old woman kept repeating, leading me to her nursling's untouched bed. 'What can be going on? And what are *you* now? . . . Maybe you'll eat something?'

On the way to bed I swallowed the supper that had been standing there since evening and fell asleep, dead to the world. . . It was around 8 o'clock of the fourth morning of the revolution.

CHAPTER 6

THE FOURTH DAY

March 2nd

BEFORE noon I entered the Palace and hurried to the Ex. Com. Scene and atmosphere as before.

I was stopped by Stankevich, a fellow-editor of the *Sovremennik*, a hopeless Trudovik or Populist Socialist, formerly a university lecturer on criminal law but now, as I called him, 'professor of fortifications and geometry' at some military college, a future member of the Ex. Com. and commissar of the northern front, and rather close to Kerensky. During the revolution he was very active in the barracks among the officers and the military in general, and overflowing with enthusiasm.

'Wonderful, my meeting you! I have a suggestion to make. Let's organize a review of troops on the Champ de Mars, and have the whole garrison marching past the Ex. Com. with a band. It will be a terrific demonstration, unprecedented in history. A demonstration to all Petersburg, all Russia, and all Europe, damn it!'

Not a bad idea at that! But it wasn't so easy to realize as Stankevich thought, and very difficult to carry off in the spirit he desired. There was much more politics in it than appeared to him; the idyllic picture would undoubtedly be ruined by snags which in his enthusiasm he ignored. For some reason I suddenly imagined Chkheidze, Shlyapnikov, and myself on horseback. We burst out laughing, and I hurried on.

The Ex. Com. was not in session, though a majority of its members were assembled. All of them, singly or in couples, were busy with 'routine matters'.

All sorts of rumours were passing around, but no one knew anything precise about either 'high policy', Rodzianko's negotiations with the Tsar, or the abdication. Work was in full swing, indispensable and unavoidable, with all its silliness and practical futility. A mass of state affairs had to be decided on one's own, or after consultation with the first comrade to turn up—when at an ordinary time a resolution would have been placed on the agenda for each of them and would have provoked heated arguments.

The 'phone rang at my side.

'Soviet of Workers' and Soldiers' Deputies? Can I speak to a member of the Executive Committee? I'm speaking for the Council of Representatives of the Petersburg banks. We want permission to open the banks at once. We think order has been restored to such an extent that there is no threat to the activity of the banks. Keeping them shut any longer would not only be harmful, it might stimulate baseless alarm and panic. . .'

Without relinquishing the receiver I called over a near-by Ex. Com. member, consulted with him for two minutes ('pro' and 'con') and asked:

'What's the attitude of the higher and lower employees towards opening the banks?'

'All the employees', was the answer, 'are ready to start working right now and are only waiting for your permission.'

I answered in the name of the Ex. Com.

'Very well, you have it. If it's needed in written form then make it up yourselves on an ordinary sheet of paper and send it to the Tauride Palace, Room 13, to be signed and stamped.'

Another call:

'Tsarskoe-Selo Railway Station speaking—Commissar of the Executive Committee on behalf of the railwaymen: Grand Duke Michael Alexandrovich in Gatchina is asking for a train to go to St. Petersburg.'

This time I answered without any consultation:

'Tell him the Executive Committee won't authorize a train because of the high cost of coal; but Citizen Romanov can go to the railway station, buy a ticket, and travel in a public train.'

* * *

The Soviet was already beginning to assemble. All of it in full session had to have an official debate now and give a final decision on the question of the Government.

Today it was impossible for the Ex. Com. to leave this session without any special attention or leadership, as it had the day before. On the contrary, we had to do our best to pave the way for and secure a harmonious and painless settlement of the political problem.

For my part I was preparing to take the appropriate steps, but I was drawn aside by Kerensky, who came over to the left wing accompanied by Zenzinov, who had become his mouthpiece, an energetic (backstage) assistant, and faithful squire. Kerensky looked comparatively rested, but excited and triumphant.

He was still after the same thing. He was ready to agree or had already agreed to accept the post of Minister of Justice. Could this be passed through the Soviet and approved by it?

I referred him to the Ex. Com. decision, taken the night before by thirteen votes to eight, not to enter the Government or send any official representatives of the democracy into a bourgeois Cabinet. I said the Ex. Com. would defend this position in the Soviet too. It followed from this that if Kerensky wanted to appeal to the Soviet for sanction, then he would have to relinquish his title of Chairman of the Soviet and act as an individual.

Personally, with respect to Kerensky, as before I thought his participation in the Cabinet might be of some use, but not as a representative of the Soviet democracy. In addition I told him I thought raising this question in the Soviet was not without danger for the settlement of the Government question in general. If Kerensky had to raise the question of what the nature of the Government was to be, then he might well receive the answer that *the power should be in the hands of the Soviet democracy*. The problem was too novel and complicated for a Soviet 'mass-meeting'; in view of the present scope of the movement the way we formulated it pointed it too sharply towards the Right, and it might very easily lurch over so far to the Left that not only all 'combinations' but the revolution itself might miscarry.

In any case, as far as Kerensky's practical objective was concerned, he either had to surrender his Soviet title and follow his own inclinations independently of the Soviet; or have it out with the Soviet in his 'private capacity' and tell it that he was determined to become a Minister, but that by virtue of the Ex. Com.'s decision he was surrendering his Soviet title and wanted its approval; or appeal to the Soviet and obtain a different decision from it about the Government than had been passed by the Ex. Com. Or finally, accomplish a *coup d'état*, and while the Ex. Com.'s decision was still unknown to the Soviet or had not been debated on by it, turn to the Soviet directly, *disregarding the Ex. Com.'s desires.*

But seeing that Kerensky had set his heart on being a Minister, I urged him to take one of the first two alternatives. He answered vaguely, pondering tactics—and rushed off to the right wing.

* * *

Before the Soviet began its session I wanted to do everything I could to secure a painless passage through the Soviet of the whole Ex. Com. 'line'. I was afraid of speeches from the Left that might easily be reinforced by the tactics of street warfare if the Bolsheviks and Left RSs were energetic enough. If a movement like this ever began, overcoming it by 'internal' means, through influence or persuasion, would be extremely difficult, if possible at all.

The point of view of the Ex. Com. *majority* (the Centre) was absolutely correct, but its position was shaky in the extreme: defending the 'property-holders' before the masses, and before the Soviet that wielded the real power, was in general the acme of difficulty. The excitement and the alarm among the soldiers increased this difficulty tenfold. But when the bourgeois, in such a situation, refused even to part with the monarchy and the dynasty, that alone would be capable of dooming the entire 'combination' to destruction—if that movement had begun.

It remained to hope, in view of the weakness of the recklessly Left groups, the indeterminateness of their position, the poor quality and lack of authority of their leaders, that it would not begin. But in any case we must do everything to forestall such a movement.

On the other hand, the militant advocates of entering the Government were extremely depressed by the Ex. Com. decision. A minority refused to submit, and talked of appealing to the Soviet.

I urged the minority leaders not to do this, saying that it would not help them and might fan a fire on the Left that couldn't be extinguished, at least not as quickly as would be necessary. I especially recall my conversation with Ehrlich, a supporter of 'coalition', who pointed out that the question of participating in the Government would be raised in the Soviet in any case by casual speakers, but promised to see to it that there was no organized intervention by the Ex. Com. minority.

Steklov was again to present our report to the Soviet. I recall my conversation with him before he made this report. A disagreeable recollection!—for it revealed those political manœuvres that characterize any clique which can rely on a safe majority and consequently allow itself dubious methods in its struggle with the minority. I urged Steklov to make his report as full and lengthy as he could, so that later it might be accepted as far as possible without discussion. I was afraid of complications or delays should there be a 'Long Parliament'; my calculation was that the report, made in exhaustive detail, would first of all convince the Soviet 'mass-meeting' and then compel it to cut the discussion so short that it would be too difficult to sway the ideas and moods of the masses to either Left or Right.

Later, when throughout the revolution I had to be in the position of an irresponsible, impotent, and numerically negligible Opposition, there was no longer any occasion for me to resort to such methods: on the contrary, I had to observe them in others and expose the dominant majority. This makes it more depressing to recall my own experience of the power of this 'dirty business' of politics, during the brief period when I found myself in the ranks of that dominant majority.

* * *

The Soviet was assembling. As usual I didn't go there or take much interest in the speeches. To begin with, I had no experience as an orator, wasn't used to addressing the masses, and had no taste for it (which I often regretted very much). Secondly, it was obvious that it wasn't there, in the general assemblies, that policy was made, and that all these plenums were of no practical importance. And thirdly there was the routine business of the Ex. Com. So I stayed behind the curtain in Room 13. As before, the Ex. Com. was not in session, and when the Soviet meeting started, the room almost emptied.

Soon Steklov's voice could be heard from the Soviet Chamber, introducing the report. The room was quiet; everyone listened intently—many for the second time—point by point to the programme of the Ex. Com. which had been submitted to the bourgeoisie and was now being expounded by the speaker in the most popular, diffuse, and watery way. The Ex. Com. room was protected by the Soviet hall from any influx of outsiders and from 'emergency matters'. And no one burst in behind the curtain from the Soviet hall, where everyone was absorbed in 'high policy', where they were having a 'great day', and where for the first time (if we omit the nocturnal rehearsal the night before in a half-empty hall) a report from the Ex. Com. was being presented. Thanks to this, after signing some papers—'certificates' and 'permits'—I finished the routine business fairly quickly and, sitting in an easy-chair behind the curtain, could enjoy a period of leisure, expansiveness, quiet, and the consciousness of duty done...

Kerensky came in again, still attended by Zenzinov, and settled himself in our midst. He didn't say why he had come, but was obviously waiting for something. He told us of the sensation produced in bourgeois circles and among the officers by Order No. 1. But he wasn't feeling specially argumentative. There was not even a trace left of his panic and spitefulness of the night before.

When asked what was going on in the right wing he replied that in spite of all the difficulties created by the Ex. Com. the work of forming a Cabinet was proceeding.

It was probably after 2 in the afternoon. Steklov had judiciously expanded his report; his torrent of words had already been flowing for more than an hour. 'Hear, hear, Steklov, very good!' I thought to myself, catching isolated words of the report, following its stages, and reflecting on the general situation.

Suddenly Steklov finished; the hall rang with applause.

Kerensky jumped up as though stung, and rushed off into the hall, once more as white as a sheet. The others, including myself, hurried after him and stood in the doorway to see what would happen.

At the opposite end of the hall, to the right of the doorway, Chkheidze was standing on the chairman's table, saying something and waving his arms in the midst of the subsiding applause. Kerensky began hurriedly making his way over there from our door. But the crowd stubbornly resisted, and after moving forward only a few steps, he climbed up on a table right there, at the end of the hall not far from the door into the Ex. Com. room. From there he asked for the floor. The entire hall turned towards him. There was some hesitant clapping.

Kerensky had chosen the very worst way to a Cabinet post—the *coup d'état*. He ignored the Ex. Com. He didn't want either to be guided by it or even to submit to its reviewing his action. Disregarding it, as a factor unworthy of any attention, Kerensky preferred to rely on the strength of his personal influence and authority, counting on the unpreparedness, the ignorance, and the herd instincts of his listeners, half of whom were purely middle class.

He began to speak in a 'failing' voice, a mystical half-whisper. White as snow, so agitated that he was shaking all over, he forced out short, broken phrases, interrupted by long pauses. His speech, especially at first, was disconnected and completely unexpected—particularly after the tranquil conversation behind the curtain.

God knows which it had more of—real frenzy or theatrical pathos! In any case it had traces of diplomatic work, testified to by some extremely skilful turns which were bound to influence the electors. (This speech of Kerensky's is quite well known: it excited lively comment at the time and later was frequently recalled.)

'Comrades!' said the new Minister of Justice *in toga candida*, 'do you trust me?'

Exclamations from the hall: 'We do, we do!'

'I speak, comrades, with all my soul, from the bottom of my heart, and if it is necessary to prove this—if you don't trust me—here and now—before your eyes—I am ready to die. . .'

A wave of amazement and emotion passed through the hall. These French oratorical flourishes, probably employed unintentionally and unexpectedly, were very unusual amongst us and produced quite a 'striking' effect. Then Kerensky took the bull by the horns and going over directly to his basic objective cut the Gordian knot at once.

'Comrades! In view of the formation of a new Government(!) I had to give an immediate reply, without waiting for your formal approval, when I was offered the post of Minister of Justice(!)'

Now, he had to justify and give an adequate explanation of his irregular action. And, remembering that he was at a mass-meeting and that there were a large number of people in the hall who had and could have had nothing in their hearts but revolutionary sentiment, political obtuseness, and devotion to him—Kerensky, 'banner' of the revolution—taking all this into account Kerensky scored a bull's eye.

'I have in my hands', he continued, 'the representatives of the former Government; I have made up my mind not to let them go.' (Stormy applause and exclamations of 'Hear, hear!') 'I accepted the proposal made to me and have entered the Government as Minister of Justice' (much less stormy applause and exclamations of 'Bravo', far from typical of the 'masses'). 'My first step was to order that political prisoners be freed immediately and that our comrades, the deputies of the Social-Democratic fraction of the Duma, be brought back from Siberia with special honours.'

Now, at the end of 1918, these 'special honours' to the champions of the proletariat have become a matter of course, just as has every form of pressure on the possessing classes in general and the representatives of the old Government in particular. But one must enter into the psychology of those days, when the process of the transformation of the former authorities into convicts had only just begun, when the amnesty itself had not yet ceased to be a 'clause in the programme', and the psychology of the masses had not yet had time to digest the new phenomena, ideas, and relationships—one must enter into the psychology of those days in order to imagine the enthusiasm which could be aroused by such declarations, which threw the people's victory into sharp relief. Why, at that time we had not even become accustomed to the sound of the *Marseillaise*, and I remember for how long I was stirred by that sound, the military band and the military honours paid to the 'illegal' hymn of freedom![1]

Kerensky's announcement of the retribution meted out to the Tsarist authorities and the honours paid to the Tsarist prisoners undoubtedly produced a great impression and heightened the atmosphere to one of enthusiasm. After this artillery barrage Kerensky could now advance to the attack. He went on:

'Since I took on myself the duties of Minister of Justice before being formally authorized by you, I resign from the duties of

[1] The *Marseillaise* was regarded until the October Revolution as an anthem of liberty; immediately afterwards it was replaced by the *Internationale* as the national anthem of the Soviet Union; the latter was replaced in its turn by a new anthem on March 15, 1944. (Ed.)

Chairman of the Soviet. But I am ready to accept that title from you again if you acknowledge the necessity of it.' (Exclamations of 'We do, We do!' and some scattered applause.)

Kerensky further spoke about his democratism, about the defence of the people's interests, for the sake of which he was going into the Government, about discipline, about support, about the revolution in general. He was positively lyrical.

He was given an ovation. Leaping from the table to a storm of shouts and applause he retired again to Room 13—knowing that he had won and confident that he had received formal approval for his entry into the Government, and that because he retained his title of Chairman of the Soviet he had become the Ministerial representative of the democracy.

Nevertheless this was not so. Having spoken in the Soviet before the debate and the decision on the question of the Government, Kerensky had merely received applause, which even a minority could make sufficiently noisy, in answer to his suggestion that he be allowed to enter the Government; and in answer to his proposal to leave him his Soviet title he had merely received exclamations ('We do, We do!'). There had been no formal ruling at all. Not only that, but Kerensky had avoided any discussion of the question—not only not asking for one but leaving the meeting-hall.

Were there any protests, the absence of which would still leave a decision without a vote, *par acclamation*, a semblance of legality? *Protests were made immediately.*

These were, to be sure, only isolated voices from the midst of the Soviet itself. The Ex. Com. leaders understood that, in the given circumstances, a debate of any scope specifically about Kerensky would mean risking brawls, muddle, and delay that were undesirable for both sides. On this ground, the majority did not think it necessary to *accept* battle any more than Kerensky had thought it necessary to *offer* it.

Nevertheless there were protests. The 'decision' by acclamation was protested against—by the whole subsequent course of the meeting and by the resolution adopted at the end of it.

Kerensky's very first phrases aroused in me a feeling of discomfort, or rather of embarrassment, dejection, and fury. Shrugging my shoulders I left the doorway, sat down on the sofa at the other end of the room, and morosely listened to the speech at the same time as I talked to two or three of my colleagues about what was to be done and what the upshot of all this would be. It was obviously pointless to give battle on these grounds about Kerensky personally. But come what might, the general line of the Ex. Com. had to be defended.

When Kerensky came back after his speech he was surrounded by a group of admirers, who filtered in after him from the hall. Among them I remember two or three British officers, of respectable and distinguished appearance. Kerensky, to be sure, made more of a fuss about them than they did about him. He drew them behind the curtain and plainly showed that he did not want anyone to interrupt their intimate conversation, which was in French.

'Look at that,' I thought, spitefully watching the new Minister; 'time now to pay attention to our gallant Allies!'

* * *

That was one ministerial speech. Another was being made at the same time. Miliukov was addressing the 'people', in the Catherine Hall, for purposes of information.

It may be that the public itself had called him away from business out of the Duma apartments. But it is quite probable that having formed a Cabinet its virtual head wanted to get an idea of the attitude of the masses of the people. In particular he may have wanted to confirm his solution of what was for him the most critical question, which was capable of becoming a source of conflict not only with the Soviet but also with his own more Leftist colleagues. This was, of course, the question of the monarchy and the dynasty. Miliukov was probably interested in getting a direct impression from the reactions of a casual but large audience to his binding of the revolution to the broken trough of the Romanovs.

Between 3 and 4 o'clock Miliukov appeared in the Catherine Hall to present himself to the people in his capacity of quasi-Minister, and introduce his colleagues in the Cabinet that was being formed. He started off with some rather demagogic onslaughts on the old régime, announced that the first people's Cabinet was in process of formation, and underlined the necessity of the bond between soldiers and officers.

The heterogeneous audience was not sparing of noisy applause. But a substantial part of it was obviously in a mood of opposition. Every now and then there would be heard from the crowd sarcastic questions and contentious sallies that Miliukov found some difficulty in picking his way through.

'Who elected you?' was one rather difficult question, to which the answer had to be given that no one had elected anyone, that there was no time for elections, that the 'revolution' had done the electing. When Miliukov called Premier Lvov the incarnation of Russian 'society' oppressed by the Tsarist régime, an exclamation was heard from the crowd: 'Propertied society!' And Miliukov answered this with a just and characteristic comment, of a piece with the considerations that governed the majority of the Ex. Com. in handing over power to the propertied bourgeoisie. He said: 'Propertied society is the only organized society, which can enable other strata of Russian society to organize themselves too.'

Concerning Kerensky, Miliukov, to thunderous applause, made a statement typical of the head of a Government forming his Cabinet:

'I have just received', he said, 'the consent of my colleague A. F. Kerensky to occupy the post of Minister of Justice in the first people's Cabinet, in which he will mete out just retribution to all the servants of the old régime, all the Stürmers and Sukhomlinovs.'

Contrariwise, at the introduction of Guchkov's name, things did not pass off without some unpleasantness, with which Miliukov himself, however, had reckoned.

'I'm going to announce a name to you', he continued, 'which will arouse some opposition here. A. I. Guchkov was my political enemy throughout the life of the Duma' (cries of 'Friend!'). 'But now we are political friends. I am an old professor accustomed to reading lectures, but Guchkov is a man of action. And at this moment, while I speak to you in this hall, Guchkov is in the streets of the capital organizing our victory. What would you say if, instead of stationing troops in railway stations last night to wait for the arrival of troops hostile to the revolution, Guchkov had taken part in our political debates, and the hostile troops, after occupying the railway stations, had then occupied the streets and finally this hall too? What would have become of you and me then?'

Such were the little tricks and distortions of the truth that Miliukov had to resort to in order to make his unexacting audience swallow Guchkov. But if uneasiness attended the name of Guchkov, a roar of laughter greeted that of Tereshchenko.[1] And really where had this gentleman sprung from, and how and why?

'Russia is vast,' the Cabinet leader answered in reply to this. 'It's hard to know the best people everywhere.' And the orator turned hurriedly to Shingarev.[2]

Miliukov was asked for the programme of the Cabinet. He was about to begin expounding, clause by clause, the programme dictated to him in our night session, indicating that this programme was the product of an agreement between the bourgeoisie and the Soviet democracy, but he was interrupted by impatient and insistent shouts:

'And the dynasty? What about the Romanovs?'

Miliukov leaped boldly into the fray, without, however, losing any opportunity of hiding his nakedness wherever possible with a screen of camouflage.

'I know', he said, 'that my answer will not satisfy all of you here, but I shall give it. The old despot who has brought the country to utter ruin will abdicate the throne or be deposed. The power will pass to a regent, the Grand Duke Michael Alexandrovich. Alexis will succeed him.'

Miliukov had not betrayed by a single word that on this point he had been trying an experiment—to see whether *his* programme would not go through *in the teeth of the Soviet democracy's demands and in contradiction to the terms of the 'agreement' laid down during the night.*

If you like it was also an attempt to effect a *coup d'état,* which ended of course with a complete fiasco. The next day Miliukov had to explain in print that his statements concerning the monarchy and dynasty reflected only his personal opinion. And a few days later nothing was left even of this personal opinion. But even then, during the speech itself, Miliukov had to retreat in disorder to the positions prepared beforehand by the Ex. Com.

[1] Tereshchenko, Mikhail Ivanovich (1888–1956): financier and sugar magnate; emigrated after the October Revolution.

[2] Shingarev, Andrei Ivanovich (1869–1918): a physician and prominent Cadet. In November 1917 he was imprisoned in the Peter-Paul Fortress and while hospitalized was killed in January 1918 by a group of sailors. (Ed.)

Tumult, outcries, and shouts of 'Down with the dynasty!' threatened to prevent the orator from finishing his speech in peace.

When he was finally able to speak again he continued in this vein: 'Gentlemen, you don't like the old dynasty. I may not like it either. But now the question is not who likes what. We cannot leave the question of the constitution of the State without a decision. We conceive of it as a parliamentary and constitutional monarchy. It may be that others will have a different conception of it. If we quarrel about this instead of deciding it immediately, then Russia will find herself in a state of civil war and the régime that has just been destroyed will come to life again. We have no right to do this, either from your point of view or our own. . .'

The audience, however, saw absolutely no reason why, in order to avoid disputes, procrastinations, and civil war, the question had to be decided in precisely Miliukov's way—i.e., in favour of the Romanovs, odious both to the people and to Miliukov himself (*sic!*). The uproar and protests, which did not abate, compelled Miliukov to effect a skilful diversion in form and to capitulate in substance.

'That doesn't mean', he went on, 'that we have decided the question arbitrarily. In our programme you will find a clause according to which, as soon as the danger is past and order is restored, we shall proceed to the convocation of a Constituent Assembly' (thunderous applause) 'elected on the basis of a universal, equal, and secret ballot. A freely elected popular representative body will decide which more faithfully expresses Russian public opinion—we or our opponents. . .'

Having arrived with his decision made, and done battle for it, Miliukov had been compelled to hide both himself and his programme behind 'some kind of' Constituent Assembly. It was plain that from here it was but a step to the Ex. Com. third point, which demanded that the right to decide the question be left to the Constituent Assembly and to it alone, and deprived the Miliukov Government of the *right to predetermine it* in one form or another.

However that might be, this programmatic speech of Miliukov's was a useful lesson to him. He had gained an idea of how the people would react to any attempts to crown the revolution with a monarchy, and how seriously they took the question of the Romanov dynasty. This part of Miliukov's speech, eclipsing all the rest in its beauty, had been carried in a flash not only all round the Palace but all round the capital. It was commented on in every possible way and exacerbated the question of the third point to an extreme degree; it aroused indignation against Miliukov and shook the prestige of the whole 'right wing', which had risked summoning the awakened people to a great festival in the stinking rags of the accursed despotism.

* * *

During those days no mass-meeting or public speeches could avoid misunderstandings on the subject of the dynasty.

I personally fell foul of it too. I don't remember why, but at about 6 o'clock that day I was making my way into the right wing through the same endless multitude. Some unknown people pounced on me, saying that a crowd of some tens of thousands of people was standing outside the Palace, and that they themselves had penetrated into the Palace in the capacity of delegates in order to call out Kerensky or at least some member of the Ex. Com. If no one came out they 'guaranteed' that the crowd would break into the Palace by force.

'You must understand,' one of them tried to persuade me; 'after all, the populace doesn't know anything about the state of affairs, the city has absolutely no news. . .'

It was impossible to go looking for Kerensky. And besides, he couldn't make speeches to the people for days on end. I was taken by the arms and dragged out into the street. From the steps, to which we could hardly get out, I saw a crowd I had never seen the like of before in my whole life. There was no end to the faces and heads turned towards me: they completely filled the courtyard, then the street, holding up banners, placards, and little flags.

Dusk was already falling, and it was snowing; the cold gripped me at once. They raised my jacket collar, put someone's fur cap on my head, and lifted me up on their shoulders, while one of my escorts introduced me to the crowd. I began talking about the situation. I don't know what part of the crowd heard my feeble voice, but as far as the eye could reach they were all straining towards me in a tense and deathlike silence.

I told them of the Ex. Com.'s decision on the problem of the régime, named the principal Ministers proposed, and expounded the programme dictated to the Lvov–Miliukov Government by the Soviet. My mention of the name of Minister Kerensky aroused the liveliest enthusiasm, but they soon began interrupting me with questions about the monarchy and the dynasty.

The same questions and exclamations were heard from all parts of the huge crowd. And I, who up to then had not ascribed any cardinal importance to this question, for the first time realized how seriously it was taken by the masses.

In answer to the shouts I said that with respect to the monarchy and dynasty there were still some differences, which had not yet been cleared up, between the bourgeois elements and the Ex. Com. I expressed confidence that the entire people would speak out in favour of a democratic republic. I thought it out of place as well as superfluous to go further and call for support of the Ex. Com.: even without that, slogans appropriate to the moment sprang up among my audience after my speech and there took place a large-scale but at the same time peaceful demonstration against the dynasty and—for a republic.

* * *

Messengers still came rushing in from the city with horrified accounts of excesses, shootings, and armed clashes. But they were less and less believed, and the hope kept increasing that all that would be dealt with even without us.

Conditions were 'returning to normal' and at the same time our routine work took on a more public, more systematic, more 'governmental', and less casual character. Moreover, the basic task of organizing the Government and creating a new revolutionary constitution was already coming to an end, and it was possible to start thinking about the new public tasks of the Soviet organization.

But before anything else it was vital somehow or other to put the organization itself in order. It was necessary to define the functions of the Ex. Com. members, create permanent departments or commissions, start thinking about finances, about a permanent staff, about the setting up of a system of propaganda and a literary section, about transport, etc. I don't remember whether there was a session of the Ex. Com. during these hours, while the debates on the Government were still going on in the Soviet. It is more likely that as before we were singly or in groups settling questions brought to us by every possible delegate, courier, and voluntary organizer, and dealt with in the order which the Ex. Com. members themselves thought best.

Around 7 o'clock the Soviet meeting was drawing to a close. The Ex. Com.'s resolution, on the Government and its programme, was already being put to the meeting. I don't remember who spoke for the Ex. Com. or whether Steklov made the final speech, but the result of the voting was splendid: *the 'line' and programme of the Ex. Com. was approved by nearly all the votes (some hundreds) to fifteen.*

It is impossible to say what elements this overwhelming majority was composed of, with respect to party allegiance or degree of political consciousness. And I don't know the proportions of Right or Left in the negligible opposition; it was probably more Right (Coalitionists) than Left (Bolsheviks). But in any case the victory of the Ex. Com. 'line', a line that was undoubtedly the most difficult for unprepared elements to assimilate, the line of maximum opposition by the masses, the line of transferring power to the bourgeoisie, of not entering the Government, and of a minimal programme—the victory of this line was decisive and complete.

* * *

The resolution on the Government was passed, the 'agreement' of the Ex. Com. with the propertied elements was approved, and the business of forming the Government had to be concluded. The following morning, whatever happened, the placards of the new Provisional Government had to be hanging in the streets, proclaiming the definitive establishment of a new era in the history of the Russian State.

Between 7 and 8 that evening I hastily collected our delegation for the final settlement of this question in the right wing. As far as I remember Sokolov was not in the Palace, and he took no part at all in this conference. Steklov was there. I started looking for Chkheidze.

The Soviet meeting was becoming completely disorganized,

but was still going on, and the hall was still full. Suddenly, as I entered the Soviet hall in search of Chkheidze, a hurricane of applause broke out, and a deafening 'Hurrah!' thundered forth. The excitement was indescribable. . . The Left Menshevik Yermansky, standing on the chairman's table with a copy of the *Russkoe Slovo* in his hands, was 'proclaiming' a telegram to the effect *that a revolution had been going on in Berlin since the previous day, that the Kaiser had already been got rid of, etc.*

No one knows how this nonsense got into a respectable, well-informed newspaper, and indeed very few people believed it, but the exposures came only later and could not diminish the enthusiasm produced by the stupendous news in the electrified crowd.

Where was Chkheidze? Elbowing my way into the hall I saw him on the chairman's table. Brandishing some crumpled papers and rolling his eyes, the old man was jumping up about a foot into the air and shouting 'Hurrah' as loud as he could. Making my way behind the platform, I called him, inviting him to come with me on more commonplace but perhaps more important business. Chkheidze, however, did not understand me very well, and was altogether rather annoyed by my interference; making an angry gesture at me, he remained on the table, breathing heavily and fiercely rolling his eyes.

* * *

But finally we were all assembled, and the three of us went off to the right wing, taking along the Soviet resolution.

The Duma working apartments presented the same scene as ours: the rooms occupied by the central agencies gradually filled up with the 'fringe', or simply the ordinary public, whom there was no getting rid of. To get a chance of doing any kind of work the leaders had to retire: they either penetrated more deeply into the inner rooms or else escaped into another corner of the Palace where their presence was still unknown.

The room where we had met the night before had already had time to be transformed into some sort of guard-room, and we were taken two rooms further in, where there were Duma leaders in great numbers, firm pillars of our bourgeois society, rank-and-file deputies of various complexions and other highly respectable people. Groups of them were sitting, walking about, arguing hotly, fussing around, conferring, and aimlessly jostling each other.

They were waiting for us and we set to work at once. But this time there was not even a semblance of an official or organizational conference at all. I can't even remember who was there: I think Rodzianko was not, and Godnev and both Lvovs were; for the first time I had pointed out to me Tereshchenko, who had not spoken. For the rest they were an indistinguishable mass.

* * *

At this time Guchkov and Shulgin were already near Pskov, where they had gone off that morning in order to persuade the Tsar to abdicate in favour of Alexis, with Michael as Regent. The Ex. Com. learned about this trip only on the following day; I don't know how it was organized technically.

But politically, from the point of view of our 'constitutional' bourgeoisie, this was the last attempt to preserve the monarchy and dynasty by way of a *coup d'état*. It was an attempt to create a Romanov centre, having rallied around it the generals, most of the officers, and thus the whole army, the functionaries, property holders, rural and urban bourgeoisie, i.e. all of 'organized society', the old state machinery, which at that time represented an enormous force, and with whom an open war on the part of a feeble and dispersed democracy would have constituted a mortal danger for the revolution.

The then monarchist leaders wanted to face Russia and the radical republican bourgeoisie, but chiefly the Soviet democracy, whose views had become clear in the course of the preceding night, with an accomplished fact. On the part of the Guchkovs and the Miliukovs this trip was not only an attempt at a *coup d'état*, but also a treacherous breach of an agreement that had actually been made between us.

* * *

Properly speaking there was no meeting: there was a conversation between Miliukov, Steklov, and myself, in which none or practically none of the other people in the room took part. Even the external arrangements of the room precluded, you might say, the idea of any kind of meeting. Miliukov was sitting and writing in a corner of the room at a table set against the wall or the window. Next to him, also facing the wall, were ourselves, the Soviet delegates. Two or three listeners from among the Duma people were also sitting there. The whole of the rest of the room was behind us and thus excluded in advance from any part in the conversations. Besides us three, someone else put in an occasional sentence.

The work itself consisted of the definitive formulation and writing down of a Government programme.

The first thing we turned to was, of course, the third point, the constitutional question. We maintained that nothing whatever would come of Miliukov's stubbornness and his attempts to thrust the Romanovs upon us except complications that would not help the monarchist cause, but at best simply destroy the prestige of his own Cabinet.

To prove this we brought up our experience of that day, during which the liquidation of the Romanovs had already become a fighting slogan. We pointed out that it was the position he, Miliukov, occupied as leader of the whole right wing, that exacerbated not only the question itself but the general situation as well. We referred to the dissatisfaction aroused by Miliukov's speech in the Catherine Hall . . .

Miliukov listened and seemed to acknowledge that we were right. He also had experienced that day's events, and may have been reflecting that the trip he had organized to Pskov had been a rather risky enterprise. . . However, to begin with, the thing was done; secondly, however risky this gamble on the monarchy may have been, it was indispensable to Miliukov and Guchkov: for a gamble on the monarchy was still less risky than a gamble on bourgeois statesmanship *without* the monarchy. Miliukov listened and reflected. . .

'You can scarcely be hoping', I said at last as a final argument, 'that a Constituent Assembly will leave a monarchy in Russia? So all your efforts will be fruitless after all. . .'

In reply to this Miliukov, squarely in the face of his Cabinet colleagues and of the Premier himself, turned to us and said, emphatically and with evident sincerity:

'The Constituent Assembly may decide as it pleases. If it pronounces against the monarchy, then I shall be able to go. But now I cannot. Now, if I am not here, there is no

Government at all. And if there is no Government, then ... you yourselves can understand. . .'

These words reflected the whole tragedy of 'thinking' but bankrupt monarchism, and all the proud self-confidence of the monopolistic leader of a whole class, a 'ruling' class but—a stupid one, whose every move had to be minutely scrutinized.

* * *

At long last the question of the third point was settled in this way: we agreed to leave out of the *governmental proclamation the official pledge 'not to take any steps to predetermine the form of government'*. We agreed to leave it to the Government, or more accurately to its individual components, to deal with the Romanov monarchy. But we stated categorically that for its part the Soviet would *engage without delay in a broad struggle for a democratic republic*. It was on this basis that we came to terms on the contents of the Government proclamation.

The formula of suppression we had found as a way out of the situation was of course a compromise. But the concession was obviously incomparably greater on the side of the monarchists than on that of the Soviet. We had not, after all, demanded that a republic be proclaimed, whereas our negotiators had insisted on the monarchy and regency. We had merely demanded that the solution of the question should not be predetermined before the Constituent Assembly met. But an official pledge of that kind would not of course have had any substantial practical significance. 'Steps', it goes without saying, would be taken (as, indeed, they were being taken even now—backstage). But a free struggle declared by us would leave all the chances on the side of the republic—not only thanks to the universal hatred of the Romanovs, the universal desire for a republic, and the material power behind that desire, but also thanks to the indubitable disloyalty of wide strata of the bourgeoisie to the 'ideals of monarchy'. The split in the bourgeoisie on that ground was even then sharply apparent, and a few days later it culminated in the assumption of the republican toga by Miliukov's own party. *Our* concessions and *our* risk were, of course, trivial. All this had made me personally neglect the question of the form of the Government, even while the programme was being worked out in the Ex. Com., when I thought it possible and desirable to leave the settlement of this question to the subsequent free struggle.

This resolution of the 'third point' brought to an end all our discussions of questions of high policy, and we now had only to draw up the first Constitution of the Great Russian Revolution, put it in order and give it to the presses. The list of Ministers already drawn up had to have the proclamation appended, and then the signatures of the Cabinet members collected below it.

The 'programme' had been written down by Miliukov the night before. We re-read it, and Miliukov obediently wrote down from dictation at the end of it: 'The Provisional Government considers it its duty to add that it is far from intending to take advantage of the circumstances of war to postpone in any way the realization of the reforms and measures described above.'

All three of us who drew up the final version of the programme were writers, and writers of considerable experience. But the revision was laborious, with many hesitations and corrections. I remember that we took a long time groping for the phrasing of this last pledge. 'Reforms and measures'—could you say that? We shrugged our shoulders and said it.

* * *

Steklov had vanished somewhere and I was left alone with Miliukov to complete the Constitution. I remember that the irregular scrap of paper on which the proclamation was written passed into my hands, and with Miliukov's help I wrote at the top of it: 'In its activities the Government will be guided by the following principles.'

Now—how should the document be headed?

'From the Provisional Committee of the Duma,' Miliukov suggested to me. But I was not satisfied. Why the Duma?

'To preserve the succession of authority,' Miliukov replied. 'After all, Rodzianko ought to sign this document.'

I didn't like any of this. I preferred to dispense with the succession, and with Rodzianko. I insisted that the document be headed 'From the Provisional Government', and said that in my view there was no need for Rodzianko to sign it.

The question was of no practical importance, but it was curious to see that it was settled in favour of punctilio by the learned representative of bourgeois monarchism, who had stuck his claws into the revolution. Miliukov clearly had no definite opinion about this.

'You don't think Rodzianko should sign?' he said dubiously. Then he tried over a few arrangements of words for the heading and said:

'Oh, very well, put down "From the Provisional Government".'

I wrote this at the top of the pasted-together scrap of paper, which had an extremely untidy look. It was essential to have it typed out and sent to the printers not later than 10 o'clock. But first the Ministers' signatures had to be collected on the original.

We went through the Duma rooms looking for them. Most of them signed on the spot, without reading it or in any case without going into details. I remember that for some reason the State Comptroller, Godnev, turned stubborn and, also without reading it, refused to sign. After spending some five minutes with him we left him in peace.

But to make up for this, Rodzianko turned up; the Ministers referred the paper to him and he himself thought it indispensable to give the revolutionary Government his blessing by signing it.

The constitution had to be sent to the printers, when we had appended to the Government declaration the Ex. Com.'s proclamation, consisting of three paragraphs and written by three hands.

'Let me send them off together,' suggested Miliukov. Then something strange happened. I don't know why, but I was suddenly seized by a doubt whether Miliukov could be trusted with it. I didn't want to leave the documents—either ours or his own—in his hands, even though no real danger, either of their disappearance or of their being altered, could arise. But how could I express these doubts of mine, completely hazy and without any foundation?

'What press will you have them printed at?' I asked.

'I don't know,' Miliukov answered. 'The printing-presses are more under your control.'

'I think we can get them printed at once in a printing-shop that is occupied by the Soviet and working for it. You probably haven't got one yet.'

'Excellent,' said Miliukov; 'in that case *you* send both documents, since you can guarantee that tomorrow morning they will be pasted up in the streets. . .'

I was embarrassed by this turn of affairs and gathering the papers together went off to have them transcribed. Quite unnecessarily, simply succumbing to my embarrassment, I decided to return the original to Miliukov together with a copy.

'Please see to it,' he called after me, 'that our proclamations are printed and pasted up on a single sheet of paper, one under the other.'

* * *

It was after 9 o'clock. Both the Soviet and the mass-meetings had long since dispersed. The Palace was almost dark and almost empty. But there were signs at hand of the new Soviet organization. Without great difficulty, I succeeded in finding a typist on duty and setting her to type out the first Constitution, holding back a courier who was ready to leave for the printing-press with some other material.

Suddenly the Soviet rooms resounded with shouts: 'The mob is destroying the University!' I did not particularly believe this, but something had to be done. One of the junior officers who had already offered his services on the morning of the 28th turned up. He assured me that he had a strong and reliable detachment of men, and undertook to set off at once for the University with them. . .

Though the city had not yet calmed down, the new order was putting forth roots with every minute that passed. The *technique* of strengthening the new régime was almost outpacing 'high policy'. But even in the realm of policy the demands of the moment were almost fulfilled. The Constitution was prepared and transcribed. I gave one copy to a comrade, a messenger, for emergency printing, having written on it the appropriate directives ('on one sheet of paper, in thick type, to be pasted up in the streets in the morning'). With another copy and the original I set out for the right wing.

The Ex. Com. had already dispersed to get some rest. I don't think any member of it was to be found. In the entrance-hall on my way over I was caught again by a 'delegation' from a crowd who were demanding that 'someone' should come out to them.

It was too much of a nuisance to run to put on my overcoat, and I went straight out into the street in my jacket, with the Constitution in my hands.

It was a cold night out of doors, and a light snow was falling. The forecourt was empty, and the crowd was being kept in the street by someone at the gate. I hurried to the gate and this time stepped up on a kerbstone, in a student's greatcoat and peaked cap. The excesses of such a crowd were in any case not to be feared: there were about four or five hundred late demonstrators, mostly intellectuals.

Showing them the original of the revolutionary Constitution, I told them in two words the state of affairs in the sphere of high policy. I was again interrupted by shouts, exclamations, and questions about the monarchy and dynasty. I appealed to them to fight for a republic and, retiring quickly, continued on my way to the right wing.

Miliukov was astonished by my 'kindness' when I handed him the copies and the original of our proclamations. So the manuscripts remained in his possession.

'The rumours about the destruction of the University have turned out to be nonsense,' I remarked in passing, as I handed over the documents.

'Yes, yes,' Miliukov replied, as though to his own thoughts, 'everything is going well. Everything's all right.'

I too thought that everything was going as well as possible. The Duma apartments also were now almost empty. The business was finished.

All the other business of the fourth day of the revolution was finished too. It was possible to think of rest and food. Miliukov and I said good-bye to each other, to meet again in the near future—by that time in the Marian Palace, and no longer as 'contracting parties' but as the representatives of two sides locked in a struggle to the death. *Our agreement was an agreement on the conditions of a duel.*

* * *

It was around 11 o'clock. At this same time Messieurs Guchkov and Shulgin, who had just arrived in Pskov, were in a parlour-car discussing with the Tsar his abdication of the throne. The Tsar had that morning, after receiving the report of General Ruzsky, who had spoken to Rodzianko in the night by direct wire, decided to abdicate. The Tsar had then composed a telegram to this effect but had not sent it, since he had received the information that members of the Duma Committee were coming to see him in Pskov. The Tsar had been expecting them in the course of the day.

And Messieurs the Deputies had gone to Pskov without the knowledge of the people, in order to persuade the Tsar in the name of the revolution to preserve the dynasty by transferring his sovereign rights to his son Alexis and the actual power to his brother Michael.

But during the day the Tsar had changed his mind, and after a long speech by Guchkov, who in an extremely diplomatic and guarded way was breaking down an open door, he announced that he himself had already decided to abdicate the throne, not, however, in favour of Alexis, from whom he could not part, but in favour of his brother, who had been put forward as Regent.

This took the Duma delegates by surprise. But they quickly calculated that for them and the groups they led this turn of events presented even more advantages; and they did not hesitate to sanction in the name of Russia this attempt to lay on the country and the revolution a more reliable Tsarist yoke. They declared that they honoured the Tsar's paternal feelings and would not object. By noon they had already left for Petersburg, carrying with them the deed of abdication in favour of Michael. In vain. . .

But from whatever point of view, the great overturn of 1917 culminated in this deed. Now the dynasty was liquidated, and the monarchy with it. Now a new revolutionary authority had been created and the foundations of a new order laid. The Russian State and the Russian people had now entered upon a new and glorious path, and new perspectives had opened before the world proletarian movement.

* * *

At this time I was walking through the empty streets of Peski to my lodging for the night. Civilian and military patrols, new militiamen, and all kinds of volunteers in the service of 'revolutionary order', with rifles, pistols, and badges, were warming themselves at the camp-fires. They conscientiously stopped the motor-cars that occasionally went by, asked for passes, and examined papers. It was reported that a black car had appeared in Petersburg, and whirled through the capital from one end to the other shooting at passers-by with a machine-gun. They were hunting it but couldn't catch it.

There was no feeling of alarm in the streets, nor any more homeless, hungry soldiers. The overturn was accomplished; the capital and the whole country with it were beginning to live a new life and proceed to the tasks of the day.

Here and there loomed up the black shapes of solitary lorries and other cars heeled over on their sides and stuck in the snow. Not a few of these had been wrecked during those days. Such sacrifices merited no attention. . .

But were not any sacrifices worth while for this magnificent victory, that still seemed like a sweet illusion and an enchanted, radiant dream?

July–November 1918.

Part II

THE UNITED DEMOCRATIC FRONT

March 3rd–April 3rd

CHAPTER 7

GETTING ORIENTED

FROM March 3rd on, the close-knit chain of my reminiscences comes to an end. Beginning with the fifth day of the revolution, gaps and voids appear which I cannot fill in. Days begin running together in confusion, then weeks as well. From now on I shall not be able to describe them in sequence.

With the help of newspapers I could, to be sure, establish a consecutive chain of events. But that is not the object of my notes: this is no history. For my personal reminiscences can lift out of this chain only isolated though numerous episodes, which I should have to link together with the help of printed materials. I should have to dilute this drama unmatched in history, this wonderful epic called the Russian Revolution, with tiresome disquisitions, in my inability to reproduce it as I saw it with my own eyes, rolling along, tumultuous, sparkling, deafening, and shot with a myriad colours like a gigantic cascade.

However, there is no need to offer the reader a 'diary' of 1917. The 'episodes' I remember make so long a chain themselves that there is some risk that the reader will not persevere to the end. Well, what of that? Let there be grains for a diligent and skilful historian to pick up! The worst is that I myself run the risk of not persevering to the end of this chain, and may never finish my reminiscences. Well, what of that? I shall go on writing them down as long as circumstances permit.

* * *

On March 3rd the proclamations 'From the Provisional Government' and the Soviet were hanging in the streets, on one sheet of paper, as agreed on. The new revolutionary order was a fact.

All available reports from the provinces said that the revolution had taken place in all principal centres and that the old régime had everywhere been more or less easily and painlessly liquidated.

The army also had speedily 'acknowledged' the new order. The Tsarist generals, seeing the hopelessness of a struggle, hurriedly began to take on protective colouring, and to pretend they had been born anew. The Black Hundred had vanished underground. In the twinkling of an eye the higher officialdom had also dissolved into thin air. Even before the formal liquidation of the Romanovs the Tsarist régime had no hope left. The counter-revolution existed, but it was disguised—like the revolution itself before the revolution. It threatened to liquidate the future conquests of the people, but it no longer threatened the revolution.

Nor was the revolution threatened any longer by anarchy in the capital, or by hunger, for all available stores were intact, and in transport the overturn had not caused even the slightest upset. A new life and new struggle were beginning.

* * *

The Ex. Com. of the Soviet had to apply itself seriously to 'organizational work'. To do this it must first construct a sound organization for itself—allocate spheres of work, eliminate overlapping and the giving of contradictory orders, select a responsible secretary, attend to the keeping of minutes, etc. The editorial board of *Izvestiya* also had to be reorganized.

Still harassed by emergency matters, the Ex. Com. formed a series of commissions from its own ranks or rather, more accurately, broke up into sections for independent decisions on various kinds of business.

The very names of these commissions may give some idea of how imperfect and, so to speak, unprincipled our organization was. The commissions were: secretarial, propagandist, literary-publishing, for the resumption of work, on licensing of newspapers and allotment of printing-shops, motor-car, financial, supply, district, and current affairs.

As we see, some of these commissions had permanent functions based, so to speak, on principle, others were provisional, technical, auxiliary, and quite specific; one was national, the rest only municipal.

In the elections to the commissions, as before, there was no sign of any intensive inter-party struggle. This reflected equally the unified spirit of the democracy and our 'unconsciousness', that is, our hazy understanding, of the future processes of the revolution, at that time.

On this March 3rd, even the politically responsible Propaganda Commission consisted of the defensist Erhlich and two Bolsheviks, Krasikov and Shlyapnikov, while the majority of the Ex. Com. were Menshevik-Internationalists.

It is even odder that the very important question of the editorial board of *Izvestiya* and its staff was entrusted to Steklov. Even then the defensist minority of the Ex. Com. was far from weak, whereas Steklov had Bolshevik origins.

This attitude of the Ex. Com. to such an important question as the editorial board of the official central organ of the revolution and of the democracy can also be explained only by the absence in the leading institution of the day of any sharp *differentiation or struggle between the parties.*

* * *

Steklov was at this time extremely prominent in the revolution and carried out a really enormous amount of most important work. With his adequate education, experience as a speaker and writer, and great revolutionary political past (both Russian and European), Steklov in those days displayed immense energy. He was indefatigable and very versatile. Other qualities of his, which later were to determine his fate, had not yet had time to show themselves.

In the first place, Steklov was always disagreeably ready to 'gravitate' to any kind of majority. From the beginning of party stratification in the Soviet, this completely discredited this useful (though not very pleasant) revolutionary worker, on whom holders of similar views could not depend in such circumstances, and from whom anything might be expected.

This characteristic of Steklov's did not result merely from personal vanity. Its fundamental reason was rather that essentially Steklov had no 'views', but at best merely 'tendencies'. Neither his erudition nor his political experience, strangely enough, had eliminated his basic qualities: political sterility, triviality, and small-mindedness.

* * *

A purely technical matter—'administration', i.e. the Secretarial Commission—was entrusted to B. O. Bogdanov. This was sound enough in the sense that Bogdanov was an extraordinarily energetic, efficient, and experienced organizer (in spite of his relative youthfulness), with a suitably heavy, not to say rough, hand.

But it would be wrong to think that Bogdanov was specially fitted for the rôle of 'administrator' in distinction from other fields of activity. On the contrary, unlike Steklov, who was destined to be one of the ideological inspirers, through *Izvestiya*, of the Soviet, Bogdanov, condemned to the secretariat, was a politician. He reasoned intensively and I should say interestingly, undergoing a curious evolution in the realm of 'high policy'.

And he was, finally, a man capable of indefatigable organizational work in various spheres. In general he was an extremely interesting figure and one of the pillars of the Ex. Com.'s work throughout the first and Menshevik-SR periods of the revolution, right up to the October insurrection itself.

I had known Bogdanov for a fairly long time and quite well, on the *Sovremennik*, in all sorts of organizations, in musical circles, and from purely personal acquaintance. He was not a brilliant or distinguished but a useful writer on special questions, though an uncommonly inaccurate one, with whom it was better for an editor not to get involved.

There was in Bogdanov a successful and unusual combination of political thinking and unflagging painstaking 'organizational' industry.

'An ox for work,' Chkheidze said of him, watching him stand for hours on end as chairman of the Soviet in an exhausting struggle with unruly elements, shaking a bell in one hand, majestically gesticulating with the other, and crying out in a hoarse voice: 'Those in favour. . . those against. . .'

An ox for work, in many circumstances irreplaceable, and at many critical moments a working centre for the Soviet organization of the capital. But his political ideas were for the most part misdirected and in the last analysis proved his undoing.

* * *

The very important matter of Soviet finances was entrusted to the old Trudovik, L. M. Bramson, the Petersburg lawyer, well known as defending counsel in political trials, an estimable and selfless worker and an excellent fellow. Unlike the other Trudoviks who failed to stand the exacting test of the revolution and almost without exception sold their 'democratic' swords to the Right wing, Bramson merged 'organically' with the Soviet and worked there unceasingly until the end. *His* democratic spirit stood the test brilliantly.

Bramson shared his duties on the financial commission with K. A. Gvozdev. This man was also one of the chief workers of the Soviet and one of the most interesting figures of the first months of the revolution.

No less an ox for work than Bogdanov, Kuzma Gvozdev, busying himself with Soviet finances and lavishing his efforts on details like the management of transport, from the very first days became the most important figure in all labour questions in the central Soviet institutions.

One must imagine all the complexity of the position of a victorious and profoundly democratic revolution which had made the proletariat the actual masters of the situation, while at the same time leaving untouched both the foundations of the bourgeois order and even the formal authority of the old ruling classes; one must understand all the complexity and contradictoriness of this position created by the revolution in order to appreciate how difficult, crucial, and ticklish the labour problem was at this period, and what experience, firmness, tact, and skill it required, between the hammer and the anvil, between the protesting rebellious workers and the employers, endlessly threatening strikes and lockouts.

Gvozdev's position was all the more difficult, since with all his qualities he still lacked the indispensable one of popularity. A proletarian by birth, he was the head of Right-wing defensism, social-reformism, and opportunism in the working-class movement during the epoch of war and revolution. This tendency was now quite discredited.

Like Bogdanov, Gvozdev was not an 'ox for work' only, nor was his 'conciliationism', like that of many 'Zimmerwaldites', stupid and flatfooted. In very many cases Gvozdev displayed not only sound ideas but also very great suppleness of thought. He was often original and always interesting as a result of this mental struggling of his. And I always, with unflagging interest and, let me say, to my considerable advantage, listened to the rather clumsy, not especially pretty or glib speeches of my constant adversary in the Ex. Com.

Not having met him before the revolution, but having heard a good deal about him, I was of course strongly prejudiced against this 'pernicious personage'. But in my first encounters with him at work and in personal acquaintance I quickly repented of my prejudice, finding in Gvozdev an excellent colleague, a good man, and a sincere Socialist, agreeable to deal with as an opponent and even more so as a comrade in arms.

He was very far indeed from being a stranger to pride, which became morbid as a result of constant baiting, his rupture with his brother workers, and his ministerial failures. He considered me, together with the *Novaya Zhizn* (New Life),[1] an arch-destroyer of the revolution and talked to me with a mournful look and sad indignation. Nevertheless I kept up pleasant personal relations with Gvozdev—unlike others—until the end, until October, when he finally transferred himself from the Tauride to the Winter Palace.[2]

Gvozdev was necessarily the principal worker on the Commission for the Resumption of Work elected on March 3rd. On the Propaganda Commission Shlyapnikov and Ehrlich, two party men, a Left Bolshevik and a Right Menshevik-Bundist, got along like fire and water.

Shlyapnikov we already know. Ehrlich too we shall meet more than once later on. He was a collaborator of the 'Socialist' *Dyen* (Day): intellectual, informed, conscientious, and energetic. Later he was sent abroad to represent the Russian Revolution and organize a Socialist Conference in Stockholm.

In the beginning he undoubtedly distinguished himself from the Soviet Right wing by his independence of thought and his attempt to keep his defensism, revisionism, and 'conciliationism' within the bounds of logic and common sense. It was often said about this defensist from a suspect newspaper that he was 'better than a Zimmerwaldite'. But when the differentiation between the elements of the Soviet finally took place and the Right wing took shape under the leadership of the 'Zimmerwaldite' Tsereteli, Ehrlich completely bogged down in it, losing his distinctive character as a 'reasonable defensist' and every other distinguishing trait as well.

[1] Daily newspaper founded by Gorky in 1917, with Sukhanov as an editor. Organ of the Social-Democratic Internationalists. It was cool to the October Revolution (see Part VI) and came to an end in 1918. (Ed.)

[2] As a Minister in the Provisional Government. (Ed.)

Such were the commissions created on March 3rd and such were their principal figures. Other prominent personalities of the Ex. Com. were not elected to these commissions: not Chkheidze, exhausted by the burden of 'representation' and spending himself in triumphal speeches; nor Skobelev, who specialized in trips to places where trouble was brewing; nor Sokolov, who was fluttering around every corner of revolutionary Petersburg, present in every nook and cranny at once and bringing back one sensational report after another to the Ex. Com.

* * *

In my absence for some reason I was appointed to the commission to examine the question of periodical publications. Then, on the next day or the 5th, two more commissions were formed—one for 'other cities' and one 'for legislative proposals'. I was appointed to both. Besides this, during these days the extremely important Labour Commission mentioned above was set up, and I became a member of this too, with Bogdanov and Gvozdev.

Alas! I practically never worked in any of these commissions. I can remember only two or at most three days of activity in the department of periodical publications and the allocation of printing-shops to them. Highly disagreeable memories!

This had quite fundamental (though completely subjective) reasons. First of all, with *Novaya Zhizn* in view, I quite consciously had no desire to be plunged into 'organic' work. Secondly, my mood, and perhaps my nature as well, were such that I had too little desire at that time for spadework in the administrative organization of the revolution.

All my efforts and thoughts were concentrated on the sphere of 'high policy'. My endeavours were directed to cutting through all 'emergency' and 'unpostponable' routine business, however urgent, and getting a bird's-eye view of the revolution. I repeat that these were my subjective inclinations. In practice they didn't come to much.

I was one of those of whom the chairman Chkheidze said later, with a spiteful sidelong glance at me: 'We have some comrades here who don't do any work, but just come here to play politics.'

And even then, in the midst of the niggling details and tedious casual drudgery, I was chiefly concerned with 'high' problems. The revolutionary Government was now formed, the general position of the democracy in the revolution was now established, the general character of the inter-relations of the Soviet and the Provisional Government was now more or less clear. In a word, the general political situation was settled and clear.

But it was essential to define without delay what had to be done, what line the Soviet had to take in the new situation. The current political line and the next practical steps of Soviet democracy in domestic and foreign policy had to be marked out.

* * *

With respect to the restoration of normality in the Soviet democracy's state machine it was naturally up to the Ex. Com. to cast its gaze towards the other side also. It had to attend to the proletarian masses, and pacify the institutions serving the workers. The strike in Petersburg was almost general. It had to be liquidated. An appeal had just been printed in *Izvestiya* to open all warehouses—supplementing the opening of the banks—and thus help start up the economic machinery, first of all, and secondly demonstrate the consolidation of the new order and of normal life in the new conditions.

The factories and workshops of the capital now had to be set in motion again—and above all, the trams. The restoration of normal street traffic in the form of the trams ought to be a clear symbol of the conclusively victorious revolution and of the beginning of a peaceful life in free Petersburg.

* * *

At 1 o'clock on March 3rd I was called to the telephone by Nikitsky, appointed by the Ex. Com. as assistant to the new Civil Governor. Nikitsky told me the prefecture was worried about the resumption of the tramway service. The Town Council and the municipal officials had bogged down in the following problem: how were soldier-passengers to be treated?

It was obvious that from then on they would be travelling not only on the platforms but also inside the cars on an equal footing with other citizens. But would they pay? If fares were not taken from them, then wasn't it obvious that the only people travelling in the trams would be non-paying passengers? The many thousands of soldiers from the garrison of the capital would create an enormous traffic movement in the city. If they need not pay, the soldiers would go by tram for the shortest distances, and get on for only one or two stops. And then good-bye to the trams for the rest of the inhabitants! Women, children, the aged, and the weak would have as much chance of getting on a tram as of flying.

Nikitsky asked me to take steps in the Ex. Com. to restrict the movements of the soldiers in one way or another, in the interests of the capital as a whole and of the trams in particular. The civic authorities thought the best way to do this was to introduce payment of fares for soldiers.

Personally I thought so too, but the Ex. Com. decided otherwise. When, after the election of the commissions, the 'resumption of work' was taken up, with the tramway service as the first item, there occurred the first clash between 'practical considerations' and the demagogy which the majority thought the situation called for. I fought for half-fare (5 copecks) for soldiers, at least inside the cars. But the majority decided against this and ordered a public announcement that soldiers were to be allowed to travel in the trams free and sit where they liked.

I don't remember who made up this majority, but there can be no doubt that if they had given a sop to demagogy, the demagogy was justified to a considerable degree by the prevailing circumstances. These were days when the revolution, freedom, and especially the Soviet, were empty sounds for the mass of the soldiery. This mass, only yesterday the blind instrument of Tsarism, had just thrown off the yoke and was threatening tomorrow to turn into just as blind a 'master of the situation', quite out of hand and capable of wreaking the most dreadful havoc. At that time it was necessary to treat the garrison with the utmost delicacy, and vital to create at all costs an undeniable authority it would consider its own and therefore obey.

So it was decided to start the trams moving. But it turned out to be technically impossible: in Petersburg there happened to be great snowdrifts during the very days of the strike. The town's spokesman said he had no hope of starting the trams moving before Tuesday, and the 3rd was only Friday. What a pity! The appearance of the trams in the streets of the revolutionary capital would not only have meant an enormous relief for the inhabitants, it would also have been a symbol of the restoration of order.

But it was characteristic that none of us had the slightest doubt in his mind that we, the Ex. Com. of the Soviet, were competent to decide the question of the trams, not only about starting them up again but also about the soldiers' fares, and that no one else had either the power or the authority to do so. Not the Town Council, not the Government, not the garrison commanders—only the Soviet of Workers' and Soldiers' Deputies. This was a cardinal question of the revolutionary situation, and here we had undisputed authority.

* * *

In the middle of the day someone brought the Ex. Com. the text of the abdication of Nicholas II. Shulgin and Guchkov had brought the document from Pskov early in the morning.

Nicholas's last 'manifesto' of course made no impression whatever on the Ex. Com. There was laughter when someone gave us the information that before his abdication Nicholas had 'appointed' G. E. Lvov Premier. Terribly prudent of the wise and solicitous monarch! Very subtle of the bourgeois diplomats who had inspired him!

We laughed at the naïve anachronism of the text of the last manifesto, but didn't pay the slightest attention to the fact of the abdication itself. It was self-evident to all of us that at this point, on March 3rd, it introduced absolutely nothing new into the general situation. The revolution was taking its course, and the new combination of forces would be established quite independently of the activities of any Romanovs. There were no Romanovs on that 3rd of March, just as there had been none the day before, the 2nd, either, or even the day before that, and just as there would be none in the future. No efforts, no diplomacy, no intrigues of the 'right wing' could change one single iota in all this. This was all clear—with the 'manifesto' just as much as without it.

The Soviet democracy had consciously tolerated a slight obscurity and lack of agreement with respect to the general question of the republic. But even so, such an attitude on the part of the Ex. Com. was possible only because the republic was secure: it was in our hands. This allowed us the luxury of silence—for diplomatic purposes.

The act of abdication was a worthless scrap of paper which might have a literary, but certainly no political, interest for us. It was another matter everywhere else in the Tauride Palace, filled as before with a motley crowd. There this scrap of paper was violently fallen on and snatched from hand to hand. It was said the same thing was going on in the city. The masses regarded the document as an important event, even against the background of everything that had happened during those days. They saw in it an essential stage and perhaps a crisis in the development of the revolution. And there were strange people, —groups, circles, and perhaps whole social strata—that saw a revolution only in this, and only in this saw the irremediable destruction of the accustomed tenor of life and only now associated the disorders that were taking place with radical changes.

Yes, the average man is stupid—as the shrewd Miliukov used to say, Miliukov, for whom this liquidation of Tsar Nicholas was not only the most self-evident necessity but also the ultimate means of avoiding these 'radical changes'.

* * *

In the right wing, however, and especially for Miliukov himself, this document caused a good deal of fuss and vexation. The trouble was not of course the fact of the abdication, but after all it had been supposed that the throne would pass to Alexis, a child, and that the Tsar's brother Michael would be Regent: Miliukov had indeed announced this publicly the night before as an accomplished fact. And here it turned out that Nicholas was most graciously conferring the succession on his brother Michael, giving him his 'blessing' on 'ascending the throne of Russia' and 'commanding' him to 'govern the country'.

From the point of view of the Right monarchists and of consistent monarchism generally, such a turn of events was in principle quite auspicious. For with a sick child and the inevitable palace machinations, what would emerge would not be a monarchy but simply a mess. Even if one hoped that this would somehow take shape, yet it must be expected in such circumstances that what took shape under the child Alexis would be not a real monarchical government but only a 'constitutional' fiction, behind whose hollow façade would lurk all the 'Left' partisans of 'democracy' and 'parliamentarianism'. Michael, a worthy son of Alexander III, was another matter. He might quite well pave the way to a real triumph of the monarchical principle.

But then the question was, what forces could place Michael on the 'throne'? For Miliukov, Guchkov, and Shulgin, Michael was obviously preferable to Alexis. They were not among those against whom he had to be defended, but among those who were ready to defend him on principle. But they did, after all, have to defend Michael not only against the entire 'left wing' of the Palace, not only against the Soviet democracy, not only against the whole people and the whole country, plus even their own Left Progressive Cadet Fronde, who had been touched by the revolutionary fervour and enthusiasm of the man in the street: Michael, unlike Alexis, had to be defended in addition against the most well-meaning elements, the most compact groups of the Progressive Bloc, the most reliable leaders of the plutocracy, who turned out to be inordinately infected by constitutional illusions.

* * *

The new Government received this surprise early in the morning of March 3rd, the day of its national début. The Ministers assembled for a conference with the Duma Committee and began discussing what to do. According to Miliukov, attempts were made to change the act of abdication and meanwhile not to publish it. All in vain!

There is no doubt that among the members of the Cabinet and on its fringes there were people with 'dizzy heads' who were extremely favourable to a republic. They were glad—even though in secret—of an occasion to make an end of their own vacillations and tear down the monarchy. But there were more who were afraid that any obstinacy in defending the monarchy and dynasty in the new arrangement would end badly for the plutocracy. And together with the new-born republicans these 'practical politicians' insisted on abandoning the monarchist position.

Kerensky was of course at the head of the anti-monarchists—

using both pathos and threats and playing on his own special position as the 'plenipotentiary representative of the democracy' in the Cabinet. Lvov and most of the monarchists of yesterday, headed by Rodzianko, inclined towards Kerensky. They all insisted that Michael Romanov should refuse the throne. There was a minority of only two, Miliukov and Guchkov, who proposed that Michael should be approved as Tsar and humbly besought to accept the throne. Eternal glory to the perspicacity of these two faithful knights of the people's freedom!

It was decided to talk things over with the candidate himself, and allow both the majority and the minority to try to sway him one way or the other to confer enormous benefits on Russia, either by accepting or by renouncing the throne.

The scene of this discussion—not entirely resembling the scene from *Boris Godunov*—was described in all the papers. But it was not reported in the papers that Miliukov, calling a country without a monarch a leaky boat and trying to persuade his colleagues to establish the firm authority of the plutocracy over the people, referred to nothing more or less than the needs of the masses of the people themselves, who were irresistibly attracted by the habitual symbol of the monarch.

Nor indeed would anyone have believed the papers if they had said that the learned leader of the bourgeoisie, who for two days had been observing the popular indignation at the slightest allusion to the Romanovs, and who during these two days should have learned how to tack and give ground under the pressure of the people's anger, could once again so quickly and completely forget all this recent knowledge, and fling himself headlong from practical politics into a world of evil fantasies and utter this manifest nonsense to the face of his own candidate for 'well-beloved' monarch. If that had been in the papers no one would have believed it.

Nor was it in the papers that Miliukov tried to convince his irresolute protégé by, among other things, an argument like this:

'There is every possibility', he said, 'of raising outside Petersburg the military force essential for the defence of the Grand Duke.'

What that meant was obvious, after all, to everyone. A military force collected to defend a Romanov from the people, and adequate for the purpose, would have meant the complete destruction of the revolution. If Miliukov were successful in mobilizing counter-revolutionary armed forces around a Romanov there could be no talk about 'some kind of Constituent Assembly' or about the very existence of the Soviets.

Alas! Miliukov was supported only by Guchkov . . . Having heard the speeches *pro* and *con*, Michael Romanov expressed a wish to have a private talk with Lvov and Rodzianko. Rodzianko was about to refuse, but Kerensky insisted. After this secret conference with Rodzianko and Lvov, Michael Romanov announced his rejection of an enterprise which would be by its very nature a fruitless and disgraceful adventure. All those present except Guchkov and Miliukov felt great satisfaction at this—but kept quiet. Kerensky, however, did not miss the chance of stepping into the limelight and in an irrepressible outburst declaimed as follows:

'Your Highness, you are a man of honour and from now on I shall always proclaim it. Your action will be appreciated by history—it is the highest patriotism and reveals your love for your country'!

Kerensky was a good and sincere man. Yet—even in this impulse of his and in the wording of the remark doesn't one sense a childish romantic impressionist, with no sense of proportion?

* * *

Wrapped up in unavoidable routine detail, we decided to stop having Soviet sessions every day. It was not only that the Soviet was 'superfluous', but its members were of no use in the Tauride Palace: they were extremely useful locally, in the districts and in their factories. Both information and contact between the Soviet and the masses were as indispensable as daily bread; but local appearances of the Soviet leaders, especially of the most important ones, were possible only on isolated occasions. It was vital for every member of the Soviet to develop agitational and organizational activity among his—*soit dit*—electors.

It is awkward to say, but it would be foolish to conceal, that there was another reason for postponing the Soviet session: the Soviet inordinately increased the hubbub, fuss, disorder, and chaos in the palace of the revolution. It had finally become intolerable for the Ex. Com. members, completely worn out even without this. Work in conditions where going from one room to another demanded an incredible amount of time and energy had become unendurable. We must, if only for a day, have a 'breather' from the Soviet and the many thousands of people it attracted into the Palace. Everyone had begun to feel this and roundly cursed this perpetual 'mass-meeting' in the Ex. Com.'s working rooms.

The next meeting was called for Saturday, March 4th, and it was decided that the members of the Soviet should devote Friday to work in the factories and institutions they represented. It was proposed to clear the White Hall galleries of prisoners and adopt the Duma hall—the hall of Miliukov and Shulgin—for the sessions of the Soviet.

* * *

Around 7 o'clock that evening I went to Dr. Manukhin's for dinner. It was only there that I learned the circumstances of Nicholas's abdication: Manukhin had seen Guchkov that day and heard about his trip to Pskov with Shulgin.

I went back to the Palace to find it empty, and all the meetings over. In the new Ex. Com. room, in the midst of the disorder and the clouds of tobacco smoke, Kapelinsky, the new secretary, was putting his minutes in order. In the corridor near this room, close to the entrance to the great hall of the Duma, at the end of a row of party stalls laid out with placards and literature, for some reason the weary Chkheidze, dressed, in spite of the heat, in a fur coat, had stopped on his way out and was sitting in an easy-chair with his feet on a chair he had drawn up, in a leisurely conversation with one of his colleagues. Nearby a number of onlookers were standing watching the famous working-class deputy. Chkheidze was relaxing after his labours in peaceful private talk, and even though desperately fatigued had a certain air of contentment.

In spite of his pernicious opinions I retain the warmest memories of this 'Papa' of the revolution. Chkheidze was not suited to be a working-class or party leader, and he never led anyone anywhere: he lacked the slightest gift for it. On the contrary, he had every talent for being led on a halter, jibbing slightly now and then. And there were occasions when his friends led him into mazes of political controversy where he was thoroughly ill at ease, but after making him into an idol, they did lead him, for he lacked the strength to take a really firm line himself. But when he had gone where he should not, he protested fruitlessly, for this 'party hanger-on', as Lenin called him, was an irreproachably honest soldier of the revolution, devoted body and soul to democracy and the working-class movement.

I went over to the group of talkers with the intention of reporting Guchkov's and Shulgin's doings in Pskov and expressing my indignation at the policy of the 'right wing' on the question of the monarchy. But I did not manage it. Chkheidze had something he wanted to talk to me about. He beckoned me over and said in my ear:

'Look here, I wanted to have a talk with you about what must be done. After all, we must publish an appeal to the European proletariat—in the name of the Soviet and the Russian Revolution.'

Of course! Like many other comrades, I had already thought of this. But there was no time: even then we didn't manage to finish this conversation; someone came running over asking that the Ex. Com. meet for 'a second'—there was 'emergency business'.

Chkheidze trudged off, everyone ran around looking for everyone else, and in a few minutes some twelve of us had collected in Room 12, the first Soviet meeting-hall.

The emergency had to do with the Baltic Fleet in Helsingfors. The revolution, in spite of the stubborn opposition of, and provocation by, the fleet and administrative officers and the police, had taken place easily and quickly; but just because of all this it had been accompanied by violence. A few naval officers had been killed and many were under lock and key.

Bourgeois sources of course gave an exaggerated account of these excesses. Pogroms and massacres were spoken of. These excesses were disagreeable and dangerous, all the more so since they were taking place at the front, one might say within sight of the enemy. No one knew the intentions and capacities of the German General Staff and it was impossible to guarantee that the Germans would not take redoubled advantage of the inevitable temporary disorders in our fleet.

In any case it was essential to take steps to 'regularize relations' among the sailors and secure the defence of Petersburg from the sea. A delegate known to the sailors and with authority over them had to be sent. We had a short discussion and sent Skobelev, who left at once, that same evening. He came back two days later and gave a report on his trip in the Soviet on March 6th. It had been not so much a mission as a triumph for the representative of the Soviet democracy both in Finland, among the Finns, and in the fleet, among the lower ranks.

The Soviet still faced a stubborn struggle for the army, but the fleet was already conquered; from then on and for ever it was faithful to the Soviet. We faced another problem now—the protection of the fleet not against the bourgeoisie but against anarchist excesses and uncontrollable elemental violence.

As for the March excesses in the Baltic Fleet, they were tiresome and dangerous, but judging by what Skobelev said about the conduct of the authorities of Helsingfors and the navy, it was astonishing that they were so inconsiderable.

* * *

We broke up until next morning. Once again I didn't go home to the Karpovka, but intended to stay the night at 'Governor' Nikitsky's. But first I decided to hurry over to the right wing to see Kerensky or one of the prospective Ministers and find out what it was intended to do, and when, to execute the new Government's programme announced that morning. I especially wanted to see how things stood with the amnesty.

My title of Ex. Com. member, when I announced it to the cadets and the glittering officer guarding the doors, had a quite good effect. I found a number of people of various sorts in one of the nearer rooms, where a typewriter was pounding away, 'papers' were being dictated, and the telephone kept ringing. Half were complete strangers, important-looking civilians and military. The other half, however, consisted of members of the well-known pre-revolutionary Kerensky *milieu*. His wife, Olga Lvovna, was also there, waiting for her husband.

While waiting I began chatting with some people about events outside the capital and at the front, and the state of affairs in the left wing and the right.

The news couldn't have been better. As for politics, I had the definite impression that all these hangers-on of Kerensky's, all these radical and 'populist' citizens, were quite unaware of what was going on in our Soviet circles, and quite uninterested.

Like the enlightened 'literary fraternity' of the great press, all these people were tacitly persuaded that the Soviet and the democracy carried very little weight as a factor in 'high policy': for them politics was all centred in the great world of glittering epaulettes and glittering ministerial names, selected by history not from the riff-raff but from the very best society. A very pleasant illusion, of course, but in the long run rather expensive for all these drawing-room democrats, the cream of the intelligentsia!

At last Kerensky came out. A few people rushed to speak to him on various matters. In spite of Olga Lvovna's pleading looks, I also decided to detain him for a few minutes.

Kerensky was excited, perhaps angry. But he greeted me unusually affectionately, with a touch of intimacy, as sometimes happened with us. I started talking to him about the amnesty, the need for a decree and precise categorical orders. His reaction was prompt and lively, and he promised to take immediate steps; then he began speaking about something else.

He was already in his fur coat, on his way out. We were standing uncomfortably against the wall near the entrance, where some people were expectantly waiting. But it was clear that he wanted to get something off his chest; he began in a rather vague way about the struggle on two fronts, the difficulties and obstacles he had to overcome in the Government 'as a Socialist', and was rather spiteful about some of his colleagues, whom he didn't name but with whom he had evidently had some friction.

It was obviously impossible to start a circumstantial conversation on this subject; I decided to limit myself to a joke, even though a trivial one: 'Of course,' I said, 'in general the position of a Minister is more difficult than that of a Governor, and your position in Guchkov's Cabinet even more so. But just wait: in two months we'll have a Kerensky Government—that'll be a horse of a different colour.'

Kerensky listened more solemnly than he should have, and doubtfully, as though to himself, muttered: 'Two months . . . Why two months? We could manage wonderfully even without these people!'

That was odd. Kerensky, who had been galloping along the broad highway of historical immortality for three days, didn't want to wait even two months! This noisy lawyer was flying high—where was he destined to alight?

* * *

I made my way along the Tauride and Suvorovsky to Nikitsky's on the Old Nevsky. I still hadn't seen the new Petersburg, not having once been home or anywhere far from the Tauride Palace. Extremely strict martial law was still being observed in the city, in the shape of frequent patrols and posts of men of the new militia, armed to the teeth, who stopped suspects and examined all motor-cars without exception.

Outbreaks by the 'pharaohs' had still not been conclusively liquidated; unfortunate incidents still took place. But there were no more disorders. Order and security had been re-established.

The self-organization of the populace was progressing not hourly but by the minute. New commissariats and district Soviets were springing up like mushrooms, widely-dispersed Socialist party organizations had appeared in a few days. Municipal reform was being prepared at full steam, and the old 'city fathers' were cogitating on the emergency patches that could be applied to the old administration in accordance with the new 'spirit of the times'.

Petersburg was in upheaval—from the top to the very bottom, and was living a full life, breathing and functioning in all its cells. Here things were going splendidly, and there could be no doubt that this organism would easily deal with all diseases, both those arising from old infections and those due to its own revolutionary growth.

But there at the end of the Tauride I came across a dense mass of people emerging from the dark Suvorovsky Prospect. It was a large military detachment of some thousands of men, at least a regiment in full formation, perhaps even two.

In complete order, as they might have paraded before the Tsar, the soldiers were marching along the street, keeping their ranks in spite of the darkness and their obvious exhaustion. They all had rifles, and the cartridge belts slung over their shoulders gave them a completely armed look.

This was not in the least a mob; it was a highly organized troop formation. But I didn't see a single officer.

I have a lively memory of the feeling of great triumph and tenderness that came over me. In these stern, fatigued, and concentrated columns no one could have seen any sign either of elemental passions, of abuse of liberty, or of disintegration. This was not a danger but a support to the revolution.

No one had brought them to Petersburg; they had come themselves. Why? Doubtless not one of them could have given a clear explanation.

I tried to find out what unit they were, where they were from, and where they were going. They answered me as they marched, as though distracted from their work. I don't remember what the unit was; they had come by rail; I don't remember where they were from either, but they were going to Okhta for the night. They weren't on quite the right road for Okhta; they evidently didn't have anyone with them who knew the capital, and I suppose they were marching more or less haphazard.

Yes, all was well; everything was going as marvellously as one might have dreamed of but hardly expected in reality.

At dinner at Nikitsky's, however, my enthusiasm was somewhat damped.

The 'Governor' had just come back from his respected institution and, sitting gloomily in a gloomy room lit by only one candle, was exchanging the impressions of the day with his old nurse. I also had the habit of interviewing Anna Mikhailovna about what people were saying; I often managed to derive a good deal of instruction from these interviews. So now I too turned first to her.

'Well, how about the queues? Have they got any smaller? Are they more orderly now or less, without the police?'

'Just the same,' said Anna Mikhailovna; 'the queues—well, the queues haven't got smaller in the least; I think they're even bigger. You stand half the day, just as before.'

'And what are they saying?'

'What are they saying? They say—liberty-flibberty, it's all the same, there's nothing to be had. They say it's just the same, the rich keep on fleecing the poor. The shopkeepers are the only ones making money.'

'Aha!'

People who used to assert that Moscow was burned down by a copeck candle were fond of repeating in 1917 that the women in the queues made the revolution. I wondered what these women wanted to do now. What would it bring forth, this talk—reaction or future Bolshevism?

Nikitsky talked of what was going on in the city and what he had seen and heard at municipal headquarters. His impressions were extremely pessimistic. He asserted that 'anarchy was in full swing'; looting, murders, and rioting were continuing as before; arrests by people acting on their own authority were increasing beyond all measure; there was absolutely no reliable disciplined force to restore order. The only thing that could help matters, according to him, was a naval detachment.

He told us of most unpleasant things, but after all it was natural for him to have lost his bearings after a whole day spent in an atmosphere of police alertness and cries for help, and in fighting excesses.

It seemed that in the new conditions the 'lower depths' were in deadly earnest about the question of prices and the struggle against the high cost of living. An enormous delegation of a hundred people had appeared before the customary authority—the Governor of the city—and demanded that 'steps be taken'. It had to be received in the street, which meant, of course, that there was an enormous mass-meeting, at which Nikitsky, who as the Soviet delegate had more authority with the masses, was forced to oppose the violence unleashed by hunger with a purely academic lecture on the laws of economic development. The crowd retorted very simply—by referring to the greed of shopkeepers. Then the two sides parted—both dissatisfied.

Night and day there was a crowd of officers at the Governor's headquarters, offering their services for the restoration of order. There were some curious types, with the most astonishing ideas about the revolution. Nikitsky's secretary, who had been sent with him from the Soviet, talking in the presence of these officers, touched on the war, and without beating about the bush explained to them that the Socialists in the Soviet were against war in general and would of course take the necessary steps to put an end to this war in particular.

The result was very queer, but quite revealing. The officers' minds were thrown into a turmoil, and after much talk it turned out that all these gallant patriots were really bitter enemies of the Soviet, and moreover would turn their backs on the revolution if the Soviet was really speaking through the mouth of its delegate at the Governor's. Nikitsky barely managed to smooth things over.

Yes, the question of the war had not yet been raised in the Soviet. But it was time to think of the line of least resistance. Something had to be said soon: silence would give the European proletariat a distorted view of the entire character of the revolution which, however, would also be confused by a clumsy *démarche* of the Soviet.

* * *

A long series of 'political' prisoners had been brought into the Governor's offices. Since no one knew what to do with them, they were crowded into the Michael Regimental Riding School, where they were rather uncomfortably accommodated. The volunteers had seized all kinds of members of the public, and practically all of them were soon allowed to go home. An enormous number of Secret Police, especially spies, were brought in. No one would have believed that there were such masses of them in the capital. Someone questioned them, sorted them out somehow, and did something with them. These wretched and filthy creatures behaved like themselves: they abjectly pleaded for mercy, said they had worked against their will for a crust of bread, and swore, after betraying the Tsar and their oath to him, in future to be faithful unto death to the people and the revolution. But one 'ideological' police spy was found. When asked about his attitude towards the revolution he answered, confused and apologetic: 'I don't sympathize. . . I served faithfully and justly. . . Very devoted too I was, loved His Majesty the Emperor. I won't betray my oath.'

I don't know what was done with this pernicious man, the only one of them all who was worthy of trust.

* * *

It was already the dead of night. This was the night that a wireless telegram flew out along the air-waves to the whole world with the news of what the Russian Revolution meant, in the opinion of Citizen Miliukov.

* * *

The morning of March 4th Frankorussky, the 'Supply Man', came looking for me.

'Agrarian business!' he said, pressing me into a corner. 'That's your department. We've just received news in the Supply Commission that in many places agrarian disorders have begun. They are sharply reflected in the grain deliveries, or at any rate may be. Something has to be done. Telegrams have to be sent out in the name of the Petersburg Soviet with the most urgent appeal not to be distracted by the sharing out of the land from the fundamental task of providing bread for the towns. Otherwise—you understand what may result. . . for the entire revolution. . .'

The reports from the Supply Commission placed before us for the first time a new agrarian problem. It was crystal-clear that in the near future it would inexorably become one of the cornerstones of the revolution. If the revolution was going to exist at all, then it would be victorious as an agrarian revolution too. The bankruptcy of the slogan 'the land for the peasants' meant the destruction of the revolution.

Just how to carry out an agrarian reform—of a scope unprecedented in history—in the most sensible, easy, and painless way, was still obscure. The thoughts of the members of the Soviet had not yet got to this point; there had been no time. But for all the then leaders of the Soviet it was absolutely unquestioned that any forcing of the agrarian problem in the coming weeks was harmful and that there was not the slightest necessity for it.

* * *

In the corridor near the White Hall I met V. G. Grohman.

'I wanted to have a talk with you,' he said. 'You're practically the only economist in the Executive Committee.'

It is true that at the university I had given considerable study to economic questions and very nearly prepared for a professorship. And after the university I devoted a good deal of time and a fair number of pamphlets to work on economic and statistical, and especially agrarian questions. But all that was some time ago. During the last few years I had gone over from economics to journalism and politics; I had forgotten what I used to know and felt like a complete dilettante in such matters.

There was, however, a shortage of economists in the Ex. Com., so Grohman wasn't far from the truth.

'For some time now, even under the autocracy,' Grohman went on, 'I've been working out a plan for an institution which I call the Committee for the Organization of National Economy and Labour. My starting-point is that the war in Russia, as well as throughout Europe, threatens the national economy with complete collapse if it continues on the old basis of private property and capitalism, with no interference or regulation by the State. There is bread in Petersburg right now for three or four days at the most. The supply situation is catastrophic. It cannot be corrected without an immediate bread monopoly. But a monopoly of bread cannot be introduced in isolation, without regulating all the other branches of economy and fixing stable prices for industrial products. Therefore the State must undertake the regulation of prices, that is, the *de facto* organization of the national economy, and thereby also the distribution of manpower. So I now propose that the Committee for the Organization of National Economy and Labour be set up. Earlier this idea was of no use to us and there was nothing practical I could do about it, but now the time has come when it is vital to realize it—with the co-operation of the Executive Committee.'

Walking with me along the crowded, noisy corridor, Grohman expounded the very theory of the regulation of industry that soon became the foundation of the entire economic programme of the democracy. To an enormous extent Grohman was its author, and he was the leader of the compact and harmonious group, that was shortly formed, of Soviet economists working in the Ex. Com. 'economic department'.

The regulation of industry—the economic programme of the democracy—was the second problem, not so radical or acute as the agrarian, but nevertheless unavoidable and insistently thrust forward by the course of the revolution.

Every 'Soviet' man we met, seeing Grohman, thought it his duty to run up to him and ask him how things were going in supply. Grohman would answer that the situation was absolutely desperate, saying there was enough bread in Petersburg for three or four days and at most some 16 million *poods* of grain en route, while 100 million were needed. . . The questioners believed this authoritative 'Supply Man' and easily caught the infection of his gloom.

But Grohman was always intolerably pessimistic and impressionable. If even a tenth of his predictions had been justified, after the next two and a half years there would have remained no vestige of Russia, the Russian State, or the Russian people.

* * *

The Ex. Com. was gathering for a meeting. There were two fundamental questions on the agenda, one of principle, the other practical. The second one dealt with the general resumption of work and was postponed for the time being. The first one had to do with the future organizational relations between the Soviet and the Provisional Government. This is more or less how I conceived it:

The revolution now consummated by the March overturn was not concluded, but just beginning. The national-liberal Government put in power was not the sum and end of the revolution, but a known and recognized brief stage in it, a means for strengthening and developing it in the hands of the democracy. It was, indeed, that Moor of Venice who should do, and—to judge by the beginning—would do, his duty and could then go. *Should* go. . .

The Constituent Assembly could be seen on the horizon. I was extremely doubtful whether it would soon be convoked. I remember telling someone that we'd have it—God willing!—by Christmas. The main thing was, however, that I was never an enthusiast for it, nor made a fetish of it, not merely as an institution, but you might say as the focal point, citadel, or banner of the revolution.

I have only a confused idea of why this was so. But I remember very well that in the course of the next few months, in spite of the most conscientious efforts, I couldn't arouse in myself that inner reverence for the Constituent Assembly that I saw all around me in large doses. My opinion was decidedly not hostile—God forbid!—but for some reason I never took an active part in anything concerning it.

In any case, however, the Constituent Assembly was over the hills and far away. And it was impossible to wait for it, what with the deepening of the revolution and the statement of its compelling basic problems.

It did not, after all, occur to anyone that the question of concluding peace could wait for the Constituent Assembly. Nor would anyone, least of all the employers themselves, expect the conditions of labour to remain the same after a revolution had been accomplished. The seizure by the democracy of further positions must of course depend not on any formal occasions but exclusively on the correlation of forces. For what we were in the midst of was a revolution, a revolution that had begun in the epoch of the collapse of world capitalism. Before the Constituent Assembly and before any changes in the Provisional Government everything possible had to be wrested from the possessing classes, and the political turn now consummated given the maximum social content.

What was needed for this? It was necessary, primarily, to dictate to the Provisional Government the democratic reforms next in turn. And for that it was necessary to elaborate them in the appropriate Soviet organizations. To elaborate them it was necessary to set up an appropriate apparatus—competent, ramified, well-equipped, and adaptable.

But there was another side to the medal. First of all, why only 'dictate' to the Provisional Government what the Soviet had worked out and thought indispensable? Why not also correct and if necessary protest against what the Provisional Government itself thought indispensable? Why not 'push', 'press', and 'regulate' it systematically?

Secondly, all this was absolutely inextricably bound up with the *control* of the activity of the bourgeois Government.

Thirdly, it was both natural and necessary for us to penetrate into every pore of the administration and gradually take into our hands the organizational work of the Government.

With respect to organizational relations with the *central* Government, this was how things appeared to me:

I thought that each of the Ministries (as before) should have a Ministerial Council; this ought to contain delegates of the Soviet in a majority or at least in equal numbers. This Ministerial Council would have no formal rights with respect to the regulation of the activity of the Ministry; at the same time the Soviet delegates, as well as the Soviet which sent them, would bear no political responsibility for the activity of the Cabinet members. But the Soviet delegates in the Ministries first of all would be conversant with the affairs of their own departments, and then would recommend to the Ministry one measure or another, as the official opinion of the Ministerial Council.

The chairmen of the Soviet delegations in the separate Ministries would combine the activity of all these delegations, forming a special board. This board, remaining, on the one hand, in close and uninterrupted contact with the Ex. Com., would stand, on the other hand, face to face with the Council of Ministers, entering into direct relations with it and applying pressure and control in the sphere of general Cabinet policy.

It was a scheme of this sort for organizational and technical inter-relationships between the Soviet and the Provisional Government that I expounded and defended in the Ex. Com. meeting of March 4th.

Even before this meeting, while 'ventilating' and formulating my ideas on this subject, I had communicated my plans right and left. I remember speaking of them the night before at dinner at Manukhin's. Manukhin then reported the whole scheme to his neighbour, D. S. Merezhkovsky,[1] who lived in the same house. Merezhkovsky translated it at once into his high biblical style: 'I see. That means it'll be like the Old Testament. There were kings, and prophets were with them. We shall have Ministers, and there will be prophets from the Soviet with them.'

Merezhkovsky was a 'type' of the right wing, but no politician. Of course he didn't appreciate the inner meaning of all these Soviet ambitions. If he had encountered them some months later, he, understanding them no better than before, would have moaned and wept in patriotic horror, if only because they issued from the Tauride Palace. At that time, a few months later, no good thing could come out of Nazareth—only something terrible, unendurable, impious! But in those days of spring everybody was predisposed to listen to all these plans with benignity and even indulgence. So fresh and sweet were the roses!

[1] Merezhkovsky, Dmitri Sergiyevich (1865–1941): author of *Christ and Antichrist*, *Death of the Gods*, *Leonardo da Vinci*, *Birth of the Gods*, etc. After the October Revolution he emigrated to Paris, where he died. (Ed.)

But in any case nothing came of all these plans of mine, or rather only stumps of them were left.

It was characteristic that almost at the very beginning, even before the formation of the petty-bourgeois-opportunist majority in the Ex. Com., the commission for exerting 'pressure' and 'control' was christened (I think by Skobelev) 'the Liaison Commission'. This was completely unwarranted, and personally I had never for a moment conceived of the tasks of this commission in this way.

To be sure its title had no effect on its activity, but of course this activity was nothing but a perversion of the original idea. During the revolution this Liaison Commission became rather well known, and I shall have occasion to refer to it often in the following notes.

The creation of the Liaison Commission was formally decreed, but the Ex. Com., distracted by other matters, postponed the actual elections, which took place only on March 7th.

Why did nothing sensible emerge from these above-mentioned plans of mine? Primarily, of course, because of the absence of any correct ideas about the actual future course of the revolution, and then because of the complexity of the general situation. This complexity did not fail to confuse the general process of debate, which was incoherent and not very sensible.

Throughout the course of the revolution, down to October, the problem of the relations between the official Government and the Soviets kept obtruding itself. This problem, however, was always conceived of and treated as a political problem, in which the question at issue was political relations. But in this case the question was concerned with the organizational and technical interrelationships (and extremely complicated ones at that).

It is natural that in the midst of a still fiercely raging struggle for the new order, not all those present at the meeting could grasp and clarify all this. And the debate was diffuse, incoherent, and confused. A whole series of speakers started talking precisely about political relations, about 'support' for the Provisional Government, 'reciprocity', 'insofar as . . .', a negative attitude towards the bourgeoisie, and so on. Consequently the talk took us back to the Ex. Com. session of March 1st, in which conditions and a programme for the future Cabinet were elaborated.

I remember especially well a speech by the Bolshevik Molotov. This official party representative only now collected his thoughts and for the first time began talking about the necessity for all political power to pass into the hands of the democracy. He didn't suggest anything concrete, but he advanced precisely this principle—instead of 'control' over the bourgeois Government and 'pressure' on it.

But it turned out that not only was Molotov speaking as an irresponsible critic, who could find fault because he was doing nothing and not suggesting anything concrete; it seemed, besides, that the opinion he expressed was not at all that of his party, or at least of those of its leaders who were available. On the following day we learned from the papers that on March 3rd the Petersburg Committee of the Bolsheviks had declared that 'it would not oppose the authority of the Provisional Government insofar as its activities corresponded to the interests of the proletariat and the broad democratic masses of the people', and announced 'its decision to carry on the most implacable struggle against any attempts of the Provisional Government to restore the monarchist régime in any form whatsoever'.

This was the official position of the Bolsheviks at that time. But the sabotaging of Right Socialists, and demagogy addressed to the masses—that was also their official position. And Molotov never missed a chance to exploit both.

The question of the resumption of work did not arouse any passion or lengthy debates in the Ex. Com. It was self-evident that the victory was definitely achieved, and that any continuation of the strikes was nothing but a senseless disruption of the already disrupted productive forces. At the same time a vital combat organization in the form of the Soviet had been created and consolidated; at the slightest danger the Petersburg proletariat (and perhaps the garrison as well) could now be mobilized in two or three hours.

Only the Bolsheviks, for the sake of appearances, principle, or because of *noblesse oblige*, thought it their duty to mumble something about the counter-revolutionary nature of the bourgeoisie, but their argument was inarticulate and frivolous. The immediate liquidation of the strikes and the transition to the new pacific status had been decided on beforehand in the Ex. Com.

But the difficulty did not lie there. The question was whether an immediate liquidation of the strikes would be successful, and how it was to be done. There was a rather strong disinclination among the masses to start work again. For one thing, the upheaval had been too violent, the excitement was still too intense, the impressions of the recent glorious holiday that had thrown the masses off the rails were still too overwhelming for them to go back easily and so soon to the workaday routine and the factory yoke. The proletariat of the capital had only just begun living a new life; it was bound by hundreds of thousands of threads to all sorts of new organizations, and had just managed to achieve for itself a new way of life from which it had to tear itself away for the old half-forgotten work-bench.

For another thing—under what conditions was work to be resumed? This question was on the lips of every member of the masses. The old ones? That was absurd, almost unthinkable. But there were still no new working conditions. No one had yet created them. And the Soviet and its Ex. Com. especially could not offer them, when they called for a liquidation of the strike.

Hence this question, clear in essence, was rather ticklish and demanded very careful handling.

The Soviet's authority was growing by the hour; but here for the first time the interests of the State and the general interests of the revolution clashed with the most 'selfish' interests of the masses. The Soviet's authority faced a serious test.

But even before the Soviet's authority was tested before the masses, the Ex. Com.'s authority had to be tested before the Soviet. Things might take a bad turn even at this stage. Heavy artillery had to be brought up: it was decided that Chkheidze should be the one to report to the Soviet on the question.

* * *

The Soviet was assembling. . . The 'resumption of work' ought to have been on the agenda, but it had been postponed until the next day.

The Duma White Hall was of course filled to overflowing. Instead of 700–800 deputies there were some 1,500 Workers' and Soldiers' Deputies. Crowds blocked the gangways, the Diplomats' Gallery, and the Gallery of the Council of Ministers —where I had spent the first night of the revolution. The Hall had never seen such an invasion or such people, 'the sweepings of the streets', within its walls. Cigarette-ends were already scattered among the nice clean desks. Men sat in their caps and fur coats. There were glimpses here and there of rifles and other military equipment. The black figures of civilian workers were beginning to be submerged in the flood of grey army greatcoats. No peasants' representatives were to be seen yet, but there were more than a few members of the intelligentsia. Above this mass of human bodies, indiscriminately filling the former Ministerial benches, the Duma officials' seats, and the Press Gallery, hung a thick cloud of smoke, which reached to the crowded upper galleries. Over the chairman's seat gaped the empty frame of the Tsar's portrait, with a crown still in position above it. Invisible electric lights shone softly and brightly from the ceiling. . .

* * *

Next day, Sunday the 5th, the Soviet met about noon. N. D. Sokolov was in the chair. He opened the session, not with unpleasant debates on the resumption of work, but ceremonially, with greetings. The first visitors had arrived: two delegates from the Moscow Soviet, a worker and a soldier, and a few other local delegations, who had been pleading for almost three days to be given the honour of appearing before the Soviet and offering it their greetings. . .

I was present in the White Hall only at the very beginning of the proceedings and then went off to the Ex. Com., and I hardly once looked in at the Soviet again all day. It was only by hearsay I learned that Sokolov, after the greetings and before turning to the resumption of work, had raised another question of a ceremonial nature, which greatly occupied the whole capital at this time. This was the funeral of the victims of the revolution. Working-class speakers made a few emotional speeches in the Soviet, after which it was decided to form a special commission to organize the funeral; the funeral itself was to take place, with the participation of the entire Petersburg proletariat and garrison, on March 10th in the Palace Square, 'where the martyrs of January 1905 had fallen, as a symbol of the downfall of the place where sat the Romanov hydra'.

I was very disturbed that evening when I learned of this

decision. And the next day, reading about it in the papers, 'all Petersburg' with the slightest interest in the artistic qualities of this wonderful city was also very worried.

In the Palace Square! The 'Romanov hydra', of course, was first-rate. But surely we could not mutilate one of the finest jewels in the crown of our northern capital? Just where in the Palace Square could they dig a common grave and put up a mausoleum? Steps must be taken at once to combat this confused thinking, and the decision must be changed in favour of the Champ de Mars.

But whom could I turn to for the preliminary agitation? Of course—Sokolov, an old Petersburger, would be the first to help; he had often enthusiastically described to me the artistic beauty of Petersburg, especially its palaces, which he knew well. Sokolov and I together could launch a concerted attack on the Ex. Com.

When I met him that evening I pounced: 'D'you know what's happened, what the Soviet decided today? They intend to bury the victims of the revolution in the Palace Square!'

'Yes,' Sokolov replied, characteristically throwing back his head and stroking his black beard, 'yes, that was while I was chairman!'

I'd completely forgotten. 'A fa-a-ateful man!' I remembered Chkheidze saying. I was too excited, and the matter seemed to me self-evident, so what I said didn't suffer from an excess of logic or persuasiveness. As for Sokolov, though he was undoubtedly affected, his position as chief criminal made him rather stubborn. I don't remember just what he said in reply. Later of course he capitulated completely and energetically co-operated in having the decision reversed. But just then he wasn't too infected by my mood. Something had to be done. . .

* * *

Chkheidze's report on the resumption of work bore traces of some basic 'diplomatic' working over, and perhaps of some basic (though completely indispensable) demagogy. These were the central points of his speech:

'The Ex. Com. has arrived at the unanimous conclusion that the moment has come to resume work in the factories and workshops. Why must this be done? Because we have decisively defeated the enemy, and can now work in peace? No, comrades, for a long time to come we shall not be in a position to carry on any peaceful work, because just now we are carrying on a civil war. While we stand at our benches we must be on the alert, ready to go into the street at the first signal. Yesterday work was still impossible, but today the enemy has been sufficiently disarmed for there to be no danger in going back to work. . .

'Under what conditions can we work? It would be absurd if we went on working under the former conditions. Let the bourgeoisie realize that. Once we have returned to work we shall immediately start elaborating the conditions under which we shall work. . .'

Opportunism? Of course. But the question is, where is the boundary beyond which a legitimate quest for the line of least resistance passes into an illegitimate submission to the force of circumstances?

The debates were quite heated. In Soviet practice later on all debates in the plenary sessions were carried on by 'fraction' speakers. The same people would speak, one or rarely two in the name of each fraction. But in the beginning this wasn't so; only independent speakers took the floor. On this March 5th the fractions themselves had not yet taken shape in the Soviet. References to party adherence were very rare. Opinions overlapped and as before were very feebly differentiated.

Also, from the fraction point of view the deputies did not sit in any kind of order. In those days there was no tendency to split up into fractions and the deputies sat as chance directed.

The question of the resumption of work was evidently being decided by the masses on a completely individual basis. It was odd that even the Soviet journalists could not distinguish the party allegiance of the speakers; in the reports in *Izvestiya* itself, when speeches 'for' or 'against' were mentioned, instead of 'Bolshevik' or 'SR' in brackets after the name, there stood 'worker' or 'soldier'!

Nevertheless an enormous majority spoke up *for* a resumption of work on the following day, March 6th. And the Ex. Com. resolution to this effect was passed in the Soviet by 1,170 votes to 30.

However, it was one thing to pass a resolution among the advanced workers' deputies, and quite another to execute it with the co-operation of the mass of the proletariat. As we shall see, the question of the resumption of work was far from settled by this resolution.

I was called out of an Ex. Com. meeting by I. P. Ladyzhnikov, Gorky's friend and secretary. He had a mysterious air. Taking me on one side he told me that he had in his possession a sheaf of papers taken from the Petersburg section of the Secret Police. Gorky had come across the papers, investigated them, and discovered an enormous list of Secret Police agents. Now it was essential for me to examine this list with him, Ladyzhnikov, and somebody else, one of the party people close to the Soviet. This was necessary because 'it appeared that some Soviet members were among the *provocateurs*. . .'

'Soviet or Ex. Com.?'

'I don't know; I think Ex. Com. Prominent people, I think.'

If there were some *provocateurs* among the Soviet deputies, it had no importance. As we know, the Soviet contained 1,200 'voting members' of every type and description, the majority of them unknown to the party centres; the leaders of the movement were not, of course, responsible for them and the movement itself could not be hurt by them in any way. But it was another matter if *provocateurs* had worked their way into the controlling centre, the Ex. Com. of the Soviet. It was almost incredible, but it would be scandalous if it were true.

I remember calling over Zenzinov, who had an enormous knowledge of the personnel of 'populist' party circles, and the three of us went out to look for somewhere secluded to sit. Ladyzhnikov unfolded the list of traitors. This was a thick notebook with hundreds of names. Indescribable loathsomeness and shame! Long strings of lawyers, doctors, civil servants, city officials, students of both sexes, writers, workers—of every origin and condition.

This shameful scroll included names, aliases, what the agent was 'investigating' and how much he received for his work. The 'investigations' involved the Socialist parties, student and intellectual circles, factories, institutions, and respectable liberal and even not very liberal groups. For all this specialists were available. How much did these conscientious people sell themselves for? For copecks: it was rare for one of them to get more than 100 roubles a month. They were worth no more. The supply seemed, at any rate at a casual glance, manifestly adequate.

We agitatedly ran through the list, afraid of coming across the name of an acquaintance or someone well known. But with a couple of exceptions I don't remember any upsetting revelations. These were the 'Bolshevik' Chernomazov, editor of *Pravda*, and an 'SR' workman, who had played a prominent part during the war and had been in very close contact with Kerensky; I forget his name. With respect to the Ex. Com. the reports were not confirmed at all. But the list brought by Ladyzhnikov was printed in the newspapers for a long time afterwards.

* * *

Late in the evening of March 5th I went home for the first time. On the Karpovka the same modest, pre-revolutionary hall-porter was explaining to someone what the new revolutionary house committee was. For the first time I was going into my own flat legally, my 'head held high', not thinking about conspiracy or permits. I looked steadily and no doubt triumphantly at the hall-porter: now what were his thoughts at meeting me, in view of all that had happened? But his face revealed nothing.

At home I had some important telephoning to do. I had to ring up Gorky, since there was no hope of a personal visit. First of all I had to warn him of the barbarous attempt on the Palace Square. Then it was necessary to get on at once with the Proclamation to the Peoples of the World, to which I ascribed great importance. It seemed to me that the worthiest and most suitable author of it might be Gorky, and I took it on myself to propose it to him. We had a thorough discussion on the 'phone. Gorky took note of the funeral business, and added that steps must be taken to protect the artistic treasures of the capital. It seems there had been some vandalism at Peterhof, and this had very strongly affected Gorky. He decided to take the matter up. As for the proclamation, he expressed some doubts, but gave a firm promise to try. The following afternoon I was to receive the manuscript in the Tauride Palace. Wonderful!

CHAPTER 8

'SELF-DETERMINATION' IN SOVIET AND GOVERNMENT

NEWSPAPERS appeared. The whole of the old bourgeois and yellow press burst out with a deafening noise on the horns and kettle-drums; during those days they poured out a whole sea of enthusiasm, emotion, and benevolence. People who had no more to do with the revolution than with last year's snows, and who regarded the working class at best as a nagging creditor, with the same mixture of fear and spitefulness—now overflowed with love of liberty, devotion to the Constituent Assembly, and compliments on the heroism and good sense of the masses of the people and their leaders.

In the Ex. Com. we looked through the bulky numbers and the rapturous leading articles of the newspapers with the condescending smile of victors, but I cannot say that the press took up much of our attention. By now it could no longer be a factor capable of changing the course of events. And in so far as the press in general could be a factor of enormous power, we in the Soviet already had a Socialist press. And we had no reason to doubt its exclusive influence on the masses—or at any rate on the workers.

* * *

Around the Ex. Com. for some time now—although the length of time was relative, for those days seemed like weeks at least and comparable in importance to years—there had been talk about the fate of the Romanovs. The former Tsar was travelling around Russia as the spirit moved him: from Pskov, after his abdication, he went to Headquarters in Mogilev, afterwards to Kiev, to his mother, and then, it was said, to the Crimea. No great importance was ascribed to all this, but some inconveniences might arise.

And now on the 6th reports were received that Nicholas Romanov and his family were leaving for England. General Alexeyev had informed the Provisional Government in his name of the desire of the Tsar's family to emigrate abroad. The Government had agreed and already opened negotiations with the British Government. Our thinking bourgeoisie of course had a very high appreciation of this solution of the problem of the dynasty and saw in it scarcely any occasion for recrimination. But the unthinking philistines from the best society naturally regarded it as nothing but a new victory for the revolution.

But Kerensky in Moscow, to the tempestuous delight of the philistine mob, spoke of it as of a matter already decided, thus:

'At this moment Nicholas II is in my hands, the hands of the Attorney General. And I tell you, comrades: the Russian Revolution has been bloodless, and I do not wish, nor will I permit it to be darkened. I will never be the Marat of the Russian Revolution. But in a very short time Nicholas II, under my personal supervision, will be taken to a port and from there go by ship to England. . .'

No, Citizen Kerensky, things are far from being as simple as that! On whether Nicholas II is to be taken to a port, and leave for England—permit us too to have our opinion!

The Ex. Com. discussed the matter on the morning of the 6th. The debate was not complicated. However little learned the Soviet leaders were in history the elementary facts were as clear to us as they had seemed to dozens of ordinary Frenchmen when they arrested not an overthrown monarch, a tattered shred of majesty wandering purposelessly around the country, ignored by everybody, but a lawful sovereign reigning in all the glory of the French kings, because he attempted to go abroad.

It was evident that letting the Romanovs go abroad to seek their fortune was out of the question. As far as I remember there was no dispute about this in the Ex. Com. The discussion was on a different level. The news was that Nicholas and his family were already fleeing abroad. The Ex. Com. Commissar for Railways reported that two special trains carrying the Romanov family were already on their way to the border—presumably with the knowledge and permission of the Provisional Government. Some sources said the Romanovs were travelling *via* Torneo, others *via* Archangel.

It was necessary to contact the Government immediately and

propose that it detain Nicholas. In view of the attitude taken by the Marian Palace[1] it was acknowledged very quickly and unanimously that the Soviet must take the Romanov question into its own hands and in any case demand categorically that no steps be taken without a preliminary agreement with the Ex. Com. The Soviet still had no permanent organ of liaison with the Government: a Liaison Commission was not elected until the 7th. Accordingly a special delegation to the Marian Palace was appointed on an emergency basis.

But what was to be done with the Romanovs? There was some argument about this. Someone, doubtless from the Left, imperatively demanded the Peter-Paul Fortress for the whole family, relying on the example of Nicholas's own Ministers and other servants. But I don't recall that it was very difficult to make the Ex. Com.'s decision less harsh. It was decided that the ex-Tsar himself, his wife, and his children should be isolated for the time being in the Tsarskoe-Selo Palace.

There was more talk about what to do with the other Romanovs—'candidates' and non-candidates. I think it was decided not to allow any of them to go abroad, and to detain all of them as far as possible on their own estates. All this was to be dictated to the Provisional Government for appropriate action.

But it wasn't enough. According to our information, after all, the Romanovs were already *en route.* It was impossible to limit ourselves to addressing demands, even in the form of ultimata, to the Provisional Government. Without much discussion or any questions about functions and rights, the Ex. Com. decided to issue an order to all railway lines that the Romanovs and their train must be detained wherever they were found, and the Ex. Com. immediately informed. Then an Ex. Com. member with a suitable escort was detailed to arrest Nicholas at the place where his train had been stopped and have the Tsar's whole family taken to Tsarskoe-Selo.

The member picked for this was Kuzma Gvozdev. It didn't especially suit his nature and took him away from duties which were far more in his line, but the meeting was influenced by his

[1] Now the seat of the Council of Ministers. 'Marian Palace' roughly corresponds to the Provisional Government, 'Tauride Palace' to the Soviet of Workers' and Soldiers' Deputies. Later the Government moved to the Winter Palace, the Tsar's former residence. (Ed.)

being an out-and-out worker, who was a particularly striking embodiment of the will of the proletariat. Gvozdev's armed detachment also consisted of reliable and well-known proletarians from the capital.

Gvozdev didn't have to carry out his mission. The Provisional Government swiftly and obediently set about fulfilling the Ex. Com.'s demands.

Contrary to rumour the Tsar was at Headquarters in Mogilev, where his mother had joined him. Commissars especially assigned by the Provisional Government from the Left Duma parties went to Mogilev that same day and safely put the former autocrat in the Tsarskoe-Selo Palace. In its turn the Ex. Com. ordered its representative to Tsarskoe-Selo to inspect everything.

Some months (which seemed like years) later on in the revolution, at times of leisure and pleasurable remembrance of battles long ago, Gvozdev used to say to me:

'And do you remember how they wrote me out an order to arrest Nicholas II?'

'Yes, what about it?'

'Nothing. I'm keeping the order. Just as a souvenir.'

* * *

In general March 6th was filled with all kinds of military questions, that is, soldiers' affairs. Personally I'd never had any taste for such questions and didn't keep abreast of the affairs of the Soldiers' Section.

That depression of spirit I felt whenever military matters were raised in the Ex. Com. (which was practically every day) I account for not only by a lack of interest in 'professional' soldiers' questions, which were deeply alien to me, but by an awareness that the soldiery was the greatest obstacle, the most harmful and reactionary element in our revolution, even though it was just the army's share in it that had secured its initial success.

The army's direct participation in the revolution was no more than a form of peasant interference in the revolutionary process. From my point of view, that of a Marxist and internationalist, it was profoundly harmful.

Greedy for land alone, and directing all its ideas of government to protecting its own interests, the peasantry, the bulk of the population, had, generally speaking, every chance of remaining neutral and not getting in anyone's way in the principal drama on the main front of the revolution. After kicking up a fuss somewhere off in the deep country, burning a few mansions, and destroying some property, the peasants would have got their patches of land and subsided into their 'rural idiocy'. The hegemony of the proletariat in the revolution would have met with no competition. And the only class that was revolutionary and Socialist by nature would have carried the revolution to the desirable limits.

But now that wasn't so. Now the peasants were dressed in grey greatcoats, to begin with, and considered themselves the chief heroes of the revolution, in the second place. Not off to one side, not off in the deep country, not in the Constituent Assembly, but right there, over the very cradle, at the very helm of the revolution there stood the peasantry, in all its terrible mass, and holding a rifle into the bargain. It was declaring: 'I am the lord not only of the country, not only of the Russian State, but of the revolution, which could not have been accomplished without me.' This was extremely dangerous. The revolution was faced with some basic tasks, very difficult ones and perhaps beyond the powers of the peasantry. These could only be successfully performed provided it remained neutral and offered no hindrance.

The principal task was liquidating the war. Here the peasantry was useless, and might be very harmful. As long as the force of inertia and the absence of a real war still kept the masses in the trenches, the peasants in their army greatcoats let the bourgeoisie lead them by the nose, listening to all sorts of chanvinist nonsense and to all the anti-German scares of the defensists. At this time it was easier to talk to them about an offensive than about peace. During the very first weeks the peasant army was still wholly in the power of the old 'martial' ideas. The soldiery of Petersburg not only didn't listen to talk about peace, but refused to allow any; it was ready to bayonet any incautious 'traitor' and 'opener of the front to the enemy'.

But later, when after months of revolution the old bogeys had lost their power and the trenches had become unendurable, these same masses, these same ignorant elements flung themselves headlong after anyone who summoned them home from the trenches to 'loot the loot'.

During the first weeks it was painful to watch the proletariat in the Soviet, at the core of the revolution, being more and more submerged amongst these impenetrable little peasants in their grey greatcoats.

These masses of course needed leadership, and leaders appeared in great numbers—in the person of all kinds of 'fellow-travellers' of the most dubious kind. At first these gentry were in clover; pouncing on the masses of soldiers in and around the Soviet, they laboured industriously at discrediting the Soviet and its Ex. Com. as a nest of 'openers of the front'. Later the bulk of these Cadet-minded 'Soviet' mass leaders vanished from the Soviet rather quickly, no one knew where; some of them crept into the Ex. Com. individually, to shape high policy.

There was still no real leader for the peasant-soldier masses. Tsereteli[1] was still only preparing to leave Irkutsk for the capital.

* * *

Around 4 o'clock I was brought a package from Gorky—with the manifesto he had promised 'to the peoples of the world'. It was superbly written, though rather more like a dissertation than a proclamation. But the point was that Gorky's text didn't contain a scrap of any sort of politics. The revolution was considered exclusively on the level of culture and of world cultural prospects: he paid practically no attention either to our reborn society or to the problem of war.

This approach to the matter was highly characteristic of Gorky, but it completely failed to achieve the Soviet's concrete purpose. It was obviously impossible to leave it in this form. To save time I was about to try throwing in a few amendments and insertions, but after working for a while with this in view I became convinced it would lead to nothing. Then I wrote another draft on the off-chance, right there on some scraps of paper, to have it in reserve and get on more rapidly with this business of the manifesto. My draft came out in a completely different way—feebly executed but more suitable to the circumstances of time and place.

[1] Tsereteli, Heraklion Georgevich (1882–1960): a Georgian; Menshevik leader. (Ed.)

I had settled myself in one of the secretaries' seats on the right, and while finishing the manifesto I listened to the debates in the Soviet, which had suddenly become very heated. They were talking about the officers, and the majority of the rank-and-file speakers were demanding nothing more or less than an elected command. The atmosphere was very highly charged. The soldiers' faces were flaming. They were pressing the deputies on an obviously sore spot, and tribunes from the deep countryside were practically in hysterics, pouring out their feelings, describing the hardships of a soldier's life, and demanding a total liquidation of the old officer corps.

The members of the Ex. Com., boldly swimming against the current, still had the support of an enormous part of the hall; but as against that another part was already raging and hooting as in the Bolshevik days later on. But by then this 'mass' was already subject to party discipline, whereas now the unruly elements had come out into the open and were showing their fangs. The tension kept growing. Going from the dais to my seat I hit up against a soldier who barred my way and, shaking a fist in front of my face, began yelling violently about the fine gentlemen who had never been in a soldier's skin.

Something had to be done. The resolution about electing officers might create trouble at the front and in the rear—real trouble, not like that over 'Order No. 1'. Sensibly or not, having gathered up my scraps of paper with the manifesto, I hurried over to the right wing to find Kerensky.

I explained the matter in two words to Zenzinov, who was stubbornly staying in the right wing and guarding the approaches to Kerensky. He immediately called his chief, who for some reason, unlike the other Ministers, still kept a base in the Tauride Palace. Kerensky came hurrying out of his retreat hobbling or anyhow moving with difficulty and supporting himself with a rather imposing walking-stick. I remembered that Kerensky not so long before had suffered a serious illness, as a result of which he had lost one kidney. At the time of this illness, which occurred in Helsingfors, the Finns did everything in their power for the leader of the Russian Left, but Gorky and Manukhin were distressed by Kerensky's losing a kidney just when Manukhin was preparing to save it.

Out of breath, I told Kerensky what was going on in the Soldiers' Section and suggested the following: 'Everything possible must be done to show the garrison that the officers will be different from before. They're demanding an elected officers' corps. Make an announcement in the name of the Government that in appointing officers the Government will be guided by the soldiers' attitude towards them; that is, in fact, the right of challenge will be exercised. Secondly, tell them the Government from now on will make admission to the corps of officers as wide as possible, for those who were formerly deprived of this possibility for reasons of origin or political unreliability. If you will make this announcement, it will certainly be oil on troubled waters.'

'But the Council of Ministers hasn't ordered anything of the kind, you know,' Kerensky objected.

'It doesn't matter,' I insisted. 'Tell them that you, the Minister of Justice, have gone to the Council of Ministers with that demand and have no doubt of its success.'

Kerensky immediately rushed off to the White Hall, forcing his way through the crowd. A door, guarded by watchdogs, was flung open in front of Kerensky and instantly shut in my face. I walked around. When I got into the hall I found Kerensky already on the dais; he had put his cane on the speaker's stand and was waiting while the chairman, who was more fluent than thoughtful, finished his speech about how a good soldier could be an officer and how this needed no special qualities or knowledge.

Kerensky was noisily welcomed, and his speech undoubtedly produced a genuine effect. After this, generally speaking, the question was somehow evaded. But the proposal to let 'politicals', Jews, etc., into the officers' corps was actually laid by Kerensky before the Council of Ministers.

* * *

That evening I sat down in a corner with Chkheidze and quietly read to him the draft of the Manifesto to the Peoples of the World. I think he also recognized all the literary quality of Gorky's text, but it was clear to him that it didn't say what had to be said in the name of the people's revolution. I also made him acquainted with my reserve text. He listened with the greatest concentration and asked me to repeat a few odd phrases:

"Yes, yes. . . Say, write it down, that the time has come . . . the time has come for the peoples to take the question of war and peace into their own hands."

From Chkheidze's words I made corrections or inserted his exact phrases in the text. In general Chkheidze thought my version all right. I had my scraps typed out immediately. Then I gave it to a few comrades, Bolsheviks, Trudoviks, and Centre, for their private information. Some approved, others criticized it radically.

The difficulties of working out this document were obvious. There were two Scyllas and two Charybdises. First of all, it was necessary on the one hand to keep to 'Zimmerwald' and carefully avoid any 'defensism'; but on the other hand it was necessary to 'go to the soldier', who was thinking about the Germans in the old way, and also to paralyse any attempt to play on the 'opening up of the front' by the Soviet, or on 'the Kaiser, who was going to gobble up the revolution'. This two-sided task, this contradictoriness of what was required, compelled me to dance along a knife-edge, afraid of slipping off to one side or the other. And of course this could not but be reflected in a disastrous way in the content of the manifesto.

Secondly, there were Scylla and Charybdis in the very conditions of passing the manifesto through the Ex. Com.: the Right inclined to open defensism and social-patriotism, which—from the point of view of the wording of the manifesto—coincided with the mood of the soldier and the average man. The Left, on the contrary, was mortally afraid of 'chauvinism', of 'defence' in general and of everything that might sanction international armed struggle. To make the manifesto acceptable to both wings at once was a task which, even if realizable, was quite puzzling. It was not so much a question of choosing the right words as of scrutinizing every comma under a microscope. This made it impossible to see the wood for the trees, and obscured the general idea in the interests of niggling phrase-making. It is this that to an enormous extent explains and perhaps even excuses the feebleness of this important document of the revolution.

On the morning of the 7th the people of Petersburg rejoiced in the long-awaited trams. The cars came out decorated with flags, emblems of every sort, or simply red cloth. Passers-by stopped and admired them.

* * *

I found the Ex. Com. debating a press question. I think it had to do with licensing the Black Hundred publications. On the basis of a Soviet decision (at its very first session on February 27) the Ex. Com.'s permission for newspapers to appear depended on their political character, and papers in the capital had been licensed even before the end of the general strike.

The debates were protracted and dull. For the Left it was a question of Black Hundred publications and of manifest enemies of the revolution, and it refused even to hear of freedom for them. The Right defended the universal freedom of the press.

I also strongly supported universal and unlimited freedom of speech. I maintained that it was impossible to destroy the principle in general, or do so with impunity in particular; and at the same time that the defence of the principle of freedom was the healthiest and most realistic policy. For the publications of the Right, even if they had in fact appeared, could never have had less moral and material support than in those days. If we welcomed the Black Hundred papers into the open arena we would force them to wither away and perish ingloriously in a few days.

Indeed, it was criminal and senseless for a democratic workers' and soldiers' body, after a victorious, brilliantly successful struggle, in full view of the bourgeois Government—tempting it by a base example—to undertake such a savage measure as a licensing system. It was just as criminal and unintelligent to use such a weapon in the given situation as to send out some stripling with a club against an enemy in an indestructible tank.

The question was decided by the Centre . . . Alas! most of the Centre lined up with the Left. I remember Chkheidze's speech. He was gloomy and confused, evidently struggling with himself. A reluctance to break away from democratic principles was struggling within him against the fear that some problematical Right leaflets might vanquish the revolution or inflict some serious damage on it. Finally the battle was over. Chkheidze leaped from his seat and, turning principally to me, started shouting furiously, rolling his eyes and gesticulating, his whole body writhing:

'No-o-o, we're not going to permit them! When a war is going on we're not going to give the enemy any weapons! When I have a rifle I'm not going to give it to the enemy! I won't tell him—here's a gun, take it, shoot me!—I won't tell him that!'

But on March 10 the ruling on the press was officially cancelled. Three days had been enough time to dissipate all the terrible fears or—think things over. In Moscow, by the way, there had been nothing like this. When the Moscow Black Hundred press appealed to the local Ex. Com. for permission to appear it received a worthy answer: We now have freedom of the press and no licences are required.

* * *

On the night of March 1st the Ex. Com. had had a collision with the self-authorized and pernicious activities of the Petersburg Interdistrict Committee—the autonomous Bolshevik organization, that had got out a proclamation against officers at a moment made risky by the danger of pogroms. Oddly enough from now on this organization was to lay down its own law on the question of its relations with the Soviet.

* * *

Gorky appeared in the Tauride Palace, where I ran into him in the corridor. He had come from the artists of Petersburg in connexion with the preservation of monuments, bringing a short appeal which he wanted pasted up in the streets the very next morning in the name of the Ex. Com.[1]

Gorky asked me to take the text and get it through as quickly

[1] *The appeal read:* 'Citizens! The old masters have gone away, and a great heritage is left behind. Now it belongs to the whole people.

'Citizens, take care of this heritage, take care of the palaces—they will become palaces of your national art; take care of the pictures, the statues, the buildings—they are the embodiment of the spiritual power of yourselves and of your forefathers.

'Art is the beauty which talented people were able to create even under despotic oppression, and which bears witness to the power and beauty of the human soul.

'Citizens, do not touch one stone; preserve the monuments, the buildings, the old things, the documents—all this is your history, your pride. Remember that this is the soil from which will grow your new national art.'

as possible. But I was determined that he should come into personal contact with the Ex. Com. The meeting, however, was breaking up, so Chkheidze's attempt to give the writer a triumphal reception failed and Gorky, hastily explaining his business, read the appeal. It was accepted in silence and sent off to the printers at once.

But of course it was impossible to limit the business to the appeal. Gorky raised the question of the funeral of the victims of the revolution in the Palace Square and presented the artists' own plan for using the Champ de Mars. It was decided that he should speak at once in the Soviet (Workers' Section).

* * *

In the White Hall the eye could relax from the grey soldiers' greatcoats among the black clothes and civilized faces of the advanced proletarians of Russia, though there was the same slovenliness and smoke in the hall.

Chkheidze came on to present the honoured guest to the Soviet and after an ovation Gorky explained his business, not very successfully, not concretely, and without attuning his voice to the hall. He was given due applause, but on the question of whether the Soviet would review its decision about the place for the funeral, the vote was negative! No one answered with objections. They just didn't feel like it, and that was all. Inscrutable are the ways of the people's movement, their mass-meetings, and their momentary impulses!

The funeral did finally take place on the Champ de Mars. I don't remember how it happened; I think it was simply decided by the Ex. Com. But from then on Gorky never appeared in the Soviet, however much I tried to provoke him into immediate contact with the central organ of the revolution.

* * *

I was called out into the vestibule, where, I was told, a 'lady', from Kerensky, was asking for me. I started for the door, but the agitated lady, a small black-clad figure, had already come into the almost empty Ex. Com. room. She was accompanied by an imposing, resplendently dressed gentleman with magnificent moustaches and a typical commercial-traveller's face.

This elegant and no longer young woman, holding out a piece

of paper towards me, began, halting and stammering, a timid and quite inarticulate speech about how Kerensky had sent her to me, and given her this paper, how she was now completely at liberty, not under arrest, how her innocence, honesty, and lack of interest in politics were completely established, etc. Not understanding what it was all about, I involuntarily looked questioningly at her companion, who bowed and said:

'This is Madame Kshesinskaya,[1] *artiste* of the Imperial theatres. I am her agent. . .'

I was afraid that the once-powerful ballerina would burst into tears as a result of all the shocks she had endured, and attempted to soothe her, assuring her that absolutely nothing was threatening her and that everything possible would be done for her. But what was it all about?

It turned out that she had come to intercede for her house, which had been requisitioned by right of revolution and was being plundered, according to her, by a vast mob staying in it. Kshesinskaya was asking that her possessions at the least be put together and sealed up in some corner of the house, and that a place be assigned her to live in her house.

A difficult affair. I was violently hostile to all seizures, unauthorized requisitions, and all separatist-anarchist action. As a Leftist I never had anything against the most radical measures *by law* and the most radical changes in the law; but I was resolutely hostile to lawlessness and to law-making by anybody who felt like it. In this respect I was prepared to go further than many Rightists and frequently made thoughtful Soviet politicians remark that there was chaos and muddle in my head, that for some reason I tossed back and forth between Right and Left, that I was an unreliable man and you never knew what I would do next.

I fought against private seizures of houses and businesses as much as I could, but I didn't have much success. In the first place the principle collided with the crying needs of the new organizations that had sprung up, which had a right to exist. Secondly, the principle was unconvincing, not only to the Left but also to many people in the Centre, and individual and arbitrary action by right of revolution was taken far and wide. I was not the only one to be shocked, for instance, by the imprint

[1] A favourite of the Tsar's. (Ed.)

of our *Izvestiya*: 'Printing-Plant of the *Izvestiya* of the Soviet of Workers' and Soldiers' Deputies'; it was there without any order, agreement, or basis whatever. The printing-plant belonged to someone else. But we could do nothing about it.

Kshesinskaya's business was difficult, and I didn't know how to help her. I asked: 'Where is your house?'

Kshesinskaya seemed to be somewhat offended. How could I not know the famous palace, the magnetic focus of the Romanovs?

'On the Embankment,' she replied; 'you can see it from Trinity Bridge, you know . . .'

'Come now!' added the 'agent': 'the house is very well known in Petersburg.'

I had to look embarrassed, and pretend that I too was familiar with it. 'And who has occupied it?'

'It's been occupied by the—Socialist-Revolutionary-Bolsheviks.'

Kshesinskaya obviously pronounced these difficult words thinking they were the most terrible things in the whole world. But what could be done? And why was it me she had been sent to?

I stopped Shlyapnikov, who was hurrying by. The house had been occupied by the Bolsheviks. Was there looting? Nonsense—all the valuable objects had been given up to the owner. Why and on what grounds had the house been occupied without authorization? Shlyapnikov burst out laughing and hurried off. . .

I promised to bring up the question in the Ex. Com. and do everything possible to regularize the matter of the premises. We would hope—but it was evident that neither she nor I could hope for anything.

* * *

On March 10th and 11th an agreement was reached in Petersburg between the Manufacturers' Association on the one hand and the Ex. Com. on the other, with respect to the new working conditions. Factory committees with wide powers in the matter of internal regulations were formed, and then factory and central conciliation boards on a basis of parity.

But this was a bagatelle compared with the third point of the agreement—the eight-hour day.

In the revolutionary situation this longed-for step, one of the slogans of the international proletariat, was achieved simply and painlessly. The Petersburg factory-owners saw the inevitability of such an agreement and were reconciled to it. But the proletariat and the entire democracy throughout Russia greeted this new victory of the revolution with enthusiasm.

The eight-hour working day was the first massive dose of the social content that had to fill the great democratic revolution. It was besides the first practical conquest from the point of view of the unthinking strata of the proletariat. But from all points of view it was a first-class achievement, which in the new situation had been accomplished easily, but which had come about precisely as a result of all those immeasurable efforts and sacrifices that had radically changed the situation.

In actual fact the eight-hour working day was not applied in Petersburg factories. The principle of shortening the working day clashed with the need for a maximum effort in the conditions of war and of decline in productive forces. What it in fact boiled down to, as a rule, was that work beyond eight hours was paid overtime. But of course this didn't prevent the patriotic bourgeoisie from starting a vicious campaign against the idleness of the workers and stirring up against them the soldiers who had to sit in the trenches and wait for death not for eight hours at a time but the whole twenty-four.

It goes without saying that the leaders of Soviet policy did not force the economic movement of the proletariat. Even without that it was pouring out in thousands of streamlets: it was obviously completely inevitable in the given revolutionary conditions, of decline in productive forces, hunger for goods, and the unavoidable lowering of real wages.

But from another point of view this inevitable movement was now hopeless: it could not raise the economic level of the working masses to the level of their political gains. Hence the Soviet leaders were right in not forcing the movement. But the point is that they did not stop there. They soon began straining every effort to restrain it, hold it back, and reduce it to zero, not only struggling against excesses but summoning the entire working class to curtail its demands. Now this was a fatal mistake—if only because it was absolutely utopian. The raising of the standard of living of the working masses was an inalienable part of the organic programme of the revolution, like 'Land to the Peasants'. And if in a situation complicated by war and destruction this programme was hopeless and unrealizable, then it was necessary not to call for it to be changed but to create a different situation. The war had to be liquidated. When the future Soviet leaders failed to grasp this and took another path they lost themselves in contradictions and led the revolution into an impassable morass.

* * *

The revolution had spread like wildfire over the whole face of Russia. From all parts there came hundreds and thousands of reports about the upheaval that had taken place easily, instantaneously, and painlessly, sprinkled with living water the oppressed and stagnant masses of the people and called them to life. Telegrams spoke of the 'recognition' or 'adherence' of the troops (together with their officers), peasants, civil servants, bourgeoisie, and people of all kinds.

It was natural that the population should split into two groups: one gravitated towards the Marian Palace, the other to the Tauride. The Centre—the petty-bourgeois strata—vacillated, but were to some extent beginning to make their choice.

In the twinkling of an eye Soviets formed everywhere, of course unmethodically and with no astute philosophizing. But they were organizations, points of support for the democracy and the revolution. Trade unions sprang up like mushrooms. *Izvestiya* was full of proclamations, invitations, announcements of all kinds of the most unexpected unions and associations. Probably hundreds of mass-meetings and organized assemblies took place in Petersburg every day.

All the parties and political groups, not excluding the microscopic and futile Trudoviks, Populist-Socialists, and Inter-districtites, flung themselves headlong into work and displayed such energy that the bourgeoisie looked on dumbfounded at this frenzied steeplechase and began expressing its fear more and more openly as time went on.

Amongst the bourgeoisie itself the Cadets swallowed up all the others. The more Rightist groups already seemed unseasonable and vanished like smoke. But that didn't change things in any way. The Cadets, the 'People's Freedom Party', became the firm stronghold of the entire plutocracy, staidly flying the banner of statesmanship and order. It was now preparing a convention and incessantly arguing about whether it was a monarchist or a republican party. Miliukov, and the March[1] Cadets, who had rushed headlong to the Right, had a hard struggle—against bourgeois flabbiness and populist enthusiasm.

The country and the democracy were organizing by the hour. The sight gladdened one's heart, and one thought: Now we must have new democratic municipalities as quickly as possible; given those, if things continue this way a bourgeois Government will soon be a superfluous luxury. Another few weeks and the Moor, doubtless, would have done his duty.

[1] i.e., Cadets associated with the Provisional Government. (Ed.)

CHAPTER 9

THE KNOT IS TIED

A WEEK had hardly gone by since the agreement between the Soviet and the new Government, and already the organs of the bourgeoisie and of the democracy were clearly defined as two contending forces. Moreover, they had defined themselves as the two sources of state power—one formally acknowledged and the other in control of all the real power.

Consequently, the *current* revolutionary policy was determined as the resultant of these two forces, but in the sphere of *general* policy, in view of irreconcilable class interests and in anticipation of decisive clashes, both sides began mobilizing their forces.

For some days, beginning modestly but swiftly developing along the entire bourgeois front, a game had been going on, based on the Germans and the danger threatening our army in the field from Hindenburg. The bourgeois press, with a Jesuitically patriotic air, was moaning and groaning about how the freedom that had been won might very easily perish if Kaiser Wilhelm, the chief enemy it had in the world, began an offensive and our army, distracted by things and ideas irrelevant to victory, failed to resist properly.

Meanwhile, according to reports in these worthy newspapers, an offensive really was being prepared, and the army really was distracted by irrelevant issues and ideas.

The agitation was in full swing. But why not have recourse to diplomatic influence too? On March 10th the Military Commander of the Petersburg district, Kornilov, the popular general and future hero of the counter-revolution, appeared in the Ex. Com., accompanied by a few officers. For the first time I saw this small, modest-looking officer with his swarthy Kalmuk face. All sorts of military men thronged endlessly into the Ex. Com. room. Amidst the clouds of smoke and stifling heat the room was crowded to the doors. But only a few took part in the long-winded, monotonous talk.

The distinguished guest, attentively and curiously watching his interlocutors from an alien world, repeated in general terms the content of ministerial announcements about the German offensive. The general demanded co-operation, discipline, solidarity, and a unified 'will to victory'. Kornilov's speech did not call forth any political talk about the war and victory; instead, some began to question the general on the state of affairs in the army, whereas others, including myself—perhaps I most of all—began to cross-examine him about what data they had on the offensive, and how such an offensive was possible during the most impassable season of the year. Kornilov was not prepared for such an interrogation and gave no articulate answers about either point. In this 'diplomatic' conversation the victory in any case was not Kornilov's, and those who had sent him failed to attain their goal. Many of those in the Ex. Com. were convinced once again that the whole hubbub raised about the German peril was nothing more than a dirty political game. This became so evident to me that I stopped listening to the long string of trivial questions addressed to the general by various respectful junior officers and loyal Cadet-minded members of the Ex. Com. More than that, I fell asleep during this boring talk and was only awakened by the noise of the chairs when it broke up.

* * *

The White Hall of the Tauride Palace could no longer seat the swollen Soviet. For a long time quarters had been sought for it. On March 10th the Michael Theatre, one of the most capacious in Petersburg, was set aside for the plenary session. The Ex. Com., either because it was paying more attention to the Soviet than before or else because it was using this as an excuse for a breathing-spell, went there almost in full strength. I recall Bogdanov dragging me there by saying that it might be possible to find a place on the agenda for the Manifesto to the Peoples of the World.

This matter of the Manifesto could no longer be put off. The Marian Palace was bringing up its entire army to the attack and the situation was threatening to become radically confused. The question was taken up again in the Ex. Com. the following day; the Manifesto had to be given its final wording and passed by the Soviet.

The basic propositions of this document consisted of the following.

First thesis: 'Aware of its revolutionary strength the Russian democracy declares that it will counteract by all its means the imperialist policies of its ruling classes, and that it summons the nations of Europe to joint decisive action on behalf of peace.'

Second thesis: 'We will steadfastly defend our freedom against any reactionary encroachments, domestic or foreign; the Russian revolution will not retreat before the bayonets of the war-mongers and will not allow itself to be crushed by military power.'

In addition the Manifesto contained a special appeal to the German proletariat, a factor of exceptional importance for war and peace, which was called upon to deal a blow to the semi-absolutist German Government, at this time victorious on the field of battle.

Thus at its very outset the Manifesto gave a general summing up of the new revolutionary situation in Russia, and by way of reply to the 'martial' declarations of the Government, and especially of Miliukov, the Ex. Com. stated officially, firmly, and clearly that the democracy was beginning a struggle against the imperialist course of the Government, which was continuing the policies of Tsarism. It was opening a struggle for peace, against the piratical aims not only of the Kaiser but also of Miliukov and his allies, against a policy that placed their obligations to Anglo-French imperialism higher than duty to the democracy, higher than peace and the brotherhood of nations. The sides were drawn up opposite each other. The knot was tied.

* * *

The Liaison Commission began operating. The first meeting took place the day after its consolidation, on March 11th, and the second on March 13th.

For these meetings we Workers' and Soldiers' Deputies went over to the Marian Palace. The background of this Palace, neither majestic nor sumptuous, but rather cosy, soft, and intimate, was not conducive to any tense political struggle but rather to private—'liaison' discussions. Nor was there ever any kind of tension there. It was always boring, lackadaisical, and rather superfluous. But it was very pleasant to wander about the small, softly glittering reception- and drawing-rooms, which though crowded and noisy during the Pre-Parliament later on, were then completely empty.

* * *

The bourgeois offensive was going ahead on all sides. On March 12th the Volhynian Regiment, one of the first insurrectionary regiments of the revolution, appeared in the Tauride Palace in full formation with all its officers, a band, and a thunderous *Marseillaise.* It had come to greet the 'Duma', the 'Provisional Government', and the 'Soviet of Workers' and Soldiers' Deputies'. Red banners flew above each unit, with inscriptions: 'Don't forget your brothers in the trenches!' 'War to total victory!' 'Long live the Provisional Government and the Soviet of Workers' and Soldiers' Deputies!'

Sokolov came out to the regiment, welcomed it in the name of the Soviet, and made a speech about the revolution, of more or less neutral content. Then after Sokolov some people from the right wing made speeches about war to the end and appealed for a victory over the enemy without. The deputies were welcomed noisily and carried shoulder-high. From the Tauride Palace the regiment made its way to the General Staff, where Kornilov came out and the same scene was repeated.

The next day the first revolutionary regiment, the Pavlovskys, appeared in the same array. The banners had, with respect to domestic policy: 'Long Live the Constituent Assembly!' 'Long Live the Soviet of Workers' and Soldiers' Deputies!' 'Long Live the Democratic Republic!' 'Land and Freedom!' 'The Eight-hour Working Day!' 'Long Live the Provisional Government!' As we see, this was a collection of slogans chosen without much consistency of principle, from all sides and for all tastes. But on foreign policy they had 'Conquer or Die!' And also: 'Soldiers to their Posts, Workers to their Benches!'

Then the Semyonovskys appeared, the Lithuanians, the Third Rifles, the Petrogradskys, and an armoured division. Their domestic slogans were lost among the foreign, which were 'Preserve Freedom and Beat Wilhelm!' 'War to a victorious end!' 'War to Total Victory!' 'Down with German Imperialism!' 'Let's Bathe our Horses in German Blood!' (from the Cossacks). And then: 'Comrades, Make the Shells!' 'Soldiers to the Trenches, Workers to the Benches!'

The Tauride Palace was transformed once again. The comparative quiet and desertion, and the comparatively small number of mass-meetings within its walls[1] were again replaced by an extraordinary animation and thunderous noise. The regiments paraded past every day, one after the other, sometimes two and three a day. The antechamber and the Catherine Hall were filled with ranks of soldiers, arms, and red flags. The *Marseillaise* kept booming out, and every minute a mighty 'Hurrah!' rolled out, winging its way as far as the remote rooms of the Ex. Com. It was beautiful, magnificent, triumphal! This was a great surge of enthusiasm; it was evident that hearts were beating high again. The glorious revolution had spread in a mighty flood and taken a deep hold on the hearts of the people.

Both 'Duma' and Soviet people went out to welcome the regiments. Rodzianko was invariably successful. At his appearances and leave-takings some officer would without fail leap up on to a table in the Catherine Hall and proclaim: 'Hurrah for the Chairman of the Duma!' which would be snatched up in unison by thousands of throats.

As far as I could see Rodzianko was neither aggressive nor tactless in his attitude to the Soviet. On the contrary, he did his best to use the most democratic forms and slogans in which to wrap up his agitation, which had one objective and struck at a single or dual point: solidarity with the Provisional Government for a struggle against the enemy without.

The demonstrators also called for members of the Ex. Com., usually Chkheidze, who also did some good work on this wretched table in the Catherine Hall. In general the people of the right and left wings alternated on it quite regularly, and in the Ex. Com. we soon began taking strict care to provide the daily soldiers' mass-meetings with our own speakers. Seeing on the banners the new slogans of the revolution concerning domestic policy and the old slogans of Tsarism with respect to the war, Chkheidze on the first day wanted to 'go to the soldiers' and in harmony with Rodzianko made a few remarks in praise of Russia and blame of the Germans. But he saw at once that the enthusiasm this aroused had a more than dubious value from the point of view of Soviet policy. So the very next day Chkheidze

[1] i.e., after the Soviet had removed to the Michael Theatre. (Ed.)

had to pass from unison with Rodzianko to determined opposition to him. It's hard to say who was the victor in the hearts of these muzhiks. But in any case an open, tense struggle was already present and went on publicly before the very eyes of the masses.

* * *

The sense of all this was absolutely clear. Before our eyes there was developing all along the front that struggle for the army between the Soviet and the propertied classes whose rudiments I described as early as February 28th, a few hours after the overturn. This struggle was decisive for the revolution, and the democracy had to win it.

The conjuncture was complicated. It demanded of the Soviet leaders far-sightedness, striking power, tact, and the skill of a tight-rope walker. What was the *goal* of the attacking bourgeoisie? Its goal was—to gain for the bourgeois Government the real power in the State, that is, to subjugate the army. The army must become the old blind instrument in the hands of the plutocratic groups, otherwise doomed to a swift though gradual withering away. The real power, in the form of the army, must be set over the Soviet democracy, and if necessary must serve as a weapon against it, or else—the authority of Russian capital would recede into the past almost without having had a present.

But what were the means of the bourgeoisie? These means consisted precisely of the mobilization of forces on the ground of the external danger, precisely of the exploitation of the 'German' as an excuse for this.

With these methods it was possible to move for quite a distance. We've seen the innocent slogans on the banners: 'Make the Shells!' and 'Workers to their Benches!' This was the beginning of a broad, deep, and menacing agitation amongst the soldiers against the workers.

First of all, the workers were idlers, betraying their brothers in the trenches, by occupying themselves with selfish interests in the rear. They had got themselves an eight-hour working day and yet the factories were making a poor job of their work for defence, while the soldiers were paying for this with thousands of lives. Secondly, the workers and their leaders were lording it in the Soviet; the Ex. Com. was full of Social-Democrats. This working-class policy issued from the Soviet; hence the weakening of the front came from the same source.

The attack proceeded along all these lines. The bourgeoisie took the only possible road to its objectives. A fight lay ahead, which the Soviet democracy was far from provoking. It did not provoke it because the situation was complicated and the fight difficult. It was difficult just because it had to be fought from positions that had not yet been worked out—the attitude to the war. Up to that time the ignorant masses, as before, were exclusively under the sway of the old officially-sanctioned ideas about the war taken from the chauvinist Tsarist press. There were still no new ideas firmly implanted in the masses by Soviet and party propaganda. What was more, the guiding nucleus of the Soviet had not yet been able to elaborate and refine them for itself. The creation here of a unifying Soviet platform was quite impossible, as history had shown. All this favoured the bourgeoisie and drove it to force an offensive.

The Soviet, of course, could have followed the line of least resistance: it could easily have won over the army by taking up a defensist position and accepting a truce on the home front, and with one blow scattered all the misunderstandings about 'pacifism', the disorganization of the army, and 'leaving the front open'. On this basis the army would have quickly and easily passed over into the complete and exclusive control of 'its own' Soviet.

But it was clear that essentially this was completely sterile and unacceptable. Let us grant that it would have precluded the destruction of the revolution, that is, the establishment of a plutocratic dictatorship by the methods of Thiers and Cavaignac; but it would doom the revolution to a future just as miserable and more inglorious, leading it into the morass of immediate coalition with the bourgeoisie, i.e., into capitulation not only on the war question but also along the whole revolutionary front.

No, it was indispensable to win the struggle for the army on our, the Soviet, Zimmerwald platform, or else the 'victory' wouldn't be worth a copeck. It was essential to conquer in the fight for the army by overcoming the inertia of the muzhik-in-barracks, the enormous density of atavism, and the primitive ingrained nationalism, together with the specific chauvinism grafted on during the past few years by the 'liberal' yellow papers and the Tsarist censors. It was vital to accept and win the battle on the platform of the Manifesto to the Peoples of the World, on the platform of an internal struggle for peace together with the defence of democratic class conquests against reactionary forces abroad. In the last analysis we were bound to win.

However, for the time being things were difficult. The bourgeoisie, its press, and especially the officers acted energetically and in concert. At the mass-meetings and demonstrations in the Tauride Palace the bourgeois military youth exploited the speeches of Right and Left orators very well, persistently watching the mood of their own units and at the slightest need leaping up on to the platform themselves. The officers skilfully stage-managed the success of the Right, at the appropriate moments ordering the *Marseillaise* to be sung, or marching out their units altogether.

The Soviet orators, surrounded by this watchfully hostile audience, and by red flags with chauvinist inscriptions, were still unable to feel out the appropriate lines or find 'genuine', 'sincere' words. An incorrect tone did great harm: in the Catherine Hall, during one of the demonstrations, a woman agitator, probably a Bolshevik, was practically torn to pieces in public by the soldiers for saying 'Down with the war'. Skobelev, a popular, experienced, far from Bolshevik-minded orator, after some days (equivalent to months), barely escaped bayoneting for an incautious word.

A difficult situation demanding all one's attention, tact, watchfulness, and energy. Well, what of that? We must find all these.

* * *

On the morning of March 14th the Ex. Com. was busy with the usual things. The question of regularizing representation in the Soviet, and reorganizing it, had reached the last stage of ripeness. The number of workers' and soldiers' deputies had kept on growing every day; the number of mandates handed out had already reached 3,000. Of these 2,000 were to soldiers and about 1,000 to workers. Such an assembly was ridiculous as a permanent legislative body. For that matter there were simply no suitable quarters for it in Petersburg.

The proportion between workers' and soldiers' representatives was also intolerable. There were two or three times as many workers as soldiers in Petersburg. The workers elected one deputy per 1,000, the soldiers one per company. That is, the soldiers had between four and five times greater representation.

All this had to be regularized. How was it to be done? Primarily, of course, by reducing the standard of representation. But the difficulty was that this standard, like the reorganization in general, had to be passed through a Soviet already in existence. That meant making a good two-thirds of the deputies resign their authority. To get together a majority in favour of self-liquidation was a practically hopeless business: we ought to have taken care earlier and not issued the mandates.

Bogdanov proposed an artificial and cumbersome way out of the difficulty: leave the existing Soviet for ceremonial, historical sessions—'without debates', but for any kind of practical work form a small Soviet out of it, with a substantially reduced standard of representation.

But neither the Soviet nor the Ex. Com. ever carried the question to a conclusion. Thus there was no single act of reorganization, in view of these technical and diplomatic difficulties. At first matters were eased simply by the routine activities of the Mandates Commission, which mercilessly weeded out the mandates and by a month and a half later had substantially reduced the Soviet. This didn't seem to provoke any particularly loud protests. After that things were helped by the re-elections on the basis of the new, narrower standards set up by the Ex. Com. Thanks to this the size of the Soviet began to be little more than a thousand people.

But what about the crying disproportion in the representation of the workers and soldiers, with the Petersburg proletariat being completely swamped by the unstable peasant-soldiers? This question too was not settled for many months, almost down to the October overturn itself. It was not in the interests of the new Soviet majority, which controlled Soviet (and state) policy, and was completely reliant on this artificial, illegitimate peasant-soldier majority. In the last analysis, however, this ostrich-like policy did not help them.

The Michael Theatre had proved too small for the Soviet, and after a lengthy search premises had been found for it at the other end of the capital, on Basil Island, in the Naval Academy. There was a huge hall there, decorated with naval emblems and enormous ship models. The hall easily held three or four thousand people, and probably even more. During the next few months it was constantly in use for Soviet meetings. Against its long wall a platform was built, always closely invested by people. Facing it there stood about a thousand chairs and a few rows of benches. The remaining deputies stood: their endless forms, faces, greatcoats, and caps receded into the distance and merged into one whole at both ends of the hall. They even seemed to be pressed in among the very models of famous ships. But the acoustics were first-rate. The inconvenience was the long and awkward journey from the Tauride Palace for the Ex. Com. Columns of our motor-cars moving along the Nevsky made the passers-by stop and look after us for a long time.

* * *

The first 'big Socialist' paper, the SR *Delo Naroda* (People's Cause), came out on March 15th. Flabby, limp, with a heterogeneous editorial board, it set its course by Kerensky and was even neutral between the Tauride and Marian Palaces. Our *Novaya Zhizn*, the organ of the 'Letopisites', was being prepared at full pressure but was not yet under way. In any case at the moment there was nowhere for me to express my views.

After some clash with Rightists in the Ex. Com., I half-jokingly said to Shlyapnikov that I would have to write an article in *Pravda* (Truth).

'Well, why not?' Shlyapnikov replied. 'I'll suggest it.'

The next day he said to me: 'Our people say: let him write, but just let him say in the beginning that he takes the Bolshevik point of view.' We laughed.

At that time *Pravda*, which expressed the Bolshevik point of view, was the muddle-headed organ of very dubious politicians and writers. Its rabid articles and appeals to passion had no clearly defined goals. There was no 'line' at all, merely a pogromist form. It was impossible to contribute to such a paper. In an extreme case, when there was absolutely nowhere else to turn, it was possible to ask for 'hospitality' for a single occasion.

A couple of days after this, on March 15th or 16th, I was called out of the Ex. Com. and told that Kamenev[1] wanted to talk to me in the Catherine Hall. Kamenev, who had arrived three days before, had not yet appeared around the Soviet but had stayed in his own party organizations 'establishing order'.

I had already met Kamenev in 1902–3 casually in Paris, but I knew him under his 'real' name, and only during the war came to the conclusion, on the basis of a few indications, that this had actually been Kamenev, who during these years had become a well-known pillar of Bolshevism. Going into the Catherine Hall I did indeed find my old acquaintance.

Kamenev had never contributed to the *Sovremennik* from abroad, but he wrote for the *Letopis* from exile in Siberia, where he had just come from now. The things he wrote were not distinguished for any great originality, deep study, or literary brilliance, but they were sensible, well-done, based on good general preparation, and interesting in substance. We shall encounter Kamenev as a political figure uninterruptedly throughout the whole course of the revolution, at least until the day I write these lines, in 1919.

As a political figure Kamenev was undoubtedly an exceptional, though not an independent, force. Lacking either sharp corners, great intellectual striking power, or original language, he was not fitted to be a leader; by himself he had nowhere to lead the masses. Left alone he would not fail to be assimilated by someone. It was always necessary to take him in tow, and if he sometimes balked it was never very violently. But as one member of a leading group Kamenev, with his political schooling and oratorical gifts, was extremely distinguished and amongst the Bolsheviks he was in many respects irreplaceable.

Personally he was gentle and good-hearted. All this taken together added up to his rôle in the Bolshevik Party.

He always stood on its Right, conciliationist, passive wing. And sometimes he would balk, defending evolutionary methods

[1] Kamenev (Rosenfeld), Lev Borisovich (1883–1936): in the revolutionary movement from 1901; a Bolshevik after the Bolshevik–Menshevik split in 1903 and one of Lenin's closest colleagues. A central participant in all Bolshevik affairs. 1917–1927 was a member of the Bolshevik Central Committee, then played a part in various Opposition movements, was arrested, 'confessed', was arrested again, and was finally shot in 1936 after pleading guilty in the first of the famous purge trials held after the assassination of the Soviet functionary Kirov. (Ed.)

or a moderate political course. At the beginning of the revolution he jibbed against Lenin, jibbed at the October Revolution, jibbed at the general havoc and terror after the revolution, jibbed on supply questions in the second year of the Bolshevik régime. But—he always surrendered on all points. Not having much faith in himself, he recently (in the autumn of 1918) said to me, in order to justify himself in his own eyes: 'As for myself, I am more and more convinced that Lenin never makes a mistake. In the last analysis he is always right. How often has it seemed that he was slipping up—either in his prognosis or in his political line! But in the last analysis his prognosis and his line were always justified.'

Here is what Kamenev wanted to talk to me about then:

'About the article in *Pravda*: our people have told you you must first declare yourself a Bolshevik. That's all nonsense, pay no attention to it; please write the article. Here is the point. D'you read *Pravda*? You know, it has a completely unseemly and unsuitable tone. It has a terrible reputation. When I got here I was in despair. What could be done? I even thought of shutting down this *Pravda* altogether and getting out a new central organ under a different name. But that's impossible. In our party too much is bound up with the name *Pravda*. It must stay. It's only necessary to shift the paper into a new course. So now I'm trying to attract contributors or get hold of a few articles by writers with some reputation. Go ahead and write. . .'

All this was curious. I began asking Kamenev what was being done in general and in which direction a 'line' was being defined in his party circles. What was Lenin thinking and writing? We strolled about the Catherine Hall for a long time, with Kamenev trying at some length to persuade me that his party was taking up or ready to take up a most 'reasonable' (from my point of view) position. This position, as he put it, was very close to that taken by the Soviet Zimmerwald centre, if not identical with it. Lenin? Lenin thought that up to now the revolution was being accomplished quite properly and that a bourgeois Government was now historically indispensable.

'Does that mean you are not going to overthrow the bourgeois Government yet and don't insist on an immediate democratic régime?' I tried to get this out of Kamenev, who was showing me what I thought important perspectives.

'We here don't insist on that, nor does Lenin over there. He writes that our immediate task now is—to organize and mobilize our forces.'

'But what do you think about current foreign policy? What about an immediate peace?'

'You know that for us the question cannot be put that way. Bolshevism has always maintained that the World War can only be ended by a world proletarian revolution. And as long as that has not taken place, as long as Russia continues the war, we shall be against any disorganization and for maintaining the front.'

At this point it seemed to me that Kamenev's practical line might be inclining somewhat to the Right. In my turn I expounded my own ideas and told him in detail of the state of affairs in the Soviet and the Ex. Com. I told him that up to then things had been going favourably, thanks to the hegemony of the united Zimmerwald centre. But just at this point, at a crisis in the bourgeois offensive and the struggle for the real power, we were beginning to be smothered numerically by philistine and petty-bourgeois elements who were following the bourgeois lead on the main question—that of the war. I said that for several days now, amongst a few members of the Ex. Com. with views close to mine, the idea had been current of rallying all anti-defensist elements and creating a Left Zimmerwald bloc. I told him that our conversation gave me very great hopes in this respect.

Kamenev agreed with everything. The prospects were really comforting. For a united Left bloc had every chance of taking with it the pulpy mass of populist-minded soldiers and flabby intellectuals. In these circumstances the struggle now developing was bound to be won. We had to be up and doing.

Kamenev did not in fact close *Pravda*, but changed its course. In a flash it became unrecognizable. The surrounding 'big press' marvelled and would certainly have showered compliments on it, if it had not been restrained by the consciousness that when all was said and done no good thing could come out of Nazareth.

* * *

Towards the middle of March the Ex. Com. was already a corporation of about forty men, if not more, and was rather cumbersome, diffuse, and fluid. The representatives of parties and other organizations often substituted for one another, going away on missions or party work or for other reasons. It was no longer possible to know all the members. At any rate, by that time I—slow at names—no longer knew the names of a good third, probably, of the Ex. Com. But there is also this to be said: all these new members did very little to distinguish themselves, and for the most part fused into one solid mass.

Around the same time we formed a habit, fairly sensible and arising from the circumstances: the Ex. Com. would invite any newcomer who had performed some special service to join it. This was the basis on which many of our well-known *émigrés* or exiles came to be in the Ex. Com. (if their party organizations did not delegate them). These comrades were given a consultative voice.

But this diluted the Ex. Com. with people whose presence was quite meaningless. More and more new faces were glimpsed in the Ex. Com. every day. They no longer attracted anyone's attention, and no one asked where they'd turned up from, what their names were, or what party they belonged to. Only the Secretariat knew this, and the Mandates Commission.

In these conditions the Ex. Com. was obviously bound to lose its former character. Most of these soldiers' and officers' delegates made a Right-democratic, or purely philistine, or simply Cadet-minded mass. In part they were people of the liberal professions and of liberal views who had hastily fastened on some kind of Socialist label, indispensable in the Soviet democratic organizations; but in part they were really soldiers put forward by soldiers' organizations in accordance with the prevailing war-mongering moods. Most of them clustered around the SR core.

I had only one name for all of them—'Mamelukes'. But—I repeat—there was still not the slightest trace of a Napoleon amongst them. They were weakly organized. They would easily waver and fall apart on small questions. And the small militant kernel with the requisite solidarity and energy, supported by the Left flank and a considerable Swamp, was able to maintain its hegemony as before and carry on a Zimmerwaldite line.

This Swamp was made up of newcomers, more or less, in politics, who were instinctively attracted towards peace and the cause of the proletariat; besides these the Swamp at that time included our tarnished 'Zimmerwaldites', headed by the binary stars Chkheidze and Skobelev. After the October Revolution they went over to the Bolsheviks, together with Steklov.

Some days before, a small, attractive-looking man, with a classical Semitic head and a black little Assyrian beard, a concentrated frown, sarcastic smile, and catlike movements had appeared in the Ex. Com. He spoke quite often, showing experience and energy, though without causing any sensation. I finally asked someone who he was. The man I asked opened his eyes wide: 'What, don't you know? That's Lieber, the famous *Bundist.*'

In the future Lieber[1] was to play a great, though not independent, rôle. Not a brilliant personality, but with a great political past, wide experience, and outstanding gifts as an orator, he quickly became, if not an inspirer, one of the mainstays of the new Soviet majority. On many occasions he was invaluable to that majority. And very often one could feel the impact of his passion, see his spare figure leap up on to the platform with two fingers raised, and hear his voice carrying his tempestuous philippics up to a high note. Lieber might have been a much more interesting political figure if he hadn't suffered from one fixed idea. In all circumstances he was *rapaciously on the look-out for what he could do or say or* invent, that would destroy or harm or annoy the Bolsheviks. When they took power Lieber broke away from all his closest colleagues and swerved far to the Right.

At this time Stalin appeared in the Ex. Com. for the Bolsheviks, in addition to Kamenev. This man was one of the central figures of the Bolshevik Party and perhaps one of the few individuals who held (and hold to this day) the fate of the revolution and of the State in their hands. Why this is so I shall not undertake to say: 'influence' in these exalted and irresponsible spheres, remote from the people and alien to publicity, is so capricious. But at any rate Stalin's rôle is bound to be perplexing. The Bolshevik Party, in spite of the low level of its 'officers' corps', had a whole series of most massive figures and

[1] Lieber (Goldman), Mikhail Isakovich (1880–1937): a Bundist and Menshevik, especially active in the Jewish working-class movement. Extremely hostile to the October Revolution; continually arrested, and finally shot. (Ed.)

able leaders among its 'generals'. Stalin, however, during his modest activity in the Ex. Com. produced—and not only on me—the impression of a grey blur, looming up now and then dimly and not leaving any trace. There is really nothing more to be said about him.[1]

I think Tereshchenko, the Finance Minister, turned up in the Ex. Com. on March 17th. He was extremely lively and charming, a very dashing, talkative young man, with unusual abilities, to my mind, and an excellently developed class-consciousness. The first news of this man's being invited into the first revolutionary Cabinet naturally caused general public astonishment. Even the reporters for a long time couldn't tell us anything about him except that his fortune amounted to roughly 80 million rubles and that he was not only an amateur of the theatre but a connoisseur. It was plain to everyone that he was no more than a political *parvenu*, a product of backstage combinations and perhaps also of internal friction among half a score of our weightiest political figures.

Tereshchenko did not find us in session. But so much the better: he went from group to group, got to know us, scattered compliments and, one might say, 'fraternized' with the representatives of Soviet democracy. He told us that in his Ministry work had already started on the reorganization of our national finances on democratic principles. He asked for eight Soviet representatives to help in this work. He had come to the Ex. Com. just for this. He invited me in particular. 'For the direct taxes, especially on land', Tereshchenko added, showing he knew my book on agrarian taxation.

The Minister was promised satisfaction in his urgent need for Soviet collaborators, and he left the Tauride Palace, satisfied with his new contacts.

Life was bubbling over.

* * *

That evening three members of the 'Zimmerwald Bloc'—Larin,[2] Uritsky,[3] and myself—started off together out of the half-empty, half-dark Tauride Palace.

[1] *Sic!* (Ed.)

[2] Larin (Lurye), Mikhail Alexandrovich (1882–1932): an active revolutionary from 1901. A Menshevik and 'liquidator' (see note, p. 15), he became a Bolshevik

'Tsereteli's arriving tomorrow,' said Uritsky; 'we mustn't forget to send workers' delegations and a regiment with a band to meet him.'

On Saturday, the 18th, Tsereteli actually arrived with a whole group of 'Second-Duma' and other exiles from Siberia. It was really necessary to organize a welcome; but I was against specially cumbersome welcomes, when they were arranged not voluntarily, but by order. A regiment, after all, is many thousands of men, who encumber the station and square. It was quite enough for a very small military unit, besides the delegations, to go out with a band. Also, these welcomes were now becoming very frequent. They had just been waiting vainly for 'Grandma' Breshkovskaya[1] who hadn't arrived. I said all this, but Uritsky acted as though offended on behalf of the eminent Social-Democrat.

'Well, you know,' he said, 'Tseretelis don't arrive every day!'

That was right. It was still right ten months later, too, when the police power in the capital lay in Uritsky's hands and Tsereteli, in order to avoid prison, was trying not to spend nights at home.

---

after the February Revolution. After the October Revolution he played a very active rôle in the internationalization of industry, in the Foreign Trade Monopoly, and in the establishing of the State Planning Commission. (Ed.)

[3] Uritsky, Moisei Solomonovich (1873–1918): a Menshevik from 1903; joined the Bolsheviks together with the Interdistrict Group in June 1917. After the October Revolution an official of the Cheka (precursor of the GPU, NKVD, MVD—the Soviet Security Police); assassinated in August 1918. (Ed.)

[1] Breshko-Breshkovskaya, Yekaterina Konstantinovna (1844–1934): one of the founders of the SR Party, and on its Right wing. A sponsor of terrorism as a method of political action. Hostile to the October Revolution, she emigrated and continued combating the Soviet régime. (Ed.)

CHAPTER 10

THE PYRRHIC VICTORY OF THE DEMOCRACY

THE mobilization of the army under imperialist military slogans was being intensified. Things were not limited to persistent demonstrations by the whole Petersburg garrison before the Soviet in the Tauride Palace; the entire bourgeoisie was systematically and energetically hammering on the same spot from various sides. Agitation was being conducted in the barracks, mass-meetings were being arranged under various auspices, etc. The whole of the big press was advancing in a solid black cloud, keeping the ordinary townspeople in the dark and creating a new 'public opinion' in the masses of the capital.

The agitation was being carried on at every street-corner, and during the last ten days of March, at every street-crossing, in the trams, or in any public place, you could see workers and soldiers in the last stages of nervous irritation, grappling with each other in a furious verbal battle. There was also actual fighting. Matters had taken an extremely alarming turn.

The workers, of course, were accused of making excessive demands, of a complete unwillingness to work and of disregarding the interests of the front. The starting point of the agitation was, among other things, the eight-hour working day. Fishers in troubled waters were gambling on the complete incapacity of the muzhik in the soldier's grey greatcoat to understand this proletarian demand. It was said that there were no such hours of work either at the front or in the village, yet factory idlers who didn't want to work any longer were buying themselves a life of freedom at the price of sacrifices in the trenches.

The soldiers were not merely demanding the curbing of the workers and control of the factories. They were threatening reprisals and the use of force. 'Just wait,' you could hear on all sides, 'we'll show you! We'll put one of our comrades with a rifle in your own workshops next to every one of your idlers. And if anything happens. . .'

Armed soldiers did in fact begin visiting factories, carrying out inspections and using force. Groups of soldiers from the nearby garrisons and even from the army in the field began arriving for this purpose. Major outbreaks might be expected from hour to hour. The revolution and its fortress, its vital nerve, the Soviet, were once again threatened by the soldiers' elemental instincts, unleashed this time by the agents of the bourgeoisie that had 'recognized the revolution'.

The situation was such that the gulled and frenzied armed muzhik might not only surrender easily into the hands of the plutocracy, but at once, without a breathing-spell, might start using his rifle against the old 'internal foe', the workers. We must act. . .

* * *

And, of course, the opposing camp, the Soviet, had already been in action for some time, or the struggle would already have been lost; but all was far from being well there.

The situation was quite favourable—from the point of view of the mobilization of forces—with respect to the relations between workers and soldiers. In these sharp clashes the Petersburg proletariat showed surprising tact and really brotherly gentleness, as well as a firm hand. It took up a defensive position. Doggedly, step by step, the Petersburg workers explained the real state of affairs to the soldiers—in private conversation, in mass-meetings, in the Soviet, in the barracks, and in the factories themselves. In every factory special meetings were devoted to 'the soldier' and the bourgeois-baiting campaign, and resolutions were passed making a special appeal to the soldier's intelligence and sense of justice. The resolutions showed that the eight-hour day was not, in fact, being put into operation, that full speed of production was held up by insufficient raw materials and not by the fault of the workers, that the demand was not only not excessive but too trivial. Proofs were given; the soldiers were told the level of wages, and freely invited to visit the workshops. Concern for the front was very clearly shown by these resolutions. In particular the Petersburg workers, on the ground of the seriousness of the moment and their responsibility to the fatherland, shortened the Easter holiday to three days.

It goes without saying that the Soviet and party centres were at the head of the movement. Special mass-meetings were arranged for the soldiers, agitators made the round of the barracks, directives were sent to the provinces. Special delegations from military units, together with members of the Soviet, went to inspect factories, and afterwards officially refuted the slanders on the workers. But for ten to fifteen days the situation was critical.

* * *

In the work of the Ex. Com. a substantial place was now occupied by all sorts of military delegations, usually consisting of two or three officers and a few soldiers, which had begun to appear every day, from the local units, from the front, and from all over Russia. They demanded to be received by the Ex. Com., and waited for hours and sometimes days. These delegations were a serious hindrance to current business. At first the Ex. Com. received them in its sessions as an emergency, later it gave them some time after 6 o'clock in the evening; then it appointed a group of people to receive the delegations at all hours of the day and night.

The delegations themselves of course asked for the few best-known and most respected members of the Ex. Com. But the comrades always tended to decline this rather monotonous and tiring occupation. However, I knew one amateur of these receptions, Sokolov, who was always assuring me of the vast interest of this living contact with the front, with the ignorant peasant-soldiery, and with unfamiliar types of officers.

It was indeed interesting, but even more, it was useful for the Soviet cause. From the depths of Russia and from the army in the field there passed through the Ex. Com. thousands of people, and they all carried back what they had seen and heard to the masses who had sent them. In such circumstances the reception of these delegations became an essential factor in Soviet propaganda.

The same delegations usually went off both to Rodzianko and to the Marian Palace. Not always, but in most cases, they had been sent to both the Soviet and the Provisional Government—to present themselves, express their views, ask questions, and see what both bodies were doing. Not all of them: there were local units or groups who had 'defined themselves' to such an extent and were so 'conscious' that they sent their delegates to one place or the other, into one of the camps, with quite categorical class instructions. But these were in the minority. As a rule one had to deal with an unprepared, ignorant, vacillating mass, well-disposed or suspicious towards both sides alike and capable of being turned one way or the other. But its composition was for the most part democratic, plebeian; this enabled the habitual prejudice, artificially induced chauvinism, and strongly corrosive spirit of bogus 'military honour' to be neutralized in the contest between the two sides.

It was the officers who usually spoke for the delegations. After greetings and rhetorical declarations of pious duty on the part of the guests, a lengthy practical talk would usually begin—on really disturbing themes. The delegation would speak of their uneasiness, based on rumours about the Soviet's attitude towards the war. They mentioned their profound disagreement with this attitude and its unacceptability to the soldiers, and repeated all the clichés of petty-bourgeois military ideology. But here they were not in the atmosphere of hatred of an enemy camp, nor in the midst of some ignorant mob incited to violence; they were standing face to face with the very 'openers of the front' themselves, with the very enemies of the fatherland and of everything sacred; and—not seeing anything terrible in them, having met reasonable, educated, and impressive people—they cleared up the question in a business-like way by a tranquil conversation. This was a more than serious test of the chauvinist phrases snatched off the street and of the whole meagre intellectual luggage of the delegates.

The March 14th Manifesto, which contained nothing terrible for any patriot (without quotation marks), was read and explained to them. The meaning of their own slogans—'War to the end', etc.—was revealed. The ideology of imperialism was still alien to the man in the street; its clarification revealed something new to him and discouraged him. Even the instability of Soviet slogans and their defensist tendencies did not prevent such conversations from being useful.

The delegations left completely different from what they had been upon arrival. If the officers, because of their caste psychology, remained of the same mind, the soldiers were thoroughly persuaded. In any case their *a priori* prejudice, their elemental distrust of the Soviet, was paralysed, as well as their subconscious belief that it was an internal enemy which at best had to be kept at a distance. A psychological if not ideological contact was always established. But it was clear that these private conversations and heart-to-heart talks could by no means replace an officially declared and systematically executed campaign against imperialist attacks on the revolution.

* * *

The delegations, individual delegates, and rural emissaries did not turn only to the Ex. Com., they very often got into the Soviet and sometimes found an opportunity to speak there, at any rate in some one of the sections, each of which packed the White Hall. The workers and soldiers liked these living accounts of remote places and gave them a warm welcome. Here too a firm and essential contact was established. But it was not only a question of news and contact—these were wonderful scenes, impossible to forget!

First of all—the orators: where did they spring from? I'm not talking about the more or less 'conscious' ones, the local political leaders who in a fortnight had already got used to the platform and the attentive crowd, but the uneducated, sometimes totally illiterate peasants, who showed no signs at all of political consciousness.

These were incomparably the more interesting, as they uttered their stormy, heroic hymns to the revolution, although they were incapable of saying what revolution meant and barely able to pronounce the word itself, yet in a self-oblivious flood of words pouring out their soul, that seemed the very soul of the *people and its revolution.* Their speeches were not always clear, they had no core nor any real content. But everyone listened excitedly and everyone understood. Everyone knew that no eloquence, adroitly phrased greeting, or solemn heart-felt vows of fidelity could replace these incoherent and not entirely understandable speeches.

They excited the audience, took possession of it, and somehow illuminated it, welding it into one by the heroic emotion of the revolution, the spirit of solidarity, and the readiness for strife and sacrifice.

I remember one fellow in a brown peasant's overcoat, with

his hair cropped all round, broad-shouldered, red-faced, and snub-nosed, a typical, primeval shepherd and not a bad model for a Russian Simple Simon. Speaking quickly in a thin voice, calling us 'brethren' and 'dears', he uttered or cried out his elemental lyrical improvisation. God knows what unendurable oppression the revolution had lifted from this barbarian—if he had been snatched from the talons of some savage noble landlord or ferocious officer and was rapturously drinking in his new freedom like a desert stallion.

The chairman didn't interrupt him. The 'conscious' politicians, the scientific Socialists, with burning eyes and fixed smiles, breathing hard and devouring every word—all listened to Simple Simon.

Peasants often climbed up on to the platform of the White Hall with their bundles on their backs. Once there came a soldier from the trenches, dragging after him a dirty sack, which he put in front of him on the dais.

Quietly, with no wasted words, he began talking about his comrades who had sent him to salute the vanguard fighters, teachers, and brothers and thank them for their great deeds and for the freedom that had been won. In the trenches they didn't know how they could play their part in the cause of the whole nation, what they could do for the revolution, or what help they could give their kinsmen in the Soviet of Workers' and Soldiers' Deputies.

'So we decided to bring you the most precious thing we had. . . In this sack are all the decorations we won with our blood; no one kept anything for himself. Here are the St. George's Crosses and Medals. I've been sent to give them to you, together with our sacred, unbreakable vow to lay down our lives for the freedom that has been won and to serve the revolution and obey without question all the orders of the Soviet. . .'

The hall was frozen rigid during these simple words, and it was a moment before a storm of applause thundered out. But later on there were more than a few such sacks full of medals dragged into the Soviet.

The eye rested with satisfaction on the rare figures of sailors with their bronzed faces, charming childish jackets and naïve little ribbons on their caps.

'From the Black Sea Fleet—greetings!'

Some speeches were simply merry, to the vexation of the business-like chairman and the great satisfaction of the whole assembly. I remember one lad from the front, not specially bright-looking, who tried for a long time to get the floor. After assuring the chairman that unless he told the Soviet what he'd been ordered to he couldn't go back to his regiment, the boy finally got on the platform. With a sly grin and sweeping gestures, he began to tell us how the trenches had greeted the revolution.

'Well, now . . . we got the news: they said the Tsar was finished, and there had begun to be a revolution. Of course we were glad. We began yelling "Hurrah!" and singing—what's it again?—"Arise, you prisoners. . ." Well! The Germans were only about as far away as that—or perhaps a bit more. They heard us and yelled over: "Hey, what have you got over there?" We yelled back: "We have got a revolu-u-ution! No more Tsar!" Well, of course they were glad too. They began singing as well, and yelling "Hurrah!" Only in the way they do it: "*Ach!*" We say "hurrah", but they say "*Ach!*" Then we yelled over: "Hey—what about you? Now you can get rid of that—what's his name?" But they yelled back: "Well now, that's something else again!" '

The satisfaction was complete—for both speaker and listeners, who warmly congratulated the grinning boy.

I was once stopped on my way out by a modest-looking soldier from the trenches. He addressed me, embarrassed and stuttering:

'Comrade, I've got an idea about something I want to tell you—I don't know whether I'm right or not—naturally, with my ignorant brain. Of course, now our Government ought to stop conquering other countries. But couldn't we go straight to the Berlin Soviet of Workers' and Soldiers' Deputies by telegraph?'

'Workers and Soldiers'—that still sounded strange and awkward even in Russia. I started explaining that unfortunately there was still no such institution in Berlin and that it could only appear with a revolution, and then peace would be secured immediately. But the soldier didn't really believe me and listened doubtfully. What? Germany, as he understood it, was an advanced country, far ahead of Russia, and suddenly they didn't have a Soviet of Workers' and Soldiers' (of course, soldiers too!) Deputies?

No, alas! they didn't—while the proletariat of backward, petty-bourgeois Russia leaped up and soared to an unheard-of height, then faltered, grew confused, collapsed, and fell in an unequal struggle beyond its strength. . .

* * *

So the second half of March was a period of an intense public struggle for power between the plutocracy and the democracy—a period of a nation-wide campaign for the conquest of the real power in the State, the army. Both sides mobilized all their forces.

The democratic side had the advantage that the army was a democracy that spontaneously gravitated towards its own class organizations, and in the process of the revolution fairly easily detached itself from the possessing classes: to a substantial degree this consolidated the army 'automatically' behind its elected Soviet. But the democratic side also had the immense defect that its political slogans—indispensable to counterbalance the battle-cries of the bourgeoisie—were completely unformulated. And in view of the unavoidable elemental chauvinism of the muzhik masses, the patriotic bourgeois playing on the foreign peril—a gamble that masked a Tsarist war programme—threatened to wrest the army away from the Soviet and make it subject to the plutocracy.

In the centres of the revolution, or if you like behind the scenes, this was the situation.

* * *

The question of 'regulating our war slogans' had not yet been put on the Ex. Com.'s agenda, or at any rate had not yet been reached. This had become unendurable. I began agitating busily in the corridors amongst the Leftists, but also appealed to a number of defensists, not without success.

On March 21st the question was put on the order of the day. A 'great day'. Everyone clearly understood the importance in principle of the question and its practical significance. But at that point scarcely anyone could have been aware that this session would be a turning point for all Soviet politics, and more than that—for the whole future course of the revolution.

I think it was the morning of that same day that I saw in the Ex. Com. a tall, lean, ox-eyed Caucasian, with a worried look and angular movements. I asked who this new face was, and was told—Tsereteli. We knew each other quite well, though not by sight. Tsereteli, after all, was also a Zimmerwaldite and used to read my things. And I knew him not only as a Second-Duma exile and famous adversary of Stolypin's, but had heard a great deal about his rôle in Siberian exile. He once sent me an article for the *Sovremennik* from there. I read it, I think without much interest. Tsereteli not only was no writer, but was no theoretician either. In this respect he was a brilliant exception to the rule that all our first-class Socialist party leaders (I leave aside Kerensky) were also writers and theoreticians.

This exceptional position of Tsereteli's, however, by no means prevented him from becoming a star of the first magnitude in our revolution. From now on these notes of mine will be fairly well filled with his name: we shall learn to know him in action.

The meeting was very crowded. Many people were sitting two to each chair or standing up clinging to the walls. The Zimmerwald Bloc was all mobilized and counted for not much less than half of the votes. Kamenev had still not appeared in the Ex. Com. and took no part in this meeting; if I'm not mistaken the Bolsheviks had sent Stalin from their Central Committee. In spite of the importance I ascribe to this meeting I don't recall its details. Here is what I do remember.

Chkheidze gave me the floor first, as the 'organizer' or 'first signatory' of the memorandum presented to the Praesidium. I referred to the March 14th Manifesto, reminded them of the pledges given to wage an internal struggle for peace, drew their attention to the mobilization of all bourgeois forces under the slogan of 'War to the end', alluded to the official declarations of the Provisional Government; and finally demanded that the Soviet begin a nation-wide, systematic campaign for peace and mobilize the proletariat and the garrison of the capital under the slogans of peace.

As for these slogans, the first of them ought to be an official rejection by revolutionary Russia of the Tsarist war programme as set forth originally in the Allies' well-known 'reply' to Wilson (in December 1915), and developed not long before by Minister Miliukov as the programme of the revolution. And then an open *démarche* jointly with the Allies, offering peace on the basis of the formula: No annexations or indemnities.

My comments on these proposals were that the present situation threatened the revolution with the greatest danger, involving it in an endless war and presaging military collapse, famine, and complete economic dissolution. Meanwhile peace overtures by the democracy, which had the greatest significance both for our revolution and for the international proletariat, did not entail the slightest risk of weakening the front or disrupting the defence of the revolution by a military disaster. On the contrary, any peace moves by Russia, since in the eyes of the masses they would purge the war of any tinges of imperialism, would only strengthen the front and weld together the masses of soldiery in the struggle against the internal danger—in case our peace moves didn't attain their goal. Only then would the army know that it was really pouring out its blood for the revolution and for freedom.

Later, throughout the next six months, I developed all these rather simple ideas dozens if not hundreds of times orally and in print. But I don't think that my speech at this meeting was successful, well-constructed, sensibly expressed, or at all convincing. That didn't prevent it from arousing great excitement.

After me the whole Zimmerwald Bloc had zealously put their names down to speak. But the Leftists, before speaking in defence of the 'peace campaign', preferred to wait for the speeches of their opponents. And an opponent was not long in presenting himself.

This was Tsereteli's first speech—and of course it became the centre of the subsequent debates.

Standing as usual, half-turned away from his adversary and never raising his eyes to his face, Tsereteli attacked me with all his strength and passion. He was very excited and indignant—and in such circumstances his fine voice rang out and a blue vein swelled up across his forehead. Reproaching me, Tsereteli also referred to the March 14th Manifesto, which he had read *en route* from Siberia, as joyful tidings inspired by the genius of the revolution; he reproached me with my own pamphlets, where I had displayed some understanding of what had now become inaccessible to me; now he considered my speech, as well as the proposed resolution, a piece of clumsy misunderstanding and a pernicious enterprise.

I listened to this philippic for a long time without understanding what the point was. But Tsereteli finally explained himself. He was perplexed and indignant because neither in my resolution nor in the memorandum was there a word about armed resistance to the foreign enemy, support for the army, or the mobilization of all vital energies in the defence of the revolution against destruction from outside.

It would have seemed that this quarrel really was based on a misunderstanding. Support of the army, discipline and fitness for battle, defence preparations, resistance to the foreign enemy—we'd been talking about all that every day and always given enough attention to it. On these questions the Ex. Com. already had a firmly established opinion that would have satisfied Tsereteli completely. As a newcomer not conversant with the tendencies within the committee, Tsereteli fell into a natural misunderstanding and had chosen the wrong moment to speak of armed defence when another question was under discussion—that of methods of fighting for peace. It would have seemed that Tsereteli's speech could be considered not a rebuttal but a continuation of what had been said by myself and others. And then this combination of a struggle for peace with the maintenance of the army's fitness for battle would have coincided with the general Soviet position in relation to the war, arising from the March 14th Manifesto.

But that's not what happened. Tsereteli's speech made a completely different impression on everyone. Tsereteli, a Zimmerwaldite, not only shifted the whole centre of gravity to the side of armed defence, but completely eliminated as undesirable any domestic political activities in favour of peace, i.e., he completely abandoned everything comprised in the word Zimmerwald. And precisely in this spirit he proposed a practical resolution in place of mine: it contained not a word about peace moves but called for the mobilization of the rear and the front for defence.

Up to then we had not heard such trenchant and plain-spoken speeches along these lines; even our extreme Right was able to adapt itself to the ruling Zimmerwald tendency. That the most authoritative Zimmerwaldite should come out so thunderously with consummate out-and-out defensism was unexpected, inexplicable, and naturally flabbergasted everyone. The Mamelukes were startled. Practically the entire Left half of the meeting began asking for the floor. Chkheidze, not knowing what to think or feel, shouted: 'Please, I ask everyone to write his name down! I can't remember everyone!'

There began long and stormy debates. The Rightists began harping on every variation on the theme of how untimely, unpatriotic, dangerous to the front, and useless to all but the Germans was any struggle inside revolutionary Russia for peace. A very great deal was said about the position of the German Social-Democracy, which wasn't doing anything for peace, but was defending the despot Wilhelm. Tsereteli had loosened all tongues. A flood of philistine vulgarity, borrowed from the gutter press, swept over the Ex. Com.

It proved to be impossible to finish the debates that day; it was decided to continue them in the morning. Going out of the Palace I met Tsereteli by accident in the office; he was sitting in his fur coat, tired and gloomy, waiting for one of his comrades. He probably saw that when all was said and done there was something that was out of place. He turned to me and said: 'So you don't support my resolution?'

'No, I don't,' I replied, and wanted to go on explaining that his resolution, correct in substance, applied only to half the question and at that the less important half at the moment.

But Tsereteli absolutely refused to listen to me. 'Oh, so you don't support it!' he said in a strange tone, and practically turned his back, pretending that everything else was clear to him without any explanations.

What a disagreeable character! I pondered, going out into the street with the gloomiest thoughts.

* * *

The next day Tsereteli came up to me before the meeting with a piece of paper in his hands. 'You know,' he said, 'I've come to the conclusion that our resolutions can be combined. Last night I misunderstood a lot of things; I think both parts should be in the resolution, both military defence and a struggle for peace. Look at this, I've made one resolution out of both parts; I think it can be acceptable to the great majority.'

One surprise after another! What was this—could an experienced politician really have got into such a mess somehow, and as an honest man simply acknowledged it straightforwardly, surrendering openly and crossing out everything that had been done? Or—was it a diplomatic move? I took the resolution. It really did speak both of the indispensable steps towards peace, and of supporting armed resistance to the foreign enemy. After some small corrections it could be voted for. But it lacked any concrete directives concerning a national peace campaign. I gave the resolution to Larin, a great expert in such matters, and suggested he work out a final text acceptable to both sides.

Tsereteli took the floor to propose the new resolution, and more or less definitely acknowledged the error he had fallen into the night before. The new resolution, made up by Larin and Tsereteli, in substance really was acceptable to the Left wing, or at least to the majority of it.

Once again the meeting was in complete confusion. The Left speakers began by saying that they had put their names down the night before in order to refute Tsereteli, but that now there was no need for it. The Right section, however, rather disappointed, continued the polemic against defeatism. In view of the academic nature of the debates they were quickly cut short. The Larin–Tsereteli resolution was passed by an enormous majority. The original question 'of regulating our war slogans' seemed exhausted. But there was also some 'diplomacy' in all this.

This resolution about peace steps, after all, also had a completely academic character. It didn't bind the Provisional Government, or the Ex. Com. or the whole Soviet democracy to anything. While correct in substance, it had no practical significance. The question at the heart of the whole political conjuncture could not, of course, be 'exhausted' by this resolution. Nor was it possible to leave matters as they were.

The Left, supplementing the resolution that had been passed, demanded official decisions about the peace campaign. Then Tsereteli, to counterbalance this, brought in a new motion: the campaign could be opened at any desired moment, but just then there was no need for it; just then the Ex. Com., in the person of its Liaison Commission, should request the Provisional Government for an official statement on the renunciation by the new Russia of all annexations or indemnities.

There was no debate, or scarcely any, on these two proposals. Tsereteli's motion gained a substantial majority of votes.

* * *

This decision, reached by the votes of a new majority, had enormous significance, which could be fully appreciated only afterwards. For the new majority this decision was of course a compromise: only the night before it had been hoping to kill the peace question entirely. But to the Soviet Zimmerwald, to the Soviet's whole policy, to the entire revolution—the vote did severe damage.

The question of peace was removed from the plane of struggle and put on the plane of a private agreement without mass participation. Theoretically speaking, it is true, the struggle could always be returned to. But in practice this was not the purpose of the new majority; it had not abandoned the appeal to revolutionary democracy in order to return the following day to mobilizing the democratic forces for a struggle against the bourgeoisie. No, this was a special, specific method of action arising from the nature of the case, the character of the functioning groups, and the position of the new petty-bourgeois majority between the proletariat and the plutocracy.

Diplomacy was now recognized as the weapon of the peace policy of the revolution—with no hope of anything to reinforce the diplomatic arts of the Soviet. The Liaison Commission was called on to stand up against all the enormous forces mobilized by the bourgeoisie. All this had great principled importance.

This dual fact—the formation of a new majority and the rejection of any appeals to the masses—had incalculable consequences for the whole history of the revolution.

The new majority was headed, in addition to Tsereteli, by our Praesidium 'Swamp', Chkheidze, and Skobelev. It was also joined (for the time being) by Steklov, who was trying to become one with the leading group, and after that by a number of Menshevik defensists. But all these leaders of the majority were 'leading' a mass known to consist of petty-bourgeois, soldiers, and intellectuals, and on it they relied entirely.

Meanwhile the new majority was still far from being either stable, strong, or substantial. It was precisely because of this that it resorted to a compromise; Tsereteli in general disliked compromises, and the ambiguities described above, based on ignorance of the situation, were quite uncharacteristic of him. The minority, headed by the Zimmerwaldites, was still very large, quite influential, and gave a very good account of itself during the coming weeks. But it was a minority. The Zimmerwald group that had begun the revolution was (with the exception of Steklov) already 'out of power' and no longer responsible for the course of Soviet policy.

* * *

By the order of March 22nd the Liaison Commission was charged with obtaining the Provisional Government's official repudiation of all aggressive policies. But that day we were unable to get an appointment with the Council of Ministers, and on the following day, the 23rd, there was the funeral of the martyrs of the revolution. The appointment was made for the evening of the 24th.

It would be an understatement to say that the funeral went off brilliantly. It was a magnificent and moving triumphal procession of the revolution and of the masses who made it. As for its size, it surpassed anything ever seen. Buchanan, the British Ambassador, watched it from his Embassy, whose windows looked on to the Champ de Mars and the Neva Embankment, and stated categorically that Europe had never seen anything like it.

But the size of the demonstration was not the most important thing on that remarkable day of March 23rd. This time the entire press without exception had to admire the standard of citizenship displayed by the masses of the people in this majestic review. All fears proved groundless. In spite of the hitherto unheard-of number of demonstrators, which undoubtedly reached a million, the order was not only irreproachable but—in the words of the same Buchanan—'unbelievable'. By some miracle a million people, with innumerable banners and with bands, moved—from early morning to the evening—across the Champ de Mars, conducting the bodies of their fallen comrades to their graves. This was no funeral but a great, unclouded triumph of the people, which long remained a grateful memory with all those who took part in it.

I did not take part in it myself, any more than in most such demonstrations. But I heard many stories about this astounding parade of the revolutionary masses. Yes, with such masses, if their will were correctly directed, really great and unprecedented victories might be achieved. But . . .

* * *

On the evening of Friday the 24th we began to assemble for the session of the Liaison Commission in the Marian Palace.

When the five of us (Chkheidze, Skobelev, Steklov, Philippovsky, and myself) had assembled, Tsereteli joined us and expressed a wish to take part in the conversations. He expressed some doubt as to his formal rights, asking whether he ought to address himself first of all to the Ex. Com. But of course all that was nonsense. He could always obtain such rights, and the Liaison Commission had full power to co-opt him. All six of us went.

The Council of Ministers was present almost in full strength; we got down to business, after greetings and compliments to the newly arrived Tsereteli. I don't recall whether Tsereteli spoke as the presenter of a report, but in any case he talked more than anyone else. I remember his highly 'diplomatic' speeches.

Tsereteli tried to be convincing to the Ministers, looking for points of departure that were close to them. Such points were the position of the army and of the rear: if things in the army and at the rear, amongst the soldiers and in the factories, were not going as well as could be desired, that could be explained to a very considerable extent by the foreign policy of the Provisional Government and its statements about war to the finish, obligations to the Allies, etc. All this was sowing alarm and discontent over the long-drawn-out character of this war for alien goals, and weakening resistance at the front as well as production in the rear. It was indispensable to make an official statement renouncing any war aims but defence. Then the general position would not only improve automatically but the Soviet would be able to mobilize all workers and soldiers and make them devote their entire strength to the defence of the revolution against the foreign enemy.

Tsereteli laid special emphasis on this last point—trying to tempt the Ministers by this generous sop. Nevertheless it was obvious that this sort of advance on our part made a most disagreeable impression on the Cabinet. At the previous meeting the Ministers had begun a concerted attack and now would obviously not mind continuing it. It was necessary to take up defensive positions.

A boring, long-winded, futile discussion started. I think G. E. Lvov, inevitably, answered first: Aggressive designs? Come, come! How was it possible to think of conquests? After all, enormous areas of our native soil were occupied by the enemy. The workers' and soldiers' deputies were actually trying to force an open door: really, you couldn't tell what they wanted from the Government. . .

Speeches like this, whose sense was of course clear to all of us—regardless of tendency!—took up a lot of time. Finally it simply had to be explained that what was necessary was a public document. And for that document to say that from now on Russia's only aims would be defence against aggressors. If that was true, and even a matter of course, then it would be all the easier to comply with our request.

When it came to Miliukov's turn he flatly, clearly, and categorically declared that he could not publish such a document and would not sign it. But Miliukov's colleagues looked on the matter differently. Another long discussion started, plainly exposing a serious split in the Cabinet. Some Ministers, without mincing words, argued against Miliukov and said that on the contrary such a document was perfectly possible and that the Council of Ministers would debate the question.

Finally we separated on the understanding that the Government would have a debate on this question and probably give us an answer the very next day. But the split in the first revolutionary Cabinet was by that time a reality and demanded attention.

In our circles the disagreements that had begun were already quite well known. Kerensky and Nekrasov had disavowed Miliukov's statement on foreign policy in print. Of course it couldn't have been otherwise: the question of war aims could not help being the most immediate source of discord within the Government: it was the natural expression of the various tendencies on this question in the various groups of the bourgeoisie.

In general, Miliukov's rabid imperialism was bound to arouse discontent amongst the propertied classes themselves; for in view of the setting of revolutionary upheaval and destruction, the unreliability of the army and the possibility of defeat—the problem of the Dardanelles and Armenia naturally began to seem to many 'untimely and out of place'.

Within the Cabinet there arose an opposition to Miliukov that included the majority of the Ministers. A Left group of seven was formed (against the Cadets and Guchkov) consisting of both Lvovs, Kerensky, Nekrasov, Tereshchenko, Konovalov, and Godnev. These seven immediately set about preparing the document we had demanded, even though it was against Miliukov.

On Sunday the 26th we got an invitation to be good enough to go to the Marian Palace in the evening, for a discussion of 'the question touched on last time'. We went, and were told that the Council of Ministers, on mature reflection, considered it possible to gratify the Ex. Com.'s wish and had already composed a draft document publicly denying all aggressive designs on the part of Russia. And indeed Premier Lvov read out an address from the Provisional Government to the citizens of Russia. The Government had determined to tell the people the whole truth frankly and straightforwardly. This 'truth' was contained in the following statement on war aims:

'The Provisional Government considers it its right and duty to declare now that the ideal of free Russia is not rule over other peoples, nor the seizure of their national property, but the establishment of a stable peace based on national self-determination. *However, the Russian people will not allow its homeland to emerge from the great struggle humbled and with its vital energies sapped.* These principles will underlie the foreign policy of the Provisional Government, unswervingly guiding the people's will and guarding the rights of our fatherland, while the obligations undertaken towards our Allies will be fully observed.'

The document passed from hand to hand; we began commenting on it. To my satisfaction there was no substantial disagreement in our estimate of it. My doubts of course had centred on Tsereteli, but he, although cautiously, said the document was unsatisfactory, adding that the Soviet would not be able to launch a campaign around such a document; it could not give the Soviet firm ground for its appeals for the supreme defence of the front, and made no direct allusions to the renunciation of annexations or of foreign territory. If that was bound up with existing Allied treaties then the document ought to refer to the necessity of a revision and a corresponding communication to the Allies. . .

This time Miliukov wanted to be more of a diplomat than the last time, when he went no further than a direct refusal to comply with our request. Now, in reply to Tsereteli, he made a statement to which I draw the reader's attention (I shall remind him of it later):

'I have in mind', Miliukov said, 'some such address to the Allies concerning a revision of the treaties. Just now I consider the moment unfavourable, but I see no obstacle to taking this step shortly.'

Another boring, fruitless, purely verbal polemic began. The document was in fact completely unsatisfactory; it naïvely sidestepped the problem and retained the usual hypocritical statements of all Governments at war. If it had been an object of contention within the Council of Ministers, the victory had been entirely Miliukov's. The majority of the Cabinet—the 'Left Seven'—had suffered a rout. Either Miliukov had been able to palm off on his colleagues a worthless scrap of paper instead of the valuable document they wanted, or else he had been able to convince them that a genuine renunciation of annexations was quite undesirable and that it was necessary to join forces and palm off this worthless scrap of paper on the Soviet. The second alternative is the more likely: the Left Seven probably constituted a rather feeble opposition to Miliukov, and there had evidently been no serious struggle in the Cabinet because of this document. In any case the Cabinet was completely united in defending its proclamation.

Primarily the Government proclamation to the people was not aimed at all at informing Europe, but was issued for domestic use. Then, not only did it not include any definite reference to the refusal of annexations, but it contained harmful allusions of another order. Defence was flatly declared to be not the sole, but the 'primary', aim of the war; a joint programme with the Allies was underlined twice. Nothing was left but a form of words—which gave rise to this small incident in the meeting:

THE SOVIETS MEET IN THE DUMA CHAMBER

MARTOV AND DAN

SIEGE OF THE TELEPHONE EXCHANGE
in the October Revolution

Wishing to illustrate the complete futility of the hackneyed phrases about Russia's not wanting 'sovereignty over others' or 'the enslavement of anyone' or 'the seizure of national property', I referred to Nicholas II's manifesto on the declaration of war. 'God sees', I quoted, 'that it is not for the sake of vain worldly glory, not for the sake of violence and oppression that we have taken up arms, but solely to defend the Russian State', etc.

I had barely finished my quotation when Tereshchenko bounded from his seat and began a high-flown speech, pretending to be profoundly upset and wounded in his finest feelings:

'What! In this room, people allow themselves to insult the Ministers of the revolution by comparing them with Nicholas II! It is absolutely intolerable. And I refuse to stay here in such circumstances!'

And in fact Tereshchenko rushed tempestuously out of the room, even slamming the door slightly. But it must be said that none of those present paid any attention to this, and the debate went on. After walking around the Palace, without seeing anyone sent after him and despairing of any satisfaction, Tereshchenko soon came back and took part in the discussion as before. The young diplomat's trick had failed.

Around midnight a servant reported that Chkheidze was being asked for on the 'phone. He was away about ten minutes. Skobelev, who was perhaps worried, went out after him. Chkheidze came back walking peculiarly and staring strangely at a fixed point with unseeing eyes. It appeared that his son, a boy of fifteen or sixteen, had just shot himself accidentally. The meeting continued. I think Chkheidze had been told the wound wasn't mortal but he evidently didn't believe it.

The meeting closed with the Soviet delegates unanimously declaring the document unsatisfactory. It was clear to the Ministers that the Ex. Com. could have no other opinion.

* * *

On March 27th the Ex. Com. debated the document. Chkheidze was at his post; we tried to leave him alone. He gave up the chairmanship but stayed in the Palace. Tsereteli, in contrast to his speeches of the night before, energetically tried to gloss things over. In the 'enemy's' camp it was one thing, but at home, when your opponents were sitting not Right but Left, it was quite different. During all those months Tsereteli had no opponents to the Right in the Soviet. From his very first appearance he consolidated the entire Soviet Right wing around his own special Siberian 'Zimmerwaldism', just as from the very first thunder-claps of the revolution the entire bourgeoisie, together with the landowners, was consolidated in the 'Left' party of the Cadets.

Tsereteli insisted that the document merely lacked clarity and a few concrete touches. If they were put in, the request of the democracy could be considered as fulfilled and a great victory as attained. But nevertheless in its present form Tsereteli did not defend the document unreservedly.

Indeed, that no doubt would have been rather too difficult. It was not a question of the document alone but of the rapid crystallization of democratic public opinion around the question of aggressive policy. The evening before, while we and Tsereteli were at the conference in the Marian Palace, an enormous meeting of the organization of the Petersburg Mensheviks had been going on, devoted to the war question, and the Zimmerwald tendency was on top.

And it was not only the Social-Democrats—someone at the Populist Socialist conference (in Moscow, March 23–25) decided to demand the renunciation of conquests. In these circumstances to defend the document of the night before in its present version would have meant an excessive readiness to compromise oneself, with no practical benefits.

The Ex. Com. said the document was unsatisfactory. The Left interestedly watched the new Right majority plunge into dejection and alarm. What was the next step? It was obvious that a new attack from the Left was inevitable.

However, the situation was resolved in another way. Tsereteli (in person!) was called to the telephone from the Marian Palace and told that a new version of the document was being sent at once to the Tauride Palace. The Government was making concessions. Miliukov could do this with no great damage. But the Right wing was so suspiciously triumphant that its attitude towards the new version of the document seemed to have been decided on beforehand. And indeed the Right majority was confronted by these alternatives: either to lead the proletariat in exerting real pressure, i.e., to begin a *struggle*, or to be satisfied by *any* wording and carry on a policy of compromise.

A packet was brought in and opened solemnly and with considerable excitement. The document contained an insertion of six words, underlined with red pencil. After the statement of what was *not* the aim of the war—no 'sovereignty', no 'annexation'—there was added: 'no violent seizure of foreign territory'. The rest remained as before.

The renunciation of conquests was set down in black and white. Nothing more had been demanded. The matter was finished. By a majority decision the document of March 27th was recognized as a great democratic victory and a long step forward in the cause of peace.

Of course, in spite of the subjective falseness of this document, objectively it was something of a concession on the part of imperialism and a certain achievement for the democracy. As it was the first action of this kind since the very beginning of the war (by any of the Powers at war) it created a new situation for further struggle. But its entire significance consisted precisely in this, that it was the starting point for further demands that arose logically; and to retain any value for this document of March 27th an immediate mobilization of forces for further action was essential.

I remember that I left the Tauride Palace that same evening of the 27th for a meeting of collaborators on the *Novaya Zhizn*, which had still not appeared. There I told them of the new document, the new situation—and there it was all received with just such conditional approval. The document of March 27th was a 'victory'.

Alas! It was in truth a Pyrrhic victory. The attitude of our new Right majority to this success bore eloquent witness of this. And this was precisely the root of the matter.

The Soviet majority had passed off this success, trivial in essence, as a major victory, and puffed it up amongst the masses. The anti-Zimmerwald majority's attitude towards the March 27th document undermined any further struggle for peace.

That was one side of the matter—the most important. But also not devoid of importance is the circumstance that the democracy was by no means indebted for the victory of March 27th to the pressure of the masses, who were not only not involved in the struggle but were not even informed of it. We owed the victory of March 27th to the tactics of peaceful compromise with the Government. Consequently, from then on the method of 'peaceful conciliation'—as opposed to appeals to the masses and the method of struggle—could be considered as approved and raised to the level of the sole rational and specifically Soviet method of action. In these conditions the March 27th 'victory' was perhaps even worse than a Pyrrhic victory. It not only tore the 'victor' away from his troops, but also propelled the 'victorious' chariot into the impenetrable swamp of opportunism and 'conciliationism'.

Only one fundamental question remains: had there really taken shape already a petty-bourgeois, opportunist majority, ready to liquidate the March 14th Manifesto and desirous of sweeping away all the previously planned foundations of Soviet peace policy and subsequently the whole projected course of the revolution?

Anyone who doubts this will find proof of it in the facts spoken of later on. But is it impossible to believe it *a priori*? Had the previous struggle of the Soviet Zimmerwaldites for the triumph of the proletarian class line in our revolution not been utopian? Was it possible for a muzhik-soldier, middle-class-intellectual majority *not* to take shape in the Soviet organs, which represented the whole democracy? This, after all, followed from the laws of history, the petty-bourgeois, peasant structure of our country, the national character of the revolution, and from the appearance in its foreground, from the very first moment, of the muzhik-soldier.

The formation of the new Soviet majority was inevitable. But that by no means implies that the task of peace-making was beyond the capacity of this petty-bourgeois majority. The task of peace-making could have been accomplished by a bloc, by the united front of the petty-bourgeois and proletarian masses against the imperialist bourgeoisie. Therefore even the struggle for a Zimmerwald line in the Soviet was not utopian or foredoomed to disaster. No, it was merely infinitely difficult, and evidently beyond the ability of those who actually took part in the struggle.

So let us not lose our tempers with the laws of history. Let us, however, be just towards those who suffered defeat in an unequal struggle for the only correct course of the revolution.

CHAPTER 11

FINALE OF THE UNITED DEMOCRATIC FRONT

AN All-Russian Congress of Soviets had been talked about for a long time now. The necessity for it was evident. To be sure, the usurpation by the Petersburg Soviet of the rights and functions of an all-Russian democratic organ had been recognized by everyone to be historically inevitable, and had not been censured by a single democratic organization. It was only the Government, in the Liaison Commission, who missed no opportunity to expose the inadequacy of our mandate. Nevertheless it was clear to everyone that an all-Russian parade of Soviets, a display of the will of the whole democracy, and the creation of a permanent, all-Russian, plenipotentiary Soviet organ, could not be postponed.

For some days the Ex. Com. had been intensifying its preparations for the Congress.

The burning questions, of course, were the war and the relationship to the Government, that is, the general character of Soviet policy, domestic and foreign.

But the Congress of Soviets didn't come off in March. Though there were about 400 provincial delegates, representing eighty-two cities and the Ex. Coms. of the armies and other military units, and the Cossack Congress had also sent eleven of its representatives, the organizing committee of the Congress (headed by Bogdanov) still considered a Congress like this incomplete and without full powers: according to its information there was still an enormous number of local Soviets which for various reasons hadn't sent their representatives. So the committee decided to consider the March Congress not a plenipotentiary Congress of Soviets, but a preliminary All-Russian Conference.

The Conference was supposed to open in the morning of the 28th, and start work at once. But of course that didn't happen. 'Grandma' Breshkovskaya had at last finished her triumphal progress, through flowers and among excited throngs of people, from Siberia to Petersburg. She had arrived in the Tauride Palace from the station, with a guard of honour consisting of Kerensky, Nekrasov, and Chkheidze.

The Praesidium was elected, and Chkheidze's speech of welcome was heard, but then the meeting had to break up until the evening. The funeral of Chkheidze's son had been fixed for 4 o'clock. The meeting, standing, saw the chairman out in deep silence, and many followed him.

There were fewer people at the funeral than might have been expected, but there were many flags and a solemn orchestra. On the stairs to Chkheidze's apartment I caught a glimpse of a well-known, round, beardless face, with a firm, chilly expression. But who this compact, short officer, already well on in years, was, I simply couldn't guess. With the constant changing from civilian to military dress and back again, these familiar strangers had now become a usual phenomenon. Nevertheless this disturbed me; finally it dawned on me. Why, it was—Dan![1] He also had returned from exile, where he had been mobilized as a physician.

I had met Dan only a few times—in 1914, before the war, when he contributed one or two articles to the *Sovremennik*, and during the days of the Austrian ultimatum to Serbia, after my banishment from Petersburg, when Dan visited me in Terioki and coldly laughed at all those who believed in the possibility of a world war. A week later the war was already a fact and Dan was being sent to Siberia under guard.

In Siberia, according to the rumours which reached me, Dan had taken up a Zimmerwald position and was even, they said, extremely Left. . . Martov had inquired from abroad why I didn't invite him to contribute to the *Letopis*.

Dan was one of the very biggest figures of the Russian Revolution, and one of the most distinguished personalities both of the Russian working-class movement and of the events of

[1] Dan (Gurvich), Fyodor Ilyich (1871–1947): a physician by profession, joined the Social-Democratic movement in Petersburg in 1896. An *émigré* from 1901 on, and active collaborator on *Iskra* (see p. 354), but afterwards permanent member of the Menshevik Central Committee and editor of all Menshevik papers and publications. After the October Revolution he was repeatedly harassed and in 1922 was exiled. He was an editor of the Menshevik *Sotsialisticheskii Vestnik* (Socialist Courier). While in emigration, he broke with the official Menshevik 'majority' in 1940. He died in New York City. (Ed.)

1917. Like Tsereteli he will occupy a good deal of our attention. His arrival at that time might of course strongly influence events. And rumours about his position aroused the most joyful hopes. Very welcome! There was only one question: wasn't this 'Siberian' Zimmerwaldism something peculiar?

* * *

The sections of the Conference began to work on the morning of the 30th. I was forced into the agrarian section, which was full of nothing but soldiers. I left without entering into the useless wrangling.

In the corridor Kamenev showed me a Bolshevik resolution on the war, which was of course doomed to defeat. It appeared to me that the Zimmerwaldites ought to vote for this resolution, and to do it to make clear the relative voting strength of the two sides. But there was a suspicious point in the resolution, to the effect that the imperialist war could be ended only with the transfer of political power to the working class. Did this mean that the struggle for peace was not necessary at that moment? Or did it mean that it was necessary, but that therefore political power had to be taken into one's own hands at once? Kamenev assured me that it meant neither the one nor the other. But he responded extremely evasively to the suggestion that this point be altered, and tried to eliminate the misunderstanding by his remarks alone. Meanwhile everyone who had read this resolution maintained that the Bolsheviks were demanding political power for the working class. Where did the truth lie?

Kamenev, giving a 'benevolent' interpretation of the resolution, was doubtless trying dutifully to retain in it the official Bolshevik idea: that the conclusion of the imperialist war was only possible by way of a Socialist revolution. But I also had no doubt that Kamenev didn't sympathize with this official Bolshevik idea, considered it unrealistic, and was trying to follow a line of genuine struggle for peace in the concrete circumstances of the moment. All the actions of the then leader of the Bolshevik party had just this kind of 'possibilist', sometimes too moderate, character. His position was ambiguous, and not easy. He had his own views, and was working on Russian revolutionary soil. But—he was casting a 'sideways' look abroad, where they had *their* own views, which were not quite the same as his.

I know very well that I'm running the risk of compromising this exalted dignitary in the eyes of his exalted colleagues, but I cannot conceal my deep conviction that if all the Bolsheviks had shared Kamenev's views—at least during the first year of the revolution—then I would have been a Bolshevik too, and a Left one at that.

* * *

Meeting Tsereteli once again on my way out of the Tauride Palace, I began to talk to him of my false position as an official speaker for the Ex. Com. I said something by way of illustration of my Left attitude towards the Provisional Government, but he interrupted me: 'Of course you'll have to talk about the necessity of a compromise with the bourgeoisie. There can be no other road for the revolution. It's true that we have all the power, and that the Government would go if we lifted a finger, but that would mean disaster for the revolution.'

Where was this ill-fated Zimmerwaldite headed for—this really fateful figure of the revolution?

* * *

Plekhanov[1] was arriving the evening of the 31st, and the Ex. Com. organized a triumphal welcome. Instead of the usual work of the Conference a ceremonial meeting was arranged in the People's House[2] between delegates from the provinces and front and the Petersburg Soviet. Plekhanov was expected to go to it from the station.

I didn't go to the station—I really don't know why, but very possibly for 'fractional' reasons: I looked on Plekhanov's arrival with some hostility, fearing his harmful rôle in future events. I had no doubt that it would be worthy of him—both quantita-

[1] Plekhanov, Georgii Valentinovich (1856–1918): a founder of the Group for the Emancipation of Labour, the first Russian Marxist organization. The first Russian commentator on Karl Marx; in the 'nineties, under the pseudonyms of Volgin and Beltov, he published the first Marxist books in Russia, which exercised a great influence on youth and for the first time created cadres of Russian Marxists. Editor of *Iskra* (see p. 354) and *Zarya* (Dawn) in 1900. An ideological adversary of Populism. A defensist during the First World War and hostile to the October Revolution. Died of tuberculosis. (Ed.)

[2] Founded by the Temperance Society to provide cheap-priced shows for poor people. Very popular in plebeian circles. During the revolution it was used for very large mass-meetings. (Ed.)

tively and qualitatively. Regardless of how high an opinion I might have had of Plekhanov, I felt alien to the present triumphal occasion.

I went straight to the People's House, and found a miserable spectacle. The vast half-dark theatre looked empty, although the whole Soviet, together with the Conference members submerged in it, was seated in the vast amphitheatre, dress-circle, and stalls, while a few anonymous soldiers from the Ex. Com., who were also directing the meeting, were sitting in the Praesidium on the stage.

There were greetings from the provinces—an infinite series. They were intolerably boring to everyone; but the meeting had nothing to do and the soldier who was chairman kept calling on one new speaker after another and asking whether there wasn't anyone else who wanted to greet the Petersburg Soviet. There was a depressing feeling that the Soviet had been completely abandoned by its leaders. Neither the Praesidium nor its usual substitutes from the Ex. Com. were present—and there were no reports and no agenda. There were only the 'rank and file'—with no 'command', which was off somewhere attending to business of its own.

But finally, after innumerable speeches of welcome at the station, Plekhanov appeared from behind the hangings on the stage. Chkheidze introduced him with several not very coherent but very warm phrases. There followed a noisy ovation which died away in the expectation that Plekhanov would say something to the meeting. But Plekhanov, exhausted by the journey and the welcomes of the commanders at the station, stood motionless in his fur coat at the back of the stage, and didn't say a word. The Soviet dispersed in silence and not in a very good mood.

Alas! This spectacle of a Soviet meeting aroused gloomy thoughts of the most general character. This isolation of the Soviet 'command' from the Soviet 'mass' was shown not only on individual occasions or in individual meetings. It had already begun to be felt generally. These 'technical' misunderstandings were henceforth a chronic phenomenon; time after time, when the Soviet assembled there was nobody to take the chair, nobody to speak on announced questions, or simply nothing to 'occupy' the Soviet with. Then the technique got better.

Chkheidze invariably took the chair, and people were organized to report to the meeting.

But the trouble was that the source of the evil did not lie in the 'technique' alone. At that time, by the end of March, the absence of any inner contact with the ranks could already be felt. Here was the beginning of the fatal split which later revealed itself.

The matter was perhaps not so much the isolation of the Ex. Com. from the Soviet, the workers' and soldiers' deputies. That fissure—among the leaders—was still kept plastered over somehow for a long time. But at this moment there were signs of dissension or lack of solder between the dominant Soviet spheres and the real masses of the Petersburg proletariat and garrison. The more observant Ex. Com. members had already realized this, the blind ones ignored it to the end. If they had not, perhaps the end would not have been so shameful for the new Soviet majority.

* * *

I think the next morning, in my absence, Plekhanov paid a visit to the Ex. Com. This was apparently his first and last visit to leading Soviet circles. Against my expectations, illness prevented him from assuming a worthy place in the Soviet and the revolution. Perhaps it was not illness alone that hindered him: there was such a sharp dividing line between Plekhanov's position and that of the Soviet that Plekhanov may have thought he had to keep away from this alien institution. I think myself that from the time of the formation of the new majority this dividing line was much less sharp: it was undoubtedly much sharper between Mamelukes and Bolsheviks. Nevertheless, the new majority also showed no inclination towards any contact with Plekhanov: it did not want to compromise itself in the eyes of the masses. It had the right idea: things may be done, but they needn't be publicized.

Plekhanov's part in the events of 1917 was limited to his writings in a tiny, little-read and completely uninfluential paper, *Yedinstvo* (Unity). His adherents constituted a small group, not represented in the Soviet precisely because of their complete negligibility.

Together with Plekhanov there had arrived some well-known and long-awaited guests—the French and British delegations:

Cachin, Moutet, Lafont, O'Grady, Thorne and Sanders.[1] We had not only been expecting them for a long time, but had heard a great deal about them. And not of a favourable kind. However honourable and well-meaning they were as citizens, or however convinced as Socialists, for us—not only for the Zimmerwaldites, but also for our Soviet defensists—these British and French representatives were really delegates from the Allied Governments and agents of Anglo-French imperialism. We were sufficiently informed of their chauvinism and their important, extremely harmful rôle in their own countries and in the working-class movement, or rather in the struggle against the working-class movement in Great Britain and France during the war.

Among other things Martov had sent us a description of these Allied parliamentary Socialists from abroad, warning the Soviet against them. But even without that we were very much on our guard.

For it was clear that these visitors had come not to express their feelings about the Russian Revolution, or to hail it, or to fraternize or learn something at first hand. Their principal aim was to agitate amongst us against German despotism, using the authority of 'more mature comrades', and to draw us into an alliance with Ribot[2] and Lloyd George in a struggle for right and justice. This was why they had been sent to Petersburg, having been selected out of the entire Socialist and working-class world of the Allied countries, as the best and most reliable from the point of view of their rulers. The others were not only not sent, but were not even *allowed* to greet the Russian Revolution.

Their 'pressure' was hopeless. We felt ourselves to be too strong, both by conviction and by authority. The 'Allied' visitors, not being friends, did not appear to us to be even worthy opponents, but rather tiresome emissaries to the victorious Russian Revolution from the frightened Allied bourgeoisie. We had no respect for them; their rôle seemed to us wretched and disagreeable.

The day after their arrival the guests paid a visit to the Ex. Com. The nervous, excitable Frenchmen and the heavy,

[1] Socialists who supported the First World War, either participating in their respective governments or backing them. (Ed.)

[2] French Premier. (Ed.)

impenetrable Englishmen were accompanied by their compatriots from the embassies. They were received in silence. They had come that day only for greetings, which were met with applause that was more than reserved, that was no more than polite. Cachin spoke for the French, O'Grady for the British. They were answered very well by Chkheidze, who took a very firm line on the tasks of the Russian Revolution in the achievement of peace. Chkheidze's speech was demonstratively greeted with lengthy applause.

One must assume that even before their visit our guests had been adequately informed of the prevailing moods in the Soviet. Now they could familiarize themselves thoroughly with the background—for their forthcoming 'business'. The volatile, smiling Frenchmen were already carrying on private conversations and getting to know people. For the time being they did nothing but pay compliments. The English were unable to do this, both by character and for linguistic reasons.

The audience did not last long, in spite of the translation of every speech. The guests were conducted to the door with every courtesy and we went back to our routine business. They doubtless left reflecting on the difficulty of their task: how, indeed, was the ice to be broken?

* * *

Around midnight Chkheidze, Dan, and I went home in a car from work in the Tauride Palace. I was going to a friend's in Peski: as before I seldom had a chance to see my home.

'Look, what's that? What's that!' Chkheidze cried suddenly, putting his head out of the window.

A crowd was standing in the street with lighted candles in their hands; we could hear singing, and the ringing of bells. 'Why, it's—Easter! The Easter service is beginning!'

All of us, especially the utterly exhausted Chkheidze, felt like celebrating and relaxing, but for the time being we had to keep on working, making no distinction between day and night, and not only not observing holidays but not even aware of them.

* * *

On Easter Sunday, April 2nd, Plekhanov and the foreign visitors turned up at the meeting of the Congress. Chkheidze, on this non-business and merely ceremonial occasion, greeted the guests much more warmly than the day before.

Cachin spoke brilliantly, briefly, powerfully, with fire, passion, and unfeigned enthusiasm. His tempestuous French eloquence, his hymn to the great revolution, revived the romance of its first days and captured the meeting. O'Grady spoke after Cachin, with a different colouring but with the same sincerity, which made him—among other things—think of God, to whom the 'working class of the whole world, their children and descendants for many generations, would pray and offer thanks for the present Russian generation and its great work'. The guests were thanked noisily and at length for their warm words.

Chkheidze then introduced Plekhanov. In the present mood of the Congress a friendly reception was certain—and the small Bolshevik section, led by Kamenev, played their full part in honouring the father of Russian Social-Democracy.

Plekhanov spoke with enthusiasm, wit and—great tact. He could not of course avoid the painful problems that had deprived him of his standing even among his own disciples. But with great skill he skirted the most dangerous reefs, softened the angles, went half-way to meet his critics, and—convinced his audience.

The ovation was renewed. Plekhanov took the Frenchman and the Englishman by the hand, wishing to represent—the united front of international Socialism in the bosom of the victorious revolution. Alas! Here there was not even a feeble semblance of it. But the atmosphere in the White Hall was festive and friendly.

The following day, April 3rd, Plekhanov made a new speech by way of bringing the Congress to a conclusion. He saw in the Congress a guarantee of the correct course of the revolution; he welcomed the decisions taken—especially the 'golden words about the war'; he called upon it to keep to the course embarked on, and not to waver.

Evil omens!

The Conference was over. It had not been able to ensure a united front of the democracy against bourgeois reaction and imperialism. But it had done all a Congress could do: it had proclaimed the united front and called on the forces of democracy to rally around the Soviet in the fight to strengthen the revolution.

More than this: the March Congress rallied the democracy around the proletarian platform of Zimmerwald. The principles of Zimmerwald, to be sure, were already evaporating from Soviet *practice*. But the decisions of the Congress still preserved the *spirit* of international class solidarity and class struggle. In the eyes of the Social-patriotic[1] working-class masses of Europe this was of unquestionable significance. And the prestige of the Russian Revolution, bearing in its hands the banner of peace, was high in the eyes of the international proletariat.

But the Congress was also fruitful in other respects. It officially formulated and confirmed in the name of the all-Russian democracy the most immediate programme of the revolution. This programme was expressed in three words—peace, land, and bread.

It was the most immediate minimum programme; and it was an *indispensable* programme, which the revolution could not help fulfilling as long as it continued to be a revolution and was not liquidated by reactionary forces.

Land—this was the age-old, unchanging cry of the 'lord of the Russian earth', the peasantry, the overwhelming majority of the Russian democracy, and the entire population of the country. *Bread* was the immutable demand of the vanguard, the leader of the revolution and its mainstay—the proletariat; it meant first a minimum living standard for the worker in the conditions of the victory he had achieved; and second the regulation of the national economy, without which bread would be unobtainable.

But the first and most important slogan of the revolution was *peace*. If the revolution didn't finish the war, the war would strangle the revolution. We knew beforehand that a dragging on of the war would deprive the people of bread, land, and the whole revolution; it would mean the destruction of the national economy, hunger, shortage of goods, reaction among the peasants, and the triumph of the counter-revolution.

[1] Words like Social-traitor, Social-patriotic, Social-chauvinist, Social-lackey, etc. refer to Socialists whose sincerity as Socialists is doubted by whoever is using the word, and whose essential political traits are considered summed up in the second half of the hyphenated word. (Ed.)

But it was clear that peace was also the most urgent demand of the country as a whole, for the revolution itself had come as a reaction against the unprecedented burden of the war. The poor, backward, disorganized country, oppressed by Tsarism, could not endure the war, and it must have been obvious even to our nationalists that ending it as soon as possible was the surest way of really defending the country.

But certain strata of the bourgeoisie were definitely trying to buy the destruction of the revolution at the price of a military catastrophe. And they were leading along not only broad bourgeois, liberal, and radical *milieux* but also democratic, Soviet petty-bourgeois strata in their struggle against the proletarian Zimmerwald line, which was the prop not only of the working-class International but also of genuine Russian patriotism. Such was the will of fate. . .

Peace, land, and bread—that was the goal. A resolute struggle for them—that was the means. The united democratic front—that was the guarantee of victory. The March Congress of Soviets planned this correctly and formulated it clearly. It would be unjust to harbour resentment against it.

But . . . the aims, of course, remained unshakeable. Readiness for the struggle? Plekhanov's parting words, and the hopes he expressed, in view of the whole context of the Congress—did not inspire much optimism. As for the united front, well——

* * *

That same day, April 3rd, the Ex. Com. was informed that Lenin was arriving from abroad that evening. An honourable welcome had to be arranged for the honoured exile. Tsereteli was chosen to represent the Soviet, but he absolutely refused. There was nothing to be done: it was unpleasant, and even somewhat strange—but the Praesidium, Skobelev and Chkheidze, had to go to the station.

It was already getting on towards evening, and time to start for the station. I decided to go too. Papa Chkheidze, the 'party hanger-on', raising his eye-brows, wagged his head afflictedly.

April–July 1919.

Part III

THE FORMATION OF A UNITED FRONT OF THE BIG AND PETTY BOURGEOISIE

April 3rd–May 5th

CHAPTER 12

LENIN'S ARRIVAL

THE throng in front of the Finland Station blocked the whole square, making movement almost impossible and scarcely letting the trams through. The innumerable red flags were dominated by a magnificent banner embroidered in gold: 'The Central Committee of the R.S.-D.W.P. (Bolsheviks)'.[1] Troops with bands were drawn up under the red flags near the side entrance, in the former imperial waiting-rooms.

There was a throbbing of many motor-cars. In two or three places the awe-inspiring outlines of armoured cars thrust up from the crowd. And from one of the side-streets there moved out on to the square, startling the mob and cutting through it, a strange monster—a mounted searchlight, which abruptly projected upon the bottomless void of the darkness tremendous strips of the living city, the roofs, many-storeyed houses, columns, wires, tramways, and human figures.

Various delegations that had failed to penetrate into the station had found places on the steps of the main entrance and were vainly trying to retain their composure and keep their places in hand-to-hand struggles with the 'private' public. Lenin's train was expected around 11.

There was a crush inside the station—more delegations, more flags, and sentries at every step demanding special authority for going any further. The title of member of the Ex. Com., however, appeased the most conscientious watchdogs, and through the mass of discontentedly grumbling people tightly packed together I made my way right through the station to a platform, and towards the Tsar's waiting-room, where a dejected Chkheidze sat, weary of the long wait and reacting sluggishly to Skobelev's witticisms. The whole square was clearly visible

[1] i.e., The Russian Social-Democratic Workers' Party (Bolsheviks). After the Russian Social-Democratic Party split into Mensheviks and Bolsheviks in 1903, both groups remained in the same party as fractions until 1912, when the Bolsheviks established a separate organization and simply added the word 'Bolsheviks' to distinguish themselves from the Mensheviks. The actual *programme*, however, remained the same until the Bolsheviks constituted themselves the Communist Party after the revolution. (Ed.)

through the heavily bolted glass doors of the 'imperial' waiting-room; the scene was extraordinarily impressive. 'Delegates' were enviously clinging to the outside of the windows, and discontented women's voices could be heard: 'Party people have to wait in the street, while they let people inside that nobody ever saw before!'

But the indignation was scarcely well-founded: I don't recall seeing any 'public', at all well known in politics, science, or literature, that was not Bolshevik. The parties hadn't sent their official representatives; indeed, of the Soviet people or Ex. Com. members, besides the Praesidium, specially detailed to go, I think there was only myself. In any case there weren't more than three or four people in the 'imperial' rooms besides ourselves, since the local Bolshevik commanders had gone to meet Lenin in Finland. While we were waiting for Lenin at the station, he in the train was already familiarizing himself thoroughly with the state of affairs from 'immediate sources'.

I passed along the platform. There it was even more festive than in the square. Its whole length was lined with people, mostly soldiers ready to 'present A-a-a-r-m-s!' Banners hung across the platform at every step; triumphal arches had been set up, adorned with red and gold; one's eyes were dazzled by every possible welcoming inscription and revolutionary slogan, while at the end of the platform, where the carriage was expected to stop, there was a band, and a group of representatives of the central Bolshevik organizations stood holding flowers.

The Bolsheviks, who shone at organization, and always aimed at emphasizing externals and putting on a good show, had dispensed with any superfluous modesty and were plainly preparing a real triumphal entry.

This time, however, they had a special reason for making a point of presenting Lenin to the Petersburg masses as a real hero. Lenin was travelling to Russia *via* Germany, in a sealed train, by the special favour of the enemy Government. Even though this was the only way for Lenin to return to his country, it was clear that the bourgeoisie and all its hangers-on would make appropriate use of it. And something had to be done to counterbalance the repulsive campaign that was already under way.

There is no doubt that without the services of the German

Government there was not the slightest possibility of getting back to Russia for all those comrades whom the police of the 'Great Democracies' chose to place in the 'defeatist' category. As early as April 11th, almost a month before his arrival, Martov informed the Ex. Com. that he had exhausted all his means, and that if the most radical steps weren't taken, then he and a group of his followers would be compelled to 'seek special means of entry'. Up to the beginning of May no agreement with the Allies had been reached by our revolutionary authorities and the Menshevik group was compelled, like Lenin, to travel in a sealed train.

Everyone understood that in meeting the interests of these Russian citizens half-way the Germans were pursuing their own interests exclusively: they were, of course, gambling on the Russian internationalists' undermining the foundations of Russian imperialism, wrenching Russia away from the Allied pirates and pushing her into a separate peace. The Russian *émigré* internationalists were fully aware of the intentions of the German authorities.

First of all, however, the aims of the Russian internationalists had by their nature nothing in common with those of German imperialism; and those of our *émigrés* who had come through Germany later showed this—by the whole character of their propaganda and their attitude towards a separate peace. Since they hadn't a semblance of an agreement with the German authorities and hadn't assumed any moral obligations in advance, the emigrant internationalists had every right to ignore with a clear conscience the speculations of the Berlin régime.

Secondly, when Allied and domestic imperialism resolutely denied Russian citizens their perfectly legitimate rights and restricted the political freedom achieved by the revolution, there was nothing for them to do but resort to the services of German imperialism or else completely renounce their just rights.

The passage through Germany was harmful, since the sealed train was bound to come under the attack of the yellow bourgeois press and incited philistia, but it was less harmful than a refusal by the Socialist party leaders to take any part in world events and their languishing abroad, as in the sombre days of Tsarist reaction.

When the reports about the first emigrant train through Germany reached the Ex. Com., it caused great regret; many thought the step a mistake, but only a few individuals condemned it. In spite of the fact that only Lenin (odious to the majority) was involved for the time being, the Ex. Com., though aware of all the ticklishness of the situation, nevertheless did not hesitate to cover the sealed train with its authority and turn its weapons against the policies of the Government, the bourgeoisie bristling with malice, and the rabble.

* * *

These were the themes, among others, that Skobelev, Chkheidze, and myself discussed during the tiresome wait, finding ourselves generally in accord. We waited for a long time. The train was very late.

But at long last it arrived. A thunderous *Marseillaise* boomed forth on the platform, and shouts of welcome rang out. We stayed in the imperial waiting-rooms while the Bolshevik generals exchanged greetings. Then we heard them marching along the platform, under the triumphal arches, to the sound of the band, and between the rows of welcoming troops and workers. The gloomy Chkheidze, and the rest of us after him, got up, went to the middle of the room, and prepared for the meeting. And what a meeting it was, worthy of—more than my wretched pen!

Shlyapnikov, acting as master of ceremonies, appeared in the doorway, portentously hurrying, with the air of a faithful old police chief announcing the Governor's arrival. Without any apparent necessity he kept crying out fussily: 'Please, Comrades, please! Make way there! Comrades, make way!'

Behind Shlyapnikov, at the head of a small cluster of people behind whom the door slammed again at once, Lenin came, or rather ran, into the room. He wore a round cap, his face looked frozen, and there was a magnificent bouquet in his hands. Running to the middle of the room, he stopped in front of Chkheidze as though colliding with a completely unexpected obstacle. And Chkheidze, still glum, pronounced the following 'speech of welcome' with not only the spirit and wording but also the tone of a sermon:

'Comrade Lenin, in the name of the Petersburg Soviet and of

the whole revolution we welcome you to Russia. . . But—we think that the principal task of the revolutionary democracy is now the defence of the revolution from any encroachments either from within or from without. We consider that what this goal requires is not disunion, but the closing of the democratic ranks. We hope you will pursue these goals together with us.'

Chkheidze stopped speaking. I was dumbfounded with surprise: really, what attitude could be taken to this 'welcome' and to that delicious 'But——'?

But Lenin plainly knew exactly how to behave. He stood there as though nothing taking place had the slightest connexion with him—looking about him, examining the persons round him and even the ceiling of the imperial waiting-room, adjusting his bouquet (rather out of tune with his whole appearance), and then, turning away from the Ex. Com. delegation altogether, he made this 'reply':

'Dear Comrades, soldiers, sailors, and workers! I am happy to greet in your persons the victorious Russian revolution, and greet you as the vanguard of the worldwide proletarian army. . . The piratical imperialist war is the beginning of civil war throughout Europe. . . The hour is not far distant when at the call of our comrade, Karl Liebknecht,[1] the peoples will turn their arms against their own capitalist exploiters. . . The worldwide Socialist revolution has already dawned. . . Germany is seething. . . Any day now the whole of European capitalism may crash. The Russian revolution accomplished by you has prepared the way and opened a new epoch. Long live the worldwide Socialist revolution!'

This was really no reply to Chkheidze's 'welcome', and it entirely failed to echo the 'context' of the Russian revolution as accepted by everyone, without distinction, of its witnesses and participants.

It was very interesting! Suddenly, before the eyes of all of us, completely swallowed up by the routine drudgery of the revolution, there was presented a bright, blinding, exotic

[1] Liebknecht, Karl (1871–1919): son of Wilhelm Liebknecht, one of the most eminent German Socialists of the end of the 19th century. A pacifist, he played an important rôle in opposition to the official Social-Democratic Party during the war. Continually arrested and imprisoned; after the German Revolution of 1919 he was assassinated, together with Rosa Luxemburg, by Rightists. He was very popular in Russia. (Ed.)

beacon, obliterating everything we 'lived by'. Lenin's voice, heard straight from the train, was a 'voice from outside'. There had broken in upon us in the revolution a note that was not, to be sure, a contradiction, but that was novel, harsh, and somewhat deafening.

Let us admit that essentially Lenin was right a thousand times over. Personally I was convinced that he was quite right, not only in recognizing the beginning of the worldwide Socialist revolution and establishing an unbreakable connexion between the World War and the crash of the imperialist system, but in maintaining that we had to steer towards world revolution and evaluate all contemporary historical events in its light. All this was beyond question.

But it was far from enough. It was not enough to acclaim the worldwide Socialist revolution: we had to understand what practical use to make of this idea in our revolutionary policy. If we didn't then the proclamation of the worldwide proletarian revolution would not merely be completely abstract, empty, and futile, but would obscure all the real perspectives and be extremely harmful.

In any case it was all *very* interesting!

The official and public part of the welcome was over. The crowd, burning with impatience, envy, and indignation, was already trying to break through the glass doors from the square. It was noisily and insistently demanding that the newly-arrived leader should come out to it in the street. Shlyapnikov again cleared a way for Lenin, shouting: 'Comrades, please! Make way there!'

To another *Marseillaise*, and to the shouts of the throng of thousands, among the red-and-gold banners illuminated by the searchlight, Lenin went out by the main entrance and was about to get into a closed car, but the crowd absolutely refused to allow this. Lenin clambered on to the bonnet of the car and had to make a speech.

'. . . any part in shameful imperialist slaughter . . . lies and frauds . . . capitalist pirates . . .' was what I could hear, squeezed in the doorway and vainly trying to get out on to the square to hear the first speech 'to the people' of this new star of the first magnitude on our revolutionary horizon.

Then I think Lenin had to change to an armoured car and

in it, preceded by the searchlight and accompanied by the band, flags, workers' detachments, army units, and an enormous crowd of 'private' people, proceed to the Sampson Bridge and over to the Petersburg Side, to the Bolshevik headquarters—the palace of Kshesinskaya, the ballerina. From the top of the armoured car Lenin 'conducted a service' at practically every street-crossing, making new speeches to continually changing audiences. The procession made slow progress. The triumph had come off brilliantly, and even quite symbolically.

* * *

On my way home I also followed along quietly at the tail end of the procession, far from its centre, together with a few people, including an old friend of mine, Raskolnikov, at that time a midshipman and later the famous Bolshevik admiral. He was unusually amiable, sincere, and honest, an unwavering revolutionary through and through, and a Bolshevik fanatic.

Raskolnikov was in raptures because of the welcome, Lenin's arrival, Lenin himself, because of everything, indeed, that had been happening before his eyes in his best of all worlds. He talked without ceasing of this leader, his personality, his rôle, his past. . .

It would have been interesting to hear what was being said now about Lenin and his triumphal entry, among 'the people', especially the soldiers; there were a great many of them both at the station and in the procession. Though I don't remember any officers with them, these soldiers were not there as individuals, but in military units. Hence there could be no question of their being Bolsheviks or Bolshevik sympathizers, or even of their knowing anything definite about Lenin and having voluntarily come along to welcome him. They were units that had been ordered out by the organizational talent of Bolshevik party workers. Hasty propaganda speeches had been made in the barracks, and in the absence of any serious objection from anyone, or of any serious reasons for refusing, a few units doubtless passed motions about the welcome without any special difficulty.

But I wondered what these soldiers were thinking and saying. Now that they had time to think, what sort of a parade was this in honour of a man without any rank or title, who was not only not in the Government but was not even a 'Duma member', not even a member of a Soldiers' and Workers' Soviet and was said, besides, to have travelled *via* Germany by the special favour of the enemy government? Moreover, now the soldiers had heard some of his speeches too—rather strange speeches, expressed in a way not heard before! During the last few days, to be sure, there had no longer been the former violent reaction on the part of the rank and file to speeches against the war. It could be felt in the air that the Soviet democracy had perhaps passed a turning-point, and in the tussle with the bourgeoisie for power and for the army it seemed as though the previous acuteness of the crisis might have passed.

But all this had just barely been accomplished, not only without any guarantees against a relapse but also without the slightest assurance that the turning-point had really been passed.

On the other hand, it is true that the very decision to take part in the parade, the very fact of the triumph, must have recommended Lenin to the soldiers honouring him, and made his credit sound enough for anything he felt like saying.

Nevertheless it would have been very interesting to hear what the soldiers marching in the procession were saying.

Until the very end, however, we had no opportunity of listening to the voice of the people. On the Petersburg Side I should have turned right, to the Karpovka, but, drawn along by my agreeable company, I nevertheless went along to the beginning of the Kronvergsky, as far as Kshesinskaya's house, which had all its lights burning and was decked out with red banners.

A crowd was standing in front of the house and from the second-floor balcony Lenin, by now hoarse, was making a speech. I stopped near a detachment of soldiers with rifles, who had accompanied the procession to its very end.

'. . . capitalist pirates', could be heard from the balcony, 'the extirpation of the nations of Europe for the sake of the profits of a handful of exploiters . . . the defence of the fatherland means the defense of one set of capitalists against another . . .'

'Ought to stick our bayonets into a fellow like that,' a soldier suddenly shouted out, in a lively reaction. 'Eh? The things he says! Eh? If he came down here we'd have to show him! And we'd show him all right! Must be a German. . . Eh, he ought to be. . .!'

I don't know why they hadn't 'shown' him before, when Lenin was making his speeches from a lower platform. I don't think they would have 'shown' him afterwards either, even if he had 'come down'. Nevertheless it was interesting.

And not only interesting: such speeches by Lenin, after all—devoid of the most elementary 'diplomacy', or any calculation of the concrete background and the soldiers' mentality—were quite risky. Now, after the turning-point had been reached, they might rapidly promote the education of the soldiery and their comprehension of the actuality of war; but there was surely a greater chance that the nakedness and clumsiness of such speeches would nullify the effects of the crisis and do great harm to the cause.

After he had got his bearings Lenin grasped this very quickly, adapted himself and took a 'diplomatic' line, generously garnishing his speeches with qualifications and fig-leaves. ('We never said we had to stick our bayonets into the ground when the enemy army was ready for battle', etc.) But now Lenin was speaking straight from the shoulder and uttering obvious truths about the war without any refinements. The reaction of the soldiers showed that this was a very dubious method.

I found myself unexpectedly near the gate, where, among the crowd who were trying to push in, a Bolshevik worker was busy making a strict selection of those who were worthy to penetrate inside the house and take part in an unofficial comradely welcome. Recognizing my face he—again unexpectedly—let me through; he may even have invited me in.

There weren't many people inside—it was clear that people were being let in only after a real screening. But the Bolshevik commanders I knew whom I met inside Kshesinskaya's apartments gave me a hospitable welcome. I am grateful to them for the impressions of that night of April 3rd.

* * *

The apartments of the famous ballerina had a rather strange and inappropriate look. The exquisite ceilings and walls were out of all harmony with the unpretentious furnishings, the primitive tables, chairs, and benches set casually about as required by business. There was very little furniture. Kshesinskaya's movable property had been put away somewhere, and it was only here and there that the remains of former grandeur were visible, in the display of flowers and a few examples of artistic furniture and ornaments.

In the dining-room upstairs tea and snacks were being prepared, and people were already being called to the table, which was set no better and no worse than our own in the Ex. Com. Triumphant and contented, the Bolshevik élite were strolling about in anticipation of their first banquet with their leader, towards whom they displayed a really extraordinary piety.

But Lenin was not in the dining-room. He had been called out to the balcony again to make more speeches. I was about to follow him, to listen, but met him before arriving at the balcony.

Until then I hadn't known Lenin personally, and had only heard his lectures and speeches in Paris in 1902–1903; at that time I was still fresh from school, while Lenin, an *Iskra*-man, was the companion-in-arms and disciple of Martov and Plekhanov. But not only did I know Lenin quite well by reputation but he knew me quite well enough too. When I stopped him and mentioned my name, Lenin, excited and lively, greeted me very affably:

'Ah! Himmer-Sukhanov—very happy indeed! You and I have had a lot of disputes on the agrarian question. Why, I followed the way you and your SRs got into a fight. And then you became an internationalist. I got your pamphlets. . .'

Lenin smiled, screwing up his merry eyes, and, wagging his untidy head, took me into the dining-room. . . Afterwards too, at my rare, accidental meetings with him, Lenin for some reason was always very cordial to me, until his disappearance after the July Days. But just then he had forgotten: it was not only on the agrarian question that I'd carried on a polemic with him. In 1914 when Lenin was irritated by my 'little magazine', the *Sovremennik*, he honoured me with his attention about other things as well ('the bare-faced lying of Messrs. the Martovs and Himmers', etc.).

We sat down at the table and went on with our talk, now on political themes. Lenin, in his characteristic way, laughed rather coarsely and without mincing words attacked the Ex. Com., the Soviet 'line' and its authors. He kept using the expression 'revolutionary defensism', which had come into use during the last few days, and attacked the three leaders of this 'revolutionary defensism', Tsereteli, Chkheidze, and Steklov. This was not quite fair, and I felt bound to defend Steklov, assuring Lenin that during the war Steklov, even though he did not say or do anything, 'thought' in quite a defeatist way, while during the revolution he kept to a definitely Left course and performed the most useful services.

Lenin, however, laughed and shrugged this aside, referring to Steklov as an arch 'Social-lackey'. But our dispute was soon interrupted by the envious disciples of the great teacher.

'Nikolai Nikolayevich!' Kamenev called out from the other end of the table, 'That's enough, you can finish later, you're taking Ilyich away from us!'

The meal, however, didn't last long. It was reported that about 200 party workers and others were waiting downstairs in the reception-room. We were asked to finish our tea quickly and go on downstairs. . .

I of course very much wanted to be present, and I asked one of those in charge whether it would be all right. After whispering among themselves they told me it would be quite all right.

On the stairs I saw Zinoviev[1] for the first time; I hadn't noticed him at all since his arrival, either at the station or there. Though quite a star himself, he was incapable of shining in the presence of the dazzling Bolshevik sun.

* * *

Downstairs, in the fairly large reception-room, there were a great many people—workers, 'professional revolutionaries', and girls. There were not enough chairs, and half the audience stood uncomfortably or sat on the tables. Someone was elected chairman, and welcoming speeches began. In general all this was monotonous and tiresome. But from time to time some characteristic traits of the Bolshevik 'way of life' and of specific methods of Bolshevik party work, all of which I found very curious, slipped out. It became quite obvious that all Bolshevik work was held within the iron framework of a foreign spiritual centre,

[1] Zinoviev (Radomyslsky), Grigorii Evseyevich (1883–1936): one of Lenin's oldest and closest collaborators. Permanent member of the Bolshevik Central Committee and the first Chairman of the Communist International. He was excluded from the Communist Party in 1927, was arrested and tried twice; he 'confessed' and was shot in 1936 together with Kamenev and others as an accomplice in the assassination of Kirov. (Ed.)

without which the party workers would have felt themselves to be completely helpless, which at the same time they felt proud of, and of which the best amongst them felt themselves to be the devoted servitors, as knights were of the Holy Grail.

Kamenev also said something rather indefinite, and finally they remembered Zinoviev, whom they applauded a little but who said nothing. At last the welcoming speeches were over.

Then the celebrated master of the order himself rose to reply. I shall never forget that thunder-like speech, which startled and amazed not only me, a heretic who had accidentally dropped in, but all the true believers. I am certain that no one had expected anything of the sort. It seemed as though all the elements had risen from their abodes, and the spirit of universal destruction, knowing neither barriers nor doubts, neither human difficulties nor human calculations, was hovering around Kshesinskaya's reception-room above the heads of the bewitched disciples.

Lenin was in general a very good orator—not an orator of the consummate, rounded phrase, or of the luminous image, or of absorbing pathos, or of the pointed witticism, but an orator of enormous impact and power, breaking down complicated systems into the simplest and most generally accessible elements, and hammering, hammering, hammering them into the heads of his audience until he took them captive.

Afterwards, about a year and half later, hearing him as head of the Government, one was bound to regret the former orator, the 'irresponsible' agitator and demagogue. After Lenin had changed from a demagogue and insurrectionary into a statesman, Lenin the orator became flat, faded, and trivial, losing both his power and his originality. His speeches became as like one another as two drops of water.

Lenin spoke probably about two hours. I shall not forget that speech, but I shall make no attempt to reproduce its original words even in a short abstract. For it would be a completely hopeless business to re-create even a feeble reflection of its impression: the dead letter cannot replace the living, tempestuous eloquence; most important of all, it is impossible to bring back the unexpectedness and novelty of its content, that now would not only not be striking, but would sound banal, and wretchedly banal at that.

* * *

I don't think Lenin, barely out of his sealed train, expected to expound in his answer his whole credo, and all his programme and tactics in the worldwide Socialist revolution. This speech was probably largely an improvization, and so lacked any special density or worked-out plan. But each individual part of the speech, each element, each idea, was excellently worked out; it was clear that these ideas had long wholly occupied Lenin and been defended by him more than once. This was shown by the astonishing wealth of vocabulary, the whole dazzling cascade of definitions, nuances, and parallel (explanatory) ideas, which can be attained only through fundamental brain-work.

Lenin began, of course, with the worldwide Socialist revolution, that was ready to explode as a result of the World War. The crisis of imperialism expressed in the war could be resolved only by Socialism. The imperialist war (Lenin said 'imperilist') could not help but turn into a civil war, and could indeed be ended only by a civil war, by a worldwide Socialist revolution.

Lenin jeered at the Soviet's 'peace' policy: no, 'Liaison' Commissions would never liquidate a world war. In general, indeed, the Soviet democracy, led by Tsereteli, Chkheidze, and Steklov, having adopted the point of view of 'revolutionary defensism', was powerless to do anything for a general peace. Lenin sharply and definitely dissociated himself from the Soviet, and hurled it completely into the enemy camp. In those days this alone, on our terrain, was enough to make his listeners' heads spin!

The worldwide Socialist revolution—that was what the Soviet Manifesto (of March 14th) called for. But what petty-bourgeois thinking! No, revolutions are not called for, they are not advised; revolutions arise out of historically established conditions, revolutions mature and grow. . . The Soviet Manifesto bragged to Europe about the successes it had achieved; it spoke of the 'revolutionary force of democracy', of 'total political liberty'. But what kind of force was this, when the imperialist bourgeoisie was at the head of the country? What kind of political liberty, when the secret diplomatic documents were not published, and we couldn't publish them? What kind of freedom of speech, when all the printing facilities were in the hands of the bourgeoisie and guarded by a bourgeois Government!

'When I was on the way here with my comrades, I thought

we should be taken from the station straight to the Peter-Paul. As we see, we turned out to be far from that. But let us not lose hope that we may still not escape it.'

The 'revolutionary-defensist' Soviet led by opportunists and Social-patriots could only be an instrument of the bourgeoisie. For it to serve as an instrument of the world-wide Socialist revolution it must still be conquered and made proletarian instead of petty-bourgeois. Bolshevik strength was inadequate for that now. Well, what of that? They would learn how to be a minority, enlighten, explain, persuade. . .

But with what goals, what programme?

First of all, if the Soviet was bankrupt, what should be said about the bourgeois-imperialist Government at the head of the revolution? As far as I recall Lenin said nothing about whether such a government had been necessary at the moment of the overturn, as the direct successor of Tsarism. But it was quite obvious that now it was unendurable. That, however, was the least of it. In general:

'We don't need a parliamentary republic, we don't need bourgeois democracy, we don't need any Government except the Soviets of Workers', Soldiers' and Farm-labourers' deputies!'

For some reason Lenin didn't use the term Constituent Assembly. This could scarcely have been diplomacy. At this point Lenin was still completely fresh, absolutely free and alien to any diplomatic ideas: he still felt himself abroad, where he was not immersed in any real political work and it was natural to say aloud whatever was in your mind. Diplomacy concerning the Constituent Assembly began later and was carried on with caution until its very dissolution: indeed, for a number of months the struggle against Kerensky and the Soviet petty-bourgeois majority was carried on under the banner of the *defence* of the Constituent Assembly.

But Lenin's constitutional system was a bolt from the blue not only for me. Up to then no one listening to the teacher in Kshesinskaya's room had ever had any inkling of anything like it. And of course every listener with any experience in political theory took Lenin's formula, fired off without any commentaries, for a purely anarchist schema.

For in the first place, the Soviets of Workers' Deputies, those militant class organs historically formed (in 1905) simply out of strike committees—however great their *real power* in the state—had up to then never been thought of as a constitutional agency; they very easily and naturally might be (and already were) the *source* of state power in the revolution; but no one had ever dreamt of them as organs of state power, and unique and enduring ones besides. In any case without the preliminary sociological groundwork of a proletarian dictatorship this whole schema was incomprehensible.

Secondly, between the militant class organs, the Workers' Soviets, there did not exist the slightest stable bond or the most primitive constitution; a 'Government of Soviets' in these circumstances sounded like a *totality of local authority, like the absence of any state in general, like a schema of 'free' (independent) workers' communes*. Moreover, Lenin didn't speak of *Peasant* Soviets, and there were no *farm-labourers'* Soviets, nor could they be formed—as must have been clear to anyone at all equipped for a 'polemic on the agrarian question'.

Later on Lenin's constitutional schema theoretically became quite comprehensible: theoretically it meant a workers' dictatorship, the 'iron broom' called upon to wipe the bourgeoisie off the face of the earth and destroy the whole edifice of capitalism. But the complete bankruptcy of this schema was also revealed as well as its unsuitability for the aims of a proletarian dictatorship—to the mind of Lenin himself; in practice this schema was never introduced (during his régime).

Later on Lenin's system turned out to be futile, but it became understandable—in the general system of Leninist principles. But for a very long time the most erudite Bolsheviks (the proselyte Trotsky most of all) floundered around in it and interpreted the slogan of 'Power to the Soviets' quite chaotically. And even then, on the day of his arrival, having fired off his formula, Lenin, who had been known up to then as a Social-Democrat, caused the more literate of his faithful disciples extreme perplexity.

Continuing his speech, Lenin also touched on agrarian affairs. He kicked aside any agrarian reform on a 'legislative plane' like all the other Soviet policies. 'Organized seizure', without waiting either for the sanction of any authority, or for any state power—such was the last word of this 'Marxist'. This was the 'approach to Socialism' of the countryside.

As for the towns, there was a vague foreshadowing of a vague new order, in which the only thing definite was that in the absence throughout the country of any Government except the Soviets, the 'armed workers' would stand at the cradle of production, at the factory benches. So much for the towns.

Then the thunderous orator came down on all those who falsely passed themselves off as Socialists. These were not only our Soviet bosses and the majority of European Socialists. He, Lenin, together with Comrade Zinoviev, thank the Lord, had passed through Zimmerwald and Kienthal[1] from the beginning to the end. Only the Zimmerwald Left wing stood guard over proletarian interests and the worldwide revolution. Contemporary Socialism was the enemy of the international proletariat. And the very name of Social-Democracy had been desecrated by treason. It was impossible to have anything in common with it, impossible to purge it: it had to be cast aside as the symbol of the betrayal of the working class.

Lenin was finishing his speech. In two hours he had said a great deal. But his speech lacked one thing—I remember this well and it's quite remarkable: it had no analysis of 'objective premises', no analysis of the socio-economic conditions for Socialism in Russia. No economic programme was even referred to. There was the embryo of what Lenin repeated many times later: namely, that the backwardness of our country, the weakness of its productive forces, did not allow it to sustain the desperate tension of the whole organism demanded by the war; this was why Russia had been the first to produce a revolution. But of how this backwardness, this petty-bourgeois, peasant structure, this extreme exhaustion and chaos could be reconciled with a Socialist reorganization independently of the West, before the worldwide Socialist revolution—not a word was said. How the Workers' and Farm-labourers' Soviets, representing a small minority of the country, as bearers of the proletarian dictatorship against the will and the interests of the majority, were to construct Socialism—about this too Lenin was completely silent. Of how, finally, his whole conception was to be reconciled with the elementary foundations of Marxism (the only thing Lenin did not dissociate himself from in his speech)

[1] The Zimmerwald conference of 1915 reassembled at Kienthal (Switzerland) in 1916. (Ed.)

—not a syllable was said. Everything touching on what had hitherto been called scientific Socialism Lenin ignored just as completely as he destroyed the foundations of the current Social-Democratic programme and tactics. Extremely remarkable. . .

Lenin ended his speech. The pupils delightedly, unanimously, lengthily applauded their teacher. On the faces of the majority there was nothing but rapture; not the shadow of a doubt. Happy, innocent souls! But the literate ones, clapping loud and long, seemed to stare strangely in front of them; or else their eyes roved about unseeingly, showing complete confusion: the teacher had given the minds of his Marxist disciples some work to do.

I looked for Kamenev, who, after taking *Pravda* in hand, had been happy three days before to vote for a united front with Tsereteli and all the 'populists'. But in answer to my question as to what he had to say about all this, he merely shrugged his shoulders: 'Wait, just wait!'

As an infidel, I turned to another and then a third of the faithful: after all, I *ought* to understand—what was this really all about? The people I talked to grinned and shook their heads, without the slightest idea of what to say.

I went out into the street. I felt as though I had been beaten about the head that night with flails. Only one thing was clear: no, Lenin and a 'wild' one like myself could not be travelling companions.

I breathed in with pleasure as much as I could of the fresh spring air. It was already quite light, the morning was beginning.

* * *

A joint session of all the Social-Democrats—Bolsheviks, Mensheviks, and independents—was scheduled the next day in the Tauride Palace. It was organized by a group of people who thought that the most urgent task of the moment was the unification of all tendencies of Social-Democracy into a single party and who did not at the same time think this task utopian. I went to the meeting with great interest.

When I turned up in the Tauride Palace the meeting had long since begun, and Lenin had already occupied the platform for more than an hour. He was no longer amongst his own disciples: most of the audience was made up of his old ideological adversaries. Accordingly he had to modify his language. Here Lenin had to emphasize the difference and irreconcilability between his position and the views of the majority: he had to talk about what he would do and call on his fraction to do in *distinction* from the majority of those present.

Thus, at this 'unifying' conference, Lenin was the living incarnation of schism; and the whole point of his speech in the given circumstances boiled down to the interment first of all of the idea of unity.

But both the content and the form of this speech as a whole reproduced the first stupefying début of the future all-Russian dictator. The Bolshevik devotees present, thinking it indispensable in all circumstances to demonstrate their solidarity and their isolation from the others, the infidels, applauded individual points of Lenin's speech even more than the night before. But the rest of the audience didn't share their feelings at all.

They weren't only stunned: each new word of Lenin's filled them with indignation. Protests and exclamations of outrage began to be heard. It wasn't only a question of the inappropriateness of such a speech at a 'unifying' conference, it was also that together with the idea of unity the foundations of the Social-Democratic programme and of Marxist theory were spat upon. . . I remember Bogdanov, who was sitting opposite me, on the 'Ministerial bench', two steps away from the platform: 'This is the raving of a madman! It's indecent to applaud this clap-trap!' he cried out, livid with rage and contempt, turning to the audience. 'You ought to be ashamed of yourselves! Marxists!'

Shouts like this of course didn't weaken but intensified the ovation the Bolshevik group gave Lenin when he finished his speech. And the cause of a unified Social-Democracy was already doomed. All speeches after that were completely devoted to Lenin. But I remember only two speeches against him.

Tsereteli constituted himself the 'official Opposition'. I don't think that before Lenin spoke he had had any special hopes of unity with the Bolsheviks or was particularly striving for it. It was clear from what had gone before that such weren't the inclinations of this leader of the Soviet Right. Nevertheless he had thought it his duty to take part in the unifying conference; and Lenin's speech gave him every chance of attacking a policy of schism and demonstrating his piety towards the cause of unity.

Tsereteli was supported by an enormous majority of the meeting, including many Bolsheviks. But the Menshevik leader, while emphasizing the absence of the objective premises for a Socialist overturn in Russia, was still far from summing up the gist of Lenin's position with as much success as a short, brilliant speech by the old Social-Democrat I. P. Goldenberg, the most active of the would-be unifiers, historically a Bolshevik but theoretically a defensist.

'Lenin has now made himself a candidate for one European throne that has been vacant for thirty years—the throne of Bakunin! Lenin's new words echo something old—the superannuated truths of primitive anarchism.'

That was one conclusion stressed by Goldenberg. This was another:

'Lenin has raised the banner of civil war within the democracy. It's ludicrous to talk of unity with those whose watchword is schism and who are placing themselves outside the Social-Democracy of their own accord!'

Further, as I see by the newspaper accounts, the future bard and ideologist of Leninist policy, Steklov, also had his say about the speech of his future commander:

'Lenin's speech', he said, 'consists of nothing but abstract constructions that prove the Russian Revolution has passed him by. After Lenin becomes acquainted with the state of affairs in Russia he himself will reject all these constructions of his.'

The real Bolsheviks also made no bones—at least in private conversations behind the scenes—about Lenin's 'abstractness'. One even expressed the idea that Lenin's speech had removed the differences within the Social-Democracy, for with respect to Lenin's position there could be no differences between Bolsheviks and Mensheviks. However, at the beginning of his speech Lenin had definitely said and even emphasized that he was speaking for himself personally, without having consulted his party.

The Bolshevik sect was still in a state of bafflement and perplexity. And the support Lenin found may underline more clearly than anything else his complete intellectual isolation, not only among Social-Democrats in general but also among his own disciples. Lenin was supported by no one but Kolontai[1] (a recent Menshevik), who rejected any alliance with those who could not and would not accomplish a social revolution! Her support called forth nothing but mockery, laughter, and hubbub. The meeting dispersed; any chance of serious debate had been destroyed.

* * *

Towards evening of this same April 14th the Liaison Commission had to go to the Marian Palace. If I'm not mistaken we were invited this time because the support of the Soviet was being demanded for the new war loan, known by the saccharinely hypocritical name of the Liberty Loan. We had to wait for the arrival of Rodzianko and his colleagues, and while Skobelev and I strolled about the room, Miliukov came up to us. The conversation turned upon Lenin. Skobelev told Miliukov about his 'lunatic ideas', appraising him as a completely lost man standing outside the movement. I agreed in general with this estimate of Lenin's ideas and said that in his present guise he was so unacceptable to everyone that now he was not at all dangerous for our interlocutor, Miliukov. However, the future of Lenin seemed different to me: I was convinced that after he had escaped from his foreign academic atmosphere and come into an atmosphere of real struggle and wide practical activity, he would acclimatize himself quickly, settle down, stand on firm ground and throw overboard the bulk of his anarchist 'ravings'. What life failed to accomplish with him, the solid pressure of his party comrades would help with. I was convinced that in the near future Lenin would again be con-

[1] Kolontai, Alexandra Mikhailovna (1872–1952): from a highly placed, reactionary *milieu*, a revolutionary from 1896 on. A Menshevik until 1915; during the First World War became a Bolshevik. Lived in Western Europe for many years and thanks to her linguistic gifts was active in the continental Social-Democratic Parties. Shortly after her return to Russia in 1917 was elected to the Bolshevik Central Committee. After the October Revolution was Minister of Social Security; very active as writer, and then as diplomat, holding ambassadorial posts in Mexico, Norway, and Sweden. (Ed.)

verted into a herald of the ideas of revolutionary Marxism and occupy a place in the revolution worthy of him as the most authoritative leader of the Soviet proletarian Left. Then, I said, he would be dangerous to Miliukov. And Miliukov agreed with me.

We refused to admit that Lenin might stick to his abstractions. Still less did we admit that through these abstractions Lenin would be able to conquer not only the revolution, not only all its active masses, not only the whole Soviet—but even his own Bolsheviks.

We were cruelly mistaken. . .

* * *

About a week after his arrival the famous First Theses of Lenin were printed in *Pravda*, in the form of an article. They contained a *résumé* of the new doctrine expounded in his speeches; they lacked the same thing as his speeches: an economic programme and a Marxist analysis of the objective conditions of our revolution.

The Theses were published in Lenin's name alone: not one Bolshevik organization, or group, or even individual had joined him. And the editors of *Pravda* for their part thought it necessary to emphasize Lenin's isolation and their independence of him. 'As for Lenin's general schema,' wrote *Pravda*, 'it seems to us unacceptable, in so far as it proceeds from the assumption that the bourgeois democratic revolution is finished and counts on the immediate conversion of that revolution into a Socialist revolution.'

It appeared that the Marxist foundations of the Bolshevik Party were firm, that the Bolshevik party mass had taken up arms to defend against Lenin the elementary foundations of scientific Socialism, Bolshevism itself, and the old traditional Lenin.

Alas! Many people, including myself, were vainly deluded: Lenin compelled his Bolsheviks to accept his 'lunatic ideas' in their entirety. How and why did this happen? I have no intention of investigating this interesting question *au fond*, nevertheless I don't think it superfluous here to note a few undoubted factors in the capitulation of the old Social-Democratic Bolshevism to Lenin's reckless anarcho-seditious system.

First of all—there can be no doubt of it—Lenin is an extraordinary phenomenon, a man of absolutely exceptional intellectual power; he is a first-class world magnitude in calibre. For he represents an unusually happy combination of theoretician and popular leader. If still other epithets were needed I shouldn't hesitate to call Lenin a genius, keeping in mind the content of this notion of genius.

A genius, as is well known, is an abnormal person. More concretely, he is very often a man with an extremely limited area of intellectual activity, in which area this activity is carried on with unusual power and productivity. A genius can very often be extremely narrow-minded, with no understanding or grasp of the simplest and most generally accessible things. Such was the generally accepted genius Leo Tolstoy, who (in the brilliant though paradoxical expression of Merezhkovsky) was simply 'not intelligent enough for his own genius'.

Lenin was undoubtedly like this too: many elementary truths were inaccessible to his mind—even in politics. This was the source of an endless series of the most elementary errors—in the period of his dictatorship as well as in the epoch of his agitation and demagogy.

But on the other hand, within a certain realm of ideas—a few 'fixed' ideas—Lenin displayed such amazing force, such superhuman power of attack that his colossal influence over the Socialists and revolutionaries was secure.

In addition to these internal and, so to speak, theoretical qualities of Lenin's, as well as his genius, the following circumstance also played a primary rôle in his victory over the old Marxist Bolsheviks. In practice Lenin had been historically the exclusive, sole, and unchallenged head of the party for many years, since the day of its emergence. The Bolshevik Party was the work of his hands, and his alone. The very thought of going against Lenin was frightening and odious, and required from the Bolshevik mass what it was incapable of giving.

Lenin the genius was an historic figure—this is one side of the matter. The other is that, except Lenin, there was nothing and no one in the party. The few massive generals without Lenin were *nothing*, like the few immense planets without the sun (for the moment I leave aside Trotsky, who at that time was still outside the ranks of the order, that is, in the camp of the 'enemies of the proletariat, lackeys of the bourgeoisie', etc.).

In the First International, according to the well-known description, there was Marx high up in the clouds; then for a long, long way there was nothing; then, also at a great height, there was Engels; then again for a long, long way there was nothing, and finally there was Liebknecht sitting there, etc.

But in the Bolshevik Party Lenin the Thunderer sat in the clouds and then—there was absolutely nothing right down to the ground. And on the ground, amongst the party rankers and officers a few generals could be distinguished—and even then I daresay not individually but rather in couples or combinations. There could be no question of *replacing* Lenin by individuals, couples, or combinations. There could be neither independent thinking nor organizational base in the Bolshevik Party without Lenin.

That is how matters stood in the Bolshevik general staff. As for the mass of party officers, they were far from distinguished. Amongst the Bolshevik officers there were many first-rate technicians in party and professional work, and not a few 'romantics', but extremely few political thinkers and conscious Socialists.

In consequence every form of radicalism and external *Leftism* had an invincible attraction for the Bolshevik mass, while the natural 'line' of work consisted of demagogy. This was very often what all the political wisdom of the Bolshevik committee-men boiled down to.

Thus the 'party public' of course quite lacked the strength or any internal resources to oppose anything whatever to Lenin's onslaught.

Lenin's radicalism, his heedless 'Leftism', and primitive demagogy, unrestrained either by science or common sense, later secured his success among the broadest proletarian-muzhik masses, who had had no other teaching than that of the Tsarist whip. But the same characteristics of this Leninist propaganda also seduced the more backward, less literate elements of the party itself. Very soon after Lenin's arrival they were faced by an alternative: either keep the old principles of Social-Democracy and Marxist science, but without Lenin, without the masses, and without the party; or stay with Lenin and the party and conquer the masses together in an easy way, having thrown overboard the obscure, unfamiliar Marxist principles. It's understandable that the mass of party Bolsheviks, though after some vacillation, decided on the latter.

But the attitude of this mass could not help but have a decisive influence on the fully-conscious Bolshevik elements too, on the Bolshevik generals, for after Lenin's conquest of the officers of the party, people like Kamenev, for instance, were completely isolated; they had fallen into the position of outlaws and internal traitors. And the implacable Thunderer soon subjected them, together with other infidels, to such abuse that not all of them could endure it. It goes without saying that even the generals, even those who had read Marx and Engels, were incapable of sustaining such an ordeal. And Lenin won one victory after another.

CHAPTER 13

THE SOVIET CONQUERS THE ARMY AND THE GOVERNMENT

LENIN'S thunder had roared and the prolonged echo reverberated in *political* circles, in party and Soviet spheres, but not amongst the broad masses. In the lower ranks of the Petersburg proletariat and garrison his arrival passed unnoticed and was not reflected in the general conjuncture. Meanwhile this general conjuncture had during the preceding few days—equal in effect to months—undoubtedly undergone some basic changes.

Beginning with the All-Russian Soviet Conference, since the very last days of March there had been signs of an important shift in the soldiers' mood. It demonstrated the fiasco of the bourgeois onslaught on the democracy in the decisive battle for the army and for the real power in the State. With the first days of April the tension in the atmosphere had begun to diminish; there were signs that the struggle was ending favourably for the democracy.

Lenin, with his devastating maximalist agitation, had undoubtedly come pat on his cue. The very possibility of such an agitation had already been prepared *before him*, by the preceding tendency of the revolution. By the time Lenin declared himself to the masses, the most difficult and important thing had already been done: the primitive instincts had been neutralized that would have swept Lenin away, and perhaps the Soviet into the bargain, if he had 'pushed in' before with his radical, naked harangues.

But now the crisis had come. With the first days of April it began to be clear that the democracy, even if it had not yet won, was undoubtedly going to win in the struggle for the army and the real power; that the revolution would not stop with the programme of the Miliukovs and Lvovs; that the army would not become a weapon in their hands against the democracy and its own interests; that a dictatorship of capital would not take root in the New Russia.

To be sure the other side of the matter, described before, must by no means be forgotten here. At that same time, at the beginning of April, the forces of the revolution and the democracy had already been undermined by the formation in the Soviet of a new petty-bourgeois opportunist majority that gravitated towards an alliance with the imperialist bourgeoisie. This cardinal fact, in the last analysis, of course altered the entire course of events; it distorted and very largely nullified the meaning of the revolutionary victory. And even now, in the first half of April, the fact of the formation of a 'conciliationist' Soviet majority to a considerable degree obscured the Soviet victory over the army, and veiled for many people the objective process of the transfer of the real forces of the revolution.

The change first became marked in the realm of the relations between workers and soldiers. I have already described in some detail the bourgeois campaign of incitement against factory 'idlers' and also the solid resistance displayed by the Soviet. The organized visits to Petersburg factories by representatives of military units soon bore fruit. Those same regiments that had turned up in the Tauride Palace ten to fifteen days before in a mood of hostility and with strict directives for the workers—had heard the reports of their specially delegated comrades on the state of affairs in the factories. They had had repeated to them the workers' moving speeches, about how, independently of any conditions whatever, they were prepared to work to supply the army for the safety of their soldier-brothers.

At the factories, instead of brawls, there was triumphant fraternization between soldiers and workers. Meetings were arranged in token of unity. First the Socialist papers were splattered with soldiers' resolutions on brotherly solidarity with the workers, and then by the middle of April the 'worker and soldier' question had completely vanished from the newspaper columns. This alone was a sign of the total liquidation of the conflict.

* * *

The army was 'conquered'. Without realizing the total *significance* of this fact, the bourgeoisie nevertheless acknowledged the fact itself; it acknowledged that the battle was lost and that a further campaign on the given terrain was pointless.

Regimental demonstrations with anti-Soviet slogans had ended with the first days of April. No more thunderous *Marseillaises* were heard in the Tauride Palace, since the hurrahs for Rodzianko were now more than dubious. The columns of the newspapers were liberated from the burden of the endless resolutions on the 'dual power', on the Soviet's catastrophic meddling in State affairs, on loyalty to the Government and to its slogan of 'war to the finish'. They had vanished completely—forever.

The state of affairs had radically changed. And perhaps its essence was expressed best of all by none other than the French visitor, M. Cachin. After travelling around the revolutionary centres, then the field army, and then returning home, in a report on his trip he gave an excellent reply to all those who were raving, ranting, and baffled in *la belle France*—as to why the gangs of workers and soldiers sitting in the Tauride Palace under the name of a Soviet and imagining themselves to be practically the Russian Government had not yet been dispersed. Said Cachin: 'Gentlemen, ten million bayonets are entirely at the disposal of the Soviet.'

Yes! On March 2nd, when Guchkov, Miliukov, and Kerensky received the power from the people's hands, the democracy, unified in the Soviet, was master of the situation—inasmuch as all available *real power* was on its side, while the propertied classes had no real support. But the point was that at that time there was no state power at all; real power was completely non-existent. The material power of the State, the *army*, was politically extinct, disorganized and neutral, whereas the *political weight* of the propertied elements, the sole organized group, was enormous. Hence the 'master of the situation' on March 2nd was master only in an extremely relative way.

The Soviet was master of the situation only in the sense that it had a free choice, and it was quite possible for it to take political power into its hands and expire beneath the unendurable burden, or else create conditions for its struggle and victory by making concessions to the Government. By transferring power to the propertied elements on March 2nd the Soviet—as I said in Part I—created for itself favourable (equal) conditions for the duel. When it entrusted the power to the first Cabinet of the revolution the Soviet was only just going into battle—for the army and the real source of authority in the State.

By April 17th, a month and a half later, it had won this battle and become the master of the situation in another sense and within different limits. Now the Soviet had in its hands a strongly organized, spiritually united army; now ten million bayonets were the obedient instruments of the Soviet, which with them had in its hands the totality of all real state power and the entire fate of the revolution.

Now the Soviet was master of the situation in the sense that it now had the integral strength to lead the army, the state power, and the revolution wherever it wished. . .

* * *

It goes without saying that the bourgeoisie, though it had lost the campaign, was far from laying down its arms. With the formation of the new Soviet majority not a few new opportunities and high hopes appeared. But it was impossible merely to count on these chances and feed on these hopes. It was necessary to do some work oneself.

There began a desperate badgering of Soviet groups and individuals, on the calculation of overcoming the whole through its parts. This creditable occupation was also carried on by bourgeois groups throughout the revolution; but it began during these first days of April after the defeat of the bourgeoisie in its basic struggle for the army.

It goes without saying that at first the entire attention of these honourable warriors was concentrated on the *Left* part of the Soviet—the Bolsheviks. If I'm not mistaken it began with the *provocateurs*. A worker Bolshevik, Mikhailov, the secretary of the printers' union, who had relentlessly and rabidly agitated against allowing the publication of newspapers, was accused of being a *provocateur*. Then the well-known Duma deputy Malinovsky[1] was mentioned. And in the columns of the newspapers—up

[1] Malinovsky, Roman Vatslavovich (1878–1918): of peasant origin, with a criminal background. For many years enjoyed the confidence of both the Bolsheviks and the Tsarist Secret Police. Finally unmasked as a police agent, but Lenin defended him as a victim of political intrigue until after the October Revolution, when the Secret Police archives were seized by the Bolsheviks and his rôle incontrovertibly clarified. He was tried, sentenced to death, and executed immediately. (Ed.)

to the most respectable—there began a frenzied war-dance of 'logical conclusions', parallels, and insinuations. 'Extremist slogans' in general, and Bolshevism in particular, were scientifically explained, historically inferred from and theoretically adapted to the activity, tasks, and ideas of the Secret Police.

Malinovsky had been the hireling of the Tsarist police. But who had defined the revolutionary line of Bolshevism in 1914? Judas-Malinovsky. And who in May of that same year, after refusing a proper investigation, had defended Judas, abusing those who had given warning as filthy slanderers and giving printed assurance of Malinovsky's political honesty? Why, Lenin, *Pravda*, the Bolshevik Central Committee. Millions of copies of newspapers carried all this every day amongst the masses of the middle class and the workers, soldiers, and peasants.

Then there began to emerge every possible kind of piquant fact about individuals. They took up Kamenev's life-history, Steklov's family situation. And for a long time, day in and day out, they busied themselves with these things.

But Lenin, of course, stood in the centre of the campaign. At this time he was isolated in Soviet spheres and had only just begun to come into power amongst the Bolsheviks themselves. Here, even for the most 'loyal' and 'democratic' journalists, with their unfailing desire to maintain decorum and keep up a show of democratic piety—the possibility of the most complete freedom of speech was opened up. And they occupied themselves with Lenin without restraint, respite, or shame. This was a really rewarding subject, and they all rushed on him at once like the rats on Bishop Hatto.

Lenin's crimes, as everyone knew, had begun even *before his arrival*, and I have already described how his trip through Germany was exploited by the entire middle class, both upper and lower. Agitation on this point poured out in a great flood and was very successful: the slogan 'Down with Lenin—back to Germany' was taken up by the broadest masses around the middle of April. It became extremely popular amongst the philistines who made up public opinion, and went not only through the barracks but through the factories too.

I have said that at the welcome to the Bolshevik leader I hadn't succeeded in finding out the opinion of the military units who had met in his honour. But now, on April 14th–16th, all the papers carried a resolution of the immemorially revolutionary sailors of the Baltic Fleet crew who had been at the station as guard of honour: 'Having learnt that Comrade Lenin came back to us in Russia with the consent of his Majesty the German Emperor and King of Prussia' (*sic*), the sailors wrote, 'we express our profound regret at our participation in his triumphal welcome to Petersburg. If we had known by what paths he had returned to us, then instead of the enthusiastic cries of "Hurrah" exclamations of indignation would have resounded: "Away with you, back to the country you passed through to us!" '

Lenin was attacked for his past, for his real opinions, for his way of life (!), etc. Kshesinskaya's palace, as though he lived there, was on everyone's lips. Every possible organization, including the Soviet ones, began to 'possess an opinion' on Lenin and his pernicious activity. The Soldiers' Executive Commission and the Moscow Soldiers' Soviet, on mature reflection, passed a resolution on *protection from Lenin* and his propaganda. The high-school students in Petersburg arranged a demonstration 'against Lenin', etc.

All this undoubtedly reached its mark: the Bolshevik leader's reputation as an enemy of Russia and the revolution was quickly established. But that was the least of it: around Kshesinskaya's house, where the magnificent flag of the Bolshevik Central Committee was flying, immense crowds of people began to assemble, especially in the evenings. They formed hostile demonstrations, agitated, threatened. In their midst, of course, real *provocateurs* were at work, repeating in their neighbours' ears all the 'conclusions' of the newspapers concerning Lenin and extending them to all Socialists and Soviet people. The papers wrote that Lenin came out on the balcony once or twice, to explain himself, 'justify himself', and assure people that he was 'being misunderstood'. It's possible that Lenin, who had learned a good deal, might really have been 'explaining' his position in a milder spirit.

But things kept getting worse. A mob began promenading around the city, stormily demanding Lenin's arrest. There were already disorders and in general a rather great, even a very great, success for the Black Hundred campaign. 'Arrest Lenin' and then 'Down with the Bolsheviks' was heard at every street-crossing. Ignoring the movement or yielding to popular indignation was impossible. You had to fight.

A broad counter-agitation was started. The Soviet *Izvestiya*, of which at that time Dan was an editor, devoted an impressive editorial to this affair on April 17th, hotly protesting both at the slanderous attacks against Lenin and at a campaign against him by such methods. 'It is hardly possible for us', wrote the editors, 'to permit the thought that in a free country, instead of open argument, violence should be employed against a man who has given his whole life to the service of the working class, the service of the insulted and oppressed!'

On April 17th there was a tremendous demonstration of war-wounded, which made a great impression on the inhabitants of Petersburg. An immense number of wounded from the military hospitals of the capital—armless, legless, in bandages—moved along the Nevsky to the Tauride Palace. Those who couldn't walk were taken in lorries and cabs. Their banners were inscribed with 'War to the End!' 'Total Annihilation of German Militarism!' 'Our Wounds Demand Victory!' Maimed men, the unhappy victims of carnage in the cause of capitalist profits, demanded, at the behest of these same capitalists, that their sons and brothers go on being maimed without end for these same goals. A really terrifying scene!

But the main thing that had mobilized the wounded was Lenin himself. With inscriptions and shouts of 'Down with Lenin!' etc. they came into the Tauride Palace to demand the arrest and exile of the future dictator. Their speeches and demands dealt for the most part with Lenin. Skobelev and Tsereteli went out and, though divided from Lenin by the whole width of the Soviet, reproached the demonstrators and protested against pogromist tendencies. But their success was not great. Shouts resounded in the midst of the tumult and excitement: 'Lenin is a spy and provocateur!' The Soviet orators were refused a hearing. Seeing this situation, Rodzianko went out to the wounded men. And he was a success, as in past disputations before demonstrating regiments.

In these exceptional circumstances Rodzianko let himself go: he not only spoke of 'War to the end' but also said 'Now there should be no attempts at shortening it.'

* * *

There was a session of the Liaison Commission on the evening of the 15th, at the Marian Palace. After the business on the agenda was finished, the Ministers began to utter reproaches by the way, concerning the 'disloyalty' of the Soviet, the indulgence of 'anarchy', and the difficulties created for the Government. . .

On the 14th of April, *Izvestiya*, without comment, had printed a resolution passed the day before by a Petersburg factory, in which an anarchist or, if you like, a Leninist programme was expounded: after the 'sweeping away' of the Government and the transfer of all power to the Soviets, the resolution spoke of the seizure of the land by the peasants, of the factories by the workers, etc. These were the first swallows of Lenin's 'Socialism'. The resolution was quite untypical, but it attracted the attention of bourgeois circles.

And now, in the Liaison Commission, Shingarev, quoting the resolution, demanded to know what was the meaning of its appearance in an official publication. The Soviet representatives expressed their regret and promised to see to it that this wouldn't be repeated.

The meeting was closed. Then, without leaving the table, Premier Lvov turned privately to Tsereteli for some advice: what measures could and should be applied in the struggle against Lenin in the present situation?

Tsereteli started to reply. For my part I thought it at least out of place and for myself inadmissible to take any part whatsoever in looking for means of fighting Lenin—jointly with Messrs. the Ministers of the Miliukov–Guchkov Cabinet. I pointedly got up and left the table, where this charming conversation was continuing. Miliukov then left and came over to me. We stopped in a corner of the room—also for a private conversation. We were joined by a silent witness, the well-known Cadet Nabokov, the Principal Secretary of the Provisional Government.

'What is this, is there a split in your Ex. Com.?' Miliukov asked, with great and unconcealed interest.

The leader of Russian imperialism (together with the imperialism itself) happened to be in difficulties. Strong allies, and some sort of support in the democracy, were as necessary to him as air. At the same time, no matter how Miliukov referred to the

Soviet in public, he could not minimize to himself the real rôle of this 'private institution', and he kept a close watch on what went on within it—hoping to find support there. I didn't like enlarging on the theme of the growing fissure within the Soviet: in those days the boats had not yet been burnt and there was still the temptation to represent the Soviet, before outsiders' envious eyes, as a unified whole, in contrast to the bourgeoisie. On the other hand—the truth will out. 'Not what you'd call a split,' I said, 'but as a matter of fact differentiations that had no significance before have begun to show. A strong tendency has emerged against Zimmerwald, and in favour of a moderate policy and solidarity with the Government. Before, these groups easily disintegrated, but now they have some coherence and possess strength. Personally, I am Left.'

'Yes, I know,' remarked Miliukov, 'I've read your books.'

In these books Miliukov had been perhaps my principal target; but properly speaking, aside from a general Zimmerwald position on the war, they still said nothing about anything: after all, Tsereteli, who had now distinguished himself as Miliukov's hope, shared the views of those books.

Miliukov's knowledge of Soviet affairs was evidently not specially profound—or else he ascribed a universal and terrifying significance to the name of Zimmerwald itself. However, I didn't wish to leave Miliukov under the impression of his victory and my defeat within the Soviet. I tried to take revenge by a reference to another basic revolutionary process that was being accomplished those days:

'But you, probably, have your eyes also on something more important than a restratification within the Ex. Com.,' I said. 'After all, the general meaning of events is that the revolution has broadened as we wanted it to and you didn't. You haven't succeeded in turning the new Russia into a plutocratic England or France, or in reinforcing the dictatorship of capital. It's already quite clear that you have no real power against the democracy, and can have none. The army, as the instrument of policy, is not going over to you.'

Miliukov interrupted me. He looked sincerely indignant and even grieved.

'But what are you saying?' he exclaimed. 'How can you put the question that way? The army is not coming over to us!

The army must fight at the front. That's our whole policy concerning the army!'

Miliukov began to speak animatedly, and apparently with complete sincerity.

'And for that matter—you surely don't think that we are really carrying on some kind of a bourgeois class policy of our own, that we are taking a definite line of some kind! Nothing of the sort. We are simply compelled to see to it that everything doesn't go to pieces once and for all. We see gaping holes everywhere, and have to rush from one to another to help, and stop them up somehow.'

Heavenly powers! Thunder and lightning! Was I dreaming? It was my turn to be flabbergasted. Miliukov, recognized by Europe as the head of Russian imperialism, the ideologist of Russia as a Great Power, one of the inspirers of the World War, the Russian Foreign Minister, the worthy partner of the Ribots, Lloyd Georges, and von Kühlmanns,[1] one of the most active and central figures in current world affairs—Miliukov *didn't know* that he was carrying out an ultra-class policy *quand-même*—balking at nothing. Miliukov, a highly-cultivated man, a great scholar, and a professor—*didn't know* he was speaking prose! Astounding! Inconceivable! Or could it simply have been a lie?

No, I'm convinced Miliukov spoke just as things seemed to him. Nor in the last analysis is this at all surprising. It was merely startling at first for an inveterate Zimmerwaldite. For this is the age-old strength of capitalism—a régime based on violence, fraud, and the exploitation of nations by a tiny minority of rulers—that it compels not merely the entire administrative machine to serve the ruling classes, and not merely culture in general, but also the most distinguished representatives of culture, who meanwhile never suspect that they are the pillars of violence, fraud, and exploitation.

We didn't have a chance to finish this conversation, to my mind extremely interesting. The Ministers and the Soviet people had got up from the table and were all going towards the door. I don't know whether they had found methods of conducting their joint fight against Lenin.

'In the next few days an important newspaper is going to

[1] Richard von Kühlmann (1873–1948): German Foreign Secretary. (Ed.)

appear, Left wing, in the former Soviet spirit,' I said to Miliukov, on the way downstairs.

'An important paper?' Miliukov asked with interest. 'What is it?'

'The *Novaya Zhizn*. Gorky and the whole crowd from the *Letopis*. We're going to do our duty.'

'Yes,' repeated Miliukov thoughtfully, 'we're going to do our duty.'

CHAPTER 14

A PETTY BOURGEOIS AND A GREAT OPPORTUNIST CONQUER THE SOVIET

THE All-Russian Soviet Conference (March 29–April 3) among other things was supposed to fulfil an important organizational (or rather, perhaps, constitutional) task: to create a permanent All-Russian Soviet organ—in place of the Petersburg Ex. Com., which up to then had been acting in the name of the entire Russian democracy. The Conference performed this task in a rather rough-and-ready way. It simply elected sixteen people to supplement our Ex. Com. and decided to consider this institution the fully authorized All-Russian Soviet organ. This decision may have been partly a sign of special confidence in and solidarity with the Petersburg Ex. Com., but it was also dictated by practical considerations—to avoid needlessly complicating the problem.

The election of these sixteen was organized in the way that from now on was usual in all (major) Soviet elections: through the proportional representation of party fractions—candidates being nominated by the fractions themselves and merely formally confirmed by the plenum. Alas! I've forgotten the names of these sixteen new members, with some exceptions, nor can I find them in the newspapers of the time.

The general character of this group and its general influence on Soviet policy can be imagined from the fact that it was a microcosm of the Conference, and faithfully reflected its composition and physiognomy. The Conference itself, with some vacillations, took the attitude of the new opportunistic majority of the Ex. Com.

A few men also came in from the Soldiers' Executive Commission—some Swamp nonentities and Rightists. The Ex. Com. was now a collegium of between eighty and ninety people.

On April 8th, at the end of a long and exhausting day of

work, the Ex. Com. learned that the SR leader Chernov[1] was arriving that evening from abroad. Another triumphal welcome was necessary. Gots[2] and I were chosen to represent the Ex. Com. On my way out of the Palace the Left SR Alexandrovich seized me by the sleeve: 'Now you just tell him straight out,' he began, holding his fist in front of his angrily flashing eyes, 'just straight out in the welcoming speech that the devil knows what's going on in the Ex. Com. And that he, he's a Zimmerwaldite, and he's got to open a campaign right away with us, against them here. Tell him that immediately, as he ought to be told, right away!'

Alexandrovich, still muttering something, rushed off. And I would not have been far from doing the same, right away, if I hadn't been a delegate of the Ex. Com. and hadn't had some doubts about Chernov's present opinions, after so many bitter disappointments.

* * *

I had heard Chernov, as well as Lenin, Martov, and Trotsky, in 1902–1903 abroad. Afterwards, in 1905–1907, I became acquainted with him personally as well, in Russia and Finland, seeing him on political but more often on literary matters. Then we separated until this ceremonial meeting—keeping up (rather feebly) a 'literary' correspondence between Moscow, Archangel, and Petersburg on one side and Italy on the other.

In spite of my extreme heresies Chernov was always glad of my contributions to the journals he edited. In general my writing owed a great deal to his encouragement.

In the creation of the SR Party Chernov had played an absolutely exceptional rôle. Chernov was the only substantial theoretician of any kind it had—and a universal one at that. If Chernov's writings were removed from the SR party literature almost nothing would be left.

[1] Chernov, Vladimir Mikhailovich (1876–1953): in the revolutionary movement since 1893; one of the founders of the Social-Revolutionary Party and its principal ideologist; a central figure in all SR affairs. Active in the Czechoslovak uprising in 1918; afterwards an *émigré* in Germany, France, and the United States. (Ed.)

[2] Gots, Abram Raphailovich (1882–1937): leader of the SR group in the Soviet. Hostile to the October Revolution, he fought the Communists until 1920. Condemned to death at the SR trial in 1920, but freed and held with others as hostages responsible for SR activities against the Soviet régime. Politically inactive after release but shot in 1937. (Ed.)

Without Chernov the SR Party would not have existed, any more than the Bolshevik Party without Lenin—inasmuch as no serious political organization can take shape round an intellectual vacuum. But the difference between Chernov and Lenin was that Lenin was not only an ideologist but also a political leader, whereas Chernov was *merely a littérateur.*

Scarcely anyone would deny Chernov's really immense literary talent. But the essential character and the basic aims of his literary creation must not be forgotten. He was always beset, after all, by the unattainable, false, and internally contradictory task of impregnating the black-earth, muzhik Russian soil with the most modern scientific international Socialism; or else wresting equal rights in the European working-class International for our black-earth muzhik, for 'independent' populism.

But Chernov—unlike Lenin—only performed half the work in the SR Party. During the period of pre-revolutionary conspiracy he was not the party organizing centre, and in the broad arena of the revolution, in spite of his vast authority amongst the SRs, *Chernov proved bankrupt as a political leader.* Here, where ideology should have yielded to politics, Chernov was fated not only to wear out his authority but also to break his neck.

Further on, in our frequent encounters with Chernov, we shall see how he lost not only his authority but also his adherents and his position as leader in the 'biggest Russian party'. We shall see how he writhed and wriggled, grew confused and lost his way among people, events, movements, and tendencies. We shall see how, under an unbearable burden, he arrived at his naïve and silly personal tactic of washing his hands of everything. We shall see the founder and leader of the SR Party in a tragi-comic position.

But one must not only be fair: the *reasons* for the tragedy (or if you like the tragi-comedy) of Chernov must be correctly understood.

Chernov never showed the slightest stability, striking power, or fighting ability—qualities vital for a political leader in a revolutionary situation. He proved inwardly feeble and outwardly unattractive, disagreeable and ridiculous. But that's only one side of the matter. I'm convinced that no less a rôle was played by the above-mentioned falsity and internal contradictoriness of his doctrine and world outlook.

While it was possible to write, and do nothing but write, things went splendidly. But in revolutionary practice how was it possible to wriggle out from under in the din of the hammer and anvil?

Chernov wanted to plant a proletarian, European, and also Zimmerwald Socialism in the Russian soil of petty-bourgeois darkness and philistinism. This was a hopeless business. But Chernov could not tear himself away either from his Socialism or from his soil. This is by no means the least important aspect of the drama of Chernov.

From the very beginning of the war Chernov had taken a Zimmerwald position. And now, on my way to the Finland Station for the triumphal welcome to the SR leader, I was thinking: Where will he get to, in this moss-covered Swamp, with his Zimmerwaldism? How is he going to manage with his internationalism against the background of the growing bloc between the imperialist bourgeoisie and his blood-brothers of the muzhik-soldier, radical-intellectual groups?

There had been bitter disillusionments already. I was far from optimistic.

* * *

The Ex. Com.'s most urgent task lay in the regulating of its organization and functions. This task had merely been postponed until the Conference, which might have radically altered the *composition* of the central Soviet organ. But now that this body had been strengthened and augmented by the Conference, it had become absolutely impossible to put off the work of organization.

The Ex. Com., in spite of the energetic labours of its numerous Commissions, was quite incapable of grappling with the vast mass of duties descending on it. This was quite understandable; it was inevitably entailed as much by the constitutional as by the political conjuncture in Russia at that time. I've already written of how the Soviet, without the slightest conscious effort, by force of circumstances and the spontaneous course of events, had been progressively broadening its functions. It was becoming more and more a State within the State.

The *populace*, with all its demands and private, group, social, and political interests, turned to it for everything. But the official Government and every kind of governmental and municipal institution also turned to it more and more for all sorts of assistance.

On the one hand the popularity and authority of the Soviet went on growing like a snowball amongst the urban and rural masses. On the other hand—not only in these masses but also in political circles and state institutions—there was taking root an awareness of the Soviet's real power and potentialities, and of the helplessness of the Government and its agencies.

The official Government machine, in one part after another, began idling more and more. Independently of what either side desired, the official mechanism was being supplanted by the Soviet.

Not only the representatives of the new Soviet majority—from 'lofty' political considerations—but I too, and other Leftists like me, for the sake of the proper economy of function indispensable for the country, and to avoid disorganization, struggled as hard as we could against this process. But it was impossible to stop it.

Just at this time agrarian affairs had begun to arouse misgivings. Excesses and disorders were not so numerous, apparently, as might have been expected and as some tried to picture them; nevertheless things were getting somewhat complicated. The Government was still keeping secret its opinion about the foundations of the future reforms. Were they being prepared? How was work proceeding, and along what lines? All this was unknown, and it disturbed the peasants.

On the other hand, land speculation was beginning. The kulaks,[1] taking advantage of the panic, were beginning to accumulate land in their capacity as 'peasants'. Estates had begun to be parcelled out on the most varied (and of course nearly always fictitious) grounds, and to be reduced to the supposed maximums of the reform. Wholesale deals with foreigners, again for the most part fictitious, began to be made. In these circumstances, there wouldn't be much left of our land resources in a few months' time.

This alone was enough to upset the peasants. Swarms of emissaries appeared in the Ex. Com.—asking, demanding, threatening. Immediate guarantees of land reform and im-

[1] A nickname for well-to-do peasants (Russian for 'fist'). (Ed.)

mediate steps to preserve our land resources from pillage were essential. There were plenty of resolutions to this effect, but still the Government took no steps. Worse still, undeniable signs began to appear that Prince Lvov's Cabinet was definitely sabotaging this business and was quite incapable of handling it. An acute conflict on this revolutionary front began to come very swiftly to a head.

The Liaison Commission's work was piling up. Some Russian citizens *en route* for Russia—our comrades Trotsky, Chudnovsky, and several other internationalists—had been arrested in Halifax by the enlightened authorities of a 'great Allied democracy'. By this action the Allied police showed how well-informed they were on the course of Russian Socialist thought, and as for the high authorities, this was how they demonstrated their declared readiness to make no distinctions between the *émigrés* and to give all of them the same co-operation in their return home.

The Ex. Com. had already sent the British Government a determined protest on the 8th. A telegram appealing to the British workers to support the Soviet protest against the British Government's medieval behaviour was also sent to the English newspapers.

On the 10th another question of the same kind arose. The Swiss internationalist, Platten, who had accompanied Lenin in the sealed train but had stayed over in Stockholm for a while, had been stopped at the Russian frontier by the revolutionary Government while trying to visit Russia. The Minister Miliukov went personally to the station to meet the French Socialist Thomas; other foreign Socialists were our welcome guests and were received with outstretched arms in the Marian Palace. Branting,[1] Cachin, O'Grady, de Brouckère,[2] and others felt themselves at home and formed a united front with our Ministers against the Soviet, while an internationalist was absolutely refused entry to Russian soil!

This was an inadmissible and intolerable action of enormous principled importance. Miliukov and his colleagues, gambling on the new conjuncture in the Soviet, were making a serious test

[1] Branting, Karl Hjalmar (1860–1925): leader of the Swedish Social-Democratic Party and one of the leaders of the Second International. (Ed.)

[2] Brouckère, Louis de (1870–1951): Belgian Socialist leader. (Ed.)

and undoubtedly understood its general political sense very well. The Soviet Opposition, headed by the Bolsheviks with their party interests, insisted that the Liaison Commission should demand Platten's immediate admission to Russia.

The Liaison Commission left for the Marian Palace. Chernov, of course, wanted to go along; he was determined to astound our home-grown Ministers with his diplomatic skill, and spoke interminably on what he had observed abroad and his views on the international political situation. Creeping up on his point, he reported his conversations with prominent French and British statesmen and assured Miliukov that the hoped-for *démarche* of the Russian Government would be received by Allied circles with every sympathy. But exactly what *démarche*?

Chernov was taxing his subtlest diplomacy to find the line of least possible resistance. Attention, please! After all, the March 27th document was addressed only to the Russian people; it had been published for domestic use only. The Allies not only had no reason to react to it, but were not even obliged to know about it. No one, of course, could doubt that the March 27th document was completely sincere on the part of the Government. But for Miliukov's own wishes to approach realization it was necessary to take a further step and bring this act of March 27th officially to the notice of the Allied Governments. Strictly speaking it was the same step. But nevertheless it went further.

In his anxiety to convince his hearers Chernov poured out a flood of words, now in an earnest and businesslike tone, now full of revolutionary patriotic sentiment and now of puns and jokes. In the Liaison Commission we were not accustomed to such broad-gauge speeches, and he was listened to with interest.

I don't remember the discussion; I only recall Miliukov's saying something to the effect that he himself, as a matter of fact, also had occasion to come in contact with the opinion of Allied ruling circles, and he expressed his profound doubt whether this kind of Russian *démarche* would be favourably received. Chernov replied that he 'had grounds' for his assertions. Miliukov said he also 'had grounds'. . .

But the question was exhausted by Miliukov's agreeing to address to the Allies a Note in connexion with the March 27th document. But would it be published in agreement with the

Ex. Com., or independently of it? As far as I recall this wasn't discussed.

The question of the arrest of Trotsky and the other internationalists was decided in two words. Miliukov said it was a simple misunderstanding and promised to take action. The *émigrés* were in fact freed, when the Russian Government had expressed its desires. The British authorities had gone too far: Miliukov had thought it diplomatic simply to keep the internationalists away from their country, whereas the British had put them in prison. This was really too much, especially since Trotsky and his comrades hadn't given the slightest occasion for any accusation of 'disloyalty'.

But Platten's case ended differently. Miliukov gave an explanation on these lines: Platten had not been allowed in because the Ministry of Foreign Affairs had some evidence concerning his relations with the German authorities; moreover, as was common knowledge, Platten had performed a friendly service for the enemy Government by arranging Lenin's trip through Germany. As for the request to change the order and admit Platten, Miliukov flatly rejected it.

There were no objections from our official speakers: the 'Praesidium Group' showed no reaction whatever.

I asked for the floor. My colleagues on the Liaison Commission, as always in such cases, frowned and pricked up their ears.

'I'm completely perplexed after listening to the explanations of the Foreign Minister,' I said. 'Platten rendered the enemy a service by co-operating in Lenin's trip. But who is Lenin? Lenin is a Russian citizen who in spite of the complete political freedom in Russia was unable to return to his country in any way whatsoever without Platten's assistance. If Lenin is a criminal why wasn't he arrested at the frontier, and why is he at liberty now? But if Lenin has full rights as a citizen then any assistance in his return to his country can only be treated as a service to him, and also to our Ministry of Foreign Affairs, which could not perform its functions in connexion with . . .'

I wasn't given a chance to finish—any more than later on at Bolshevik meetings. The Ministers raised a hubbub, their faces expressed indignation, regret, and embarrassment. They shrugged their shoulders, waved their hands at me, made exclamations of protest and consternation. As far as I recall, Nekrasov got more excited than the others and shouted louder:

'That's enough! Look here, Nikolai Nikolayevich, stop it! We don't agree! We just don't agree! Stop!'

My comrades lowered their eyes and kept a deathly silence. *Not a soul* supported me. Obviously from the point of view of the Soviet members also I had committed a major gaffe—neither for the first nor the last time.

* * *

This time a report to the Ex. Com. on the meeting of the Liaison Commission was inevitable. Tsereteli got the floor: he painted everything in the rosiest colours—the Government, as always, was willing to compromise on everything. The Note to the Allies would be prepared in the next few days. To be sure, the Government had refused to let Platten into Russia: but it seemed that the Ministry of Foreign Affairs had some evidence as to his relations with the German Government.

I asked for the floor for a supplementary report.

'The Liaison Commission, which reflects the general inter-relationships of the Soviet and the Provisional Government, is in a very bad way,' I said. 'The Liaison Commission has been dealing with the Ministerial Council in a kind of private, intimate way, especially recently. We put questions to the Government and make requests just as any organization or group might. The Ministers hear us out, report facts, express their views and by and large turn down our requests. We show no reaction whatever to this and don't even report our discussions to the Ex. Com. In general the Soviet never reacts to Government actions which go against its wishes. Therefore I think it necessary to pay special attention to the activity of the Liaison Commission, and moreover I insist on the necessary practical steps. First of all, the Ex. Com. should at once come to a decision obliging the Commission to make constant detailed reports, and secondly, to give an official character at once to its activities, if only by keeping official minutes of 'Liaison' sessions and a precise record of all its decisions and the replies of the Government.'

Then, after expounding the Platten affair, I insisted that the

Ex. Com. ought to react to this inadmissible precedent and use all its authority to secure Platten a permit.

Tsereteli objected. He said my interpretation of the Liaison Commission's activity was completely false: the Government agreed more often than it refused, and when it did refuse it had good reasons for it, and in general was extremely well disposed.

But the main thing Tsereteli objected to—with his usual flat-footed 'manliness'—was the official minutes. Why? In the first place, with less formality you could get more; secondly, conversations off the record were generally more fruitful and useful: the Ministers would never say what they would have said off the record, if they knew that every word of theirs was going to be taken down.

It sounds unlikely, but it is a fact that Tsereteli's argument ran just like this. Now it was no longer a question of the charm of this primitive, 'cynical' line of reasoning. What was important here was something else: just how did Tsereteli interpret the reciprocal relationship of the Soviet and the Government? How did he conceive of the place of the Ex. Com. and the Liaison Commission itself *vis-à-vis* the Miliukov–Guchkov Cabinet?

These ideas had an enormous importance just then for the revolution. For Tsereteli was the exponent and the leader of the philistine mass that constituted the majority of the Ex. Com. This mass regarded as real wisdom his vulgar, flabby little notions, that concealed the impenetrable quagmire prepared for the revolution.

We tried in vain to persuade the Mamelukes that the Liaison Commission was not a commission of journalistic ferrets who thought they must creep into the souls of their exalted interlocutors and extort state secrets from them, and that the Soviet delegation did not exist for intimate conversations with highly-placed personages. In vain we reminded them that the Liaison Commission was simply a technical mediator between class enemies. All in vain.

My suggestions were rejected. It was simply decided that the members of the Liaison Commission—should keep minutes themselves!

* * *

On April 19th, I left the Ex. Com. with the intention of not returning. I was supposed to get out the *Novaya Zhizn* that day and would have to go straight to the printers' from the editorial offices.

I rang up the Ex. Com. to see whether there was anything special. Someone from the Opposition gave me a sensational piece of news: the Ex. Com. had received the text of the long-awaited Note prepared by Miliukov and already despatched to the Allies, in fulfilment of the promises given the Ex. Com. delegates by the Government.

The new Note completely annulled everything the revolution had accomplished on behalf of peace up to then. It assured the Allies that Russia's aims in the war remained as before, under the Tsar, and that the revolution had changed nothing in them—just like the document published on March 27th for home consumption.

I stood at the telephone utterly taken aback.

'But what about the Ex. Com.? What are they saying, and what are they going to do?'

There was a meeting scheduled for that evening. . . What were they saying? The Left wing thought, first of all, that this was a total liquidation not only of the significance but of the very fact itself of the revolution, from the point of view of foreign policy and peace. Secondly, the Left wing thought it an impudent and cynical mockery of the Soviet and the people. They felt that Miliukov ought to be liquidated within twenty-four hours. As for the Right wing, it was rather confused; it was trying to calm us and make us believe that nothing special had happened.

I still couldn't recover my senses and simply *understand* what it was all about. If a Note like this had been published by the Government independently of our demands, that would have been simply a continuation of Miliukov's customary imperialist policy. But how could such a document appear in *answer* to our demands, and as the fulfilment of the promises given? What was it—a misunderstanding, *naïveté*, the demonstrative gesture of a victor who thought he could lightly disregard the people's will? Or—the most natural idea of all—was it a conscious provocation of popular wrath and civil war?

I returned to the editorial offices and reported all I'd heard. It had an unexpected effect.

Bazarov—so mild and yielding a personality, who wouldn't hurt a fly and was inclined to explain everything people did in the best possible light—leaped to his feet as though stung and rushed towards me waving his arms.

'Aha!' he bellowed, completely beside himself, brandishing his fists in my face, 'then you just tell them that tomorrow we'll start a revolt!'

But who was this 'we' who were going to start a revolt, and *how* would 'we' do it? And how could Bazarov be imagined leading a rebellion?

But actually nothing could express the very essence of the situation better than Bazarov's language. 'They' had thrown down the gauntlet; it was up to 'us' to pick it up.

* * *

It is well known that hypocrisy is vice's tribute to virtue. On March 27th Miliukov had agreed to pay this tribute, but on April 18th he refused.

In March the leader of the bourgeoisie had been playing a sort of diplomatic game, hypocritically and with stacked political cards. In April he would have nothing to do with veils, haziness, deception, or fig-leaves. He clearly thought it no longer worth the trouble.

The diplomats of the Marian Palace had removed their gloves, and flung one of them at the feet of the people and the Soviet. There was nothing left for the people and the Soviet to do but pick it up.

* * *

The next day, April 20th, the new Homogeneous Bureau[1] of the Ex. Com. was at work before the meeting. But organic work was going slowly: everyone was obviously thinking primarily of the 'Note' and 'high policy'.

A motor-car raced up to the entrance, visible from the window, and a soldier ran out of it and rushed to the door. Some time later he ran into the room of the Bureau and hastily related the following.

An immense crowd of workers, some of them armed, was

[1] A sub-grouping within the Ex. Com. initially composed of about 10 men of different tendencies, formed as a sort of counter-weight to the Star Chamber (see p. 359). It was an informal conference that met every day. Sukhanov was invited to join by Lieber, and did so despite his view that the Bureau was fundamentally submissive to the new Right-wing Soviet majority. (Ed.)

moving towards the Nevsky from the Vyborg Side. There were also a lot of soldiers with them. The demonstrators were marching under the slogans: 'Down with the Provisional Government!' 'Down with Miliukov!' Tremendous excitement reigned generally in the working-class districts, the factories, and the barracks. Many factories were idle. Local meetings were taking place everywhere.

All this on account of Miliukov's Note, which had appeared that day in all the newspapers.

People began running into the Palace square. Passers-by stopped one another, and gesticulating told each other something. A second courier ran in and reported that crowds were assembling and impromptu meetings being held on the Nevsky. You could hear speeches and shouts there aimed at Miliukov and the Provisional Government. Great agitation prevailed everywhere—on account of the Note.

What should we do in the Bureau, the centre of the Soviet organization and the heart of the revolutionary democracy? First of all, skirmishes and bloodshed must be prevented. We were told that two volunteer working-class detachments were already on the spot and blazing with violence. If there must be civil war, then at least let it not be in the form of a senseless casual scrimmage between Nevsky strollers and Vyborg workers. The demonstration from the Vyborg Side had to be stopped at once and if possible turned back; then we could come to grips with 'high policy' and settle the general question of the situation.

Chkheidze was in the Palace. He was hunted up immediately and a few minutes later was on his way, with two or three nameless comrades, to intercept the demonstration. He caught it somewhere near the Champ de Mars. As far as I recall there was some rather stormy wrangling, but nevertheless Chkheidze apparently managed to calm and disperse the demonstrators. He pointed out that the Ex. Com. was going to discuss the situation at once, and in case of need would then call for organized action, whereas fragmentary actions would show us to be weak and merely hurt the cause.

Meanwhile, we continued our discussion in the Bureau. In the midst of it, more sensational news arrived. The Finnish Regiment, with banners and placards—'Down with Aggressive Policy!' 'Dismiss Miliukov and Guchkov!'—had moved on the

Marian Palace, surrounded it, and occupied all its entrances and exits. . . The Finns were followed by other regiments—the Moscow and the 180th. The soldiers were terribly excited: they said they intended to arrest Miliukov and the entire Provisional Government.

Like lightning Skobelev was ordered over to the Marian Palace. With a speech like Chkheidze's he succeeded, if not in quieting the soldiers completely, in making them give up their intention of 'squeezing' the Provisional Government by arms and physical violence. The Soviet would announce what must be done to defend the democracy and when.

The regiments started to disperse from the Marian Palace, but they continued demonstrating against Miliukov and the policy of aggression in favour of peace and the Soviet.

Who had summoned the regiments from the barracks—with such an impressive aim? All these actions had of course taken place on the initiative of Left party elements. In particular the siege of the Marian Palace was ascribed to the excess energy of a certain Bolshevik, a soldier called Linde, a former member of the Ex. Com. The arrest of the Provisional Government of course far exceeded the rights or powers of any party or group; besides, this easily realizable act was completely out of accord with both the views of the Soviet and the needs of the moment.

* * *

The Note of April 18th did not stir up the capital alone. Exactly the same performance took place in Moscow too. Workers left their benches, soldiers their barracks. The streets and squares were seething with passion and tempestuous demonstrations. The same mass-meetings, the same slogans—for and against Miliukov. The same two camps and the same solidarity of the democracy. The Moscow Soviet, like that of Petersburg, was calling for calm and endurance, issuing warnings against isolated actions and requesting the workers and soldiers to wait for the Soviet's orders.

Newspapers, especially the *Novaya Zhizn*, were inundated with dozens of factory and regimental resolutions concerning the Note—with unequivocal demands for the immediate dismissal of Miliukov or of the Provisional Government.

But it was not merely slogans and moods that were taking

form: the enormous strain on the people's will and energy was becoming clear. In spite of Soviet agitation against the street movement, in spite of the appeals for calm and passivity—the excitement did not diminish at all. Everyone knew about the negotiations with the Government and about the Soviet's decisions. But this didn't make the workers and soldiers refrain from a direct and active part in events.

On the morning of the 21st the streets of Petersburg looked just as they had the day before. That was the least of it: the movement kept growing and was already about to overflow its banks. There was as yet no news of any excesses, but here and there free fights might be expected to break out at any moment. If not civil war, then civil bloodshed seemed to be approaching.

The agitators of the bourgeoisie had assembled on the Nevsky large cadres of demonstrators in favour of Miliukov. Everyone possible was mobilized and called out into the street. The speeches at mass-meetings of the 'better' public became more outspoken. The slogans on placards and banners of the day before now had dozens of variants, sharper in their expression of both points of view, *in favour* of Guchkov–Miliukov, the war and the Allies, and *against 'anarchy'*, Lenin, and German militarism.

In spite of all the eloquence of Tsereteli's friends, the workers and soldiers simply could not watch all this scene with indifference. In such conditions, as ought to have been expected, Soviet agitation against demonstration was useless. The soldiers and workers had also come out into the streets in dense masses, and some of them had made for the Nevsky.

The atmosphere was getting thicker; bloodshed was imminent. Then the first shots rang out. Somewhere near the Nevsky a number of people were killed and wounded by shots from among the crowds of demonstrators. Of course the bourgeoisie and its press, without waiting for investigation or trial, howled that it was Leninists who had shot at unarmed citizens, but it is far more likely that it was the handiwork of *agents provocateurs* from former Tsarist police circles, venting their impotent spite.

However that may be, the carnage had begun. The situation could no longer be endured for a single moment. It was absurd from all points of view. These street actions must be liquidated at once, by one decisive blow. And—*it was done.*

But who did it, and by what means? The autocratic, national Provisional Government, or the valiant General Kornilov? It was, of course, the Soviet, which alone possessed the authority and the real power. Miliukov's Cabinet was the *source* of the 'civil war', but it had absolutely no means of stopping it except by resigning.

As soon as the Ex. Com. got the news of the armed fighting it issued an appeal to 'all citizens'—'in the name of safeguarding the revolution against the disturbances that threatened it'. Calling for trust in the Soviet, which 'would find the road towards the realization of the people's will', the Ex. Com. addressed the workers and soldiers separately. It urged the workers not to take arms to meetings and demonstrations; as for the soldiers, it told them 'not to go out into the street armed'; that 'they were under the orders of the Ex. Com. alone, which must give written authorization for the appearance in the streets of any military units'.

As we see, the 'loyal' Soviet leaders, and those closest to the Government, in these exceptional circumstances, didn't think twice about demonstrating the full power and authority of the Soviet in the broad light of day. And of the presence of this power and authority neither they nor the Opposition could have the slightest doubt. For them, as well as for all Leftists, it was obvious that here the Government was absolutely helpless and powerless, that in no circumstances could it control the people, and that without the Soviet's help it would become the victim of the people's wrath. And the Soviet clearly and simply told the army, the real support and strength of the State: '*We alone have the right to give you orders*'. Which was incontrovertible.

This appeal, however, was inadequate. Military units might not go into the street, but enough bloodshed could be arranged even without them. If crowds of people and mutually hostile demonstrations were to continue, there would be a broad field left for provocations. Consequently the Ex. Com. decided on a heroic measure.

First of all, it declared 'a traitor to the revolution anyone who called for armed demonstrations or fired a shot even in the air', and secondly, 'to avert the discord threatening the revolutionary cause' *it forbade any street meetings or demonstrations for two days.*

This order was drawn up by the Ex. Com. and submitted to the Petersburg Soviet, which had met at 6 o'clock. The Soviet passed it unanimously. Then the Ex. Com., on its own authority, extended it for another day, to include Sunday, April 23rd.

And that was all. The Soviet took no further measures. But these were quite enough. The spectre of civil war dissipated like smoke. In the twinkling of an eye the agitated city resumed its normal appearance. For these three days there were no street meetings or demonstrations. Neither the working-class suburbs nor the Nevsky Prospect disobeyed the Soviet's order. Complete and irreproachable order had come in a flash.

Will the future historians of the revolution and of this brilliant episode in it—the April Days—pass over this fact? If the people's movement itself was amazing in its strength its liquidation was even more so.

Two months before, the conception of the Soviet had still been completely alien to everyone, and the word unknown; only a month before the Soviet was alien and hostile to a good half of the democracy. And now it was lightly directing popular movements and passions; its word commanded the elements. This was where the real strength and power of the people was demonstrated.

* * *

The April Days were a remarkable episode in the revolution. It was not for nothing that Lenin, much later, in a speech on the occasion of the dissolution of the Constituent Assembly, said that it was just these April Days that really opened his eyes for the first time to the true meaning and rôle of a popular uprising.

Lenin learned from the April Days, completed his education, and steeled his fighting spirit. But in April neither Lenin himself, nor the party he had won over, were yet setting in motion the new Leninist science. Bolshevik elements, to be sure, were forcing the movement against the Provisional Government. At this time Lenin's party had already put forward its programmatic slogan: 'All Power to the Soviets'. But it had no serious intention of realising this programme during the April Days. The position of the Bolsheviks was then neither firm nor effective.

In spite of the enormous temptation, in spite of his over-zealous comrades' anticipation of events, Lenin, as we shall see, was projecting all his plans and hopes into the future. But his plans were firmly grounded, and during the April Days his hopes soared. It was not for nothing that he had a good word for these magnificent lessons when he was in power, and thrusting an aspen stake into the Russian democratic republic.

The April Days marked a boundary and a turning-point: they infinitely deepened the crack in the Soviet; having broken the petty-bourgeois away from the proletarian groups, they—on the other hand—almost closed the gap between the petty and the big bourgeoisie; they created a hitherto unprecedented contact between them and gave a firm foundation to a united bourgeois front against the proletariat, Zimmerwald, and the revolution.

* * *

[*Part of the Political Spectrum*]

Just as it was impossible to find a line of demarcation between the 'responsible' and the 'irresponsible' circles of the bourgeoisie, so it was impossible to tell where the bourgeoisie ended and the democracy began. Bourgeois-radical groups passed over directly into Right-Soviet ones. The figure of Kerensky embodied even a personal union. In general the 'Populist' groups—Socialist Populist, Trudoviks, SRs—served as a connecting link. The middle strata—practically speaking, the intelligentsia—were organized around these interstitial groups. And behind them stood the vast Russian peasantry. The peasantry was incontestably and almost exclusively dominated by the SRs from the very beginning. Of course these were the *Right* SRs, who controlled the land-holding peasants.

In the very first days of May an All-Russian Peasant Congress was scheduled in Petersburg. Both the bourgeois and the 'Marxist' parties scarcely touched these representatives of the Russian blacklands, amongst whom there was a mass of 'populist' intellectuals, but also quite a few rural kulaks, shopkeepers, and various people from the Co-operative Movement.

But however that may have been, this was where the principal force in Russian society and the revolution was assembling. It was just this petty-bourgeois middle, which had not passed through the furnace of capitalism, that unfortunately was and remains the master of the Russian land and in the last analysis determines the course of events. And now it served as the basic lever of Soviet policy, for the interstitial populist parties were no longer bourgeois but Soviet parties, in the camp not of the Marian but of the Tauride Palace.

* * *

In the Soviet, however, by the side of the SR Party itself stood the Right Mensheviks, constituting with it a stable and indivisible bloc. It was this Right Menshevik group, of course, that headed and controlled the SR mass, which lacked enough skilled leaders of its own.

Of the Mensheviks themselves these Soviet leaders had hitherto been quite untypical. Menshevism as a whole was *internationalist* not only before the revolution, under its old leaders—the Zimmerwaldites Martov and Axelrod;[1] at the beginning of the revolution too the Menshevik majority maintained its Zimmerwald position. The Right Mensheviks, defensists and opportunists lording it in the Soviets, represented the minority of the party and did not express its opinion at all.

Now, however, at the end of April, things had changed. The Menshevik opportunists had begun to gain more and more ground within the party. The Petersburg organization was still in the hands of the internationalists, but in the provinces the party was entirely taken over by the opportunists.

This was of course aided primarily by the immense activity (throughout Russia) of the Menshevik leaders of the Soviet. It was no wonder that in the eyes of the masses, newcomers in politics, Menshevism came to be identified with the 'line' of Tsereteli, Dan and Chkheidze. No wonder that in such conditions the party began to grow in the provinces and the army precisely amongst petty-bourgeois philistine elements. Headed by a group of talented and authoritative leaders, these *parvenu*

[1] Axelrod, Pavel Borisovich (1850–1928): began his revolutionary career as a member of populist and anarchist groups. In the emigration from the end of the 'eighties, where together with Plekhanov and V. I. Zasulich he founded the Group for the Emancipation of Labour—the first Russian Social-Democratic and Marxist organization. One of the founders and editors of *Iskra* from 1901 on. After the 1903 split between Bolsheviks and Mensheviks he became a Menshevik, which he remained until his death. Very hostile to the October Revolution, he emigrated to Berlin in 1918 and died there. (Ed.)

March Social-Democrats already made up the *majority* of the party, and had changed the physiognomy of Menshevism.

'Populists' and Right Mensheviks now constituted a stable majority of the Soviet and completely determined its 'line'. These were the 'responsible' elements.

Further to the Left were the 'irresponsible' Soviet groups, parties and tendencies. And in the democratic camp this line of demarcation was drawn much more precisely. All the Left-wing opposition to Tsereteli was called irresponsible. Essentially, however, it was far from homogeneous.

There were, first of all, the Menshevik-Internationalists, whose influence extended over about 20–25 per cent. of the advanced proletariat of Petersburg and Moscow. This consistently Marxist Socialist group was, however, very feebly represented in the Petersburg Soviet; and by now it was also getting completely lost in the Ex. Com., where at one time it had constituted, together with associated elements, the central core.

To this period belongs an attempt to organize in the Ex. Com. these associated *non*-Menshevik internationalist elements. To increase the striking force of the Opposition, a number of representatives of the Left Centre tried at this time to create from them a group of extra-fractional Social-Democrats. It was joined by people of old Bolshevik origins, who were afraid of the name of Menshevism, but had nothing in common with the present party of Lenin. It was also joined even by some former Mensheviks. In the Ex. Com. it had about fifteen to eighteen people, including myself, behind it.

However, no one paid very close attention to this group and, in view of the existence of the Menshevik-Internationalists, it found no support outside the Ex. Com. Indeed, it fairly soon fell apart as an organized unit even within it.

Further to the Left were the Bolsheviks, who made up the most powerful part of the 'irresponsible' Soviet Opposition. Under the influence of various subjective and objective factors this party was growing swiftly and irresistibly. And it was growing almost exclusively amongst the proletariat. It was still far from having a majority of the Petersburg proletariat behind it, but by the first days of May it certainly had already about a third. This was reflected in the composition of the Petersburg Soviet, and even more in its Workers' Section.

Some partial re-elections were taking place in the factories, and giving greater weight to the Bolsheviks, who had begun realizing their programme of conquering the Soviet. The Soviet majority looked somewhat askance at these re-elections. But nevertheless it was not much alarmed: first of all, having concentrated all its attention on a compromise with the bourgeoisie, and having been reassured as to its unshakeable strength after the April Days, the Soviet majority was altogether too little concerned about the masses; secondly, Soviet leaders were already accustomed to look for support not to the workers but to the soldiers and the comparatively ignorant countryfolk that made up (even though illegitimately) the overwhelming majority of the Soviet plenum.

The Bolshevik fraction in the Ex. Com. and the Soviet was led by the moderate Kamenev. Lenin and Zinoviev and their assistants were busy with party affairs, *Pravda*, and mass agitation. But Kamenev was by now not very representative of his party's viewpoint, for Lenin had already scored a most decisive victory over his Bolsheviks.

It was just at this time, in the last days of April, that the All-Russian Bolshevik Conference took place in Petersburg, in Kshesinskaya's Palace. Its resolutions, passed almost unanimously by 140 delegates, were nothing but Lenin's famous Theses. They were passed almost without amendment. What Plekhanov had called raving, and what the oldest Bolsheviks a month before had thought wild and absurd, now became the official platform of the party that was hourly capturing more of the Russian proletariat. A very few old party figures could not endure it and left. The rest accepted Lenin's anarchism and shook the dust of Marxism off their feet as though they had never thought anything else, as though their own views of the day before and their own former doctrines had always been in their eyes a bourgeois fraud and Social-traitors' delusion.

I consider this Lenin's most important and fundamental victory, and it was won in the first days of May.

* * *

One would have thought it impossible to go further than Lenin in socio-political radicalism. Nevertheless the Leninists did not stand at the extreme Left of the motley and colourful political life of the time. The anarchists and their specific Russian variety, the Maximalists (historically a development of the SRs), were busy, not without some success, amongst the working-class masses.

They were badly organized and had neither wide popularity, clear and independent slogans, nor, I think, a periodical. Nevertheless they swarmed in the entrails of revolutionary Petersburg, and in particular had made themselves a nest amongst the sailors of the Baltic Fleet.

They had representatives in the Soviet also. One Bleichman used to speak at almost every meeting in the name of the Anarchist-Communists; his naïve demagogy would meet with semi-ironical sympathy in a certain part of the audience. We shall encounter the Petersburg anarchists later on.

CHAPTER 15

THE LEGAL NUPTIALS OF THE BIG AND PETTY BOURGEOISIE

THE Provisional Government was completely powerless. It reigned, but could not *rule*. In Guchkov's words it possessed 'none of the attributes generally characteristic of a State'. For, running counter to the objective course of events, the machinery of civil administration was *idling*, useless and unnecessary.

But this was only one aspect of the matter. The Provisional Government did not rule, but it *reigned*. Its rôle was not limited to serving as the intellectual and organizational centre for the entire bourgeois campaign against the revolution. The rôle of this helpless and non-functioning Government was also expressed in something else. It was an official sign-board, a company—primarily to carry conviction to Europe, and secondly to *declare* its counter-revolutionary policy.

All real power and authority was in the hands of the Soviet. The many millions of the army submitted to it; hundreds and thousands of democratic organizations acknowledged it; the masses obeyed it.

But the Soviet was now identified with its petty-bourgeois, opportunistic majority. This majority did not want power and was afraid of it. But it had it in spite of itself. And then it was obliged to apply all its energies to hand over to the Government the totality of its power and lay it at its feet. This was the Soviet 'line'.

The masses of the people obeyed the Soviet without question; but that doesn't mean they obeyed *willingly*, completely convinced that it was in the right. We have seen the mood of the masses in the April Days, and how it differed from the Soviet 'line'. There is not the slightest doubt that at this time the masses were outstripping the Soviet majority. Not only did the spontaneous course of events demand the realization of the minimal programme of the revolution, but the masses themselves had assimilated and formulated this programme, which the bourgeois Government couldn't and wouldn't realize.

There were widespread demands for peace, land, and bread amongst the masses. The Government could not and would not grant them. And in this class struggle the Soviet was on the side of the Government. It passed off the Government's sabotage as the realization of the programme, while it exhorted the masses to tranquillity and loyalty. *That is, the Soviet was fighting against the people and the revolution and for the policy of the bourgeois Government.*

The masses obeyed the Soviet for historical reasons, because of the general monopolistic rôle of the Soviet in the revolution and because of the absence of any other democratic centre that might have replaced it. The masses were still obeying it through inertia. In addition, they were partly unenlightened and unaware, and partly petty-bourgeois. But with all this they were *already* diverging from the Soviet and already obeying it with reluctance.

Here is a small but quite good illustration. The peasants arriving at their All-Russian Congress turned up as usual at the Ex. Com.—demanding a law to stop dealing in land. As usual they were sent to the Government. They were reluctant to go into these alien spheres, but obeyed. On the day scheduled for the reception I got a telephone call in the Ex. Com. from the People's House, where the peasants' preliminary meetings were taking place. As head of the Soviet agrarian department I was asked to be present at the reception of the deputation in the Marian Palace—so that their demand might seem to be made in the name of the Ex. Com.

I was in the Marian Palace at the appointed time. The peasant deputation was not the only one in its circular hall. In addition, a rather large group of soldiers up from the front had been assembled there, waiting for the Ministers. They were headed by an officer in dress uniform, with an expressionless wooden face. The group had evidently come to greet the Provisional Government and express the feelings of some military unit. The officer who would have to make the speech was visibly excited.

Premier Lvov came into the circular hall with Kerensky, Tereshchenko, and perhaps someone else. The officer stood to attention and began slowly reciting his speech, pronouncing jerkily and with difficulty the unaccustomed words, undoubtedly learnt by heart. He spoke of his devotion to the revolution and readiness to lay down his life for it.

'We have been charged'—he hacked away—'with a greeting to the Provisional Government and the Soviet of Workers' and Soldiers' Deputies. We have been commissioned to inform the Provisional Government that we honour it, trust it, and support it to the extent and in so far as it fulfils . . .'

But this was too much. The gentle and considerate Lvov turned squarely on his heel and swiftly left the deputation, without hearing the 'greeting' to the end. I recalled the Russian vassal envoys who appeared before the luminous eyes of the mighty Tatar Khan and greeted him with the words: 'Hail Kalin, dog of a Tsar!'

Yes, these were no longer the former deputations nor the former greetings, which were nothing but a demonstration against the Soviet. Now the intolerable formula about supporting the Government *in so far* as it supported the Soviet had sunk deep into the consciousness of the masses once and for all. The Government itself, however, was very well aware of the impossibility of this kind of existence, which everyone knew to be *by permission of the Soviet.* The naïve officer had struck the chief of the Cabinet on a sore spot.

The Ministers turned to the peasant deputations. I had no desire to play an active part here and kept as far as possible in the background. The head of the deputation, a grey little peasant, began urgently and almost tearfully asking the Ministers for a law to preserve the land resources. He was impatiently interrupted by the pale and agitated Kerensky.

'Yes, yes, that will be done. The Provisional Government is already taking steps. Tell them there is nothing to worry about. The Government and myself will do our duty.'

One of the deputation, however, obviously mistrusting the Minister's assurance, tried to put in the remark that the law had been promised long since but that nothing was happening. The others were obviously in sympathy. By now Kerensky was furious and began a thorough tongue-lashing, practically stamping his foot:

'I said it would be done, that means it will! And—there is no need to look at me so suspiciously'!

I give this *verbatim*—Kerensky was right, the little peasants were looking *suspiciously* at the famous people's Minister. The delegation of peasants had finally arrived at the same point as the delegation from the front.

Yes, it was impossible to live like that any longer!

* * *

Public opinion was proposing as the only possible way out the creation of a *Coalition Government* of representatives of the bourgeoisie and the Soviet democracy. Since the first days of the revolution the Right 'Populists', the Populist Socialists, and the Trudoviks had been insisting on the formation of a Coalition Government. They had now returned to the attack in the Ex. Com., and were joined by the Soviet SRs.

A part of the big press—the more Left and less efficient—also took up the idea of a Coalition. In general the Right-wing democracy and the Left bourgeoisie gave this idea wide popularity during the last third of April. It was talked of everywhere. And against the background of the April Days, with their consequences, it very quickly penetrated the Government itself.

Even earlier, in the Liaison Commission, the Ministers had more than once raised the question of the entrance of Soviet leaders into the Cabinet. Now, restlessly looking for a way out of the intolerable situation, the Provisional Government published an address to Russian citizens, which officially raised the question of the reconstruction of the Government. It was published on April 26th.

On the same April 26th, Kerensky for his part published a statement in which he quite definitely put the 'coalition' question on a practical basis. Kerensky was addressing the Ex. Com. and the SRs, his party comrades: Up to then (he said) he had been representing the democracy in the Government on his own responsibility, but now the situation had radically altered; in the present critical circumstances the organized democracy ought no longer to decline responsibility and the guidance of the State.

In conclusion Kerensky said that he would make his further participation in the Government dependent on the decision of his party and presumably of the Soviet.

In any case, by this action of his Kerensky forced both the

Soviet and his own party to take a stand on the coalition question—the decision of the largest Soviet party thus being known in advance.

Finally, on April 27th Chkheidze, the Soviet representative, received an official letter from the Premier: the Ex. Com. now had to decide.

* * *

It was evident that now the entire bourgeois front was longing for a Coalition and demanding it, you might even say was provoking the Ex. Com. into entering it. And there could be no doubt that from its own point of view it was right.

This may have seemed to it a sorry turn of events, nevertheless it was the lesser evil and the only way out for the bourgeoisie. They could not remain suspended. They could not be so flatly ignored by the populace. They could not tolerate being recognized simply out of loyalty to the Soviet. They could not exist with their castrated administrative machine. It was vital to acquire all the attributes of power—even at the price of a compromise, even at a very high price. For this there was only one real means.

This was—a formal marriage to the petty-bourgeois Soviet majority. Love was absent—but there was clear and obvious calculation. In itself the Soviet was not, of course, desirable; but it was a question of the *dowry*. And as a dowry the Soviet would bring the army, the real power, immediate confidence and support, and all the technical means of administration.

This was the natural point of view of the bourgeoisie. But how did things stand in reality? How should it be judged from the point of view of the interests of the democracy and the revolution?

First of all—*objectively*, from *all* points of view, *things could no longer continue as they were*. After the April Days the liquidation of the first revolutionary Cabinet was a foregone conclusion. The country was becoming disorganized without a real government, and its organic work—supply, transport, local administration, labour—could no longer make the slightest progress, as a result of the decay of the government machine.

None of this, however, meant that for the democracy and the revolution the right way out of the situation lay in the formation of a Coalition Government. The Social-Democratic press, in the person of *Pravda* and the *Rabochaya Gazeta* (Workers' Newspaper), had spoken out *against* a coalition. But *Pravda* did not for the moment advance any practical solution of the problem: it insisted only on preparations for the transfer of power to the Soviet. The *Rabochaya Gazeta* also stood, practically speaking, for the maintenance of the *status quo*, advancing against the Coalition the classical argument of the International against Socialist Ministers being responsible for bourgeois policy and the blunting of the weapons of the proletarian class struggle through their participation in the Government. It was pointed out that in wartime, in the conditions of international struggle against imperialism, a coalition with the bourgeoisie might prove especially pernicious.

Apart from this argument's not settling the question, it did not seem to me convincing in substance either. The conditions of our revolution were quite exceptional and had not been foreseen by the International. We had, as master of the situation and *de facto* holder of state power, not the bourgeoisie but the democracy. Therefore the responsibility for the policy and for the very existence of *any* cabinet *already* lay on the Soviet. If the spontaneous course of events had allowed Miliukov to remain in power, the Soviet would still have been responsible, in the eyes of the country and of the world proletariat, for everything he did. Any discussion of the responsibility of Socialists or their having a free hand, *in our then situation*, was no more than a hollow game of make-believe. The war, of course, did not alter matters: the Soviet had long been responsible for the policy of war and peace also.

But wouldn't the course of policy change for the worse if Soviet representatives entered the Government? This would have been a substantial argument against the Coalition. But what grounds were there for assuming this result? The Soviet majority, after all, had *capitulated to Miliukov*. What was worse than that? Why, in entering the Government, would our 'responsible' Soviet elements become worse without Miliukov and in alliance with the more Leftist representatives of the bourgeoisie?

Blunting the edge of the class struggle? But once again—how would that differ from the existing situation? The Soviet, indeed, in the person of its majority, was doing everything possible to blunt it. If the leaders of this petty-bourgeois majority were to be formally linked with the Government, in the eyes of the masses their words about support would be not more, but perhaps *much less* convincing. . .

But wouldn't the Soviet discredit itself by a coalition? Possibly. But events had, after all, long been driving the proletarian groups and parties headlong down this path. In the struggle for the revolution they had long been fighting against the official Soviet. In general—the question of the *class struggle* had long since been reduced by events to the level of a *struggle against the Soviet majority*. And if this now formally became part of the Government, the struggle against both taken together would be not confused but made clear, and appear as the proletarian class struggle.

The real way for the revolution to move forward, independently of the form of government, consisted only in the conquest of the Soviet by genuinely democratic proletarian groups. A coalition could change nothing here, and wherever it could it would be a change for the better. The arguments of the Social-Democrats *against* coalitions in general didn't convince me at all.

But what could be said convincingly in *favour* of coalition—from the point of view of the revolution? If changes in the construction of the Government were absolutely inevitable, two solutions were theoretically conceivable: a coalition, or the transfer of all power to the Soviet. In the given situation in the Soviet, a Soviet Government could not be in reality a *dictatorship of the democracy*, that is, of the peasantry and the proletariat. For the all-powerful Soviet majority was and remained a prisoner of the bourgeoisie. Hence the *content* and direction of the policy of a Soviet Government could scarcely have been distinguished from the policy of a coalition.

Besides, the *form of a coalition had all the advantages*—from another point of view. Bourgeois authority was far from outworn in the eyes of the interstitial groups of the populace. The intelligentsia, the officialdom, the Third Estate, the officers—in a word all those strata that propped up the state apparatus, headed by the Soviet leaders themselves, were entirely unreconciled to the idea of a purely democratic Government, and refused to conceive of a State which had not the 'best people' in liberal society at its head. Meanwhile the state machine could not stand still for a moment; it had to work at full speed. This was what constituted the basic idea of reconstructing the Government, and for this reason the Government had to be reconstructed with, or not against, the will of these enormous strata that served the state machine. All these could recognize only a coalition; and to the extent that they were active they stood behind it at this moment. And they insisted on including representatives of the liberal bourgeoisie in the Government.

A Coalition Government had no other significance. It was a concession to organic function and to the interstitial strata. In addition the country in general and the democracy in particular were still not sufficiently organized. The democracy still lacked the fundamental institutions that perform the important work of the State: it lacked democratic organs of self-government. In three to five weeks the country would have to be covered with a dense network of democratic state institutions and in the near future the interstitial strata would have to reconcile themselves to the inevitable under the pressure of the iron logic of events. The Coalition was a concession to special temporary circumstances.

By then there would be no Coalition, and no bourgeoisie in power—they would be altogether unnecessary. Then the inevitable and legitimate time would be at hand for a purely democratic Government. I had no doubt that a Constituent Assembly would bring about precisely such a worker-peasant régime.

Could a coalition satisfy the demand the bourgeoisie was making of it—could it be a stable, strong Government? It could not. It was abolishing the dual power by uniting the Government and the Soviet majority. But a coalition was incapable of setting up a firm régime.

The Government could be strong and stable only if its policy really corresponded to the demands of the revolution and kept pace with them. Then it would be strong and stable by virtue of the nation-wide confidence and the lively support of the revolutionary people. The bourgeoisie counted on the Soviet's bringing it this dowry. Nor was it mistaken, in so far as the Soviet majority itself enjoyed these advantages. But in so far as a cruel class struggle was developing *within the Soviet democracy*, to that extent the Soviet could not confer the requisite strength and stability on its coalition with the bourgeoisie.

Consequently the Coalition Government could only be regarded as a temporary and even a very short-lived way out of the situation. It was known to be an unstable and transitory combination. But this known instability and transitoriness could not disqualify it as the sole way out of the situation. For in the sense of stability and strength, after all, this was all a Government of the petty-bourgeois Soviet could give. Such was the immutable logic of events.

My reasoning may have been right or wrong. But it was obvious that no reasoning at all could change things by one iota. A coalition remained the only solution. *It could not fail to come about*: the previous status had already been destroyed and the Soviet majority did not wish to take the power into its own hands, nor could it be forced to. Consequently, anything but a coalition was utopian. Reasoning was superfluous.

* * *

The wine was poured—it had to be drunk.

On the morning of April 28th the question of a Coalition Government was on the Ex. Com. agenda.

The hall was full. The debates were violent and lasted several hours. But they presented nothing new or essential.

They were finally cut short. In a very tense atmosphere the question was put to the vote. The Praesidium Group gave the preponderance to the *opponents* of the Coalition, but their majority was only of two votes. I personally, not afraid of a sensation, voted together with the 'Populists' *for*. I repeat, I may have been cruelly mistaken; but in any case my vote was an attempt to lighten the 'birth pangs of history'.

The Coalition was turned down, but its Soviet partisans were not downhearted. Neither I nor the others had any doubt that having driven the Coalition out of the door we should have to let it in by the window.

* * *

For the next couple of days, however, the question was not raised again. Everyone felt the provisional nature of the decision and the extreme instability of the situation, but no occasion had yet been found to change it.

Two days later, however, Guchkov, the Minister of War, resigned. His resignation didn't arouse much regret. On the contrary, even bourgeois circles and their press bowed him out rather coldly. Everyone knew very well it was either the Coalition or Guchkov.

His departure gave the Provisional Government an opportunity, after the refusal of the Ex. Com., to renew the proposal of the Coalition.

What aims Guchkov himself was pursuing by his resignation remains obscure. He may have been hoping to blow up the whole Cabinet, in order to sow panic amongst the Soviet leaders, force them to make every possible concession and by this method create a new situation. He may simply have wanted to expose the Government crisis formally, so as to shift the situation from its dead point—regardless of the direction. He may even have wanted to ease the birth of the Coalition after the delays in the Ex. Com. In any event, whatever Guchkov himself intended, objectively he created an opportunity for a review of the Ex. Com.'s decision of April 28th.

I haven't the slightest doubt that unofficial negotiations between the Marian Palace and the Praesidium Group were being carried on at this time with great intensity. Kerensky in particular, after his statement of April 26th, could no longer remain in his former position. He must either resign or hastily try to win over the Soviet leaders and hope for a swift success. The 'Populist' part of the Soviet majority also, of course, helped Kerensky and the other Ministers—in the backstage persuasion of the Social-Democratic part, which had obstructed the Coalition on April 28th.

Echoes of these private negotiations were heard once in the official meetings of the Ex. Com. On one of these days Tsereteli, *à propos* of something or other, declared at the meeting that that morning, before he left home, either Lvov or Tereshchenko had rung him up and told him something, made some proposal, and so on. Someone (on the Left) made a dissatisfied and ironic remark that Tsereteli was carrying on confidential negotiations with the Government, when, after all, the official Liaison Commission existed for that purpose.

'It's not my fault,' exclaimed Tsereteli angrily, the vein on his temple swelling up. 'I live with Skobelev, and the Ministers know his 'phone number. What can I do if they ask to speak to me?'

'Leave the receiver off!' squeaked a voice from the back of the room. It was Larin, who never balked at the most radical solutions of any problem. . .

* * *

On the very cold morning of May 2nd we raced from the Tauride Palace in two cars over to the Alexandra Theatre, where G. E. Lvov lived, to construct the new Government. The delegation was made up of the Mensheviks Chkheidze, Tsereteli, Dan, and Bogdanov; the Trudoviks Stankevich and Bramson; the SRs Gots and, I think, Chernov, whom, however, I completely fail to recall throughout this affair. Delegates from the Opposition were the Bolshevik Kamenev, the Interdistrictite Yurenev, and a non-fraction man—myself. Tedious and nerve-racking proceedings began, which lasted for three whole days.

Agreement was very quickly reached on the *platform* of the Coalition Cabinet, but the interest of the situation lay elsewhere. First of all, the Council of Ministers as such had not appeared at the meeting, which—officially—had not taken place. Secondly, their absence rather fitted in with the general tone of the conversations with those Ministers who were there, who were clearly not aiming at a coalition as such but wanted to see themselves masters of the situation, and counted on having the future Soviet Ministers as their *hostages* once again.

This semi-private conversation made it clear above all that the old Cabinet envisaged giving three or four portfolios to Soviet people, including Kerensky as Minister of Justice. These portfolios were Labour, Posts and Telegraphs, and I forget which one besides. When the Soviet delegation began feeling out the terrain with respect to Miliukov, it was explained that in any case Miliukov was not expected to remain as Foreign Minister.

They began telephoning to the remaining members of the Cabinet. It was arranged to meet again at either 2 or 4 o'clock, and until then we each went off about our own business.

* * *

Our delegation decided it wasn't worth while returning to the Tauride Palace; we went to a nearby restaurant, where we spent most of the time talking about the portfolios while we waited for the old Ministers to assemble. I don't think any of the Soviet people had any plans about who could and should be given Miliukov's portfolio. But it had been decided in Soviet circles to leave this—the most important ministerial post—to the bourgeoisie. The bourgeoisie had also firmly decided to hang on to it.

Suddenly Skobelev turned up, straight from the station. He was already informed about the general state of affairs. Turning as usual his simple, open, merry face into a terribly serious, gloomy, demonic mask, he told us that in public affairs he had always been accustomed to be guided, in the first place, by his hot-blooded emotions, but, in the second place, by his cold-blooded reason. Now his cold-blooded reason told him to become a Minister. But his hot-blooded emotions said—nothing. What was to be done? The situation, that is to say, was unusual, and of course, very puzzling. Nevertheless everyone hoped that his difficulties would somehow blow over. . .

We rang up Lvov's flat, but the Ministers had not assembled at 2 o'clock, or at 4 o'clock either. Our delegation had to stay in the restaurant until it was almost dark. At last we arranged to meet Lvov at about 8 o'clock. But an emergency session of the Petersburg Soviet had been called for that day. The Coalition, after all, had to be passed by it. The leaders never for a moment doubted their complete success, but nevertheless the heavy artillery had to be brought up. And around 6 o'clock the Praesidium Group left for the Naval Academy, where the Soviet had already assembled.

Tsereteli's report to the meeting was brief. He spoke of anarchy and ruin, the machinations of the Right bourgeoisie, the desire of the Left bourgeoisie for solidarity with the democracy, and the necessity of creating at all costs a strong unified Government, which would enjoy the complete and unqualified support of the masses of the people. His words fell on prepared ground: in the eyes of the masses changes were inevitable and the Coalition was already popular with all non-Bolsheviks. And as for the Bolsheviks, there were still only a few of them.

Zinoviev spoke for the Bolsheviks—for the first time, I think, in the Soviet. He referred to the lessons of history, proving that only the bourgeoisie profited by the Coalition, and proposed that the Soviet should take all power into its own hands. There were objections. Voitinsky[1] made a row, finding nothing better to do than infer from Zinoviev's words that the Bolsheviks were trying to get a separate peace. This was, unfortunately, the ex-Bolshevik's usual method in controversy.

Then Tsereteli thought of beating the Bolsheviks with their own weapons: after all, he said, the Bolsheviks wanted to give the power to the majority of the population, but the majority of the population was the peasantry—that is, the petty bourgeoisie; the bourgeoisie could not be 'swept out' of power.

'Europe', he said, 'will look upon our entry into the Provisional Government as a new victory of the revolution. . .'

None of this was particularly convincing nor even, I should think, especially witty. But that didn't prevent the Soviet from approving all the Ex. Com.'s steps with respect to the Coalition—by an overwhelming majority against 100.

I write of this Soviet session from newspaper and other accounts. I wasn't there. I had gone straight to Lvov's flat. Going into the Premier's study through a throng of reporters I found a number of Soviet people there having a political argument with the Procurator of the Holy Synod, V. N. Lvov. He was holding forth loudly and complacently, drawing a parallel between events at home and the French Revolution. However odd it may seem, he preferred *our* revolution—pointing out that 'there had been terrible party strife there', which we didn't have. Altogether the Procurator was feeling optimistic. So there still were such people. But of course they were thorough philistines.

On that same night of May 2nd Miliukov was 'pushed' out of the Government. He put up a tenacious fight and refused to leave—in the name of great Russia. But—alas!—this man, who would have had to be called the Cadets' Lenin, if he hadn't been a professor—was quite unthinkable in a Government based on 'full confidence and unconditional support'. Plucking up

[1] Voitinsky, Vladimir Savelyevich (1887–1960): former Bolshevik, then defensist; an economist. Close to Tsereteli, with whom he was associated in the Menshevik Caucasian Republic. After its repression he emigrated, eventually to America. At present (his name spelt Woytinsky) he is professor of economics at Johns Hopkins University and an economic analyst of international repute. (Ed.)

their courage the 'Left Seven'[1] flatly told him so, and Miliukov left the Council of Ministers, never to return.[2]

* * *

By 2 o'clock in the morning of May 5th everything was ready. The portfolios had been quickly assigned, and all the doubtful points settled in this way: Kerensky got the War Ministry and the Admiralty, Pereverzev the Ministry of Justice; Peshekhonov Supply, Skobelev Labour, Tsereteli Posts and Telegraphs.

The Coalition had been created. The formal union of the Soviet petty-bourgeois majority with the big bourgeoisie had been ratified in a written constitution.

* * *

The inevitable had come about. Well, what of that? Let history accomplish as quickly as possible what was predestined for it. . . Now only the last act remained, the final chord, the apotheosis. This was the Soviet's sanction—an empty formality, mere wedding congratulations.

That day in the Ex. Com. I caught a passing glimpse of a new face. Familiar piercing eyes, familiar wavy hair, but an unfamiliar little beard. Well—Trotsky! He had arrived unnoticed during this turmoil. Fifteen years before, in 1902–3, I had often met him in Paris and listened to the papers he read. But I didn't know him. Before the revolution he had sent things to the *Letopis*, and now he was one of the contributors to the *Novaya Zhizn*. But it was just in order to avoid talking about his work on the *Novaya Zhizn* that I didn't go over to him and introduce myself. First I had to discover what his position was in the present circumstances.

The official speakers didn't arouse much interest. While they were speaking, I was sitting at a table on the platform, toiling in the sweat of my brow over a leading article for next day's issue of the *Novaya Zhizn*—on our attitude to the new Government. But I couldn't get on. . . Accidentally turning around I saw

[1] See p. 249.

[2] After the October Revolution Miliukov actively fought the Bolsheviks, but despairing of the struggle emigrated to Paris, where he published an influential newspaper, and losing his monarchist inclinations—always moderate—founded the *émigré* Russian Democratic Organization. He died in France. (Ed.)

Trotsky behind me. Chkheidze, behaving differently from the way he behaved with his *friends*, ignored Trotsky's appearance and didn't propose a welcome to the distinguished revolutionary, who had, moreover, just returned from imprisonment. But Trotsky had already been pointed out, and the hall resounded with cries of: 'Trotsky! We want Comrade Trotsky!'

It was the famous orator's first appearance on a revolutionary tribune. He was warmly greeted. And, with characteristic brilliance, he made his first speech—on the Russian Revolution and its influence in Europe and overseas. He spoke of proletarian solidarity and the international struggle for peace; but he also touched on the Coalition. In mild and cautious terms, not characteristic of him, he pointed out the practical fruitlessness and erroneousness in principle of the step that had now been taken. He called the Coalition a capture of the Soviet by the bourgeoisie, but he didn't think the mistake very serious.

Trotsky was visibly disturbed at this *début* under the neutral gaze of an unknown crowd and to the accompaniment of the hostile exclamations of a couple of dozen 'Social-traitors'. From the outset he did not expect any sympathy. And to make it worse—his cuff kept constantly shooting out of his sleeve and threatening to fall on the heads of his nearest listeners. Trotsky kept on settling it back in place, but the wilful cuff would shoot out again—and it distracted and irritated him.

The Socialist Ministers argued against him. Peshekhonov and Tsereteli were livid. Skobelev, demonic, pronounced his sacramental formula about a hot-blooded heart and a cold-blooded mind. As for Kerensky—he, of course, had not turned up at all.

I was struggling with my leading article in the sweat of my brow. But nothing came. I was quite incapable of thinking up or expressing an attitude towards the new Government. Complete and unqualified confidence? But after all I didn't have a shadow of such confidence *in the Soviet majority*. Should I say that the Coalition had been born dead and was rotten, and ephemeral? But that could be said any day. I didn't want to say it just now. I wanted to think of something positive and encouraging. But nothing came out.

Nothing ever came out. The next day, May 26th, the *Novaya Zhizn* appeared without a leading article on the new Government. It was painful to have to make this confession of impotence. Indeed, this whole business of the Coalition was painful.

Late that night after the meeting I was walking to the printers' from the Soviet, in utter dejection. The narrow, empty streets of the Petersburg Side were peaceful—just as though there were no revolution. Only from a distance strange singing could be heard, like the roaring of a huge beast. I wandered dejectedly along a dead side-street and turned the corner. A lanky figure was staggering towards me on the other side of the street, waving his arms and chanting in *basso profundo* like an archdeacon:

'Let us pra-a-y to the Lord, for pea-a-a-ce for the wo-o-rld, without annexations or inde-e-emnities! . . .'

August–October 1919.

Part IV

THE TRIUMPH OF THE REACTION

May 6th–July 8th

CHAPTER 16

THE COALITION

WITH the birth of the Coalition Government events slowed down and lost their former dizzy speed. However urgently *history* continued to move forward, the *revolution* had begun to mark time. Between May and October tremendous events took place, but the *phase* of the revolution did not change and constituted a single unified period. The line of development was as straight as an arrow. Two attempts to turn it aside interrupted this straight line, but did not change its direction: the revolution quickly and easily returned to its previous course both after the *July Days* and after the *Kornilov putsch.*

This evidently means that towards the beginning of May 'political relations' in the revolution were completely crystallized, and had arrived at some sort of stable point. The bloc of the big and petty bourgeoisie was completely stable, unshakeable, and even formal—from the beginning of May until October; and the policy of the united bourgeois front was the suffocation of the proletariat, Zimmerwald, and the entire revolution. It moved along a straight road to liquidation.

This was the obverse side of the Coalition period. The reverse side was simply the enormous growth of discontent amongst the masses of the people, headed by the proletariat of the capital. Worn out by the war, hunger, and chaos, disillusioned by the policy of the Government, thirsting for the fruits of victory—the masses of the people rallied in the struggle for the revolution and prepared themselves for new and decisive battles.

Anyone looking at the policy of the Coalition was also seeing the success of Lenin, for these were two sides of the same medal. And amongst the genuine revolutionaries from the beginning of May on it was already being said: 'Bolshevik mole, you're digging magnificently!'

* * *

Soon after the March revolution the whole of the Russian plutocracy was consolidated in the Cadet Party. And the Cadets, while Miliukov was a Minister, were of course a completely

Government party: any differences within the party were then expressed externally only in the degree of exasperation with the democracy and the Soviet.

After the April Days, with the liquidation of Miliukov and the formation of a Coalition Government, things changed. The Coalition was a sort of external expression of how far the revolution had advanced.

The Coalition had been created against the will of the leading Cadet circles. The Cadets, consequently, could in the nature of things no longer be a Government party as before. The course of events had left them *behind* the official Government. They became the *Right Opposition*—an officially reactionary, counter-revolutionary force. And the differences within the Cadet Party were now expressed externally in the degree of opposition to the *Government.*

There were, to be sure, still some members of the party left in the Cabinet. The Cadets neither could nor wanted to break with the official Government. Since they were no longer capable of disrupting the Cabinet, and a boycott by them could no longer be dangerous to the revolution, the situation compelled them to cling to the Government with the utmost tenacity. Their opposition could only be 'diplomatically' disguised. They had to promise the new Cabinet their confidence and support, even though with an unmistakably sour expression. But in the nature of things there could be no question here of any real support—since there was no confidence.

* * *

The Cadets were the big bourgeoisie, together with the liberal professional classes who served them. The specific gravity of this party was of course very great. It was precisely with these strata that the revolutionary democracy had formed a Coalition. And their relationship to the new Government was characteristic.

But of course the largest party at this time was the SRs. They were the petty-bourgeois democracy—peasants, shop-keepers, Co-operators, minor officials, the Third Estate, the great mass of the indigent intelligentsia and all the unthinking ordinary people and odds and ends who had been stirred and shaken up by recent events. The intellectual SR circles, who shouted so loudly for 'Land and Freedom' were based in the cities on a dense stratum of soldiers of peasant origin and even of workers who had not been fully digested by the cauldron of the factories. And in the country this exclusive SR slogan had won exclusive control of all the peasantry.

Generally speaking, in our peasant country this peasant party occupied its rightful place, and already it seemed to have laid the foundations of future supremacy. Growing at the beginning of the Coalition like an immense snowball, it had lately become the last word of fashion and begun to overflow far beyond its natural limits, encompassing spheres completely alien both to 'Socialism' and to 'revolution'. This, the largest party, had attracted into itself both some of the temperamental upper bourgeoisie and some of the effusively liberal landowners, and in the footsteps of the highly popular new War Minister, Kerensky, solid masses of military people—regular officers and even generals—had begun to enter the party. Two and a half months before, presumably, not one of the latter would have hesitated to shoot or hand over to the executioner any passer-by he even suspected of being an SR. But—my God!—what cannot 'public opinion' and disinterested devotion to duty do with a man?

And now this party, the biggest and most powerful in the revolution, was, in the person of its majority, giving the new Government the whole weight of its confidence and support, both in words and in deeds. . . The intermediate intellectual strata, as we know, had from the very first days of the revolution insisted on a coalition. Now their dreams were coming true; the philistines were revelling in their victory, and the unattached nondescripts wallowed in beatitude.

The SR Party, the biggest and most powerful, at that time had two centres—one more Right, the other more Left. One centre was Kerensky, the other Chernov. In addition, there was a tiny little centre in the person of the Bolshevik sympathizer Kamkov. Even before this, however, people like him had been invisible to the naked eye amidst the limitless sea of SR philistinism. But the whole of this mass was drawn towards the new Cabinet by these first two centres; for both Kerensky and Chernov were Ministers. The biggest party, having rightfully gathered under its banners the bulk of our petty-bourgeois country, was giving itself up entirely to the support of the new Government.

It would have seemed that the Coalition was standing on the firmest of foundations. But alas! the leaders of the petty-bourgeois SR masses proved faithful to the nature of their party. Flabby creatures without political personality, caught between the mighty millstones of capitalist society, they were bewildered by the dizzying events and failed to grasp their meaning. Buffeted by the tempest and shackled by the traditions and fetters of capitalist dictatorship, they cravenly renounced their own minimum programme and surrendered, with the revolution and the popular masses into the bargain, to the mercy of the bourgeoisie. But in doing this they also lost these popular masses, who rejected their leaders and trampled them into the mud. When the masses saw with their own eyes that their leaders were incompetent and deceitful, and were not leading them forward, the petty-bourgeois political docility of the masses turned into a petty-bourgeois elemental outburst, and these same masses threw themselves headlong into the open arms of the Bolsheviks.

At that time the SR Party was the biggest and the most powerful. But it was a colossus with a head of clay; it was not destined to become a really firm foundation for the new Government. The SR Party gave itself up entirely to the Coalition, it gave it everything it had. The loveliest girl in France could have given no more. But giving everything doesn't mean giving enough. And in the end Kerensky's and Chernov's million-headed flock in city and country was of no assistance to the Coalition.

* * *

The question of the Mensheviks' attitude to the Coalition was not settled so simply. The Mensheviks, to be sure, had also given the new Cabinet two Ministers—and, what is more, one of them was very important and the other very clever. But here of course there could not be the same ingenuousness, the same triumph, nor the same simple-minded confidence and support as those with which the petty-bourgeois populists greeted the Coalition. I've already related how during the birth-pangs of the new Government, at luncheon in the restaurant and afterwards on the platform, Skobelev vainly appealed to his hot-blooded heart and only under the irresistible pressure of his cold-blooded mind was compelled to accept a ministerial portfolio. Tsereteli had, one might say, simply yielded to force, and as Minister of Posts and Telegraphs considered himself the victim of an unexpected chain of circumstances that had formed against his will. And the Menshevik chairman of the Soviet, Chkheidze, had resisted to the last ditch and was only reconciled in the face of an already accomplished fact.

The then leaders of the Mensheviks, bound by international Socialist traditions, were in general inclined to shun this whole dubious enterprise. Perhaps the principal reason for this was doubt as to how the Menshevik party masses would accept these Social-Democratic portfolios. The doubt was justified; for the Menshevik section of the ruling Soviet bloc had somehow its special character, distinct from that of the SRs, and its own special fate.

It's true that from the beginning of the revolution a mass of philistine elements, 'former' people, and the casual public, with nothing in common with the proletarian movement, had flooded the Menshevik Party as well as the SRs. Nevertheless, unlike the SRs, the Mensheviks had been protected up to a point by their reputation as a proletarian class party and their ties with the International. Hence the influx of obviously bourgeois and reactionary elements into this party was substantially smaller. And its proletarian core, which before the revolution had given an enormous preponderance to the Zimmerwald tendency in Menshevism, was incomparably stronger. And we know that *after* the revolution Zimmerwald continued to dominate the Menshevik Party up to the April Days themselves. Up to that time, even during the Coalition, the organizations in both Moscow and Petersburg were overwhelmingly Left and Internationalist. It was only the provincial fellow-travellers who took their line from Tsereteli and succeeded in dragging many organizations into the quagmire of patriotism and conciliationism.

The attitude of the Mensheviks to the Coalition Government and to the acceptance of portfolios by party members was still unclear, and aroused the fears of the Menshevik Ministers themselves. The decisive word was to be pronounced by the All-

Russian Conference of Mensheviks, which opened in Petersburg on May 9th.

* * *

The Conference got off to a flying start, and the very first morning session on May 9th settled the hash of the central problem of the whole Conference, the attitude of the party to the Coalition, and the entry of members into the Cabinet. The debate was fierce and on both sides blows rained down heavily. But the results were fatal.

A resolution approving of the Menshevik entry into the Coalition and promising the new Cabinet complete confidence and support was passed by a majority of 44 votes to 11, with 13 abstentions.

This meant that the Menshevik–SR–Liberal bloc had definitely taken shape. The Mensheviks, like the SRs, had conclusively and officially become a Government party. And moreover, in spite of the passionate onslaught of the minority, the Conference had settled its basic problem very easily and swiftly. Conclusively and officially—the hegemony of opportunism and capitulationism in the Menshevik Party had been confirmed in some two or three hours.

That same day I too went to the evening session of the Menshevik Conference. At that time I had, as before, no formal connexion with this party. To be sure, being present even as a spectator at meetings which were to decide the fate of Menshevism in the revolution was far from uninteresting. But this was not what drew me to the Conference: I went to see Martov, whom I hadn't seen for just three years.

Martov had arrived that same day, about 2 o'clock. A rather large group had come with him, including those eminent leaders of our movement and future distinguished figures of the revolution: Axelrod, Lunacharsky,[1] Ryazanov,[2] and others.

[1] Lunacharsky, Anatol Vasilyevich (1875–1933): educated in Switzerland; in the revolutionary movement from the age of seventeen; a Bolshevik from 1903, but with highly personal opinions, especially in philosophy. People's Commissar for Education after the October Revolution. (Ed.)

[2] Ryazanov, (Goldendach) David Borisovich (1870–1938): celebrated as scholar of Marxism; founder and director of Marx-Engels Institute. Joined Bolsheviks in July 1917 together with Interdistrictites. After the 1931 Trial of the Mensheviks he was removed from all his posts and left for the countryside, where he died. (Ed.)

All of them, like Lenin but more than a month later, had passed through Germany in a 'sealed train'.

A triumphal welcome at the Finland Station had been arranged for them, as for the leaders of the other parties. But, though I very much wanted to, this time I couldn't get to the station, because of their daytime arrival. For the same reason—doubtless—the welcome was less crowded and impressive than that for the SRs, and especially for the Bolsheviks. I was a little vexed for Martov—not only because of my personal weakness for him, but also because of his incontestable objective importance. Moreover, while awaiting his arrival I had for some days been scowling with jealous spite at the 'ministerialized' Soviet Menshevik chiefs, who were awaiting without special enthusiasm or impatience, but rather with alarm and ill-will, the appearance in the revolutionary arena of the acknowledged ideological leader of the Mensheviks.

It had been demonstrated more than once during the preceding weeks that Martov occupied as before a consistent internationalist position, sharply inimical to the ruling Soviet bloc. There was no doubt that he would take a firm stand against those participating in the Coalition. Truly an untimely guest.

Now, when the basic question was being decided at the Conference and the correlation of forces was still unclear—God knew in which direction the party ship might be turned by the influence of this old, experienced, most authoritative and popular helmsman! In any case the ministerial question appeared so urgent that it seemed completely impossible to delay the debate on it. Axelrod, the founder of Russian Social-Democracy, and Martov, its leader, were faced by the Conference with a *fait accompli*—just as the Conference itself had been faced with the *fait accompli* of the Coalition. How could one fail to be reminded of the Latin legal maxim: *beati possidentes*?

I was late for the evening session and it was already breaking up when I arrived. The spacious hall and its corridors were filled by a dense crowd. The external aspect of the Conference was extremely imposing. A guest like myself might easily not even have been allowed into the meeting-hall, but they let me in anyhow, though without much pleasure. But Martov was surrounded by a dense barrier; 'seeing each other' was clearly out of the question, we had to limit ourselves to a handshake and a few words, hoping to renew our former friendly relations.

It appeared that Martov had already spoken and rebuked the Soviet majority, now the party majority as well, both for the policy of compromise and for the Coalition. As in his telegrams from abroad he had defended the irreconcilable proletarian position, the position of class *war*, the position of a real struggle for peace, and not sugary hypocritical lisping about peace.

But in spite of the passionate support of the minority, Martov's isolation from the compact group of Menshevik leaders, his former followers, friends, and disciples, and simultaneously his rupture with the party majority, stood out in full relief. Tradition prevented the partisans of Dan and Tsereteli from attacking Martov directly: that was still left for the near future. But the prevailing mood of hostility had already completely crystallized, and coldness was already evident at the first reunion.

Martov, the begetter of Menshevism, its incomparable, almost its sole theoretician, its most authoritative and popular chieftain—was now no longer the leader of his own party. Philistine notions and their exponents had led the Menshevik Party away from Martov—far away, into neither more nor less than the camp of the bourgeoisie. Only a small group remained with Martov. It was a catastrophe.

It didn't shake Martov. He stood his ground, with his small group and without the old Menshevik Party, until October. After October a reconquest of the Menshevik Party by Martov began, and by a year after October he had returned to his customary position as the generally acknowledged leader of Menshevism. But that was too late.

* * *

Martov—a vast theme. I won't attempt a thorough-going treatment of it, in view of my constant references to him: we worked side by side both before and after October. Nevertheless it's very tempting now to note his basic traits, to establish, so to speak, the general pattern of this distinguished figure, not only of our own but of the European working-class movement. All the more so since there was relatively little interest in him during the revolution. The fates decreed that he should not play a prominent part in the events of these last years, but nevertheless he was and remains a star of the first magnitude, one of the few whose names were characteristic of our epoch.

I had seen Martov for the first time in Paris in 1903. He was then 29 years old. At that time he, with Lenin and Plekhanov, made up the editorial board of *Iskra*, and he gave propaganda lectures to the Russian colonies abroad, waging a bitter struggle against the SRs, who were increasing in strength. He was already famous among the expatriates and lived somewhere on Olympus, amidst other such deities, and people in the Russian colony, meeting his spare, hobbling figure, would nudge one another.

Although I was not convinced by his arguments at that time, I remember very well the enormous impression made on me by his erudition and his intellectual and dialectical power. I was, to be sure, an absolute fledgeling, but I felt that Martov's speeches filled my head with new ideas; without sympathizing with him, I watched him emerge victorious in his bouts with the populist chiefs. Trotsky, in spite of his showiness, did not produce a tenth of his effect and seemed no more than his echo.

In those days Martov also revealed his qualities as an orator. These are rather singular. He has not a single external oratorical gift. A completely unimpressive, puny little body, standing if possible half-turned away from the audience, with stiff monotonous gestures; indistinct diction, a weak and muffled voice, hoarse in 1917 and still so now; his speech in general far from smooth, with clipped words and full of pauses; finally, an abstractness in exposition exhausting to a mass audience. Tens of thousands of people retain this impression of him. But all this doesn't prevent him from being a remarkable orator. For a man's qualities should be judged not by what he does but by what he may do, and Martov the orator is, of course, capable of making you forget all his oratorical faults. At some moments he rises to an extraordinary, breath-taking height. These are either *critical* moments, or occasions of special excitement, among a lively, heckling crowd actively 'participating in the debate'. Then Martov's speech turns into a dazzling firework display of images, epithets, and similes; his blows acquire enormous power, his sarcasms extraordinary sharpness, his improvisations the quality of a magnificently staged artistic production. In his memoirs Lunacharsky acknowledges this and says that Martov was the incomparable master of the summing up. Anyone who knew Martov the orator well can confirm this.

In our Paris days I didn't know him personally. Then, in 1904–5, cooped up in the *Taganka*[1] in Moscow, and carefully studying *Iskra*,[2] I perceived other qualities of Martov's—as a remarkable writer and journalist. Our foreign, illegal, Social-Democratic press, thought to be beyond the pale of Russian journalism, introduced a whole group of first-rate writers—Plekhanov, Martov, Trotsky, and perhaps Lenin. All these of course should stand in the front rank of our journalistic history. But surely Martov must be given the palm; no one had a pen like his; no one showed himself so completely its master in the full meaning of the word. He was capable, when necessary, of giving his writing the brilliant wit of Plekhanov, the striking power of Lenin, the elegant finish of Trotsky.

One of Martov's basic traits is effectively illustrated in his writing. Here, however, it may not appear uniquely exceptional; but in any personal encounter with him, whether private or concerned with public affairs, it leaps to the eye at once. This trait is a *mind* of extraordinary power and development. In my time I've had the fortune to meet not a few remarkable contemporaries—scientists, artists, and statesmen with world names. But I have never doubted for a moment that Martov is the most intelligent man I've ever known.

It used to be said of our ancient magicians that they saw three yards into the earth beneath you. Martov constantly reminds you of this. An incomparable political analyst, he has the capacity of grasping, anticipating, and evaluating the psychology, train of ideas, and sources of his interlocutor's argumentation. Hence a conversation with Martov always has a special character, as with no one else in the world, and always provides a peculiar enjoyment, however disagreeable the theme, however sharp at times the disagreement and virulent the recriminations. When you talk to him, it does not occur to you that you won't be *understood*; you can feel no doubts on this

[1] A gaol in Moscow, for both criminal and political offenders. (Ed.)

[2] A Social-Democratic paper founded in 1900 by Lenin, Martov, and Potresov, under the sponsorship of Plekhanov, Axelrod, and Vera Zasulich; after the Social-Democratic split into Bolsheviks and Mensheviks in 1903 it was in Menshevik hands until 1905, when it ceased publication. In 1917 Martov started a bulletin also called *Iskra*. (Ed.)

score. Here the slightest hint or gesture is enough to provoke a response that pierces to the very hub of the question and forestalls any further arguments around its periphery.

Martov is an incomparable political thinker and a remarkable analyst because of his exceptional intellect. But this intellect dominates his whole personality to such an extent that an unexpected conclusion begins to thrust itself on you: Martov owes not only his good side to this intellect, but also his bad side, not only his highly cultivated thinking apparatus but also his *weakness in action.*

Of course it's impossible to blame only his omnivorous intellect for his incapacity for practical combat. A lot must be ascribed to other general qualities. Nevertheless, in speaking of Martov, it would be perfectly just to develop the theme of *Woe from Wit.*[1]

First of all, to understand everything is to forgive everything. And Martov, who always has an exhaustive understanding of his opponent, is to a substantial degree condemned by virtue of this very understanding to that mildness and submissiveness to his ideological adversaries that characterizes him. To a considerable extent it is precisely Martov's breadth of view that ties his hands in intellectual combat and condemns him to the rôle of critic, of perpetual 'Opposition'.

Secondly, it must be said that since the birth of the most famous of analysts, Prince Hamlet, analysis, as the supreme quality of a character, is never divorced from Hamletism. That is, an intellect that dominates everything is a source of softening of the will and of indecisiveness in action. With Martov, who is a thinking apparatus *par excellence*, the centres of restraint are too strong to allow him the free and reckless acts of combat, the revolutionary feats that no longer demand the reason, but only the will.

'I knew,' Trotsky said to me much later, not long before these lines were written, 'I knew Martov would be destroyed by the revolution!'

Trotsky expressed himself too one-sidedly. His words actually mean that in a revolution Martov could not occupy a place corresponding to his specific weight, for reasons inherent in

[1] A famous satirical comedy by Alexander Sergeyevich Griboyedov (1795–1829). (Ed.)

himself. This is not so. Reasons outside himself had much greater significance. But it is true that Martov's sphere is theory, not practice. And when this epoch of fabulous exploits, of the greatest deeds in history began, then this star of the first magnitude of the underground period, the equal of Lenin and Trotsky, was eclipsed by the light even of comparatively minor luminaries like Dan and Tsereteli. There are a number of reasons for this—as we shall see later on. But again the same paradoxical reason stands out among them: Martov was *too* intelligent to be a first-class revolutionary.

His excessive, all-embracing analytical thinking apparatus was no help and was sometimes a hindrance in the fire of battle, amidst the unprecedented play of the elements. And later we shall see—even in my account, the account of a follower and apprentice—to what criminal inactivity Martov was condemned more than once by his Hamletism and his ultra-refined analytical web-spinning at moments demanding action and aggressiveness. These moments—critical moments!—will always remain my bitterest memories of the revolution. For the consequences of his errors in these critical moments were enormous, if not for the revolution as a whole, at least for his party and for himself.[1]

* * *

The Menshevik Conference had given the victory to the petty-bourgeois, conciliationist Soviet majority and turned the Mensheviks into a Government party. But the differences within the party were too great: the internationalist minority at the Conference, headed by Martov, stood, so to speak, on the other side of the barricades, side by side with Lenin's party. The party split.

This was, to be sure, more *de facto* than formal, and was seen principally in the big centres, remaining unknown and obscure to the many thousands of converts in the remote provinces.

It goes without saying that the Central Committee elected was conciliationist. Its decisions, however, did not commit either the party minority or its (two or three) internationalist members to anything whatever. The extremely influential and

[1] After the October Revolution, to which Martov was hostile, he was exiled (in 1921). He was one of the founders of the so-called '2½ International', and together with Dan edited the *Sotsialisticheskii Vestnik*. He died of tuberculosis. (Ed.)

very large Petersburg organization was entirely in the hands of the internationalist minority, and was sharply hostile to the Central Committee. The defensist minority in the capital, loyal to the Central Committee, was hostile to the Petersburg Committee and didn't recognize it. In the Soviet fraction the Internationalists were in a minority and formed a completely independent group. They always voted with the extreme Left against Dan and Tsereteli, who led the majority; they introduced their own independent resolutions, sometimes in concert with the Bolsheviks. And the line of the Soviet struggle—the struggle of the united big and petty bourgeoisie against the proletariat—lay at that time just between the Menshevik majority and the Menshevik-Internationalists.

The only thing needed for a definitive formal split was the departure of the Internationalists from the Central Committee and the formation of an all-Russian Internationalist centre. Throughout the whole summer there were endless debates in the Petersburg organization about a definitive split, but fear of the provinces delayed matters amongst the minority. Aside from this the minority was, generally speaking, in quite a 'winning' position: it lost only from polemical reproaches for its formal alliance with Tsereteli. But while it retained the possibility of a struggle 'within the party' it really enjoyed at the same time the most complete freedom of action and didn't submit to any decision of the majority. The position was, of course, quite false and ridiculous, but in point of fact it was the majority who found it intolerable. There were standing discussions amongst them also, about excluding the Internationalists, but all the same they weren't excluded.

All this shilly-shallying was unendurably tedious for both Left and Right. The more resolute Internationalists carried on an energetic agitation for a split. With Martov's arrival after the Conference, I was personally convinced that a definitive split was a question of the immediate future. Martov, however, who was living with his sister, Dan's wife, although not yielding an iota of the essence of his internationalist principles, was *against* a split. In mild and cautious form, with constant references to prematurity, he upheld the existing unnatural status. In those days Dan would say: 'I'm working on defence night and day. Every night I talk to Martov until four in the morning.'

A few days after the Conference, foreseeing a definitive split of the Mensheviks, I finished at last with my 'wild' situation, that had already dragged on so long, and registered in the Petersburg organization of the Menshevik-Internationalists. My party sponsor, who introduced me, was of course Martov.

* * *

Thus the Cadets, the SRs, and the official Mensheviks—some from fear, others from conscience, some with sincere feeling, others with a sourly scornful smile—brought their 'confidence and support' to the cradle of the Coalition.

The Menshevik-Internationalists, in view of the particularly strong desire to emphasize that devotion to the new Government was nation-wide, would be disregarded as simply a party minority. Every family, after all, has its black sheep. . .

Unfortunately, though, there still remained the Bolsheviks. But these were in the first place also notoriously black sheep, and secondly, black sheep outside the family, who were not worth talking about. This was how the faithful Coalition press reassured itself in those days, thinking it was brushing aside a gang of malefactors, and not the immutable course of history. . .

* * *

In the Soviet itself and the Ex. Com. things were completely satisfactory. But beyond their walls the efforts of the Compromisers collided with an indifference of the masses that was no better than downright hostility. Of course, resolutions of confidence were successfully carried even in working-class districts, but they fairly regularly alternated with enactments of this kind: 'We, the workers of the *Nevka* factory, having debated in general assembly the question of the entry of the Mensheviks and Populists into the Coalition Cabinet, consider such entry directly inimical to the international proletarian movement. We consider that the right method of combating the supply crisis and of ending the fratricidal war most rapidly is not entry into a bourgeois imperialist Government, but the transfer of all power to the Soviet. We demand that the representatives of the democracy leave the bourgeois Government at once.'

* * *

Relations within the Soviet and the Ex. Com. were now conclusively defined. The Ex. Com. had fallen into sharply hostile camps which never agreed on anything and one of which dictatorially and mercilessly oppressed the other with all its weight. And generally speaking in the Soviet at this time all the 'i's had been dotted in the dictatorship of the conciliationist Menshevik–SR Praesidium. This merely consummated a process long since begun. But now, after the Coalition, this process was completed by a certain formal crystallization of the dictatorship of a narrow little circle of opportunists.

First of all, the Praesidium of the Soviet, from being an organ of internal order, as it should have been, was definitely converted into a substitute for the Ex. Com., and began to replace it in its executive and legislative functions. Proposals to refer to the Praesidium were very often heard both in trivial and important matters—most of these proposals emanating from the Praesidium Group itself.

Secondly, the Praesidium Group from now on was concentrated into a continuously operative, quasi-official though still backstage institution, that had been given the name of Star Chamber. It consisted not only of the members of the Praesidium but also of a kind of camarilla, loyal intimates of Chkheidze and Tsereteli. At that time I was so far from these ruling spheres that I never knew exactly, and still don't know just who was in this Star Chamber. The official members of the Praesidium themselves, Chkheidze and Skobelev, were of course in it—but more *ex officio*, and they were, of course, not its controlling personages. Its leading spirit was, of course, Tsereteli. Consequently half of the Soviet dictatorship and all the corresponding honour, and all the odium—must be laid to his account.

But life in the Ex. Com. had not changed. In particular its whole pre-Coalition organization survived. To be sure, the Liaison Commission, now permanently transferred to the Marian Palace, was abolished—that is, as far as I recall, it died a natural death without any special decision.

Of the new members Trotsky used to attend, though not often. He had joined the Interdistrictites, the autonomous Bolsheviks; together with Lunacharsky, who had not yet appeared in the Ex. Com. at all, Trotsky had already begun holding numerous meetings and was looking for a literary organ. In the Ex. Com., against the grey, tedious background, he did not attract much interest, and he himself showed even less interest in the central Soviet institution.

At that time I personally avoided making the acquaintance of Trotsky, for quite specific reasons: Trotsky had many grounds for entering into more or less close relationship with the *Novaya Zhizn*, and he himself was counting on this. My getting acquainted with him would indicate an immediate discussion of this subject. But his contributions might prove quite unsuitable. Indefinite rumours were circulating about him, while he was still outside the Bolshevik Party, to the effect that he was 'worse than Lenin'. Before we could discuss the *Novaya Zhizn* this new star had to be inspected.

* * *

This is what the new Government said in its official statement of May 6th: 'In foreign policy, while rejecting, in accord with the entire nation, any thought of a separate peace, the Provisional Government openly sets as its goal the attainment of a general peace, without annexations or indemnities, on the basis of the self-determination of nations.'

But concretely? Methods? Guarantees?

'The Provisional Government will undertake preparatory steps towards an agreement with the Allies on the basis of the statement of March 27th.'

That was all. Even in words, even in naked promises, the Coalition went no further. Let anyone who can be satisfied by that.

On the other hand, 'persuaded that a defeat of Russia and her Allies could not only be a source of the greatest disasters, but would also make impossible the conclusion of a general peace on the basis indicated, the Provisional Government firmly believes that the revolutionary army of Russia will not allow German troops to destroy our Allies in the west and attack us with the full force of their arms. The strengthening of the foundations of the democratic army, and the organization and strengthening of its fighting force for offensive as well as defensive operations, will be the chief task of the Provisional Government.'

This was what the new Cabinet said about the first and basic point of the immutable, indispensable, and inevitable programme of the revolution—the question of peace.

* * *

Now, in the two capitals and in the provinces, as though at a signal, there began an orgy of chauvinism and a frenzied war-dance of journalists and mass-meeting orators demanding an immediate renewal of the slaughter. The whole of the big press set up a fiendish howl, playing variations on the patriotic slogan 'Take the offensive!' The gallant Allies who had inspired the campaign helped it not only with gold but with their personal participation. In huge, specially organized meetings advertised in the bourgeois yellow press there appeared, together with Kerensky and various counterfeit 'sailor' adventurers, the representatives and even ambassadors of the Allies. The agents of Anglo-French financial interests, Thomas and the newly-arrived Vandervelde,[1] again began turning up in the Ex. Com., demanding blood, and they now entered into more and more intimate contact with the top leaders of the Soviet majority.

At army Headquarters, at an officers' meeting, Alexeyev, the Commander-in-Chief, declared the 'Government' formula—'without annexations or indemnities'—to be a utopian phrase and demanded an offensive for the sake of total victory.

All this began at one stroke on the very day the new Cabinet was formed. And it was all directly connected with this. The atmosphere had suddenly become imbued with a chauvinism not hitherto seen in the revolution. Militaristic attacks rained down from all sides with a long-forgotten effrontery.

On May 14th Kerensky published an Order to the army—concerning an offensive. Properly speaking, it was not quite an order to attack but only a preliminary official proclamation. . . 'In the name of the salvation of free Russia,' Kerensky said, 'you will go where your commanders and your Government send you. On your bayonet-points you will be bearing peace, truth, and justice. You will go forward in serried ranks, kept firm by the discipline of your duty and your supreme love for the revolution and your country. . .' The proclamation was written with verve and breathed sincere 'heroic' emotion.

[1] Vandervelde, Emile (1866–1938): Belgian Socialist leader. (Ed.)

Kerensky undoubtedly felt himself to be a hero of 1793. And he was of course equal to the heroes of the great French Revolution, but—not of the Russian.

At this time Kerensky displayed astonishing activity, supernatural energy, and the greatest enthusiasm. Of course he did everything within human power. And not for nothing does the chilly and malevolent historian Miliukov, in whose interests Kerensky was working at this time, recall, with a shade of tenderness and gratitude, the 'comely figure of the young man with a bandaged arm' appearing first at one point then at another of our limitless front (apparently everywhere at once) and calling for great sacrifices, demanding that the wayward and indifferent rabble should pay tribute to the impulses of idealism.

Kerensky, who as Minister of Justice had put on a dark-brown jacket in place of his sports coat, now changed it for a light-coloured, elegant, officer's tunic. His hand had been bothering him nearly all that summer, and in a black sling gave him the appearance of a wounded hero. I have no idea what was wrong with Kerensky's hand—it was a long time since I had talked to him. But it is just like this that he is remembered by tens and hundreds of thousands of soldiers and officers from Finland to the Black Sea, to whom he addressed his fiery speeches.

Everywhere, in the trenches, on ships, at parades, at meetings at the front, at social gatherings, in theatres, town-halls, Soviets —in Helsingfors, Riga, Dvinsk, Kamenets-Podolsk, Kiev, Odessa, Sebastopol—he kept speaking about the same thing and with the same enthusiasm, with sincere and unfeigned emotion. He spoke of freedom, of the land, of the brotherhood of nations, and of the imminent glowing future of the country. He called upon the soldiers and citizens to defend and conquer all this by force of arms, and show themselves worthy of the great revolution. And he pointed to himself as a guarantee that the sacrifices demanded would not be in vain, and that not one drop of free Russian blood would be shed for other, secondary goals.

Kerensky's agitation was (almost) a complete triumph for himself. Everywhere he was carried shoulder-high and pelted with flowers. Everywhere scenes of unprecedented enthusiasm took place, from the descriptions of which breathed the legendary air of heroic ages. Men flung their Crosses of St. George at the feet of Kerensky, who was calling on them to die; women stripped off their valuables and in Kerensky's name laid them on the altar of the (for some unknown reason) longed-for victory...

Of course a sizeable portion of all this enthusiasm was generated by the middle classes, the officers and the philistines. But even amongst the front-line soldiers, in the very trenches, Kerensky had an enormous success. Tens and hundreds of thousands of fighting soldiers, at tremendous meetings, vowed to go into battle on the word of command and die for 'Land and Freedom'.

There is no doubt that the army had been roused by the agitation of this Minister, the 'symbol of the revolution'. The commanding officers cheered up and said good-bye to Kerensky with assurances that now the army would justify the hopes of the country...

By May 19th Kerensky had already telegraphed the Premier: 'Report: I have seen situation on south-eastern front and come to positive conclusions I shall communicate upon arrival. Position in Sebastopol highly favourable...'

There was some 'roughness' too, some of it substantial and important: we shall speak of it later. But there were also grounds for Kerensky's positive conclusions. The whole bourgeoisie had leapt to its feet: the agreeable smell of blood was in its nostrils again, and once again almost abandoned imperialist illusions had revived.

The Coalition had grouped itself around the offensive; it regarded the offensive as its central task, and it was *only* in the organization of the offensive that the new Government manifested itself. What with Kerensky's agitation the situation was becoming unendurable.

* * *

As soon as the new Cabinet's statement was wired to Europe, a question was asked in the British Parliament on the 'Russian formula' for peace. Philip Snowden proposed that Russia's renunciation of annexations and indemnities be welcomed. Robert Cecil, the Foreign Secretary, replied to this with extreme disapproval. He called it senseless and misplaced. But he added: if there were any question of Russia's renouncing its obligations to the Allies, Great Britain would know what to do.

The Cadet *Rech* was, of course, delighted. It had already drawn the conclusion that the Coalition would never think up anything beyond the continuation of the policy of Miliukov.

Nor did either Lvov, or Tereshchenko, or Tsereteli, or even Skobelev, really think up anything more. And every now and then Tereshchenko gave renewed proof of his fidelity to Miliukov's policy. It goes without saying that our whole Diplomatic Corps stayed on at their posts, as they had under the Tsar and Miliukov. Tereshchenko's closest collaborators and advisers were on the one hand the Star Chamber of the Soviet, and on the other Rasputin's protégés (almost). And now, against the background of Kerensky's agitation in the army, Tereshchenko started direct relations with the Allied Governments. He sent a wire to Ribot, the French Premier, in which there was not a word about any peace, or about any requests on the part of the new Russian Government: nothing but compliments, raptures, and assurances of unshakeable fidelity to everything as it had been before.

When Ribot read aloud this wire in the Chambre des Députés he aroused the liveliest sensation. He couldn't find appropriate words to congratulate the Russian Government, 'made up of prominent, bold and energetic statesmen, but subject to outside influences'. And Ribot concluded correctly that nothing had changed for the worse—'Coalitionary' Russia was true to the Russia of the Tsar and of Miliukov.

The next day a similar scene took place in the British House of Commons. Questions were put from the Left about the unfavourable impression made in Russia by Robert Cecil's reaction to the 'Russian formula' for peace. But this worthy gentleman explained that (apart from intriguers and anarchists) there had been no unfavourable impression. Quite the contrary—all was well. . .

All these facts, that deeply discredited the Russian Revolution, practically liquidated the question it had raised about peace. They strengthened, of course, not only Allied imperialism, but also that of Austria and Germany, and on the other hand generated the deepest depression in the advanced proletariat of all countries.

The overt formulation of the old rapacious war programme of the Entente automatically placed the German command on its own kind of 'defensive' positions, reinforced the idea of 'national self-defence' and once again rallied the masses, longing for peace, around the Kaiser, Kühlmann, and Hindenburg. The aggressiveness and chauvinism of the 'great democracies' were extremely favourable to the German imperialists, who set all their hopes on the naked power of arms.

The Austro-German diplomats and military chiefs did not of course cease to be interested in an 'honourable' separate peace with Russia, nor did they cease to take steps to achieve it—steps that were sometimes quite risky. A German agent, a certain D. Rizov, Bulgarian Ambassador to Berlin, had the nerve to write a letter to Gorky proposing that he should become mediator for a separate peace; he gave humanitarian considerations as his motive. Rizov's letter, with a postscript by Gorky, was printed in the *Novaya Zhizn* and caused a stupendous sensation, which fed the whole gutter-press for several days.

* * *

A bitter struggle developed in the press. The bourgeois press examined all the Bolshevik leaders in turn, accusing them of every possible crime. Every day whole tubs of filth were poured over Gorky because of Rizov's letter and for other reasons, some connected with the *Novaya Zhizn* and some not. I personally became the favourite target of the *Rech* and was never called anything but 'dear to the German heart', or 'so highly appreciated by the Germans'. I began getting letters almost every day from the capital, the provinces or the army: some contained admonitions and jeers, others questions: 'How much did you get?'

An extraordinary amount was done to inflame the chauvinistic atmosphere by the Entente agents who had arrived in Russia, Thomas, Vandervelde, and Henderson.[1] The first two were quite familiar to us. We could not say that about Henderson at this time, since his policy speech in the Ex. Com. shed an unexpected light on his—one can't say impudence so much as a unique kind of *naïveté*. Henderson, calling a spade a spade, expounded the war programme of British finance—including the liberation of Mesopotamia, Africa, Constantinople, and

[1] Socialists who supported the First World War, either participating in their respective governments or backing them. (Ed.)

Armenia from the German or Turkish yoke. For all these idealistic goals he demanded from the Russian Revolution cannon-fodder and practical self-immolation. Henderson talked for two hours, but alas! he merely confused even the Mamelukes.

At this same time the representatives of still another gallant Ally, Italy, had appeared in Petersburg. I don't think there were any Ministers in the delegation, but as 'Socialists' the Italian 'patriots' who came, Arturo Labriola, Giovanni Lerda, Orazio Raimondo, and Innocenzo Cappa, were perhaps even more dubious than the above-mentioned trio. At the same time the position of Italy in the World War was the most nakedly piratical. These gentry, with nothing in their minds but the badgering of neutral Italy into the war and the struggle against the honest Italian Socialists, presented themselves to the Ex. Com. only once and 'hailed' the revolution more in Ministerial circles, but they did their bit to intensify the chauvinist atmosphere by their interviews and public speeches.

The French Social-patriotic delegates, Cachin, Moutet, and Lafont, kept the promise they had given the Ex. Com., and after they got home insisted on the French Social-chauvinist majority's taking part in the Stockholm Conference.[1] This resolution was passed by the National Council of the French Socialist Party. It was based on an effort to confine the mighty Russian Revolution within definite limits and keep it from any radical measures and within the sphere of Entente influence. For this it was essential to meet the Soviet, which controlled the army, half-way. The honourable Citizen Cachin, agitating amongst the Socialists, tried to persuade his own ruling bourgeoisie to get along with the Soviet and refer to it as little as possible in public as a gang of vagabonds and German agents—which for that matter was quite untrue, since the Soviet was now headed by quite statesmanlike patriots.

It was the same thing in England. The radical press maintained that it would be dangerous for the Allies to forbid the Stockholm Conference, but the Government decided that it would nevertheless be better not to let the British Socialists go to the Conference. There was a united conference of the Independent Labour Party and the British Labour Party in Leeds

[1] An international conference of Zimmerwaldites scheduled for June 25th, but never held. (Ed.)

during the last third of May. More than a thousand delegates backed the 'Russian formula' and decided to take part in the Conference. This was an impressive force, and it was awkward for the Government of the 'Great Democracy' simply not to 'allow' it, in the face of the aroused proletariat. A slippery path was chosen. They staged 'workers' demonstrations of protest' against the trip of MacDonald and other delegates to Petersburg —*via* Stockholm. The Seamen's Union was induced to refuse to service the ship in which MacDonald was to travel to Russia. The trip of the British workers' minority was prevented, while the majority refused of its own accord to take part in an 'International with the Germans'.

It was the same everywhere in Europe. Some parties—the British and French minorities, the German independents, the Czech, Hungarian, Austrian, and Italian—backed the Russian formula and were ready to go to the Conference, but they were not allowed to and were attacked in their own countries for their attitude.

CHAPTER 17

IN THE DEPTHS

'OUR country is definitely turning into some sort of madhouse with lunatics in command, while people who have not yet lost their reason huddle fearfully against the walls.' (*Rech*, May 17th.) 'Russia is turning into a Texas, into a country of the Far West.' (*Rech*, May 30th.)

The bourgeois gutter-press, without respite or repose, in creative self-forgetfulness and patriotic rapture, played variations on this theme in all conceivable styles—sorrowful, menacing, and playful. 'Anarchy' in large letters made its appearance as a standing headline. This press was now filled with descriptions of every possible excess and disorder. 'Arbitrary arrests', 'lynch-law', 'collapse', 'riots'. The struggle of the bourgeoisie against the revolution had expanded to its full scope.

There were indeed many excesses, perhaps more than before. Lynch-law, the destruction of houses and shops, jeering at and attacks on officers, provincial authorities, or private persons, unauthorized arrests, seizures, and beatings-up—were recorded every day by tens and hundreds. In the country burnings and destruction of country-houses became more frequent. The peasants were beginning to 'regulate' land-tenure according to their own ideas, forbidding the illegal felling of trees, driving off the landlords' stock, taking the stocks of grain under their own control, and refusing to permit them to be taken to stations and wharves. The terrific destruction of a great lord's estate in the Mtsensk district caused a special uproar in the first half of May. Quite a few excesses were also observed amongst the workers—against factory administration, owners, and foremen. But more than anything else of course it was the unbridled rioting soldiers who were 'destroying law and order'.

In the idle garrisons of the capital and the provinces, in an atmosphere of unprecedented freedom, military discipline naturally collapsed. The iron shackles had weakened. The ignorant wantonness of the grey mass made itself felt. All garrison service in the rear became more or less disrupted; there was almost no training; orders were frequently ignored, sentries not stationed. There were masses of deserters both in the rear and at the front.

The soldiers, without leave, went off home in great floods. They filled all the trains, hectored the administration, kicked out the passengers, and threatened the entire transport system with catastrophe. The deserters were given a period of time to report back, then this time was extended and reinforced by threats. The soldiers flowed through the countryside from the rear and the front, recalling a great migration of peoples. In the cities they blighted the trams and boulevards, and filled all the public places. There were reports here and there of drunkenness, rowdiness, and disorder.

In Russia generally, under the Coalition, in the summer of 1917, there was very little order. The man in the street, following bourgeois initiative, began complaining about it menacingly and grumbling ill-naturedly about the revolution as such. It was precisely the fact of the revolution that he held responsible for our not having any law or stable authority. Once again Miliukov's catchword came to mind: the man in the street is stupid.

The same thing took place amongst the soldiers. There were not only *excesses* here, but also a profound process, a shift in mood, a movement only the blind could fail to notice. . . We have seen how the minds of the soldiers reflected the problem of war and peace two months before. The mere notion of peace would have made them impale 'traitors and openers up of the front' on their bayonets. I have noted an embryonic shift as early as a month after the revolution, around the time of Lenin's arrival. Now, two months and a bit later, against the background of the Coalition, the soldiers' temper began turning into its opposite.

This process was obscured in the eyes of the Soviet leaders by the fact that the mass of the Petersburg soldiery was in this respect far behind the provinces. In the Soviet the soldiers as before were in an extremely patriotic mood (they were, by the way, better protected than any of the others against despatch to the front). But in Moscow and the provinces this upheaval in the minds of the soldiers gradually made its presence felt. As early as May 9th Thomas met with a petty unpleasantness in the Moscow Soviet: he was publicly told in the name of the soldiers that our army was tired and wanted peace; that there was no party in Russia for a *separate* peace, but if the war was going to drag on it was impossible to vouch for the consequences. Thomas 'experienced an uncomfortable impression'.

But with Kerensky these little unpleasantnesses went still further. While agitating at the front he began meeting with argumentative resistance from the soldiers. It's true that these were isolated cases, and that the impression was smoothed over at once by patriotic enthusiasm. But after all the surroundings were also exceptionally unfavourable for any argument against an offensive. In the last week of May, in the loyal Twelfth Army, Kerensky came across a minor scandal. Under the pretext of asking a question, a soldier declared the Government ought to conclude peace very soon. Kerensky interrupted the soldier with a thunderous exclamation of 'Coward!' and ordered him to be dismissed from the army. The regimental commander, however, asked permission to dismiss, together with the unsuccessful debater, several others who 'dishonoured the whole regiment' with these same thoughts on war and peace.

Once at the end of May, from the balcony of the *Novaya Zhizn*, looking out on the Nevsky, we watched a strange demonstration. Its beginning and end were lost in the distance; the demonstration stretched for practically two-thirds of a mile. Rows of elderly men were moving along in vaguely military uniforms. They were walking slackly with their heads bowed, in an unusually deep, glum silence. They had no banners, but wretched little signs with inscriptions: 'The land has no one to work it!' 'Our land isn't sown!' 'We can't get bread for the workers!' 'Our families are starving on the land!' 'Let the young men fight!'. . .

These were soldiers over forty years old. For a long time they had been demanding to be demobilized, with no success. And now this morose demonstration, organized by no one knew whom, showed they were beginning to lose patience. . . The 'over-forties' were on their way to the Marian Palace. There Minister of Agriculture Chernov, closest to their hearts, was ordered out to them. He made them a long, flowery speech promising something and nothing at the same time. The over-forties dispersed unsatisfied and definitely resentful.

The war was becoming more and more intolerable. The elemental forces against war, against support of it and against its entire organization, were accumulating drop by drop and day by day.

* * *

The names of Lenin and his companions-in-arms, daily spattered with filth, were still heard with hatred and suspicion by the ignorant masses. At an Officers' Congress on May 20th his arrest was demanded; it was said that otherwise the people would kill him. But that same day Lenin appeared at the Peasant Congress. Generally speaking Lenin held himself aloof in those days, like some great noble. He was never seen either at Soviet sessions or in the lobbies; as before he was staying somewhere 'underground', in intimate party circles. Whenever he appeared at a meeting he would ask for the floor out of turn, upsetting the agenda. An attempt of this kind a few days before at the Peasant Congress, as though he were a Minister, had failed, and he had to leave: it was against his principles to wait for the floor. But now, on the 20th, with the absorbed interest of the Peasant Congress, Lenin developed his programme of 'direct action', his tactics of land seizure regardless of the legally-appointed limits. It would seem that Lenin had landed not merely in a camp of bitter enemies, but you might say in the very jaws of the crocodile. The little muzhiks listened attentively and probably not without sympathy. But they dared not show it. . .

Around this time we in the Ex. Com. once heard that Lenin was making a speech to the Soldiers' Section in the White Hall. This was the most faithful support Chaikovsky[1] and Tsereteli had—the Praetorian Guard of the Coalition. Lenin was not likely to get on well. I hurried over. He had already been on the platform a long time and was making the same speech as at the Peasants' Congress. I sat down in about the seventh row, in the heart of the soldier audience. The soldiers were listening with the greatest interest as Lenin berated the Coalition's agrarian policy and proposed that they should settle the matter on their own authority, without any Constituent Assembly. . . But the speaker was soon interrupted by the chair: his time was up.

[1] Chaikovsky, Nikolai Vasilyevich (1850–1926): prominent in Co-operative movement. After the October Revolution he joined the 'White reaction' against Bolshevism. (Ed.)

Some arguing began about whether to allow Lenin to continue his speech. The Praesidium evidently didn't want to, but the assembly had nothing against it. Lenin, bored, was standing on the platform wiping his bald spot with a handkerchief; recognising me from a distance he nodded to me gaily. I heard comments around me: 'Talks sense, hey? Hey?' one soldier said to the other.

By a majority vote the assembly ordered that Lenin be allowed to finish speaking. The ice was broken: Lenin and his principles had begun penetrating even the nucleus of the Praetorians.

Trotsky and Lunacharsky were not of course members of the Bolshevik Party at that time, but these first-class orators had already succeeded in the course of two or three weeks in becoming most popular agitators. Their successes began, perhaps, in Kronstadt, where they very often played guest rôles. By the middle of May, Kerensky, who was preparing the offensive, already figured in Kronstadt under the epithets: 'Socialist-plunderer and blood-drinker'.

The 'Bolshevik question' was coming to the surface as the current problem of state, though the Soviet leaders in the Tauride Palace were calmer about it than anyone else. Tsereteli himself was blind as an owl in the dazzling light of the revolution, and he blinkered his neighbours' eyes too. In the Tauride Palace the Soviet leaders, yawning, repeated endless platitudes about how they personally were shaping the country's fate and saving the revolution in the name of the 'whole democracy'.

Meanwhile the facts spoke more and more eloquently for themselves. If in the Soldiers' Section they were still no more than listening to Lenin with sympathy, in some regiments of the capital, recently loyal to Rodzianko, they were solidly *obeying* the Bolsheviks. In particular, Lenin already had the allegiance of the 1st Machine-Gun Regiment, where a certain 2nd Lieut. Semashko was active. At the end of May, when the latter was accidentally arrested, the entire Machine-Gun Regiment turned out in full formation, freed Semashko, and carried him shoulder-high out of the Commandant's headquarters. Here already was *military power* in the hands of the Bolshevik Central Committee.

But of course it was first and foremost the Petersburg *proletariat* that rallied to the banner of Bolshevism.

* * *

On May 30th a conference of the Factory Committees of the capital and its suburbs opened in the White Hall. The Conference grew up from the bottom; it was planned in the factories —without the participation either of the official organs of labour or of the Soviet institutions. It was initiated and organized by the Bolshevik Party, which was making an appeal to the masses directly, and quasi-directly, obliquely, to the Soviet. It was inspired by Lenin, and carried out primarily by Zinoviev.

Unlike the Workers' Section of the Soviet, whose composition was changed, not very quickly, by a series of partial elections, the members of the Factory Committee Conference had just been elected *en bloc* and reflected with precision the real physiognomy of the Petersburg proletariat. The Conference really represented it, and workers from the bench in great numbers took an active part in its labours. For two days this workers' parliament debated the economic crisis and the ruin throughout the country. And of course it combined economics with politics. The Government Mensheviks, and also a few Internationalists, sponsored the organization of economy by the *State*—ignoring the question of *just which* State. But the Bolsheviks, Lenin and Zinoviev, with the support of the worker speakers, now for the first time developed their slogan of 'workers' control'.

When the vote was taken, 335 of the 421 workers voted for the Bolsheviks. The victory of Bolshevism was complete. In conclusion the Conference of the Factory Committees resolved to 'organize in Petersburg an all-city centre of the representatives of all factory committees and trade unions; this centre must play the leading rôle in the realization of all measures indicated above (control *et al.*) within Petersburg'.

This centre, which fell completely into the hands of the Bolsheviks, was naturally bound to become from now on altogether the most authoritative centre for the Petersburg proletariat. It was bound to supplant the conciliationist Soviet. If this didn't happen it was for only one reason: the Soviet Workers' Section—both in Petersburg and Moscow—was day by day irresistibly filling up with Bolsheviks. They still had no majority, and it was impossible to say when they would have. But it would come, and in the not too distant future—there could be no doubt of that.

Meanwhile Kerensky was harvesting laurels in Moscow. Crowds thronged into the streets he passed through. Flowers were showered on his car. Standing up in it Kerensky hailed 'the people'. He was at the peak of his popularity. He was a hero and object of adoration—for philistines and nondescripts. Meanwhile Lenin with a firm tread was striding on and on, strengthening each step with the steel of proletarian ranks and anchoring himself in the sole unshakeable basis of the revolution.

* * *

One fine day during the last week of May I heard that three generals of the revolution wanted to have a talk with the editorial board of the *Novaya Zhizn* about their more intimate association with it. These were the three non-party Bolsheviks, Trotsky, Lunacharsky, and Ryazanov. Lunacharsky and I had had a rather intensive correspondence during the period of the *Sovremennik*, for which he did a good deal of writing. I knew him of course as a most talented writer, of great culture and many-sided gifts. I naturally not only valued his contributions, but actively sought him out, and in spite of the dubiousness of the *Sovremennik* with respect to fees, so necessary to an *émigré*, Lunacharsky gladly responded to my suggestions. Without any prompting from me he often sent me agreeable notes, such as an expression of sympathy for my activity in Russia during the war years. Accordingly I not only had a high regard for him but also felt myself drawn to him before seeing him.

After he arrived in Russia on May 9th, together with Martov, he at once, and quite naturally, came to the *Novaya Zhizn*. There we became personally acquainted and quite soon intimate. He didn't appear immediately in the Ex. Com. and didn't come often: he was not yet in Lenin's party and had a rather 'soft' disposition; we still felt ourselves to be comrades-in-arms in politics as well as literary collaborators.

But we also became rather close friends on purely personal grounds. You might say I spent almost all my unoccupied time with Lunacharsky. He often spent days and nights with us in the *Letopis*, where my wife and I had a *pied-à-terre*. Sometimes at night he would come to see me at the printer's, to have a little more talk and look at the next day's edition. And when we were detained in the Tauride Palace we used to spend the night at Manukhin's and again talk away endlessly.

We discussed everything: regardless of the theme, Lunacharsky's talk, stories, and repartee were interesting, clear and picturesque, just as he himself was interesting and brilliant, glittering with every hue and attractive through his culture and the astonishing inborn talent that permeated him from head to foot.

I remember hearing a woman I knew, who didn't know Lunacharsky, tell of her trip home from some boring meeting. Sitting opposite her in the tram Lunacharsky, also on his way back from the same place, was telling his neighbour about the meeting. Though the meeting had bored her to death the entire evening, it now, as reported by Lunacharsky, flashed and glittered, adorned with colours whose existence had not been suspected by the average person there. Lunacharsky's account of it was more interesting than the reality itself. Lunacharsky was like that always and in everything.

The great people of the revolution—both his comrades and his opponents—almost always spoke of Lunacharsky with sneers, irony, or scorn. Though a most popular personality and Minister, he was kept away from high policy: 'I have no influence,' he once told me himself.

In a word—*suum cuique*. Lunacharsky is not one of those who can create an era or an epoch. The lot of Lenin and Trotsky is not for him. In general his *historical* rôle in world events is comparatively small. But it is small only in comparison with these cosmic titans. After them, of course, for a long, long, long time there is nothing. Then it is no longer individuals that are visible, but groups, constellations. Among these Lunacharsky of course is one of the first. But that is his *historical* rôle; for brilliance of *talent*, to say nothing of culture, he has no equal in the constellation of the Bolshevik leaders.

It is said that when he became a Minister Lunacharsky more quickly and completely than others acquired a ministerial manner, with its negative qualities. I don't know. After the October Revolution I completely broke with him, unlike what happened with many others. For two and a half years, down to this very moment, I've only had a few fleeting encounters with him, and not very agreeable ones at that. He really took a ministerial air with me. But I don't know how much he was to blame for all this, and I know very well how much I was, with my rather disagreeable character. My continual polemics were really bitter and unendurable, when we ceased to be companions-in-arms and became political enemies.

We shall have to deal further on with the little human foibles of this most important figure of the revolution, and with some of his blunders, that everyone, small and great, thought ridiculous. But these spots on the sun cannot in any way obscure for me, now an alien, indifferent, and polemically disposed man, either the brilliance of this remarkable figure or the attractive personal qualities of the man with whom I spent the summer of 1917.

* * *

In order that the editorial staff might all be present, the conference was arranged for the evening of May 25th in the *Novaya Zhizn* printing-house. I don't remember that the conversation was particularly interesting. I was silent, busy with an article, and the conversation was almost over when I spoke, and I daresay definitely turned the tide against any editorial alliance. The talk had been chiefly about the most immediate political perspectives and the fate of the Coalition. I said that however negative my feelings towards it, as shown by daily articles, I didn't think it right to hasten its liquidation and the transfer of all power to the Socialists: it was obvious that the country and the democracy had still not digested the idea of a Socialist Government, while the Coalition in any case would collapse very shortly without any urging, through the spontaneous course of events. In general, I said, with respect to high policy I was closer to Martov than to Trotsky.

Trotsky spoke last and briefly; everything was clear for him. For his part he sharply dissociated himself from Martov, who 'while in the Opposition was only on the side of the defensists', and he considered the position of the *Novaya Zhizn* to be really an approach to Martov, but not to 'revolutionary Socialism'. Trotsky finished with some rather remarkable words, which made a strong impression on me, and which I remember more or less as follows:

'Now I see there is nothing left for me to do but found a newspaper together with Lenin.'

Afterwards, almost three years later, just a short while before I wrote these lines, Trotsky corrected the wording.[1]

'Not "nothing is left for me to do",' he answered when I gave him my account of this episode, 'but "it remains for me and Lenin to make our own newspaper".'

Trotsky explained that he and Lenin had agreed beforehand to make an attempt to 'conquer' the *Novaya Zhizn*, and in case of failure to create their own organ jointly. Of course I won't dispute this. . .

But at that time Lenin and Trotsky did not create their joint organ. Soon after this, to be sure, Lunacharsky started telling me about projects for a big newspaper with Bolshevik editors (the trio of Lenin, Zinoviev, and Kamenev) and Interdistrictites (Trotsky and Lunacharsky). But no such newspaper saw the light. Instead Trotsky and the Interdistrictites founded a little magazine *Vperyod* (Forward), where he worked independently of Lenin. This made a very small audience for Trotsky and was rather thankless work for him.

I think we left the *Novaya Zhizn* conference without any special regrets, at least on our side. Only Steklov, on his way to the composing-room with me, expressed his chagrin at the results of the talk. 'We've lost some useful collaborators,' he said.

But the question had nothing to do with acquiring new collaborators. Lunacharsky went on working on the paper on the old arrangement, together with many other Bolsheviks. But Trotsky we never saw inside our walls again.

[1] Trotsky corrects it still further in his own version of all this, given in Appendix III, Volume I of his *History of the Russian Revolution.* (Ed.)

CHAPTER 18

THE FIRST ALL-RUSSIAN CONGRESS OF SOVIETS

THIS was properly not the first, but the second Soviet Congress. The first one assembled, as we know, at the end of March. This March Congress, which was very far from dull, had been a sufficiently full and authoritative exposition of the contemporary moods of the democracy. But at that time these moods had still been wavering, whereas now the course was quite definite—towards an unrestricted capitulation to the bourgeoisie. There was absolutely no question but that the Compromisers and the Praetorians of the Coalition would have a decided advantage at the Congress. If only for this reason it was impossible to expect anything decisive from the forthcoming Congress, or any change in direction. All its activities would be reduced to 'support' of the Government and a struggle against the Left 'irresponsible' minority. Nevertheless the Congress was of enormous interest as a large-scale review of the forces of the revolution.

The general physiognomy of the Congress and its results were clear in advance, but the review of the revolutionary forces might come out in various ways, depending on the specific weight of the Opposition. The SRs were assured of a majority, but the eyes of all the thinking elements of the Tauride Palace were fixed on the Bolshevik and Menshevik-Internationalist fractions. It was plainly an absorbing question, what Bolshevism had done in the provinces.

For me, however, another question was just as interesting: what would be the situation within the Menshevik Party?; how many would be Right and how many Left?; what section of the Menshevik Swamp would join Martov's independent internationalist fraction and take the chance of splitting from the conciliationist majority?

Alas! the reality disappointed even the pessimists. Out of 777 delegates definitely committed to a party, 105 proved to be Bolsheviks. But with the Mensheviks the position was quite unexpected: the Internationalists among them didn't even number thirty-five; all the rest were the troops of Tsereteli and Tereshchenko. It was a stunning and bitter outrage. The whole Menshevik-Internationalist fraction, headed by Martov and the group that had come with him from abroad, together with those present in an advisory capacity, didn't even amount to one-sixth of all the Mensheviks.

Besides this there was at the Congress the fraction of the 'United Internationalists', which Steklov was trying to turn into a party and which the Interdistrictites led by Lunacharsky and Trotsky had joined. But this fraction didn't have more than from thirty-five to forty people either.

* * *

The SRs had just concluded their third All-Russian Party Conference, which had produced absolutely nothing new or interesting. At the Soviet Congress these same SRs proved a decisive force. They did not have an absolute majority, but together with the Right Mensheviks they made up five-sixths of the Congress. The Opposition fractions, taken together, including delegates without votes, did not amount to more than 150–160; while in the voting not more than 120–125 hands were raised against the ruling bloc. They formed a narrow strip extending from the left side of the chairman's platform along the wall and not going further than the middle of the hall. Looking at it from the platform itself, this strip was divided from the remaining mass by its external appearance also: it wore almost exclusively *civilian* clothes, and especially *workmen's* jackets.

The remaining mass was almost all military. There were 'real' soldiers, peasants; but there were more mobilized intellectuals. There were more than a hundred junior officers, who still represented a great part of the army in the field. And what figures they cut! It goes without saying that they were all 'Socialists'. It was absolutely impossible to represent the masses or appeal to them without this label. But judging by their sympathies, and by quite intangible factors, it was not only the *secret* Cadets, Octobrists, and anti-Semites that had joined the SRs or Mensheviks; there were also people there *known* to be liberal, and even not very liberal lawyers, physicians, teachers, landowners, and government officials, in the guise of 'populists' or 'Marxists'.

* * *

The Congress opened on June 3rd at 7 in the evening. On the following day the question of the relationship to the Provisional Government was taken up. The debate went on for five whole days.

With complete *naïveté* Lieber and Tsereteli sang the praises of the Coalition Government, the 'all-national' Government of all the living forces, all the responsible elements of society, the only one possible, which had completely justified itself. This blind and vulgar bragging about the Coalition's counter-revolutionary policy did not, of course, nauseate only the Bolsheviks. But there was nothing either novel or interesting here.

The novelty and interest began when Lenin himself spoke in rebuttal, having left his underground cave for the light of day. In unaccustomed surroundings, face to face with his ferocious enemies, surrounded by a hostile crowd that looked on him as a wild beast—Lenin clearly felt himself insignificant and had no special success. In addition, the cruel fifteen minutes allotted to a fraction speaker weighed on him. But Lenin wouldn't have been allowed to speak at all except for the enormous curiosity every one of the provincial Mamelukes felt for this notorious figure. His speech was not very well arranged and had no central pivot, but it contained some remarkable passages for whose sake it must be recalled.

In it Lenin gave his own solution of the question of the Government, and also a general 'schematic' outline of the programme and tactics of this Government. Hear ye! Hear ye!

'The citizen Minister of Posts and Telegraphs', said Lenin, 'has declared that there is no political party in Russia that would agree to take the entire power on itself. I answer: There is. No party can refuse to do this, all parties are contending and must contend for the power, and our party will not refuse it. *It is ready at any moment to take over the Government.*'

This was novel, interesting, and very important. This was Lenin's first open statement of what the slogan 'All Power to the Soviets' meant in his mouth. Lenin's proletarian party was struggling for the *entire* power. The other aspect of the matter was that Lenin was ready to accept all power *at any moment*, that is, when his party was known to be in a minority. This was no less interesting and important.

In general this fragment of Lenin's speech is unusually rich in content; it comprises a complete political system that now replaced, developed, and interpreted Lenin's original schema of April. At *that* time the Bolshevik leader had enjoined his party to learn how to be in the minority, to have patience, to win over the Soviets, to get majorities in them and transfer all power to *them*. Now Lenin, without patience, without having got a majority or won over the Soviets, was demanding all power against their will, and a dictatorship for his own party alone. It's possible that in the recesses of Lenin's mind there had never been any other interpretation of the original April slogans, and that only now for the first time he thought it appropriate to proclaim them.

And now—what would Lenin have done if at any moment he had found himself in power?

'The first step we should take if we had the power would be to arrest the biggest capitalists and smash their intrigues. Without that all the phrases about peace without annexations and indemnities are the emptiest of words. Our second step would be to announce to the nations, independently of their Governments, that we hold all capitalists to be plunderers, both Tereshchenko, who is not one whit better than Miliukov, just slightly more stupid, and the French capitalists, and the British, and all of them. . .'

Lenin didn't enumerate any further steps, being distracted by random ideas. He simply said further that a Bolshevik Government would come forward with a proposal for a *general peace*. But the first and the second steps in any case were enough to make the entire hall gasp at the unexpectedness and absurdity of such a programme. Not that the prospect of arresting a hundred of the biggest capitalists definitely displeased the majority of the respected gathering: let's not forget that very many of the then Mensheviks were future 'Communists', nor that nearly a majority of the peasant SRs became *Left* SRs in the near future. Arresting capitalists—that was very pleasant, and as for calling them plunderers—quite right.

Aside from junior officers, liberal lawyers, and similar people, the class instinct of the workers' and peasants' section of the meeting may even have been on Lenin's side, though prejudice prevented their displaying this while their most authoritative leaders lingered in the embraces of these same capitalists. But as a *programme* for a future Government, both of Lenin's 'steps' were really absurd, and didn't seem the least bit attractive even to the tiny Left sector, where both the faces and the talk reflected an absolutely unambiguous bafflement at Lenin's speech.

At the end of this session I remember meeting Trotsky on the stairs; as usual he had been 'with the masses' and had come after the fair. He stopped me with 'Well, what's happening there? Debates interesting? Have I missed much?'

'Nothing,' I said; 'Lunacharsky was best of all; he was really wonderful.'

'Yes?' Trotsky's eyes flashed with satisfaction. Lunacharsky, after all, was the second biggest star in the tiny Interdistrict group.

Peshekhonov, the Minister of Supply, was another of the Socialist Ministers who spoke at the Congress; unlike the others, however, he didn't touch on high policy in his speech, which was entirely devoted to supply. Here is his philosophy of the supply problem.

'The productivity of the working class understandably fell after the revolution; . . . the scope of its demands is far more than normal. With the raising of wages the value of money falls, the cost of commodities goes up, and the situation must again be ameliorated by raising wages. But after all, a time will come when that will be impossible. *The whole difficulty lies, not in overcoming the resistance of the bourgeoisie, which gives way in everything, but in winning over the toiling masses, who must be summoned to the most exacting labour and the indispensable sacrifices.* If we succeed in overcoming these psychological difficulties of the masses, and drawing them after us, then we shall solve our problems.'

That's what Peshekhonov said. One scarcely knows what to be more amazed at—this 'Socialist Minister's' theoretical innocence or his political cynicism. No one, however, noticed any of this in his speech, while Trotsky, who succeeded him, spoke as follows:

'I have listened to Peshekhonov's speech with enormous interest, since it's always possible to learn from one's theoretical opponents. What should come next is the collaboration of the Ministers of Labour and Industry, but Konovalov has left, after sabotaging the organization of industry. For three weeks a replacement has been looked for, but can't be found. Put twelve

Peshekhonovs in power, and that would already be an enormous step forward. Find another Peshekhonov to replace Konovalov.

'You see that I'm not proceeding from fractional considerations, but only from the point of view of efficiency. The working class must know that its own Government is at the top, and it will not try to snatch crumbs for itself but will deal with the Government considerately. We are not undermining your régime, but are working to prepare tomorrow for you. We say that your policies of procrastination may sap the foundations of the Constituent Assembly. We criticize you because together with you we suffer from the same pains.'

In this speech Trotsky called the Coalition Government an Arbitration Court. But he himself spoke at the Congress as a kind of arbitrator.

I remember very much later, when Trotsky, after reading the first part of these Notes of mine, made fun of me:

'You had *conversations* with Kerensky!' he exclaimed, sarcastically histrionic. 'You tried to "persuade" him, the known creature of the bourgeoisie, the representative of an enemy class. Well, don't tell me you're not a *Zemstvo* liberal! Only one path is permissible for a revolutionary: to go to his *own* class and call on it to fight!'

In his speech about the Government at the first Congress Trotsky did not, as we see, follow these sage principles. On the contrary, he generously lavished the most opportunistic, *Zemstvo*-liberal 'persuasions' on the servants of the bourgeoisie. In the Ex. Com. I too had recommended putting some Peshekhonov or other (or still better a Socialist without quotation marks) in place of Konovalov—a fortnight before this. But for me such a Peshekhonov was only an unavoidable element, the extreme Right wing of a democratic Government, and in my eyes a *dozen Peshekhonovs* could never be the workers' 'own' Government.

From my point of view the Government that succeeded the Coalition would be a Government of the worker-peasant bloc, where the representatives of the petty bourgeoisie, the Peshekhonovs, Chernovs, and Tseretelis, would be allied with the real leaders of the proletariat, with Lenin, Martov, and Trotsky. Even though the former would be in a majority, and would tend as before to a 'procrastinating' bourgeois policy, still the proletariat, to make up for that, would be the master of the revolution. The right course of events would be ensured by such a régime, and *only* by such a régime.

In any case the above-quoted excerpt from Trotsky's speech would seem to indicate very clearly that in spite of Lenin Trotsky did not put the question of the Bolshevik seizure of power on the order of the day. By 'Power to the Soviets' he would really seem to have meant just that. There are no signs here of any seizure of power by the minority of the Petersburg proletariat. In what sense are Trotsky's words to the *Novaya Zhizn* to be understood, that from then on his path lay solely with Lenin? Hadn't I made a thoughtless mistake that time, when the three generals swooped down on our paper, in refusing an alliance with Lunacharsky and Trotsky?[1]

* * *

The concluding act of the Congress was to create a new plenipotentiary Soviet organ, in place of the former Petersburg Ex. Com. The body it set up was called the All-Russian Central Executive Committee of the Soviets of Workers' and Soldiers' Deputies (the Central Ex. Com.). It was to consist of 300 members, of whom half were to be elected by the Congress from anyone it liked—of the 'most worthy'. One hundred members had to be local provincial workers: they were supposed to return home or to specially designated points at once to carry on their work as plenipotentiaries of the Central Soviet organ. The remaining fifty people were to be taken from the Petersburg Ex. Com.

The Central Ex. Com., minus its 100 provincial members, was to be permanently active with 200, while on special occasions it was supposed to convoke an emergency plenum. This was most convenient for the ruling clique: any decision it liked could be declared so important or so controversial that it would have to be shelved 'until the plenum of the Central Ex. Com.'

The Central Ex. Com. membership included, of course, both Kerensky and Lenin. But they never came once. In general a good half was made up of dead souls, who scarcely ever appeared

[1] For Trotsky's comments on this see Appendix III to Volume I of his *History of the Russian Revolution*. (Ed.)

in the Soviet centre. No importance was ascribed to it, and it was not taken seriously; no one felt that this body could have any effect on the destinies of the revolution.

Having left in its place its plenipotentiary organ to guard the revolution, the Congress had finished its programme. It quietly closed on June 24th, after working for three weeks and a few days.

CHAPTER 19

THE COALITION SPLITS UNDER STRESS

All over the country disorders, anarchy, seizures, violence, and 'republics' still continued; people took the law into their own hands, soldiers mutinied, and regiments disbanded.

In Petersburg, among other things, the anarchists were intensifying their 'activity'. They had a territorial base on the Vyborg Side, in the distant and secluded villa of the former Tsarist Minister Durnovo. They had seized this villa long before and held it firmly. This anarchist nest enjoyed an enviable reputation in the capital as a sort of Brocken, where the powers of evil assembled, witches' Sabbaths were held, and there were orgies, plots, dark and sinister and doubtless bloody doings. Of course no one doubted that Durnovo's mysterious villa was stocked with bombs and all sorts of weapons. The official and Soviet authorities understandably looked askance at this indecent spot in the heart of the very capital, but—without sufficient courage, they waited for an excuse and meanwhile were patient.

The anarchists had recently begun to find not a few supporters amongst the working-class masses densely settled throughout the Vyborg Side. At the same time they began to undertake offensive operations. Up to then in Petersburg they had tried to seize only dwelling-houses, from which they were quickly evicted. But on June 5th they decided to make an attempt to set up an anarchist régime in some industrial enterprise. For this experiment they chose the magnificent printing-plant of the muddle-headed yellow paper *Russkaya Volya* (Russian Freedom).

About seventy armed men appeared at the printing-plant, occupied all the entrances and exits, and told the local workers that from now on the plant was theirs. The workers, however, were not sufficiently sympathetic, and the authorities, in the person of some Ex. Com. members, turned up at the spot of the anarchist revolution.

The anarchists arrested the management, dismissed the

workers, and refused to leave the plant. While negotiations were going on they printed their own proclamation, in which they declared they were killing two birds: liquidating a vulgar newspaper and giving its own property back to the people. An enormous excited mob collected around the building. Two companies of soldiers were sent; they occupied the adjacent street and didn't know what else to do.

Then the matter came, not very appropriately, before the Soviet Congress itself. The Congress immediately passed an emergency resolution—condemning the seizure and suggesting the evacuation of the occupied premises. That evening the anarchists 'surrendered' under the double pressure of the Congress and a passive siege. A few dozen men were disarmed, arrested, and brought to—the Military Academy, where they were kept under guard. The next day the *Rech* flew into a rage: why had the prisoners been brought to the Congress? Surely there were more suitable premises? Weren't there any lawful authorities, a lawful court and justice? But these were all empty questions.

* * *

In any case, after this the legal authorities decided to act. On June 7th the Minister of Justice prepared to evict the Anarchist-Communists from the Durnovo villa. They were given twenty-four hours' notice.

On the morning of June 8th twenty-eight factories on the Vyborg Side came out on strike, and crowds, processions, and armed workers' detachments began moving towards the Durnovo villa. An enormous mass-meeting formed, and delegates were sent to the Ex. Com. to ask it to take steps against the eviction and secure to the 'toiling people' the possession of the villa. The Ex. Com. met the delegation quite coldly. Then another delegation was sent from the Durnovo villa, this time with a declaration that the anarchists would defend the villa themselves, if necessary by force of arms.

This might not have been an empty threat: the Vyborg Side was in the right mood and had enough arms. Then the Ex. Com. once again referred the question to the Congress.

Meanwhile the direct executor of the sentence, the Procurator Bessarabov, arrived at the Durnovo villa. He got into the building without much difficulty and found an unexpected sight. He discovered nothing either dreadful or mysterious: the rooms were in perfect order; there was nothing dilapidated or broken, and the only disorder was that a great number of chairs and arm-chairs had been put into the largest room and destroyed the harmony of the ministerial background by their heterogeneous appearance: the room was meant for lectures and meetings.

The crowd showed no aggressiveness, giving the Procurator another surprise. The Durnovo villa, empty and deserted, really had been occupied by the Anarchist-Communists; but now there were all kinds of organizations there that had nothing to do with the anarchists: a bakers' trade union, a People's Militia organization, etc. They had nowhere else to go. The villa's enormous garden, always thronged with children, served as a resting-place for the whole workers' district nearby. All this explained a good deal of the popularity of the Durnovo villa on the Vyborg Side.

So the 'legal authorities' had to go back on their word, explaining that the Minister's decision did not concern either the garden or any organization except the anarchists, amongst whom lurked 'criminal elements'. The authorities also muttered something about provocation by irresponsible people, who were exciting the workers and attempting to force the authorities to shed blood. But for the time being it was best to smooth over the affair. These problematic criminal elements were obviously not worth a wave of strikes and excitement in the capital.

But the affair was already being aired in the supreme organ of the whole democracy. Through the efforts of the zealous servant of 'the legal authorities', the All-Russian Congress again interrupted its labours to turn to police functions.

The hue and cry was raised. As usual it had by no means the results counted on by the sage politicians of the petty-bourgeois majority. The anarchists did not submit but stayed on at the villa; and amongst the Petersburg proletariat the police exploits of the 'Congress of the whole democracy' of course had a depressing effect. In the eyes of the workers the Soviet majority and its leaders were changing hourly from a theoretical adversary into a class enemy. Lenin was reaping a rich harvest.

* * *

The Bolshevik Central Committee controlled most of the Workers' Section in the Soviet, as well as the majority of the Petersburg proletariat. In addition, the organizations closest to the workers—the Factory Committees—were now united in a single centre, completely forgotten by the official Soviet and fully in the power of the Bolsheviks. They acted as feelers among all the working class of the capital.

But from one hour to the next a similar situation was being produced amongst the troops of the Petersburg garrison. For some time now the Bolshevik *Military Organization* had been successfully operating under the careful supervision of Lenin himself. This organ did not restrict itself to propaganda and agitation: it had managed to spread a fairly good organizational network over both capital and provinces, as well as at the front. It had also made a good many converts amongst junior officers. And in Petersburg, in addition to the 1st Machine-Gun Regiment, the Bolsheviks now had others too: the Moscow, the Grenadiers, the 1st Reserve, the Pavlovsky, the Michael Artillery School with its big guns, and others. There were also Bolshevik organizations in the other regiments. If these were as a whole against Lenin, they were not for Chernov-Tsereteli, and even less for the Provisional Government. They were 'for the Soviet' in general. There's no doubt of this.

In any case the Petersburg garrison was no longer fighting material. It was not a garrison but half-disintegrated military cadres. And in so far as they were not actively for the Bolsheviks, they were—with the exception of two or three regiments—indifferent, neutral, and useless for active operations either on the foreign or on the domestic front.

The ruling Soviet bloc had already let the masses of the soldiers slip through its fingers: the Bolsheviks had taken a strong hold on some sections and were hourly penetrating deeper into the others.

* * *

And now things began to happen. . . At the evening session of the Congress on the 9th Chkheidze took the floor for an emergency statement. He said big demonstrations were scheduled in Petersburg for the next day, Saturday June 10th; the Congress might have to sit all night; if it didn't take the right steps the next day would be fatal.

Chkheidze's statement, though not quite clear, was extremely impressive, and aroused the greatest excitement amongst the delegates. There was a great hubbub, exclamations, questions from the floor. Everyone demanded information about exactly what had happened. To calm the delegates and give them information privately an adjournment had to be announced. The delegates separated into fractions and groups, and this is what they found out about the situation in the capital.

The disturbances on the Vyborg Side had not subsided since the day before. And indeed these disturbances had not begun the day before, with the eviction of the anarchists: they were tied up with the general dissatisfaction of the workers and their distressing condition. For some days now obscure rumours had been going around the city about some sort of 'demonstrations' by the Petersburg workers—against the Government and its supporters. Now the unrest had seized all the working-class parts of the capital, and especially Basil Island, where the Congress was in session. And in the Durnovo villa there sat a special assembly of workers' delegates, which had announced an armed demonstration against the Provisional Government for the next day. Kronstadt had also sent representatives to this meeting.

But it goes without saying that matters were not restricted to the kindling of the workers' elemental instincts. Without the interference of solid workers' centres the situation could not have become so acute at this moment.

And the Bolsheviks, of course, were such a centre. On June 9th proclamations signed by the Bolshevik Central Committee and the Central Bureau of the Factory Committees were pasted up in the working-class districts. These proclamations summoned the Petersburg proletariat to a peaceful demonstration against the counter-revolution at 2 o'clock on June 10th.

This proclamation was very important. It won't hurt to become familiar with it. First, in powerful fighting language it gave an acute and accurate description of the general state of affairs and of the Coalition Government. Then, referring to the rights of free citizens, it called for a protest against the policy of the Coalition. The slogans of the demonstrations were these: 'Down with the Tsarist Duma!' 'Down with the Ten Minister-Capitalists!' 'All Power to the All-Russian Soviet of Workers',

Soldiers' and Peasants' Deputies!' 'Long Live the Control and Organization of Industry!' 'End the War!' 'Neither a Separate Peace with Wilhelm nor Secret Treaties with the French and British Capitalists!' 'Bread, Peace, Freedom!'

I don't know whether the proclamation was in the hands of the Congress delegates on the 9th. But in any case, it was known to them that the 1st Machine-Gun Regiment, the Izmailovsky, and some others had decided to take part in the demonstration. Consequently, the demonstration proved in fact to be *armed.* This naturally heightened the excitement.

It must be said, however, that the bulk of the delegates were wrought up largely through the efforts of the Praesidium, the ruling circles, and their hangers-on in the capital. These circles had really fallen into a panic and tried to infect the Congress with it, but they lacked enough facts. News came to the Star Chamber that the demonstration was supposedly known to be armed. Then there were obscure rumours about some special plans of the Bolsheviks. The main source of this information was said to be Lieber. But nothing at all definite was known. Meanwhile a pacific demonstration by no means seemed such a dreadful thing to the mass of delegates. All Russia, after all, was constantly demonstrating in those days. The provinces had all become accustomed to street demonstrations. And in Petersburg too, in those same days, the 'over-forties' and the women were demonstrating—in general everyone was demonstrating who wasn't too lazy! No permission was required. Up to then the Soviet hadn't stopped anyone (aside from some special cases in April) and any group could come out into the street and 'enjoy the rights of free citizens'.

The cause of the alarm amongst the leaders was not entirely clear to the mass of delegates. Those who were not particularly timid soon expressed their dissatisfaction: the All-Russian Congress had not met to deal with one local affair after another; if any disorders were being prepared it was up to the local Petersburg Soviet, not to the Congress, to prevent them.

And, of course, this was an elementary truth. Between the masses in the capital and Soviet circles there was not only no ideological contact or organic ties, there were no relations at all. The Ex. Com., quietly expiring in the Tauride Palace, was absolutely impotent. And it was appealing to the Congress as the last resort.

For its part the 'legal Government', on the evening of the 9th, was taking steps. It 'enjoined calm on the populace', and promised to 'suppress' any attempts at violence with all the strength of the State.

This, of course, was all nonsense. They had no strength. But patrols were driving about the city, showing the state of alarm in the capital.

At the same time it was asserted that it was not only a question of the Bolsheviks, but that monarchist elements were also preparing to 'come out' simultaneously. 'Rumours' kept coming from all sides. The delegates, wandering about the rooms and corridors, were excited and worn out in the heated atmosphere.

The Congress met again in the Military Academy at 12.30 a.m. The Bolshevik fraction showed some confusion. It was evidently rather at sea about the affairs of the capital and of its own leaders. And the leaders were absent. Lenin, Zinoviev and Kamenev were busy with important matters elsewhere. Trotsky was also absent. Krylenko[1] was on the platform of the Praesidium for the Bolshevik fraction, and the Interdistrictite Lunacharsky was acting on its behalf.

The Chairman proposed to create a bureau for resolute action against any who declared war on the Congress. Lunacharsky entered it, but he said he would leave if it started a direct struggle. He added that the Bolsheviks had empowered him to emphasize the pacific character of the proposed demonstration. Krylenko for his part protested against the actions of the Congress: why was it carrying out its decisions without entering into negotiations with the Bolsheviks, who would gladly meet it half-way?

Kerensky said unequivocally: 'The rumours about troops drawn into Petersburg from the front, to fight against the workers, are completely false. There is not a single soldier in Petersburg who does not belong to the garrison of the capital.

[1] Krylenko, Nikolai Vasilyevich (1885–1937): leader in the student movement (1905–08). Repeatedly arrested; after the October Revolution, in which he played an active part, became People's Minister of Justice, and then State's Attorney. Was Prosecutor at many state trials, including the 1931 Trial of the Mensheviks. Vanished in 1937. (Ed.)

The troops, on my orders, are moving and will move only from the rear to the front, to fight against the foreign enemies of the revolution. But the other way round, from the front to the rear, to fight against the workers—never!'

Splendid. We'll keep that in mind. . . Martov also spoke, against the disorganizing activities of the Bolsheviks, but exhorting the Congress to calm and *sang-froid.*

Then, of course, a new proclamation to the soldiers and workers was passed, followed by an appeal that no one should go to the demonstration the next day and by a ban on street meetings and processions for the next three days.

This did not finish the work of the Congress on the eve of June 10th. The delegates were divided up among the Petersburg districts and sent out to the factories, regiments, and companies to prevent the demonstration. The delegates worked all night. It was agreed to meet at the Tauride Palace at 8 o'clock that morning for an accounting. At 2 o'clock in the afternoon a meeting was also scheduled there for all battalion committees of the capital garrison—on the question of armed troop demonstrations.

But it will be asked what the chief heroes of the day and the authors of the turmoil were doing at this time. To summon a pacific demonstration with any slogans they liked was their inalienable right. But for some hours now the sharply negative will of the Congress and of the Soviet majority concerning their enterprise had been absolutely clear.

Now, how were the Bolsheviks reacting to this? The activity of the Bolshevik centres was of course cloaked in deep secrecy. No one knew anything of what Lenin, Zinoviev, Kamenev, and Stalin, who had been hiding away from the Congress somewhere, were doing or thinking. And, by the way, where was Trotsky, who two days before had been calling for twelve Peshekhonovs, and now had also vanished from the Congress to avoid taking a stand on the question of the demonstration? None of them, of course, was sleeping that night. But Catiline did not report his machinations to Cicero.

* * *

Early next morning the Congress delegates learned of some of the results of the nocturnal labours of the Bolshevik leaders.

Krylenko had obviously known what he was saying that night at the Congress: the Bolsheviks really came half-way to meet the ruling Soviet majority. That night their Central Committee *cancelled* the demonstration.

At 9 o'clock in the morning of June 10th, the delegates who had spent the night among the Petersburg masses began crowding into the Tauride Palace: a conference opened in the White Hall. The first part, dealing with 'principles', was brief but extremely typical. Lunacharsky reported the cancellation of the demonstration and told the history of the whole affair. The demonstration had actually been initiated at the Durnovo villa, where a self-appointed committee representing ninety factories was in session. As for the Bolsheviks, they were against it, and in any case today there wouldn't be one. The incident was liquidated; now they ought to put a stop to the inter-party quarrel, forgetting the mistakes of the past for the sake of the tasks ahead.

Lunacharsky's information was clearly not authentic. The Bolshevik centre had made no bones about leading him astray. But his conclusions were not only honest and humanly sensible but also the only correct ones politically. However, he was immediately attacked by Dan—not for his information, but precisely for his conclusions.

'After everything that's happened unctuousness is out of place,' declared the venerable member of the Star Chamber. 'Once for all we have to finish with a situation in which such unexpected complications are possible. There must be a careful investigation to show who is to blame. . .'

Dan's speech was drowned in applause. Lunacharsky tried to explain again that it was not a question of who was responsible, nor of the Bolsheviks, pursuit of whom would simply exacerbate the situation. The most profound discontent among the workers had been aroused by general causes, which ought to be paid attention to.

Summed up before us in a nutshell were the classic inter-relationships between the Government and the Opposition, or—between a rootless dictatorship and the champions of democracy. The situation was acute; but for the blind rulers there was no doubt of the correctness of their path to the truth and no obstacles except malefactors.

THREE BOLSHEVIK LEADERS: TROTSKY, LENIN, KAMENEV

THE 'JULY DAYS'

A demonstration is fired on in the Nevsky Prospect

Trotsky was now there too. He was vigorously urged to the platform, but he held his tongue and didn't go. Why?

The second, *informational* part of this conference was equally interesting. The delegates who had spent the night among the Petersburg masses reported on the situation in the regiments and factories. These reports seemed to leave no doubt that the Coalition's cause could not be improved by looking for the malefactors or taking reprisals against them. About fifteen speakers succeeded one another on the platform—supporters of the Coalition and of the ruling Soviet bloc. They all said roughly the same thing:

The delegates were met everywhere with extreme unfriendliness and allowed to pass only after lengthy disputes. On the Vyborg Side there was nothing but Bolsheviks and Anarchists. Neither the Congress nor the Petersburg Soviet had the slightest authority. They were spoken of just like the Provisional Government: the Menshevik-SR majority had sold itself to the bourgeoisie and the imperialists; the Provisional Government was a counter-revolutionary gang. In particular people at the Durnovo villa had declared that the decision of the Congress didn't mean anything and that the demonstration would take place. On Basil Island it was the same thing. 'Demonstrating' was extremely popular amongst the workers, and held out the only real hopes for a change. Among the regiments the Congress was proclaimed a gang of landlords and capitalists, or their hirelings; the liquidation of the Coalition Government was considered urgent. Only the Bolsheviks were trusted, and whether the demonstration took place or not depended solely on the Bolshevik Central Committee. The Socialist Ministers were sneered at as traitors and hirelings.

There was hardly any information of a different character; one or two exceptions served to confirm the rule. In any case the delegates' impressions boiled down to this: there was no possibility of holding back the working-class masses; if the demonstration were prevented today, it was inevitable tomorrow; there could be no contact, reconciliation, or agreement between the working class of the capital and the ruling Soviet bloc.

The foundation of the Coalition was splitting at every seam.

* * *

Nevertheless June 10th passed without any demonstrations. In the course of the day the Ex. Com. and the Star Chamber received a whole series of reassuring reports. In many factories and military units resolution against the scheduled demonstration were passed. There were even a few reluctant expressions of loyalty to the All-Russian Congress of Soviets.

The spirits of the Star Chamber went up. It evidently took the exceptions to be the rule, and the military organizations for the masses of the soldiers, while the Socialist Ministers laid confidence in the Congress to their own account, that is, the account of the entire Coalition.

But did the Soviet leaders pull themselves up? Did they think of taking advantage of the breathing-spell to change the Coalition policy and proceed resolutely towards the fulfilment of a programme of peace, bread, and land?

Alas! The wisdom of the Star Chamber was accessible to only one kind of measure. Having overcome their panic and plucked up their courage, the Menshevik-SR leaders flung themselves into an offensive against the Bolsheviks.

On Sunday June 11th, around 5 in the afternoon, in one of the classrooms of the Military Academy, a closed joint session of the highest Soviet Institutions, the Ex. Com., the Praesidium of the Congress, and the Bureau of each of its fractions, was called. In all about 100 people were there, including the majority of the Soviet party leaders. Trotsky was there too; I don't remember Zinoviev, but Lenin of course was absent.

It will be remembered that the object of the meeting was known only to the intimates of the Star Chamber. But the atmosphere was extremely tense and saturated with passion. There was no longer merely excitement here, but also bitter hatred. It was obvious that the ruling clique was preparing some surprise.

At the chairman's table, the teacher's desk, sat Chkheidze; he announced that the question of the demonstration that hadn't taken place the day before would be debated. Some of his intimates, or simply pushful people, were sitting on primitive benches or standing around the chairman, in an untidy-looking fashion. The others, distributed at the pupils' desks, were waiting in concentrated silence to see what would happen.

It seemed that a 'Special Commission' had been formed to prepare this conference. Dan spoke in its name.

'The Bolshevik action,' he said, 'was a political adventure. In future, demonstrations of individual parties ought to be permitted only with the knowledge and approval of the Soviet. Military units as such may take part only in demonstrations arranged by the Soviets. Parties which do not submit to these requirements ought to be excluded from the Soviets.'

The point of all this was elementary. In the Soviets the Bolsheviks were in a minority; by introducing a licensing system for demonstrations the 'Special Commission' was putting Bolsheviks in the power of the Mensheviks and SRs and practically depriving them of the right to demonstrate. This was done to stop the Bolshevik criminals from using the right of demonstration for uprisings like the one in April, or for any other schemes against the ruling bloc. It was actually a special decree directed against the Bolsheviks.

The wisdom of the Star Chamber was incapable of devising anything more for the salvation of the revolution. But Dan had forgotten Camille Desmoulins's winged words: A decree cannot prevent the seizure of the Bastille. If it was a question of an uprising, then—good God! how comical it was to try to fight it with a decree, even a special one.

But Dan also forgot something else, no less vital. As ironical exclamations, protests, sarcasms and laughter began in the hall, a very Right-wing Menshevik, the worker Bulkin, reminded him of this elementary fact. He said that times change, and today's majority might turn out to be tomorrow's minority. It might turn out that it was preparing to repress itself and introducing into revolutionary practice methods of political struggle that would result badly for their initiators.

This, of course, was the sacred truth, but still not all: the transformation of the majority into a minority and *vice versa* was not only possible; it was *inevitable* in the very near future. And for those who knew the Bolsheviks as well as Dan and his comrades knew them, one would think it must have been clear that in the event of a real victory of Lenin the ruling bloc would not have too good a time of it. . . But nothing was clear to the Menshevik-SR leaders. They were blind as owls at high noon.

The conference wanted to hear the Bolsheviks themselves.

Kamenev responded. He tried to be calm, sober, and ironical—under the gaze of a majority filled with hatred and contempt. He even tried to take the offensive. What—in reality—was all the fuss about? A pacific demonstration had been scheduled, which flowed out of the right of the revolution and had never been forbidden before by anyone. Then the demonstration had been cancelled, simply because the Congress wished it. Where, in all this, was there even the shadow of illegality in the first place, or disloyalty in the second?

I think Kamenev's argument was completely clear and convincing. It evidently appeared incontestable to a very great many. But for some reason his irony was unsuccessful. One would have thought he knew how to be in the minority and was used to glances of hatred, but he was strangely pale and agitated, and his state of mind was communicated to the whole group of Bolsheviks.

Kamenev was asked a series of questions. But Tsereteli leaped up and demanded that the questioning should cease: it was not a matter of details, and the entire problem required to be stated quite differently. Tsereteli was just as pale as Kamenev, and, agitated as never before, was hopping violently from one foot to the other. He was plainly preparing to say something really out of the ordinary.

And as a matter of fact it was already out of the ordinary for Tsereteli to speak against Dan in public: in the 'Special Commission' he had evidently been in the minority and was now appealing to the meeting. Dan's resolution was of no use at all; Tsereteli waved a contemptuous hand at it. What was needed now was something else, also very much out of the ordinary.

'What has happened', he cried, the vein on his temple swelling up, 'is nothing but a plot against the revolution, a conspiracy for the overthrow of the Government and the seizure of power by the Bolsheviks, who know that they can never get this power in any other way. The conspiracy was rendered harmless when we discovered it. But it may be repeated tomorrow. They say that counter-revolution has lifted its head. That's not true. Counter-revolution has not raised its head, but lowered it. Counter-revolution can penetrate to us only through one door: through the Bolsheviks. What the Bolsheviks are doing now is no longer ideological propaganda, it is a plot. The weapon of criticism is being replaced by criticism with weapons. Let the Bolsheviks accuse us as they will, now we shall go over to other methods of struggle. Those revolutionaries who cannot worthily wield their arms must have those arms taken away. The Bolsheviks must be disarmed. We will not permit any conspiracies. . .'

Tsereteli sat down. A tempest swept over the meeting—complete consternation. Some were overwhelmed by the extraordinary content of Tsereteli's words, others by their strangeness and lack of clarity. The Opposition demanded an explanation. Kamenev cried out: 'Mr. Minister, if you're not talking wildly don't confine yourself to words, arrest me and try me for plotting against the revolution!'

Tsereteli was silent. The handful of Bolsheviks all noisily got to their feet and left the hall protesting. . .

But even without the Bolsheviks there was still someone left to pick a bone with Tsereteli. The Interdistrictite Trotsky remained in the hall. Martov asked for the floor at once. But even amongst the majority the mood was far from favourable to Minister Tsereteli. Some officer, completely shaken up by what had happened, let out hysterical shrieks. A general attack was launched on two fronts: both against the Bolsheviks and against Tsereteli.

First of all—what special information had Mr. Minister in fact? If definite information of an attempt at a *coup d'état* exists—then communicate it. If not, don't draw these conclusions. Then, what do you mean by conspiracy? Is it the malevolence of a clique towards the Provisional Government and the existing order? In your blindness you can think as you please, but to anyone with eyes it's obvious that we are faced by a vast popular movement, that this can only be a question of an uprising on the part of the proletarian and soldier masses of the capital, and that no repressing of *cliques* or even of *parties* can help. What is needed here is a change of régime, martial law and an iron hand with the workers. The only logical thing now is a *bourgeois dictatorship*, and the end of the revolution.

Tsereteli proposed '*disarming the Bolsheviks*'. What did that actually mean? Removing some special arsenal that the Bolshevik Central Committee possessed? Nonsense—the Bolsheviks, after all, had no special stores of arms: all arms were in the hands of the soldiers and workers, the great mass of whom followed the Bolsheviks. Disarming the Bolsheviks could only mean disarming the proletariat. More than that, it meant the troops. This was not only bourgeois dictatorship, but also childish nonsense. Perhaps it meant setting brother against brother in the workers' camp, dividing the proletariat into white and black, handing out arms according to party labels—or perhaps creating special cadres of Praetorians for Tsereteli and Tereshchenko?

Well, all right. Let us grant that this is a splendid programme. But the question arises how to realise it. Was Tsereteli going to take arms away from the proletarian-soldier masses with his own hand, to throw them at Tereshchenko's feet? 'We shall go over to other methods.' But how?

In Petersburg there were of course very many workers and even more soldiers who would not take part in a Bolshevik conspiracy, or overthrow the Coalition by armed force. But where was there even a shadow of reason to think that with these arms they would advance against their comrades, the soldiers and workers of the neighbouring factories and regiments?

It was even plainer that the *Bolshevik* workers and units would not willingly hand over the rifles given them by the revolution. They could be disarmed only by *force*, which didn't exist. Mr. Minister's programme was a utopia.

In the course of the debate Martov recalled Cavour's remark that any donkey could govern by means of a state of siege. That's how the Bolsheviks governed later on. Alas! It would have been beyond Tsereteli's capacity even with the help of a siege.

I don't remember all the course of this 'historic' meeting. But in any case it should not be thought that the Minister of Posts and Telegraphs was left without support. Still in the same taut atmosphere, saturated with passions, there came to his aid the sworn Bolshevik-eater, the rabid Lieber, on the point of bursting. He was undoubtedly the principal source of information concerning the conspiracy. I have no idea where he got his information, or just what he'd heard. But here at the meeting, in any case, he had no more to tell than Tsereteli. His support didn't consist of any new information but in deepening the statesmanlike wisdom of his leader. Raising two fingers, he fell on the Bolsheviks with the ferocity of a famished beast, in a sort of sensual ecstasy. Hopping on the tips of his toes, shrilling away and working on the nerves of his audience, he frenziedly demanded the most 'decisive measures'—the repression, eradication, and punishment of all the disobedient workers with all the means at the State's disposal.

Suddenly, from the bench where Martov was sitting, there was heard the word 'Merzavets!' [scoundrel].

The hall gasped and then froze, and so did the chairman and the speaker himself. The atmosphere was incandescent, this kind of 'exchange of ideas' in the revolution was still unheard of.

Later it appeared that the epithet Martov had hurled at Lieber was not 'merzavets' but 'versalets' [i.e., Versaillean]. It was not a term of abuse, but a description. And an absolutely accurate one.

The debates lasted many hours, to the point of total exhaustion. But the results were not clear. The meeting was interrupted and not re-opened until night. The passage of Dan's resolution was secured, but Tsereteli refused to be reconciled and insisted on the acceptance of other, non-verbal measures. He fought with characteristic energy, one might say desperately. Unceremoniously abusing his ministerial position he was continually taking the floor out of order. Finally I could no longer endure it and shouted at him some phrase like the one flung by Louvet at Danton, when the latter began to speak without the Chairman's permission: 'You are not yet king, Danton!' Tsereteli was silent for a few seconds, shuffling from one foot to the other, not knowing how to express his contempt, then he snapped, shrugging his shoulders, 'I'm not speaking to the Sukhanovs!'

Nevertheless he failed to convince the others either. I don't recall exactly how the meeting ended, at early dawn: but the fact is that in general it agreed with the *majority* of the Star Chamber and not with its extremist leader.

* * *

At the end of the June 12th session Bogdanov took the floor for an emergency resolution in the name of the Praesidium. His resolution was interesting; I later learned that Dan had originated it. It was proposed to organize an 'official Soviet' workers' and peasants' peaceful demonstration the following Sunday, June 18th, in Petersburg, and in other cities as far as possible. At this tense moment of internal struggle in the Soviet it ought to illustrate the unity of the democracy and its strength in the face of the common enemy. The slogans of this demonstration ought to be only those common to all Soviet parties. In the opinion of those proposing the resolution these slogans were: the unification of the democracy around the Soviets, peace without annexations or indemnities, and the earliest convocation of the Constituent Assembly.

The idea of this demonstration revealed the triumph of a softer line within the Star Chamber with respect to the Bolsheviks. In any case the June 18th demonstration was the tribute of vice to virtue. The resolution was, of course, passed in the absence of the Bolsheviks. It goes without saying that the Bolsheviks had no grounds for objection either. Let us see what came of it.

* * *

At that time, in the summer of 1917, the truth about the abortive demonstration of June 10th seemed to be exactly what I have described in the preceding pages. But now, just three years later, I can add the following. What the Bolsheviks said at meetings, and what *Pravda* printed, was in any case not the entire truth about the demonstration. A few people 'instinctively' divined the real truth, but nobody knew it except a dozen or so Bolsheviks. I personally learned it very much later, not before 1920.

There was no real *conspiracy*. Neither strategic dispositions nor plans for the occupation of the city and its individual points and institutions were worked out. Nor on the other hand do I think the *political* intentions of the insurgents were any more developed. Nevertheless the smoke was not without fire.

It is essential to understand clearly that a Bolshevik 'plot' or uprising, if it had taken place at that time, would have had an irrefragable logic. What objective goal could it have had? Of its *negative* aspect there could be no doubt—the Coalition must be annihilated, a thing which could not have been easier in itself. But from a positive point of view? This was—verbally—expressed by the words: 'All Power to the Soviets'. But the

Soviets, after all, were all at hand, in the form of the Congress. They stood *for* the Coalition and were categorically refusing power. To force power on them against their will was impossible. An uprising *might* have pushed them into taking power, but it was more likely that it would have rallied Soviet-bourgeois elements against the Bolsheviks and their slogans. In any case it was obvious that if an uprising were to be started it would have to be started not only against the bourgeoisie, but also *against the Soviet democracy*, embodied in the Congress that was its highest authority. The Petersburg proletariat and the Bolshevik regiments, as the minority that began it all, with their slogan of 'All Power to the Soviets', would have had to advance against the Soviets and the Congress. That meant that with the liquidation of the Provisional Government, the power could have passed only to the *Bolshevik Central Committee*, that had initiated the uprising.

But the Bolsheviks had not begun an uprising aimed directly at this goal. The dense smoke that went on curling around us for a long time after June 10th came from a little fire burning around Lenin in the conspiratorial chambers of the Bolshevik Central Committee. This was the situation: Lenin's group was not directly aiming at the seizure of power, but *it was ready to seize it in favourable circumstances, which it was taking steps to create.*

Speaking concretely, the target of the demonstration scheduled for June 10th was the Marian Palace, the residency of the Provisional Government. That was where the working-class detachments and the regiments loyal to the Bolsheviks were to make their way. Specially appointed individuals were to express 'popular discontent' while the Ministers were speaking, and work the masses up. When that mood was at the right temperature the Provisional Government were to be arrested on the spot. The capital, of course, was expected to react to this at once, and the Bolshevik Central Committee, under that or another name, depending on the character of the reaction, was to declare itself in power. If in the course of the 'demonstration' the mood was sufficiently favourable and the resistance of Lvov–Tsereteli was not great, that resistance was to be crushed by the force of Bolshevik regiments and arms.

According to the data of the Bolshevik 'Military Organization', it was assumed that action against the Bolsheviks would be taken by these regiments: the Semyonovsky, the Preobrazhensky, the 9th Cavalry Reserve, the two Cossack regiments, and of course the military cadets. The Bolshevik centres regarded the four Imperial Regiments of Guards—the Izmailovsky, the Petrogradsky, the Cuxholm, and the Lithuanian—as wavering and doubtful. The Volhynian Regiment also looked unreliable. But in any case these regiments were considered not an active hostile force but merely neutral. It was thought they wouldn't come out either for or against a revolt. The Finnish Regiment, which not long before had been the chattel of non-Bolshevik internationalists, ought to observe at least a *benevolent* neutrality. The Armoured Division, an extremely important part of the garrison and a first-class factor in an uprising, was in those days evenly divided between Lenin and Tsereteli; but if the matter was decided by a majority of its personnel then the workshops definitely gave Lenin the advantage.

As for the regiments that were completely loyal to the Bolsheviks, and ready to serve as an active force in the revolt, they were the following: the 1st and 2nd Machine-Gun Regiments, the Moscow, the Grenadiers, the 1st Reserve, the Pavlovsky, the 180th (which had a substantial number of Bolshevik officers), the garrison of the Peter-Paul Fortress, and rank-and-file of the Michael Artillery School, which *had the artillery*. It must be remarked that all these units were located on the Petersburg and the Vyborg Sides, around the Bolshevik centre, Kshesinskaya's house. In addition, active support for the uprising ought to come from the suburbs: first, Kronstadt; then Peterhof, where the 3rd Army Reserve Regiment, which the Bolsheviks controlled, was stationed, and Krasnoe Selo, with the 176th Regiment, where the Interdistrictites were firmly established. If necessary these units could have been summoned to Petersburg at once.

All these 'insurrectionary' regiments, taken together, were to crush the resistance of the Soviet-Coalition armed forces, terrorize the Nevsky Prospect and the lower middle classes of the capital, and serve as the real support of a new Government. The above-mentioned leader of the 1st Machine-Gun Regiment, 2nd Lieutenant Semashko, was appointed commander-in-chief of all the armed forces of the 'insurrectionaries'.

On the military-technical side the success of the revolt was practically assured. In this respect the Bolshevik organization was already competent even then.

In the *political* core of the 'uprising', the Central Committee, the matter was put, as we have seen, conditionally, optionally. The revolt and the seizure of power ought to be accomplished, given a favourable conjuncture of circumstances. Here there was embodied in action what Lenin had said at the Congress three days before: that *the Bolshevik Party was ready to take power into its hands alone at any moment.* But *readiness* to take power into one's hands means only a mood, a political attitude. It still does not mean a definite intention to take power at a *given moment.* The Bolshevik Central Committee could not make up its mind to put the question in *that* way. It had simply decided to create conditions favourable to a violent reversal of the situation. And this excellently reflected its vacillations during those days. It was willing, but hesitant. It was both ready, and not ready; it could and it could not.

The waverings of the Bolshevik Central Committee reflected the position of its individual members, the focal personalities of the Bolshevism of the time. It is understandable that the more their temperament and will to action dominated their common sense the less they wavered. Stalin, supported by Stasova and also by all those who, while not in central positions, were in the know, and thought that a whiff of powder would not pollute the revolutionary atmosphere, stood inexorably for the overthrow of the Government. Lenin occupied an *intermediate*, most unstable and opportunistic position—the same as the official position of the Central Committee. Kamenev, of course, and I think Zinoviev, were *against* the seizure of power. Of this pair of cronies one—*soit dit*—had been a Menshevik and the other, in addition to his great abilities, possessed the well-known qualities of the cat and the rabbit. I don't know who else of the Bolshevik leaders determined the fate of the overturn at that time.

On the night of the 9th, when 'the conspiracy was discovered', the persons mentioned, in accordance with the plan they had adopted, were discussing the question of *cancelling the demonstration.* Stalin was against cancellation; he thought that the opposition of the Congress by no means altered the objective conjuncture, and that Cicero was to be expected to 'forbid' Catiline to act. From his point of view Stalin was right. On the other hand, the 'cronies', of course, stood for submission to the Congress and for cancelling the demonstration. But it was naturally Lenin who decided the matter. In his opportunistic mood he was given a push and—indecisively held back. The 'demonstration' was called off.

What was the Interdistrictite Trotsky's rôle in all this business? I don't know anything about it. Two or three days before the 'demonstration' Lenin had said publicly that he was ready to take the whole power into his own hands, but Trotsky said at the same time that he wanted to see twelve Peshekhonovs in power. There's a difference there. Nevertheless I think Trotsky was attracted to the affair of June 10th. I have no other grounds for this than some features of his behaviour: while they may be insufficient to characterize his attitude they show very clearly that he was *informed*, and also that Lenin even then was not inclined to enter a decisive battle without this dubious Interdistrictite. For Trotsky, like Lenin, was a monumental partner in the monumental game, and in Lenin's own party, after himself, there was nothing for a very, very, very long time.

Such was the June 10th affair, one of the most significant episodes of the revolution.[1]

It was 'favourably' liquidated by the Star Chamber with the help of the Congress and the Petersburg Soviet. But obviously this changed nothing in the general political conjuncture. The leaders didn't recover their sight, the rulers did not change, the temper of the masses remained as before. The capital was plainly living on a volcano. The Government was 'ruling' in the Marian Palace; the Congress and its sections were carrying on 'organic labours' in the Military Academy. All this, however, could hide the real perspective only from the most case-hardened philistines, while the essence of the situation lay in this, that now, in the cracks that had split the democracy asunder, the shadow of the barricades could be most distinctly seen.

Passions went on seething in the Military Academy. Both sides were preparing for a review of strength in the official Soviet demonstration of June 18th.

* * *

[1] Trotsky has some special comments on this episode in Appendix III to Vol. I of his *History*. (Ed.)

Around this time Dr. Manukhin turned up in the Military Academy, and sought me out among the throng on urgent business.

Manukhin, as a trustworthy and well-known figure, was the prison physician at the Peter-Paul Fortress. There had already been a number of instances where Manukhin, recognizing that conditions in the Fortress were deadly for the prisoners, had demanded the transfer of some of them to other places of detention. Now he was demanding that Vyrubova, the Tsarina's famous lady-in-waiting, be transferred from the Peter-Paul. The Procurator had agreed and made all the necessary arrangements, but the Fortress garrison had said that regardless of what the practice in the past had been, in the future it would not allow any of the Tsar's servants to be transferred from the Fortress: it didn't trust the Government and didn't see any other guarantees that justice would be done on its hangmen than keeping them in the Fortress, guarded by its own bayonets. This was a sign of the times, a product of the decay of the Coalition.

The agitated Manukhin hastily explained to me why emergency measures were necessary. A mood was finally becoming defined in the garrison in favour of dealing with the prisoners arbitrarily. A kind of plot had been discovered, of which the first victim was to be Vyrubova. Only that night a number of the sentries' revolvers had been missed. A massacre was hourly to be expected.

Manukhin heatedly insisted that I go off with him to the Peter-Paul Fortress at once. As an Ex. Com. member I ought to impress on the garrison the complete inadmissibility of this kind of action, pacify it, and personally conduct Vyrubova out of the Fortress. The excursion upset my plans, but nevertheless I needed no lengthy urging. I had never yet set foot in the famous Fortress. I was tempted by the opportunity of visiting it, while the task didn't seem difficult to me. I thought the garrison would yield before the name of the Ex. Com. For greater assurance I invited Anisimov, a member of the Soviet Praesidium I ran into, to go with me: as a completely official personage it was up to him to defend Coalition law and order. A member of the Soviet Praesidium might prove more authoritative for the 'loyal' part of the garrison, while I might be useful as a representative of the Left Opposition, which was protesting in my person against the soldiers' usurpation of authority. Essentially I had no doubt that the Government, of course, deserved no confidence; as citizens, the soldiers could and should protest against its activities and try to get rid of it, but while it was still in power, they, as *soldiers*, were obliged to execute its orders. In any case the arbitrary behaviour of individual groups should cease; workers and soldiers could make policy only according to the will of the Soviet. That had always been my line.

In awe and trepidation I passed through the gates of the Russian Bastille, past stalwart sentries who spent a long time studying our papers. In my capacity as one of the 'authorities' I was behind the walls where the vanguard of many a Russian generation had drained their cups. Manukhin was very worried about how the garrison would meet us, and what would come of our expedition; he even doubted whether the guard would allow us into the Trubetskoy Bastion. But I was more occupied with observing my surroundings.

Everything, however, went off perfectly. The commandant, a recently-appointed, modest, young, disabled soldier, with one arm, was summoned to the crude, gloomy commandant's quarters. It was clear that he had no real contact with a garrison which was inclining towards Bolshevism, and he was quite unable to vouch for its temper. His detail hadn't expected our arrival, and had scattered in various directions on their own affairs. The commandant collected the representatives of the separate sections of the garrison, and we members of the Ex. Com. made admonitory speeches to them. Our listeners did not argue, and if they did not agree, at any rate they were ready to submit. It is true that they hinted, with a tinge of censure, at the mood of their units, which, they said, got excited over nothing and might call them to account for taking the decision on themselves. But they finally accepted the responsibility for releasing Vyrubova from the fortress—if the sentries in the prison itself would only agree.

We all had to make our way at once into the Trubetskoy Bastion. There was absolutely nothing either menacing, frightening, or gloomy in the broad grass-covered square or the surrounding buildings. Led by the commandant past some tumbledown carts, rusty kettles, and other quite prosaic objects, we came to the crude and unimpressive gate of the Trubetskoy Bastion. The sentry let us through quite indifferently.

Manukhin, who was used to these surroundings, was still uneasy; he kept hurrying on and distracting me with talk about the affair in hand. He didn't understand me; I was completely absorbed in studying the prison, fell behind the procession, and worried the slightly perplexed commandant with questions. But in a way I was quite disappointed with the prison.

We were taken to an office to which Vyrubova was also to be brought. There were two or three rooms which looked not merely unprisonlike, but even unofficial, with their shabby, almost homelike furnishings. There we had to wait for some special personage who had got lost somewhere and who was the only one who had the right to penetrate under the sacred vaults, to the cells themselves.

The two-storey prison building formed a triangle. At this time only the cells of the second floor, where the office was also located, were occupied by Tsarist dignitaries. Perhaps it was in this cheerful little office that newcomers were searched with extraordinary thoroughness. A triangular little garden, overgrown with thick grass, could be seen from its windows, which looked on the interior of the triangle. A boarded walk was laid out along the walls of the triangle, around the little garden, where prisoners were walking about. In the corner, under a tree, a tiny hut could be seen, looking quite pastoral: this was the bath-house.

While waiting for the supervisor, I expressed a strong desire to go into the cells themselves and see the very entrails of the prison. The guard on duty, a soldierly-looking fellow, didn't object for his part, and merely expressed doubt that the sentry standing at the iron gate opposite the office would let me pass. But after a few words the latter did so. We entered a broad corridor that went along the outer side of the triangle, and were met by a warder who according to the old custom was in silent felt boots. He was practically the only one in all three wings. The duty guard suggested that we go into the cells and talk to the prisoners. But that would perhaps have been awkward and unsuitable, although not without interest, and I declined. But I couldn't help looking through the peep-hole into a number of the cells. The guard and Manukhin, who was at home here, told me the names of their occupants.

For myself, quite used to imprisonment, this looking through a peephole at someone caged up was also perfectly matter-of-fact. How many friends and comrades had I seen in the course of my life *only* through a peephole! And now, when my own gaolers were before me, curiosity easily overcame squeamishness. I remember that Protopopov was sound asleep with his back to the door. Stürmer was sitting on a bunk holding a small book. And then I heard the name of an old friend of mine, Vissarionov, one of the most talented and pernicious of the Tsarist Secret Police. While he was an assistant Procurator in Moscow he used to visit my cell in the *Taganka*. Later, during the war, when he was the chief Petersburg censor, I had to turn hastily away whenever he appeared, when I visited the censor's office on *Sovremennik* and *Letopis* business: I was living in the capital illegally, and the keen eye of the Secret Policeman might have recognized me even after ten years.

Now Vissarionov, sitting at a table, was attentively reading a sheet of note-paper.

A denunciation! flashed through my mind, though in the circumstances such an occupation would have been quite meaningless.

On my request an empty cell was opened. Splendid cells in the Peter-Paul! Light, clean, and about twice as large as in a 'model' prison.

'This isn't too bad!' I summed up my impressions. 'We've seen a lot worse.'

Then we heard that Vyrubova was now ready to go. We went to her cell. A pretty young woman, with a simple, typically Russian face, got up to meet us, very excited at the imminent change, as is always the case in prisons. She was on crutches, I think as a result of a railway accident.

'But I haven't a coat!' she said, naïvely and confusedly.

She had to go without one. Manukhin was extremely excited: our slow-moving procession had to get past a whole series of sentries. Indeed, the times were such that a sentry was no less important than the Minister of Justice. The sentries watched our procession rather gloomily and suspiciously, but made no attempt to detain it. Manukhin insisted that we should personally conduct Vyrubova outside the gates of the fortress and into a prison hospital. Everything went off all right.

* * *

In the preparations of the Soviet parties for the June 18th demonstration, the ruling bloc took part without undue urgency. First of all, it had no doubts as to its victory—under an 'official Soviet' banner; secondly it had neither the proper attraction to the masses, nor any skill in dealing with them. In general, the Menshevik-SR bloc was at that time a model of a decaying Government, congealed in its assurance and self-satisfied blindness. The Bolsheviks, on the contrary, were feverishly busy in the entrails of the proletarian capital, ploughing up virgin soil and forming their converts into fighting columns.

But the masses were rushing to battle. The June 10th affair, not having given their temper a vent, had only exasperated them. An official Soviet demonstration, of course, did not satisfy the Bolshevik workers and soldiers in the least. Objectively—it ought to have served as a sort of safety-valve against explosion: an official Soviet demonstration was obviously of no use *against* the Soviet. But for some reason it was subjectively unsatisfactory: the worker-soldier masses, while accepting June 18th as an excuse to *display* their strength, were hoping to *employ* it in the near future.

I don't recall that the Ex. Com. made any special preparations for its own official demonstration; when the matter was raised it was in the following, peculiarly characteristic manner. On Saturday June 17th, the eve of the demonstration, in the heat of the 'organic labour' of the Congress, the Ex. Com. assembled in one of the uncomfortable rooms of the Military Academy. A lot of members were there, most of them on their feet with nowhere to sit, squeezing around a crude table and two or three ancient benches. The heat was suffocating, and there was an atmosphere of irritation.

I think all the leaders were present; but it was Lieber who brought up the subject of the demonstration. Once more, with uncontrolled fury, he began to tell us of the Bolshevik 'preparations' and the dangers that threatened freedom and the existing order. Bolshevik detachments of workers and soldiers were preparing to come armed; excesses, bloodshed, attempts to attack the Government, were inevitable, and had to be nipped in the bud by the most determined measures: under no circumstances must arms be allowed in the streets. For this a reliable detachment must be placed at the gates of every doubtful barracks and every factory from which the demonstrators would come; if they showed themselves with weapons the reliable detachments must disarm them.

This is how the Menshevik-SR bankrupts of the Coalition, in the person of Lieber, defended freedom and order. I don't recall who else spoke for the Right in support of the Lieber recipe, but I myself lost my calm and attacked Lieber with as much fury as he had the Bolshevik traitors and plotters. I acknowledged the risk of senseless bloodshed and unauthorized activities if the streets of Petersburg were filled with arms. But it was obvious that Lieber's statesmanlike wisdom and his methods by no means prevented this, but on the contrary, made it all inevitable. After all, it was ridiculous to imagine that a detachment of workers or soldiers leaving an assembly point with arms in their hands against the Soviet's orders would hand over these arms without a struggle to a Lieberite 'national guard'. A clash was made absolutely inevitable by the very presence of a detachment blocking the way. And ten such clashes would mean tremendous bloodshed, the beginning of an absurd rebellion, and civil war created by panic and political stupidity. This was the purely practical side of the matter. As for the principle of it, things were no better.

I made a practical proposal, in view of the alarming mood of the masses, that we should at once scatter through the factories and barracks, directly explain the significance of the next day's demonstration, and try to persuade our hearers not to take arms with them, in order to avoid senseless accidental bloodshed. I was supported by many, including, if I'm not mistaken, Chernov. And that's what was decided. 'Danger' points were determined at once and two or three comrades assigned to each one, the Bolsheviks also taking part. It was decided to assemble again in the Tauride Palace that evening at 10 o'clock for each delegation to report on its expedition.

I was sent to the most ticklish spot, the Durnovo villa. I left for the mysterious nest of the terrible anarchists full of doubts. Would they let me in? Would they talk? Or, if they had any serious plans for the following day, would they not hold me as a Soviet hostage? The mission, however, was concluded quite safely.

We went into the shady courtyard of the villa unhindered. On the steps there were no sentries, no passes were demanded, and nobody took notice of us. It was evident that outsiders who wished to could come in with complete freedom and that they often did so. We asked where we could converse officially, in the name of the Soviet, with the official representatives of the anarchist organization. We were invited into the club. The news of our arrival had spread instantaneously and we were surrounded by curious faces, with rather ironical expressions. The rooms were in order and completely furnished, though with total confusion of styles. While we waited for the official spokesmen we settled ourselves in a large room, converted into an auditorium and adorned with black banners and other anarchist emblems.

Bleichman, whom we knew as a habitual Soviet speaker, fairly quickly appeared as the representative of the local leaders. He had with him a number of people of different kinds, both workers and intellectuals. I explained the purpose of our visit, laying the main emphasis on the possibility of unfortunate incidents, unintentional excesses, and guns going off of their own accord. I told them what the Soviet insisted on and asked for an account of the intentions and views of the anarchists themselves. Bleichman replied without wasting words: for the anarchists the Soviet was quite without authority; if the Bolsheviks chose to join in its decisions that meant nothing—the Soviet was essentially the servant of the bourgeoisie and the landlords; the anarchists had no definite intentions for the next day; they would take part in the demonstration—with their black flags; and as for their coming armed—they might not, and then again they might.

The dialogue got rather long-winded. I couldn't get a more definite answer: had they decided to go armed or unarmed? Nor did either my diplomacy or my attempts at persuading them to leave their arms at home have any definite success. I kept coming up against a quite simple and yet insurmountable obstacle: it was, they said, just because they would not submit to anyone but acted as the good Lord inspired them that they were anarchists. It was only when the official conversation became private that my interlocutors began to emit rather more soothing sounds.

'Don't worry, we're not that sort; everything will go off all right,' they said directly or obliquely.

They took us off as private guests to show us their premises. We went out into an enormous shady garden where large groups of workers were quietly strolling about. The lawns were overrun with children. There was a kiosk at the entrance where anarchist literature was sold or given away. A speaker was standing on a tall stump making a naïve speech about the ideal structure for society. Not very many people were listening to him. There was obviously more relaxation here than concern with politics. The very widespread popularity of this anarchist nest amongst working-class circles in the capital was quite understandable.

I would not have minded starting a general conversation with the local public, or perhaps even climbing up on the stump in my turn, but a warm, heavy shower started to fall; accompanied by a large and benevolent group of people, we found our car and went home.

That night the Ex. Com. reassembled in the Tauride Palace. There was quite a large crowd. The delegates reported on their visits to the unreliable places. All the reports were optimistic: the mood everywhere was 'loyal'; no excesses were expected; people were not preparing to go armed. The most doubtful point remained the Durnovo villa; but—it was hoped that 'everything would go off all right'.

I don't know just why, but suddenly, under the influence of these favourable reports, Tsereteli triumphantly addressed the Bolsheviks, especially Kamenev, in an indignantly didactic speech:

'Here we have before us now an open and honest review of the forces of the revolution. Tomorrow there will be demonstrating not separate groups but all the working class of the capital, not against the will of the Soviet, but at its invitation. Now we shall all see which the majority follows, you or us. This isn't a matter of underhand plots but a duel in the open arena. Tomorrow we shall see. . .'

Kamenev was discreetly silent. Was he as confident of his own victory as Tsereteli of his? Was he holding his tongue for secrecy, or because he was not confident in the results of the review? I myself was not quite confident in them when I left late that night to sleep on the Petersburg Side, in the *Letopis* offices.

* * *

The next day, Sunday the 18th, I left the house around noon. As usual, I had no intention of taking part in the procession—even though it had been decided that the Congress would go in full force. . . I left for Gorky's nearby. He or some literary friend might go with me to watch the demonstration. But there were no literary people around, and Gorky said: 'The demonstration's a failure. I've heard from a number of places; only handfuls of people are marching. The streets are empty; there's nothing to see. I'm not going. . .'

Hm! Somewhere someone already had his conclusions ready. At the same time these conclusions, if correct, could be interpreted in two ways. The demonstration was a 'failure' because the revolutionary energy of the masses was drying up; they no longer wanted to come out when the Soviet called them and demand peace, etc., but to pass on to peaceful labour and finish the revolution—in spite of the exhortations of Soviet demagogues and loudmouths. It was obvious which circles, thirsting for the reaction, had been anticipating just these conclusions. . .

But there might be another interpretation: the democracy of the capital remained relatively indifferent to the demonstration because it was official, 'Soviet', and its slogans did not correspond to the mood of the masses; the revolutionary energy had perhaps long since definitely rolled past the boundary at which the Star Chamber had been trying to stop it.

But one moment! the failure of the demonstration might be utter nonsense. All the Soviet parties, after all, had decided to take part in it, and prepared for it! I went out alone, turning towards the Champ de Mars, through which all the columns were to march. In the Kamenno-ostrovsky Prospect, near Kshesinskaya's house, near Trinity Bridge, it was really rather deserted. It was only on the other side of the Neva that detachments of demonstrators were visible. It was a magnificent day, and already hot.

There wasn't a dense crowd blocking the Champ de Mars, but thick columns were moving towards me.

'Bolsheviks!' I thought, looking at the slogans on the banners.

I went over to the graves of those who had been killed, where familiar Soviet people were standing in compact groups taking the salute. Apparently the demonstration was rather behind time. The districts had started from the assembly points later than schedule. It was still only the first detachments of the Petersburg revolutionary army that were parading through the Champ de Mars. Columns were still on the way from every part of Petersburg. There was nothing, however, to be heard of any excesses, disorders or upsets. No arms could be seen amongst the demonstrators.

The columns marched swiftly and in close order. There could be no question of a 'failure', but there was something *peculiar* about this demonstration. On the faces, in the movements, in the whole appearance of the demonstrators—there was no sign of lively participation in what they were doing. There was no sign of enthusiasm, or holiday spirits, or political indignation. The masses had been called and they had come. They all came—to do what was required and then go back. . . Probably some of those called from their homes and private affairs this Sunday were indifferent. Others thought this was a government demonstration, and felt that they were doing not their *own* business but something compulsory and perhaps superfluous. There was a businesslike veneer over the entire demonstration. But it was on a magnificent scale. All worker and soldier Petersburg took part in it.

But what was the political character of the demonstration?

'Bolsheviks again,' I remarked, looking at the slogans, 'and there behind them is another Bolshevik column.'

'Apparently the next one too,' I went on calculating, watching the banners advancing towards me and the endless rows going away towards Michael Castle a long way down the Sadovoy.

'All Power to the Soviets!' 'Down with the Ten Capitalist Ministers!' 'Peace for the hovels, war for the palaces!'

In this sturdy and weighty way worker-peasant Petersburg, the vanguard of the Russian and the world revolution, expressed its will. The situation was absolutely unambiguous. Here and there the chain of Bolshevik flags and columns was interrupted by specifically SR and official Soviet slogans. But they were submerged in the mass; they seemed to be exceptions, intentionally confirming the rule. Again and again, like the unchanging summons of the very depths of the revolutionary capital, like fate itself, like the fatal Birnam wood—there advanced towards us: 'All Power to the Soviets!' 'Down with the Ten Capitalist Ministers!'

An astonishing, bewitching slogan, this! Embodying a vast programme in naïve and awkward words, it seemed to emerge directly from the very depths of the nation, reviving the unconscious, spontaneously heroic spirit of the great French Revolution.

At the sight of the measured advance of the fighting columns of the revolutionary army, it seemed that the Coalition was already formally liquidated and that Messrs. the Ministers, in view of the manifest popular mistrust, would quit their places that very day without waiting to be urged by more imposing means.

I remembered the purblind Tsereteli's fervour of the night before. Here was the duel in the open arena! Here was the honest legal review of forces in an official Soviet demonstration!

A few steps away from me Kamenev's stocky figure was visible in the thin crowd, rather like a victor acknowledging a parade. But he looked more perplexed than triumphant.

'Well, what now?' I said to him. 'What sort of Government is there going to be now? Are you going into a Cabinet with Tsereteli, Skobelev and Chernov?'

'We are,' Kamenev replied, but somehow without real assurance.

The programme of action in the minds of the Bolshevik leaders was evidently completely vague. And Kamenev himself was vacillation incarnate.

A detachment was approaching with an enormous, heavy, gold-embroidered banner: 'The Central Committee of the Russian Social-Democratic Workers' Party (Bolsheviks)'. The leader demanded that, unlike the others, the detachment be allowed to stop and go right up to the graves. Someone who was acting as master of ceremonies tried to argue with them, but yielded at once. Who and what could have stopped the victors from allowing themselves this trifling indulgence, if that was what they wanted?

Then a small column of anarchists appeared. Their black flags stood out sharply against the background of the endless red ones. The anarchists were *armed*, and were singing their songs with a fiercely challenging look. However, the crowd on the Champ de Mars merely greeted them with ironical merriment: they didn't seem at all dangerous.

Such was June 18th in Petersburg. It was a stinging flick of the whip in the face of the Soviet majority and the bourgeoisie. It was an unexpected revelation to the Star Chamber and its purblind leader. But as a matter of fact what could a blind man make of a blow on the head from an axe-butt in the dark?

The bourgeoisie and the politically-minded man in the street evaluated things better. But what could they do? The men in the street, tormented by forebodings, simply whispered among themselves. And the bourgeoisie? Its Ministers, of course, didn't retire voluntarily. In the given circumstances they would have gained nothing by that and lost everything. It was after all really impossible, while retaining a bourgeois dictatorship, to take seriously the trust or mistrust of the masses of the people. It was after all really impossible to abandon power voluntarily when it might pass easily and painlessly into the hands of enemies. The experiment of resigning would be permissible only when it created difficulties, disorganized the enemy camp, and served to strengthen the reaction and the bourgeois dictatorship. But what could be done, when the lower depths of the revolutionary capital appeared before their very eyes?

It was obvious what could be done. First of all, take no official notice. Secondly, prove by means of 'public opinion'—i.e., the big newspapers—that the demonstration had been a failure, and that the miserable fragments of the 'revolutionary democracy' who had been in the streets with their demagogues and loudmouths reflected precisely nothing. Thirdly, hide from them behind the real 'revolutionary democracy', behind its overwhelming majority: not the Bolsheviks of the capital, but the All-Russian Congress; not Lenin and Trotsky, but Chaikovsky and Tsereteli. To be sure, these must be kicked at once, to teach them their place; nevertheless it must be hoped that they wouldn't give up. The 'big press' harped on all these themes.

* * *

The capital was seething. The temper of the masses and the desire for decisive action were growing daily. In the capital there was no longer any need to agitate against the Coalition.

Everywhere, in every corner, in the Soviet, in the Marian Palace, in people's homes, in the squares and boulevards, in the barracks and factories, everyone was talking about some sort of 'demonstrations' that were expected any day; nobody knew exactly who was going to 'demonstrate', or how or where, but the city felt itself to be on the eve of some sort of explosion.

On Sunday July 2nd, a splendid sunny day, I spent the morning chatting amiably and strolling about with Lunacharsky, who had stayed with us overnight. At this time I had already moved from the *Letopis* to my own place in the Karpovka. That morning the Bolsheviks were arranging a mass-meeting for their 1st Machine-Gun Regiment in the huge hall of the People's House. Lunacharsky was obliged to speak there, with Trotsky and others: the Bolshevik powers thought this meeting very important.

Lunacharsky went to the People's House; but after speaking returned and we went for a walk. We admired the beauties of Petersburg, and then the three of us—Lunacharsky, my wife, and myself—went to dinner in the famous 'Vienna'. The restaurant of literary Bohemia now swarmed with political figures of the more or less democratic camp. I had a short talk with Chernov, who was now very chilly towards me.

There was to be an all-city conference that day of the Interdistrict Party. Lunacharsky, one of the leaders of the group, thought it very important. After dinner we set off on foot for the conference, somewhere far down the Sadovoy. Lunacharsky tried unceasingly to make a convert of me; my wife was already converted.

The conference agenda included, among other things, the question of uniting the Interdistrictites with Lenin's party. It was a foregone conclusion. . . Lunacharsky had invited me to the conference as a guest; he had no doubt that sooner or later

I would join the Bolsheviks; but we didn't know whether I should be let in.

After some preliminary negotiations by Lunacharsky, they willingly let me into the little hall, which held about fifty delegates and roughly as many guests. The star performer, sitting near a chairman I did not know, was Uritsky. Trotsky was also among the delegates, and he was delighted to have me sit by him. Steklov was also there as one of the guests. But the majority were workers and soldiers unknown to me. There was no doubt that here—despite the miniature quality of the conference—the authentic worker-soldier masses were represented.

We arrived during the 'reports from the floor'. They were listened to with interest, and really were interesting. Party work was being feverishly carried on and its successes were perceptible to everyone. There was one hindrance: 'What distinguishes you from the Bolsheviks, and why aren't you with them?' All the speakers reiterated this, ending with exhortations to flow into the Bolshevik sea.

I well remember the report of the representative of the garrison of Krasnoe Selo. He said that they had a monopoly of influence there; and the 176th Regiment was fully at the disposal of the central organs of the group—*for any purpose*, at any time. The report was clear, full of interesting details, and important in its implications.

The discussion of principles began. I think the question of uniting with the Bolsheviks was settled then and there while I was present. But I particularly recall the debates on the new programme of the party. Here glances turned, naturally, to Trotsky.

Around this time Lenin had composed his draft of the Bolshevik party programme. I don't think it had yet been published, but it was passing through a few hands in the form of a printed pamphlet. It contained a detailed elaboration of *political* questions: parliamentarism, the Soviets, the judiciary, the remuneration of officials and specialists. Here were collected all the elements of that utopian structure of the state which Lenin afterwards passionately defended in his pamphlet *State and Revolution*, and then later still—soon after the bitter lessons of practice—threw overboard as childish delusions and worthless rubbish. It was quite remarkable. And it was even more remarkable that side by side with this detailed working out of the *political* side the *economic* programme was allotted only the most perfunctory attention. It hardly existed. Its place was evidently taken simply by a proposal for 'direct creation from below' and 'expropriating the expropriators'.

I was amazed when at the Interdistrict Conference the party programme was arrived at: Trotsky repeated Lenin. He took Lenin's draft as a basis and introduced a few amendments. Incomprehensible! It's true that Trotsky, Lunacharsky, and Uritsky were not economists. But they were highly educated and the most advanced Socialists in Europe. Why wasn't it clear to them that Socialism is primarily an *economic* system and that without a strictly worked out programme of economic enterprises nothing could come of a dictatorship of the proletariat? It was precisely from their point of view that a party programme must necessarily contain a detailed, purely practical, and concrete schedule of economic reforms. For their programme was the programme of the liquidation of capitalism.

Let us grant that at a mass-meeting this disregard of real economic tasks was tolerable. But here, when dispositions were being elaborated for the guidance of the revolutionary staff itself? I, a guest, a member of another party, was itching to ask for the floor—at least to put some puzzled questions. And they might have given it: there were no theoreticians present, and the discussion was lackadaisical. Nevertheless it was out of place for me to speak, and I didn't like to ask. Lenin and Trotsky, by the way, were here disregarding just those urgent problems they were to come up against a few months later when they were the Government. But the political system that absorbed all their attention wasn't the slightest use to them then. They at once abandoned all their constructions in this field.

I had to leave: some Commission or other was to meet in the Tauride Palace. I went out into the street alone—with strange feelings, honestly not understanding how people's minds worked. Tired by my earlier walk, I plodded off to the distant palace of the revolution.

* * *

The first Coalition against the revolution, not waiting to be swept away by an explosion of popular wrath, broke up as a result of internal crisis. It had survived exactly as long as the first Guchkov–Miliukov Cabinet.

It goes without saying that there was only one sensible solution of the problem of power, the establishment of a dictatorship of the democracy. In place of the Coalition of the big and petty bourgeoisie against the proletariat and the revolution there must be created a new coalition: a coalition of the Soviet parties, the proletariat, and the peasantry—against capital and imperialism. There was no other solution. But this solution could be arrived at only by a united front, by the united will of the Soviet.

All power had long been in its hands. The dictatorship of the Soviet democracy could have been established—*formally*—by the simple proclamation of a Government of the Soviet bloc. The overturn could have been consummated with complete ease, without shedding a drop of blood. And the dictatorship of the democracy would have been created as a fact simply by the realization of the effective power and the accomplishment of the programme of peace, bread, and land. Here the road seemed smooth, but only if the Soviet *came out* for the overturn.

In any case the question was now posed in all its scope—by the internal collapse of the Coalition. But at this point, on Sunday July 2nd, while I walked slowly to the Tauride Palace from the Interdistrict Conference—nothing was known about this. It was not until late that evening that the rumour that the Cadets had left the Coalition Government began to get all over the city by 'phone.

Now, as before, the city was saturated with other rumours—about various 'demonstrations' by the Bolsheviks, the workers, and the regiments—against the Government and the Soviet. The capital was seething. The slogan of the turbulent masses was also—'All Power to the Soviets'. It might have seemed that events were hitting the same target from various directions. It might have seemed that the movement of the masses, expressing the 'public opinion' of the worker–soldier capital, would serve as a favourable factor for the correct solution of the problem of power. But this wasn't so.

The elements were rising without restraint or reason. And those who led them, by continually proclaiming these same slogans of Soviet power, radically undermined the possibility of a correct solution of the crisis. For they were known to be acting *against* their own slogans, *against* the Soviet, and not in a united Soviet front against the bourgeoisie. Their aim was to hand the power not to the Soviet, in the form of a bloc of Soviet parties, but to an 'active minority' in the form of the Bolshevik Party alone.

In such conditions the movement of the Petersburg 'depths' infinitely confused the situation. Now the mounting tide of popular passion could not serve the revolution as it had in the April Days. Then the Soviet had ruled the elements; now they had gone beyond any obedience. If anyone still retained some little power over them, it was the Bolsheviks, who were mixing up all the cards and in the *name* of the Soviet directing the elements *against* it.

But the power of the Bolsheviks over the elements was not great. In the heart of the capital, still invisible to the outsider's eye, the tempest was raging irresistibly. Tens and hundreds of thousands of workers were really plunging towards an inevitable outbreak; it was impossible to hold them back. This outbreak threatened to be fatal. That was just how I estimated it at that time, in view of all the circumstances, and that is just how I estimate it now, three years later, looking at its consequences *sub specie aeternitatis*.

But then as well as now, independently of political results, it was impossible to look on this stupendous movement of the masses with anything but enthusiasm. Even if you thought it fatal you could only rejoice in its gigantic elemental sweep.

Tens and hundreds of thousands of proletarian hearts veritably burned with passion, hatred, and love combined, and with yearning for some vast and intangible exploit. They were rushing to sweep away all obstacles with their own hands, crush all enemies and build a new destiny then and there. But how? Just what destiny? This the elements did not know. But they surged out, all aflame; they *had* to come out. Such was the decree of the historical destiny that ruled the elements. It was a magnificent spectacle; only blind men could fail to sense its greatness.

And what came of it all? An 'episode' heavy with consequences, that will go down in history as the *July Days*.

CHAPTER 20

THE 'JULY DAYS'

Monday, July 3rd. The next day I went to the Tauride Palace in the morning. In spite of the comparatively early hour I found a great deal of excitement. In the Ex. Com.'s rooms there were almost as many people as during the whole summer. There was no session, but Mameluke and Opposition groups seemed to have shaken off their torpor and were conferring excitedly here and there.

Amongst these groups I also noticed the members of my own fraction, the Menshevik-Internationalists, headed by Martov. They had already had time to arrange an impromptu session and even to pass an important political resolution.

Martov, having learned the night before that the Cadets had left the Coalition, had drawn it up beforehand. The resolution stated that it was *imperative to create immediately a purely democratic Government, made up solely of 'Soviet' parties.*

It was only now, after the 'spontaneous' collapse of the Coalition, that the Menshevik-Internationalists had decided to say this. It was only now, a month after the opening of the All-Russian Congress of Soviets, that Martov thought it possible to authorize this slogan for his group. He was not too late—contrary to his habit—only because from that day on events took a very special turn.

This was the day when the famous July week began. The story is not only very important and interesting, but very complicated, and also very obscure and confused. As usual I shall not assume the slightest obligation to disentangle it; I shall write it down as I personally recall it.

I think it was announced that morning that a session of the Central Ex. Com. was to be held that afternoon, when the Socialist Ministers had finished their business in the Marian Palace and the Star Chamber. It was said that the Star Chamber already had a plan ready for settling the crisis.

The Coalition Cabinet had collapsed—through internal bankruptcy. The 'living forces of the country' in the person of the entire organized bourgeoisie embodied in the Cadet Party, had now left the revolution formally, officially, and openly—for the camp of its enemies. But our revolution, after all, was 'bourgeois'. This the Star Chamber knew very well, and that was all it knew. Its special logic pushed these deep thinkers to the conclusion that the bourgeoisie *must* be in power. And the only plan the Star Chamber could have was this: if there was no Coalition, it would have to be invented. If the Cabinet of May 5th had now crumbled, a new one must be concocted in its likeness. If the real, the organized bourgeoisie had gone, leaving in the Cabinet only a few individuals representing no one but themselves, then at all costs substitutes for it must be found, deceiving the country, the democracy, the plutocracy, and oneself.

But it wasn't so easy to do all this: the desired Capitalist Ministers were not to be picked up in the street. Meanwhile it was impossible to prolong the interregnum in the stormy atmosphere prevailing. The masses might take a hand; the Opposition might take advantage of the interregnum, and who knew what that might threaten the principle of the Coalition with?

It was impossible to leave the situation vague. And this is what the wily Tsereteli had thought up.

The decision of the question of the Government was to be declared outside the jurisdiction of the available personnel of the Central Ex. Com., when a whole third of the members elected by the Congress were in the provinces. Loyalty, constitutionality and democratic principles demanded that the question of the future composition of the Government and of the replacement of the members who had left should be decided by a plenum of the Central Ex. Com. A plenary session could be arranged in two or three weeks; meanwhile the Star Chamber proposed not to replace the missing Cadet Ministers at all, but to appoint in their places suitable heads of departments for 'organic' work while the *political* Cabinet would be left at its present strength, of eleven Ministers (with a 'Socialist' majority of one!).

Rumours of this plan had spread throughout the Tauride Palace and the delegates were hotly discussing it. The Opposition was filled with rage and contempt, and indeed the 'plan' merited rage and contempt. It was, of course, a ruse, and predetermined a new Coalition just as surely as two and two make four. Objectively, to be sure, the question would be decided with the most intimate participation of the masses of the people, but, while it *knew* that those forces existed, the Star Chamber did not *believe* in them, and within the confines of parliamentary Soviet machinations its game was almost unbeatable.

The whole difficulty consisted in the one fact that there were waverers among the majority—under the influence of the enormous movement of the rank and file; especially among the ignorant Rightist masses of the *Peasant* Ex. Com., very many could not understand why they should strive for a bourgeois régime; not having mastered the 'Marxist' theories of Dan and Tsereteli they were not at all averse from taking the whole power into their own peasant hands and personally unleashing anarchy. After all, it was obvious that the bourgeois government would not give the peasants land without payment; nothing had been accomplished in the agrarian question—except sabotage. It wouldn't be at all a bad idea to seize all the power, in order to seize all the land. Then the peasants would start to establish exemplary order themselves, to squeeze the Kaiser's partisans, put a stop to the unreasonable demands of the workers and—beat up the Yids.

This was how many of the 'ignorant masses' who had overrun the central Soviet bodies thought and spoke. Speaking *generally*, these little SR peasants constituted the most reliable foundation of the Star Chamber. But *specifically*, in this matter of the composition of the Government, the 'Marxist' leaders had to be very careful with them. The whole difficulty for the Star Chamber lay in the mood of these little peasants and the waverings of the more Left elements of the Soviet majority.

Nevertheless the Star Chamber's game was almost unbeatable. In the two or three weeks before the plenum met they could do their best to convince the waverers (Right and Left). During this interval they could rout out some sort of Capitalist Ministers and present the plenum with an accomplished fact.

* * *

The Star Chamber appeared around 2 o'clock, when the small former Ex. Com. room was quite full. Members of the peasant Central Ex. Com. were also present—some looking like professors, some like seminarists, and some like shopkeepers. In all there were about 200 people present. The hall, buzzing like a beehive, had long since forgotten such a bustle.

Tsereteli of course took the floor. He made a short report which included all the known facts and, at the end, the plan described above. I immediately rose on a point of order: Tsereteli, by uniting two questions with nothing in common, wanted to push one through with the help of the other; these two questions should be decided separately. But I don't know the fate of the point of order in the debates that it started. Unfortunately—for a reason which had nothing to do with the political crisis—I had to leave the meeting for about an hour.

I needed a car for that hour and painfully tearing myself away from the—*soit dit*—'historic' meeting, excited by the great day and the new events of the revolution, I feverishly bustled about after one, so as not to be late for my business and to return as quickly as possible. Hurrying through the next room, which was empty, I heard a ring from the telephone booth. I hurriedly picked up the receiver.

'Is that the Ex. Com.?' said a voice, obviously a worker's. 'Call some member of the Ex. Com. Hurry up; it's urgent!'

'What's the matter? Quick! This is a member of the Ex. Com. speaking.'

'This is the *Promyot* Factory. A few workers and soldiers have just come in here, and they say that all the factories and regiments have already demonstrated against the Provisional Government, and others are demonstrating now. They say ours is the only factory that isn't demonstrating. In the Factory Committee we don't know what to do. Tell us, what are the Ex. Com.'s instructions? Should we go and demonstrate or detain these people as *provocateurs*?'

I answered: 'The Ex. Com. is unconditionally against the demonstration. Anyone telling people to go out into the street is acting on his own initiative, against the Soviet. The Ex. Com. has no knowledge of any demonstrations by factories or regiments. It's probably not true. The people who have come to you talking about other factories and regiments are simply trying to get you out into the street. Don't go anywhere till the Ex. Com. orders you. Don't try to keep those people there, but be sure to try and find out who they are and who sent them. Tell them and the factory that the Ex. Com. is in session right now debating just this question of the new Government and the transfer of all power to the Soviet. Ring back again later.'

I thought it essential to hurry back to the Ex. Com. for a moment and tell them about this conversation. I don't recall whether I succeeded, but at the meeting I found the whole picture changed. The political discussion had been suspended. In my absence information had been received that the 1st Machine-Gun Regiment had already come out into the street and was now making its way towards—no one knew where. In a flash the whole appearance of the meeting had changed. Most of the faces showed anger, irritation, and boredom: this was the old atmosphere of 'demonstrations' which had become quite customary during the preceding weeks, and which was supposed to have been changed by 'high policy' but was now so inopportunely renewed.

The Ex. Com. knew by rote what it had to do, and was already behaving by rote: it decided to send someone at once to intercept the Machine-Gun Regiment and persuade it to go back. But the question was, *whom* to send? Though I was late and agitated, nevertheless for a few minutes I watched the meeting lackadaisically talking things over, choosing between candidates.

Who, indeed, should be sent? Representatives of the Soviet majority, partisans, or members of the Star Chamber? But they were not in the least likely to persuade anybody. No one would listen to them, and perhaps they might be arrested. Even they themselves realized this. The Bolsheviks of course would have been persuasive. But it was impossible to send them—*they couldn't be trusted*: God knew where Kamenev or Shlyapnikov would lead the intercepted regiment—to the barracks or to the Marian Palace?

No candidate was found and nobody was sent while I was there. The atmosphere of demonstrations had become habitual. The minds of the leaden 'authorities' were turning over slowly and heavily. I left, and during my mad rush in the car thoughts were dancing about in my head, one interrupting the other, about the political crisis and the demonstration that had begun. Great events were beginning!

* * *

My recollections of that day begin again at about 6 or 7 in the evening. At 7 o'clock a meeting of the Workers' Section of the Soviet began in the White Hall. The overwhelming majority was Bolshevik. Was this meeting connected with the movement that had begun, and what, in general, was the Bolshevik Party's relation to it? I don't know for certain. According to all the data, the Bolshevik Central Committee did not organize a demonstration for July 3rd—unlike what had happened on June 9th. I know that the temper of the masses was considered somewhat 'worse', a little softer, less well-defined, than three weeks before. It was somewhat dejected by the fiasco of the 9th and by the official Soviet demonstration of the 18th. An uprising, of course, was considered inevitable, for the capital was seething and the general situation was unendurable. The Bolsheviks were getting ready for it—technically and politically. But it was clear that they had not scheduled it for July 3rd. And the Bolsheviks in the Soviet, after meeting during the day, agreed to go to the factories and barracks to agitate against the demonstration.

From various outskirts of the city, beginning with the Vyborg Side, masses of workers and soldiers were moving towards the centre. The workers had left their benches in thousands and tens of thousands. The soldiers were coming out armed. Both had banners bearing the slogans that had predominated on the 18th: 'Down with the Ten Capitalist Ministers!' 'All Power to the Soviets!'

It was reported that some workers' detachments and two regiments, the 1st Machine-Gunners and the Grenadiers, were approaching the Tauride Palace. An enormous agitation began in the hall. The aisles and the seats for the public, empty up to then, as at ordinary sessions, suddenly filled up with people. Kamenev suddenly leaped up on to the speaker's platform. And this indecisive Right Bolshevik was the first to give official sanction to the uprising.

'We never called for a demonstration,' he cried out, 'but the popular masses themselves have come out into the streets, to show their will. And once the masses have come out our place is with them. Our task now is to give the movement an organized character. The Workers' Section must here and now elect a special body, a Commission of twenty-five people to control the movement. The others should go to their own districts and join their detachments.' There was no doubt that Kamenev's resolution would be accepted. Whether on his own initiative or according to instructions received, Kamenev was far from trying to isolate the Bolsheviks as the instigators of the uprising; as always, he acted conciliatorily. But I cannot find in my memory the slightest trace of any activities during the July Days of the newly-elected 'Commission'.

* * *

Meanwhile the movement was already pouring through the city. The tempest was unleashed. Everywhere in the factories the same thing as had been reported by the *Promyot* worker on the 'phone was going on: workers' and soldiers' delegations would turn up, refer to 'all the others', and demand in someone's name that they 'come out'. Only a minority, of course, demonstrated, but everywhere work was abandoned. Trains ceased to leave from the Finland Station. In the barracks short mass-meetings took place, and then from all sides enormous detachments of armed soldiers made their way towards the centre—some of them to the Tauride Palace. Some started shooting into the air: the rifles went off by themselves.

From early evening, lorries and cars began to rush about the city. In them were civilians and soldiers with rifles at the trail and with frightened-fierce faces. Where they came hurtling from and why—no one knew.

The city fairly quickly took on the look of the last days of February. Since then four months of revolution and liberty had passed. The garrison of the capital, and even more the proletariat, were now strongly organized. But the movement appeared to have no more 'consciousness', discipline, or order. Elemental forces raged.

One of the insurgent regiments, led by a Bolshevik lieutenant, was moving along the Nevsky, from the Sadovoy towards the Liteiny. It was an imposing armed force. It was probably enough to hold the city—unless it came up against a similar armed force. The head of the regiment had started to turn into the Liteiny, when some shots were heard from Znamensky Square. The commander of the column, who was riding in a car, turned around and saw the heels of the soldiers, running off in all directions. A few seconds later the car was left alone in the middle of a jeering crowd on the Nevsky Prospect. There were no casualties. . . I was told all this by the commander himself—now a well-known Bolshevik military leader. Something similar was going on at this time at various points of the capital.

The insurgent army didn't know where it should go, or why. It had nothing but a 'mood'. This wasn't enough. The soldiers led by the Bolsheviks, in spite of the complete absence of any real resistance, showed themselves to be really worthless fighting material. But not only Bolsheviks led the soldiers' groups that 'came out' on July 3rd: unquestionably there were also some completely obscure elements present.

The 'over-forties' also came out: that day their representatives had again seen Kerensky and again pleaded to be allowed to go home to work on the land. But Kerensky refused: after all, the offensive against the insolent enemy still continued, for the glory of the gallant Allies. So the 'over-forties' gladly joined the 'uprising' and in enormous numbers for some reason moved on to the Tauride Palace.

* * *

We hurried out of the meeting of the Workers' Section, through the crowd that filled the Catherine Hall and the ante-chamber of the palace, into the rooms of the Central Ex. Com. But there was no meeting, simply disorder, excitement, and incoherence. No Bolshevik leaders were there: after the meeting of the Workers' Section they had hurried off to their own party centres.

Crowds kept coming to the Tauride Palace until late at night. But they looked 'disorganized'. They were capable of excesses, but not of revolutionary action, conscious and purposeful. They plainly did not know why they were in that particular place. And because they had nothing to do they called for speakers—members of the Soviet. The speakers went out to them. Chkheidze tried to persuade them to disperse, referring to the forthcoming meeting of the Central Ex. Com., but he was unsuccessful and was interrupted more than once by hostile shouts. The crowd was in a nasty mood. Voices were heard: 'Arrest the Ex. Com., they've surrendered to the landlords and the bourgeoisie!'

But there was no one to do any arresting, nor any reason for it. They were saying in the crowd that the Provisional Government had already been arrested. But nothing of the sort had taken place. More than that, evidently nothing of the sort had been intended for that day.

The remnants of the Government, with the 'Socialist' majority, were having a meeting in the undefended apartments of Prince Lvov. Any group of ten or twelve people that wanted to could have arrested the Government. But this wasn't done. The sole attempt at it was completely futile.

Around 10 o'clock a motor-car with a machine-gun and ten armed men dashed up to the Premier's house, where they asked the hall-porter to hand over the Ministers. Tsereteli was summoned to negotiate with them, but before he got to the entrance the men in the armed motor-car had vanished, contenting themselves with taking Tsereteli's own car with them. It was obvious that this was a completely 'private enterprise'. But through all the July Days there were no other attacks on the Capitalist Ministers.

In general, contrary to what had been expected on June 10th, the Marian Palace, where the Provisional Government was supposed to be, had not proved to be at all a centre of attraction for the demonstrating masses. It was in fact to the *Tauride*—the residency of the central *Soviet* bodies—that they were attracted. And it was precisely against these, as we see, that their ire was directed.

Around the same time some speakers of the Soviet Opposition, proclaiming the transfer of power to the Soviet, also came out to the square of the Tauride Palace. These met with a completely different reaction—especially Trotsky, whose speech aroused vociferous enthusiasm. But with the darkness the crowd thinned out a great deal. The detachments melted away, scattered, and went off somewhere. There were fewer people in the halls of the Palace too. The 'uprising' seemed to be coming to an end.

* * *

Around midnight some faces from the Star Chamber finally became visible in the Tauride Palace. They had a very triumphant and rather provocative air: they must have been going to propose something special, which in fact they did.

The halls were fairly empty. At a few points some soldiers, standing or lying down, were grouped around stacks of rifles like patrols. And the representatives of the regiments of the capital, loyal to the Soviet majority and without the least authority over the masses, were wandering about with nothing to do, having been summoned by telephone messages. . .

The deputies were beginning to be summoned into the White Hall, when news came about a brawl and the first casualties on the Nevsky, around the Town Council. The Council session, where Lunacharsky, among others, had also spent the evening, had just finished. When the Town Councillors went into the street they encountered volleys of machine-gun fire going on without rhyme or reason between two groups of armed people who had taken each other for enemies. Just then some motor-cars with machine-guns also passed by. This was enough to produce panicky and random firing. Some wounded were brought into the Town Council. These, of course, were not part of the 'demonstration'. The Town Councillors went back to the meeting-hall and hurriedly got out an appeal—to refrain from further bloodshed. The total number of casualties was unknown.

The joint session of the Central Ex. Com. probably opened around one in the morning. The White Hall had a look unusual in the revolution: it was not full. About 300 deputies occupied at most half the seats, while the remaining chairs were not taken up by the crowd. No crowds were standing about the corridors or clustering around the platform, nor was there a soul in the galleries. Exceptional measures had been taken to keep the session really closed. It was sedate, as in the good old Duma. And it was quiet.

There was a feeling of great tension in the air. The deputies were gloomy and taciturn. Everyone was waiting to see what surprise the Star Chamber sitting on the platform had thought up. Chkheidze, pale and morose, was chairman. He had been assigned the presentation of the surprise by the Star Chamber, and opened the meeting with something like this:

'This is an exceptionally serious occasion,' he said, slowly, with difficulty and with many pauses. 'The Praesidium has taken an exceptional decision. We declare that the decisions which will be taken at once must be binding on every one. All those present must undertake to carry them out. Those who refuse to undertake this obligation should leave the meeting-hall.'

Chkheidze stopped. His assignment was evidently limited to this. The hall was motionless for some seconds—a part waiting for something further, a part stunned by surprise.

But Chkheidze sat down. And from the benches on the extreme right, where the Interdistrictites were located, there began a movement towards the way out on the left—Trotsky, Ryazanov, Uritsky, and Yurenev, followed by Steklov. Not wishing to undertake such an obligation 'in the dark' they were obediently leaving the meeting. The hall was silent.

To my own surprise, I rushed on to the platform from the topmost bench on the left, where I had been sitting with Martov and others. Chkheidze failed to stop me.

'In extraordinary circumstances,' I said, 'you may take any extraordinary steps you like. But be aware of what you're proposing. You, the majority, did not appoint us to our deputies' seats. We were sent here by the workers and soldiers. We will answer to them for our acts, but you cannot deprive us of our rights. You can remove us illegally—without our having committed any crime. But we will not give you any promises nor will we leave the hall voluntarily.'

My closest comrades were in accord with me, while the Praesidium was perplexed and didn't react at all. At that point there appeared on the platform the diminutive figure of the famous Spiridonova. As a Left SR she had joined the Kamkov group as soon as she got back from Siberia. The Peasant Congress had elected her to its Central Ex. Com. But amongst ourselves, in Soviet circles, she was speaking for the first time. I didn't even know her by sight and asked who was following me on the platform. . .

In the midst of the stillness and tension Spiridonova cried out hysterically:

'Comrades! A terrible crime is being prepared! Our Minister-leaders are demanding complete obedience from us before explaining what is at issue. It's clear that they are going to propose a decree against the people. They are preparing to shoot down our comrades, the workers and soldiers!'

The Praesidium group was discomfited. It was plain to everyone that the Star Chamber had blundered and that nothing would come of its stupid trick.

In the silence and embarrassment Chkheidze's 'resolution' was voted on. Hands were raised. Against it there were only twenty-one votes—ourselves, the Menshevik-Internationalists and the Left SRs. According to the resolution and the vote we ought to undertake the obligation required of us or leave. But of course we didn't do one or the other. We were left in peace—as, indeed, we were bound to be. The meeting went on. Nothing had come of this stupid enterprise.

When Tsereteli got the floor I went off to look for the Inter-districtites who had gone out. They were conferring nearby on what they should do. They were already coming to the conclusion that they had left in vain and ought to return to the hall. I too urged them to do so, and they really did return at once. Trotsky made the following statement in their name:

'Chkheidze's resolution is illegal and nullifies the rights of the minority. In order to defend the rights of their electors the Interdistrictites are returning to the meeting and will appeal to the proletarian masses.'

The debates were endless. One speaker followed another, all saying the same thing—either about the crimes of the Bolsheviks or about the salvation to be found in the Coalition. The 'little peasants' demanded martial law and similar nonsense. The SR intellectuals, finding the setting appropriate, gave vent to their patriotic feelings.

But the meeting, on this 'exceptionally serious occasion', had no positive content.

Meanwhile the sun came up. The hall filled with bright daylight. The plenipotentiary organ of the revolutionary democracy was wasting its time in idle talk. . .

Bogdanov came on to the platform with a practical proposal:

The meeting was to be stopped. The worker–soldier section of the Central Ex. Com. was to remain in the Palace. All those with any capacity at all for speaking in public were to share out the factories and barracks at once and leave immediately on their missions, before the city woke up, in order to persuade the workers and soldiers on the spot to refrain from any demonstrations. The deputies were to stay in the factories and barracks as long as necessary for this purpose.

And on this the meeting dispersed.

* * *

Pale and hungry, we moved off to the rooms of the Central Ex. Com., while the peasants dispersed homewards.

Aided by two or three people, Bogdanov, with a list of factories and barracks, peremptorily 'billeted' the deputies present —a hundred and a few—on factories and troop units. There was a furious clatter of typewriters, on which whole packets of credentials were being written. Cars were hastily got ready. The deputies scattered like shadows. Not only the Opposition, but also those faithful to the Coalition showed neither enthusiasm nor any desire to embark on this doubtful course after a sleepless night.

Bogdanov called out the names—two for each point. The Interdistrictites declined to go. Gots and myself were sent to the Preobrazhensky Regiment. But Gots had disappeared somewhere. After waiting a quarter of an hour I went alone. The battalion I was going to was quartered quite near the Tauride Palace, at the corner of the Zakharevsky. I went on foot and going out under the colonnade of the porch breathed in the fresh air with pleasure.

It was probably 7 o'clock. A magnificent morning was coming up. The square was empty. On my left there loomed up two or three armoured cars, with no sign of an attendant. The adjoining streets were silent. There was no sign of any uprising or disorders.

Apparently there had been no new shooting during the night. The crowds had dispersed and the streets were empty.

In the Preobrazhensky Regiment—I forget which battalion—my task was not difficult. This regiment was considered reactionary and wasn't on the side of the Bolsheviks. It was likely that it wasn't going to demonstrate and would not have demonstrated regardless of my intervention.

Life in the battalion was just beginning. The sleepy soldiers were just beginning to wander about the huge courtyard. I called out the commander, asked about their mood and what 'steps' were required. The young officer, although he had stood watch all night, was sure of his battalion. He thought there was no need for a general meeting and we decided to assemble only platoon representatives. Some solid, heavy-set little peasants assembled, looking like nothing less than revolutionaries. I explained the political situation to them and told them by what strange methods the movement had been called forth, how dark and obscure its origins were, and what harm it was bound to do. I asked that no one go out into the street armed without a summons from the Ex. Com. . . .

The soldiers' representatives listened respectfully: but none of this was necessary—they were not going anywhere.

My audience didn't show much interest in politics. The attempts of the soldiers to get into conversation with me were limited to a few malicious remarks aimed at Lenin and the Bolsheviks, and at once I had to switch over to the other front—go to the defence of Lenin and his friends, as a proletarian party that was carrying on a legal and necessary struggle for its principles and the interests of the proletariat. The soldiers' uncalled-for attacks were an out-and-out repetition of the filthy, slanderous phrases in the gutter press about all internationalists generally.

My task in the Preobrazhensky Regiment was fulfilled. I could leave with an easy conscience. . .

It was 8 o'clock. I didn't want to start a row at Manukhin's, and I went to the Old Nevsky to 'Comrade Governor' Nikitsky's, to rest a couple of hours. Nikitsky wasn't home: he had been at the Town Council all night in case of an alarm. But what could the Town Council have done about it?

* * *

While dozing off I remembered that during the night the party Bolsheviks had not been either at the meeting or in the Tauride Palace.

That night their Central Committee had a stormy and feverish debate about what to do. . . In general the situation was the same as on the night of June 9th. The debates and plans were apparently also the same. One way or the other, whether started by the party, or spontaneously, or by some unofficial party groups—the movement had begun and assumed enormous dimensions. Should they continue it, by placing themselves at the head of the rebellious masses? Or should they capitulate again to the conciliationist majority of the Soviet and deprive the movement of their sanction?

This was the first question that confronted the Bolshevik Central Committee.

It was apparently decided contingent on the strength and character of the movement. This was a question of fact—that is, of judgement and calculation. And here the outlook was uncertain. First of all, the movement had calmed down during the night; the overwhelming majority of the masses had slept peacefully and shown no desire for action. Secondly, the movement *had begun in a dubious way*; the Bolshevik Party was far from controlling it, and God knew who was at the head of a great many detachments. Thirdly, the movement had shown quite clearly its internal feebleness and rottenness. The uprising had no striking power, nor any real fitness for battle. The outlook was dubious. Now the chief hope lay in the Kronstadters, whose arrival was expected hourly. But in general—was it worth taking *this* movement into one's own hands? It is true that at the session of the Workers' Section Kamenev had already tied the Bolshevik Party to it, but nevertheless it was quite possible to change front as on June 9th. It was a question, after all, of the following day, Tuesday July 4th.

This was the first question that confronted Lenin and his comrades that night. And I think it was the only one that demanded an answer. For the second was probably already decided. This was the question of *where to lead the movement.* This was not a question of concrete fact but of party position. And that had already been determined—a month before. We recall what it reduced itself to: *the movement was beginning as a peaceful demonstration*, and if it developed adequately it would at a favourable conjuncture pass over into *the seizure of power by the Bolshevik Central Committee*, which would rule in the name of the Soviet, with the support at the given moment of the majority of the Petersburg proletariat and the active army units. *This* question was doubtless decided this way now too: a renewal of the debates concerning it was hardly timely now, in the smoke of an uprising.

But how was the first point decided: Whether to take over the movement? Speaking concretely this meant: Should they call for a continuation of the 'peaceful demonstration' in the name of the Central Committee of the Party? According to all the evidence this point made the Bolshevik leaders go through tormenting doubts and vacillations the whole night.

In the evening the question was decided *positively*. Corresponding local orders were given. And a corresponding sheet was prepared for the first page of *Pravda*. The Bolsheviks officially and definitely put themselves at the head of the uprising.

But later the mood changed. The lull in the streets and the districts, in connexion with the firm course of the Star Chamber, inclined the scales to the opposite side. Irresolution came to the fore. And in this irresolution the Bolsheviks held back once again. The type for the first page of *Pravda* was not only set up, but in the matrix: it had to be cut out of the stereotype machine. The Bolsheviks *countermanded* their summons to a 'peaceful demonstration'. They *declined* to continue the movement and stand at its head. . . On July 4th *Pravda* came out with a yawning blank strip on the first page.

I have been speaking of the Bolsheviks of Lenin's party. But the Interdistrictites headed by Trotsky were in the Tauride Palace that night. Evidently neither Trotsky nor Lunacharsky took part in the wakeful night of the Bolshevik Central Committee or shared Lenin's torments. But during the night, I don't remember when, I happened to run across Uritsky, one of the Interdistrict leaders. I asked whether *their* group was calling for a 'peaceful demonstration' the next day. It may be that Uritsky yielded to my somewhat ironic tone, and he answered with emphasis and a certain irritation:

'Yes, we're calling a demonstration tomorrow!'

Well, everyone to his taste, I thought, dropping off to sleep on Nikitsky's bed and turning over in my mind the events of the first 'July Day'.

* * *

Tuesday, July 4th. I went out into the street around 11 o'clock. At the first glance it was obvious that *the disorders had begun again.* Clusters of people were collecting everywhere and arguing violently. Half the shops were shut. The trams had not been running since 8 o'clock that morning. A tremendous excitement was felt—tinged with anger, but not with anything like fanaticism. It was just this that distinguished July 4th from February 28th in Petersburg's external aspect. They were saying something in the groups of people about the *Kronstadters*. . . I hurried to the Tauride Palace.

The nearer I got the more people there were. Around the Palace—enormous throngs, but as it were no demonstrations, no detachments, no columns, nothing organized. A mass of armed soldiers, but split up, solitary, with no command. The square was so packed it was hard to pass through. Ugly black armoured cars as before towered above the crowds.

The halls looked exactly the same as in the first days of the revolution. But the heat was stifling. The windows were open, and armed soldiers were climbing in. With some difficulty I forced my way through to the rooms of the Central Ex. Com.

The open windows looked out into the luxuriant Potemkin Garden, and armed soldiers were jostling one another to look in. The hall was quite crowded, and very noisy. Lunacharsky, whom I hadn't seen all the previous day, was standing at the other end arguing violently with someone. He turned abruptly away from his companion and hurried to my end of the room. He was clearly excited and irritated by the argument. And as though continuing it he flung out at me, without saying good morning, in the angry tone of a challenge, some naïve words of justification:

'I've just brought 20,000 *absolutely peaceful people* from Kronstadt.'

In my turn I opened my eyes wide. 'Really? You brought them? Absolutely peaceful?'

The Kronstadters were unquestionably the chief trump of Lenin's party and the decisive factor in his eyes. Having decided the night before to summon the masses to a 'peaceful demonstration', the Bolsheviks were of course taking steps to mobilize Kronstadt. During the hours of nocturnal wavering, when the movement began to die down, Kronstadt became the sole trump of those members of the Bolshevik Central Committee who sponsored the uprising. . . Then they countermanded the insurrection. But they had evidently not taken the appropriate steps with respect to Kronstadt—or else one Bolshevik hand didn't know what the other was doing. I don't know exactly what the facts were.

But in any case this is what happened: at around 10 o'clock in the morning there came up to the Nicholas Embankment, where there was a tremendous concentration of people, upwards of forty different ships with Kronstadt sailors, soldiers, and workers. According to Lunacharsky some 20,000 of these 'peaceful people' had landed. They were armed and their bands came with them. Landing at the Nicholas Embankment, the Kronstadters formed columns and made their way—to Kshesinskaya's house, the Bolshevik headquarters. They evidently had no precise strategic plan, and only quite a vague idea of where to go or just what to do. They were simply in a mood definitely hostile to the Provisional Government and the Soviet majority. But the Kronstadters were led by Roshal and Raskolnikov—and led to Lenin.

Once again the chances of a new revolution had risen extraordinarily high. Lenin must have very much regretted that the summons to the Petersburg proletariat and garrison had been cancelled as a result of his overnight vacillations. At this point it would have been quite possible to lead the movement as far as he liked. And it was also quite possible to bring about the desired overturn, that is, at least to liquidate the Capitalist Ministers, and the Socialist Ministers and their Mamelukes into the bargain.

In any case Lenin must have begun wavering again. And when the Kronstadters surrounded Kshesinskaya's house, expecting to receive instructions, Lenin made an extremely ambiguous speech from the balcony. He didn't demand any concrete action from the impressive force standing in front of him; he didn't even call on his audience to continue the street demonstrations—even though that audience had just proved its readiness for battle by the troublesome journey from Kronstadt to Petersburg. Lenin merely agitated strongly against the Provisional Government and against the Social-traitors of the Soviet, and called for the defence of the revolution and for loyalty to the Bolsheviks.

According to Lunacharsky, he, Lunacharsky, had been passing Kshesinskaya's house at exactly that time. During the ovation given Lenin by the Kronstadters, Lenin called him over and suggested that he speak to the crowd. Lunacharsky, always ablaze with eloquence, didn't wait to be urged and gave a speech on roughly the same lines as Lenin's. Then he led the Kronstadters towards the centre of the city, in the direction of the Tauride Palace. On the way this army was joined by the workers of the Trubochny and Baltic Factories. They were in a truculent mood. In the columns, headed by bands and surrounded by the curious, there was some extremely strong language directed at the Capitalist Ministers and the Compromisers of the Central Ex. Com. It was clear that Kronstadt had come out as one man to save the revolution, bringing ammunition and equipment; only the old and the young had been left at home.

But just where they were going or what for, they didn't really know. Lunacharsky had said he had 'brought' the Kronstadters. But in my opinion they had got stuck somewhere on the Nevsky or near the Champ de Mars. I don't think Lunacharsky *brought* them to the Tauride Palace; as far as I remember they only appeared there around 5 o'clock in the afternoon.

The movement was also pouring out again apart from the Kronstadters. From the early morning the working-class districts were stirring. Around 11 o'clock a unit of the Volhynian Regiment 'came out', followed by half the 180th, the whole 1st Machine-Gun Regiment and others. Around noon firing began at various points of the city—not skirmishes or fights, but firing: partly into the air, partly at people. There was shooting on the Suvorovsky Prospect, Basil Island, the Kamenno-ostrovsky, and especially on the Nevsky—near the Sadovoy and the Liteiny. As a rule it began with a chance shot; panic would follow; rifles began to go off at random. There were dead and wounded everywhere. . .

There was absolutely no sign of any plan in the movement of the 'insurrectionaries'. But there could be no question of systematically localizing or liquidating the movement. The Soviet and Government authorities despatched loyal detachments of military cadets, Semyonovskys, and Cossacks. They paraded and encountered the enemy. But no one dreamed of a serious battle. At the first shot both sides panicked and scattered helter-skelter. Passers-by of course got the great bulk of the bullets. When two columns met each other neither participants nor spectators *could distinguish where either side was*. Perhaps only the Kronstadters had a distinctive look. As for the rest it was all muddle, spontaneous and irresistible. But the question is, were the first shots that started the panic and fighting accidental or not?

Small, isolated pogroms began. Because of shots from houses, or with them as a pretext, mass-searches were conducted by soldiers and sailors. The searches were a pretext for looting. Many shops suffered, mainly wine and food shops and tobacconists. Various groups began to arrest people on the streets at random.

Around 4 o'clock, according to rumour, the number of people wounded or killed already amounted to hundreds. Dead horses lay here and there.

* * *

The Tauride Palace was packed, stifling and full of disorder. Some mass-meetings were going on in the Catherine Hall, but there were no sessions.

At 2 o'clock, in the midst of the disorder, a session of the Soldiers' Section opened in the White Hall, packed with various armed people. I was detained by some business in the Central Ex. Com. and wasn't there. Dan reported on the situation and, to judge by the newspapers, did so in definitely Rightist tones. But there is no doubt that a good half of these old Soviet praetorians had a contemptuous and plainly hostile attitude towards what Dan said. The movement against the Coalition was gathering too much momentum. The only thing that helped the Star Chamber was that by the will of fate it was directed simultaneously at the Soviets. It was this fact too that ought to make the 'rebels' and their Bolshevik inspirers lose their footing.

The Soldiers' Section dispersed without having taken any practical decisions, and the White Hall had to be cleared for a joint session of the Worker–Soldier and the Peasant Central Ex. Coms. From the city, as before, came news of more and more demonstrations, clashes, shootings, people killed.

I was not at the beginning of the meeting but stayed in the rooms of the Central Ex. Com. It was reported that a workers' army of 30,000 men was coming out of the Putilov Factory. There was talk of two enormous fighting columns with artillery and machine-guns on the Nevsky and the Liteiny. The situation had become extremely grave; there was no apparent way of preventing a possible general pogrom and tremendous bloodshed.

But suddenly a heavy downpour fell on Petersburg. One minute—two—three, and the 'fighting columns' succumbed. Officers who witnessed it told me later that the insurgent soldiers ran off as though under fire and filled up all the doors and gateways. Rain had routed the insurgent army. The demonstrating masses could no longer find their leaders, nor the leaders their sub-commanders. The officers said that the army could no longer be reorganized and that the last chance for any systematic operations had completely vanished after the downpour. But the unruly elements remained...

It was around 5 o'clock. Someone hurried into the Ex. Com. rooms and reported that the Kronstadters had come to the Palace. Under the leadership of Roshal and Raskolnikov they filled all the square and a large part of the Shpalerny. They were in an ugly, fighting mood. They were asking for the Socialist Ministers, and a whole mass of them was pouring into the Palace.

* * *

I went to the meeting-hall. From the windows of the crowded corridor looking on to the square I saw an endless multitude packing the entire space as far as the eye could reach. Armed men were climbing through the open windows. A mass of placards and banners with the Bolshevik slogans (of June 9th) rose above the crowd. As before in the left corner of the square the black, ugly masses of armoured cars loomed up.

I forced my way into the ante-chamber, which was completely packed; lines and groups of people, in the midst of the noise and clanking of arms, for some reason or other were excitedly pushing back and forth. Suddenly someone tugged at my sleeve. Lesha Emelyanova, an old SR friend recently back from prison and now on the staff of *Izvestiya*, stood before me. She was pale and trembling violently.

'Go quickly—Chernov's been arrested—the Kronstadters—here in the courtyard! Quickly, quickly... They may kill him!'

I rushed towards the doors. Just then I saw Raskolnikov pushing his way towards the Catherine Hall. I seized him by the arm and pulled him back with me, explaining on the way what the trouble was: if Raskolnikov couldn't pacify the Kronstadters, who could? But it wasn't easy to get out: there was a crush in the porch. Raskolnikov followed me obediently, but answered me ambiguously. I was perplexed and began to lose my temper. We had already pushed through to the steps when Trotsky, shouldering aside the crowd, overtook us. He was also hurrying to Chernov's rescue.

It seemed that this was what had happened. When the Central Ex. Com. was told that the Kronstadters were demanding the Socialist Ministers, the Praesidium sent Chernov out to them. No sooner had he appeared at the top of the steps of the entry-way that the Kronstadters became very aggressive; shouts arose from the armed crowd of many thousands: 'Search him! See whether he's armed!'

'In that case I won't speak,' Chernov declared, and started back into the Palace.

Then the crowd got relatively calm. Chernov made a short speech about the Government crisis, sharply condemning the Cadets who had left the Government. The speech was interrupted by shouts of a Bolshevik character. And towards the end some enterprising person in the crowd demanded that the Socialist Ministers at once declare the land national property, etc.

There arose a frantic din. The crowd, brandishing its weapons, began to surge forward. A group of people tried to get Chernov inside the Palace, but strong hands seized him and put him in an open car standing close to the steps at the right of the porch. Chernov was declared under arrest as a hostage.

A group of workers immediately rushed off to report all this to the Central Ex. Com.; bursting into the White Hall they produced a panic by shouting out: 'Comrade Chernov has been arrested by the mob! They're tearing him to pieces right now! To the rescue! Everyone out into the street!'

Chkheidze, restoring order with difficulty, proposed that Kamenev, Martov, Lunacharsky, and Trotsky should hasten to rescue Chernov. I don't know where the others were, but Trotsky got there in time.

Raskolnikov and I had stopped on the top step near the right side of the porch—when Trotsky, two steps below us, climbed up on the bonnet of a car. The mob was in turmoil as far as the eye could reach. Around the motor-car a number of sailors with rather savage faces were particularly violent. Chernov, who had plainly lost all presence of mind, was in the back seat.

All Kronstadt knew Trotsky and, one would have thought, trusted him. But he began to speak and the crowd did not subside. If a shot had been fired nearby at that moment by way of provocation, a tremendous slaughter might have occurred, and all of us, including perhaps Trotsky, might have been torn to shreds. Trotsky, excited and not finding words in this savage atmosphere, could barely make the nearest rows listen to him. But what was he saying?

'You hurried over here, Red Kronstadters, as soon as you heard the revolution was in danger! Red Kronstadt has once again shown itself to be the champion of the proletarian cause. Long live Red Kronstadt, the glory and pride of the revolution! . . .'

Nevertheless he was listened to with hostility. When he tried to pass on to Chernov himself, the ranks around the car again began raging.

'You've come to declare your will and show the Soviet that the working class no longer wants to see the bourgeoisie in power. But why hurt your own cause by petty acts of violence against casual individuals? Individuals are not worthy of your attention. . . Every one of you has demonstrated his devotion to the revolution. Every one of you is ready to lay down his life for it. I know that. Give me your hand, Comrade! Your hand, brother!'

Trotsky stretched his hand down to a sailor who was protesting with especial violence. But the latter firmly refused to respond, and moved his hand—the one which was not holding a rifle—out of reach. If these were people alien to the revolution or outright *provocateurs*, to them Trotsky was just as bad as Chernov, or much worse: they might be waiting only for an opportunity to settle accounts with both advocate and defendant. But I think they were Kronstadt naval ratings who had, in their own judgement, accepted Bolshevik ideas. It seemed to me that the sailor, who must have heard Trotsky in Kronstadt more than once, now had a real feeling that he was a traitor:

he remembered his previous speeches and was confused. Let Chernov go? Then why had he been summoned?

Not knowing what to do, the Kronstadters released Chernov. Trotsky took him by the arm and hurried him off into the Palace. But I, remaining on the scene of events, made a row with Raskolnikov.

'Take away your army at once!' I demanded. 'You must see that the most senseless fights may occur. What can be the *political* objective of their staying here, and of this whole movement? They have made their *will* clear enough, and there's nothing to be done here by *violence*! You know the question of the Government is being debated, and everything going on in the streets is simply killing the possibility of a favourable decision.'

Raskolnikov looked at me angrily and mumbled some monosyllables. He obviously didn't know just what more he could do at the Tauride Palace with his Kronstadters, but he clearly didn't want to take them away.

I understood quite well what a spontaneous movement was. But I completely failed to understand Raskolnikov at that moment. He had obviously not finished saying something he knew but didn't want to tell me. I failed to understand him just because at that time I didn't know the real position of his commanders, the Bolshevik Central Committee: I didn't know that for at least a month the Bolsheviks had been completely prepared (not in words, but in deeds) to take all power into their own hands 'in favourable conditions'. Raskolnikov had his instructions.

However, though the movement was tremendous, the overturn didn't come off. This reflected the whole futility of vacillating and half-hearted decisions at critical moments. In view of the Chernov incident and Trotsky's speech, Raskolnikov could now no longer lead his army straight to the Central Ex. Com. and liquidate it. The moment had passed, the mood was destroyed, the impulse was confused; the affair might miscarry—especially in view of the armoured cars looming up to the left. Raskolnikov and Roshal, after all, had received only conditional, not direct, orders. But it was also impossible for the crowd of many thousands, who had been fetched to 'save the revolution', to stand still and do nothing. The mood might easily turn against the Kronstadt generals themselves, as it might have turned against Trotsky.

Irritated by my brush with Raskolnikov, I was on the point of climbing up on the bonnet of the same car, even though I knew it would do no good. But at that moment Roshal jumped up there himself. Lisping like a child, in ingratiating language, he extolled the Kronstadters for having performed their revolutionary duty—and then invited them to go away and rest at points shown to them, where the army would be given food and shelter. But the gallant Kronstadters must remain on the alert: at any moment they might again be needed by the revolution and they would be summoned once more.

I didn't wait for the results. I left for the room where the Central Ex. Com. met.

* * *

But I quickly got bored and went out to 'the people'. The crowd in the Catherine Hall seemed to be getting a little thinner, but generally speaking there was the same scene of crowded, senseless fuss. The square was also emptier: the Kronstadters really had vanished somewhere. But there were new crowds. . .

Just then a particularly dense crowd appeared at the left-hand gates opening on to the Shpalerny. Columns of soldiers with a rather special appearance were entering the square. Dirty and dusty, the soldiers, soaked by the rain, had a look of active service, with their packs on their backs, their rolled-up greatcoats slung round their shoulders, their mess-tins and cooking-pots. The crowd made way before their dense columns. Taking up the whole courtyard of the palace, from one gate to the other, the detachment halted and began settling itself in the most businesslike way: they stacked their rifles, shook out their wet coats, and piled up their belongings.

This was the 176th Reserve Regiment, the same as I had heard a detailed report of two days before at the above-mentioned Interdistrict Conference. This was another Bolshevik 'insurrectionary' army. At the request of the Bolshevik organizations, the regiment had marched from Krasnoe Selo—to 'defend the revolution'.

Well, and what did this remarkable regiment intend to do?

And where were the leaders who had called it out for some purpose or other? The leaders were invisible. And the regiment once again had no idea of what it should do. Doubtless after its hard march it would not object to a rest. But nevertheless it must have been aware that this was not what it had been summoned for. No one, however, ordered it to do anything.

Dan appeared at the door of the palace. It was evidently to him that a delegation of the regiment, sent to reconnoitre, had spoken. Dan had come out to 'welcome' the regiment. And he gave it something to do. The regiment, of its own free will, had performed a difficult march to defend the revolution? Splendid. The revolution, in the person of the central organ of the Soviet, was really in danger. Reliable protection for the Central Ex. Com. must be organized. And Dan personally, with the co-operation of the officers of the 'insurrectionary' regiment, posted some of these mutinous soldiers as sentries at various points in the Palace, for the defence of those against whom the insurrection was aimed.

Yes, such things happen in history! But it's hardly likely that history of that kind will repeat itself. Dan didn't know what sort of a regiment this was and why it had come, and he found a use for it. And the regiment didn't know what it was to do when it reached its destination, received no other orders, and unprotestingly put itself at the service of the enemy. Now it was all over: the regiment was scattered, its soldiers' minds were hopelessly muddled and it could not be turned back again into a fighting force of the uprising.

* * *

This was around 7 o'clock. I went back to the meeting. There was nothing new there. Suddenly like an arrow the news sped through the meeting: the men from the Putilov Factory had come, 30,000 of them, bearing themselves extremely aggressively; some of them had burst into the Palace looking for Tsereteli, who at that moment was not in the hall. They were said to have hunted all over the Palace for him without finding him. The hall was full of excitement, hubbub and frenzied yelling. Just then a crowd of about forty workers, many of them armed, burst in tempestuously. The deputies leaped from their seats. Some failed to show adequate courage and self-control.

One of the workers, a classical *sans-culotte*, in a cap and a short blue blouse without a belt, with a rifle in his hand, leaped up on to the speakers' platform. He was quivering with excitement and rage, stridently shouting out incoherent words and shaking his rifle:

'Comrades! How long must we workers put up with treachery? You're all here debating and making deals with the bourgeoisie and the landlords. . . You're busy betraying the working class. Well, just understand that the working class won't put up with it! There are 30,000 of us all told here from Putilov. We're going to have our way. All power to the Soviets! We have a firm grip on our rifles! Your Kerenskys and Tseretelis are not going to fool us!'

Chkheidze, in front of whose nose the rifle was dancing about, showed complete self-control. In answer to the hysterics of the *sans-culotte*, pouring out his hungry proletarian soul, the chairman tranquilly leaned down from his height and pushed into the worker's quivering hand a manifesto, printed the evening before:

'Here, please take this, Comrade, read it. It says here what you and your Putilov comrades should do. Please read it and don't interrupt our business. Everything necessary is said there.'

The manifesto said that all those who had gone out into the street should go back home, otherwise they would be traitors to the revolution. The ruling Soviet clique and Chkheidze could think of nothing else to propose to the rank-and-file at a moment of extreme tension.

The baffled *sans-culotte*, not knowing what else to do, took the appeal and then without much difficulty was got off the platform. His comrades too were quickly 'persuaded' to leave the hall. Order was restored and the incident liquidated. . . But to this day I can still see that *sans-culotte* on the platform of the White Hall, shaking his rifle in self-oblivion in the faces of the hostile 'leaders of the democracy', trying in torment to express the will, the longings, and the fury of the authentic proletarian lower depths, who scented treachery but were powerless to fight against it. This was one of the finest scenes of the revolution. And with Chkheidze's gesture one of the most dramatic.

* * *

The speakers were holding forth again. It was as boring as before in the hall: everybody was conscious of the total futility of all these polemics.

It was interesting to watch the mood of the little peasants. Like the praetorians of the Soldiers' Section, they were not in the least averse from driving the bourgeoisie from power and furthering the revolution, that is, strictly, the agrarian revolution. All power, after all, had long been in Soviet-peasant hands—so why be afraid of proclaiming the fact? This is how the little peasants talked in intimate corners. But that was only one side of the matter. The other was that they were mortally afraid of the Bolsheviks and the Internationalists, traitors to the fatherland, lackeys of the Kaiser, universal destroyers, atheists, who talked gibberish about class war and international proletarian solidarity. The peasants were peasants, and the more substantial they were the more clearly their speech and whole appearance showed their old reactionary anti-Semitic principles.

It was this fear of Bolshevism that the leaders of the Soviet majority were playing on. They could not explain their theories to the peasants, but it wasn't so difficult to scare them with Lenin and anarchy. They clung tight to the Star Chamber without understanding its politics—in order not to fall into the maw of the Bolsheviks.

I was called away from the meeting to talk to somebody. The corridors and rooms had become much less crowded by evening. The Putilov workers had soon gone away. On their way to the Palace they had been caught in the rain and were wet to the skin, and this probably influenced them more strongly than any arguments. The great majority of the Kronstadters had also gone directly from the Tauride Palace to the Nicholas Embankment, boarded their ships and gone home. Only two or three thousand of them were left, with Raskolnikov and Roshal in command; they were somewhere around Kshesinskaya's house and the Peter-Paul Fortress.

Altogether, according to the rumours that reached the 'centre of the revolution', by evening the streets had quickly grown calm. The blood and filth of this senseless day had had a sobering effect by evening, and evidently evoked a swift reaction. Nothing was heard of further 'demonstrations'. The 'uprising' had definitely crumbled. There remained only the *excesses* of a wanton mob. There were some 400 killed and wounded.

* * *

Our session still continued. The speeches dragged on. The darkness drew on imperceptibly, and in the glass roof invisible little lamps began to burn brightly all round the hall.

Martov was speaking, as intelligently as usual, and persuasively, but in an 'unrevolutionary' tone, trying to persuade the Soviet majority to take power.

In the endless list of speakers my turn came. I spoke in support of Martov, so badly, boringly, and confusedly, that it's painful to recall.

I don't remember that Trotsky spoke, but he was there, sitting in a small group with Lunacharsky and some others on the extreme upper right benches. This little cluster had been the target of savage catcalls and ferocious looks from the rest of the hall throughout the day. But now the little group had melted away. I saw that Lunacharsky was left alone. Something stirred in me, a spirit of protest and solidarity: under the spiteful looks of the Mamelukes I went right across the hall to Lunacharsky, sat down beside him and began to talk to him.

'Why don't you speak? After all, they'll take this for the meekness of a schoolboy who has been up to mischief.'

'I'm on the list,' he replied, 'but I don't feel like speaking. Do you think I ought to?'

'Without any doubt.'

Lunacharsky went over to Chkheidze to see whether his turn was coming soon. Only two or three people were before him. We sat and waited, idly chatting.

Suddenly a rifle-shot rang out, very close, and then another. Someone yelled out hysterically from the empty galleries something about some shootings. The hall was filled with panic and hubbub. The little peasants and the intellectuals jumped up and dashed wildly about. It was ludicrous and disgusting to see the scared 'leaders of the revolution'.

These shots were all that happened. It was explained later that they were accidental: apparently some horses had broken loose in the square and caused an alarm in the midst of which a few rifles had gone off of their own accord.

Chkheidze gave the floor to Lunacharsky. He spoke well, as he always did, but without conviction or fire. He attributed the popular movement to general causes and demanded their removal by a decision on the Government question. He looked exhausted and dejected. He was evidently beginning to suffer a real hangover.

A break was announced, and everyone made for the garden, or filled the buffet and the cool rooms of the Ex. Com. It was about 11 o'clock. The Tauride Palace looked as it did during the first days of the revolution, in the dead of night. Along the endless walls of the Catherine Hall and the ante-chamber, soldiers slept beside their stacked-up arms.

* * *

There was a crush in the buffet, around the tea and sandwiches. I had squeezed myself into a seat at the table when Lunacharsky hurried over to me. Just then I was talking to some outsider about the day's events. Without sparing either irony or merriment, I turned to Lunacharsky:

'So, Anatol Vasilievich, those 20,000 were completely peaceful people?'

Lunacharsky turned on his heel and walked away from me. More than once that day I had already poked fun—a bad habit I have—at his *début* as a regimental commander. But just now my joke evidently was out of tune with his mood. I followed him and asked what it was all about.

It was something really sensational. Nothing more nor less than that reports had been received about Lenin's connexion with the German General Staff. The newspapers had documents intended for publication the next day.

The Praesidium was hurriedly taking steps to prevent it—before the 'responsible' Soviet spheres considered the matter. Tsereteli and others were feverishly conferring on the 'phone with Premier Lvov and the newspaper editors.

It goes without saying that not one of the people really connected with the revolution doubted for a moment the absurdity of these rumours. But—my God!—what talk began amongst the majority, the hangers-on, and the average ignoramuses from town and country. In any case our Star Chamber correctly evaluated both the degree of seriousness and the essence of this contemptible affair.

* * *

The session reopened. Only three or four regular speakers were left. But there were also some emergency ones: to the stormy patriotic raptures of the Mamelukes, with their angry glances directed at us, there spoke 'a representative of the 12th Army', just rushed in by car from Dvinsk at a summons from the Soviet authorities. This was the fairly well-known Right Menshevik Kuchin, who was daring to speak in the name of the army. Making an impression by his martial 'trench-like' appearance, he called the demonstrations, organized against the Government and the Soviet itself by irresponsible and sinister elements, a stab in the back of the army, which was straining all its efforts in the struggle for the freedom of the fatherland. He spoke of the readiness of the front to 'defend the revolution' by all its means, stopping at nothing in order to liquidate the disorders.

Oho! The front was getting involved!

Kuchin's speech was not the only one of its kind. Other couriers from some units stationed in the suburbs also spoke along the same lines. . .

Around then someone reported that two or three hours previously the Bolshevik *Pravda* had been destroyed. It was plain that the affair was taking an abrupt turn.

The initiator of the attack on *Pravda* was the conscientious Minister of Justice, Pereverzev. He thought it timely to pick the evening of July 4th to give an order for the liberation of the printing-shop occupied (I think on my order) by *Pravda* in the first few days of the revolution.

No sooner said than done. Then and there a detachment had been sent to the printing-shop and offices; they arrested everyone present, confiscated manuscripts, documents, etc. All this was taken to the Staff in a district where the Minister of Justice himself resided. He probably did this in connexion with the reports at hand of Lenin's having been hired by the German General Staff.

After the legal authorities the mob began lording it on the

Pravda premises. 'War-wounded' and other Black Hundred elements completely destroyed the editorial offices; they tore down, smashed, and burnt everything.

It was plain that things had taken an abrupt turn.

Numerous arrests were reported to be taking place that night throughout the city. From everywhere dozens of all kinds of people 'suspected of shooting' and of inciting to riot were being taken to the same General Staff. Soldiers, workers, and sailors especially were being seized on the streets and at home. They were interrogated there and sent to different prisons. Weapons were being brought in from all sides—revolvers, rifles, and machine-guns.

* * *

The session continued. The speakers were already coming to an end. Suddenly a noise was heard in the distance. It came nearer and nearer. The measured tramping of thousands of feet was already clearly audible in the surrounding halls. . . The hall again grew agitated. Faces looked anxious, deputies leaped from their seats. What was it? Where was this new danger to the revolution coming from?

But Dan appeared on the platform as though out of the ground. He was so filled with glee that he tried without success to conceal it, at least partially, by assuming a somewhat more serene, objective, and balanced expression.

'Comrades!' he called out, 'be calm! There is no danger! Regiments loyal to the revolution have arrived to defend the Central Ex. Com.'

Just then in the Catherine Hall a powerful *Marseillaise* thundered forth. Enthusiasm in the hall—the faces of the Mamelukes lit up. Squinting triumphantly at the Left, they took hands in an outburst of emotion and standing with bared heads ecstatically chanted the *Marseillaise.*

'A classic scene of the beginning of a counter-revolution!' Martov snapped angrily.

The Left sat there motionless, watching with scornful faces the triumph of the victors.

Certain 'loyal' units had indeed appeared in the Tauride Palace—I think a battalion of the Izmailovsky Regiment, and of course the Semyonovskys and the Preobrazhenskys. As a matter of fact this had very little value. At night, when the capital was completely tranquil, they could be brought over to the Tauride Palace in complete safety—'to defend the revolution and protect the Soviet'. We know that these were units as yet untouched by Bolshevism, who were against any 'demonstration', in spite of the change in mood that was taking place. Bringing them over was worth very little.

But it was also quite useless. The revolution, in the person of its 'plenipotentiary organ', was not threatened by anyone at all. But in case of real danger, of an attack—these regiments would doubtless not have endured a single volley. The 'classic scene of counter-revolution' was not a cause but merely a symptom of the radical change in the situation. But facts remained facts.

The commander of the newly-arrived units mounted the platform. The deputies, with sidelong glances at our little group, gave him an enthusiastic reception. And he replied with a speech about their devotion to the revolution and readiness to defend it with their blood. It was a most remarkable speech: it reflected all the absurd contradictions and incomparable confusions in the relationships of this revolutionary period.

The commander spoke of his loyalty to the *Soviet* and his readiness to defend it with his life: he called the Soviet the sole authority to which the army owed obedience. No party centres or separate groups! Only the central Soviet organ, which was called to decide the fate of the revolution. Not a word about the Provisional Government, Lvov, or Tereshchenko, as though they had never existed. All power was laid at the feet of the *Soviet*. But did not the 'rebels' insist on this very point?

What was confusing here was only the *form*. For in essence the 'rebels' were demanding a dictatorship of the Soviet which would carry out their immutable programme: peace, bread, and land. They demanded all power for it, and insisted that it use that power as a worker-peasant Government should, while the 'loyalists' acknowledged the Soviet as a dictator without conditions; they *blindly* followed their blind leaders and were ready to do (without risk to themselves!) absolutely everything it commanded.

As on the evening before, the Bolsheviks were not present at this session. Their leaders again spent the night at their Central Committee. This was a very hard night for them. *Pravda* had been destroyed; the slandering of Lenin was taking unheard-of forms and the movement for which they had accepted practical responsibility was obviously and very ingloriously collapsing.

That night in their Central Committee the Bolsheviks came to the decision 'to end the demonstration, in view of the fact that the workers' and soldiers' actions of July 4th and 5th have forcefully emphasized the danger in which the country has been placed by the disastrous policy of the Provisional Government'(!).

So everything was over. The Mamelukes had triumphed. For the time being the only thing to do was disperse and go home. Through the glass roof the hall had been full of daylight for some time. It was about 4 o'clock.

The courtyard, drenched in the rising sun, was empty and calm. The armoured cars were no longer there; they had been moved into the garden behind the Palace. Nor were there any signs on the streets of the recent tempest.

I don't remember where I spent the 'night' that morning.

* * *

Wednesday, July 5th. That day all the Petersburg newspapers actually did come out without the material prepared in the editorial offices on Lenin's treachery. Only one newspaper disobeyed Lvov and Tsereteli, so that the material on Lenin became public property that day anyhow, and on the next day it was reprinted by the whole bourgeois gutter press.

But just what kind of material had zealots of the truth got hold of in connexion with this monstrous affair? And what were they called, those patriots who had unmasked Lenin as a traitor?

One was Pankratov, an old inmate of the Schlüsselburg Fortress, now an SR, known in the '17 revolution for nothing more than this; and the other was the Second Duma-ite Alexinsky,[1] whose name speaks for itself and with exhaustive

[1] Alexinsky, Grigorii Alexeyevich (1879– ?): an ex-Bolshevik, the most popular speaker for the Bolshevik wing of the Social-Democratic fraction in the Second Duma and a former collaborator of Lenin's. At the outbreak of the First World War he made a sharp turn to the Right, becoming a 'Social-patriot' and even working with monarchists. In 1917 he was refused admission into the Soviet, and went to extreme lengths in his struggle against the Bolsheviks. He left Russia in 1918 and became an ideologist of the 'White' reaction to Bolshevism. (Ed.)

fullness characterizes the value of the material *a priori.* I refer to them to show the level of baseness of our liberal press, which now began to speak of Lenin's venality as documentarily established.

Messrs. Alexinsky and Pankratov were publishing a thoroughly 'official' document. This was the record of the interrogation of a certain Lieut. Yermolenko in Staff Headquarters, dated May 16th, 1917. Yermolenko testified that he had been 'transferred' by the Germans to our rear in order to agitate for an immediate separate peace. He accepted this assignment on the insistence of some 'Comrades'. But he was informed in the German General Staff that such an agitation was already being carried on in Russia by other German agents, among them Lenin. Lenin had been commissioned to try by all his means to 'undermine the confidence of the Russian people in the Provisional Government'. Money for agitation and instructions were being received from someone in the German Consulate in Stockholm. . .

No one knows whether an obscure person by the name of Yermolenko, who agreed to become a German agent, ever really existed, or whether this kind of document was ever really sent to the staff of the Minister of War, Kerensky, from the head of the General Staff. It may have been fabricated completely in Palace Square, where Black Hundred officers swarmed around Kerensky. But helpful hands evidently got hold of this paper from there for Alexinsky. *He* surely had an established reputation! *He* would surely put the paper to the right use!

And Alexinsky published the document as an incontrovertible proof of Lenin's treachery.

It would seem to have been unusually strange for such a 'record' to serve as a proof of this kind in the eyes of the 'public'. It would seem that any conclusions might be drawn from this document except that of the Bolshevik leader's corruption. It would seem, in particular, that it added precisely nothing to the daily tubs of slander from the gutter press.

But against the background of the July events, and the frenzied malice of bourgeois and Right-Soviet elements, against the background of the terrible hangover of the 'insurgents'—the published document made a quite special and very powerful impression. No one wanted to study it in substance. *There was a document about corruption*—and that was enough. And for the *reaction* that had begun it served as just such a factor as had the senseless bloodshed of the day before.

No further material at all was published during the days that followed. But for the period that was beginning even this proved sufficient. No quotations are needed for one to imagine the war-dance that began in the bourgeois press, based on the proof of Lenin's corruption. The Tsarist Secret Police and real agents of the German General Staff were undoubtedly trying to play on the July disorders. All sorts of riff-raff in the capital were trying to exploit the confusion, muddle, brawls, and shifts in mood of the day before. But of course it was the Bolsheviks who were unanimously declared to be the culprits for all crimes. And on July 5th, the first day of the reaction, the 'big press' was filled with a campaign of Bolshevik-baiting.

That day the *Novaya Zhizn* came out with only a few copies, looking very miserable: the printing-shop had been seized the night before, and another one had given us refuge. I was disturbed at not going to the editorial offices for a second day. That day I decided to appear without fail.

* * *

This is how that Wednesday reappears to me now, three and a half years later:

There were no trams, but generally speaking the streets had gone back to normal. There were almost no crowds or street meetings: the shops were almost all open. Now and then patrols, led by officers, would be met. In the shops and in the streets there was talk of the German money Lenin had received. Bitter anger with the Bolsheviks was sharply expressed.

The Tauride Palace also looked almost ordinary. I think the encampment in the Catherine Hall of the evening before was gone by around noon. But the armoured cars with their crews and guards were still standing in the garden behind the Palace.

There was no session of the committee, but the Bureau was to meet. There were lots of deputies in the Central Ex. Com.'s rooms, again unoccupied. Some reports came in that armed people were again appearing at the factories and demanding that work be stopped. Dan insisted that someone at once write an appeal to the workers—against strikes and new demonstrations: he, Dan, was too exhausted to write the proclamation himself.

Someone took it in hand and for about twenty minutes plugged away at it. But Dan, without mincing his words, declared the result unsuitable and as a last resort insisted that I write the appeal, which I did. Dan seized the sheet of paper and hurried off with it. I think this was the sole instance during the six months of the Coalition in which I collaborated with the Soviet majority.

As before there were no Bolsheviks in the Palace. As far as I recall neither Trotsky nor Lunacharsky was visible. The Left was weakly represented. . .

But suddenly there was an outburst of indignation amongst the Left wing. It appeared that the *summoning of the troops from the front for the pacification of Petersburg was an accomplished fact.* Some 'scratch detachment', of unknown composition and leadership, was moving on Petersburg.

We recall Kerensky's solemn declaration that troops were moving and would move only from the rear to the front to defend the freedom that had been won, and never in the opposite direction, against the citizens of a free country. This was how these phrases were now being justified.

* * *

In the Bureau an extraordinary commission was of course appointed to investigate the events of the preceding days. The question of calling out troops to pacify the capital was raised.

There were only two of us Menshevik-Internationalists in the Bureau—Martov and I. We fought stubbornly and well. In the given situation, when the 'mood' might easily lead at any moment to an anti-Bolshevik, and then an anti-Soviet pogrom, there was no question but that front-line troops *might* serve as a factor in the insurrection and the source of a blood-bath: after all, we knew neither the composition of these troops, their leaders, nor their 'mood'. Martov and I demanded that they should be stopped and sent back.

Once more there were no Bolsheviks at the meeting, but Zinoviev turned up in the midst of the debates on the troops. Without sitting down he went straight to Chkheidze and asked for the floor on an emergency matter. He looked wretched, upset and confused, and was plainly in a great hurry.

'Comrades, a horrible thing has happened. A monstrous slander has appeared in the press and is already having its effect on the most ignorant and backward strata of the masses. There is no need for me to explain to you the meaning of this piece of baseness and its possible consequences. This is another Dreyfus affair, which Black Hundred elements are trying to stage. But its significance is hundreds of times greater. It is bound up not only with the interests of our revolution, but also with the entire European working-class movement. There is no need for me to try to prove that the Central Ex. Com. ought to take the most resolute measures to rehabilitate Comrade Lenin and suppress all the conceivable results of this slander. I've been charged to come here in the name of the Central Committee of our party.'

Zinoviev ended, and without sitting down waited for the majority's reaction. Many faces had an ironical look, others showed complete indifference. But the answer of the whole Central Ex. Com. was already predetermined by the Star Chamber's preventive measures of the night before. Chkheidze replied that the situation was clear to all present and that all measures within the Central Ex. Com.'s power would of course be taken without delay. Chkheidze's tone was icy—as though he were addressing a grown-up schoolboy in disgrace. But there was nothing left for Zinoviev to do but express satisfaction at the assurances he had received. Then he hurried off; we never saw either him or Lenin again in Petersburg until 'October' itself.

Yet another investigating Commission was formed then and there, for Lenin's rehabilitation. I don't know anything about its activities. But I recall that two days later there were discussions of some other elections to this Commission: the 'inconvenience' emerged that its original membership consisted only of Jews, five in all—including Dan, Lieber, and Gots. The rehabilitation of Lenin by a Commission like *that* could serve only as the source of another Black Hundred campaign—against the whole Soviet for concealing high treason. . .

However, I don't think there were any new elections, and the matter died down of itself. In any case, the Commission understood that what it had to investigate was not the question of whether Lenin had sold Russia, but only the sources of the slander. . . There was much talk in those days, amongst other things, about the extreme disorder of *Pravda*'s finances; the sources of its income in the shape of donations and collections could not always be established with precision; and the possibility could not be excluded that unknown elements, even of German origin, gambling on the Bolsheviks, might palm off some sum of money or other on them without their knowledge. That was always possible with any party or newspaper in the situation of the Bolsheviks and *Pravda*. A complete rehabilitation in this respect too would have been an indispensable result of the activities of an investigating commission, but as far as I know nothing like it was ever established concerning Lenin and his party.

* * *

Meanwhile rumours had begun to come in that the mob, with a Black Hundred tendency, was again getting out of hand in the city. Certain groups were beginning to seize Bolsheviks in the streets. It was said that some had been beaten up.

Some units from the city and suburbs began to appear in Staff Headquarters to place themselves at the disposal of the 'legal authorities', and throughout the day these 'legal authorities' carried out numerous arrests. Russian gaols, after a pause of four months, were again filled with 'politicals'. And Dr. Manukhin, who until now had been treating only Tsarist dignitaries, was now enriched by a great many new prison patients from amongst the Bolsheviks.

Alarming news also came in about the Kronstadters. We know that most of them had gone off home in their ships the night before, but two or three thousand had remained in Petersburg. After hanging about in Trinity Square for a while, around Kshesinskaya's house, the Kronstadters, led by Raskolnikov and Roshal, decided that it would be a good idea to go to the Peter-Paul Fortress. Of course they were not admitted, but without much difficulty they occupied the Fortress by force and became masters of the situation there. But exactly what was to be done with the conquered Fortress, once again neither the army nor its leaders had any idea. It was a 'base', just 'in case'. They broke into the arsenal, duly armed themselves, and put their weapons into readiness for battle. But there was nothing else to do, and the Kronstadters spent the night quite peacefully.

Nevertheless the seizure of a fortress under the leadership of Bolshevik fighting commanders was a manifest and very important 'disorder'. The Fortress must be freed. And in the morning the Soviet authorities began to busy themselves with this. In the name of the Central Ex. Com., General Lieber was sent off to retake and pacify the fortress; but he didn't go alone. He found Kamenev and asked him to go too, in the firm belief that it would be easier for him to talk to Roshal and Raskolnikov. Kamenev went with Lieber: his Central Committee, in the early morning atmosphere of July 5th, obviously endorsed this without any difficulty.

But getting into the Peter-Paul was not so easy. Although the bridges were open, the entire district from the Palace Square to the Peter-Paul was held by troops 'loyal to the legitimate Government' and to 'order', who wouldn't let anyone go from any point to any other without special passes from the Staff. This was all very impressive, but I wonder what these 'loyal' troops would have said if they had been ordered to *take* the Peter-Paul Fortress. . .

In any case Kamenev and Lieber had to go to the General Staff to get a pass. While Lieber was fussing about there, the rumour spread amongst the soldiers that the famous Bolshevik Kamenev was in their midst, and they arrested him without thinking twice. The sensation filled practically the whole district. They began demanding an immediate investigation and trial—there was even a danger that both might be dispensed with. Lieber rushed to the rescue. But—*horribile dictu!*—he was taken for Zinoviev and also arrested; the officers behaved even worse than the soldiers. It was with difficulty that the prisoners were got into the Staff, where the misunderstanding was cleared up. The square held by the 'loyal' troops remained in a state of agitation for a long time. Kamenev and Lieber, somehow making their way out of the Staff, went off on their mission.

They arrived at the Peter-Paul Fortress around 3 o'clock. Its garrison had already managed to be 'assimilated' by the conquerors and, incited by Raskolnikov and Roshal, were not averse from showing their readiness for some warlike action. Their hearts had simply been set on fire by the fighting speeches of their ardent leaders. Nevertheless Kamenev and Lieber were able to make an agreement 'honourable to both sides' with the garrison. It was achieved at the price of the great disappointment of Raskolnikov and Roshal, but without much trouble: Kamenev, after all, had brought instructions from the Central Committee itself, to the effect that the game must be considered irredeemably lost. The Kronstadt leaders declared that the sailors, machine-gunners and all the outsiders would leave the Fortress and return the weapons taken from the arsenal. But at the same time they demanded that their own arms should be left to them, and that they should be guaranteed an unimpeded and honourable journey home. The Central Ex. Com. delegates made a vague reply to this. But in any case agreement to restore order in the Fortress was considered to have been reached.

Lieber told us all this at this same session of the Bureau, arriving at the very end of it. He felt like a hero: he had taken the Fortress, pacified the Kronstadters, and at the risk of his life saved his bitter enemy from lynching.

* * *

There were reports of more fighting and bloodshed somewhere on the Liteiny. And there was no doubt that it had been originated by certain 'loyal' units. Lunacharsky had been arrested near the Staff. He was detained for about two hours, vouched for and released. In general they were now arresting in the street anyone who said a word in favour of the Bolsheviks. It was no longer possible to say that Lenin was an honest man: you'd be arrested.

Towards evening complete calm had been restored in the streets. The weather was wonderful. A huge, gay, bourgeois throng poured into the Nevsky. I can't remember at all where I spent these hours, but around 11 o'clock I went back again to the Tauride, which looked just as it had the day before. There were not many people in the halls or at the buffet. The windows were open, but the air was bad; the floor was dirty; there was no real order; the recent presence of a crowd of outsiders could be felt. The buffet was still selling tea and sandwiches, but there were hardly any customers. What was happening in the Ex. Com.?

I went in and saw something quite extraordinary. Lieber was sitting at a table in the Chairman's place. He looked like a conquering hero, but was trying, with very poor success, to put on a dour, stony expression. Bogdanov, tranquil and slow-moving as usual, was sitting on Lieber's right, while Anisimov could be seen on his left. Further off at the table or on sofas and in arm-chairs along the walls, there were a few deputies, who were evidently only looking on. A handful of men, huddled together, stood facing Lieber. They were Raskolnikov, Roshal, two or three sailors, and two or three workers.

The whole group recalled wolves at bay—or, perhaps more precisely, rabbits driven into a corner. Raskolnikov, gesticulating in his sailor's oilskins, was making an anxious, excited, and incoherent speech on their behalf, pleading with the trio sitting in front of him:

'Comrades, after all, you can't—you must—— We can't do that, comrades, you must understand—— Comrades, after all, you must make some concessions. . .'

What I saw in front of me was evidently some kind of unprecedented court of justice. The presiding judge, listening to his victim, had an immobile, stony expression. He was trying to appear inexorable and deaf to entreaties, but his eyes flashed with the enjoyment of power, and his lips struggled with a triumphant smile.

'Eh! Lieber is playing Marshal Davoût,' I thought, remembering Pierre's trial in *War and Peace*. I sat down at the end of the table to see what would happen.

It was a question of the Kronstadters. After giving up the weapons taken from the arsenal, some of them had stayed on in the Fortress, while others remained in the open not far off, waiting to be sent home. But the reaction had grown stronger, and the material strength of the Soviet-bourgeois bloc was growing hourly. Whatever agreement had been arrived at in the afternoon, the 'lawful authorities' were now demanding the *disarming* of the Kronstadters. Raskolnikov naturally refused to agree to depriving his army of their 'military honour' and was begging Lieber and his colleagues to let them take their arms back with them. He swore that this would not cause the slightest danger to anyone, and that disarming the Kronstadters could have no practical result whatever, except their humiliation.

Only Lieber spoke for the court. He was implacable. He kept saying the same few phrases over and over again:

'I suggest that you should consent at once and go to your army to make them comply with our request. This decision is final. There can be no changes or concessions. But in two hours it will be too late. In two hours decisive steps will be taken; they won't be in your interests.'

Lieber didn't explain exactly *whose* decision this was, or what had provoked it, or what kind of steps would be taken and by whom. This actually was more effective. Let us have mysterious hints and frightening words! Just let these cornered rabbits try to argue with us!

Raskolnikov and his comrades could not oppose anything to this but a plea for forgiveness. It was intolerable to see and hear. Neither side, in the given situation, in fact aroused much sympathy: all the same, for me one of them was the age-old enemy, the other a schoolboy who had made a fool of himself.

The fruitless, hollow, and tiresome disputes had already lasted a quarter of an hour. Suddenly Lieber announced that he had that moment received new instructions and could no longer give the respite of two hours he had promised before. Now Lieber-Davoût could only give ten minutes. If at the end of that time the response was unsatisfactory, then 'decisive steps' would be taken at once. The reaction was attaining its full strength.

Raskolnikov asked for a pause to consult with his comrades who were present. The handful of Kronstadters huddled in a corner. I went out to the buffet. . . There I saw a group of Bolshevik leaders sitting at a table in the corner, Kamenev, Trotsky, and three or four others. I never, either before or after, saw them in such a miserable, confused, and dejected state. They were evidently not even trying to cheer up. Kamenev was sitting at the table completely overwhelmed. Trotsky came over to me: 'Well, what's going on there?'

I reported the trial in two words.

'But what do you think should be done? What would you advise?'

I shrugged my shoulders in perplexity. I had not the slightest idea what to do. It was impossible to say whether Lieber could or couldn't take decisive steps—involving bloodshed or the most extreme forms of humiliation. But one ought not to go in for bloodshed oneself or try to break through by force. Perhaps it would be better to surrender and hand over the arms.

I don't remember that Raskolnikov and Roshal conferred with Trotsky and Kamenev during the interval, but when the trial was resumed, Raskolnikov, as before, would not give a definite answer, but again made incoherent attempts at persuasion. He finished by saying that the Kronstadt leaders would go off to their army at once and 'do everything possible'. The judges rose again. Lieber finally gave up trying to maintain his rôle and broke into a smile.

Raskolnikov looked round, perplexed, for sympathizers and friends amongst us. His glance rested on me; he came over to ask a favour of me. He was extremely agitated and afraid of being arrested, if not on the spot, then in the street; he had no hope of reaching his Kronstadters. It was essential that he should be given an escort, or at least reliable documents to allow him to make his way freely about the city. They had been told that Bolsheviks were being seized and beaten up. And if they were recognized. . .

Those around were amused by the excitement of the youthful commanders. No escort was needed; they would get through. But they could have passes. They went into the next room, the office, which was dimly lit and extremely untidy. Passes were typed out. I was stopped by Roshal, whom I hadn't known before. Lisping and mumbling like a child, he asked me to look after his Browning: if they caught him with a weapon it would be worse.

A fine business indeed!

I went off to spend the night at Manukhin's. Lunacharsky was already lying on a bed made from some arm-chairs tied together, next to my sofa. He was very shaken by all that had happened. Lying in the dark we had a long talk. I was irritated, and our conversation was not especially agreeable.

'Well, Nikolai Nikolayevich,' he asked me hesitatingly: 'what d'you think? Ought I to leave Petersburg?'

This made me furious. Leave? Why? What for? Was the situation so clear that there was nothing left but flight from the field of battle? Had an irresistible terror already begun? Was anything serious threatening Bolshevik heads? And if not, surely they must unravel the knot they had tied themselves?

To whom will you leave the masses, whom you have just led or dragged along after you? What will they think and feel when they see themselves abandoned? Or will you take your masses with you as well?

Lunacharsky made no rejoinder. For a long time we went on tossing about on our couches.

Later I was told that the homeless Kronstadters had wandered about the whole night, not knowing where to go. Their leaders weren't with them. They were the irresolute, uncomprehending fragments of an unsuccessful experiment, left to the mercy of fate. . .

* * *

Thursday the 6th. From early morning on, troops withdrawn from the front were arriving in Petersburg at the Warsaw and Nicholas Stations. There arrived a part of the 14th Cavalry Division, the 177th Izborsky Regiment, the 14th Don Cossacks, etc.—in a word, quite enough to take the capital. They were drawn up in Palace Square. They were received there by the Socialist Minister Skobelev and someone else from the Star Chamber. The triumphant Soviet victors admired their Praetorian Guards and made welcoming speeches to them from the windows.

These troops were called a 'scratch detachment', and it was quite obvious they were a very rich soil for Black Hundred propaganda. If any enterprising groups were on hand to annoy this beast, then the blood-bath in Petersburg might turn out to be far from a joke.

Meanwhile, during these days Black Hundred elements became very familiar with the whole charm and all the advantages for the cause of reaction of the 'disorders' and killings. And now, upon the liquidation of the revolt, they did everything they could to prolong and renew the disorders. Looting, violence, and shooting continued here and there in the capital on Thursday the 6th too. . . There was still no 'pacification'. And all the excesses, now aimed *at the Left*, were inspired exclusively by the fragments of Tsarism.

The Soviet victors could rest content: once again the Coalition was set on firm foundations. Moreover, it looked as though the General Staff might at any time initiate a *coup d'état*.

However transitory, a great counter-revolutionary upheaval was nevertheless quite possible. But the Soviet authorities had not yet turned their gaze to the Right.

On the morning of that same day Gots and Avksentiev[1] had led a scratch detachment to Kshesinskaya's house and the Peter-Paul Fortress. The first point was the citadel of the Bolsheviks, and Kronstadters or other pernicious elements might still remain in the second. Crossing Trinity Bridge, they were about to begin a regular siege, and were ready to open fire when it turned out that the Bolsheviks had already abandoned Kshesinskaya's house. Bursting into the quiet, empty rooms, the soldiers arrested a dozen people who happened to be wandering around the rooms, and thus brought the expedition to a victorious conclusion. As for the Peter-Paul Fortress, there too there was nothing to justify the campaign. The Kronstadters had left, the garrison had lost its head and 'repented'; the Fortress was 'taken' without a shot, and order was restored without the slightest trouble.

The Durnovo villa was taken in the same fashion during the afternoon. The anarchists had left. A few weapons and a great deal of literature were found there.

The mood of the workers was indefinite. On the one hand only half the factories were working; the workers were still keeping up their previous positions by a strike. In particular the Putilov Factory was idle, and there were even some unimportant attempts to come out again into the streets in a demonstration. But, on the other hand, depression was taking more and more hold of the proletarian masses. Mass-meetings, which passed resolutions condemning the 'instigators' of the rebellion, were taking place in the factories. The advanced groups were isolated. The Petersburg proletariat was once more scattered and unfit for battle.

It was much worse among the soldiers. These ignorant masses, having received a stunning blow, flung themselves headlong into the arms of the Black Hundreds. Here all shades of reactionary agitation were already bearing rich, ripe fruit. Hundreds and thousands of yesterday's 'Bolsheviks' had been swept out of the

[1] Avksentiev, Nikolai Dmitriyevich (1878–1943): one of the oldest SR leaders. Very hostile to the October Revolution, he emigrated in 1919, and continued actively fighting the new Soviet régime. (Ed.)

reach of any Socialist parties whatever. And in the eyes of the garrison even the *Soviet* banner had definitely begun to waver. There were mass-meetings in the barracks too, where out-and-out pogrom speeches were beginning to be heard. The whole force of anger and 'patriotism' was of course coming down on the Bolsheviks. And the other Socialist elements as well were now definitely tacked on to the Bolsheviks.

As for the petty bourgeois, philistines, and 'intelligentsia'—there things were really abominable. These strata not only deliberately lumped together the Bolsheviks and the whole Soviet, but were also prepared to use any and every method of struggle against everything Soviet. Here feigned panic and unfeigned spite reached their extreme limits. A military dictatorship, perhaps even a restoration, would have been accepted, if not with enthusiasm at least without any attempts at resistance.

The word 'Bolshevik' had already become synonymous with scoundrel, murderer, Judas, and anybody else whom it was essential to seize, maul, and beat up. And to make it more vivid a charming phrase was coined in the twinkling of an eye and put into circulation: an 'ideational Bolshevik'. This was the unhappy creature who through *naïveté* and obtuseness had fallen from decent society into the clutches of a gang of bandits and deserved to be treated indulgently. But there were extremely few of these.

* * *

Around 9 o'clock on the evening of the 6th, Kerensky came back from the front and went straight to the session of the Provisional Government. At this time a formal decision had already been taken to put all instigators of and participants in the uprising of July 3rd–4th on trial. But although many hundreds of people had been arrested the Bolshevik leaders were still at large. . . On his arrival Kerensky immediately displayed great aggressiveness and demanded that decisive measures should be taken against the Bolsheviks, especially their leaders.

An order was at once issued for the immediate arrest of Lenin, Zinoviev, Kamenev, and others. Besides this an order was drawn up and signed by Lvov for the disbanding of all army units which had taken part in the revolt and their reassignment at the discretion of the Minister of War.

At about 2 in the morning the militia came to Lenin's flat, but it was empty. Lenin, like Zinoviev, had vanished.

Lenin's disappearance under the threat of arrest and trial is noteworthy in itself. No one in the Central Ex. Com. expected Lenin to 'get out of the situation' in just this way. His flight produced an enormous sensation amongst us and was hotly discussed for a long time in every possible aspect. There were some Bolsheviks who approved of Lenin's action, but the majority of the Soviet people were sharply against it. The Mamelukes and the Soviet leaders loudly boomed forth their noble indignation. The Opposition kept its opinion to itself. But this opinion reduced itself to a definite censure of Lenin—from a political and moral point of view. And I personally was completely in accord.

I've already said (in connexion with Lunacharsky) that—first of all—in the given circumstances the shepherd's flight could not help but be a heavy blow to the sheep. The masses mobilized by Lenin, after all, were bearing the whole burden of responsibility for the July Days. They had no means of ridding themselves of this burden. Some remained in their factories or in their districts—isolated, slandered, in sick depression and unspeakable confusion of mind. Others were under arrest and awaiting retribution for having done their political duty according to their feeble lights. And the 'real author' abandoned his army and his comrades, and sought personal salvation in flight!

Why was it necessary? Was he in any real danger? Absurd, in the summer of 1917! There could be no question of lynch-law, of the death penalty or of hard labour. However biased the court, however minimal the guarantees of justice—nevertheless Lenin risked absolutely nothing but imprisonment.

Lenin of course may have prized not his life or health, but his freedom of political action. But in a prison of the time could he have been more hampered than in his underground retreat? He could unquestionably have written his fortnightly *Pravda* articles from prison, while from the point of view of the political effect the very fact of Lenin's imprisonment would have had an enormous positive significance. His flight had only a negative one.

The example of Lenin's comrades completely confirms all this. Many of them were arrested and put on trial for the same crimes. They safely sat out six weeks or two months in prison and went on with their writing there. With their martyrs' haloes they served as an inexhaustible source of agitation against the Government of Kerensky and Tsereteli. And then, without the slightest evil consequences for anyone, they returned to their posts.

From a political and moral point of view the flight of Lenin and Zinoviev, devoid of any practical sense, was reprehensible. And I'm not surprised that this example was not followed by their own comrades.

But, as is well known, there was another circumstance that heightened the odium of Lenin's flight a thousandfold. For after all, besides the accusation of insurrection, a monstrous slander, which was believed by hundreds of thousands and millions of people, had been directed at Lenin. Lenin was accused of the crime, vile and shameful from every point of view, of being in the pay of the German General Staff. . . It was impossible *simply to ignore this*. And Lenin had not ignored it; he had sent Zinoviev to the Central Ex. Com. to defend his honour and his party. This was not at all difficult to do. After a little time had passed the nonsensical accusation went up like smoke. Nobody had adduced anything in its support and people ceased to believe it. There was no longer the slightest risk that any charge would be brought on this count. But Lenin *went into hiding* with *such* a charge hanging over him.

This was something quite special, unexampled, and incomprehensible. Any other mortal would have demanded an investigation and trial even in the most unfavourable conditions. Any other mortal would personally and publicly have done everything possible, as energetically as he could, to rehabilitate himself. But Lenin proposed that others, his adversaries, should do this, while he sought safety in flight.

I consider that the fact of Lenin's disappearance must lie at the very root of any description of the personality of the future ruler of Russia. In the whole world only he could have behaved thus.

* * *

That same night the session of the Provisional Government was succeeded by a meeting of the Soviet Star Chamber. Towards 2 o'clock in the morning Kerensky arrived at Skobelev's flat, where Tsereteli was living. Dan, Gots, and Chkheidze were also there. . . In the presence of the newly-arrived Kerensky the Star Chamber revised its judgement of the state of affairs.

The Right was evidently represented by Kerensky (probably together with Gots) and the Left by Dan and Chkheidze. The Right carried on the line of reaction and repression, the Left the line of restraining the repressions. Kerensky insisted on the liquidation of the Bolsheviks as a party. Dan insisted on the freedom of parties and on the responsibility of individuals. Tsereteli was in the centre. The result was that Dan was formally on top, but Kerensky was given satisfaction in fact.

* * *

Friday the 7th. Early in the morning the Menshevik Central Committee met. Dan and Tsereteli probably went there straight from the session of the Star Chamber. The Menshevik leaders were definitely beginning to display an understanding of the conjuncture: they continued a line of halting the counter-revolution. And by 7 in the morning the Menshevik Central Committee had already passed a resolution directed *against the Right.* I can say with assurance that Dan initiated it.

The Provisional Government, following the lead of the ruling Soviet bloc, also met very early, at about 8.30. I don't know whether it was a stormy session, but in any case it was 'dramatic': what was in question was forcing the resignation of the revolutionary Premier, that visionary intellectual and humane landowner, Prince Lvov.

The campaign had doubtless been prepared the night before, at Skobelev's flat. The 'Marxist' section of the ruling group had evidently managed to unite the entire Star Chamber.

Why had the SR part of the Star Chamber agreed to this? I think there is only one way to explain it: Kerensky was now convinced that it was time for him to become Chief of State. And for him concessions to the democracy, however undesirable and 'untimely' in themselves, were a means of exerting pressure on Lvov which the latter, God willing, would be unable to sustain. Thanks to this pressure from the Left, there must be new upheavals in the Cabinet, and then Kerensky could not fail to get the Premiership.

I even think it was precisely Kerensky, the SR, who was the direct or indirect *initiator* of the 'Left' campaign against Lvov. In Kerensky's present mood he was quite unconcerned with counter-revolution or the struggle against it. He was interested only in bringing about changes in the Government and setting up his *own* Cabinet. For the 'Star Chamber' Menshevik Dan, on the contrary, it was necessary to stop the reaction. As for changes in the Government, it was, after all, only two days earlier that Dan and Tsereteli together had wholeheartedly insisted, before the entire revolutionary democracy, on the lack of authority to decide these questions until a plenum of the Central Ex. Com. could meet, and on the maintenance of the *status quo* as the last word in statesmanship. And now, suddenly, the campaign against Lvov!

In any case, the Star Chamber SRs and the Mensheviks had arrived at the same 'platform' from different directions. The first wanted changes in the Cabinet, the others a strengthening of the Soviet 'line' against the counter-revolution. The result was the joint campaign to force the resignation of the head of the Government.

The session ended at about 1 o'clock. And it ended with the resignation of the first revolutionary 'Premier'. Lvov had announced his resignation. Now he had to be replaced. This was done without any delay or difficulty. I do not think I am mistaken if I say that during the night the Star Chamber had not only worked out its campaign but also redistributed the portfolios.

Lvov had occupied two posts: Premier and Minister of the Interior. Kerensky, while remaining War Minister, was 'appointed' to the first at once, and Heraklion Tsereteli, while remaining Minister of Posts and Telegraphs, to the second.

This was at 1 o'clock in the afternoon.

At 2 o'clock the Bureau slowly began to assemble in the Tauride Palace. But the leaders were not to be seen. The deputies dejectedly wandered about, argued lazily, or sat about in arm-chairs, hiding behind newspapers. God knew when the Praesidium would appear.

Just then it was reported that one of the units that had come from the front had been fired on by machine-guns not far from the Nicholas Station. The firing still continued; it could be heard from the windows of the Tauride Palace.

Eh! This was a serious business, and might end badly. This monstrous provocation could only be the work of German agents—to disorganize the Government in Petersburg in the interests of an offensive at the front; it might have been carried out by the Black Hundreds, the Tsarist servitors who were already convinced of the advantages of a street brawl, and who could not but be tempted by the possible results of a provocation of front-line troops. A direct attack on the pacifiers might really be a match thrown into the powder-keg. The pacifying troops might shatter working-class Petersburg to smithereens rather than entrust some upstart with power over them for five minutes. Nor was this an accidental shooting: it was a well-organized attack, complete with machine-guns.

The firing did not begin to die down until evening, and it was renewed during the night. The militia reported shooting in eleven different districts of Petersburg.

There is no doubt that on Friday the 7th we lived through a critical moment. The ordinary people, after all—the petty bourgeoisie, the 'intelligentsia', and the soldiery—were again blaming the Bolsheviks for the new bloodshed. The disorders on that day did an excellent service to the profound and thoroughgoing reaction. Nevertheless the acuteness of the crisis, and the danger of a counter-revolutionary catastrophe, vanished quite swiftly.

Around noon an important meeting of garrison representatives, arranged the night before, took place in the Tauride Palace. The delegates of the newly-arrived troops also came. The meeting was supposed to reveal the state of mind of the garrison of the capital after the July Days. Had the blow it had received really thrown it back into undisguisedly bourgeois hands?

I don't know just what happened at the meeting, but its results proved favourable enough. Both the speeches and the resolution showed that the garrison would do its best to keep its promise of loyalty to the Soviet. The resolution stated that the garrison 'submitted unconditionally to the Central Ex. Com. and would unquestioningly obey all its orders'. Even the Mamelukes sighed with relief.

* * *

The Bureau session probably began around 3 o'clock.

It was, of course, Tsereteli who reported on the situation. I shall not undertake to say just how he explained the change of front. Doubtless, while announcing the successful liquidation of the insurrection, he pointed out the danger of a reaction which went too far, and consequently the necessity for resolutely carrying out the programme of the All-Russian Congress, for Lvov's resignation, and for the formation of a new Cabinet—temporarily, of course, until a decision could be reached by a plenum of the Central Ex. Com. Tsereteli also named the new Ministers. I remember his being unable to keep back the embarrassed smile of a schoolboy who has distinguished himself, when he said: 'Minister of the Interior—Tsereteli. . .'

Properly speaking, nothing particularly bad had happened in reality. But *how* it had all happened! A tiny handful of people had been whirled about by the irresistible caprice of the revolution, flung now to one side, then to the other. It was not only the masses who had had no part in their machinations, but even their 'authorized representatives', who had handed over to the Star Chamber all their rights and duties, were obedient, silent servants of their masters. This was a sign of the profound weakness of the revolution, and the source of a profound reaction. It was a depressing picture.

But it was interesting to look into the real nature of the affair too. Kerensky's new Cabinet was, after all, a *Soviet* Government. At its head was a member of the Central Ex. Com. Socialist Ministers formed its most important kernel. They not only *could* shape, but in fact did shape the whole Government as they saw fit. They announced that the Government was to act in accordance with the instructions of the Congress of Soviets. They also formally and in practice acknowledged the Congress and the Central Ex. Com. as the sole sources of power. Indeed, there were now no others at all. If one adds to this that the real power and authority were as before in their hands and in their hands alone, then the situation would seem to be clear: no matter how the Soviet leaders had refused power before, now they had formally received it.

So it seemed. At the same time another side of the matter was also plain. The new Chief of State, a member of the Central Ex. Com., the Soviet protégé Kerensky—would not have anything to do with any Soviet. He had become Chief of State not as a representative of the organized democracy, but by himself, seeing himself as a being above class who had been called, and was able, to save Russia. And Kerensky, together with his 'Soviet' colleagues, was of course using his newly acquired rights primarily in order to return the bourgeoisie to power formally and in fact. This 'Soviet' Government would of course make its chief concern the creation of a new Coalition against the revolution. It was a depressing picture.

* * *

In the heat of the debates there was a sudden commotion and tumult. The stunning news flew round the room like lightning. It was the news of the defeat at the front of the attacking Russian army. On the preceding day, the 6th, our lines had been pierced on a front of twelve versts near Tarnopol to a depth of ten versts. The enemy was continuing his advance.

No well-informed person had had any doubt that our offensive was not only bound to collapse in the immediate future, but might end in a tremendous disaster. There were many army people amongst the Right Soviet deputies who had scented the truth from the very beginning. But none of them had wanted to display anything but patriotic enthusiasm. And now the news of the rout hit the whole Tauride Palace like a thunderbolt.

It was as patriots that the Mamelukes were shaken, but the Opposition was well aware that a defeat at the front would free the hands of internal reaction still more. After all, no matter how well aware Kerensky was that a wretched ending to his enterprise was inevitable, he blamed the *Bolsheviks* and the July uprising for it, both to himself and aloud. Of the Mamelukes, the yellow press, and the petty-bourgeois mass, there is no need to speak. For them the Tarnopol defeat and the collapse of the whole longed-for offensive was the work of Bolshevik hands from beginning to end. And indeed, in the official communiqués from Headquarters Bolshevik agitation was directly blamed for the defeat.

There was consternation in the Central Ex. Com. Even the most honest Right-wing deputies, on hearing of the collapse of the front, turned their thoughts and glances primarily on these same Bolsheviks. The less honest ones, greatly exaggerating the danger of the position, definitely hinted that there was now no reason to object to a rightful settling of accounts with the traitors.

* * *

Towards evening a joint session of the Central Ex. Com. and the Peasants' Central Ex. Com. was held. It was expected to listen once more to the same old speeches on the subject of the Government. But first it had to concern itself with other things. During all this time arrests had been going on in the city as before, and the prisons were being filled to overflowing. In the working-class quarters the proletarian detachments and individual workers were being disarmed. It was not only the spontaneous reaction of the masses that was in full swing, but a governmental and police reaction as well.

The Menshevik-Internationalists did everything in their power to fight it. Before the Central Ex. Com. got to the fundamental item on the agenda, the Government, Martov asked for the floor for an 'emergency statement', and made a short speech protesting against the arrests. A statement over our signatures was later published in the papers. Just now it would have been possible not to answer an 'emergency statement', but nevertheless the brave Tsereteli spoke in reply. He said what he had said many times before. Why did these second-class Bolsheviks exist at all, when there were first-class ones? He, Tsereteli, preferred to have to do with Lenin rather than Martov. With the former he knew how to deal, but the latter tied his hands. As for the repressions and arrests, they were called for by necessities of state and the interests of the revolution. 'Irresponsible groups' ought to hold their tongues.

'I take the responsibility for these arrests,' said the new Minister of the Interior, clearly and distinctly, amidst the silence.

Indeed, Citizen Tsereteli? You're very bold. You're sowing excellent seeds. What will you reap?

* * *

Once again on a sunny morning, around 6 o'clock, I left the Tauride Palace and went off to Manukhin's to spend the 'night'. As usual, they had been expecting me since the evening. A bed had been made up for me on the sofa in the study. And Lunacharsky, stretched out on his arm-chairs next to it, was sleeping the blameless sleep of youth. He hadn't turned up that day in the Tauride Palace, and it seemed as though I hadn't seen him for a long time.

My coming in woke him up; he asked where I'd come from. Full of despair and rage I congratulated him on the new Coalition and told him of the events of the last day. We talked over the whole of the July Days, united by our awareness of the catastrophe and hatred of the victors. Both of us forgot about the 'authors' of the defeat, in our preoccupation with the general calamity. And then Lunacharsky told me the unknown details of the July uprising. They were unexpected.

According to him, on the night of July 4th Lenin was definitely planning a *coup d'état*. The Government, which would in fact be in the hands of the Bolshevik Central Committee, would officially be embodied in a 'Soviet' Cabinet made up of eminent and popular Bolsheviks. For the time being three Ministers had been appointed: Lenin, Trotsky, and Lunacharsky. This Government would at once issue decrees about peace and land, thus attracting the sympathies of the millions of the capital and the provinces and consolidating its power. An agreement of this kind had been come to between Lenin, Trotsky, and Lunacharsky. It was concluded while the Kronstadters were making their way from Kshesinskaya's house to the Tauride Palace. The *coup d'état* itself was to proceed in this way: the 176th Regiment (the same one Dan had posted on guard in the Tauride Palace), arriving from Krasnoe Selo, was to arrest the Central Ex. Com., and at about that time Lenin was to arrive on the scene of action and proclaim the new Government. But Lenin was too late. The 176th Regiment was intercepted and became disorganized. The 'rising' had failed.

This is what Lunacharsky told me—that is, this is the form I remember it in, and in this form I pass it on to anyone into whose hands this book happens to fall. It may be that the content of this story is not a fully-established historical fact. I may have forgotten, confused, or distorted the story. Lunacharsky may have been 'poeticizing', confusing, and distorting the reality. But the precise establishment of an historical fact is the business of historians, and I'm writing my personal memoirs; I pass this on as I recall it. . .

How things were in reality I will not undertake to say. I didn't investigate the matter. Only once, much later, I asked another candidate for the triumvirate—Trotsky—about it. He strongly objected when I gave him Lunacharsky's version. Among other things he brushed aside Lunacharsky as a person completely unsuited for this kind of action.

'The belletristic side of the plot,' Martov said later, when I reported my conversation with Lunacharsky. So be it. But if the Bolshevik Central Committee, in organizing the *coup d'état*, had provided for the creation of a centre to direct the fighting and take the first steps, that centre could really only have been the triumvirate—Lenin, Trotsky, and Lunacharsky.

But none of this proves in any way that on July 4th Lenin was definitely and directly aiming at a *coup d'état*, that he had already distributed the portfolios, or that it was only because he came too late that he did not command the 176th Regiment! Some elementary facts tell against Lunacharsky's version. For instance, the Kronstadters were present in addition to the 176th Regiment. They undoubtedly constituted the principal—not only technical but you might say political—force. And on July 4th at 5 in the afternoon, the 'triumvir' Trotsky stood face to face with them. What did he do? At the risk of losing his popularity, if not his head, he freed Chernov, whereas by putting the conspiracy into effect he could have stood at the head of the Kronstadters and, to their utter joy, liquidated the Central Ex. Com. in five minutes.

Besides, Trotsky later arranged, so to speak, a confrontation with Lunacharsky, addressing a puzzled question to him. Lunacharsky said that I had mixed up and distorted my conversation with him. I'm inclined to maintain that I remember the conversation well, and that Lunacharsky had mixed up the events. But let industrious historians sort it all out.[1] If in the preceding

[1] As a result of Trotsky's inquiry, Lunacharsky sent me a letter, maintaining that I had distorted his story. But I can't give his second version *instead of* the first. The principle I'm adhering to in these Notes is to write down everything I recall *as* I recall it. This does not become a historian; Lunacharsky is right there. But I'm not writing a history. All I can do to 're-establish the truth' is to print his letter of March 30th, 1920. I do this gladly.

'Dear Nikolai Nikolayevich,

'Yesterday I received from Comrade Trotsky the following note: "N. N. Sukhanov has told me that in his book on the revolution there is an account of the

pages I have not described historical *events*, then perhaps this page may serve as a description of historical *personages*.

At that time, in the early morning of July 8th, lying on my sofa, I listened to Lunacharsky's account in utter dejection. The devilish grimacing mask of the July Days, looming over me like a nightmare, passed before my eyes. So then, there had been not only the spontaneous course of events but a malevolent political blunder.

'Peaceful demonstration' and—distribution of portfolios. 'Down with the Capitalist Ministers' and—an attack on the Socialist Ministers. 'All Power to the Soviets' and—the arrest of the supreme Soviet body. And as the result blood, filth, and the triumph of reaction. . .

At that moment, while Lunacharsky and I were talking about the days that had just passed, in the Palace Square the disarming and vilifying of the 'insurgent' Bolshevik army was proceeding.

It was already about 8 o'clock. Lunacharsky began dressing and left me alone.

* * *

July Days in which he relates, in your words, that in July the three of us (Lenin, you and myself) wanted to seize power and set about doing so!?!?!?"

'It is clear, Nikolai Nikolayevich, that you have fallen into a profound error, which may have disagreeable consequences for you as well as for the historian. In general reference to personal conversations is bad documentation. In this instance, if you've really written something of the kind, your memory has completely distorted our conversation. It never, of course, occurred to Comrade Lenin, Comrade Trotsky, or myself to agree on the seizure of power, nor was there even a hint of anything in the nature of a triumvirate.

'In the minds of all the leaders of the movement the July Days had only the meaning we put forward with complete frankness: "All power to the Soviet of Workers', Soldiers', and Peasants' Deputies."

'Of course we did not conceal from ourselves that if the Menshevik–SR Soviet had seized the power, it would have slipped away to more resolute revolutionary groups further to the Left.

'Your error was probably caused by my telling you that at a decisive moment of the July Days, I told Trotsky in conversation that I should consider it calamitous for us to be in power just then, to which Comrade Trotsky, who was always far more resolute than I and surer of victory, replied that in his opinion that would not have been so bad at all, since the masses would of course have supported us.

'All this was said merely by way of weighing up the situation in a private conversation at a flaming moment in history.

'I beg you to take this letter of mine into account in the final version of your history, so that you yourself do not fall into error or lead others into it.

'People's Commissar

'(signed) A. LUNACHARSKY

'30-III-1920'

Yes, the reaction was triumphant. Everything gained by the revolution in the past months had gone to rack and ruin.

Before the July Days the Coalition with the bourgeoisie had been shaken, and had crumbled of itself. The spontaneous course of events led immutably to the liquidation of the ruling bourgeois bloc and to the dictatorship of the authentic worker-peasant democracy. The conquest of the Soviets by this authentic democracy was a matter of the immediate future. And the end of the reign of the bourgeoisie was bound to come in conditions that favoured the further course of the revolution while preserving its enormous and still fresh energies.

But a 'political blunder' intervened—naturally, a 'logical' one. The Coalition was on firm ground again and strengthened for a long time. The vast energies of the revolution had been squandered in vain and cast to the winds. The revolution had suffered a profound strain and been flung a long way back.

March–December 1920.

Part V

[COUNTER-REVOLUTION AND THE DISSOLUTION OF THE DEMOCRACY]

July 8th–October 20th

CHAPTER 21

[AFTER 'JULY': THE SECOND AND THIRD COALITIONS]

HEROES have indeed their destiny! For Kerensky democracy was an absolute good; he sincerely saw it as the goal of his service to the revolution. He had selflessly served it under the Tsarist autocracy, ever since he had appeared before the world as the ardent champion and, if you like, the *poet* of the democracy.

Now, after the July Days, Kerensky had become the head of the Government and the State. And this epoch—the Kerensky epoch—was an epoch of *dissolution, stifling, and destruction of the democracy*. Of this epoch Kerensky was the most active and responsible hero.

His premiership began in an evil hour and ended badly. It began under the sign of the birth-pangs of counter-revolution and its attacks on the democracy. These attempts failed: the revolution still retained too much accumulated strength and the plutocracy lacked everything but rage, slanders, and the miserable shattered remnants of Tsarism. The counter-revolution failed in the July riots, but a firm, stubborn, and profound reaction set in.

There had been this reaction before, at the beginning of the First Coalition; now, under Kerensky, the reaction became dynamic. Before, the reactionary classes had been defending themselves; now the bourgeois bloc had passed to the offensive. Before the July Days the reaction expressed itself in random sabotage; now, under Premier Kerensky, the *active* liquidation of the achievements of the workers and peasants began.

* * *

The Second Coalition, created on July 7th under Kerensky's leadership, didn't last long—a fortnight in all. This term was quite inadequate either to 'save' or to destroy the revolution, but quite enough to reveal itself properly.

This was done with complete success.

First of all the new Government energetically continued the searches, arrests, disarmings, and persecutions of all kinds that had already been begun. Self-appointed groups of officers, military cadets, and I think the gilded youth too, rushed to the 'help' of the new régime, which was obviously trying to present itself as a 'strong Government'. It was not only the mutinous regiments and battalions that were disarmed: almost more attention was devoted to the working-class districts, where the workers' Red Guard was disarmed. Enormous quantities of arms were collected.

Every Bolshevik that could be found was seized and imprisoned. Kerensky and his military friends were definitely trying to wipe them off the face of the earth, but the Soviet restrained the patriotic enthusiasm of the victors, and an attempt at the formal outlawing of Bolshevism as such was a failure. Repressions, however, came directly down only on the Bolshevik 'officer-corps' and rank-and-file. I think only Kamenev, of the *generals*, was arrested during the July Days; then a few days later, on her way back from Stockholm, Kolontai was arrested at the border—naturally with 'important documents' on her; finally the same fate overtook Roshal. Lenin and Zinoviev had officially, so to speak, gone into hiding. Trotsky, Stalin, Stasova, and many others meanwhile avoided spending nights at home and their whereabouts were 'unknown'. Raskolnikov was staying in Kronstadt, under the protection of his own army. But it must be said that the police apparatus of this Government of the revolution, even though it was being restored, was still very weak; the authorities simply did not know the secondary Bolshevik leaders, whose names did not appear in the newspapers.

In one way or another all the Bolshevik leaders temporarily vanished from the horizon after the July Days. Lunacharsky and Ryazanov remained, and in addition Nogin, one of the most important figures of the Moscow Soviet, and one of the oldest Bolsheviks—rather negligible, however, in substance—was sent from Moscow as a representative on the Central Committee. At this time Steklov was disavowing the Bolsheviks right and left, paying vigorous court to us, the Menshevik-Internationalists, and trying to persuade us, in view of the rout of Bolshevism, to unite with its remnants and take over the leadership of the extreme Left. But Steklov's diplomacy was inadequate.

Nor was Steklov himself helped by his equivocations. On the night of July 10th, when a high-spirited detachment of military cadets was looking for Lenin at Bonch's Finnish villa, they didn't find Lenin, but were satisfied with another toothsome morsel in the person of the famous Steklov, who was taken by a reinforced guard directly to the General Staff in Petersburg. Since he had 'absolutely nothing in common with the Bolsheviks', he was quickly let go. But he didn't go home. Many days later he could be seen wandering about like a shadow in his Tauride sanctuary at the most unseasonable hours, replying to astonished questions: 'I'm not budging from here night or day. They'll kill me. You know what there is against me.'

But the military cadets didn't hunt down only Steklov, who had 'nothing in common with Bolshevism'. After destroying the Bolshevik organizations, which were legal, they went further and executed a raid on the Government Mensheviks themselves, whose party was headed by the Minister of the Interior. Was this excessive? But it was completely compatible with the 'general mood', and especially with the line of the bourgeois press. This press evidently considered that the Bolsheviks were done for; and after despatching the humiliated, fallen, and despised enemy, the Cadet *Rech* and its gutter-press imitators began striking out more and more Rightwards: at Chernov, Tsereteli, the Mensheviks and SRs, and at the Soviet generally. This was inevitable, quite consistent, and far-sighted. In the interests of the bourgeois dictatorship that had become so imminent and possible, it was precisely the *Soviets* that must be wiped off the face of the earth. For after all, from the point of view of the plutocracy, they were just what constituted the original sin of the revolution, the source of 'dual power' and the root of evil. The campaign had begun to develop quite openly.

* * *

Now the question that naturally and inevitably arose was that of a *dictatorship*. Indeed, three days after Kerensky's 'appointment' as Premier, the Star Chamber appeared before the Central Ex. Com. with a demand for a dictatorship.

The groundwork was thoroughly prepared. For after the July Days the reaction and despondency of the masses of the people were enormous. They had penetrated deep into the vanguard itself, the most reliable prop of the revolution—the thick of the Petersburg workers. During the July Days themselves we had already seen some factory resolutions against the Bolsheviks. That was a shock. Now it was worse. A whole series of factories, dissociating themselves from the Bolsheviks and following the army units, ardently supported a new Coalition.

We had been thrown a long way back. The enormous store of revolutionary energy had been scattered to the winds. The masses were humbled and enfeebled. The bourgeoisie had plucked up heart and was eager for battle. The atmosphere of deep and lasting reaction could be plainly felt by everyone. The ground was favourable for a real dictatorship.

The entire period of the Second Coalition was spent in an uninterrupted, frenzied, self-forgetting *hunt by Kerensky and Tsereteli for new bourgeois Ministers.*

The Second Coalition had organized itself 'on its own authority', but it was incomplete; there were some Ministerial vacancies. After the July blow, Kerensky, having become head of the Cabinet, with quite childish enthusiasm set about forming 'his own' Government. Swiftly losing all sense of proportion, he began displaying his capriciousness in these operations. Without waiting for any 'authority' from the Central Ex. Com. he started looking for 'supplementary' lieutenants and colleagues immediately after July 7th. And when the Central Ex. Com. formally untied his hands he had already set himself the straightforward goal of forming a completely new cabinet—the Third Coalition—to his own taste.

By the 23rd a Cabinet was ready. Kerensky had left himself the Army and Navy Departments, and named as his deputies for naval and military affairs Savinkov[1] and Lebedev, both SRs, but especially offensive to the democracy. Nekrasov, Deputy Chairman in the Council of Ministers, was given Finance. Tereshchenko, Skobelev, and Peshekhonov stayed where they

[1] Savinkov, Boris Viktorovich (1879–1925): famous SR terrorist and writer. After the October Revolution worked against the Soviet Government; caught by GPU on secret trip to Russia, tried and sentenced to gaol for ten years, where he died. Winston Churchill thought him one of the most extraordinary men he had ever met. (Ed.)

were. Yefremov got Public Welfare, Prokopovich Industry and Commerce, and Avksentiev Internal Affairs. The Minister of Justice was now Zarudny, a non-party radical and a personal friend of Kerensky's. Nikitin, a lawyer who was considered a Social-Democrat but was actually no nearer to being one than Prokopovich, was summoned from Moscow for Posts and Telegraphs. Then there came four longed-for Cadets: Kokoshkin—Comptroller of Finances, Kartashev—Procurator of the Holy Synod, Yurenev—Communications, and Oldenburg—Education. And to crown it all—the Zimmerwaldite and defeatist Chernov.

Such was the Third Coalition. *It did not publish the briefest programme* or declaration.

* * *

On the night of July 22nd, in the very heat of the shuffling of portfolios, Trotsky and Lunacharsky, accused of the July uprising, were arrested at home.

* * *

For the first time I tore myself away from the centre, away from the inferno. I had not yet seen the New Russia. And as a matter of fact I was not to see it during my 'furlough'. I stayed in the country near Yaroslavl, giving myself over to literature, sun, and sloth. My impressions of the province were casual and meagre. I visited, in the Governor's house on the banks of the Volga, the local Soviet—which was in the hands of the Mensheviks. I did not attend any meetings, nor did I see the masses. But I was at the Ex. Com., in the centre, the laboratory, and with my own eyes witnessed the provincial scarcity of workers and the extraordinary concentration of party-functions in the hands of two or three men. It was clear that if you took them out of the city, all the activity of the Soviet would die away, agitation would cease, the Soviet would close down, and candidates for the Town Council and the Constituent Assembly would vanish. Meanwhile all local power was in the hands of the Soviet, without which the provincial commissar and all the other official authorities would have been mere puppets.

Generally speaking, the July disturbance had touched the provinces very little. Its echoes were to be found in the psychology of the *leaders*; the masses, who had not seen with their own eyes what had happened, reacted feebly. Here the 'normal' process of the conquest of the masses by the Bolsheviks still went on.

More particularly I, as an inhabitant of the capital, was astonished at the extensive street life of the ordinary people: in this respect the capital had long since shrunk and in its 'July' atmosphere begun to resemble old Petersburg. In Yaroslavl my eye was gladdened by free demonstrations of workers, 'prohibited' among us and obsolete.

A provincial Menshevik conference took place there around then. It was a rather pitiful spectacle. The handful of people who had convened displayed an extremely low level of political and party consciousness. Among other things the local leaders were incapable of distinguishing between the official Mensheviks and the Menshevik-Internationalists. Dan was easily distinguished from Lenin, but not from Martov. This seemed rather strange to me: I thought that—if not theoretically, then *historically*, *practically*—it was easier for them to confuse Martov with Lenin than with Dan (as all the bourgeoisie did). But no, it was evident that it was the word Menshevik as distinct from Bolshevik that had the decisive significance here. They knew the *word* quite well, but were unprepared for a deepening of the concept and had no interest in it.

This was a surprise to me. And I may say I was at my wit's end when I thought about a Menshevik *schism*, which in the capital appeared to me inevitable and indispensable. It was clear that for these provincials a schism at this moment would have been incomprehensible, indigestible. And consequently unrealizable. After my return to Petersburg I told Martov all this—to his great satisfaction.

* * *

The July events had destroyed Bolshevism. But a month passed and the joint labours of Kerensky and Tsereteli revived it again. Recuperating from the rout themselves, the masses poured life and vigour into the Bolshevik Party. They grew together with it: it grew together with them.

By the end of July a new Bolshevik congress had met. It was already a 'united' conference where the party of Lenin, Zinoviev,

KERENSKY ARRIVING IN MOSCOW FOR THE STATE CONFERENCE

LENIN SPEAKS TO 'THE PEOPLE'

and Kamenev formally coalesced with the group of Trotsky, Lunacharsky, and Uritsky. The leaders couldn't attend—they could only inspire the congress from afar. But somehow things were managed even without them.

At this congress the Bolsheviks put their post-July ideology in order. Its general framework, of course, remained as before, but the Bolshevik fighting slogans underwent some characteristic changes. 'All Power to the Soviets' was discarded. This slogan, which before 'July' the masses had become used to and regarded as their *own*, was replaced by one more diffuse and less refined: 'A Revolutionary Dictatorship of the Workers and Peasants', etc. . . The reason for this was twofold. First of all, 'All Power to the Soviets' had become very shabby in the July events; secondly, the contradiction between this slogan and the unavoidable *de facto* struggle against the existing Soviets had become too flagrant. The 'Soviets', after all, in the form of the Central Ex. Com., had definitely embarked on the support of the counter-revolution. It was not worth while to demand power for *such* Soviets.

A characteristic fact, almost the only one of its kind: Martov's fraction addressed a welcome to this Bolshevik Congress which underlined our differences (Bolshevik anarcho-Blanquism), but expressed our solidarity in the struggle against the Coalition and a protest against the persecution of the party of the proletariat.

I've already mentioned that the defeat of Bolshevism in July affected mainly the capital, touching the provinces very little. The provincial delegates to the Congress, by their accounts of continuing successes, poured a great deal of energy and good cheer into the party, which again reckoned up its assets and was once more ready to develop the struggle to its full extent. Its seeds must have fallen on excellent soil. And the work amongst the masses was already proceeding at full speed.

The results of this work were soon made known within the Petersburg Soviet, too, where now only the secondary Bolshevik leaders were active—Volodarsky,[1] Kurayev, Fedorov, and others. *The Workers' Section* of the Soviet set up its own

[1] Volodarsky (Goldstein), Moisei Markovich (1891–1918): a revolutionary from the age of fourteen. Lived in USA (1913–1917) where he was a member of the American Socialist Party. (Ed.)

Praesidium, which it hadn't had before. And this Praesidium proved to be Bolshevik—headed by Fedorov. Actually, the composition of the section remained as before—that is, it had an enormous majority of deputies elected under the Bolshevik banner. But we have seen the great depression and instability in the behaviour of the Workers' Section after the July Days. One might have thought that the Bolshevik fraction was routed and disorganized and that its members had betrayed the party. But in the last analysis that had not happened. The election of the Praesidium put the leadership of the section into firm Bolshevik hands.

Finally, on August 7th, the second Conference of Factory Committees opened in Smolny. It wasn't as showy and noisy as the first one in May. Its scope was substantially less. Its formulation of questions was more modest, more businesslike, less politico-demagogic. This was a tribute to the defeat that had compelled insurgents and utopians to shrink into themselves. But again the *composition* of the conference was Bolshevik. Once again the leadership was completely in the hands of Lenin's party.

In general, towards the date of the Moscow Conference, a little over a month after the July Days, it was already quite clear that the movement of the popular masses had resumed its former course. The Third Coalition, like the one before it, was hanging in the air. The Menshevik–SR Soviet was being followed by quite compact groups of burgherdom, but not by the masses of the workers and soldiers. The rank-and-file of the people as before were turning their eyes to the Bolsheviks alone—while Tsereteli and his friends came before bourgeois-landlord Russia and proletarian Europe in the name of 'the whole democracy'.

CHAPTER 22

THE SCANDAL IN MOSCOW

FROM the beginning of August the whole bourgeoisie and the 'whole democracy' were preparing for the sensational 'State Conference'. But no one could tell why this strange and unwieldy affair was undertaken just then. The press was strenuously trying to make the man in the street take an interest in this enterprise—not without success. The man in the street, like everyone else, saw that something was decidedly out of tune in our revolution. No matter what they tried in the Marian and Winter Palaces—still nothing happened. Well, maybe the Moscow Conference would 'produce' something.

Before the Central Ex. Com. delegation actually left for Moscow the news came out that Savinkov, Kerensky's deputy in charge of the War Department, had resigned. Savinkov was hand in glove with Kornilov: together they had just handed Kerensky a report demanding that the army committees be dissolved and capital punishment be introduced at the rear. Kerensky was vacillating between Headquarters and the Star Chamber, which didn't agree and was exerting pressure through the SR Central Committee. Hence Kornilov decided to go his own way, and Savinkov resigned. But the resignation wasn't serious; it was simply a household mutiny, for Savinkov, after all, was Kornilov's *alter ego*, and was not a Cadet but his own man—a Socialist Minister and famous SR terrorist.

On the evening of the 11th I left the Yaroslavl countryside for Moscow. I got into a train at one of the stations *before* Yaroslavl, but the train was already overflowing, and in all classes you had to stand up all night. In Yaroslavl, by using my title of Central Ex. Com. member, I penetrated into an almost empty military carriage. I was delighted at my success, but something rather disagreeable happened as a result. I was naïve enough to remove my boots, which were gone when I happened to wake up an hour or two later. The extraordinary stupidity of my situation prevented me from going to sleep again.

In Moscow, astounding the crowd with my stockinged feet, I made my way to the station-master and spent about two hours telephoning to people at random, to see whether some friend could bring a pair of boots to the station for me. This was all quite typical of travelling at this time.

I finally found someone with a spare pair of boots. But bringing them proved to be more difficult than could have been expected. The trams in Moscow had stopped, and there were almost no drozhky-drivers in the streets either. There was a strike, not a general one, but very impressive and sufficient to manifest the will of the masses. A number of factories and works were on strike, as was every municipal undertaking except those satisfying the daily needs of the population. Restaurants, waiters, and even half the drozhky-drivers were on strike. This whole working-class army was following the Bolsheviks *against its own Soviet*! Towards evening the demonstration would become still more perceptible: Moscow was to be submerged in darkness, since the gas works was also on strike.

In somebody else's enormous boots I set out on foot to look for the Soviet delegation. *En route* I dropped into the journalists' office (somewhere near the post-office), to see the *Novaya Zhizn* correspondent assigned to the Conference. The journalists' office was a tower of babel: whole crowds of them were struggling, each one against all the others, for a place at the Conference. The hubbub, excitement, and play of passions attained absolutely extraordinary limits. In this street it was a real holiday and a great day. And this one picture of frenzied reporters was enough to define the historical importance of the Moscow State Conference. A good two-thirds of its weight, after all, depended on the journalists' interest in it.

The magnificent hall of the Bolshoi Theatre was glittering with all its lights. From top to bottom it was filled with a triumphal and even brilliant crowd. Oh, here in truth was all the flower of Russian society! Only a few accidental unfortunates were missing from among the big and little political 'names'. Keeping guard around the theatre was a dense column of military cadets—Kerensky's only reliable force. A niggling control-system stopped one at every step inside the theatre too. Nevertheless, going into the stalls, I could scarcely make my way to my seat through the dense throng of supers crowding round the doors. . .

I was late for the opening. But even before catching sight of Kerensky, I heard him emotionally holding forth on the high notes in his first speech for the Provisional Government.

I shall not, of course, follow the course of this 'State Conference'. It was foredoomed to contribute nothing whatever to the formation of a Government: the Government had already been formed, everyone was content with it, and nothing more was asked. Nor was the Conference supposed to replace a parliament. Why should it? Kerensky and his colleagues, after all, were responsible only to their own consciences. To discover and say something new about 'the needs of the country'? Come now, this was, after all, a time of the flowering of a thousand-voiced press, which it was clearly unthinkable to surpass. Only one thing was left: to crush the opinion of the 'whole democracy' by means of the opinion of the 'whole country'—for the sake of a definitive and complete liberation of the 'all-national Government' from the tutelage of all the workers', peasants', Zimmerwaldite, half-German, half-Jewish, hooligan organizations. To compel the Soviets to efface themselves once and for all before the overwhelming majority of the rest of the populace, which demanded an 'all-national' policy. And perhaps at the same time to enforce silence on the handful of upstarts on the Right, who were shouting too immoderately about General Fist as the sole recourse. It was all bizarrely trivial and naïve, but I could find no other explanation in history for this stupidity.

CHAPTER 23

THE UNITED BOURGEOISIE DEMONSTRATES

ELECTIONS for the central Petersburg Town Council were scheduled for Sunday, August 20th. Up to then our 'commune' had been composed provisionally of the delegations of the district councils elected in May. Now its final composition was to be determined by city-wide direct elections.

All the parties naturally ascribed enormous importance to these elections. No one knew what turn the revolution would take. And circumstances might arise in which the capital's 'commune' might play a decisive rôle, as in the time of Robespierre. But at the same time indications of the fatigue and apathy of the masses of the people came from everywhere; many abstentions were expected. The Right Soviet elements and newspapers pointed this out with especial frequency.

And in some strange inscrutable way the conclusion they drew from it was that in such conditions it was impossible to disown the Coalition or struggle against it; in such circumstances nothing was left but to support it. Wouldn't one have thought the contrary? Fatigue, disillusionment, depression, had been engendered, after all, precisely by the Coalition policy, that had brought the revolution into an impassable bog. One would have thought that the end of the Coalition would mean a renaissance, towards which no other paths even existed. But no, burgherdom and the Mamelukes reasoned otherwise.

In any case all the parties had long been frenziedly preparing for the elections.

The Mensheviks had a single list of candidates. And it was entirely *internationalist*. On the eve of the election Larin proposed that we should all go to various parts of the city to do some electoral campaigning for the Menshevik ticket. I personally was assigned to two places: first to the proletarian Vyborg Side, then to the bourgeois Mokhovoy. I was to speak at one SR and one Cadet meeting. Influenced by the talk about apathy I was in a rather slack mood. And as a matter of fact, in spite of the animation of the dusty 'democratic' streets of the Vyborg Side, I found in the meeting-hall a boring little group of workers sleepily listening to an SR speaker. It would have been tiresome and futile to speak. I thought the bourgeoisie would be mobilizing far more energetically. But when I arrived at the Tenishevsky School, I looked in vain for the meeting scheduled there. It evidently was not taking place at all. Unbearably fatigued I glumly wandered back to the newspaper offices.

The election results, however, were unexpected. The voters were fed up with meetings, but that did not mean at all that they were neglecting their civic duties. In all 549,400 votes were cast on August 20th. There is no doubt that the *overwhelming majority* turned out to the poll.

But it was not the *activity* of the masses that was the chief blow; that was still to come. The SRs kept the first place with 37 per cent of the votes; in comparison with the May elections, however, this was no victory but a substantial setback. The victors of July, the Cadets, had also held their ground since the district elections: they got one-fifth of all the votes. Our Menshevik list got a wretched 23,000 votes. The others simply did not come into the reckoning.

But who was the sole real victor? It was the Bolsheviks, so recently trampled into the mud, accused of treason and venality, utterly routed morally and materially, and filling till that very day the prisons of the capital. Why, one would have thought them annihilated for ever. People had almost ceased to notice them. Then where had they sprung up from again? What sort of strange, diabolical enchantment was this?

In the August elections in the capital the Bolsheviks got just short of 200,000 votes, i.e., 33 per cent. A third of Petersburg. Once again the whole proletariat of the capital, the lord of the revolution! Citizens Tsereteli and Chkheidze, leaders of the all-powerful organ, orators of the whole democracy—*now* do you see the Bolsheviks? *Now* do you understand?

No! *Still* they see nothing, *still* they don't understand what is going on around them. . .

* * *

Miliukov, Rodzianko, and Kornilov—they saw and understood something. In any case their press was stunned by the success of the Bolsheviks. And these gallant heroes of the revolution began, at express speed, though in secret, to prepare their own 'demonstration'. To cover it up they began shouting loudly that the Bolsheviks were on the point of 'demonstrating'. Sometimes, it is true, their tongues slipped. For instance, the respectable Cadet *Rech*, in response to the hearty tone of the Kronstadt Soviet newspaper, in an uncharacteristic colloquial style, snapped back with two excellent Russian proverbs: 'the birdie sang before the cat sprang', and 'he laughs best who laughs last'.

The cat about to spring was preparing to have a good last laugh. But this couldn't be said to be so very easy. A plot was hatched by some monarchist elements, with the participation of the Romanov Grand Dukes, in the middle of August, but it was discovered in time and the participants were arrested together with the Romanovs. The bourgeois press, for its own reasons, didn't make anything very sensational of this plot. But the masters of this press had been warned, nevertheless, that you can't take a republic with your bare hands, and that they must make solider preparations. But this slight warning had no effect on the sleepy, half-disorganized 'national' Central Ex. Com. . .

* * *

Around then I glanced into Smolny Institute, the school for daughters of the nobility, which the Central Ex. Com. had started moving into on July 18th, the same day the Provisional Government moved to the Winter Palace and the Premier took up residence there. I wanted to see what was going on in the new quarters of the 'all-powerful organ'. But I received little satisfaction and still less benefit. I did not like Smolny at all, and never ceased to regret the loss of the Tauride. This famous place was located on the outskirts of the capital and consumed an enormous amount of everyone's time in getting back and forth. It was all right to keep 'young gentlewomen' in, but not for making a revolution with the proletariat and garrison of the capital. But I don't know whether the young ladies and the children liked it there, either. There were, to be sure, magnificent architectural monuments nearby, especially the monastery: I remember gasping and standing stockstill on seeing it for the first time. Smolny also had a remarkable, divinely clean, harmoniously finished assembly hall: from now on this was the principal, as it were *internal*, arena of the revolution. But those interminable, dark, gloomy, gaol-like, monotonous, stone-floored corridors! Those arid, barrack-like classrooms, with nothing in them to rest the eye! It was dreary, uncomfortable, and uninviting.

Life was concentrated for the most part on the second floor, the lightest and most handsome. There the big assembly hall, holding 1,500 or 2,000 people, took up the whole right wing. This was where the Soviet sections and plenum, the Central Ex. Com., and the Second All-Russian Congress of Soviets held their sittings. Near it there was an uncomfortable buffet with rough tables and benches and extremely meagre food: not far off was the office of the Praesidium. All the other classrooms were occupied by sections of the Central Ex. Com. The furniture was manifestly inadequate. There was neither order nor cleanliness.

Remembering the Tauride, I wandered sadly around the new citadel of the revolution. It was deserted and melancholy. Both in the sections and in the meeting of the Bureau there were oddly few people. But it seemed to me that amongst them there were oddly many new faces. Chkheidze was enthroned in an extraordinary wing-chair, but this failed to lend any solemnity to the session. Why it had assembled, what it talked about—I simply don't remember. But I very well remember feeling that what was talked about there made no difference at all.

* * *

Sunday, August 27th, marked the end of six months of revolution. It was a rather wretched jubilee. It was not only not showy and noisy, but it passed almost without notice in the repulsive atmosphere of those days. The whole affair was limited to a few mass-meetings and a 'ceremonial' session of the Central Ex. Com., which I did not attend; nor indeed did almost anybody else.

On that day, at 10 in the morning, I was giving a workers' lecture in a cinema not far from the Nicholas Station. I've just now seen in one of the newspapers that the topic of my lecture was 'The Moscow Conference'. This seems strange to me. To be sure, the lecture given on the 27th had obviously been scheduled for around the 20th, immediately after my arrival from Moscow. But nevertheless—why was it necessary, in the midst of all that was happening, for me to speak to workers about this silly business? It was obviously the fashion.

After the lecture, I went to the Petersburg Side to the *Cirque Moderne*, where Lunacharsky was giving a lecture on Greek art. A huge working-class audience was listening with great interest to the popular speaker and his unfamiliar stories. The lecture was already almost over. We had actually agreed to meet only in order to lunch and spend the holiday together.

The two of us, together with my wife and someone else, strolled to the 'Vienna', then wandered about the streets and quays for a long time, talking about aesthetics and 'culture'. . . There was a breath of autumn already in the sky. The unforgettable summer was ending, and the sun set early in the sea. We could not sufficiently admire our marvellous Petersburg. Already tired, we strolled homewards to the Karpovka across Trinity Bridge and along the Kamenno-ostrovsky. We sat there till dark, chatting over tea.

The 'phone rang. Someone from Smolny:

'Why are you at home? You know the Bureau's been sitting since morning, and a plenum of the Central Ex. Com. is just going to begin. Smolny is full. . . Why aren't you here?'

'But what's the matter?'

'What? Don't you know? Kornilov is moving on Petersburg with troops from the front. He's got an army corps. . . Things are being organized here. . .'

I dropped the receiver. In two minutes Lunacharsky and I had already left for Smolny. I related to him the few words I'd heard on the 'phone; they gave both of us an equal shock. We scarcely discussed the stupefying news. Its meaning was instantly apparent in its full scope and in the same light to both of us. A deep, extraordinary sigh of relief escaped from both of us. We felt excitement, exaltation, and the joy of liberation.

Yes, this was a threat that would clear the unbearably oppressive atmosphere. This was the starting point for a radical transformation of the whole conjuncture. And in any case it was a full revenge for the July Days. The Soviet might be reborn!

The democracy might take new heart, and the revolution might swiftly find its lawful course, long lost. . .

That Kornilov could attain his goal we didn't believe for a single second. That he might get as far as Petersburg with his troops and there establish a real dictatorship we so thoroughly disregarded that I don't think we even mentioned it on our way to Smolny. There was still enough powder left in the magazine to prevent that! If not one Tsarist echelon got to Petersburg at the moment of the March revolution, in the complete chaos of ideas and in spite of the old discipline, the old officers, the age-old inertia, and the terrible and unknown *novelty*—a Tsarist general could not now seize the army and the capital. Now we had a new, democratically organized army and a powerful proletarian organization in the capital. Now we had *our own* commanders, ideological centres, and traditions. . .

Kornilov, the Tsarist general, had of course all the organized bourgeoisie behind him. He might also have behind him a small military apparatus in Petersburg, with its centre in the Staff and controlled by his accomplices.[1] But he had no real power. Kornilov could have had only a scratch detachment, even though a very big one. But *Petersburg* would meet him as it should—if the field army did not settle him on the spot.

There was no danger from this quarter. Here the revolution would lose nothing; but how much it would gain from the fact that Kornilov, Rodzianko, and Miliukov behaved like Lenin, Zinoviev, and Stalin! In July, to be sure, the Bolsheviks had been in a hurry to pluck the unripe fruit and got poisoned. The fruit would have ripened, and then have benefited the revolution. The Kornilovites had not committed so gross a blunder: their fruit was quite ripe, but it might turn rotten, or the revolution might at any moment pull the tree up by the roots. Unlike the Bolsheviks, the Kornilovites had reason to be afraid of allowing the moment to pass, and to consider the present conjuncture the *most* favourable for a 'demonstration'.

But this subjective side of the matter has no meaning. *Objectively* Kornilov and his friends, when they lost the game,

[1] General Lukomsky, in his memoirs (Vol. 5 of the *Archives of the Revolution*), reports that the Staff really did have a military apparatus in Petersburg consisting of officer and cadet cadres, which even numbered many thousands. This would have been an adequate force, if only . . .

would accept all its consequences, like the Bolsheviks in July. The *coup* of the generals and financiers, with the consequent opening of the front to the Kaiser, shifted the centre of gravity of the whole situation to the opposite side—a feat which the Bolsheviks could not accomplish a millionth part of. And as for the rest. . . It's true that the rest was still unknown, but after all it depended to an enormous extent on ourselves alone. . . To Smolny, then, as quickly as possible!

* * *

Smolny was indeed full. Strings of people were scurrying about the corridors, dimly lit as always. Only the assembly hall, with its snow-white columns, was shining brightly. This was now the centre of Smolny. But there was no meeting of the Central Ex. Com., though a great many deputies and nearly all the leaders were there. There were impromptu meetings in the hall, groups formed, people wandered about in pairs. Tsereteli, downcast and dejected, was walking up and down with one of the Bolsheviks. As I appeared I heard him say listlessly: 'Well! Now you have a holiday in your Bolshevik alley, you'll be taking the bit between your teeth again. . .'

Indeed! So Lunacharsky and I hadn't been mistaken. Tsereteli felt depressed, foreseeing the same results of the Kornilov rising as we had. So we really could pluck up heart again.

* * *

Rumours of the Kornilov *coup* had reached Smolny that morning, I think while I was giving my lecture in the cinema near the Nicholas Station. There were a few people there at this time who were about to set out for mass-meetings to celebrate the first six months of the revolution.

They tried to call the Bureau together. It proved to be a miserable session with scarcely a quorum. It 'completely approved the decision of the Provisional Government and the steps taken by A. F. Kerensky'. Just what steps these were I don't know, and the Bureau, *in concreto*, must also be thought not to have known. But the 'decision' that had been approved referred to Kornilov's dismissal.

The Bureau, assembled in a small casual conclave, actually couldn't take any other decision. Not only because it was its natural 'line' to support the Coalition and associate itself with it in every way, but also because it did not, after all, even suspect the real state of affairs. In Smolny only one thing was known: that General Kornilov, who had just surrendered Riga to the Germans, had 'come out' against the Provisional Government as a pretender to power, while Kerensky had declared him a rebel and was taking decisive steps against him. Obviously, this could only be approved.

Kornilov, with his civilian and military friends, had been crystal clear to us from the very beginning. He was the 'mathematical centre' of the bourgeois dictatorship, relieving the sham dictatorship in order to liquidate the revolution. It was only Premier Kerensky, the head of the Third Coalition, who baffled us. But even this perplexity had only a partial and local, not a general, character. His *general* rôle, of course, needs no clarification, hardly even a brief formulation.

Kerensky, just like Kornilov, had set himself the goal of introducing a bourgeois dictatorship (even though, also like Kornilov, he didn't understand this).

These two 'mathematical centres' had fallen out over the question of which could be the bearer of this dictatorship. One represented the Stock Exchange, capital, and the rentiers; the other the same, plus the still to a large extent indeterminate groups of petty-bourgeois democratic artisans, intelligentsia, the Third Estate, and the paid managers of home industry and commerce.

But Kornilov and Kerensky each needed the other, so great was the yet undissipated power of the masses. The contending sides had been forced into an *alliance*, but they *still remained* contending sides.

Each was trying to use the other for his own aims. Kornilov was striving for a pure dictatorship of finance, capital, and rentiers, but had to accept Kerensky as hostage of the democracy. Kerensky was aiming at a dictatorship of a bloc of the big and petty bourgeoisie, but had to pay heavy tribute to his ally as the *wielder of the real power*. And each was trying to ensure that at the finishing post he would be the actual and formal master of the situation.

Hence came all the 'interrelationships' of the two enemy allies, which were sometimes strange, absurd, and incomprehensible.

This was the source of the 'lack of clarity' of this dirty but not obscure business.

* * *

Now the Central Ex. Com. came on the scene. I have a rather dim recollection of the night session to which Lunacharsky and I had hurried. I recall only a certain amount of hubbub in the hall and disorder in the conduct of the meeting. One would have thought the deputies ought to have got ready, pulled themselves together, and been filled with revolutionary energy and consciousness of the gravity of the moment. But none of this was to be seen. No one here believed in any real danger, and since the revolution people had become accustomed and inured to dramatic situations. The Commander-in-Chief's march on Petersburg and the beginning of a civil war under the nose of the advancing German Army had neither more nor less effect on the imagination than at one time a street demonstration against Tsarist arbitrariness.

The debates proceeded along two lines. The first led to the formation of a new Government, the second to the organization of the defence of the capital against Kornilov's troops.

The second was by far the more important and interesting. Only the night before, the Right Menshevik Weinstein had proposed, in the name of his fraction, that a special 'committee for the struggle against the counter-revolution' be formed. But what should this special committee do? Its initiators were not quite clear about that. In any case it must give every kind of technical aid to the official organs of government in the struggle against Kornilov.

The Menshevik resolution was of course passed. Later the new body received the name of Military Revolutionary Committee. It was this institution that bore the whole brunt of the struggle against the Kornilov campaign. It was this, and only this, that liquidated the conspiracy (if we leave aside the generally unfavourable atmosphere that precluded Kornilov's success, independently of the activity of any institutions at all). . .

But, in spite of the exceptional rôle of the Military Revolutionary Committee in liquidating the Kornilov revolt, we must assume that the Soviet bloc would not have taken on itself the initiative in the matter if it had foreseen what that rôle would be in the future. From now on we shall do our best not to lose sight of this Military Revolutionary Committee, which did not die after the Kornilov revolt, but simply fell into a state of suspended animation, to revive on different foundations later on and tower aloft in October.

Anyone capable of penetrating the general situation at this time must grasp a basic point: the Bolshevik attitude towards this new body. It was precisely the Bolsheviks who were to define its whole character, fate, and rôle. The Star Chamber and its Mamelukes more or less failed to see this, but so it was. The Military Revolutionary Committee, in organizing the defence, had to set in motion the masses of workers and soldiers, and these masses, in so far as they were organized, were organized by the *Bolsheviks* and followed them. At that time theirs was the only organization that was large, welded together by elementary discipline, and united with the democratic rank-and-file of the capital. *Without* them the Military Revolutionary Committee was impotent; without them it could only have passed the time with makeshift proclamations and flabby speeches by orators who had long since lost all authority. *With* the Bolsheviks, however, the Military Revolutionary Committee had at its disposal all organized worker–soldier strength, of whatever kind. What attitude, then, did the Bolsheviks adopt?

The evening before, the Bolsheviks had declared that their party had already taken steps to inform the masses of the danger that threatened them, and had set up a special commission for the organization of defence. This commission would establish contact with the newly created organ of the Central Ex. Com. The Bolsheviks sent their representatives into the Military Revolutionary Committee, although they were bound to find themselves in a negligible minority there. And then, in the morning, when a resolution to give Kerensky a free hand was being voted on, the Bolsheviks, voting *against* it, declared that if the Government was really going to fight against the counter-revolution, they were ready to co-ordinate their entire activity with that of the Provisional Government, and conclude a military-technical alliance with it.

The beginning was excellent. The Bolsheviks had shown extraordinary tact and political wisdom, to say nothing of devotion to the revolution. To be sure, when they entered into an uncharacteristic compromise they were pursuing certain special goals their allies did not foresee, but this made their acumen all the greater.

* * *

The same night and morning of the 28th the Central Ex. Com. issued a series of proclamations and instructions to the various organizations of the democracy. First of all—to committees and Soviets of the army and at the front. Then to the railwaymen, the postal and telegraph workers, and the Petersburg garrison. These addresses gave an account of what had happened and asked people not to obey orders from Headquarters, to watch the movement of counter-revolutionary troops and put every kind of obstacle in their way, to detain the conspirators' letters, and to obey at once the orders of the Soviet organs and the Provisional Government. They also pointed out that the conspiracy lacked deep roots and could be overcome by solidarity and dash. And then the Provisional Government, which was of course taking most resolute steps and hence ought to be the centre of such solidarity, was given a puff.

The Military Revolutionary Committee, speaking generally, had not a particularly brilliant array of names, but the composition of the collegium was rather typical: the Right Soviet bloc, in the person of their stars of the first magnitude, continued to operate primarily in the sphere of 'higher policy' on the parquets of the Winter Palace; while in the Military Revolutionary Committee the *well-known* names were Leftists. And despite their being in the minority it was quite clear that in the Military Revolutionary Committee *control was in the hands of the Bolsheviks*. This followed from the nature of things. First of all, if the committee wanted to act *seriously*, then it had to act *revolutionarily*, that is, independently of the Provisional Government, of the existing constitution, of the acting official institutions. Only the Bolsheviks could operate like this, not the Soviet Compromisers. Secondly, only the Bolsheviks had the material means for revolutionary activity, in the form of control of the masses.

On August 28th the Military Revolutionary Committee began with the investigation and localization of all possible Kornilov bases in Petersburg: these were, of course, all the military academies and officers' organizations—undoubtedly strong counter-revolutionary cells that had to be paralysed. To the Soviet emissaries, however, the gallant military cadets energetically painted themselves in coalitionary and Right-Soviet colours. Arrests were still exceptional. . .

Then steps were taken to cut off the Kornilov troops. Some orders to this effect may have been given by Kerensky, though this is more than doubtful. In any case, however, the railwaymen's organizations were completely at the disposal of the Soviet.

But perhaps the most effective measures taken that day were for arming the workers. It goes without saying not only that this was on the initiative of the Bolsheviks but also that they issued an ultimatum on the subject. As far as I know it was a condition of their participation in the Military Revolutionary Committee. The majority of the committee could not help accepting this condition, if it took a serious view of its tasks. But it had an excellent appreciation of the principled significance of this measure, and did not yield without a struggle. The Military Revolutionary Committee resolved, in view of the necessity of 'opposing the armed forces of the counter-revolution by mobilizing the forces of the workers, that the arming of individual groups of workers for the defence of the workers' districts and factories, under the closest guidance of the district Soviets and the control of the Committee, be considered desirable. In case of necessity these groups would join field army units and be completely subject to the general army command.'

The swiftness and thoroughness with which the Military Revolutionary Committee entered into the rôle of the real headquarters and core of the besieged capital may be seen, for instance, in the following manifestations of its 'organic labours' on that same August 28th: it received reports on the supply situation in the capital from Nikitsky, the 'Governor', and Grohman, the chairman of the Central Supply Committee. It also ordered the mobilization of all supply organs for especially intense activity under the control of the corresponding trade-unions—and the reduction of the *bread ration in the capital to half a pound per food-card.*

The democratic, military, and trade-union organizations in the suburbs of Petersburg wired the Military Revolutionary

Committee their readiness to place themselves completely at its disposition. Without any superfluous words the Kronstadt Soviet eliminated the post-July authorities and installed their own commander in the fortress. The Central Committee of the Fleet also went over to a revolutionary position and was ready for battle—on sea or land—at the first demand from the Central Ex. Com.

That same night and early morning the Bolsheviks had begun to display a feverish activity in the workers' districts. Their military apparatus organized mass-meetings in all the barracks. Everywhere instructions were given, and obeyed, to remain under arms, ready to advance. By and large Smolny was meeting Kornilov with all its lights blazing.

* * *

But what was going on in the Winter Palace? Was the head of the State, the sole hope of the revolution, doing anything at this terrible hour?

Kerensky, to save the revolution and liquidate the Kornilov rising as quickly as possible, insisted on a Directory. And there and then, on August 28th, as a beginning,[1] he conferred Directory portfolios on the following indubitable Kornilovites—Savinkov, Tereshchenko, and Kishkin.[2]

But the same irritating and tiresome people, who actually had no business having been born at all, even if they were party comrades, kept interfering. Tsereteli and Gots turned up from Smolny and began arguing again: 'How can you?' said they.

Kerensky's 'superhuman' wisdom was impossible for simple people to grasp. As far as can be judged from a great deal of evidence, he answered at first: 'Well, all right—we can leave a sixth place in the Directory for some representative of the revolutionary democracy, say Nikitin'. But the tiresome people from Smolny persisted in demanding closer relations with the Soviet and the representation of SRs and Mensheviks in the Directory.

But the deal was spoilt, and the head of the State appointed

[1] Later Kerensky also declared himself Commander-in-Chief. (Ed.)

[2] Kishkin, Nikolai Mikhailovich (1864–1930): physician; Cadet; member of Provisional Government; Commissar of Moscow in summer of 1917. Arrested a number of times for political reasons after the October Revolution, but spent last years of his life in the People's Commissariat for Health. (Ed.)

Savinkov Governor-General of Petersburg and its suburbs. In addition, all troops in the area were subject to him. Thus the entire official weight of the struggle against Kornilov rested on Savinkov, while on Kerensky rested the entire responsibility for this—incomprehensible choice. Kerensky, after all, *knew* Savinkov to be a Kornilovite; the latter had very often declared his solidarity with the General, and handed his resignation to the Premier, who disagreed, and even now, on August 28th, continued to insist on the Kornilov programme. Let us allow that the head of the State was really incapable of regarding Tereshchenko or Maklakov (both frequenters of Supreme Headquarters) as Kornilovites, but you would have thought there could be no possible doubt about Savinkov.

All this only *seems* unnaturally absurd. As a matter of fact it was the logic of Kerensky's position, which he himself, of course, was unaware of. For he really couldn't, after all, start a serious struggle against Kornilov instead of this unworthy and distasteful game. He felt this without understanding it, for he himself was a Kornilovite—on condition that he himself head the Kornilov rising—and all the people he looked to for support were unconditional and unqualified Kornilovites. In these circumstances Kerensky could do nothing else in fighting the plot but appoint someone known to be one of the plotters, as the fully authorized and official commander of all the forces mobilized for its liquidation.

But why didn't *Smolny* declare that this was manifest treason? Or was the Star Chamber too in the plot with Kornilov? Oh no—it was decidedly not guilty of that. The point is that Smolny didn't know anything about the quibbling and pettifogging in the Winter Palace. As before it knew only one thing: that Kornilov was marching on Petersburg with troops to set up a military dictatorship, while Kerensky had declared him a rebel and was taking decisive steps to defend the revolution. It was only by degrees that the truth began, in the midst of the tumult, to filter through, and then only in the following days.

* * *

But it's time to take a look at how the 'revolt' was getting on. What was being done at the Headquarters and on the new Petersburg front of the civil war on August 28th?

'Coming out openly' on the night of the 27th, the official chief of the rebels immediately set about consolidating the whole field army behind him. He sent a proclamation and an order throughout the front to the commanding generals to support his *coup*. For the front commanders there was undoubtedly nothing unexpected in this; there was probably not one non-Kornilovite among them. Nevertheless it was evident that a majority had not been calculating on a war with the *Government*, but on the destruction of the revolution with the '*maximum of legality*'.

Kornilov's appeal was responded to at once by Kaledin, the Cossack ataman, then by the even better-known Denikin, the commander of the south-western front. Finally the commander of the very important north-western front, General Klembovsky, Kerensky's worthy choice, appointed by Kerensky himself to Kornilov's post, came over to the side of the rebels.

But it would seem that the dissemination of Kornilovism in the army ended there. At least there seemed to be no other outward show of it. Here, of course, it was Kerensky's demonstrative action that played the primary rôle; in declaring the Kornilov coup to be a rebellion against the legitimate Government and in outlawing it, Kerensky was demanding an open active insurrectionary move from the Kornilovite generals. The majority couldn't make up their minds to this, and this introduced confusion, vacillation, and disorganization into the Kornilovite *milieu*. However they may have sympathized with Kornilov and despised the Premier, they had not expected to take *such a form* of action and were not prepared to do so.

The highest command did not place itself at Kornilov's disposal, and this inflicted a cruel blow on the Kornilov revolt at the most decisive hour. Other commanders began asking *Petersburg* what they were to do. Some went back on their word immediately and began to work 'in contact' with the Government commissars, while the official Kornilov adherents simply undertook no action and lost precious moments.

But the army itself? The rest of the commanders? The officers? The soldiery? We know that on the night of the 27th the Central Ex. Com. had already circulated instructions to its army organizations, which forestalled the Kornilov *coup* in the army as a whole. Kornilov's orders were in the hands only of the staffs at the front, where they were held up by Soviet agency and didn't reach the army. On the contrary, the position of the supreme Government and of the Soviet was widely popularized amongst the officers and soldiers by the concerted efforts of the army organizations from the morning of the 28th on. Here the results were manifest. The army units took no action *against* Kornilov, since they had received no instructions, but there could be no question of any *support* for the revolt. If Headquarters cannot be said to have been isolated, at any rate its rebellion was localized at the very first, decisive moment.

In the last analysis the practical calculations of the rebels could be based now only on the 3rd Cossack Corps, which was marching on Petersburg. The Corps should have been stationed in the suburbs of Petersburg by the evening of the 27th. Those were the directives given to Krymov, the commanding officer. But they were not carried out: Krymov was late for technical reasons. In particular the 'Savage Division' got stuck at the Dno junction.

With the morning of the 28th the Kornilov echelons began arriving in the town of Luga. There were eight echelons in all, led by Krymov himself. The troops occupied the town, the municipal and government offices, the premises of the Soviet; but everything was orderly and calm. There was no resistance. The Soviet didn't show itself. There was nothing there for Krymov to do, but it was impossible to go any further because the line had been torn up.

The newly-arrived units mingled with the Luga garrison. The local party and Soviet elements at once started most extensive agitation amongst the Kornilovites; while Krymov, out of touch with Headquarters, hesitated to liquidate them and begin on his own personal initiative a serious policy of iron rule. Amidst the inaction and agitation Kornilov's Cossacks naturally became disorganized, and it was fairly simple to get at them.

It goes without saying that their commanders, in so far as they had prepared them for the march, had cited riots started in Petersburg by the 'Bolshevik German agents'. But the Soviet agitators had documents to show that the rebel general was leading the 3rd Corps against the *legitimate* Government, and that there had been no riots in Petersburg. The complete bewilderment of the Kornilovites was inevitable. Decisive action, with *no time to think*, might have helped, but there were no instructions for that.

The local Soviet authorities had quickly begun to raise their heads. Around 8 o'clock in the evening the local Ex. Com. assembled, together with delegates from the army units. It became clear that more echelons were on their way to Luga. It was decided to stop them at all costs, even by joining battle. It was already too late to liquidate *now* the Luga Soviet and garrison. It was no longer possible with the available echelons. Krymov was in quite an absurd position.

So on the morning of the 28th the echelons of the Savage Division left Dno Station on another line. At 4 o'clock in the afternoon two echelons had got within forty-two versts of Petersburg, where the line was cut and timber-wagons had been overturned. A small reconnaissance detachment left the Kornilov train. From the other direction a special delegation of Muslims and Caucasians, specially sent by the Central Ex. Com., went to meet them, to influence their kinsmen in the Savage Division. The delegates suggested that they be taken to the echelons. The detachment willingly agreed, and gave their word of honour that those sent to parley should not be touched. *En route* they had time to talk, always on the same simple theme.

But a group of Kornilovite officers who had left the train refused to allow the delegation to see the echelons. After long and stormy arguments the delegates had to go back, since it was already after 9 o'clock. But they had already done enough to undermine the morale of the detachment: the 'Savages' had been informed of the real state of affairs. Later they told of how they had been lured to Petersburg: first they had been told they were being taken north of Riga to repel the Germans; after Dno they were assured that the Bolsheviks were slaughtering people in Petersburg, and that these traitors had to be repressed. To make things more convincing a *provocateur* threw a bomb at the echelon not far from Dno, which heightened morale. But simple information made it fall again. After August 28th, while Miliukov and Kornilov were asserting they had all the real power, that real power, in the form of an isolated Corps, was already coming apart at the seams.

On the evening of the 28th all roads were barred to Kornilov not only by the destruction of all the railways, but also by men. The garrisons of all the nearby cities—Gatchina, Pavlovsk, Tsarskoe, Krasny—having been put under arms, were spread out in a fighting front on the railways and roads. Units of the capital garrison were stationed around Petersburg, mixed in with the workers' Red Guard. The Military Revolutionary Committee had called out a few units from Finland to reinforce them. I myself watched them arrive at the Finland Station, and mingled with the mob of soldiers; a part of them, apparently the smaller, were consciously going to the defence of the revolution; the others, with a businesslike look, were simply carrying out orders. The thinking proletarians were in the minority: most of them were rugged, clumsy country boys; but the minority served as a sufficient cement for the whole army.

The Petersburg suburbs had been turned into an enormous camp. Smolny commissars visited the regiments. Intense, unflagging activity continued day and night in the heart of Petersburg itself. The workers were being armed. Where had the weapons come from? From wherever they could be found. Nobody asked about legal principles. It was quite enough that the arming went on systematically under the direction of the Military Revolutionary Committee agents. Quite a lot of weapons were found, especially in the Putilov Factory, which gave them all to Smolny to arm the Red Guard. The official authorities of the General Staff, around the Kornilovite Savinkov, grumbled, snorted, became indignant, and lost their tempers. But this had no importance; people had other things to think about. Not the slightest excesses were observed in Petersburg.

It was quite clear that Kornilov's hours were numbered. On the morning of the 29th news came that he had been arrested with his staff. Then it was learned that Pskov, Vitebsk, and Dno were in the hands of troops loyal to the Government. And, finally, the advance on Petersburg had definitely been stopped.

* * *

A favourable turn in the revolution, a thorough revenge for the July Days, and especially the strengthening of Bolshevism, as a result of the Kornilov uprising, not only were obvious to Lunacharsky, Tsereteli, and myself, but now, after the collapse of the adventure, had become obvious for Kerensky, Miliukov, and the whole reaction too. Now, in the eyes of the united plutocracy, this Bolshevik 'peril' came to the fore.

While Kornilov was still at the gates, the newspapers were already making a bogey of the Bolsheviks, as once again seizing the streets, calling for battle and arming the workers. 'In the streets', *Rech* announced with horror, 'groups of armed workers have already appeared, frightening peaceful citizens. In the Soviet the Bolsheviks are energetically demanding the release of their arrested comrades. In connexion with all these facts everyone is profoundly convinced that as soon as General Kornilov's enterprise is definitely liquidated, the Bolsheviks, whom the Soviet majority has now once again ceased to consider traitors to the revolution, will use all their energy to force the Soviet to embark on the realization, even though partial, of the Bolshevik programme.'

In these rather naïve terms the general conjuncture is depicted not at all badly. But the conclusions? Obvious. Barrages, bastions, barricades must be built at once. There must be emergency reinforcement of the positions adopted after July, at the Moscow Conference, before the Kornilov revolt. How could this be done? The details would become clear later, but for the time being it was necessary at all costs to retain a maximum of power in the hands of the post-July, i.e., Kornilovite elements. And the *Cadets*, at the head of the stock-marketeers, business men, industrialists, and generals, pestered the remains of the Government, demanding power. They clamoured that they would not refuse to make this sacrifice for their country, and presented their conditions: (1) that representatives of the army should be invited to accept the military posts in the Cabinet, i.e., the generals should be given political power; (2) that representatives of commerce and industry (over and above the Cadets themselves) should be invited into the Cabinet; (3) that the Kornilov revolt should be crushed without destroying the unity of the army, i.e., without reprisals against the counter-revolutionary generals. It was all very consistent.

* * *

Only a few small illustrations of the Directory's great deeds are warranted.

The day after it began ruling a report appeared in the papers, as a 'rumour', that the Government was moving to Moscow.

This idea was far from new. The Petersburg proletariat was the most dangerous internal enemy—during the revolution as well as before—and after the fall of Riga the danger from without was a good pretext. It was essential for the all-national Government to get away from the Bolshevik city. During the State Conference Moscow, to be sure, showed that it was not benevolent either—nevertheless . . .

For some days the theme of evacuating the Government was harped on in every key. But on September 7th the Moscow Soviet also passed a Bolshevik resolution [like one passed by the Petersburg Soviet on September 1st]. The ancient capital was in the hands of the Bolsheviks too. There was no place to flee to. A denial of the 'rumours' followed: the Government was not preparing to go anywhere.

But then the same goals were approached by other routes. The *removal of excess manpower from Petersburg* was taken up in detail for some weeks. If it was impossible to escape from the enemy—was it also impossible to remove the enemy?

This was a long-drawn-out business, but it didn't have much success. Led by the Bolsheviks, the workers, both in the Workers' Section and in the Government institutions, resisted firmly. The political lining of the project was swiftly and easily unmasked; its technical unfeasibility and economic incoherence were explained—while incidentally a mass of spicy details about the ruses and speculations of the industrial and financial magnates was disclosed. No workers were removed, but this affair has its place among the good intentions of the Directory.

* * *

On August 31st, at Smolny, I learned that Palchinsky, the 'Governor-General', had ordered two Petersburg newspapers, *Rabochii* (The Worker) and *Novaya Zhizn*, to be shut down. The first was the central organ of the biggest proletarian party, the Bolsheviks, and the other was a non-party independent organ that had been carrying on a consistent policy of internationalism and of proletarian class struggle. They had been shut down at the moment when the revolution was being defended from the attacks of Tsarist generals and Stock-Exchange magnates, at a moment of solidarity of the whole Soviet democracy.

There had been no formal occasion, no apparent reason, for shutting down the papers. It was such a blatant and impudent affront that it brought protests from quite disinterested circles remote from the proletariat. It was an affront first to the whole Russian working class, which had rallied as one man to the defence of the revolution and of Kerensky himself, and secondly to the entire free, independent press. The next day even the *Izvestiya* called this act of the Government, in black and white, a filthy provocation. Meanwhile it soon became clear that Mr. Palchinsky was simply the executor of instructions given by Kerensky. Wonderful!

On the morning of September 1st I went to Smolny, principally on *Novaya Zhizn* business. I was met on the stairs by Karakhan, who said by way of greeting: 'Aha! One of the best representatives of the petty-bourgeois democracy!' I goggled, but Karakhan laughed and passed on. The same thing happened when I met various other people. Upstairs it was cleared up: a copy of *Rabochii* was thrust into my hand, with a long article by Lenin devoted to me, which started off by calling me one of the 'best representatives of the petty-bourgeois democracy'. My *Novaya Zhizn* articles had given Lenin, in his hiding-place, an opportunity for some lofty theoretical constructions.

At that time the article, entitled the 'Root of Evil' (a shot at me), did not seem of any special interest. But now, on the contrary, it seems to me instructive in the highest degree; perhaps I shall still return to these thoughts of the great revolutionary later on.

In the small hall where the Bureau usually sat I saw Avksentiev, the Minister of the Interior, and decided to question him about the *Novaya Zhizn*. Round him stood a group of people asking about what was going on in the Winter Palace.

'And what d'you think of Kerensky's treachery?' one of the Left workers naïvely blurted out.

Avksentiev, quite taken aback, was silent for a moment. 'Treachery? I don't understand. How can there be any question of treachery?'

Avksentiev, from the Winter Palace, really failed to grasp

something generally acknowledged in the working-class suburbs of the capital.

He was also in complete confusion concerning the *Novaya Zhizn*. Not only had he had no part in closing it down, but he had no information about it and was in no position to give any help. I ought to discuss it with the 'Governor-General', Palchinsky. I knew that myself. I was also being urged to do so on the paper. But I didn't want to. To go and talk to an ambiguous *parvenu* from the semi-Kornilovite Staff, an impotent dummy impudently playing at supreme command—for *me*, a member of the Central Ex. Com. etc.—was decidedly out of harmony with my dignity and self-esteem. I refused as long as possible. However, pressure was put on me, and I left Smolny for the General Staff where the so-called Governor-General was to be found.

Philippovsky, the chairman of the Military Revolutionary Committee, and I went off together by car. And I was given one more opportunity to convince myself of the acute shift the Kornilov revolt had brought about in the minds of the 'loyal' elements.

'When you get to the Staff', said Philippovsky, 'you'll see the insolent vileness of the place. Talking to Palchinsky will get you nowhere. But why do you hesitate? After all, *Rabochii* has come out again. You just take 30 Kronstadt sailors and get the paper out tomorrow. They will be very willing to go. . . Anarchy? Inconsistency? The hell with all that! That's over with now. . .'

At the Staff I was immediately plunged into an atmosphere of the most impudent bare-faced counter-revolution. First I went to the room of our Soviet delegation, where two or three of our Smolny military people were on duty. These were people from the majority, my opponents. And they surprised me by their friendly reception, which I explained by the fact that here, on the territory of the Winter Palace, they felt they were in a profoundly hostile atmosphere. Here these people, who were breaking their necks on 'support and confidence' for the 'unrestricted' Coalition, were definitely thrown back on the united democratic front of Smolny.

They were on 'duty' in the Staff; but they actually did nothing—they simply grew depressed and spiteful at their impotence.

Here on the terrain of the supreme legal authority they were ignored and even slighted—just as this sham supreme authority was ignored and slighted throughout the territory of Russia.

The rooms were noisy and disorderly, and somewhat faded since the revolution. Inscrutable, exquisitely polite cadet sentries. Long-forgotten, sulky, arrogantly obsequious, *ancien-régime* functionaries' faces. Glossy, brilliant officers slithering over the dubious parquet. Inquisitive glances of contempt were shot at me from all sides, as though I were some alien body. I mechanically drew myself up at once and assumed an extremely haughty air. I gave my name to the adjutant who had turned up at my elbow and asked that it be given to Palchinsky, refusing to explain the point of my visit. Much whispering; the looks multiplied. I was pointed out to the passing officers and generals by glances. . . But Palchinsky did not keep me waiting.

Visibly aware of the fullness of his power, he was sitting at a desk, somewhat strangely placed in the *front* of a huge study. I sat down opposite. The conversation was extremely brief, but not without some characteristic features.

'D'you intend to cancel your order to close down the *Novaya Zhizn*?'

'No, that order was actually given at the Premier's personal request. Your paper can't be tolerated. In these difficult hours it's carrying on its former bitter opposition to the State, and appealing for out-and-out disorders. . . And your methods! Somehow your paper is always—emphasizing . . .'

Palchinsky resorted to a gesture; his face showed unfeigned hatred of the newspaper which had hounded him personally quite often. . . However, there was no reason for me to maintain the conversation on this level.

'Well,' I said, 'after all, you know we can publish the same newspaper tomorrow under another name. And of course we will. Consequently if anyone loses it will be . . .'

Palchinsky looked rather pleased at this.

'Aha! You want to publish again? But have you read the decree which I signed specially for such a case? According to that decree you'd be liable . . .'

I hadn't read any decree—but in any case it was obviously futile to continue the conversation. I got up without hearing the end of the speech about the punishments lying in wait for me.

Just then the 'phone rang, and Palchinsky, not without triumph, as though concluding an audience, told me: 'The Premier wants me to go to him.'

We went out of the study at the same time and separated. When I had reported to the office the question stood thus: whether to publish the *Novaya Zhizn* next day under the old name, or change the name for the same paper. In either case (in view of the new 'decree') an indispensable condition of publication was an armed detachment at the printing-press. This could be got at Smolny without any difficulty. . . The person formally responsible, Gorky, was not in Petersburg. To act in a sharply *revolutionary* manner could only be done with his knowledge and consent. So it was decided to act more mildly—to publish the paper *in spite* of the decree, but under *another* name. . .

A concluding act of the Kornilov episode was taking place just then at Smolny. Going there around 8 o'clock in the evening I met Martov on the stairs.

'Hurry,' he said, 'there's an interesting spectacle. The Savage Division has arrived with a confession of guilt. The Praesidium and others are receiving delegates from it.'

The 'Bureau' was packed tight with Caucasian greatcoats, fur caps, felt cloaks, galoons, daggers, glossy black moustaches, astounded prawn-like eyes, and the smell of horses. This was the *élite*, the cream, headed by 'native' officers—in all perhaps 500 men. The crowd kept the deepest silence while the delegates of the individual units, with their caps in their hands, made broken speeches in the names of those who had sent them. On the whole they all said one and the same thing. In naïvely grandiloquent language they extolled the revolution and talked about their devotion to it to the tomb, to the last drop of their blood. Not one man in their units, not one of their people had gone or would go against the revolution and the revolutionary Government. A misunderstanding had taken place, dissipated by the simple establishment of the truth. The 'Savages' were the bearers of solemn vows.

Not one of the speakers missed a chance of emphasizing their special pride, that the Russian Revolution was headed by their countrymen, who were now receiving them in the name of the 'great' Soviet. Every one of them devoted a part of his speech, and sometimes a good half of it, to the Chairman Chkheidze, and especially to Tsereteli; some of them even addressed him as 'thou', calling him 'great leader . . .'. Tsereteli answered his countrymen in a very sympathetic speech. His characteristic oratorical quality, and the very poverty of his vocabulary, which to my mind reflected his entire intellectual range, was this time compensated for by an extraordinary warmth of tone. And of course Tsereteli also spoke not only as a Soviet leader; he welcomed the 'Savages' also as Caucasians, as natives of those same hills he came from himself.

Kamenev was also sitting at the Praesidium table, and behind him Ryazanov was standing in a group of Soviet people. I elbowed my way through the crowd and tried to persuade Kamenev that he absolutely must speak for the Bolsheviks. He too was aware that that was vital, but couldn't make up his mind. The 'Savages', now in contact with the Soviet and identifying it with the 'legitimate Government' and with the revolution, still, as before, imagined that the *Bolsheviks* were evil-doers from some alien universe. They would have been ready to fling themselves on the *Bolsheviks* with their former violence even now. It was essential, then and there, while the air was being cleared, to expose the hollowness of the bogey to them; they must be given a rudimentary understanding of the Bolshevik Party, which represented the interests of the working class; and it was especially necessary to emphasize the united Soviet front with the Bolsheviks in the face of the Kornilov revolt. As far as I recall, Kamenev didn't speak, but Ryazanov made a very emotional and explosive speech.

* * *

This was how the Kornilov 'manifestation' was liquidated. The Winter Palace farce retained its previous character; as before, the bourgeoisie was advancing, attempting to strengthen its pre-Kornilov and post-July positions, and convert its formal dictatorship into a real one. The Kerensky and Tereshchenko clique were aiming as before at liquidating any influence of the organized democracy and establishing the dictatorship of capital. . . While Smolny, the Star Chamber, and the Soviet majority were as before betraying the revolution into the hands of the bourgeoisie.

Both the Winter Palace and Smolny retained their positions

after the Kornilov campaign. But this was merely on the surface, and shouldn't conceal from us the essence of the matter. The enormous impetus from the Right given by Kornilov definitely disengaged the revolution from the atmosphere of the July reaction; it threw it far to the Left and gave it a big push forward.

CHAPTER 24

THE DISSOLUTION OF THE DEMOCRACY AFTER THE KORNILOV REVOLT

THE course of the revolution had been defined even before the Kornilov rebellion, but this gave it a tremendous push forward. And the wretched floundering of the 'reigning' capitulators and reactionaries merely formed the setting of a basic historical process—the mass movement of the people.

The news of the bourgeois *coup* profoundly stirred the surface and the depths of Russia. The entire organized democracy rose to its feet. All Soviet Russia bristled and took up arms, not only metaphorically but quite literally. Hundreds of thousands and millions of workers, soldiers, and peasants rose up in arms, for defence and for attack, against the class enemy.

Their desire for a decisive battle grew irresistibly, hour by hour. Here there was class instinct, a small portion of class consciousness, and the influence of the ideas and organization of the gigantically growing Bolsheviks: but more than that there was weariness of war and other burdens; disappointment in the fruitlessness of the revolution, which up to then had given the masses of the people nothing; bitter resentment against the masters and the wealthy rulers; and a yearning to make use of the sovereignty that had been won.

In any case, directly after the Kornilov upheaval the mood grew extraordinarily firm; and the formation of fighting columns correspondingly began at a feverish tempo—against the Coalition and the bourgeoisie, against Kerensky and the Compromisers, against the official régime and its loyal servants, the traitors to the working class.

In the provinces the Bolsheviks already controlled a great many Soviets. That is, the administrative authority, which moreover was quite unlimited, was virtually in the hands of Lenin's party. In such cities the bristling Soviets formed purely Bolshevik local Military Revolutionary Committees, which during the Kornilov revolt put out their sharp, though clumsy claws, and refused to pull them in again afterwards.

At this time the Bolshevik centres revived their slogan of 'All Power to the Soviets!' It was a matter of course in these conditions for the general Kornilov situation to be reflected in the simple minds of the local Bolshevik leaders. Almost mechanically, without any clear conception of the significance of their own actions, the local Bolshevik–Soviet organs began to 'annul' the official 'power' and make use of their opportunities on the widest possible scale. This, from the point of view of the 'Directory' and all the loyal elements, was a vast new explosion of 'anarchy'. But whatever the process is called, one thing is clear: after the Kornilov revolt Bolshevism began blossoming luxuriantly and put forth deep roots throughout the country.

Even before the Kornilov mutiny, before the fall of Riga and after the Moscow Conference, the entire bourgeois press had sounded the alarm about the Bolshevik peril, in connexion with 'reliable reports' about forthcoming 'demonstrations' by the Bolsheviks. But that was a false alarm, with the object of putting public opinion on to a false scent and covering up the conspiracy of Headquarters.

Now the press was once more full of panic and rage. But now this panic and rage were quite sincere. The peril was at hand. By now it was not only the central Soviets of the capital and the leaders of all the others that were *in Lenin's hands*—that alone now had decisive importance. But the army in the field! And the garrisons in the rear! All this, after all, meant a brimming over of all real power and State sovereignty no longer even to the tame, enfeebled, and self-stultifying Soviets, but into the hands of the Bolshevik 'outsiders' firmly united with the masses. There was something to sound a real alarm about.

* * *

The Kornilov incident, however, not only accelerated the Bolshevization of the Soviets and the worker–peasant masses, but was also sharply reflected in the current policies of Lenin's *Soviet opponents*. The Mensheviks and SRs who ruled in the Central Ex. Com. were just as far from Bolshevism as before; but they too had shifted their positions and swung further Left.

Martov's group, the Menshevik-Internationalists, still had

nothing in common with the central organ of the Mensheviks, but we had no ideological grounds for moving Left under the influence of the Kornilov revolt. Our fraction had already stood for a long time for a *dictatorship of the Soviet democracy*. We were divided from the Bolsheviks not so much by theory, as by practice, which made itself felt later on; we were divided not so much by slogans as by a profoundly different conception of their inner meaning. The Bolsheviks reserved that meaning for the use of the leadership and didn't carry it to the masses. This had to do not with Lenin's *Leftism*, but with his methods. The Kornilov episode could not graft these on to us.

However, it did not pass without having had some effect on the Menshevik-Internationalists. They had in their hands the entire Menshevik organization of the capital: the Petersburg Committee consisted of Martovists only. The working-class districts, especially Basil Island, had long since insisted on a formal split with official Menshevism. The affair dragged on all summer, and you might say was sabotaged by the efforts of old and influential Mensheviks, close to Martov. But now Tsereteli & Co. became unendurable to many Petersburg leaders and to the solid working-class cadres in the districts. A mass exodus from the organization began. An example was set by Larin, who was followed by more than ten active figures. Almost all of them went directly over to the Bolsheviks. And then, in the first part of September, a split took place in the strongest of our working-class organizations, on Basil Island. At the time of the Democratic Conference practically the entire district went into Lenin's party. This provoked a ferment in other districts too, which was carried into the provinces. The crisis of Menshevism began all along the line and developed rapidly.

It was reflected rather strongly in the political 'new formation' familiar to us—in the party of the *Novaya Zhizn* people, officially the United Internationalists. This 'party' (of which the renowned Steklov was also a member from now on) began growing quite strongly at the expense of the Mensheviks, thanks to that irreplaceable medium, a big and widely read newspaper. Our editorial board began intensifying its 'party' activity. And in the near future an All-Russian conference of provincial *Novaya Zhizn* groups was being prepared.

* * *

As for the Bolsheviks, they also had nowhere to shift Leftwards. Their business was simply to gain time to form the ranks of their army, which was growing by the hour. But after the Kornilov revolt it was possible—for an attentive eye—to observe that the Bolsheviks had again begun to anticipate, you might say touch, the power snatched away in July. Lenin and Zinoviev, taking advantage of their leisure, began deepening their current programme and tactics—tactics of finished Jacobinism and a programme of general explosion, as an example to proletarian Europe.

In one of the first numbers of *Rabochii Put* (Workers' Way) (which had replaced *Rabochii*, *Proletarii*, and *Pravda*), Lenin proposed a 'compromise'. Let the Menshevik–SR bloc, having driven out the bourgeoisie, set up a régime unconditionally responsible to the Soviets. The Bolsheviks would not create any obstacles on condition, first of all, of complete freedom of agitation, and secondly, of the transfer of all power to the local Soviets. It is quite clear that for the knights of the Coalition this was a 'compromise', but what Lenin's 'compromise' amounted to, on the other hand, is not particularly clear. The principal perspectives, however, that presented themselves to Lenin's mind are quite obvious. If the Bolshevik Party was now growing like a snowball and becoming a decisive force, Lenin was assured of a majority in the Congress of Soviets in the very near future. Apart from 'freedom of agitation' this would be furthered by the entire objective course of events, and especially by the inevitable marking time to please the bourgeoisie that the Mensheviks and SRs would undertake if they agreed to the 'compromise'. Then it would be possible to drive the ruling bloc out of power (or even further) without resorting to the risky experiments of June 10th and July 4th. Lenin's party would have 'full power' painlessly and safely. Well, and what would it do? We are familiar with its programme in general. But now, in *Rabochii Put* Zinoviev filled it out and made it concrete: One of the first steps of any Government which had broken with the bourgeoisie would be to refuse to pay any debts contracted in connexion with the war. The second step would be the partial expropriation of the 'richest people' in favour of the State.

This was unquestionably highly alluring. And note—in the absence of an elementary economic programme, and given the systematic replacement of Marxist concepts by anarchist slogans ('organized seizure', 'workers' control', etc.)—what terms are used by Citizen Zinoviev: Rich people! This is both scientific and statesmanlike, and—it can be understood by any lumpen-proletarian. This is why the Bolsheviks' correct theoretical formulas about the worker-peasant dictatorship could not draw into Lenin's party the extreme Left Marxist elements. During those days I personally used to say that if it hadn't been for these persistent suspicious and nasty notes in their 'ideology' then I too might have entered the Bolshevik Party. But I didn't, and a good thing too. . .

CHAPTER 25

THE LAST COALITION

THE 'Democratic Conference' should have opened on the 12th, but was postponed until September 14th, just a month after the Moscow State Conference. It proceeded on its futile, tiresome business: a debate on whether we should have a Coalition or a purely democratic Government. Not one of the speeches deserves to be expounded here. Everything had been heard or read already.

We were back in the old *post-July, pre-Kornilov* situation. A fourth, irresponsible Coalition was revived, which once again confirmed the formal dictatorship of the bourgeoisie. This 'sovereign' bourgeois régime was formed exactly two months after the Third Coalition, one month after the Kornilov *coup* and one month before—but let's not anticipate events. I shall simply recall something that apparently does not require any special explanation. The dictatorship of the Stock Exchange was formally evident, though as before this was nothing but a sham. But, unlike the last time, when some attributes of power were in the hands of the *friends and accomplices* of the bourgeois 'dictators'—*now* the whole power was in the hands of their known class enemies. In July and August the petty-bourgeois Soviet had still preserved some fragments of its power; but now all the power, and the Soviets into the bargain, had gone over to the Bolsheviks. The whole situation was more absurd and intolerable than before. There was no state power, and no State.

This was so clear that even the yellow bourgeois press did not exult. The new Coalition was greeted without enthusiasm. The Right wing of the democracy demonstratively, though not convincingly, rejoiced over its infant. To make up for this the Left, Internationalist section set to work at once and, without giving it a breathing spell, took a direct line toward the overthrow of the new 'Government'.

* * *

Trotsky had been released from prison on September 4th, just as suddenly and causelessly as he had been arrested on July 23rd.

Now he became chairman of the Petersburg Soviet; there was a hurricane of applause when he appeared. Everything had changed! Since the April Days the Soviet had gone against the revolution and been the mainstay of the bourgeoisie. For a whole half-year it had served as bulwark—against the people's movement and their wrath. It had been the Praetorian Guard of the Star Chamber, at the disposal of Kerensky and Tsereteli. Now it was once again a revolutionary army inseparable from the popular masses of Petersburg. It was now Trotsky's guard, ready at a sign from him to storm the Coalition, the Winter Palace and all the citadels of the bourgeoisie. The Soviet, re-united with the masses, had once again recovered its enormous energies.

The conjuncture, however, was no longer the same as it had been before. Trotsky's Soviet did not act like an acknowledged State power carrying on a revolution. It did not act by methods of opposition, pressure, and 'liaison'. It was a latent potential revolutionary force, gathering together the elements for a general explosion. This hidden potentiality blinded the wretched sham 'rulers', the man in the street, and the old Soviet majority. But that didn't alter anything: the success of the forth-coming explosion was assured. Nothing could withstand the new destructive power of the Soviet; the only question was where Trotsky would lead it. For what did it contain but destruction? Well, we shall live and learn.

In his first speech as chairman Trotsky said that actually he had not taken Chkheidze's place, but, on the contrary, Chkheidze had been occupying his (Trotsky's) place: in the 1905 Revolution the chairman of the Petersburg Soviet was Trotsky. Now, however, the perspectives were different; the new Praesidium had to form part of a new upsurge of the revolution, which would lead to victory. . .

But then he added a few words, not thinking that in time he would have to disregard them and create a theory to justify their opposite. He said:

'We are all party people, and we shall have to cross swords more than once. But we shall guide the work of the Petersburg Soviet in a spirit of justice and complete independence for all fractions; the hand of the Praesidium will never oppress the minority.'

Heavens! What liberal views! What self-mockery! But the point is that about three years later, while exchanging reminiscences with me, Trotsky, thinking back to this moment, exclaimed dreamily:

'What a happy time!'

Yes, wonderful! Perhaps not one person in the world, not excluding himself, will ever recall Trotsky's rule with *such* feelings.

At the session on September 25th the Soviet passed this resolution on the new Government by an enormous majority: 'The new Government will go down in the history of the revolution as the Government of the civil war. The Soviet declares: "We, the workers and the garrison of Petersburg, refuse to support the Government of bourgeois autocracy and counter-revolutionary violence. We express the unshakeable conviction that the new Government will meet with a single response from the entire revolutionary democracy: 'Resign!'"'

Such was the unusual greeting of the Petersburg Soviet to the new Government.

As we went down the Smolny stairs, discussing the new events, someone called up from below: 'Eh, Volodarsky, where is it tomorrow?'

'Tomorrow?' answered Volodarsky, who was going out with me, 'at the Patronny plant.'

Yes, the Bolsheviks were working stubbornly and without let-up. They were among the masses, at the factory-benches, every day without a pause. Tens of speakers, big and little, were speaking in Petersburg, at the factories and in the barracks, every blessed day. For the masses they had become *their own people*, because they were always there, taking the lead in details as well as in the most important affairs of the factory or barracks. They had become the sole hope, if only because since they were one with the masses they were lavish with promises and sweet though simple fairy tales. The mass lived and breathed together with the Bolsheviks. It was in the hands of the party of Lenin and Trotsky.

* * *

Around this time new elections on a proportional basis took place for the Petersburg Ex. Com. Of the forty-four members elected two-thirds were Bolsheviks. The Mensheviks numbered five in all, whereas our group, the Menshevik-Internationalists —the group that had made up the fundamental core of the *first* Ex. Com., which had begun the revolution—did not get a single seat.

This may have been distressing for us, but it was not at all surprising.

It was not actually because we had to take the blame for official Menshevism, with which the Martov group had not yet conclusively broken, or because the group still didn't have a literary organ, a basic instrument of agitation. Nor was it, finally, that we, the leaders, had abandoned work in the Soviet, hardly showed ourselves in Smolny and were separated from its rank-and-file.

The cause was something basic: our position, at least in its positive part, was superfluous for the masses. In its *negative*, critical part we—Martovites and *Novaya Zhizn* people—were in accord with the Bolsheviks. In the arena of the struggle going on at that time against the Coalition and the bourgeoisie we stood at their side. We did not fuse with them because a number of features of the positive creative strength of Bolshevism, as well as its methods of agitation, revealed to us its future hateful countenance. It was based on an unbridled, anarchistic, petty-bourgeois elemental explosion, which was only smothered by Bolshevism when once again it was not followed by the masses. We were afraid of this elemental explosion.

But the masses were not afraid of it, for they could neither perceive it nor appreciate its significance.

Our Marxist theories were incomprehensible and irritating to the masses, which had just barely tasted the blessing of free political development. Our logical proletarian class ideology was useless and offensive to the workers and soldiers of our petty-bourgeois country. The disappointed, weary and hungry masses swept over our heads—from SR-opportunist philistinism to the devastating fury of Bolshevism. Our proletarian Marxist outlook did not find a place for itself amidst the turbulent elements. Our 'interstitial' group was easily pounded to bits by the gigantic oncoming billows of the imminent civil war.

In the new Petersburg Ex. Com., where we had once played a

leading rôle, we now did not get a single seat. However, in the kaleidoscope of the dizzying events, the masses not only did not remember, they did not *know* about our rôle in the first period of the revolution. Only the leaders knew about it, and, evidently in remembrance of the first magnificent weeks, the Bolshevik Ex. Com. at its first session resolved to co-opt our group with a consulting voice: Sokolov, Kapelinsky, Sokolovsky, our leader Martov, I think Steklov, and myself.

* * *

During those days I remember one session of our—Martovite—'centre' devoted to the elections for the Constituent Assembly. We had gathered in a place that was new to me—on the third floor of Smolny, near the galleries giving on to the big hall. I raised the question of a bloc with the Bolsheviks. There were some sympathetic responses, but Martov rebelled outright and said, among other things:

'At the present moment a drift to the Bolsheviks is absolutely out of place. Now the revolution is endangered not by the Right, but by the *Left*!'

Martov may have shown great acumen here, but I must admit that to me personally, after the Kornilov *coup*, the Democratic Conference, and the restoration of the bourgeois dictatorship, a movement from the Left did not seem a peril but salvation.

As far as I recall, the question of a bloc with the Bolsheviks was never finally settled: it came up against the consideration that under no circumstances would the Bolsheviks agree to enter a bloc with us; they were too strong and 'self-sufficient' for that, and were carrying on their preparation for the elections too energetically, having already put forward everywhere prepared lists of candidates, headed in most instances by Trotsky himself.

I don't think it superfluous to remark that my differences with Martov at this time had become more or less systematic. Two tendencies had begun to reveal themselves in our group. Martov had with him the group of old Menshevik *émigrés*—Semkovsky, Astrov, Martynov—who had gravitated to the old core of the party. But on the Left, together with me, were the Petersburgers and especially the active workers of the old Ex. Com. Martov rather jealously guarded his influence and the representation of the entire organization by elements close to him.

* * *

On the day, I think, when we discussed the Constituent Assembly, I went to Smolny after working in the evening on the newspaper. I wanted to see Trotsky and 'feel out the ground' concerning an electoral bloc of the Bolsheviks and the Martovites. Trotsky was at Smolny, but at a meeting in the Bureau, at a council of 'Elders' of the forthcoming Pre-Parliament.[1]

I went into the committee-room to see Trotsky, my hated face shocking all these 'Elders' so familiar to us. Didn't this Sukhanov want to put something indiscreet into his paper? The Bolsheviks (Trotsky and Kamenev) were sitting to one side, in their usual places to the right of the chairman. Trotsky looked a bit different from usual, in a long grey overcoat and spectacles with metal rims instead of pince-nez.

He spoke politely of the bloc with the Menshevik-Internationalists, but with such reserve that the outcome was clear. I sat down at his side to listen to what the 'Elders' were saying and hear Tsereteli's philippics. Even the Stolypin Duma under Rasputin's boot seemed the ideal of an all-powerful Parliament, filled with grandeur, compared with the Pre-Parliament, that unspeakable product of stupidity and treachery.

I recall this evening very well. I had never yet suffered such a sharp and unendurable feeling of dejection and shame: to what a point they had led the great revolution! I remember that I began choking, partly with anger, and partly with something else, that blocked up my throat.

'What's going on?' I said, naïvely and 'unconsciously' turning to Trotsky.

But Trotsky merely laughed his soundless laugh with his mouth half-open. At the time I didn't understand his indifference, but actually it was obvious. For Trotsky, after all, all questions had by then been settled. He was already living on the *other* side, and as for what was being done on *this* side—that didn't concern him. Perhaps the worse it was, the better.

I returned to the *Novaya Zhizn* in the Shpalerny to get out the

[1] Decided on at the Democratic Conference. Sukhanov uses the word 'Elders' ironically. (Ed.)

paper. At this time we were implacably and with unusual energy bombarding Kerensky, the Konovalovs, and their whole beneficent Government. There was an excellent atmosphere on the paper, and more and more attention was being paid us —by both enemies and friends.

In general, as far as I recall, I derived some satisfaction from the paper, more than previously. But I also remember the physical strain. I was still living on the Karpovka, and the endless trips there in the damp Petersburg autumn nights after publication now come to mind quite differently from the enchanting walks through the streets of the Petersburg Side into the roseate, carolling mornings of that unforgettable spring. . .

* * *

'Disorders' were taking on absolutely unendurable, really menacing proportions in Russia. Anarchy was really getting under way. The city and the countryside were both in revolt. The first was demanding bread, the second land. The new Coalition was met with hunger riots and savage pogroms throughout Russia. I happen to have in front of me reports of such riots in Zhitomir, Kharkov, Tambov, Orel, Odessa, etc., etc. Troops were sent everywhere, Cossacks whenever possible. There were repressions, shootings, martial law. But nothing helped. Petersburg was quiet; it simply hungered and—waited.

But the peasants, finally losing patience, began settling the agrarian question at first hand—by their own methods. It was *impossible* not to give them land: it was *impossible* to torture them any longer by uncertainty. It was *impossible* to make speeches to them about the 'regulation of rural relations without the destruction of the existing forms of land-holding. . .'

But this was the *essence of the Coalition.* And the peasants began acting on their own. Estates were divided up and tilled, herds were slaughtered and driven off, country-houses were destroyed and set on fire, arms were seized, stores were plundered and destroyed, trees and orchards were chopped down, there was murder and violence. These were no longer 'excesses', as they had been in May and June. It was a mass phenomenon—tidal waves heaving and billowing throughout the country.

Worst of all, however, was the position in the field army. This was as before the root and core of the entire situation.

Famine was assuming horrifying proportions at the front. It was obvious to any honest observer that our army, even though it was pinning down 130 German divisions on the Eastern front, could not hold out the winter, nor even the autumn.

As early as September 21st at a Petersburg Soviet session an officer who had been at the front made a speech saying:

'The soldiers in the trenches don't want either freedom or land now. They want only one thing now—the end of the war. Whatever you may say here, the soldiers are not going to fight any more. . .'

This caused a sensation even in the Bolshevik Soviet. Exclamations were heard: 'Even the Bolsheviks don't say that!' But the officer, no Bolshevik, calmly waited, conscious of duty done.

'We don't know and we don't care what the Bolsheviks say. I'm reporting what I know and what the soldiers have sent me to tell you.'

It was impossible to go on like this. This 'Government' had to be torn out by the roots. I harped on this over and over again, every day, in the paper. And I was right.

But how could such a situation be ended? Martov said, during those days: 'I know only two methods of forming a Government: either the citizen's gesture of throwing his ballot into the voting urn, or the citizen's gesture of loading his rifle.' It happened that the last Coalition had been created by a *third* method, but now we were confronted by the two first. In the immediate future one of these was going to decide matters.

* * *

The Pre-Parliament was going to open—powerless, sickly, alien, and repugnant to every revolutionary principle. But compared with the comic-opera Government it was a *de facto* power. It *could* have decided the fate of the 'ruling' Coalition by the first method—the *parliamentary* method. The results—were another question. But there could be no doubt as to the *possibility*.

And if not? Then the capitulationism of Smolny and the provocative attitude of the Winter Palace would do their work. The real democracy of Russia, after all, had already loaded its guns.

CHAPTER 26

THE PRE-PARLIAMENT

THE official title conferred on the Pre-Parliament was: 'The Provisional Council of the Russian Republic'. The opening was scheduled for October 7th. Premises were looked for. Something fitting was wanted—not too primitive or provincial, for the Government itself and the most respectable social elements (not workers or soldiers) would have to be there often. But not too ceremonial or official either, for this wasn't the State Duma or any plenipotentiary organ. The *Rech* thought the Smolny Institute would be a very suitable location. And as a matter of fact, it was quite free: only the Central Ex. Com. and the Petersburg Soviet, which should never have seen the light of day, were there. But could the Bolsheviks be cleared out of Smolny. . .? The row of dots meant: 'Oh, for Kornilov!' But suitable premises couldn't be found, and the Marian Palace had to do.

The 'democratic' majority consisted of 308 people, of whom sixty-six were Bolsheviks, about sixty official Mensheviks, and 120 SRs, about twenty of whom were Leftist. Then there were some Co-operators in the 'democracy', who included extreme Right Mensheviks and SRs.

Our fraction, the Menshevik-Internationalists, numbered about thirty. We had never had so many; with such a 'mass' we could at any rate produce enough of an uproar, or start verbal obstruction.

At the beginning the bourgeois representatives demanded 120 seats, but then they increased that to 150. Then I think they did some more bargaining, of no particular interest to us. They, like the democracy, had heaped up the most improbable social classes, strata, and groups, and the unlikeliest combinations. Well-to-do peasants were affiliated with propertied elements. . . There were about seventy-five Cadets. The majority of the rest, sent by every possible organization of industrialists and landowners, was more Right: old Octobrists and Nationalists. For some reason they were still stubbornly fighting against formally pouring their streamlets into the Cadet sea. But in practice they acknowledged Cadet hegemony and had the same programme: the iron dictatorship of the plutocracy.

But there were also 'intellectuals' amongst the propertied elements, for instance the 'academic' delegation. Others were divided up this way: the Society of Journalists was represented in the democracy, while the Society of Editors got a place amongst the propertied elements.

This Pre-Parliament was officially powerless, a concoction unworthy of the revolution and pathetic as an institution. But it had an interesting quality, unlike perhaps most real parliaments. Its composition was exceptionally brilliant. It concentrated within itself, indeed, the flower of the nation. It owed this precisely to the unprecedented method of its selection. All the political parties and other associations sent their *best people*, without subjecting them to the risk of losing their place in an election to the popular but insignificant hero of some provincial ant-hill. Hence there were rather few people who did not have an all-Russian reputation. And all the 'names' were included. All the party Central Committees were represented in the Pre-Parliament *in corpore*; exceptions were few, accidental and unimportant. This in itself proclaimed the concentration of all the country's political *strength* and the quintessence of all its political *thought*.

Some individuals were absent. Plekhanov, old, ill, and ignored by events, wasn't there; he had played no part in the revolution. Nor was Lenin there: our powerful and forthright Government kept renewing its orders for his arrest every week; as before he was hiding 'underground', though unlike Plekhanov he played a part, a very powerful part, in current events. But Lenin's place was successfully taken by Trotsky. The time had now passed when in the Bolshevik Party, as in the First International, after the Thunderer himself—there was nothing for a long, long, long time. Now Trotsky was side by side with him. He was quite different, and speaking generally quite unfitted to replace Lenin, but, I'm inclined to think, he was no less important a man, whom Lenin could not have replaced either, and without whom the forthcoming events could not have come about.

There was one other who was absent—Tsereteli. He had gone away to the Caucasus to rest—for 'a few weeks'. He was not to return—politically. His rôle was played out, finished. He had botched and ruined as much as one able man could. And he had gone away. . . Enough of him; I shall not speak of him again—it has all been said.[1]

* * *

On October 7th at 5 o'clock, amidst rain and slush, Kerensky opened the Pre-Parliament. This was no mere democratic conference! This time Kerensky wasn't late. Also, something unheard of in the revolution happened: the Pre-Parliament opened on time. No one could have foreseen that. And that, it was said, was why there were not very many people in the hall and it was just as boring and dreary in the Marian Palace as in the streets of Petersburg.

It was quite late, and happening for some reason to go in by a way I didn't know, I wandered about for a long time through the endless corridors and rooms of the Palace. I came out somehow into the Press Gallery, from which I heard the end of the speech from the Throne. The head of the Government and the State was speaking in hollowly official but loftily patriotic tones. I don't remember, nor can I extract from the newspaper accounts, one living concrete idea. In any case the entire speech was full of the 'war dangers' under the impact of the latest events at the front and the news, just received, that the Germans were threatening Reval. . . But really, all the political interest of the opening of the Pre-Parliament revolved around the Bolsheviks.

Their whole large fraction arrived late, almost at the same time as I did. They had had an important and stormy meeting at Smolny, which had only just ended. They had been making a final decision on what to do about the Pre-Parliament: stay or go? After a first session, at which the question was left hanging in the air, they had had a bitter dispute. This, as a piquant incident in Smolny circles, was of great interest. The opinions of the Bolsheviks were almost evenly divided, and it wasn't known which way the majority would go. It was reported that Lenin was demanding that they should leave. Trotsky also defended

[1] After the October Revolution Tsereteli was one of the leaders of the Menshevik Caucasian Republic, after the repression of which by the Soviet Government he emigrated, eventually to New York City. (Ed.)

this position with great vigour. Ryazanov and Kamenev were fighting against it. The Right wing was demanding that the rupture with the Pre-Parliament be postponed at least until the moment the Pre-Parliament exposed itself on some issue, for instance refused to make some important decision in the interests of the working class. They said the rupture would otherwise not be understood by the people. But Trotsky, for whom all questions were settled, insisted that there should be no obscurities, that the boats should be conclusively and publicly burnt. Let both hostile armies see and understand!

In an interval, a sensational rumour circulated in the corridors of the Marian Palace: Trotsky had won by a majority of two or three votes, and the Bolsheviks would leave the Pre-Parliament immediately. That was the least of it; the Menshevik and SR leaders, very disturbed, were saying that before they left the Bolsheviks would create a tremendous row. The most unlikely rumours passed from mouth to mouth. A kind of panic began. One of the officials was told off to make private enquiries of the Bolsheviks.

'Nonsense!' answered Trotsky, standing not far off from me in the rotunda adjoining the meeting hall, 'nonsense, a few pistol-shots. . .'

But Trotsky looked rather nervous—in anticipation of the shots. The Right Bolsheviks, around Ryazanov, were grumbling angrily. This whole affair was very disagreeable to me, and I didn't go over to Trotsky.

At the end of the session Trotsky was given the floor for an emergency statement. There was a sensation in the hall. For most of the bourgeois the famous leader of the bandits, idlers, and hooligans was still a novelty.

'The officially stated aim of the Democratic Conference', Trotsky began, 'was the elimination of the personal régime that fed the Kornilov revolt, and the creation of a responsible Government capable of liquidating the war and promoting the convocation of a Constituent Assembly at the appointed time. Meanwhile, behind the back of the Democratic Conference, directly contrary results have been achieved by way of the backstage deals of Citizen Kerensky, the Cadets, and the SR and Menshevik leaders. A Government has been formed in and around which both avowed and clandestine Kornilovites play the leading rôle. The non-responsibility of this Government [to the Council of the Republic] has been formally established. The Council of the Russian Republic has been declared a consultant body. Propertied elements have come into the Provisional Council in numbers to which, as all elections throughout the country indicate, they are not entitled. Despite this it is precisely the Cadet Party that has made the Government independent of the Council of the Republic. Propertied elements will undoubtedly occupy a much less favourable position in the Constituent Assembly than in the Provisional Council. The Government cannot help but be responsible to the Constituent Assembly. If the propertied elements were really preparing for the Constituent Assembly in a month and a half, they would have no grounds for defending the non-responsibility of the Government now. The whole point is that the bourgeois classes have set themselves the goal of preventing the Constituent Assembly . . .'

There was an uproar. Shouts from the Right: 'Lies!' Trotsky tried to show complete indifference, and didn't raise his voice.

'In the fields of industry, agriculture, and supply the policy of the Government and the possessing classes is aggravating the havoc produced by the war. The propertied classes, who provoked the uprising, are now moving to crush it and are openly steering a course for the bony hand of hunger, which is expected to strangle the revolution and the Constituent Assembly first of all.

'Nor is foreign policy any less criminal. After forty months of war the capital is threatened by mortal danger. In response to this a plan has been put forward for the transfer of the Government to Moscow. The idea of surrendering the revolutionary capital to German troops does not arouse the slightest indignation amongst the bourgeois classes; on the contrary it is accepted as a natural link in the general policy that is supposed to help them in their counter-revolutionary conspiracy.'

The uproar grew worse. The patriots leaped from their seats and wouldn't allow Trotsky to go on speaking. Shouts about Germany, the sealed car and so on. One shout stood out: 'Bastard!' I make the point now that *throughout* the revolution, both before and after the Bolsheviks, neither in the Tauride, nor in Smolny, however stormy the sessions and however tense the atmosphere, there was *never once* such an outcry at the meetings of our rank-and-file. But it was enough for us to come into the fine society of the Marian Palace, the company of polished lawyers, professors, financiers, landowners, and generals, for the tavern atmosphere of the bourgeois State Duma to revive immediately.

The chairman called the meeting to order. Trotsky was standing there as though none of this were any concern of his, and finally found it possible to go on.

'We, the Bolshevik fraction of the Social-Democratic Party, declare that with this Government of national treachery and with this "Council" we——'

The uproar took on an obviously hopeless character. The majority of the Right got to their feet with the obvious intention of stopping the speech. The chairman called the speaker to order. Trotsky, beginning to lose his temper, and speaking by now through the hubbub, finished:

'—that we have nothing in common with them. We have nothing in common with that murderous intrigue against the people which is being conducted behind the official scenes. We refuse to shield it either directly or indirectly for a single day. In leaving the Provisional Council we call upon the workers, soldiers, and peasants of all Russia to be stalwart and courageous. Petersburg is in danger, the revolution is in danger, the nation is in danger. The Government is intensifying that danger. The ruling parties are increasing it. Only the nation can save itself and the country. We appeal to the people: Long live an immediate, honourable democratic peace, all power to the Soviets, all land to the people, long live the Constituent Assembly!'

Trotsky got off the platform, and a few dozen men of the extreme Left left the hall amidst hubbub and shouting. The majority gazed after them disdainfully, waving their hands—good riddance! The majority saw nothing: after all, this was only sixty specimens of a peculiar breed of wild beast who were leaving the society of mankind. Just the Bolsheviks alone. Good riddance! It was calmer and more agreeable without them.

But we, the closest neighbours of the Bolsheviks and their companions-in-arms, sat there utterly depressed by all that had happened.

* * *

Despite all the power and brilliance of his speech Trotsky, as we see, was far from having *proved* the necessity of the break. He had not proved it because he didn't wish to finish what he had to say. But from their point of view the ones who left were logical enough. If they were *on the other side* of this entire order, then there was really nothing for them to do in the Pre-Parliament.

But this was just how the matter must be understood: if there was nothing for them to do there and they left, consequently—they were *on the other side*. There was only one road for them out of the Pre-Parliament—to the barricades. If they cast away the 'electoral ballot', they must take up the rifle. And that, indeed, is what happened. But the majority didn't understand this, didn't see it, didn't believe it. We, their neighbours and companions-in-arms, did understand it. But we thought it wrong.

'Just the Bolsheviks alone.' For the Pre-Parliamentary majority they were a handful who could be liquidated by repression. For *us* they were an overwhelming section of a proletariat straining into battle and nourished on class hatred, and also of the tormented soldiery, and of the peasant depths that had despaired of the revolution. They were a vast landslide of people. They were millions. Repress them? And with our comic-opera Government!

For us Internationalists the question was not posed on that plane at all. It was not a question of its being impossible to liquidate the Bolsheviks. The point was that the proletariat, the soldiery, and the peasant rank-and-file, led by the Bolshevik Party and finding themselves outside the existing 'political order', were now taking up arms against the entire old world, to raze the millennial bourgeois system to the ground. By the strength of their own proletarian vanguard party alone, surrounded by millions of casual and unreliable fellow-travellers, they wanted to create a new unheard-of proletarian state and an unprecedented social and economic order. They wanted to do this in our ruined, half-wild, petty-bourgeois, economically-shattered country. They wanted to do this against the organized petty-bourgeois elements, after putting an end to the united front of the democracy for ever.

This was a fateful mistake. It was a disastrous programme and tactic for the revolution.

A new revolution was admissible, an uprising was legitimate, the liquidation of the existing régime was indispensable. But all this was so—*on condition of a united democratic front.* That meant an armed struggle *only* against big capital and imperialism. It meant *only* the liquidation of the political and economic rule of the bourgeoisie and the landowners. It did *not* mean the definitive destruction of the old State and the rejection of its heritage. It meant the plenipotentiary participation of the petty-bourgeois, *Menshevik–SR* groups in the construction of a new State *together with* the proletariat and the peasantry. These were all *unconditionally essential* elements of the new society that was springing up on the ruins of the empire of the exploiting minority. And in the conditions of our revolution this was the only correct formulation of the problem.

But the leaders of the Bolshevik Party were hostile to all this. They formulated the basic task of the revolution *incorrectly*. And they continually carried on, *not* a policy of alliance, but the contrary policy of rupture, split, and mutual isolation.

The Bolshevik departure from the Pre-Parliament was an important step. In flinging aside their voting papers the Bolsheviks, in the eyes of all those with eyes to see, were taking up their rifles. They had no chance of arousing the sympathy of the Mensheviks and SRs by this demonstration and every chance of repelling them far away. The Bolshevik leaders were heading straight for this and calculating on it.

What we Internationalists were depressed by was not that the Bolsheviks had taken to the barricades to make a legitimate revolution. It was not the burning of the boats that disconcerted us. What was depressing was that with the declaration of civil war the democratic front was almost hopelessly disrupted by the Bolsheviks, and that they were turning their weapons against elements *vital to themselves* and to the realization of the tasks of the revolution as correctly formulated.

Well, and what would have happened if the Bolsheviks had *stayed* in the Pre-Parliament? What would have happened if in liquidating Kerenskyism they had shown an inclination for a *rapprochement* with the old Soviet bloc, as had happened in the short period of the liquidation of the *Kornilov* revolt?

Let us note two circumstances. First of all the new Coalition, like every product of 'Kerenskyism', was quite unfit for survival.

Its fate was pre-determined by the whole conjuncture, and especially by the fact that the real power was already in the hands of the Bolsheviks. Secondly, the Bolsheviks would have been a very strong inspirational minority in the Pre-Parliament; together with the Internationalists and the allied SRs this minority could have amounted to 30 per cent; if the situation ever became more acute and there was a split in the Menshevik–SR bloc (as had happened in Smolny during the Kornilov revolt), the *majority* of the Pre-Parliament would have been on the side of the former Soviet Left.

All these abstract calculations would have been significant i the Bolsheviks hadn't been Bolsheviks.

* * *

Rumours of the internal collapse of the Coalition kept growing stronger and stronger. The loyal elements were beginning to lose patience. . . And they were egged on by various factors from all sides.

On the one hand a Congress of Soviets was already assembling at Smolny. Here the Bolsheviks were completely sovereign; the Congress was a rather serious factor, while the intentions of the Bolsheviks—in any case promised unpleasantness.

On another side the Cossacks, who had been attracting attention for a long time, began to allow themselves absolutely infamous conduct: in Kaluga, on the 20th, a Cossack detachment had besieged the local Soviet and demanded its surrender, but when the surrender took place, nevertheless opened fire and killed a few members of the Soviet. Kaluga today, Poltava tomorrow, Moscow the day after. . .

From a third side, the internal collapse of the Coalition was progressing before everybody's eyes.

The official Menshevik leaders, widely at variance with each other, had been trying up to now to contrive a *Left-Centre* bloc, cutting off the Martovites and the Left SRs on the Left, and finding alliances on the Right. Now the orientation had changed. Instead of the Left-Centre bloc Dan was fussing about trying to concoct a *Left* bloc. He was stretching out a hand to Martov. That meant he was ready to sacrifice the Centre and was calculating on finally drawing the SRs into the Opposition.

But we didn't have time to finish our debates. The Left Centre was creeping further and further towards the Left with every step. Events were dragging along behind them the hopeless interstitial ordinary people who had no class backbone—dragging along those who would not go along of their own free will. We didn't have time. . . Do you miss my point, Reader? Then I'll try to explain it all to you now, as well as I can.

January–July 1921.

Part VI

THE OCTOBER INSURRECTION

October 3rd–November 1st

CHAPTER 27

THE SOFTENING-UP

IN the softly glittering halls of the Marian Palace there was no revolution at all. It was all in Smolny, in the working-class sections of the capital and in the provincial towns and districts. And that revolution was racing down an inclined plane to a *dénouement*. . . The Bolsheviks had definitely embarked on a violent revolutionary destruction of the Coalition and its replacement by 'Power to the Soviets'. They had embraced the cause of a *coup d'état.*

We shall have to deal with three groups of problems, for every *coup d'état* has, in the first place, its ideology or philosophy; secondly, its politics; and thirdly, its strategy. Perhaps this can be expressed more concretely and less pretentiously: we shall be dealing with the *programme* of the overturn, its *tactics*, and its *organization.*

From the last days of September on, the salient points of spoken and written Bolshevik propaganda were the following. First of all, this last Coalition of ours was a gang of usurpers, who had seized autocratic power through private agreement among a couple of dozen men. This was the incontestable and shameful truth which the Bolsheviks strove to make every worker and soldier aware of. Apart from a resolution of the Petersburg Soviet refusing support to the newly born Coalition, a wave of mass-meetings swiftly poured over both capitals and the whole country; hundreds of thousands of workers and soldiers protested against the very fact of the formation of a new bourgeois Government, and demanded power for the Soviets.

Moreover, the existing Government was not only a gang of usurpers; it was a Government of *counter-revolutionary rebels.* That Kornilov was such a rebel everyone knew: it had been officially announced. But by now, after all, the whole affair had been sufficiently exposed. Kerensky had been in league with Kornilov, and he himself had summoned the Third Corps to destroy the Soviets, and agreed to enter Kornilov's Cabinet. The Bolsheviks had raised the question of the Kornilov revolt;

and the Central Ex. Com. Bureau had supported them; but the Ministers didn't even consider explaining themselves.

Further—it followed from this that the existing Government, Kornilovite by nature, could not help but prepare a *new* Kornilov revolt. Any day now it might launch a decisive onslaught on the revolution, and then—good-bye to everything that had been won! It was necessary to defend oneself.

On the other hand, this Government of conspirators and counter-revolutionaries was allowing itself a base mockery of the working class, its press, and its representatives. In the Kornilov affair exactly five men had been arrested, who were in the custody of their own guard of honour, and could escape when they saw fit, while the real gaols were full of Bolsheviks on hunger-strike, incapable of obtaining either their release or any coherent charges.

The shameful attempt at evacuating the Government to Moscow was taken up with special fury. The plotters were betraying the revolutionary capital! Incapable of defending it, they did not even want to do so. . . The Germans were continuing their naval operations, the sailors were staking their lives, while the Allies, not lifting a finger to help, were covering our heroes with dirt. And the Government? It was not only fleeing to Moscow, but preparing the surrender of Petersburg.

The new Government had issued orders to clear the revolutionary *troops* out of the capital; these orders were also directed to the same aims. Things were serious at the front, and reinforcements were needed. That we believed. But was there even one worker or soldier who would believe that Kerensky was removing these troops without any political end in view? No, after the Kornilov revolt it would have been stupid and criminal to believe this. We would all go to the front. But we would go when we were sure that this would close the road to the Germans and not open it to the counter-revolution. . .

But in that case what about defence? There was only one solution: we must take it *into our own hands*. We were ready to defend the revolution from the Germans, as our brothers, the sailor-heroes and the Lettish Rifles, had defended it. But we could not say to the garrison: put yourselves in the hands of Kerensky, who will turn you against the working class. The situation was absurd and unendurable. Yes—and the only way of changing it was to liquidate the Government of national betrayal. . .

The following fact was characteristic both of the state of defence and of the mood of the politically active masses. Our 'commander-in-chief' addressed the sailors in his usual tactless shout: the fleet was becoming disorganized, it was unreliable, it must expiate its crimes against the revolution, and so on. In reply the Second Congress of Sailors of the Baltic Fleet produced this resolution: '. . . to demand from the Central Ex. Com. of the Workers, Soldiers, and Peasants the instant removal from the ranks of the Provisional Government of the Socialist, with and without quotation-marks, the anti-political adventurer Kerensky, as a blackguard who, by his shameless political blackmail on behalf of the bourgeoisie, is destroying the great revolution and with it the whole revolutionary people. As for you, Kerensky–Bonaparte, traitor to the revolution, we send you our curses, while our comrades are being slain by bullets and shells or drowning at sea, calling for the defence of the revolution, and while we all as one man are prepared to lay down our lives for liberty, land, and freedom, and perish in battle against the enemy without, or on the barricades against the enemy within, calling down curses on you, Kerensky, and your gang. . .'

A document undoubtedly not without a certain eloquence.

These were the principal points of Bolshevik agitation during those weeks. This agitation met with no opposition whatsoever. But there was one special point that had to be concentrated on. That the Coalition was unendurable and criminal had been proved a million times, and was clear without proofs. But that wasn't enough. . . If it was impossible to endure the *Coalition*, then let the Constituent Assembly assemble soon—*that* would provide salvation, and peace, bread, and land. So the worker, the peasant, and the soldier might think. That was where all their hopes lay.

This would not do. Faith in the Constituent Assembly had to be destroyed. That is, it had to be proved that under a Coalition it was impossible. It was just this the Bolsheviks were directing their special attention to.

The bourgeoisie and the Coalition were undermining the Constituent Assembly! Not one Bolshevik speech, resolution, statement, or newspaper article could dispense with this. It might have been said that their whole agitation was being carried on under the banner of the Constituent Assembly and its defence.

To those conversant—but not specially conversant—with affairs, this might seem somewhat odd. Lenin, after all, only an hour after his arrival, had attacked the parliamentary republic and rejected any Government except that of the Soviets. Nor did the slogan of 'Soviet power', which had later become the cornerstone of Bolshevism, suggest that the Soviet Government would be a *Provisional* Government. The Constituent Assembly seemed definitely *excluded* by all this. . .

But no—the Bolshevik Party put the matter otherwise: down with the Coalition and long live a Soviet régime in the name of the Constituent Assembly!

I have noted in its place that it was actually not the Bolshevik Party as a whole that had to keep quiet about the Constituent Assembly, but merely its head, Lenin, who did not show his cards within the confines of the Bolshevik Party. Lenin conspired away from the party, and the party, not putting two and two together, accepted the Constituent Assembly at its face value and sponsored it whole-heartedly. That was how it had been at first. . . But that could hardly have continued until now? What sort of Asiatic perfidy on the part of the leader was this? And boundless innocence of the party's 'officer-corps'?

There was here, of course, a substantial degree of both one and the other. But that didn't exhaust the matter. The point was that Lenin, after first giving the Constituent Assembly a kick, and then deciding to keep a diplomatic *silence* about it, had soon arrived at the idea of *exploiting* it. No sooner thought of than done. The Constituent Assembly began to conceal 'Power to the Soviets'. Lenin not only did not keep silent but shouted with the party; in his central organ he would write about how 'to ensure the success of the Constituent Assembly'.

But could there really be people in the world who could fail to remember Lenin's thrust at the parliamentary republic and the Constituent Assembly? What could be done about that now, before fighting began? Very simple: 'Our opponents maintain that Lenin was against the Constituent Assembly and for a Soviet republic. This assertion is obviously false. Lenin was never "against" the Constituent Assembly. From the very first months he, together with our whole party, has exposed the Provisional Government for delaying the Constituent Assembly. Events have now demonstrated that these accusations of ours were right.' That was all, as explained by the *Rabochii Put.*

Well, but how about a new constitutional theory? For after all it's impossible to count indefinitely on everyone's being as trusting as a child and as short-sighted as a sheep. It was necessary, after all, to have some kind of 'theory', to conceal the secrets of diplomacy and plaster over the yawning logical vacuum. Of course! And such a theory was created—just as easily as the malicious inventions about Lenin's position were refuted. 'A Soviet republic,' said this theory, 'far from excludes the Constituent Assembly, just as, conversely, a Constituent Assembly republic doesn't preclude the existence of Soviets. If our revolution is destined to conquer, then in practice we shall see a combined type of Soviet republic and Constituent Assembly.' And that was all.

This article in the *Rabochii Put* of 4 October was not signed by the modest author. But—oh, gallant Zinoviev! I should recognize your inimitable boldness of thought, your celebrated courage in defending difficult positions a thousand miles away! It is true that besides a central newspaper the Bolshevik Party in those days had a *draft programme.* It was impossible to find in it any signs of a 'combined type'; what it contained was simply the Soviet *worker–peasant dictatorship*, which excluded the bourgeois-parliamentary Constituent Assembly. But that doesn't matter. Everyone understands that a theoretical document for oneself is one thing—and a practical idea for general use is another.

In all this both the perfidy of the shepherd and the innocence of the sheep are evident. But we see that both the one and the other, in spite of our initial impressions, have here not a crudely primitive but, on the contrary, a highly qualified character. As we see, it's not a question here of a comparatively minor and private deception aimed at one's own friends and companions-in-arms, or of a simple childish readiness to be deceived. Here the deception has a general mass character and a national scale. Mass slaughter on a national scale, of course, is not a reprehensible action, but gallantry and heroism. Deception in such circumstances is called diplomacy or tactics, or politics. For the subject of the deception it must be considered in the aspect of statesmanship—*sui generis*—and for its objects in the aspect of intellectual solidarity and party discipline—also *sui generis*.

* * *

So 'Down with the Coalition' and 'Long live a Soviet régime'—in the name of the Constituent Assembly! Only when the Soviets have the power will the fate of the Constituent Assembly be in safe hands. Well, and what *else* will the power of the Soviets give us?

A Soviet Government, it was said, is not only the guarantor of the Constituent Assembly, but also its *mainstay*. First of all, 'capitalists and landowners might not only jeer at the Constituent Assembly, but also dismiss it, as the Tsar dismissed the first two Dumas'. The Soviets wouldn't allow that. Secondly, the Soviets would constitute an apparatus for putting into practice the plans of the Constituent Assembly. 'Suppose that on November 30th it decrees the confiscation of all land-holdings. What could the municipal and rural local authorities do for the effective realization of this demand? Practically nothing. But what could the Soviets do? Everything.' (*Rabochii Put*, 3 October.)

Further: it goes without saying that the Soviets were called to realize everything the masses could no longer live without, and which the Coalition couldn't give them: peace, land, and bread. This was so simple and obvious, and filled all the articles and speeches of the Bolsheviks at this time so naturally, that there is no need to dwell on it. It was simply the other side of the struggle against 'Kerenskyism'.

The question could only lie in exactly *how* and *when* the Soviets would give land, peace, and bread. Here the question of land was extremely clear: the Soviets would give the land to the peasants *immediately*. The question of peace was not so clear-cut: a Soviet Government would at once propose peace to the countries at war, appealing to the ruined and destroyed nations; with full confidence it could be expected that we would obtain a just and general peace.

But the question of *bread* was completely vague: it was an involved complex of ideas (collecting actual bread from the countryside, raising real wages, and so on) and this demanded a system of correspondingly various measures; but in the process of agitation this complexity was not without its advantages, since it allowed everyone to chatter on and on without saying anything. . . For in the last analysis, after all, to go into details and explain just how and what would be done, was not at all obligatory. In the given circumstances it was quite enough to show the party's firm intention of realizing the most vital demands of the people.

But it was quite clear that all these conditions and the whole character of the campaign of agitation made irresistibly for the most unprincipled *demagogy*, which the Bolsheviks, inflaming the atmosphere, plunged into. Their demagogy was brazen and unbounded. It had nothing to do with science, elementary truth, or common sense. And it was not only the rank-and-file agitators, who lacked all these, who proved themselves in the demagogic arena. The leaders behaved with the same primitive lack of self-restraint.

Lenin, by 'giving the peasants the land at once' and preaching seizure, was in fact subscribing to anarchist tactics and an SR programme. Both one and the other were pleasing and understandable to the peasant, who was far from being a fanatical upholder of Marxism. But both one and the other had been railed at night and day by the Marxist Lenin for at least fifteen years. Now this was flung aside. To please the peasants and be understood by them Lenin became both an anarchist and an SR.

Trotsky too in one breath resolved all supply difficulties with the utmost boldness. The Soviet Government would send out a soldier, a sailor, and a working girl (at dozens of meetings for some reason Trotsky said 'working girl') into every village; they would inspect the stores of the well-to-do, leave them as much as they needed and take the rest gratis for the city or the front. . . The Petersburg working masses hailed these promises with enthusiasm.

It is obvious that all these 'confiscations' and 'seizures without payment' scattered left and right with regal lavishness were captivating and irresistible in the mouths of the friends of the people. Nothing could withstand them. Hence the spontaneous and irresistible development of this method of agitation. . . There are rich and poor; the rich have a lot of everything, the poor have nothing; everything will belong to the poor, will be divided amongst the have-nots. This is the message of your own working-class party, followed by the millions of poor of the city and country,—the sole party fighting against the rich and their Government for land, peace, and bread.

All this flooded the whole of Russia in endless waves during the final weeks. Every day all this was listened to by hundreds of thousands of hungry, tired, and angry people. This was an inalienable element of Bolshevik agitation, even though it wasn't the official programme.

* * *

But a delicate question arises—was there any Socialism in this 'platform'? No. I maintain that in a *direct form* the Bolsheviks never harped to the masses on Socialism as the object and task of a Soviet Government; nor did the masses, in supporting the Bolsheviks, even think about Socialism. But in an *indirect*, confused form the problem of 'immediate Socialism' was nevertheless posed. In general the central leaders of Bolshevism were evidently firmly bent on carrying out a Socialist experiment: this was demanded by the logic of the situation. But once again —before the eyes of the masses—they did not dot any of their 'i's.

Socialism is, of course, primarily an *economic* problem. I have indicated that the Bolsheviks were weak on this. Neither Lenin, elaborating the programme of his party, nor Trotsky, doing the same for the former Interdistrictites, appreciated the significance of an *economic* programme as such, or gave it priority; indeed, they simply almost forgot about it. Even now, in October, the new Bolshevik convert, Larin, loudly complained that in place of an economic programme the Bolsheviks had 'almost a vacuum'. (*Rabochii Put*, 8 October.) He was asked to fill it as an emergency measure. He proposed the cancellation of the national debt, compulsory collective contracts, the extension of working-class legislation to domestic servants, annual vacations for workers, and much more, all very fine. But there is no question here of Socialism proper. The Soviet Government is based on the existence of private property.

If we turn to the official statement read by Trotsky at the Democratic Conference, the economic programme of a Soviet Government is expounded as follows: only a Soviet Government is 'capable of introducing a maximum of planning into the economy at present disintegrating, helping the peasantry and rural workers to exploit the now available means of agricultural production, limiting profits, establishing wages and, in conformity with the regulation of production, assuring real labour discipline, based on the autonomy of the workers and their centralized control over industry'. This is all very obscure and insubstantial, but is quite alien to utopianism. The statement is far from placing Socialism on the agenda of a Soviet régime. In essence its content does not go beyond the limits of the May 16th economic programme which was accepted by the old Ex. Com. to be carried out by a Coalition Government. The Coalition could not, of course, carry it out, for this programme undermined at its root the economic hegemony of capital. For Konovalov that was the same as Socialism, but essentially it was a far cry from it.

This was the economic platform of the Bolshevik Party on the eve of its decisive *coup*.

Nevertheless there was a point in it that has special significance for us. This was the *workers' control* over production. This was a fighting point at all proletarian meetings. As a specifically *working-class* demand it was figured equally with *land*. And, if you like, it was *here and only here* that the Bolshevik leaders approached a public declaration of Socialist principles. However, this 'Socialism' was extremely timid and modest: in their theory the Bolsheviks, while moving along a different road, went no further than the Right Menshevik Grohman, with his programme of the 'regulation' or 'organization of national economy and labour'.

So the masses were politically prepared for the liquidation of Kerenskyism and ready for a Soviet régime. They were awaiting the summons to technical action, but speaking generally were not thinking about it at all. They were being told: 'Let's wait—for what the Congress[1] decides on October 20th or 25th'.

I detected a different note for the first time that same October 7th, the day the Bolsheviks left the Pre-Parliament. But this was no more than a *note*—a suggestive one to be sure, but not as yet burning the smallest boat or binding anyone to anything. In a stormy article devoted by Lenin to a peasant uprising we read: 'There's not the slightest doubt that if the

[1] i.e., the Second All-Russian Soviet Congress. (Ed.)

Bolsheviks allowed themselves to fall into the snare of constitutional illusions, "faith" in the convocation of the Constituent Assembly and the "expectation" of a congress of Soviets, etc.—there is no doubt that such Bolsheviks would be miserable traitors to the proletarian cause.'

Lenin considered that a peasant uprising embracing all Russia would decide matters. 'To allow the crushing of a peasant uprising at such a moment means falsifying the elections to the Constituent Assembly even more, and more grossly, than the Democratic Conference and the Pre-Parliament were falsified. The whole future of the Russian Revolution is at stake. The whole future of the international working-class revolution is at stake. The crisis is at hand.'

Trotsky, leading his army out of the Pre-Parliament, had definitely set course towards a violent overthrow. Lenin had declared that it was criminal to wait for the Congress of Soviets. As yet nothing more. The masses were still in the same position. But it was clear that within the party the question of *how* had been placed next in order. It ought to be decided at once.

On October 10th it was posed by the supreme authority. The Central Committee of the Bolshevik Party assembled in full strength. . . Oh, the novel jokes of the merry muse of History! This supreme and decisive session took place in my own home, still at the Karpovka. But—without my knowledge. As before I would very often spend the night somewhere near the office or Smolny, that is about eight versts from the Karpovka. This time special steps were taken to have me spend the night away from home: at least my wife knew my intentions exactly and gave me a piece of friendly, disinterested advice—not to inconvenience myself by a further journey after work. In any case the lofty assemblage had a complete guarantee against my arrival.

For such a cardinal session not only did people come from Moscow, but the Lord of Hosts himself, with his henchman, crept out of the underground. Lenin appeared in a wig, but without his beard. Zinoviev appeared with a beard, but without his shock of hair. The meeting went on for about ten hours, until about 3 o'clock in the morning. Half the exalted guests had to sleep somehow in the Karpovka.

However, I don't actually know much about the exact course of this meeting, or even about its outcome. It's clear that the question of an *uprising* was put. There was evidently also a question about its relation to the Soviet Congress: should it depend on the time and circumstances of the Congress? The question of the revolt was decided in the affirmative, and evidently it was decided to raise it as quickly as possible—depending on the course of its speedy technical preparation and on the most favourable external conditions. It was possible to confront the Congress of Soviets with an accomplished fact; political conditions allowed of this, and there could be no doubt of the support and sanction of the Congress. But aside from that, because of weighty considerations the Congress *ought* to be confronted by an accomplished fact. For it was, after all, clear to the enemy camp that the Congress would *decide* to take power and—at least—*make an attempt to realize that decision.* It would be absurd for a Government which was not prepared to yield voluntarily to the Bolsheviks to await that moment. It was clear that it would attempt to forestall the action of the Congress, doing everything possible either to forbid or to disperse or shoot down the Congress. If an uprising had been decided on, then it was absurd to wait for this to happen. Common sense demanded that the people in their turn forestall the Government's offensive. This was elementary tactics and strategy.

It was decided to begin the uprising as quickly as possible, depending on circumstances but not on the Congress.

In the Central Committee of the party this decision was accepted by all but two votes. The dissenters were the same as in June—Kamenev and Zinoviev. . . This of course could not confound the Thunderer. He had never been confounded even when he remained practically alone in his own party; now he had the *majority* with him. And, besides the majority, *Trotsky was with Lenin.* I don't know to what degree Lenin himself valued this fact, but for the course of events it had incalculable significance. I have no doubt of that. . . The 'cronies' were for the time being left to their own opinion, but without any attention from the others. The order was accepted and matters followed their course.

* * *

The decision put events on a new footing. The boats had been burnt. Now direct preparations for an uprising were started—

politically and technically. It is clear that an uprising against the Coalition, and its destruction, were incumbent on the Petersburg proletariat and garrison. Hence the official agency of the uprising was the Petersburg Soviet. The political and technical work had to proceed from there.

But it goes without saying that the decision of the party Central Committee was not brought to the knowledge either of the Petersburg masses or of the Soviet. The *political* change was expressed only in a few additions to the earlier agitation. 'Further delay is impossible.' 'It's time to pass from words to deeds.' 'The moment has come when the revolutionary slogan of "All Power to the Soviets" must be realized at last.' Etc.

It was clear that an uprising was necessary. 'Action' was plainly imminent. The proletariat and the garrison had to be ready at any minute to obey revolutionary orders. . . Such was the new political phase of the movement.

It may be asked whether the Petersburg proletariat and garrison was ready for dynamic action and bloody sacrifice, just as it was for the acceptance of a Soviet Government and all its blessings? Was it capable not only of passing a menacing resolution, but also of really going into battle? Was it burning, not only with hate, but with a real longing for revolutionary exploits? Was its mood firm?

There are various answers to all this. It is quite fundamental. Not because the outcome of the movement depended on it—the success of the overturn was assured because there was nothing to oppose it. But the mood of the masses who were to act is important because in the eyes of history this is what determined the *character* of the overturn.

Personally, as a witness and participant in the events, I have no single answer. *There were various moods.* The only common ones were hatred for 'Kerenskyism', fatigue, rage, and a desire for peace, bread, and land. . . During just these weeks I, more than ever before, made the rounds of the factories and spoke to the 'masses'. I had the definite impression that the mood was ambiguous, conditional. The Coalition and the *status quo* could no longer be endured; but whether it was necessary to come out, or necessary to pass through an uprising, was not clearly known. Many well remembered the July Days. What if once again nothing came of it?

I'm speaking of the mood of the *average* rank-and-filer. That doesn't mean that the Bolsheviks could not have assembled, summoned, and launched into battle as many revolutionary battalions as they wanted. On the contrary: they had a sufficient number of advanced, active cadres ready for sacrifice. The most reliable were the workers and their Red Guard; then the sailors. There was enough fighting material. But good-quality fighting material made up a small part of the Bolshevik following at this time. On the average, the mood was strongly Bolshevik, but rather slack and wavering with respect to action and a rising.

So, after the decision of the Bolshevik centre on October 10th, the masses were told that it was time to pass from words to deeds. For the time being they were told nothing else. This was quite natural. The main results of the vote on October 10th could not be spoken of. Policy might remain almost the same; but now it had to yield its primary position to *strategy*. The direct preparation of the uprising now had to pass to the *Staff*. It was impossible to work out dispositions before the whole army, before the eyes of the enemy. The enemy was to be left in the dark, while the army stood at the ready, working up steam.

* * *

During those days, in view of the acute situation at the front, discussions were going on everywhere about defence; on October 9th, before the decision of the party Central Committee, this question was raised in the Petersburg Ex. Com. also. It was, of course, provoked primarily by political considerations. And the discussion itself was tied up with the question of evacuating troops from the capital. It was said that the Staff demands for troops to be sent to the front had, as always, a political motivation, and that in general it was impossible to trust the Government in matters of defence. Consequently it was necessary first of all to organize *control over the Staff* and determine the evacuation of troops as circumstances demanded, and secondly to take the defence question into one's own hands and create a special organ for it—a committee of revolutionary defence.

The Mensheviks and SRs talked of the dual power and the inappropriateness of forming a Staff of one's own. But seeing the weakness of their position they gave in and themselves proposed a resolution which was accepted by the Bolshevik Ex. Com., demanding, in the main: (1) the creation of a board of representatives of the Petersburg Soviet and the Central Committee of the Fleet, to be informed of the evacuation of any given unit; (2) extraordinary measures for the purging of the General Staff; and (3) the formation of a committee of revolutionary defence, which would clarify the question of the defence of Petersburg.

That same day the question was taken before the plenum of the Petersburg Soviet. However, the Ex. Com. resolution proposed by the Mensheviks was turned down. A *Bolshevik* resolution was passed, which spoke of the need for a Soviet Government that would propose immediate peace; of the necessity, before the conclusion of peace, of taking the defence of the capital and the whole country into the hands of the Soviets; and of the necessity of arming the workers for defence. And the Ex. Com., the Soldiers' Section and the garrison deputies were charged with the organization of a revolutionary committee of defence which 'would concentrate in its own hands all data relevant to the defence of Petersburg'.

'All data'—rather happily put. But nevertheless we see that things were still going along under the banner of *military defence.* All this was *before the Bolshevik Central Committee session at my flat.*

On October 12th a new meeting of the Ex. Com. was held to execute the Soviet resolution. It was a closed meeting. In a matter such as defence (*sic!*) the Bolsheviks thought it necessary to violate the principles they were still continuing to fight for. But this wasn't secret diplomacy—it was a plot. However, it must be kept in mind that it could not be fully realized; in this closed session there could be no freedom of discussion, for there were a few 'Social-traitors' in the Ex. Com. So one thing was said and another meant. Nor did the published decision, as a matter of fact, have the same inward meaning as appeared to the world in the lines below.

This was the decision:

'A Military Revolutionary Committee is being formed by the Petersburg Ex. Com. and is its organ. It is composed of: the Praesidiums of the plenum and of the Soldiers' Section of the Soviet, representatives of the Central Committee of the Fleet, the Railwaymen's Union, the Union of Post Office and Telegraph Employees, the Factory Committees, the Trade Unions, representatives of the party military organizations, the military section of the Central Ex. Com., and the workers' militia, as well as individuals whose presence is thought necessary. The Military Revolutionary Committee's first tasks are the allocation of combat and auxiliary forces, necessary for the defence of the capital and not subject to evacuation; then the registration of the personal composition of the garrison of Petersburg and its suburbs, and also the registration of supply sources; the elaboration of a working plan for the defence of the city; measures of protection against pogroms and desertions; the maintenance of revolutionary discipline amongst the working class and soldiery. . .'

We can see that none of this is honest or legitimate *co-operation* in defence. It is, in essence, the illegal *elimination* from defence affairs of the 'legitimate' agencies of the Government and the transference of all their functions to the Petersburg Soviet. But that was the least of it: under the banner of defence against the foreign enemy the Ex. Com. concentrated in its own hands *all military power* in the capital and the provinces. That is, it officially arrogated to itself all real power whatever.

In fact, of course, this power had long belonged to the Bolshevik Soviet. Does this mean that the decrees of October 12th made the overturn an accomplished fact? No, it doesn't. But only because the Bolsheviks themselves said that there was nothing in it but co-operation for external defence. They gave such explanations right down to October 23rd.

But the Mensheviks, in the closed session of the Ex. Com., revealed the true meaning of these decrees. The Military Revolutionary Committee was an apparatus for the overthrow of the Government and the seizure of power by the Bolsheviks.

* * *

And on October 16th this 'motion' was presented to the Soviet plenum for approval. There were heated protests from a Menshevik orator, whose fraction, in this meeting of a thousand men, numbered fifty people.

'The Bolsheviks won't answer the straight question whether or not they are preparing a *coup*. This is either cowardice or lack of confidence in their own strength' (laughter in the audience).

'But the projected Military Revolutionary Committee is nothing but a revolutionary staff for the seizure of power. . . We have many local reports that the masses are out of sympathy with a *coup*. There is a 'Provisional Military Committee' attached to the Central Ex. Com., whose object is real co-operation in the defence of the northern front. The Petersburg Soviet ought to send its representatives there and reject the proposal for a military revolutionary committee.'

Trotsky got up. In this gathering his task was not especially difficult.

'The Menshevik representative is preoccupied with whether the Bolsheviks are preparing an armed demonstration. In whose name has he asked this question: in the name of Kerensky, the counter-intelligence, the Secret Police, or some other body?'

This was a tumultuous success. But even without this the resolution on the Military Revolutionary Committee would have been passed by an overwhelming majority of the Soviet that session of October 16th.

The Military Revolutionary Committee was created and rapidly got to work. Both the Mensheviks and the Right SRs refused to go into it. The Left SRs did enter it. Its principal figures were Trotsky, Lashevich, then the leaders of the Bolshevik Military Organization, Podvoisky and Nevsky, Yurenev, Mekhonoshin, the Left SR Lazimir, and others, until then less well-known.

* * *

The camp of the bourgeoisie and the interstitial groups grew alarmed. Outcries and complaints about 'proposed Bolshevik *coups*' had actually never ceased. They were permanent. But now, apart from 'rumours', they had real grounds. The general atmosphere was so oppressive that the country and the masses were plainly stifling. The crisis was manifest to everyone. The movement of the masses was clearly overflowing its banks. The workers' districts of Petersburg were boiling over before everyone's eyes. Only the Bolsheviks were listened to. At the famous *Cirque Moderne*, where Trotsky, Lunacharsky, and Volodarsky appeared, you kept seeing endless queues and throngs of people for whom there was no longer room in the enormous crowded circus. Agitators were calling for deeds, not words, and promising the imminent achievement of a Soviet régime. And in Smolny, finally, they were working on the creation of a new and more than suspect organ of 'defence'. . . There were real grounds for alarm.

It was not that they were afraid of a Bolshevik victory. It was something else. Amongst the Right, in the bourgeois newspapers, this was the basis of an agitation in favour of immediate decisive repressions, in favour of the assumption of the 'attributes of a real Government' (let us recall Guchkov's golden words!), that is, in favour of a new Kornilov revolt. As for the SRs and Mensheviks, the press alarm meant a real fear—not of the success of the Bolshevik enterprise, but of new July Days.

Besides the written and spoken agitation there appeared a series of appeals in the names of parties, a few institutions, and, of course, the Central Ex. Com. These appeals were all in the same spirit: street action under a separate Bolshevik banner would play into the hands of the counter-revolution. One such appeal was also published by a group of Martovites—over a few of our signatures. On October 18th Gorky came out with a flaming article: 'Rumours are being spread more and more insistently about a Bolshevik *coup*. The repellent scenes of July 3–5th may be repeated. That is—once again lorries tightly packed with people holding rifles and revolvers in hands trembling with fear, and these rifles will go off at random into the windows of shops and at people. They will fire only because the people armed with them want to kill their own fear. All the dark instincts of the mob, infuriated by the destruction of life and the lies of politics, will flare up and begin to smoke—people will kill each other, unable to overcome their own bestial stupidity. In a word, there will be a repetition of that same senseless bloody carnage which we have already seen and which has undermined the moral significance of the revolution throughout the country. It is highly likely that this time events will take on a still more bloody and destructive character. . . The Bolshevik Central Committee has done nothing to confirm the rumours of a *coup*, though it hasn't refuted them either. . . It is its duty to refute them, if it really is a powerful and freely acting political organ capable of directing the masses and not the passive toy of the moods of a savage mob, or a tool in the hands of shameless adventurers or unbalanced fanatics. . .'

* * *

But what was the Government thinking and doing? All hopes, after all, were on it! Moreover, it had once been entrusted with 'limitless power' and even been called the Government of the 'salvation of the revolution'.

It had had a debate on the 'disorders' on the day when the Military Revolutionary Committee was finally approved, October 16th. 'The most resolute measures would be taken and were already being taken.' What these were simple mortals didn't know. What measures our Government could take *at all* was also a mystery to everyone.

However, *there was no alarm*. The tranquil assurance of a powerful Government reigned there. First of all, the *coup* was considered doubtful, once the plans had been disclosed. Secondly, all these plans were very well known to the splendidly organized Government. The Chief of Staff of the Petersburg region reported to the head of the Government: the Bolsheviks were preparing a 'demonstration of protest against the Government': the 'demonstration would have a peaceful character, but nevertheless the workers would come out armed'. The Chief of Staff reported on the measures he 'was prepared to take to forestall the possibility that the demonstration would turn into disorders'. The measures were evidently excellent, since they were approved by the head of the Government.

In general only the man-in-the-street could fall into a panic, while there was no reason at all to be distracted from serious state affairs because of this gossip. In the last analysis this was only the Bolsheviks, while against them was the whole country, which—was with the Government.

Speaking seriously, it is possible to explain the failure of our comic-opera Government to attempt any serious measures of self-defence at this time only by its complete *naïveté* and childishness. Kerensky couldn't, of course, win, but he could and ought to have made an attempt. It was, after all, not May and not June outside. Now he had nothing to lose. He had to take a risk, and play all or nothing.

Kerensky wasn't making any political concessions—out of

considerations of the highest statesmanship. Consequently his only method was—*Kornilovism.* Kerensky was of course ready for this: wasn't he with the whole country and its democracy against its enemies? But he was weak. The 'Commander-in-Chief' had no troops at all. He wouldn't be able to carry his Kornilovism through. . .

Very well. But a risk had to be taken. He had a thousand military cadets and officers in Petersburg. There were even a few more. That was a force. An attempt could be made to paralyse the Bolshevik centres, decapitate the party, and arrest a hundred men in suitable conditions. That might smash the movement. . . In May and June this method was unsuitable. Only the man-in-the-street, wise after the event, lamented this without understanding the point. In May and June, even in July, repressions and violence only *helped the rise* of the movement. But the atmosphere then was *completely different*, the revolution had not yet delivered point-blank its irrevocable ultimatum: either the total destruction of Bolshevism, or its total victory. Now, when there was nothing to lose and it was vital to take a risk, an attempt to smash the movement by a bold and stormy onslaught was the only solution for those who called themselves the Government.

But for this it was necessary to understand at least something. The inflated puppets of the Winter Palace understood nothing. Thinking themselves strong they felt no alarm, and busied themselves with more important affairs of state. They told each other that steps had been and would be taken, and composed decrees to tell the entire nation that the most resolute measures, including . . . etc., etc.

And nothing else.

* * *

On the grey and gloomy afternoon of October 14th there was a session of the Central Ex. Com. in the great hall of Smolny. During the period of the Pre-Parliament the sessions of the Central Ex. Com. plenum had almost ceased: only the Bureau was in session. There were very few delegates even now, and hardly any public; the hall was empty. I remember that the Bolsheviks for some reason were not sitting in their places but were clustered along the left side of the platform in a small group, as though entrenched there in their camp, against the besieging majority. But neither Trotsky nor Kamenev was there. The group was headed by Ryazanov.

The 'defence of the capital' was on the agenda. Dan, of course, reported to the meeting. He began quickly and resolutely to deal with 'the dissension in the heart of the democracy'.

'Exactly at this time, in these days of danger, an agitation is being carried on by the Bolsheviks that is sowing confusion amongst the worker and soldier masses. We must definitely ask our Bolshevik comrades why they are carrying on this policy. Do they know how their agitation is being received by the soldiers and workers? Will they take the responsibility for the consequences? I demand that the Bolshevik Party give a straightforward and honest reply to this question: Yes or no?'

Dan concluded his report on the defence of the capital with this resolution: all workers, peasants, and soldiers were to remain calm and do their duty, while any kind of *coup* was completely inadmissible and could only unleash a destructive movement and thus lead to the wreck of the revolution.

The atmosphere in the hall was very tense. Heads turned towards the cluster of Bolsheviks, from whom protests and contemptuous exclamations were heard. This made the Right lose its temper. The Bolsheviks, after a two-minute consultation, sent Ryazanov to the platform to get away from the question of the *coup* and concentrate attention on defence.

There arose a long argument on procedure, which simply infuriated the majority. The Bolsheviks saw they had to explain themselves on this point, and asked for a break to discuss the resolution, which they hadn't known about up to then. In the absence of their leaders the position of the little group was not easy. An exhausting and boring interval dragged on till evening. Still no leaders. . .

The session was resumed and there was Ryazanov on the platform again, agitated and pale as never before. He was the victim of party duty, but his performance was heroic. What, however, could he say? He was confronted, after all, with the task of explaining himself without giving a straightforward reply. He began:

'I'm sincerely sorry we're debating such a serious question in an empty hall. But I have no desire to have recourse to formalities and raise the question of a quorum. I should merely like to recall our sessions in June and July.'

But the chairman was not to be bamboozled: he wouldn't allow any indulgence in reminiscences and asked him to stick to the point. Ryazanov came a little closer to it and beat about the bush for about an hour.

'As long as the matter of defence is in the hands of the Coalition it will be in the same miserable state it's in now. Starting from this point, we set up the Military Revolutionary Committee, which the Mensheviks voted against. You haven't the resolution to say to the Government "hands off!" Consequently don't say you seriously want to defend the revolution. We are asked whether we want to organize an uprising, but Dan knows that we are Marxists and do not prepare uprisings. The uprising is being prepared by the policy you have supported for seven months. The uprising is being prepared by those who are creating despair and apathy in the masses. If the policy remains the same in future, and if as a result there is an uprising, then we shall be in the first ranks of the insurgents.'

Lenin complimented Ryazanov highly on this speech. The audience, however, was more indignant than satisfied. But what could they do? That was that; you can't squeeze out answers by force.

Fraction speeches followed. Bogdanov spoke for the Mensheviks: 'Ryazanov hasn't given a definite reply, but in any case it's clear the Bolsheviks are preparing an armed uprising; the masses, however, will not go out into the streets. Only handfuls will go, who will be crushed by the Government; Dan's resolution is feeble and colourless, it counts on Bolshevik support, but it should be voted for.'

For our fraction Martov declared that he also would vote for the resolution, though disagreeing with the Bolshevik appraisal of the situation. He also thought street demonstrations a hazardous undertaking. To say that in the interests of defence it was necessary to change the structure of the régime was self-delusion. Civil war would not help defence; for this reason it was impossible now to regard insurgent elements as a method of creating the régime we needed. Ryazanov was right—it was the Government that was preparing the uprising. But each party was also a political factor. We were bound to fight against any attempts at unleashing the elements and we ought to warn the masses. We could not depend on the Bolsheviks' listening to us, but to do our duty we ought to tell the masses that an uprising would be a source of counter-revolution.

Not only the Right but also the *Left* SRs supported Dan's resolution. One more resolution. . .

And the leaders of the old Soviet majority turned to current tasks. . .

* * *

Ryazanov's speech at the Central Ex. Com. enquiry and his references to Marxism called forth an immediate response in the *Novaya Zhizn*, from our accredited theoretician, Bazarov. This began what I may call a *theoretical discussion* of the theme of the uprising. It was rather pathetic. But its political significance lay in the fact that it was *only here* that all the 't's were crossed and it was officially acknowledged that 'going from words to deeds' meant—making an uprising. But even this acknowledgement was at first indirect and academic, and for the masses changed nothing. It was not until October 21st that, by way of closing the discussion, Lenin said in straightforward language that he was calling for insurrection. It was not until then that the political preparation was finished, and only technical instructions remained. It would seem that this was a little too late. But no matter—it came off. The fruit, after all, was so ripe it fell into one's hand by itself.

Bazarov (in his article of October 17th) in reality produced very little theory: 'Ryazanov', he wrote, 'declared that "we" would lead the insurrection; if "we" means individuals, then it is nobody's business; if "we" is the party, then it is a crime, for the party, which embraces the entire working class, will be crushed together with the insurrection, which will lead to the total collapse of the revolution. Violence is inevitable because the "despair and apathy" proclaimed by Ryazanov has never yet been victorious, for Marxism demands an objective calculation of the chances of an insurrection. Amongst the Bolsheviks themselves there are numerous and authoritative dissenters; it is their duty to come out before the masses and fight against this adventure in public, but they have done no more than issue a manuscript leaflet that is being passed from hand to hand.'

As we see, none of this was at all terrible, while the *Novaya Zhizn* attack on Bolshevik plans and methods was far from the first. Each pin-prick from our newspaper, however, had a greater effect on the Bolsheviks than the tempestuous fire of all the rest of the press put together. They were *enemies*; their attacks were merely a source of clarity and strength. But up to now we had been *allies*; this was 'obfuscation' and deadly sabotage. The Bolsheviks broke into a frenzy. Every effort had to be made to trample the *Novaya Zhizn* into the mud in the eyes of the proletariat: our paper was read and considered *their own* by many thousands of advanced Petersburg workers.

The propagandists of *Rabochii Put* took up the cudgels at once. The very next day, amidst a tub of filth, they displayed an interesting quotation from Marx, thinking it was in their favour. Marx's pamphlet, *Revolution and Counter-Revolution in Germany*, gives two important and eloquently expressed directives: 'First, don't undertake an insurrection until you are fully prepared to deal with the consequences; and secondly, once embarked on a revolution act with the greatest resolution and as the attacking side.'

On the basis of this the Bolshevik theoreticians evidently thought their position sound: they were preparing to attack and to act with resolution. And that was as correct as 2 plus 2 makes 4. But the whole point was in that '*once embarked*', that is, if it was necessary. *Was it necessary?* When was it necessary? When was it possible? Only when you were 'fully prepared to deal with the consequences'.

This was not so at all. Bazarov at once seized on this the following day in a new article. But once again, to my mind, he did not focus attention on the heart of the matter. He spoke again of the chances of success and failure of the insurrection; again he indicated the inadequacy of material and moral strength. These assertions were no more than the writer's own pessimism, but could not serve as the theoretical ground of his conclusions.

Nevertheless Marx's statement was at the very core of the Bolshevik position and damaged it mortally. For you had to be ready to deal with the consequences. The consequences of victorious insurrections can be and have been in history extraordinarily varied. The working class has not always raised an insurrection in order to take the state into its own hands. This time that's just what it was. In spite of all the chances of victory of the uprising, the Bolsheviks knew in advance they could not deal with its consequences, knew in advance that, in view of the whole complex of circumstances, they could not perform the consequent tasks of state.

This was shown in practice, but only later; at this time there had been no practice. But at this time there should have been *theory*; the Bolsheviks should have had clear ideas and precise plans as to what they would do with the State they had won, how they would run it, and how in our conditions they would perform the tasks of a new proletarian State and satisfy the immediate, day-to-day needs, which had produced the insurrection, of the labouring masses. I maintain the Bolsheviks had no such plans. And personally, both in speeches and in articles, I directed attention precisely to this aspect of the matter.

I maintain the Bolsheviks had no other ideas than the immediate handing over of the land for seizure by the peasants, readiness to propose peace at once, the most confused ideas about 'workers' control', and the most fantastic notions of methods of extracting bread, with the help of the 'sailor' and the 'working girl'. . . Lenin had more 'ideas', borrowed whole from the experience of the Paris Commune and Marx's pamphlet on it, and also—from Kropotkin.[1] These of course included the destruction of the system of credit and the seizure of the banks; the thoroughgoing revision of the whole government apparatus and its replacement by administrators from among the working class (this in peasant, limitless, and half-savage Tsarist Russia!); the liability to election of all officials; compulsory parity between specialists' wages and the average worker's. And there were some other fantasies, which all vanished at the first contact with reality. But all these 'ideas' were, first of all, so disproportionately few in comparison with the immensity of the tasks, and secondly were so unknown to anyone in the Bolshevik Party, that you might say they were completely irrelevant.

Lenin's pamphlet, *State and Revolution*, was very soon to become gospel. But first of all this gospel, as always, served merely as something to swear by—God forbid that anything

[1] The celebrated philosopher of anarchism. (Ed.)

should be done in accordance with its visionary words!—and secondly it had not yet been published.

So far only 'materials' for a programme were present. And these materials, as Larin put it, revealed a vacuum instead of a financial-economic plan.

The Bolsheviks didn't know what they were going to do with their victory and the State they would win. They were acting *against* Marx, *against* scientific Socialism, *against* common sense, *against* the working class, when by way of an insurrection, under the slogan of 'Power to the Soviets' they attempted to hand over to their own Central Committee the totality of state power in Russia. The power of a single isolated proletarian vanguard, though it was based on the confidence of millions of the masses, obliged the new Government and the Bolsheviks themselves to perform tasks they knew to be beyond their strength. This was the core of the problem. The Bolshevik Party was utopian in undertaking to perform these tasks. It made a fateful error when it started an insurrection without thinking about them.

* * *

But let us return to the 'discussion'. Bazarov had mentioned the manuscript leaflet of two prominent Bolsheviks, who were protesting against the insurrection. Bazarov surmised (quite rightly, of course) that there was in the party a group which dissented from the official line. But the *Rabochii Put* said at once there was nothing of the sort—the authors of the sheet remained in splendid isolation. These were none other, of course, than the well-known 'cronies', Kamenev and Zinoviev.

Once the garbage was out of the house and there was nothing to lose, Kamenev decided to give a public explanation. For this, of course, they didn't allow him into the *Rabochii Put*. The 'communication' appeared in the *Novaya Zhizn*. He, Kamenev, and Zinoviev appealed to the largest party organizations in a letter, and in it they expressed themselves 'decidedly against the party's taking on itself the initiative of any armed moves in the immediate future. Everyone understands that in the present situation there can be no question of anything like an armed demonstration. The question can only be *of the seizure of power by force of arms*: any kind of mass demonstration can be undertaken only after clearly and definitely setting before oneself the task of an armed insurrection. Not only Comrade Zinoviev and I, but also a large group of our fellow practical workers think that taking the initiative of an armed insurrection at the given moment, with the given correlation of forces, independently of and a few days before the Soviet Congress—would be inadmissible, and fatal to both the proletariat and the revolution.' The Bolshevik Party, of course, was striving towards the realization of its programme with the help of the state power already achieved. It would not, of course, shrink even from an insurrection. But 'now it would be doomed to defeat'. 'To risk the fate of the party, the proletariat and the revolution and rise up in the next few days—would be to commit an act of despair. And the party is too strong, too great a future lies ahead, for it to take such desperate steps.'

Not especially profound, but quite eloquent. In any case we see that Kamenev's argumentation says no more and no less than what the Socialists of the other parties were saying at that time. Here, too, attention was focused on the chances of the insurrection and its destruction in unfavourable conditions. This is attested by the fact that no basic questions about what would happen *afterwards* were given priority even by Bolshevik opponents of the insurrection. But in any case this evaluation of the chances was very convincing in the mouth of a Bolshevik.

* * *

Lenin was living in those days somewhere a few hours' journey away from Petersburg. He received the *Novaya Zhizn* number with Bazarov's article that same October 17th, at 8 o'clock in the evening. At that time he was finishing a very long 'Letter to the Comrades' to counterbalance the 'cronies'' letter. He hadn't intended it to be printed and hence didn't intend to pronounce the word 'uprising' publicly in connexion with the party's plans. But Bazarov's article made Lenin indignant. Seeing the reference to the manuscript leaflet, which had fallen out of party hands into those of the 'fools on the *Novaya Zhizn*', Lenin made arrangements to have his letter, too, printed at once. 'If that's how things are, we must agitate even *for* an insurrection.'

The letter was printed in three long instalments (October 19th–21st). Lenin was afraid the 'cronies' would create confusion in the ranks of the party, and hastened to intervene—in spite of his having been 'placed by the will of fate a little to one side of the main stream of history'. Oh, of course, *that* could not stop Jupiter! But the point is that this document, intended to clarify the minds of the comrades in the hour of destiny, *adds precisely nothing* to the 'theory' of the insurrection. If we leave aside some sour notes produced with Lenin's inherent violence, the rest of this document is a complete vacuum. And the letter might be ignored if it were not a document of the epoch, a memorial to a great act of history. Just take it as it is.

'Rejection of the insurrection is rejection of the transference of power to the Soviets and a placing of all hopes in the well-meaning bourgeoisie who have "promised" to convoke the Constituent Assembly. Either an open rejection of the slogan of "All Power to the Soviets", or else insurrection. There is no middle way. Either idly fold your useless arms and wait, vowing fidelity to the Constituent Assembly, while Rodzianko & Co. surrender Petersburg and smother the revolution, or else insurrection.'

Meanwhile these are merely menacing preliminary remarks; Lenin is only causing a fright with the terrible words 'There is no middle way'. Further on, however, he comes to grips with his opponents' *arguments*. Well, let's listen. It's our duty.

Lenin quotes his opponents: 'There is nothing in the international situation that actually obliges us to demonstrate at once; we should, rather, harm the cause if we allowed ourselves to be shot.'

Here is Lenin's reply to this 'magnificent argument, which Scheidemann himself could not have improved on':

'The Germans, with Liebknecht alone, without newspapers or mass-meetings, made an insurrection in the fleet, and we, with dozens of papers, a majority in the Soviets and so on—are to refrain from insurrection! "Let's demonstrate our good sense. Let's pass a resolution of sympathy with the German insurgents, and overthrow the revolution in Russia".'

Hard to resist this: it's very powerful. But it's not enough—*comparaison n'est pas raison.*

The following argument: 'Everyone is against us. We are in isolation. Both the Central Ex. Com. and the Menshevik-Internationalists, both the *Novaya Zhizn* and the Left SRs have published and are publishing proclamations against us.'

Lenin's answer to 'this most powerful argument':

'Up to now we have fought the vacillators, and this is what has won us the sympathy of the people and gained us a majority in the Soviets; shall we now exploit the Soviets we have won in order to go over ourselves into the camp of the vacillators? What a splendid career for Bolshevism! On account of the betrayal of the peasant insurrection by the Martovs, the Kamkovs, and the Sukhanovs, it is now proposed that we betray it too. This is what the policy of ogling the Left SRs and the Menshevik-Internationalists boils down to.'

Evidently, for the comrades who were the objects of the agitation, this was enough to convince them of the safety and even utility of their isolation. Let's make a proletarian State against the parties, that is, against the subjective will and the objective class interests of the overwhelming majority of the population. Well, all right, do so!

Further: 'But we haven't even firm ties with the railwaymen and postal employees; is it possible to win without them?'

Lenin's answer: 'It's not a question of stocking up on ties beforehand, but of the fact that only a victory of the proletarian and peasant insurrection can satisfy the masses of railwaymen and postal employees.'

Here the simplification is quite childish! No, it is not the *victory* of the insurrection that will satisfy these masses, but the *right organization* and functioning of the new State. Is that as easy as it is to win an insurrection with dozens of newspapers and a majority in the Soviets? Or is it somewhat harder?

Argument: 'There is bread in Petersburg for two or three days. Can we give the insurgents bread?'

Lenin's answer: 'Sceptics can always doubt, and nothing but experience will convince them; it is precisely the bourgeoisie that is preparing the famine; there is not and cannot be any other means of salvation from hunger than an insurrection of the peasants against the landlords in the country and the victory of the workers against the capitalists in the cities and the capital. Any delay in the insurrection is like death—that is the reply that must be made to those who have the miserable courage to watch the growth of chaos and dissuade the workers from insurrection. . .'

This plainly needs no comment. Let's go on.

Argument: 'The situation at the front is not yet dangerous; even if the soldiers concluded a truce by themselves it would still be no calamity.'

Lenin's answer: 'But the soldiers are not concluding any truce; for this the state power is necessary, and it cannot be obtained without an insurrection. The soldiers are simply running away. Waiting is impossible without making it easier for Rodzianko to come to an agreement with the Kaiser.'

Now this would have been true—if, instead of a Bolshevik insurrection with utopian aims, it had been a question of a dictatorship of the Soviet democracy proceeding to replace the Cadet–Kornilov Coalition in order to fulfil the real programme of the revolution.

Argument: 'And if we take power and obtain neither a truce, nor peace, then the soldiers might not come along into a revolutionary war. What then?'

Here the Thunderer lost patience: 'One fool', he replied, 'can ask ten times as many questions as ten wise men can answer. . . We have never denied the difficulties of ruling, but—we will not allow ourselves to be frightened by the difficulties of revolution.'

Lenin devoted three columns to the argument we have met with not only from the 'cronies' but also from other Soviet people and parties: 'the masses, as everyone reports, are not belligerent'.

Lenin, 'placed to one side of the stream', makes a correction: first of all, everyone says that the mood is one of 'concentration and expectancy'; secondly, the workers do not want to come out for a manifestation, but 'there is the approach of a general struggle hovering in the air'; thirdly, the 'broad masses are near despair, and it is on this soil that anarchism is growing'; fourthly, 'excitement' is not necessary either, what is necessary is just a 'mood of desperate concentration. . .'

Well, now you can take your choice. Personally I have absolutely never agreed that the mood of the masses excluded a successful insurrection. The only question was rather how many of them might go to the barricades. But I see no need to linger over Lenin's verbiage, even though it is directed towards the same conclusion.

This was the final argument of his opponents: 'A Marxist

party cannot reduce the question of an insurrection to the question of a military conspiracy.'

In essence this is correct. But this time Lenin too was right, that this was quite irrelevant. To talk about a military conspiracy instead of a national insurrection, when the party was followed by the overwhelming majority of the people, when the party had already *de facto* conquered all real power and authority—was clearly an absurdity. On the part of the *enemies* of Bolshevism it was a *malicious* absurdity, but on the part of the 'cronies'—an aberration based on panic. Here Lenin was right... But even on this basis I can by no means renounce the estimate I placed on the entire document: I'm not responsible for the fact that the 'cronies' said some absurd things.

So—the arguments are exhausted. And the theoretical material of this time is also, I think, all exhausted. Now we are familiar with the whole philosophy of the insurrection at that time. There was no other. He who has ears, has heard.

As for the 'cronies', it was as though they had simply been waiting to be called to heel. Two days later Zinoviev published a letter—that he was 'postponing the dispute until more favourable circumstances', and 'closing the ranks'. Kamenev announced the same thing in the Soviet, the same day his views were published in the *Novaya Zhizn*.

Everyone was asking: and what about Lunacharsky? What does he think? Wasn't he probably against 'all that'? Personally at this time I saw him rarely. The party command had long since forbidden him to write in the *Novaya Zhizn*. He was spending a lot of time in the Town Council, where he was a colleague of the 'Governor's'. He was beginning to get involved in cultural and municipal work, and told me he wanted to go over to it entirely. The reason for this was primarily the fact that the party didn't let him into 'major policy' and was treating him badly. I don't think I ever spoke to him at this time about Bolshevik activities and plans, and I don't know what he thought. But because of all the newspaper rumours libelling his position he declared in print, neck and neck with Zinoviev: I stand with the party.

But it's time to leave 'ideas'. In those days, actually, there was no time for them.

CHAPTER 28

THE FINAL REVIEW

THOSE were the days of the final mobilization and final review of strength. Everywhere in the provinces at this time there were Soviet congresses, and almost everywhere they gave predominance to the Bolsheviks, while in Moscow a movement again began going out into the streets. On the 15th a large manifestation took place—with the most violent slogans, especially from the soldiers: 'We would rather die in Moscow on the barricades than go to the front!' In the Soviet and the Ex. Com. it became evident that it was no longer possible to hold back the Moscow masses. In other corners of Russia, even where there was no peasant uprising, the movement, under the slogans of 'Soviet power', was clearly sweeping over the countryside.

In general there was no doubt that Moscow would lend complete and active support; the greater part of the provinces would give support; the rest would be 'assimilated'.

The *front* was more doubtful. Here party influence was diverse, but, generally speaking, they had no time there for politics: they refused to know or think of anything but peace. What worked *against* the Bolsheviks was their not letting the Petersburg garrison out of the capital as reinforcements. But the Bolsheviks had every hope of immediate peace proposals. It was scarcely possible to assemble any real force against any Government that proposed peace. No one would have marched against Petersburg. And nothing more was needed.

But even at the front there were substantial Bolshevik organizations. Corps, divisions, batteries, and other units were sending to the papers a multitude of Bolshevik resolutions. There were also congresses that took place under the exclusive influence of the Bolsheviks.

I should like to mention just this about the front. Once more strings of delegations from the front were not only filing into Smolny, appearing at big Soviet meetings with their messages and speeches: besides this they were stubbornly seeking *intimate conversations* and authoritative direct explanations from the old

Soviet leaders. But there was no time for them. They were almost never received. When they did succeed in getting hold of a leader they could get no satisfaction from him. Non-party or SR-minded delegates, disappointed and angry, immediately turned to the Bolsheviks. They poured out their hearts to them at Smolny, and at the front became conductors of their influence. Our editorial office (and others too no doubt) was literally swamped at this time with letters from the trenches. These were remarkable human documents. Pouring their souls out to the dregs, the soldiers showed what the unbearable suffering of wartime had turned them into. If only it would end: nothing else mattered—parties, politics, or revolution. Anyone would be supported who produced even a ghost of peace.

There was nothing there to be afraid of. Though the front might give no active *support*, it would not be actively *hostile*. Though it might not be helpful, it wouldn't be harmful. The non-party and SR mass would easily be assimilated by the Bolshevik minority. And doubtless even 'scratch detachments' would not easily be turned against the Bolsheviks in this atmosphere.

Besides the Soviet organizations there were also some *municipalities* in the hands of the Bolsheviks. One way or another in such conditions the overturn definitely did not recall either a military conspiracy or a Blanquist experiment.

But the active and deciding rôle belonged to Petersburg, and partly to its suburbs. Forces were mobilized here most of all, in the main arena of the drama.

Trotsky, tearing himself away from work on the revolutionary staff, personally rushed from the Obukhovsky plant to the Trubochny, from the Putilov to the Baltic works, from the riding-school to the barracks; he seemed to be speaking at all points simultaneously. His influence, both among the masses and on the staff, was overwhelming. He was the central figure of those days and the principal hero of this remarkable page of history.

* * *

On the evening of October 18th, after a speech by Miliukov in the Pre-Parliament, I went to Smolny. The Soviet was in session. The great hall was glittering brightly with its chandelier and snow-white columns. It was packed. The mood was obviously exalted. In the stuffy, smoky air an endless mass of excited faces was looking up at the platform from out of clouds of tobacco smoke. The aisles and the seats behind the columns were packed with disorderly groups.

The file of men from the trenches had already long since passed by. When I got there Trotsky was on the platform talking heatedly about something.

I pushed my way to the platform stage. I had something quite special in mind. An anniversary of Gorky's was coming up on Sunday the 22nd—his twenty-five years as a writer. The importance of this, especially to the Petersburg worker-soldier Soviet, seemed self-evident to me, but almost no one knew about it. I wanted the Soviet to pass a motion and send him greetings.

But how could this be done? If I spoke in my own name it would only produce embarrassment, and might end in a scandal. The meeting would look questioningly at the leaders—and what would they say? The point was that the Bolsheviks had now been subjecting our paper, and Gorky, its director, to a particularly heavy fire. And it happened that Gorky had picked just that day to come out with an article against the uprising.

I knew very well what the Bolshevik traditions were, and that this wasn't a moment when the Bolsheviks would distinguish between the world-famous writer, the artistic ideologist of the proletariat, and—their political antagonist on a current question of tactics.

I began looking for someone on the platform with whom I could make arrangements beforehand. I didn't want to appeal to Trotsky: we hadn't met for about three weeks, during which our paths had radically diverged, and the question was rather delicate. I looked around, and hit upon someone highly suitable.

That was Ryazanov. I had no doubt of his sympathy. But to my surprise he began to give me hurried evasive answers and seemed somewhat embarrassed. He refused to speak himself, but promised to tell Trotsky when the latter had finished his speech. I waited. . .

But what was Trotsky so hot about? Why were the soldiers' faces so excited?

Trotsky had exposed a scandal. He was resisting an impudent *encroachment on the soldiers' vital interests. That's why he was* so emotional and why the hall was aroused.

The Petersburg Town Council, in order to help out its totally ruined exchequer a little and rescue its tram-cars from rapid deterioration, had decided to ask the soldiers to pay a fare of about five copecks instead of the twenty paid by all simple mortals, not excepting even the workers. Up to then the completely idle Petersburg garrison had been riding around without paying, packing the trams even for only one or two stops. Both the populace and the municipal finances suffered bitterly. Finally a reform was decided on, that went directly counter to the interests of the revolution.

I saw a group of Bolshevik Town Council members, led by Joffe, the future famous diplomat and ambassador, on the platform. These council-men had already explored the question in the Town Council and admitted that the proposed measure was completely sensible. Nevertheless they had appeared in the Soviet to give Trotsky authoritative backing. Everything else had to stop for considerations of higher policy!

But Trotsky, who was carrying on this higher policy, was describing to the soldiers the whole outrageous injustice of the five-copeck fare in vivid colours and demanding its abolition.

In his demagogy the future ruler did not hesitate to preach the most primitive capriciousness and anarchy. A rather miserable scene—an episode in the softening-up.

I couldn't stay long enough to propose that Gorky be honoured. Trotsky was obviously out of sympathy. The Soviet passed over the anniversary of the writer who had brought down on his head innumerable blows, filth, and slanders—for his revolutionary services.

* * *

It was already late at night when my wife and I left the meeting. Outside we were met by pitch darkness, with a downpour into the bargain. We were in a bad mood. And now another delight! How to get to the other end of the city, to the Karpovka, with my tubercular wife, who couldn't resist going to this meeting and missing all the trams. There was quite a crowd in the darkness of the gardens quarrelling about a couple of snorting motor-cars the Bolshevik Soviet had succeeded in getting away from the Menshevik–SR Central Ex. Com. The cars of course were out of the question: Trotsky was about to go up to one of them, but after standing there a moment and looking at it he laughed, splashed off through the puddles, and vanished in the darkness.

About to start off on foot, we found out that some special trams, standing in the square, had been supplied for the delegates. We rushed over. Another success! The tram for the Petersburg Side had already left. The only thing we could do was to ride to the corner of Sadovoy and Inzhenerny. But it was still a good five versts from there.

Standing on the platform of the tram I was extraordinarily irritable and gloomy. A short fellow with a modest look was standing near us, with a pince-nez, a black goatee, and flashing Jewish eyes. Seeing my mood he set about cheering me up, and tried to distract me with some advice about the route. But I answered him disagreeably and monosyllabically.

'Who's that?' I asked, when we left the tram.

'That's our old party worker, the Town Councillor, Sverdlov. . .'

In my bad temper I should undoubtedly have cheered up and laughed a great deal if someone had told me that in a fortnight this man would be the titular head of the Russian Republic.

* * *

The Petersburg garrison was the primary and most important factor. This was obvious to everyone. During this period the Soldiers' Section was being 'dealt with' practically every day. But this wasn't enough: the garrison had to be sounded out and strengthened in every possible way.

That same day, the 18th, the Military Department of the Petersburg Soviet had wired all units: (1) To refrain from any unauthorized action; (2) To carry out regional Staff orders *only after their approval by the Military Department.* And the telegram carried an invitation to come to Smolny that same day for personal explanations.

This wire was held up in the Central Ex. Com. Nevertheless representatives of most of the units appeared at Smolny. In the name of the Central Ex. Com. the meeting was declared incompetent. As you like! It took place anyhow, and of course Trotsky took the floor. One of the Central Ex. Com. members asked for the floor at this incompetent meeting, but didn't get it.

The unit delegates, however, had not been gathered together to be agitated at again, but to be listened to. The 'speeches from the floor' were in the last analysis all alike: the Izmailovskys, Chasseurs, Volhynians, Grenadiers, Cuxholms, Semyonovskys, Rifles, Pavlovskys, the Electro-Technical Battalion, the Moscow Regiment, the 89th, and others—all said the self-same thing: Power to the Soviets; they would come out at the first call; mistrust and contempt for the Government—and sometimes for the Central Ex. Com. into the bargain. Of those present only the *cavalry* units declared either their passivity or their refusal to come out at all. This was 'neutrality'—a term often used at this time.

The next day, the 19th, the Central Ex. Com. convened another, 'competent', garrison meeting. This time the organizers obviously preferred to *talk*, not listen. Dan thought it necessary to say that a Soviet Congress in his opinion was now 'unsuitable', although no one was thinking of disrupting it. But for the most part of course he spoke of the 'unsuitability' and calamitousness of a demonstration. He was opposed by Trotsky—in the customary spirit. But the delegates themselves spoke up, showing the Star Chamber the same scene as the evening before: *we shall obey the Petersburg Soviet absolutely and come out only on its summons.*

Finally, on Saturday the 21st there was another meeting—of the regimental and company committees of all units. Once again—Trotsky. Again the everlasting 'current moment', but three decisions.

First of all, the Soviet Congress was assembling and would take power in order to secure land, peace, and bread; the garrison solemnly promised to place all its forces down to the last man at the disposal of the Congress.

Secondly, the Military Revolutionary Committee was now formed and in operation; the garrison welcomed it and promised it full support in everything it undertook.

Thirdly, the following morning, Sunday the 22nd, the Day of the Petersburg Soviet, was a day of the peaceful muster of forces; the garrison, without demonstrating anywhere, would watch over order and in case of need resist any provocative attempts of the bourgeoisie to carry discord into the revolutionary ranks.

Some minor misunderstandings arose with the Cossack delegates, who referred to Lenin's articles, in alarm about a possible uprising the following day; they were actually preparing for a ceremonial procession, and moreover would never bend the knee to the Germans for peace. There was a hubbub at first, but then a 'common language' was found: an appeal was made to the Cossack brethren inviting them as dear guests 'to our meetings on the holiday of our peaceful muster of forces'.

No one voted against Trotsky's resolution. Only fifty-seven people remained neutral and abstained. It seemed that one could remain calm. Things were firm enough here.

On October 21st the Petersburg garrison *conclusively acknowledged the Soviet as sole power, and the Military Revolutionary Committee as the immediate organ of authority.*

Two days earlier the District Commander had again reported to the Premier: 'There is no reason to think the garrison will refuse to obey the orders of the military authorities'.

One could remain calm. The Winter Palace was calm. 'Steps had been taken.'

* * *

I spent that night in the Karpovka because I had to speak the next day at noon at a mass-meeting in the People's House.

The decisive day came. The Cyclopean building of the People's House was packed to the doors with a countless throng. They filled the enormous theatres to overflowing in the expectation of mass-meetings. The foyer, buffet, and corridors were also full. Behind the scenes people kept asking me: Just what did I intend to talk about? I replied—about the 'current moment', of course. Did that mean—*against the coup*? They began trying to persuade me to speak on foreign policy. After all, that was my speciality! The discussion with the organizers took on such a character I absolutely refused to speak at all. But that was no use either.

Irritated, I went out from backstage, to watch events from the hall. Trotsky was flying along the corridor towards me on to the stage. He glanced at me angrily and rushed by without any greeting. That was the first time. . . Diplomatic relations were broken off for a long while.

The mood of the people, more than 3,000, who filled the hall was definitely tense: they were all silently waiting for something. The audience was of course primarily workers and soldiers, but more than a few typically lower-middle-class men's and women's figures were visible.

Trotsky's ovation seemed to be cut short prematurely, out of curiosity and impatience: what was he going to say? Trotsky at once began to heat up the atmosphere, with his skill and brilliance. I remember that at length and with extraordinary power he drew a picture (difficult through its simplicity) of the suffering of the trenches. Thoughts flashed through my mind of the inevitable incongruity of the parts in this oratorical whole. But Trotsky knew what he was doing. The whole point lay in the mood. The political conclusions had long been familiar. They could be condensed, as long as there were enough highlights.

Trotsky did this—with enough highlights. The Soviet régime was not only called upon to put an end to the suffering of the trenches. It would give land and heal the internal disorder. Once again the recipes against hunger were repeated: a soldier, a sailor, and a working girl, who would requisition bread from those who had it and distribute it gratis to the cities and front. But Trotsky went even further on this decisive 'Day of the Petersburg Soviet'.

'The Soviet Government will give everything the country contains to the poor and the men in the trenches. You, bourgeois, have got two fur caps!—give one of them to the soldier, who's freezing in the trenches. Have you got warm boots? Stay at home. The worker needs your boots. . .'

These were very good and just ideas. They could not but excite the enthusiasm of a crowd who had been reared on the Tsarist whip. In any case, I certify as a direct witness that this was what was said on this last day.

All round me was a mood bordering on ecstasy. It seemed as though the crowd, spontaneously and of its own accord, would break into some religious hymn. Trotsky formulated a brief and general resolution, or pronounced some general formula like 'we will defend the worker-peasant cause to the last drop of our blood'.

Who was—for? The crowd of thousands, as one man, raised their hands. I saw the raised hands and burning eyes of men, women, youths, soldiers, peasants, and—typically lower-middle-class faces. Were they in spiritual transports? Did they see, through the raised curtain, a corner of the 'righteous land' of their longing? Or were they penetrated by a consciousness of the *political occasion*, under the influence of the political agitation of a *Socialist*? Ask no questions! Accept it as it was. . .

Trotsky went on speaking. The innumerable crowd went on holding their hands up. Trotsky rapped out the words: 'Let this vote of yours be your vow—with all your strength and at any sacrifice to support the Soviet that has taken on itself the glorious burden of bringing to a conclusion the victory of the revolution and of giving land, bread, and peace!'

The vast crowd was holding up its hands. It agreed. It vowed. Once again, accept this as it was. With an unusual feeling of oppression I looked on at this really magnificent scene.

Trotsky finished. Someone else went out on to the stage. But there was no point in waiting and looking any more.

Throughout Petersburg more or less the same thing was going on. Everywhere there were final reviews and final vows. Thousands, tens of thousands and hundreds of thousands of people. . . This, actually, was already an insurrection. Things had started. . .

* * *

At about 5 or 6 o'clock, I don't remember just why, a meeting of our Pre-Parliament fraction was scheduled in the Marian Palace. But almost no one was there. In the reading-room I came across two or three comrades, in deep arm-chairs, lazily exchanging remarks. I began to tell them what I had seen and heard that day. But I don't think it made much impression. Dr. Mandelberg, coming to the point, began talking about what was going to happen in the Pre-Parliament on Tuesday or Wednesday.

'What?' I stopped him. 'D'you think there's still going to be a Pre-Parliament on Tuesday and Wednesday? Don't delude yourself! In two or three days the Pre-Parliament will no longer exist. . .'

But they ironically waved me aside. Two hours passed. The time assigned for our fraction meeting had already gone by. I didn't go away because at about 8 or 9 o'clock an *inter-fraction* meeting was scheduled on the question of a peace formula. While waiting I wandered about the empty half-dark rooms. All at once a group of people from other fractions appeared—Peshekhonov, Kuskov, Skobelev, and someone else. They were already looking for the other delegates in order to begin the conference. Well, what had they seen and heard today? What did they think? I went up to them and abruptly flung out: 'So the insurrection's begun! What are your impressions?'

For a long moment the group looked at me in frowning silence, not knowing what to say. Insurrection? No, they didn't know a thing. Should they believe me? How should they reply? Whether you believed it or not you shouldn't get into this sort of conversation. After all, if the insurrection really had begun Sukhanov of course would be in it. . .

The inter-fraction meeting began, but we didn't have time to finish. We were interrupted by a group of people who had rushed over from Smolny with extraordinary news.

CHAPTER 29

OVERTURE

IN actual fact the overturn was accomplished the moment the Petersburg garrison acknowledged the Soviet as its supreme authority and the Military Revolutionary Committee as its direct command. Such a decision, as we know, was made at the meeting of the garrison representatives on October 21st. But in the unprecedented setting this act may be said to have had an *abstract character*. No one took it for a *coup d'état*.

And no wonder. The decision, after all, did not really change the situation: even earlier the Government had had no real power or authority. The real power in the capital had already been in the hands of the Bolsheviks of the Petersburg Soviet long before, and nevertheless the Winter Palace had remained the Government, and Smolny—a private institution. Now the garrison had declared officially, *urbi et orbi*, that it did not recognize the Government and was subject to the Soviet. But did it matter what was said in Smolny, where there was nobody but Bolsheviks?

Nevertheless, this is a fact: by October 21st the Provisional Government had already been overthrown, and was non-existent in the territory of the capital. Kerensky and his colleagues, calling themselves Ministers, were still completely at liberty, busy with something or other in the Winter Palace; in many parts of the country they were still recognized as the Government (wherever the Soviets were not Bolshevik), and in addition they might still have some real support outside the capital and theoretically speaking have been able to destroy the Bolsheviks and their Petersburg garrison together. The main thing, however, was that no new power had been proclaimed, and the situation was transitional. It was the same as on February 28th, when the capital garrison turned against the Tsarist Government but there was no new Government; when Tsar Nicholas was at liberty and busy at Headquarters; when his authority was still recognized in many parts of the country and he could still find loyal troops to crush the insurgent capital.

Nevertheless the Government was already overthrown on October 21st, as Tsar Nicholas had been on February 28th. What remained now was essentially to *complete* what had been done—first of all, to make the overturn official by proclaiming a new government, and secondly, to liquidate *de facto* the pretenders to power, thus achieving general acknowledgement of the accomplished fact.

The significance of what was accomplished on October 21st was obscure not only to the man-in-the-street and the spectator; it was not clear to the revolutionary leaders themselves. Glance into the memoirs of one of the chief figures of the October Days, Antonov-Ovseyenko,[1] secretary of the Military Revolutionary Committee. You'll see a complete 'unawareness' of the internal evolution of events. This gave rise to a lack of system and orderliness in the external, military-technical measures of the Bolsheviks. It might have ended for them much less successfully if they had been dealing with a different adversary. It was luck that the adversary was not only unaware, but completely blind; and not only blind, but equal to zero with respect to real power...

But here's what must be taken into account: neither Smolny nor the Winter Palace could be fully aware of the meaning of events. It was obscured by the historical position of the Soviet in the revolution. A confusion of ideas inevitably flowed from the fact that for half a year the totality of real power had been in the hands of the Soviet, while at the same time there existed a Government, and indeed an independent and sovereign one. The Soviet, by tradition, did not acknowledge that it was a government; and the Government, by tradition, did not acknowledge that it was a mere sham... How many times, after all, had even the garrison passed resolutions almost identical with its vote on October 21st? How many times had it sworn allegiance to the Soviet, both after the July events and during the Kornilov revolt? And this, after all, had not only not been an overturn, but had even been made in honour of the Coalition. How could one tell that now something completely different had taken place?

[1] Antonov-Ovseyenko, Vladimir Alexandrovich (1884–1938): a Bolshevik from 1903; of a military family; a leading figure in preparation of Bolshevik insurrection in October. Member of Trotskyite opposition, 1923–28; sent to Spain by Soviet Government during the Spanish Civil War; on his return to Russia was shot. (Ed.)

In the Winter Palace it was quite impossible to tell. But Smolny didn't appreciate it either. If it *had* been possible to tell in the Winter Palace, one would have thought that a desperate attempt to destroy Smolny then and there would have been inevitable. If Smolny had appreciated it, one would have thought that the inevitability of such an attempt on the part of the Winter Palace should have been manifest; and it would have been vital to liquidate the Winter Palace at once, at one blow, in order to forestall it.

But no, both sides thought the business of an overturn had not yet begun. The Winter Palace didn't care a rap for the vote of October 21st, while Smolny silently, gropingly, cautiously, chaotically, moved on to something that in essence appeared to be an overturn, but was actually only its formal recognition.

* * *

A few hours after the meeting of the garrison, on Saturday night, October 21st, representatives of the Military Revolutionary Committee went to see the District Commander, Polkovnikov. They demanded the right to countersign all Staff orders to the garrison. Polkovnikov categorically refused. The Smolny delegates withdrew.

The General Staff was—*the General Staff of an enemy army*. The correct tactics (according to Marx) required that the insurgents, being the attacking side, destroy, shatter, paralyse, and liquidate this centre of the whole enemy organization in one annihilating onslaught. A detachment of 300 volunteers—sailors, workers, party soldiers—could have done this without the slightest difficulty; at that time the possibility of such a raid had not even entered anyone's head.

But Smolny acted differently. The Bolsheviks went to the enemy and said: We demand power over you.

The action of the Military Revolutionary Committee on the night of October 21st was completely superfluous. It might have proved extremely dangerous, if it had provoked a proper response from the Staff. But it turned out to be completely safe: the District Commander didn't understand this action and didn't respond adequately. He could have arrested the delegates of a 'private organization', which (like Kornilov on August 26th) was demanding power over the highest military authority and was definitely embarking on a revolt. Then Polkovnikov might have collected 500 military cadets, officers and Cossacks, and made an attempt to destroy, shatter, and paralyse Smolny. At that moment he had more than a few chances of success; in any case, it would seem, nothing else was left for him to do.

But the Staff understood nothing. Indeed, as a matter of fact this was not the first time the Soviet had wished to countersign its orders. During the April Days, after all, something similar had been announced by the garrison without any warning: that the commander was not to take troops out of the barracks without the permission of certain Soviet Mensheviks and SRs. And there was no revolt and no overturn at all there. The matter was very satisfactorily settled with Miliukov and Guchkov in the Liaison Commission. So why should they think of overturns or revolts now? Polkovnikov categorically refused: the delegates left empty-handed. All was well.

The next day, Sunday, the District Commander gave the journalists an authoritative explanation of the inwardness of the conflict that had taken place. The point, you see, was that the Government refused to confirm a Commissar sent to the Staff by the Petersburg Soviet. The Government would not recognize a Bolshevik in such a post. Besides, there was already a Commissar on the Staff, sent by the Central Ex. Com. In addition, in the units of the Petersburg garrison recently new elections for unit Commissars had been energetically proceeding: Mensheviks and SRs were being thrown out and replaced everywhere by Bolsheviks. The Government protested against the elections. That was the essence of the conflict. But it was to be hoped that it would be smoothed over.

The whole attention of the Winter Palace and the Staff was fixed on street demonstrations. It was in case they happened that 'steps had been taken'. But there were no demonstrations. Hence, all was well. It was possible to occupy oneself with current business.

On Sunday, October 22, the Council of Ministers was occupied with it. Kerensky, however, also went into the question of the preservation of order. He had an excellent command of the essence of the conflict between the Staff and Smolny. Polkovnikov had given him a detailed report. You can't baffle sensible, statesmanlike people: Moscow once burned because of a copeck candle; not so long ago, the World War had begun because of the assassination of an Austrian Crown Prince; and the conflict between Smolny and the Staff arose from the non-confirmation of a commissar. . .

It was all clear enough, but all the same Kerensky, according to reports, insisted on the definitive liquidation of the Military Revolutionary Committee. He was determined. But—Polkovnikov persuaded him to wait a little: he would fix things! Kerensky began waiting.

* * *

Meanwhile the Soviet began assembling in Smolny for an emergency session. The delegates arrived haphazardly. Most of them had been holding mass-meetings in the factories and elsewhere. But the point was not the deputies, it was the representatives of the regiments, who had again been assembled as an emergency measure. Trotsky flew to them and explained the new state of affairs. It seemed the Staff did not agree to submit to the control of the Military Revolutionary Committee. Very odd, what? But one way or another it imposed a 'further step'.

The further step was in the form of a telephone message, sent out at once to all units of the garrison in the name of the Soviet; it read: 'At a meeting on October 21st the revolutionary garrison of Petersburg rallied around the Military Revolutionary Committee as its governing body. In spite of this the Staff of the Petersburg military area has failed to recognize the Military Revolutionary Committee, and refuses to carry on work jointly with the representatives of the Soldiers' Section of the Soviet. By this very fact the Staff has broken with the revolutionary garrison and the Petersburg Soviet. By breaking with the organized garrison of the capital, the Staff has made itself the tool of counter-revolutionary forces. The Military Revolutionary Committee divests itself of any responsibility for the actions of the Staff. . .

'Soldiers of Petersburg! The defence of revolutionary order against counter-revolutionary attacks is incumbent on you, under the leadership of the Military Revolutionary Committee. No orders to the garrison, not signed by the Military Revolutionary Committee, are valid. All Soviet orders for today, the

Day of the Petersburg Soviet, remain in full force. Vigilance, firmness, and unwavering discipline is the duty of every soldier of the garrison. The revolution is in danger! Long live the revolutionary garrison!'

The premises of this document are completely hollow: merely awesome agitational words with very naïve content. But the *conclusions* are extremely substantial—the garrison was not to execute the orders of the legal authorities.

Now this was definitely an *insurrectionary act.* Hostilities had definitely begun—before the eyes of the whole nation. But, at the same time, weren't troops moved up to occupy the Staff, railway stations, telegraphs, telephones, and other centres of the capital? And detachments also sent to arrest the Provisional Government? After all, you can't declare war unequivocally and definitely before the country and the army and not begin combat activities, to anticipate the initiative's passing into the hands of the enemy.

This, however, was just what had happened. War had been declared in unmistakable terms, but combat activities were not begun. No one attacked either the Staff or the Provisional Government. . . This, to put it mildly, was not according to Marx. And nevertheless this kind of conduct proved quite safe.

After receiving the declaration of war, without being either arrested or hampered in their movements, did the Staff take the initiative into its own hands? Did it fling itself on the mutineers in a last desperate attempt to defend the State and the revolution against the seditious Bolsheviks? The Staff did nothing of the sort.

Instead of combat activities Polkovnikov scheduled a Staff meeting. Representatives of the Central Ex. Com., the Petersburg Soviet, and the regimental committees were invited to it. Smolny sent the well-known Bolshevik second-lieutenant Dashkevich with two or three representatives of the garrison meeting that had just ended. Dashkevich tersely repeated the decision of this meeting, that is, the content of the telephone message given above: all Staff orders to be countersigned, otherwise they would not be executed. . . Then the Smolny delegation withdrew, having refused to listen to their opponents.

At the Staff they began chattering about what to do. A few representatives from the garrison committees reported on the mood of their units. They, of course, couldn't tell the district commander anything reassuring. But then the Staff began reassuring itself: the conflict, after all, had arisen because of the non-confirmation of a Commissar; that was nothing; it had happened only because someone selected by the Central Ex. Com. had already been confirmed. Somehow things would be smoothed over. . . In the newspapers we read: 'After a brief exchange of opinions no definite decisions were taken; it was considered necessary to wait for the resolution of the conflict between the Central Ex. Com. and the Petersburg Soviet.' (*Rech*, No. 250.)

Very good. But really—were the Bolsheviks timid, unconscious, and clumsy, or did they know whom they were dealing with? Was this a criminally light-minded risk on their part, or were they acting on a certainty?

* * *

Now, what forces did Kerensky have? There was, of course, first of all, the garrison of the capital in general. After all, all power was in the hands of the Provisional Government; the local army authorities were at their posts, and we are familiar with their reports: 'There are no grounds for thinking the garrison won't obey orders.' Without this conviction, of course, the entire picture of the conduct of the Winter Palace and Staff would have been different.

But nevertheless *specially* reliable units, which could be depended on without any risk and to any extent, might have to be used against the Bolsheviks. This had been acknowledged, after all, even in August, when the 3rd Corps had been called back from the front. And since then specially reliable cadres which might be needed against the internal enemy had been sought. This same 3rd Corps, at the head of which Kornilov himself had placed the arch-reactionary General Krasnov, was stationed in the suburbs of Petersburg. Kerensky, at the beginning of September, in a coded telegram in Krasnov's name, had ordered this corps to be stationed in Gatchina, Tsarskoe, and Peterhof. Part of the corps had recently been distributed in the nearer parts of the province—for the pacification of the rebellious garrisons. Nevertheless Krasnov's Cossacks would have been a grave threat to the Bolsheviks—if the neighbouring Bolsheviks had not done some serious work amongst them and promised them peace and immediate departure to their beloved Don. . .

But in any case these units were considered especially reliable. Once again, as in August, Kerensky turned to them first of all. The Bolsheviks, however, had taken their own measures. The northern district Soviet Congress had sufficiently strengthened their military organization. The movements of the Cossacks met with every possible technical obstacle. And in the course of the next three days the Cossacks failed to reach Petersburg. But I'm not saying that on the night of the 22nd Kerensky ordered the Krasnov men to advance; rather, he simply told them to stay at the ready.

Besides the Cossacks, the military cadets were of course considered especially reliable. The Bolsheviks—partly through persuasion and threats, partly through technical means—had had an effect on them too. Not many of them came to Petersburg from the provinces on Kerensky's order. But in any case, from the 23rd on the Winter Palace was guarded primarily by military cadets.

That same night Kerensky and Bagratuni[1] gave orders for a bicycle battalion to be called to Petersburg. The battalion was about to move, but then decided to ask Smolny: why were they being called up and must they go? Smolny, 'with fraternal greetings', replied, of course, that it was quite unnecessary. . .

In general this question of calling up specially reliable troops was not easy at all. But there was nothing to be particularly alarmed about. After all, it was only just in case. . . There might be no demonstration. 'Soviet Day' had passed without excesses. . . The Bolsheviks, to be sure, had executed their decision: Staff orders really were being controlled by local unit Commissars. Nevertheless, orders were being obeyed.

But just what orders did the Staff give that night and the following day? Orders about sentries and uniforms. They were checked on, but obeyed. And the sentries and uniforms in those days may be said to have been brilliant. Hence, all was well.

* * *

In the Pre-Parliament, from the morning of Monday the 23rd on, in a rather empty hall, boring debates on foreign policy flowed on peacefully. There had been some alarm the day

[1] A general who replaced Colonel Polkovnikov as District Commander. (Ed.)

before—it was the stormy 'Soviet Day'—but everything passed over and serious people went back to their current business. . . Various microscopic fractions talked. Yawning deputies lazily heckled the speakers.

I don't recall any liveliness in the corridors either. I don't recall any special reaction to the extraordinary events. Bolsheviks? Oh well, after all, *them*. . . I attacked my fraction comrades and demanded a debate on the general political problem. But in spite of the sympathy of many nothing came of it. As before Martov thought untimely a resolute offensive and the line of immediate and thoroughgoing liquidation of 'Kerenskyism'.

* * *

In Smolny during those hours everything pursued its course. The Military Revolutionary Committee was in session, and the work was ceaseless; but only the Bolsheviks worked. Smolny had changed considerably during those days. The sections of the Central Ex. Com. were doing hardly any work and their second-floor rooms were shut up. But Smolny hummed with a new crowd, quite grey in aspect. Everything was dirty and untidy and smelt of cheap tobacco, boots, and damp greatcoats. Armed groups of soldiers, sailors, and workers scurried about everywhere. Grey wolves lived in Smolny now, and they were going on with their work.

The Military Revolutionary Committee passed on to the next point on the agenda. This was of special importance: the Commissar assigned to the Peter-Paul Fortress turned up with the information that the Commandant refused to recognize him and had threatened him with arrest. Thus the Fortress must be considered to be in the hands of the Government. This created enormous difficulties—apart from the fact that the Peter-Paul had an arsenal of a hundred thousand rifles. To take the Fortress by force *after* the beginning of military action was more than risky; besides, the Government might hide there until troops arrived from the front to rescue them.

It was necessary to take the Peter-Paul quickly, before the Government stopped debating and started doing something to protect itself. Two methods were proposed for taking over the Fortress. Antonov proposed to bring in a reliable battalion of the Pavlovskys immediately and disarm the garrison of the Fortress.

But in the first place this involved a risk; secondly, it was essentially an act of war, after which it would be necessary to attack at once and liquidate the Government. Trotsky had another proposal, namely, that he, Trotsky, go to the Fortress, hold a meeting there, and capture not the body but the spirit of the garrison. In the first place there would be no risk in that, secondly it might be that even after this the Government would go on living in Nirvana and allow Smolny to extend its authority further and further without let or hindrance.

No sooner said than done. Trotsky set off at once, together with Lashevich. Their harangues were enthusiastically received. The garrison, almost unanimously, passed a resolution about the Soviet régime and its own readiness to rise up, weapons in hand, against the bourgeois Government. A Smolny Commissar was installed in the Fortress, under the protection of the garrison, and refused to recognize the Commandant. A hundred thousand extra rifles were in the hands of the Bolsheviks.

What the Government thought about all this, and what they were saying about it on the General Staff—I have no idea. But neither in one place nor the other *did they do anything* in the course of that whole day, until far into the night.

* * *

After an interval, in the early evening hours, the debates in the Pre-Parliament on foreign policy were resumed. I don't recall any talk in the corridors about what was going on; I don't think anything was known about the taking of the Peter-Paul. But in the hall it was somewhat more cheerful. There were lots of deputies. The certified Soviet diplomat Skobelev made a curious speech: in vulgarly threadbare, empty generalities he 'expounded' the diplomatic wisdom of Ribot and Bonar Law. It was comical to listen to.

But the centre was Martov's speech. This was perhaps the most brilliant speech I ever heard him give. Indeed, even the Right had never heard such a speech from its golden-tongued orators in the Duma. They got angry and interrupted. But this poured oil on the fire; Martov got off a whole pyrotechnical display of images welded into a firm artistic monolith. It was impossible not to be gripped by his oratorical power. And the audience gave it due appreciation.

But what did Martov talk about? He spoke of the revolution, and of the crisis, its cause and conditions. It was not only brilliant, but also remarkable for intellectual grasp and profundity. The content of the speech far overflowed the confines of foreign policy; this was the *philosophy* of the moment. And it was a passionate accusation of the ruling circles. But—it was not the *political* act the moment demanded. It lacked the right political conclusions. It by-passed the stupendous current events. At the critical moment of the revolution Martov failed to find the indispensable words or perform the indispensable act he was capable of.

I listened, paying tribute to Martov the orator, but—made deeply indignant in the last analysis by this speech. . . Tereshchenko spoke—a toothless polemic. But the hall was already thinning out. It was near evening. In the ministerial seats the white, exhausted face of Kerensky was glimpsed and vanished. He didn't speak. About 8 o'clock the meeting closed.

'What a brilliant speech Martov made!' Lapinsky said to me in the corridor, with even a note of surprise.

I angrily shrugged my shoulders.

* * *

While the Pre-Parliament was sitting in the Marian, the garrison representatives had gathered again in Smolny. But there was no reason for it. They had been assembled only for liaison and contact. Those who had come were invited to the Soviet session, which opened at 7 o'clock and was very crowded.

It began with the usual type of agitation, not at all reminiscent of the start of the 'final decisive battle'. Only Antonov recalled one to current events, reporting on the activities of the Military Revolutionary Committee.

An odd scene. The chief of staff of the insurgent troops was making a resounding report on all the measures and tactical steps of his staff—listened to not only by his own army, but also by the enemy army and its staff. The commander of the insurgent troops was announcing publicly: we have begun to conquer and disarm the enemy this way and that, and we're going to go on as we see fit.

Antonov reported: the Military Revolutionary Committee officially began operations on the 20th. Since then it had taken the following steps (of a definitely rebellious nature): (1) All 'suspect' printing orders now required its sanction; (2) there were Commissars in all the garrison units through whom all Staff orders had to pass; (3) there was also a Commissar in the Peter-Paul Fortress and the Fortress arsenal was now available; (4) arms in all the factory stores and others would be given out only on the Military Revolutionary Committee's orders.

He went on to say: the Commissars were objected to by the Staff, but that didn't change anything. Yesterday the Staff suggested that the Military Revolutionary Committee start negotiations with it, but these conversations didn't change anything either. Today the Staff had demanded the cancellation of the telephone message about the preliminary control of its orders; besides this, the Staff proposed to form a Staff Council without the right of veto instead of the Military Revolutionary Committee; but the Military Revolutionary Committee had rejected these demands. And today the Commissars had been holding mass-meetings in all units; the garrison had reaffirmed its adherence to the Military Revolutionary Committee.

He was asked: did he know that troops loyal to the Government had been summoned to Petersburg from various points at the front and from the suburbs? What steps was the Military Revolutionary Committee taking? Antonov replied: the calling up of the troops and their movements were known; some of these troops would be held up, others were themselves refusing to march; it was only a few military cadet detachments there was no information about.

So everyone had heard how the insurrection was going. Did anyone feel like expressing his opinion?... The Mensheviks and SRs said that an insurrection was going on, that the Bolsheviks were seizing power and that all this threatened disaster. The Menshevik-Internationalist Astrov, a very bitter controversialist, specially emphasized the disastrousness of the split within the democracy: this was unjustified if only because the Bolsheviks themselves were not unanimous on the question of the insurrection; nothing would come of it but a bloody skirmish. Astrov worked up the meeting to such a point that Trotsky refused to continue as chairman. Trotsky's success as speaker, however, was all the greater.

'Yes,' he said, 'an insurrection is going on, and the Bolsheviks, in the form of the Congress majority, will take the power into their own hands. The steps taken by the Military Revolutionary Committee are steps for the seizure of power.'

Had everybody heard? Or was it still not clear enough?

A resolution was passed: the Military Revolutionary Committee's measures were approved; it was also charged with taking steps against riots, plundering, and other attempts to destroy order and the safety of the citizenry.

That same evening Smolny got a wire from Helsingfors, from the Baltic Fleet. The Fleet said it was attentively listening for every movement of both camps. At the first call from Smolny it would move its forces against the counter-revolution. This was not only a reliable Bolshevik force, but an active one. A decisive blow without this force would have been risky in the extreme. But—for the time being—Smolny didn't summon it.

* * *

Around 11 o'clock I was sitting in the newspaper office hurriedly finishing my leading article. It was on the same theme I had formulated an hour before at a session of the Bureau. The overturn which was giving the power to the Bolshevik Party was a dangerous adventure. It could only be forestalled and the revolution corrected by a decisive change of front on the part of the Menshevik–SR ruling circles.

An odd little incident arose from this leading article. I read it to Bazarov and Avilov,[1] who were waiting for me to finish. Avilov, who had long since moved far from Lenin, abruptly objected strongly to the expression 'The Bolsheviks are preparing a *coup d'état*.' This still seemed to him doubtful, and such an expression tactless. This made me lose my temper; Bazarov supported me, but Avilov persisted. We were all tense. Bazarov began shouting at Avilov, Avilov at Bazarov, both of them at me, and I at both of them. I flung the article into the waste-paper basket, but it was needed. We got it out and, continuing to shout at each other, went to the door. Avilov and Bazarov went home, and I to the printers' to get out the paper.

* * *

[1] Avilov, Boris Vasilyevich (1874–1938): a Bolshevik until February 1917, later an editor of *Novaya Zhizn*. (Ed.)

During that night of the 23rd work was going on at the General Staff too. Kerensky again went there for the night. But what could he do? It must have seemed time to act. Whatever his thoughts, and however he concealed the danger from himself, it was evidently impossible to wait any longer. The Peter-Paul had been taken, the arsenal had been seized, the Staff's demand that the Commissars should be removed had been refused, and it had been announced in unmistakable terms: 'I, Smolny, will certainly gobble you up, Kerenskyism, whenever I feel like it.' He must act—now or never.

The specially reliable units had now all been called up. If they didn't come, there was nothing to be done about it. Nevertheless detachments had been formed for the defence of the Winter Palace; guard-duties were being performed. In the city, of course, there *were* loyal elements, if not troops. It might be possible to form a detachment of several thousands from military cadets, the women's services, engineers, and Cossacks. A scratch detachment like that might be quite effective. But a firm decision to *act and attack* had to be made.

The Staff had made no effort to form a scratch detachment. It was muddled and vacillating. And it began to 'act'—in the habitual way, quite safely for the adversary, and not involving any risk whatever for itself. That night the Staff wrote a whole pile of orders. First, to avoid the seizure of motor-cars by the insurgents, all owners were ordered to place their cars at the disposition of the Staff; the 'full rigour of the law' was promised for disobedience, but it goes without saying that not one loyal bourgeois responded to this, and during the day the Staff lost even those cars it had. Secondly, all demonstrations were again prohibited 'on pain of arrest for armed rebellion'; execution by the troops of 'orders' emanating from 'various organizations' was also prohibited. Thirdly, an appeal to company, regimental, and brigade committees also announced that the District Commander's orders had to be obeyed: 'there are Central Ex. Com. Commissars on the Staff and therefore (!!) non-execution of orders would cause the disorganization and shattering of the revolutionary garrison'. For his part the Central Ex. Com. Commissar 'seconded the execution of the Staff's orders', pointing out that 'they were issued with his knowledge'.

Are you laughing, reader? Does the picture seem too pathetic?

I can't help it. The sovereign Government could emit only this empty babbling.

But is it possible that it didn't even dare call its enemy, not by an allusion, but by his real name? Can it be possible that it did not even permit itself in the Cabinet—confidentially, between Kerensky and Polkovnikov—to write down something with greater real content? Paper, after all, will stand for anything. Bolder, bolder!

Kerensky and Polkovnikov wrote: 'In view of the illegal activities of the representatives of the Petersburg Soviet assigned as Commissars to the units, institutions, and departments of the War Office, I order (1) all Commissars of the Petersburg Soviet to be removed until their confirmation by a Government Commissar of the district, (2) all illegal activities to be investigated for submission to a court martial, (3) all illegal activities to be reported to me instantly with an indication of the name of the Commissars. Polkovnikov.'

You can see that despair gives courage. The 'court martial', of course, was rhetoric as before. And as for removing the Commissars—who would remove them? In the units, after all, the order would fall into the hands of those very Commissars, who had already removed everyone who didn't obey them. So though it may have been bold enough, it wasn't very businesslike.

But the activity of the Staff that night was not limited to this. Towards morning the Staff had finally grown bold, or else desperate. And it decided to start fighting... What, did it send a detachment to seize Smolny, where there was no longer the democracy but only Bolshevik rebels? No, that would have been too much. The Staff did something else. I emphasize: in principle this was no less a destruction of constitutional guarantees and liberties and no less an act of violence than the seizure of mutinous Smolny would have been. But to make up for this the measure undertaken was first customary, secondly facile and cowardly, thirdly empty and futile. This was just as much as the wisdom and efficiency of the Provisional Government were equal to.

At 6 in the morning, on Polkovnikov's order, a few military cadets, headed by a Commissar of Militia, appeared at the offices of the Bolshevik papers *Rabochii Put* and *Soldat* (The Soldier) and announced that the papers were shut down. The responsible editor met the 'legitimate authorities' with wide-open eyes: what? did Polkovnikov still exist, or any Government at all except the Military Revolutionary Committee? He was assured that they did, and the cadets ruined the matrices, sealed the printing-presses, and destroyed the numbers already printed.

This was what it was equal to! After this, to pass off its cowardliness as democratic spirit and its simple-mindedness as respect for freedom was impossible (as indeed it had been before). The Bolshevik papers, you see, *were calling for an insurrection*, and so were destroyed, only to revive the very next day, while Smolny and the unit Commissars had already *made the insurrection* long ago, and they didn't lay a finger on them—out of democracy and love of liberty!

Nevertheless all the data indicate that the scene in the printing-shop could have been successfully repeated in Smolny too. There too they had so little belief in Polkovnikov that a good scratch detachment wouldn't have had much trouble. Some resistance would probably have been shown, and the affair wouldn't have come off without skirmishing, but the liquidation of Smolny was *possible*.

And the same question again: Why didn't the Military Revolutionary Committee attack and strike a decisive blow? If there is some reason to believe that Smolny could have been smashed, there can be no doubt at all that it would have been easy to occupy the Staff and seize the Ministers. In the last analysis there could be only one answer: from *political considerations* they were postponing the final blow until the Congress on the 25th. This was a tremendous risk which I think it would have been impossible to take on a cold calculation of all possible chances. But it reveals the most characteristic trait of this whole unprecedented insurrection: the insurgent camp, seeing no real strength in its adversary, acted with absolute irresponsibility, allowing itself something that is impossible in war, in manœuvres, or in a chess game.

In those pre-dawn hours of October 24th, when Kerensky started combat activities by swooping down on the Bolshevik press, two torpedo-boats came into Petersburg from Helsingfors. They had been sent by the Baltic Fleet to support the insurrection. Smolny—for the time being—hadn't called them. But the sailors themselves had sent them, under the pretext of 'greeting the Congress'.

CHAPTER 30

OCTOBER 24TH

EARLY in the morning of the 24th the Military Revolutionary Committee learned of the destruction of its press. It immediately set to work. It occupied the city, the Staff, and the Winter Palace, didn't it? Oh no—this is what it did.

First it sent a telephone message to all army units: 'The Petersburg Soviet is threatened; during the night counter-revolutionary conspirators ('very good!') attempted to call out the military cadets and the shock battalions; we order a regiment in battle readiness to be brought up and await further orders. . . For the Chairman, PODVOISKY. Secretary: ANTONOV.'

Then detachments of Lithuanians and Sappers were sent to the printing-presses of the shut-down newspapers. The printing-presses were unsealed and set in motion under the protection of the Military Revolutionary Committee's troops.

Further, two proclamations were drawn up. One said: 'The enemies of the people passed over to the attack during the night and are contemplating a treacherous blow against the Soviet; therefore the regimental and company committees and the Commissars must meet at once; no one must leave the barracks; firmness must be maintained, doubts avoided. The people's cause is in firm hands.' The second proclamation spoke of the struggle against riots and disorders: the Military Revolutionary Committee was on guard; the criminal pogromists and agents of the counter-revolution would be wiped off the face of the earth; the populace was called upon to restrain hooligans and Black Hundred agitators.

But alongside all this the Military Revolutionary Committee thought it necessary to publish this ruling of its own on October 24th: 'In spite of all kinds of rumours, the Military Revolutionary Committee states that it definitely does not exist to prepare and execute a seizure of power, but exclusively to defend the interests of the Petersburg garrison from counter-revolutionaries and pogromist attacks.' A *Novaya Zhizn* reporter asserts that this motion was passed unanimously. This was a special jibe at the Provisional Government. No one could have believed it any longer.

Finally, together with the order to the garrison about battle readiness, still another important step was taken. Over Sverdlov's signature a telegram in code was sent to Smilga, the chairman of the Finnish district committee in Helsingfors: 'Send regulations.' This meant: send 1,500 picked sailors and soldiers to our aid. But at best, if no one and nothing hindered them, they could not be in Petersburg until twenty-four hours later.

And it was only now, during the day and evening of the 24th, that armed detachments of Red Army militia-men and soldiers began to rally to Smolny to defend the staff of the insurrection. It's impossible to say how staunch or reliable they were. As we know their spirit was only moderate. The soldiers were well-disposed, but scarcely reliable. The workers were reliable, but scarcely steadfast, never having smelt powder in their lives. However, towards the evening of the 24th the defence of Smolny began to look like something.

* * *

And that morning the Provisional Government assembled in the Winter Palace. They busied themselves with 'organic work', supply, etc. Then they proceeded to the 'situation that has arisen'. Kerensky again insisted on the arrest of the Military Revolutionary Committee. But the Minister of Justice, Malyantovich, and someone else objected. Then Kerensky decided to appeal to the Pre-Parliament and immediately set out for it. This was quite unnecessary and absurd. Limitless powers were available. Practice, tradition, and custom also allowed any arrests or attacks to be carried out: after all, hundreds of Bolsheviks were sitting as before in the gaols, going hungry, vainly awaiting inquiries and the formulation of charges; as before, people were being seized and locked up for agitation as opportunity presented itself. So why had a special question arisen about the arrest of a few Bolsheviks who were the core of a clear-cut revolt that had already started? Was it because there was a risk there—of fighting and bloodshed? Nonsense! After all, they had equipped an expedition against the Durnovo villa—with devastation and bloodshed. . . No, here there was simply a lack of resolution or boldness, just the decrepitude and impotence of 'the sovereign Government'.

But in any case some further combat measures were decided on. Which ones? Those within their capacities. Orders were given to raise all the bridges, except the Palace Bridge, in order to hinder marchers. They had enough forces for this; it had been tried once before—on July 5th; it was futile, and even harmful.

The raising of the bridges at once produced in the city the circumstances of a *coup d'état* accomplished and disorders begun. The whole capital, hitherto quite tranquil, became agitated. Crowds began gathering in the streets. Armed detachments started moving; the bridge-raising had to be stopped, and where it had already taken place to be reversed. For these operations the Military Revolutionary Committee moved up workers and Red Army men. There were some small clashes at the bridges, or rather quarrels and friction. Neither side felt like a serious brawl. Depending on numbers, now the Red Army men would yield, now the military cadets. The bridges were lowered and raised again several times that day.

Excitement and crowds were the sole result of the Government's new measure. Nevertheless there were no disorders. Shooting wasn't seen anywhere. To make up for that the most alarming 'reports' flew around the city all day. On the 24th everyone thought the *coup* had begun.

* * *

Between 12 and 1 o'clock the Pre-Parliament opened. That too started off with 'organic work'. Nikitin, the Minister of the Interior, was making a report on local anarchy and the seizures of supplies in transit. But while he was speaking Kerensky appeared and hurried on to the platform immediately after Nikitin. White, excited, his eyes red with sleeplessness, but a little triumphant, he said the Government had instructed him to make a statement.

But he made a lengthy speech: the Constituent Assembly and the consolidation of the revolution were imminent. The Provisional Government was protecting the freedom and rights of the populace. But enemies of the State—Right and Left—were leading to disaster by invoking dictatorship and insurrection.

The Bolsheviks were preparing a *coup d'état*. There were incontestable proofs of it. Kerensky proved this at length, quoting *Rabochii Put* and the articles of the political criminal Lenin-Ulyanov we are familiar with. Then he made a diversion: and all this while the Government, three weeks before the Constituent Assembly, 'was debating in a final form the question of transferring the land to the hands of the rural committees' and sending a delegation to Paris where 'amongst other questions steps for bringing nearer the conclusion of the war would be submitted to the attention of the Allies'. Then the Premier gave an account of the current conflict between Smolny and the Staff. The Government proposed, in the form of an ultimatum, the cancellation of the telephone message on control of the Staff. 'Even though all data were available for immediate recourse to rigorous measures, the military authorities thought it best first to give the people every opportunity of rectifying their conscious or unconscious error' (exclamation from the Right: 'But that's just what's bad!)'. 'We had to do this also because no material consequences of this order were noticed amongst the troops the day it was announced.'

'In general,' said Kerensky, 'I prefer the Government to act more slowly but, to make up for that, more correctly, and at the necessary moment more resolutely too.' But Smolny had delayed its reply to the ultimatum. It was not until 3 o'clock that morning that a vaguely conditional reply had been given. It was accepted as a declaration that the 'organizers had committed an illegal act, which they were repudiating'. (Miliukov from his seat: 'Highly original!') But of course this was a ruse on the part of Smolny: the cancellation of the telephone message was not announced to the regiments. And now Kerensky discovered that a part of the Petersburg population was in 'a state of insurgence'. The Government had begun a 'judicial investigation'. Also, 'appropriate arrests were proposed'. 'The Provisional Government prefers to be killed and annihilated, but it will never betray the life, honour, and independence of the State'.

Kerensky was given an ovation. The audience in the galleries and the entire hall stood up and applauded—except the Internationalists. In his enthusiasm the Cadet Adzhemov ran forward, and cried, pointing his finger at us: 'Take a picture of them sitting down.' Kerensky went on: 'The Provisional Government is being reproached with . . .'

'Silliness!' Martov shouted out, amidst hubbub and excitement. The chairman called Martov to order. Kerensky went on:

'. . . with weakness and extraordinary patience. But in any case no one has the right to say that for the whole time I've been at its head, and before that too, it has resorted to any measures of pressure whatever until the State was threatened with immediate danger and destruction.'

Kerensky spoke further of his firm support at the front. He had a whole series of telegrams demanding decisive measures against the Bolsheviks and promising support. Then Konovalov came over and handed him the new telephone message of the Military Revolutionary Committee, already known to us: it demanded the immediate preparation of the regiments for battle. Kerensky looked at the document and then read it aloud. 'In legal language this is called a state of insurrection.'

There followed a patriotic statement about the menace of the foreign foe, and more about the virtues of the State and Kerensky's devotion to the principles of democracy. Finally the Premier finished his speech—a warning on the one hand, and on the other, a demand addressed to the Pre-Parliament.

Again everyone stood up and applauded—except the Internationalists.

In general Kerensky's speech, as we see, was quite superfluous. From a *formal* point of view the Government was fully sovereign, and its most 'decisive' steps were lawful. And in *fact* contact had been achieved in the usual conversations with the Star Chamber: there might be conflict with that on *any* ground, but in the given circumstances the usual arrests of Bolsheviks would have passed off without a hitch. Kerensky made a speech simply because there was nothing else he could do. He made a speech *instead* of doing anything real.

Nevertheless, read his speech: this man, after all, really believed he was doing something, just as he believed that in fact it was out of democracy and a feeling of legality and so on that he failed to destroy Smolny. Such was his nature.

After Kerensky's speech the agenda was of course disorganized. It was decided to make an immediate reply to the head of the State. But for this an interval and consultation and agreements between the fractions were essential. Everyone got up, amidst excitement and hubbub. I had stopped with someone at the end of the long middle aisle leading from the rostrum, and from a distance saw Kerensky, pale and morose, accompanied by his adjutants, advancing straight towards me from the depths of the auditorium.

Step aside and avoid a face to face encounter? For some months we hadn't come across one another. Between us now there were the barricades, *sans phrases*. I had berated him daily in the press. He had shut down my press. From a distance Kerensky, his eyes narrowed, caught sight of me. We looked at each other, like Peter I and the musketeer in Surikov's famous picture. Coming up within a couple of paces, Kerensky evidently didn't know what to do. Then, rather abruptly, with a resolute gesture, but a glum look, he stretched out his hand.

I never saw him again.[1]

* * *

The interval dragged on several hours, almost till evening. I must say I have no recollection at all of what *our* fraction decided. The Mensheviks and SRs turned to us and proposed that we should collect a majority under a *Left wing, Opposition* formula. By tacit consent the former delegates, Martov and I, were sent to this conference of Left fractions. We assembled below, doubtless in the apartments of the SR fraction. A gloomy rainy day of Petersburg late autumn looked into the huge windows facing out on Isaac Square. I think Martov was scribbling out a draft for a general Left formula. But the meeting didn't begin. First one of us, then another, then all of us together, were distracted by the alarming rumours from the city and outskirts. There was talk about outbreaks beginning—now here, now there.

But there were none. We know that the Central Ex. Com. Commissar on the Staff had forbidden the soldiers to go out into the streets. But the very same order had been given by the Military Revolutionary Commission, and finally, by the troop

[1] After the October Revolution Kerensky emigrated, eventually to New York City. He wrote a number of articles and books, including *Prelude to Bolshevism* (1919), *The Catastrophe* (1927), etc. He remained a leading figure in émigré circles until his death in 1970. (Ed.)

commander too. Whichever order seemed most convincing to the troops, they didn't leave the barracks. Personally I ascribe this primarily to their *mood*. It was on the side of the Bolsheviks, but there was no intention of *demonstrating* and *acting*, i.e., taking a chance. Without an order in any case they would never have come out. It would be well if volunteers could be found to come out on Smolny *orders*, when armed masses were needed!

But nevertheless there was alarm in the streets. The raising of the bridges, and the cadet patrols, provoked some panic in the central sections of the city. There were not only groups of cadets on guard at the bridges, arguing with small groups of the workers' Red Guard; tiny detachments of them were posted in the railway stations too and at various points of the city, in the power station, the Ministries, etc. Cadet pickets were standing in the main streets, stopping and requisitioning motor-cars and sending them to the Staff.

As a result, at about 2 o'clock government offices and shops began closing. The Nevsky crowd hurried home. In the midst of the tumult some hooligans appeared and began looting with great boldness, tearing clothing, footwear, and valuables off the passers-by. . . Towards evening, with the onset of the early autumn dusk, the streets were completely empty. But rumours took on the most monstrous forms.

It was in the atmosphere of these rumours that our inter-fraction commission met. As far as I recall, Martov proved to be *beatus possidens*—the happy possessor of a ready-made formula, which naturally was the basis of the discussion. It contained nothing like the confidence and support Kerensky demanded. It laid it down that the movement of the Bolsheviks had been provoked by the policy of the Government, and therefore peace had to be proposed immediately and the land transferred to the rural committees. As for the struggle against anarchy and possible pogroms, this struggle had to be assigned to a special Committee of Public Safety; it should be composed of representatives of the municipality and the organs of the revolutionary democracy, and should act in contact with the Provisional Government.

This did not, of course, satisfy Kerensky's party comrades. But it didn't satisfy me either. Gots and Zenzinov were demanding at least some kind of 'support', while I was insisting on immediate liquidation. . . As far as I recall we never came to a final settlement.

* * *

The session of the Pre-Parliament was resumed at 6 o'clock. . . I had just stopped by the office for a moment and then hurried off for a bite to eat at the 'Vienna', two steps away from the Marian Palace.

The Pre-Parliament hall wasn't crowded, but was very lively. Kamkov was on the platform and, to an uproar from the Right, was demanding the resignation of the Provisional Government and the formation of a Government of the democracy. Quite sound conclusions, which no one else formulated from the Pre-Parliament rostrum.

But the most interesting to us were the official representatives of the Menshevik–SR groups. Dan spoke in the name of the entire bloc:

'The bulk of the working class will not embark on the criminal adventure the Bolsheviks are urging on it. . . But while we wish to struggle against Bolshevism in the most decisive way, we do not wish to be an instrument in the hands of that counter-revolution which is trying to gamble on the crushing of this uprising. . . It is the duty of everyone to do everything possible for a peaceful settlement of the conflict. . . It is essential to cut the ground away from under the feet of the Bolsheviks. First of all, the outcry of the masses of the people for peace must be satisfied. Not out of weakness, but out of revolutionary strength we must say that we are demanding immediate steps towards peace negotiations. Further, we must raise the question of the land in such a way as to leave no one in any doubt. . . We don't want any government crisis, and we are ready to defend the Provisional Government, but let it make it possible for the democracy to rally round it.'

This was the contribution of the interstitial groups at the final hour: We don't want to be an instrument of the Kornilovites, but we shall defend the Government (and are already doing so).

Limping on one leg Martov came on to the platform.

'Minister in the future Bolshevik Cabinet' was heard from the Right.

'I am shortsighted', retorted Martov, 'and can't see whether that wasn't a former Minister of Kornilov's Cabinet!'

'In no circumstances', he went on, 'shall we collaborate with Kornilovites. The words of Kerensky, who permitted himself to talk about a rabble, when it is a question of the movement of a considerable part of the proletariat and the army, even though it is being directed towards mistaken goals—those words are a summons to civil war. But I have not lost hope that the democracy that is not taking part in the preparation of an armed demonstration will not permit the victory of those people who are trying to prevent the development of the revolution. . . The democracy must tell the Government that it will receive no support from them unless it gives immediate guarantees that the most vital needs of the country will be realized. . . I am sure that the senseless policy of repression and of hasty measures may provoke a desperate attempt on the part of the masses to join an uprising which they do not want. . . Therefore our fraction is appealing to all elements of the democracy to force the official circles now ruling in the name of Russia to carry on a democratic policy and thus prevent civil war.'

In essence Martov said *almost* everything he should. But this 'almost' was the main point. 'Force those ruling . . .' But was this really possible in the final hour? In form this was parliamentary diplomacy—did it have a place amidst the flames?

The official speaker for our fraction, limping on one leg, *was not up to the occasion.*

To make up for it he had a parliamentary success. . . A short interval was announced. And the Left fractions agreed, as an emergency, to vote for Martov's formula. In general we are already acquainted with it. First of all, it expressed a negative attitude to the Bolshevik uprising; secondly, it laid it down that it was the policy of the Government that had prepared the ground for the uprising, and called for immediate guarantees concerning peace and the land; thirdly, it proposed that the technical measures of combating the uprising be entrusted not to the Government, but to the Committee of Public Safety acting in 'contact' with the official authorities.

The other formula—of the Cadets and Co-operative people—'declared confidence in', 'supported', and demanded decisive measures against the uprising.

The tired deputies were nervous, excited, and wrangling with each other. . . The interval brought a whole series of alarming rumours. The Bolsheviks had begun. . .

The voting began. Martov's formula was passed by a majority of 122 to 102. . .

A storm of applause on the Left. The Right was thunderstruck. First of all, that morning, after all, the Internationalists had been completely isolated—everyone else had taken part in the ovation for Kerensky. Secondly—what was to be done?

The session ended at 8.30. But the deputies did not disperse. The hall was filled with hubbub and mass-meetings. The Right wing fell on the Mensheviks and SRs. What had they started? They had been asked for support, which they were waiting for in the Winter Palace. And what they had done in essence was to express a lack of confidence! The Government now ought to resign. At a critical hour it was left without support, and the country without a Government.

This view of the formula was fundamentally correct. But the Mensheviks and SRs, under the pressure of the Cadets, lost no time in getting confused and began hastily retreating. Come, come! We meant to put no such idea into the formula. We think a crisis untimely. We just wanted—well, after all, the programme promised should be put into effect. . .

* * *

But in the Winter Palace they were waiting for a formula. It was, after all, necessary for 'decisive measures'. . . At 9 o'clock in the evening the Government assembled in the Malachite Hall. The Chairman of the 'Council of the Republic' hurried there with the formula.

The Premier, after a quick glance, expressed surprise. Why wasn't there the usual parliamentary vote of confidence? Avksentiev didn't have to grope for a reply: it was missing by an oversight. The Premier, reading more carefully, exclaimed: 'Why, in a concealed form there's actually *no* confidence!' Everyone in the Malachite Hall was stupefied. No one had expected a surprise like this. No one had had any doubt that the overwhelming majority of the Pre-Parliament would be an adamantine wall around its powerful Government and would emphasize the complete isolation of the handful of Internationalists.

Kerensky declared that in these circumstances he thought it

necessary to surrender his mandate. Let the Praesidium of the Pre-Parliament form another Government. But by now the Chairman of the Council of the Republic was at a loss.

'Wait,' he said, 'I'll ask for the assistance of a couple of friends.'

No sooner said than done. Fifteen minutes later the assistance was in the Malachite Hall. All three began to prevail upon Boris Godunov: the terribly able Avksentiev, the terribly influential Gots, and the terribly cautious Dan. Come, come, we meant nothing of the sort! Kerensky himself had declared that morning that the Government would concern itself with the land and with peace. We support this. We emphasized it only to steal the Bolsheviks' thunder, and also to destroy the legend that the Government and the Pre-Parliament were enemies of the people. . .

Kerensky listened, but continued gently reprimanding the mischievous schoolboys: 'Yes, but these satisfactory comments do not change the formula; the country, after all, would understand it only as a lack of confidence, and the Government's prestige would be destroyed.'

This was reasonable. Here Dan was evidently at a loss, even though he thought a 'government crisis untimely'. Judging by the papers, the weight of this last argument fell to the SRs.

The formula, they declared, was the result of a general misunderstanding. Not one of the SRs could have had any thought of a lack of confidence. It was unsuccessful phraseology—the result of haste.

Kerensky said he would consult with his colleagues. And the colleagues assembled to consider decisive measures against the Bolsheviks—on the basis of a formula expressing support. The Minister conferred, and by virtue of patriotic considerations decided to forgive the Pre-Parliament this time in order not to leave Russia without a strong Government at a perilous moment. The Cabinet decided to remain at the helm. All's well that ends well—says the people's wisdom.

* * *

The representatives of the 'whole democracy' had barely dispersed from the Winter Palace when the Premier got a report that all was well in the streets, but that a detachment of twelve sailors, led by a very well-armed Commissar, had occupied the Government telegraph agency. The Commissar was already lording it there and imposing a censorship on wires to the provinces. . .

The Government immediately took 'decisive steps'. A detachment of military cadets with an armoured car was sent to the telegraph agency. Outnumbered by the enemy, the twelve sailors surrendered without a struggle. And then another decisive step was taken at once. On the order of the authorities the telephone central exchange cut off all Smolny's telephones. The Military Revolutionary Committee found itself cut off from the garrison. Communication was only possible through couriers—a very substantial inconvenience.

As we see, these two decisive steps were highly indicative of the course of the uprising and its character. There is no doubt that the affair had been formulated by Smolny without sufficient seriousness. The twelve sailors, of course, were not much, but to relinquish such a cardinal point as the telephone exchange meant a general delay in the development of fighting action. It was only permissible *when confronting this particular adversary*. But one way or another carelessness was manifest.

* * *

But what was happening all this time in Smolny? Smolny now had a quite impregnable look. Detachments of sailors, soldiers, and armed workers were posted around and inside the enormous building. There were quite a few machine-guns in the square, besides the cannon. Lorries, on which were crowded people with rifles and other weapons, were making a deafening racket. Now it was no longer possible to arrest the Military Revolutionary Committee, or bring up a detachment of 500 men to *occupy* this nest of insurgents. Now Smolny could only be *besieged and stormed*. This would no longer have been a simple 'measure' of a powerful Government, but an act of civil war. If the Government had massed enough strength, with artillery and the activity and skill of Government troops, I don't think success would have been completely excluded as yet. The chances, however, had grown infinitely smaller. The moment had been missed. It was probably impossible to collect forces in the capital for a siege and storm.

While the Pre-Parliament was voting on Martov's formula, a Soviet session was opening in Smolny. There were very few deputies, but the hall was filled with Congress delegates, representatives of regiments, and all sorts of onlookers. The session was declared informational—only for a report on the events of the past night and that day.

Trotsky presented the report:

Both the night and the day had been uneasy and full of events. During the night negotiations were going on with the Staff (already familiar from what has gone before). Towards morning they were broken off. In place of a definitive answer from the Staff, information was received that shock-troops had been summoned from Tsarskoe and from the junior officers' school at Oranienbaum, and artillery from Pavlovsk. The Military Revolutionary Committee had taken steps. Agitators had been sent out in large groups of thirty to fifty men each. As a result the shock-troops and the artillery refused to come out, and the junior officers split, a minority coming out. The printing-presses of the Bolshevik papers were being protected by reliable detachments; the papers' publication was assured. The cruiser *Aurora* was in the Neva, near Nicholas Bridge; its crew was loyal to the revolution. The Government had ordered the cruiser to leave the Neva waters; but the *Aurora* had not obeyed and was standing on guard. In the Pre-Parliament Kerensky had called the proletariat and the garrison of the capital a rabble; he demanded co-operation in the decisive struggle against the Soviet. The Bolsheviks didn't intend to strike a final blow on the eve of the Congress. The Congress itself would do whatever it decided, and take power into its own hands. But if the Government used the remaining twenty-four hours to enter into an open struggle, then the Soviet would give blow for blow and steel for iron.

Trotsky was questioned. For how many days was there bread in Petersburg? For three days. Were the rumours true about the constant searches? Unauthorized searches and looting would not be permitted, but there would be inspections of warehouses and other places, with the aim of requisitioning the excess on behalf of the people and the army. . .

Then the informational session was closed.

* * *

There was a united session of the worker-soldier and the peasant Central Ex. Coms. scheduled in Smolny at 11 o'clock in the evening. After hurrying over to the newspaper office again, I went to Smolny around 10 o'clock. Both outside and inside this armed camp passes were demanded. However, a determined look and the statement 'Member of the Central Ex. Com.' was enough to get inside. The stairs and corridors were packed with an armed mob. In the large hall for some reason the lighting was dimmed. But the hall was full, and there was an extraordinary number of all kinds of arms.

Making our way through the unknown crowd, new to Smolny, Martov and I found two empty seats in the second or third row. Hardly any Central Ex. Com. members were visible amongst the mass of newcomers, who didn't yield their seats to the members of the 'supreme Soviet organ'. In front, at the sides, and at the back we saw the greatcoats and grey features of the Bolshevik provinces. The mood too was grey. Faces were tired, dull, even gloomy. There was no enthusiasm.

The meeting began around midnight. Gots was sitting alone at a table on the large, dimly lit platform. He gave Dan, of course, the floor for a report on the 'current moment'. But with his own eyes Dan saw he was not in a meeting of the united Central Ex. Coms. at all, but amongst the direct participants in the insurrection, and it was precisely to them that he addressed his speech. His arguments were rather feeble. They were more of a plea—to refrain from a disastrous *coup* and not obey the Bolsheviks. The audience listened without any special objections, but also without any interest.

'Weak,' I said to Martov. 'He plainly has nothing to say. It's impossible to convince anyone with a naked plea.'

And from the hall there rang out some lazy but angry exclamations: 'All right! We've heard all that! We've stood it for eight months!'

Again they spoke up through yawns: 'We've been listening for eight months! You and your blood-sucker Kerensky! The *provocateur*!'

Dan tried to 'meet them half-way'. He was aware that the Soviet peace policy had been dragging somewhat, and he promised to go forward by 'another, quicker path'. Then he tried to frighten them with hunger, and predicted an immediate Bolshevik attack, transfer of power to the unruly elements of the populace, the triumph of the counter-revolution. . . In vain! From the hall there came an indifferent: 'Too late! We've heard all that!'

Trotsky came out against Dan; though really brilliant, he failed to arouse much enthusiasm in the tired audience. His position, against the background of Dan's attempts to keep up with the revolution, was completely tenable. After all, this was something basic and elementary which the Bolsheviks had been saying for ages, and which was going to realize the power of the Soviets the very next day. This power would be genuinely of the people. For every worker, peasant, and soldier, this was *his* régime. The Soviets would continuously renew their composition. They could not break with the masses and would always be the best exponents of their will. All attempts to frighten them with civil war were in vain.

'There will be none, if you don't falter, since our enemies will capitulate immediately and you will take the place that is rightfully yours, the place of master of the Russian land.'

* * *

And while in the dead of night the interstitial groups were talking this way, neither enemy camp was asleep. One was acting, the other trying to act. At midnight Sverdlov's wire was received in Helsingfors: 'Send regulations.' On the instant work came to the boil. In some two hours the echelons were made up. In place of the 1,500 promised, 1,800 armed sailors with machine-guns and ammunition were already on their way to Petersburg.

But in the Winter Palace around midnight Kerensky was receiving a deputation from the Union of Cossack Troops, headed by the chairman Grekov. The deputation insisted on a struggle against the Bolsheviks and promised its co-operation on condition that the struggle was decisive. Kerensky very willingly agreed: yes, the struggle had to be decisive. Then a telegram was written and sent at once to General Krasnov on the northern front: to bring up his cavalry corps to Petersburg at once. This was, as we know, the same corps that Kerensky had once asked Kornilov for, and which was then declared insurgent. Kerensky was now summoning it again, but Grekov signed the telegram as well, just in case.

However, no Winter Palace signatures at all were valid. Without the name of the Soviet, and under the banner of the Provisional Government, no troops *at all* could now be mobilized on the front for a march on Petersburg. And in this decisive hour Kerensky had to mobilize again the forces loyal to the Soviet. I don't know just when or how this took place. But in view of the obvious inadequacy of his order to the corps commander, on the night of the 24th a parallel order was sent from Petersburg—by the Star Chamber to Voitinsky, the Soviet Commissar of the northern front. It was only through the name of the Soviet and with the closest participation of an authoritative Soviet personality that it was possible to organize an attack on the revolutionary capital by front-line troops.

On the night of the 24th Gots talked to Voitinsky over a direct line. He demanded the immediate despatch of a reliable army against the Bolsheviks. Voitinsky was not sufficiently informed about the state of affairs in Petersburg, and asked whether the order was issued in the name of the Central Ex. Com. Gots asked him to wait until he talked to whomever he had to (Dan, Avksentiev, Skobelev?). A few minutes later Gots said on the direct line that the order was issued in the name of the Praesidium of the Central Ex. Com. Voitinsky acted at once. But he really had no choice; very quickly it was narrowed down to that same Cossack corps of the loyal Tsarist servant Krasnov.

Voitinsky himself told me all about this a few years after the events. The rôle of Voitinsky himself is of relatively little interest here, but it ought to be known just who did most to attack the revolutionary capital and the legal representatives of the workers, peasants, and soldiers. This was the Star Chamber, acting by means of a forgery—of the name of the Soviet, which it knew for certain was not behind it.

That night the Provisional Government left the Winter Palace rather early, at around 2. Kerensky may have taken a rest, but not for more than an hour. He hurried to the Staff.

There very alarming news had been received. It was decided on the spot to send the Cossack troops stationed in the capital into action. But would they go? A telephone message was sent to the 1st, 4th, and 14th Don Cossack Regiments: 'In the name of freedom, honour, and the glory of the fatherland come to the aid of the Central Ex. Com., the revolutionary democracy and the Provisional Government.'

But the Cossacks did not obey. They got up a mass-meeting and began bargaining. Would the infantry go with them? It was explained at once by authoritative, competent people that in no circumstances would the infantry move for the Government or the Central Ex. Com. Then the regiments declared that they refused to make a living target out of themselves, and would therefore 'abstain'.

Nor did the Staff hope for anything special from these regiments. This is evident from the very text of the order: first, it is propaganda, and secondly, the sovereign Government timidly hides behind the Central Ex. Com. But in any case these regiments were the *last* hope. The cadets and women's shock-troops, taken all together, might have served for the defence of a single point, but weren't enough to defend the whole city.

Indeed, were even the privileged, *ancien-régime* cadets of the capital reliable? The Pavlovsky Academy also refused to come out; the cadets were afraid of the Grenadier Regiment stationed nearby (which was undoubtedly still more afraid of them).

Not one unit came from the suburbs. There was a report that half the armoured cars had gone over to the side of Smolny; the others—no one knew. . . The city lay *undefended.*

CHAPTER 31

OCTOBER 25TH

THE decisive operations of the Military Revolutionary Committee started around 2 in the morning.

Three members of the Military Revolutionary Committee were assigned to work out the dispositions: Podvoisky, Antonov, and Mekhonoshin. Antonov says it was his plan that was accepted. It consisted in occupying first of all those parts of the city adjoining the Finland Station: the Vyborg Side, the outskirts of the Petersburg Side, etc. Together with the units arrived from Finland it would then be possible to launch an offensive against the centre of the capital. But of course—that was only in an extremity, in case of serious resistance, which was considered possible.

But no resistance was shown. Beginning at 2 in the morning the stations, bridges, lighting installations, telegraphs, and telegraphic agency were gradually occupied by small forces brought from the barracks. The little groups of cadets could not resist and didn't think of it. In general the military operations in the politically important centres of the city rather resembled a changing of the guard. The weaker defence force, of cadets, retired; and a strengthened defence force, of Guards, took its place.

From evening on there were rumours of shootings and of armed cars racing round the city attacking Government pickets. But these were manifestly fancies. In any case the decisive operations that had begun were quite bloodless; not one casualty was recorded. The city was absolutely calm. Both the centre and the suburbs were sunk in a deep sleep, not suspecting what was going on in the quiet of the cold autumn night.

I don't know *how* the soldiers behaved. According to all reports, with no enthusiasm or spirit. Occasionally they may have refused to move. A fighting mood or readiness for sacrifice could not be expected from our garrison. But now this had no significance. The operations, gradually developing, went so smoothly that no great forces were required. Out of the garrison of 200,000 scarcely a tenth went into action, probably much fewer. Because of the presence of the workers and sailors only volunteers could be led out of the barracks. The staff of the insurgents was cautiously feeling its way—you might say too cautiously and *feebly*.

It was natural to try above all to paralyse the political and military centre of the Government, that is, occupy the Winter Palace and the Staff. First and foremost the old authorities and their military apparatus had to be liquidated. Otherwise the insurrection could by no means be considered consummated; and the two powers—one 'legitimate', the other merely future—would have been able to carry on a civil war, with chances greatly favouring the former. So it had to be annihilated first of all. The telegraphs, bridges, stations, and the rest—would take care of themselves.

Nevertheless, throughout the night the insurrectionaries did not even try to touch either the Winter Palace, the Staff or individual Ministers. The objection may be made that the liquidation of the old régime is the *conclusion* of an insurrection. It is very hard and hazardous, for this is the centre of the defence. But was this so in the special conditions of our October insurrection? Had the ground been adequately felt out by Smolny in its cautious movements? Was even the most primitive reconnaissance carried out—by sending a courier to the Staff and to the Winter Palace? No. For the defences of the empty Winter Palace in those hours were absolutely fictitious; while the General Staff, where the head of the Government was located, was not protected at all. As far as can be judged from the scanty data, there was not even the usual pair of sentries at the entrance. The General Staff, together with Kerensky, could have been taken with bare hands. For this few more people were needed than the Military Revolutionary Committee itself contained.

That's how it went on the whole night and the whole morning. It was not until 7 o'clock in the morning, when the telephone exchange was occupied, that the *Staff telephones were cut off*. There you are—revenge for the same operation against Smolny! . . . In general it was all quite frivolous. But in any case let us recall one absolutely credible fact. Kerensky (like all the Ministers, who were at home) might have been seized in the

Staff without the slightest difficulty. This could of course have been done before: now I'm thinking of the period *after the beginning* of decisive combat activities.

In the early morning the troops began to form lines along a few streets and canals. But there was no artillery. And the idea of this operation was more or less obscure. It would seem there must have been some notion of a siege of the Winter Palace and the General Staff nearby. But in any case this wasn't accomplished. The ranks, as I saw them personally, looked not so much like a fighting as a policing force: they did not besiege, at best they surrounded. But they performed even this police task very feebly and without the slightest understanding of its rationale.

* * *

At 5 o'clock in the morning Kerensky summoned to the Staff Manikovsky, the War Minister, who had to come from the Petersburg Side.

At 9 o'clock he hurriedly summoned all the Ministers. As before the Staff was still undefended in any way by anyone. Whole strings of military people were going in and coming out of the entrance. Who they were and why they had come—no one knew. No one asked either for passes or for identification papers. The people going in might all have been agents of the Military Revolutionary Committee, and have declared whenever they liked that the General Staff had passed into Smolny's hands. But this didn't happen.

The head of the Government was in the Staff, but the passers-by didn't know where he was and were not interested in him. The officer on duty ought to have known, but he was not at his post.

Kerensky remained in the study of the Chief of Staff. At the doors there were neither sentries, nor adjutants, nor attendants. The door could simply have been opened and the Premier taken by anyone with the energy.

Kerensky was walking around in an overcoat. He was calling the Ministers together for final instructions. The American Embassy had lent him a car, and he was going to Luga, to meet the troops coming from the front for the defence of the Provisional Government.

* * *

Here is the Smolny estimate of the situation. When all the important points of the city were occupied without any resistance and the ranks, so-called, were placed not very far from the Winter Palace and the Staff, the Military Revolutionary Committee struck the bell. By 10 o'clock in the morning it had already written and had sent to be printed this proclamation: 'To the citizens of Russia: The Provisional Government is overthrown. The state power has passed into the hands of the organ of the Petersburg Soviet of Workers' and Soldiers' Deputies, the Military Revolutionary Committee, which stands at the head of the Petersburg garrison and proletariat. The cause the people have been fighting for—the immediate proposal of a democratic peace, the elimination of private property in land, workers' control of production, and the formation of a Soviet Government—is assured. Long live the revolution of the workers, soldiers, and peasants! . . .'

Roughly the same thing was broadcast by wireless to the whole country and the front. There it was also added that the 'new Government will convoke a Constituent Assembly', and that 'the workers were victorious without any bloodshed.'

To my mind all this was premature. The Provisional Government was still not overthrown. It still existed in the form of the acknowledged official authority and was organizing defences within the capital and the crushing of the rebellion outside. At 10 o'clock in the morning of the 25th the position, to my mind, was no different from what it had been the night or the week before. By the use of its *de facto* influence Smolny had brought the troops out of barracks and distributed them at various points in the city. The Government, having no *de facto* authority, could not hinder this, either the previous night or the week before. But it would be overthrown only when it either was captured or ceased calling itself the Government and *de facto* declined to govern. Now, on October 25th, this was more difficult to attain than the night or a week before: the head of the Government had left for the field army to organize a march on Petersburg, while his colleagues were surrounded by defences they'd never had before in their lives. . . Hence, it was too early to talk about a victory at all, and especially about a bloodless one.

* * *

Soon after 12 o'clock I walked to the Marian Palace along the Nevsky and the Moika. The streets were animated, but not alarmed, even though everyone was watching the 'demonstration that had begun'. But some of the shops were shut and others shutting down. The banks, that had hardly opened, were finishing their operations. Government offices were closed. It may be that no alarm was noticeable because the 'demonstration' didn't look at all terrifying. As before there was neither fighting nor shooting anywhere.

In the middle of the Moika I came up against a line of soldiers barring the way. What unit it was I have no idea. There may have been machine-guns there too: since the revolution the eye had become so accustomed to these terrible objects it no longer noticed them. But in any case the soldiers, bored, were standing at ease, and for that matter not close together. This column was not terrifying, not only to any organized military force but to a mob either. Its activity was limited to not letting anyone pass.

But I showed persistence. The Commander hurried over to me —one of the new ones, elected and dependable. I had various credentials on me, including the blue members' card of the Petersburg Ex. Com., signed by Trotsky. But I presented the card of the counter-revolutionary Pre-Parliament, saying that was where I was going. The Commander thought this convincing. He not only willingly ordered me to be let pass, but offered to give me a soldier as escort: he said there was another column to stop me before the Marian Palace. I refused the escort, and as far as I recall wasn't stopped any more. But the Commander, in letting me go, was not averse to a chat and said: 'Incomprehensible! The order was to march. But why—no one knows. Against one's own people, after all. All rather strange. . .'

The Commander smiled with embarrassment, and it was evident that he was indeed rather baffled by everything. There was no doubt about it: there was no spirit; such troops would never fight; they would scatter and surrender at the first blank shot. But there was no one to do any shooting.

I went over to the Marian Palace. There was a lorry standing at the portico steps, and in the portico itself I found a group of some fifteen to twenty sailors and workers. One of them recognized me. They surrounded me and told me they had just driven the Pre-Parliament out. There was no one in the Palace any more and they wouldn't let me in. But they wouldn't arrest me. No, they didn't want me. Generally speaking they weren't touching members of the Central Ex. Com. By the way, did I happen to know where the Provisional Government were? They had looked for them in the Marian Palace, but hadn't found them. They had to arrest the Ministers, they just didn't know where they were. But just let Kerensky or anyone show his face! The conversation, however, was quite amiable.

* * *

This is what had happened in the Pre-Parliament in my absence. Everything went off very simply. By noon very few deputies had assembled. They were exchanging news with the journalists. This place was occupied, that was occupied. . . Suddenly it was revealed that the Marian Palace telephones had been cut off. Smolny had taken yesterday night's lesson of the Winter Palace to heart.

But the session didn't begin. Fractions were conferring in corners. Then there was a meeting of the expanded Council of 'Elders'. As always, the fateful question was put: What shall we do? But they didn't have time to decide. It was reported that an armoured car, some detachments of the Lithuanian and Cuxholm Regiments, and the sailors of the Guards crew had arrived at the Marian Palace. They were already lining both sides of the staircase and had occupied the first hall. Their commanders were demanding that the Palace premises be cleared immediately.

The soldiers, however, were in no hurry and didn't seem aggressive. The 'Elders' had time for a hasty debate on the new situation and the elaboration of a resolution for the plenum. Then the 'Elders' came to the conference hall, where there were about a hundred deputies. The chairman proposed a motion: that (1) The Council of the Republic had not ceased, but merely temporarily suspended its activities; (2) The Council of the Republic, in the form of its Council of 'Elders', would enter a Committee of Safety; (3) The chairman was charged with launching an appeal to the nation; (4) The deputies would not leave and would assemble at the first opportunity. Then, of course, there was voiced a protest against violence; and finally it was decided by fifty-six votes to forty-eight with two abstentions to yield to force and go home.

The soldiers and the commanders were patiently waiting. The deputies, having done their duty, began dispersing.

As we see there was nothing theatrical or dramatic about all this; eye-witnesses said so too. You will say that the Thermidorians showed far more energy and quality on the 18th Brumaire. But that was a *revolutionary* bourgeoisie, as it had always openly professed to be. Our bourgeoisie, however, from the first day on, was in the camp of the counter-revolution and had always carefully concealed this. The Right section of the Pre-Parliament voted *against* the voluntary 'temporary' dissolution, but didn't undertake anything further. Those weren't its traditions or spirit. But the Left section, for all its moral indignation, was politically in a difficult situation. On the one hand it was impossible to submit to Smolny's order without protest. On the other, it was impossible, with Gen. Alexeyev, to stand shoulder to shoulder and face the Bolshevik onslaught without palaver.

Perhaps the most interesting thing was at the exit, when the deputies went down the magnificent staircase between the lines of sailors and soldiers. The detachment officers were requesting the deputies' cards and examining them with unusual care—both upstairs and at the actual exits. It was thought there would be arrests. The Cadet leaders were already prepared to go off to the Peter-Paul. But they were let through with the most thorough-going, indeed insulting, indifference. The inexperienced new rulers were carrying out only the letter of the carelessly given order: arrest the members of the Provisional Government. But not one Minister was there. What was to be done? For it was, after all, very important to arrest them. Releasing Miliukov, Nabokov, and other Kornilovite aces, the commanders jumped on the Right Menshevik Dubois; his papers read: Assistant Minister of Labour. One caught! But then a dispute began. After all, he's a Socialist—been in gaol, etc. The soldiers insisted: it was highly necessary to catch a Minister. But excuse me, after all it was this Dubois who arrested Guchkov at the front during the Kornilov days! They couldn't hold out against that, and released this peculiar Minister. But where were the others? They were really wanted; and nobody knew where they were.

And indeed, where were they? This was a first-class puzzle for the Military Revolutionary Committee.

* * *

From the Marian Palace I headed for Smolny. There were no lines of soldiers across the Morskoy. Near the Nevsky, around the arch rising above the Palace square, it was said cadets were holding out near the Palace and were supposed to be shooting. I didn't hear a single shot, but small units were going here and there. The streets seemed to be growing more and more lively. The rifles might begin to go off of their own accord, but the mood was not truculent. The rifles didn't go off.

I got to Smolny around 3 o'clock. It still looked much the same. But there were even more people, and the disorder had grown. There were many defenders, but I doubt whether the defence could have been firm or organized.

I went straight along the dirty, sombre corridor into the great hall. It was packed, without the slightest sign of order or decorum. A meeting was going on. Trotsky was chairman. But it was hard to hear from behind the columns, and armed people were thrusting back and forth.

When I came in an unknown, bald, clean-shaven man was standing on the platform making a heated speech. But he spoke in a strangely familiar, loud, hoarse voice, with a throaty note and a very typical stressing of the ends of sentences. . . Eh—Lenin! He had appeared that day, after a four-month stay underground. So this was the final celebration of victory!

The Petersburg Soviet was once again in session. Opening it, before my arrival, Trotsky, in the midst of applause, hubbub, and disorder, had said this: 'In the name of the Military Revolutionary Committee I declare that the Provisional Government has ceased to exist. Individual Ministers are under arrest, the others will be arrested in the next few days or hours. The revolutionary garrison has dispersed the Pre-Parliament. We were told that the insurrection would provoke a pogrom and drown the revolution in torrents of blood. So far everything has gone off bloodlessly. We don't know of a single casualty. I don't know of any examples in history of a revolutionary movement in which such enormous masses participated and which took place so bloodlessly. The Winter Palace has not yet been taken, but its fate will be decided in the course of the next few minutes. At the present time the Soviet of Soldiers', Workers', and Peasants' Deputies faces the historically unprecedented experiment of the creation of a régime which will have no other interests but the needs of the workers, peasants, and soldiers. The State must be an instrument of the masses in the struggle for their liberation from all bondage. It is essential to establish control of industry. The peasants, workers, and soldiers must feel that the national economy is their economy. This is the basic principle of the Soviet Government. The introduction of a universal labour draft is one of our most immediate tasks.'

* * *

These programmatic perspectives were not at all clear and were no more than agitation. But don't they reflect a rather bold and swift advance towards Bolshevik Socialism? It was as though the nearer he got to power the more this benevolent process was taking place in Trotsky's mind. A trivial but accurate saying—*noblesse oblige*. . .

Then Trotsky 'introduced' Lenin to the meeting and gave him the floor for a speech on the Soviet régime. Lenin was given a tumultuous ovation. . . While he was speaking I moved forward and stood with someone I knew behind the columns to the right of the entrance. I couldn't hear very well what Lenin was saying; I think I was more interested in the mood of the crowd. In spite of Trotsky's expansive remarks I didn't notice either enthusiasm or a festival spirit. People may have become too accustomed to dizzying events. They may have been tired. They may have been a little confused as to what would come of all this, and doubtful that anything would.

'Well, Comrade Sukhanov?' a low, effeminate voice, with a slight lisping accent, came from behind me; 'you didn't expect the victory to be so quick and easy?'

I turned around. Behind me stood an unknown man with a beard and close-cropped hair, with his hand outstretched. On close examination, or rather when I remembered whose agreeable contralto this was, I finally recognized Zinoviev. His appearance had radically altered.

'Victory?' I answered. 'Are you celebrating a victory already? Wait just a little longer. Just liquidate Kerensky, who has gone off to organize an expedition against Petersburg. Besides, in general you and I will hardly find ourselves in complete agreement.'

Zinoviev said nothing but looked at me a moment in silence, then walked away a couple of steps. After all, he had just expressed himself, and even tried to carry on a campaign *against* the insurrection, for fear it would be crushed. And suddenly the thing was going so smoothly! On the other hand, he really had forgotten about Kerensky and much else, and had been in too much of a hurry to congratulate an outsider. Zinoviev's mind was undoubtedly in a whirl.

'No, no, I'm not going to speak now,' I heard the contralto saying, in reply to a suggestion that he speak, brought from the Praesidium.

Meanwhile Lenin was saying:

'The oppressed masses themselves will form a Government. The old state apparatus will be destroyed root and branch, and a new administrative apparatus will be created in the form of the Soviet organizations. Now begins a new era in the history of Russia, and this third Russian revolution must finally lead to the victory of Socialism. One of our routine tasks is to end the war at once. But in order to end this war, closely bound up with the present capitalist order, it is clear to everyone that our capitalism itself must be conquered. In this task we shall be helped by the worldwide working-class movement which has already begun to develop in Italy, Germany, and England. Within Russia an enormous section of the peasantry has said: Enough playing around with the capitalists; we will go with the workers. We shall win the peasants' trust with a single decree which will annihilate landed property. We shall institute a genuine workers' control of industry. We have the strength of a mass organization that will triumph over everything and bring the proletariat to the world revolution. In Russia we must set to work at once on the construction of a proletarian Socialist State. Long live the worldwide Socialist revolution!'

The programme of the new régime, which the chief was addressing to his guard, was not very clear, but it was very suspicious. Suspicious because of the transparent disinclination to take two circumstances into account. First of all, the current tasks of state administration: utterly to destroy all the old state apparatus in the desperate conditions of war and famine meant to consummate the destruction of the productive forces of the country, and not to fulfil the most urgent tasks of peaceful construction aimed at the cultural and economic elevation of the lȧbouring masses. Secondly, how things stood with the general foundations of scientific Socialism: to construct (not merely a Soviet) but a 'proletarian Socialist State' in a vast, economically-shattered peasant country meant taking on oneself tasks known to be utopian. Now, in the mouth of a Lenin whose mind had not yet digested the jumble of Marx and Kropotkin, this was not yet clear. But it was extremely suspicious.

Then Zinoviev appeared on the platform to give greetings: Lunacharsky also congratulated the Soviet. It was decided not to debate Lenin's speech. Why cloud the triumph by Menshevik speeches? A motion was passed directly: 'The Soviet expresses its confidence that a Soviet Government will firmly advance towards Socialism, the only salvation of the country. The Soviet is convinced that the proletariat of Western Europe will help lead the cause of Socialism to total victory.'

Capital! A long step forward towards Socialism! But meanwhile Trotsky made this statement: 'A telegram has just been received that troops are moving on Petersburg from the front. Commissars from the Petersburg Soviet must be sent to the front and throughout the country at once to tell the broad masses of the people what has happened.'

Voices from the body of the hall: 'You're anticipating the will of the Congress!'

Trotsky: 'The will of the Congress has been anticipated by the tremendous fact of the insurrection of the Petersburg workers and soldiers, which has taken place tonight. It simply remains for us now to develop our victory.'

* * *

It was getting dark when I broke away from the commotion in Smolny and went home. I had left my Karpovka place around then and moved to the Shpalerny, closer to the office, Soviet–Smolny circles, and—the Constituent Assembly, for which the Tauride Palace was already prepared. I went home to eat, anticipating another sleepless night at Smolny. A very characteristic fact, this dining by the light of a candle-stub in a room not quite ready for habitation. Formerly, amidst similar events, this strange idea of leaving the cauldron for even two hours to sit down to dinner couldn't have entered my head. Now it came into my mind rather easily. It was a question, and not for myself alone, of the blunting of perceptions. People were very used to every kind of happening. Nothing had any effect. But at the same time a feeling of impotence also made itself felt. Of course something *had* to be done; it was impossible not to fight. But it meant so little! The arena was occupied almost in its entirety. The course of events was predetermined by the volcanic eruption of the depths of the remote countryside and by the monopolists of the moment.

* * *

It was around 8 o'clock when I returned to Smolny. There seemed to be even more chaos and disorder. As I went in I met old Martynov, of our fraction. 'Well?'

'The fraction's in session. Of course we shall leave the Congress. . .'

'What? How, leave the Congress? Our fraction?'

I was thunderstruck. Nothing like this had ever entered my head. It was thought possible that the Right Mensheviks would apply a specifically Bolshevik tactic and subject the Congress to a boycott. But for *our* fraction such a possibility seemed to me absolutely excluded.

First of all, no one contested the legality of the Congress. Secondly, it represented the most authentic worker–peasant democracy; and it must be said that not a small part of it consisted of the participants in the first Congress in June, the members of the 'Corps of Cadets'. Of that grey mass of delegates who had once followed the Menshevik patriots, many had been enticed away by Lenin, while most of the Right SRs were becoming Left SRs, if not Bolsheviks. Thirdly, the question was: *Where* would the Right Mensheviks and the SRs leave the Congress for? Where would they go from the Soviet?

The Soviet, after all, was—the revolution itself. Without the Soviet it never existed, nor could it. It was in the Soviet, the combat instrument of the revolution, that the revolutionary masses were always organized and rallied. So where could one go from the Soviet? It meant a formal break with the masses and with the revolution.

And why? Because the Congress had proclaimed a Soviet régime in which the minute Menshevik–SR minority would not be given a place! I myself considered this fatal for the revolution, but why link this with abandoning the supreme representative organ of the workers, soldiers, and peasants? The 'Coalition', after all, was no less odious to the Bolsheviks than a 'Soviet régime' was to the old Soviet bloc; the Bolsheviks, not long ago, under the dictatorship of the Star Chamber, themselves constituted the same impotent minority as the Mensheviks and SRs now, but they did not and could not draw the conclusion that they had to leave the Soviet.

The old bloc could not swallow its defeat and the Bolshevik dictatorship. With the bourgeoisie and with the Kornilovites—yes; but with the workers and peasants whom they had thrown into the arms of Lenin with their own hands—impossible.

The sole argument heard from the Rightists was this: the Bolshevik adventure would be liquidated from one day to the next; the 'Soviet Government' would not hold out more than a few days, and at such a time the Bolsheviks had to be *isolated* in the eyes of the entire country; they had to be smitten now by every possible means and driven into a corner with whips and scorpions.

I too was convinced that the power of a Bolshevik régime would be ephemeral. A majority of them themselves were at that time convinced of the same thing. I also thought it useful and necessary to *isolate their position* and oppose to it the idea of a united democratic front. But for this why was it necessary to get out? That was the least of it: how was it possible to achieve this by getting out of the Soviet, away from the organized masses, away from the revolution? It could be achieved only in the arena of Soviet struggle.

But the point was that it was not the united democratic front that was opposed to the Bolshevik position. The Mensheviks and SRs—at least their leaders—today just as yesterday kept on opposing the same *Coalition* to the Soviet régime. This of course considerably changed matters. If yesterday it was blindness, today it was—practically—definite Kornilovism. It was the programme of a bourgeois dictatorship on the ruins of the Bolshevik régime. That was now the *only way the Coalition could be restored.* If that was so, then of course it was not a question of the Soviets, the revolution, or the masses. . . If that was so, then the arguments in favour of getting out of the Congress had their rationale and did not seem so senseless.

However, only a few *Right* Soviet elements, after all, former adherents of the Coalition, could reason this way. But what connexion could all this have with *our* fraction? Avksentiev and Gots would leave the Soviet for wherever the bourgeoisie was. Would even leave for that luckless Committee of Safety, which was supposed to take on itself the liquidation of the Bolshevik enterprise—'without the bourgeoisie, by the forces of the democracy alone'. Let us admit that out of traditional solidarity Dan would follow Avksentiev out of the Soviet. But where would Martov go? Where would *we* go—partisans of the *dictatorship of the democracy*, opponents of the Coalition, close allies of the proletariat and its fighting organization? We had nowhere to go; torn out of Soviet soil we should perish like a snail torn from its shell.

I didn't formulate all this after my encounter with Martynov, in the midst of the fuss and hubbub of Smolny. But it had long been firmly fixed in my mind. Martynov's communication absolutely stunned me. I rushed off to look for the fraction, and Martov especially. The fraction was not then in session, and Martov wasn't around, but I was told that many of us wanted to get out, and Martov, even though not very resolutely, was also inclined to follow the example of Dan and Avksentiev. A bad business!

My indignation was shared by many—not only the Left section of the Pre-Parliament fraction, but also the provincials. The fraction had not yet come to a final decision. The session had been a joint one with the Rightists. As for us, no one yet knew which side the majority would be on. The fraction had to be assembled.

* * *

I and some others who shared my views called together the fraction of the Menshevik-Internationalists. It assembled in a big unfamiliar room. Rather a large number of people crowded around a rough table with simple rude benches. There were probably more than a few of the official Mensheviks, of the *Novaya Zhizn* people too, and of the Left SRs who were trying to maintain contact with us. I think Martov arrived towards the end. On the question of getting out he wavered and twisted. But some of his closest lieutenants were definitely for getting out. If I'm not mistaken, Abramovich[1] made a heated speech for leaving. But we on the Left fought hard and didn't yield.

It was learned that the Menshevik Central Committee had resolved that 'responsibility for any completely military overturn be lifted from the party, that it take no part in the Congress, and that it take steps to negotiate with the Provisional Government on the formation of a régime based on the will of the democracy'. Besides this, the Menshevik Central Committee had resolved to form 'a commission of the Mensheviks and SRs for joint work on questions of common security'. The Right SRs had also, of course, decided to leave the Congress.

This news had various effects on the members of our conference. Some recoiled Rightwards—from motives of solidarity and discipline. Others, on the contrary, clearly saw in all this the bankruptcy of the Rightists and their complete rupture with the revolution; any possibility of solidarity with these elements was excluded for them, and this reinforced their *Left* position.

In general there was no definite decision taken on getting out. Martov deflected matters somewhat by proposing this solution: the fraction would demand from the Congress an agreement to create a democratic régime from representatives of all the parties in the Soviet; until the results of the requisite party negotiations were clear the Congress would suspend its functions. A majority of the votes settled on this. The question of getting out was postponed: it was to be decided in due course, depending on events.

The delegates nervously hurried through the rooms and corridors, gathering in clusters, getting in the way, and packing the buffet. Rifles, bayonets, and Caucasian fur-caps could be glimpsed everywhere. The exhausted guard were dozing on the stairs; soldiers, sailors, Red Guards, were sitting on the floor of the corridor close to the walls. It was stifling, filthy. . . The Congress opened in a far from triumphal setting; it opened under

[1] Abramovich, Raphael (1879–1963): prominent Bundist and Right Menshevik. Emigrated after October Revolution, eventually to New York City. (Ed.)

fire and seemed immersed in the most urgent and primitive drudgery.

* * *

It was not until 11 o'clock that bells began to ring for the meeting. The hall was already full, still with the same grey mob from the heart of the country. An enormous difference leaped to the eye: the Petersburg Soviet, that is, its Workers' Section in particular, which consisted of average Petersburg proletarians, in comparison with the masses of the Second Congress looked like the Roman Senate that the ancient Carthaginians[1] took for an assembly of gods. With masses like *that*, with the vanguard of the Petersburg proletariat, I think it really was possible to be enticed into an attempt to illuminate old Europe with the light of the Socialist revolution. But in Russia this incomparable type is an exception. The Moscow worker is as different from the Petersburg proletarian as a hen from a peacock. But even he, as familiar to me as the Petersburger, is not altogether benighted and homespun. Here at the Congress, however, the hall was filled with a crowd of a completely different order. Out of the trenches and obscure holes and corners had crept utterly crude and ignorant people whose devotion to the revolution was spite and despair, while their 'Socialism' was hunger and an unendurable longing for rest. Not bad material for experiments, but—those experiments would be risky.

The assembly hall was filled with these morose, indifferent faces and grey greatcoats. I pushed my way forward through the dense crowd standing in the aisle to where a place should have been kept for me. It was either darkish again in the hall or else the clouds of tobacco smoke obscured the bright light of the chandelier between the white columns. On the platform, unlike the emptiness of the night before, there were far more people than elementary orderliness permitted. I looked about for Lenin, but I don't think he was on the platform. I had got to my seat in one of the front rows when Dan came on to the platform to open the Congress in the name of the Central Ex. Com.

Throughout the revolution I don't recall a more disorderly and muddled session. In opening it Dan said he would abstain from any political speech: he asked people to understand this

[1] *Sic.* Sukhanov means Gauls. (Ed.)

and remember that at this moment his party comrades were self-sacrificingly doing their duty under fire in the Winter Palace.

Avanesov, sent by the Bolsheviks, had a list of the Praesidium ready. But the Menshevik and SR representatives refused to participate in it. In the name of our fraction someone made a statement that we were 'abstaining for the time being' from participating in the Praesidium, until a number of questions had been cleared up. The Praesidium was composed of the principal Bolshevik leaders and the half-dozen Left SRs. They could scarcely find seats, the platform was so packed and disorderly. Kamenev was in the chair throughout the Congress. He announced the agenda: (1) the organization of a Government, (2) war and peace, and (3) the Constituent Assembly.

Martov asked for the floor on a point of order:

First of all, a pacific settlement of the crisis must be assured. There was blood flowing in the streets of Petersburg. Military activities on both sides must be halted. A pacific settlement of the crisis might be attained by the creation of a régime which would be recognized by the entire democracy. The Congress could not remain indifferent to the civil war now developing, which might lead to a menacing flare-up of the counter-revolution.

Martov's speech was greeted with tempestuous applause from a very large section of the meeting. It was manifest that a very great many Bolsheviks, not having assimilated the spirit of the teaching of Lenin and Trotsky, would have been happy to take precisely this path. But now Lenin and Trotsky were completely at one. Of course we recall the difference between them at the *First* Soviet Congress and much later, but now, in October, Trotsky, lapsing into his 1905 ideas, flew irresistibly into Lenin's open arms and merged with him completely.[1] The Bolshevik mass, however, still insufficiently understood the majestic ideas of its leaders and quite amicably applauded Martov.

Martov's motion was upheld by the *Novaya Zhizn* people, by a front-line group, and—most important—by the Left SRs. Lunacharsky answered for the Bolsheviks: the Bolsheviks had absolutely nothing against it; let the question of a peaceable settlement of the crisis be made the first item on the agenda. Martov's motion was voted on: against it—nobody.

[1] See Introduction. (Ed.)

Here there was no risk whatever for the Bolsheviks. At the Congress, just as in the capital, they were the masters of the situation. But nevertheless things were taking a quite favourable turn. Lenin and Trotsky, meeting their own following half-way, were simultaneously cutting the ground away from under the feet of the Rightists: to leave the Congress when the majority had agreed to a joint debate of the basic questions, which had been considered already predetermined, was not only a blatant rupture with the Soviet and with the revolution for the sake of the same old, decrepit, bankrupt counter-revolutionary ideas; it was simply the senseless stubbornness of counter-revolutionaries. If the Mensheviks and SRs left *now*, they would simply write *finis* to themselves and infinitely strengthen their opponents. One would have thought the Right wouldn't do this *immediately*, and that the Congress, though with a wavering majority, would be set on the right road to the formation of a united democratic front.

But the Mensheviks and SRs did do it. These blind counter-revolutionaries not only failed to see that their 'line' was counter-revolutionary, but also failed to realize the complete absurdity and unworthy childishness of their behaviour. . . *After* Martov's resolution was passed, but *before* the debate was begun, Khinchuk, a pedant and future Bolshevik functionary, spoke for the Menshevik fraction:

The only solution was to start negotiations with the Provisional Government for the formation of a new Government that would be based on all strata. (A terrible din filled the hall; it was not only the Bolsheviks who were indignant, and for a long time the speaker wasn't allowed to continue.) 'The military conspiracy has been organized behind the back of the Congress. We divest ourselves of all responsibility for what is happening and leave the Congress, inviting the other fractions to meet to discuss the present situation.'

This brilliant speech immediately turned the mood against the Compromisers. The Bolshevik mass pressed tightly around Lenin. Indignation was expressed very stormily. You could hear shouts of 'Deserters! Go over to Kornilov! Lackeys of the bourgeoisie! Enemies of the people!'

In the midst of the hubbub the SR Geldeman appeared on the platform, and in the name of his fraction, repeated the same statement. The temper of the hall rose still higher. Stamping, whistling, and cursing began.

Ehrlich was on the platform: in the name of the [Jewish] Bund he supported the SRs and Mensheviks. The hall began to overflow. The 'pure-in-heart' were going out in small groups, but this was almost unnoticed. They were accompanied by whistles, jeers, and curses. Even the semblance of order finally disappeared. On the platform, where Martov remained because it was impossible to get away or move, the mob, which soon so completely surrounded the orator that you could not see who was speaking, was leaning over the shoulders of the members of the Praesidium.

* * *

The 'pure-in-heart' had left. Well—would Martov's resolution now be debated without them? Now it had lost most of its sense, but it seemed there was no time for that now. 'Emergency statements' hailed down, on behalf of every kind of organization and of individual speakers themselves. The notorious Right Menshevik Kuchin, always accepted as speaking for the front, was also accusing the Bolsheviks of a military conspiracy against the people, and with his 'front-line group' was also leaving the Congress. As usual, he was unmasked: he had been elected to the Army Committee eight months before and for half a year had no longer expressed the army's opinion. The front was going along with the Congress majority. In addition to the front-line Menshevik, a front-line SR also spoke. But by now the meeting was beginning to lose patience.

Abramovich came on—'for the Bund group'. First, he repeated what Ehrlich had said. Secondly, he reported that firing on the Winter Palace had begun; the Mensheviks, SRs, peasant Central Ex. Com., and Town Council had decided to go there and face the bullets.

This was very effective and dramatic, but completely failed to arouse any sympathy. Jeers could be distinguished amidst the tumult, some of them coarse, others venomous. . . Up to then, nevertheless, shooting had not been an everyday occurrence in our revolution, and Abramovich's news made a painful impression on a great many people.

It was dissipated, however, by Ryazanov, who declared in the name of the Military Revolutionary Committee: 'An hour and a half ago the Mayor came to us and offered to undertake negotiations between the Winter Palace and its besiegers. The Military Revolutionary Committee has sent its representatives, thus doing everything to forestall bloodshed.'

Ryazanov was known to everyone as a man averse to bloodshed, and he was believed. But when would Martov's resolution be debated?

It was begun by Martov himself when he got the floor amidst an endless series of emergency statements.

'The news that's just come——' he began.

But the meeting, which an hour before had passed his resolution unanimously, was now very irritated with every species of 'compromiser'. Martov was interrupted: 'What news? What are you trying to scare us for? You ought to be ashamed of yourself!'

In some detail Martov analysed the motives for his resolution. Then he proposed that the Congress pass a decree on the necessity for a peaceable settlement of the crisis by forming a general democratic Government and electing a delegation to negotiate with all Socialist parties. . .

Martov's reply came from Trotsky, who was standing at his side in the crowd that packed the platform. Now that the Rightists had left, Trotsky's position was as strong as Martov's was weak.

'A rising of the masses of the people', Trotsky rapped out, 'needs no justification. What has happened is an insurrection, and not a conspiracy. We hardened the revolutionary energy of the Petersburg workers and soldiers. We openly forged the will of the masses for an insurrection, and not a conspiracy. The masses of the people followed our banner and our insurrection was victorious. And now we are told: renounce your victory, make concessions, compromise. With whom? I ask: with whom ought we to compromise? With those wretched groups who have left us or who are making this proposal? But after all we've had a full view of them. No one in Russia is with them any longer. A compromise is supposed to be made, as between two equal sides, by the millions of workers and peasants represented in this Congress, whom they are ready, not for the first time or the last, to barter away as the bourgeoisie sees fit. No, here no compromise is possible. To those who have left and to those who tell us to do this we must say: you are miserable bankrupts, your rôle is played out; go where you ought to be: into the dustbin of history!'

'Then we'll leave,' Martov shouted from the platform amidst stormy applause for Trotsky.

No, excuse me, Comrade Martov! Trotsky's speech of course was a clear and unambiguous reply. But rage at an opponent, and Martov's emotional state, still did not bind the fraction to a decisive and fatal act. Martov, enraged and upset, began pushing his way off the platform. And I called an emergency conference of our fraction, scattered throughout the hall.

Meanwhile Trotsky was reading aloud a harsh resolution against the Compromisers and against their 'wretched and criminal attempt to smash the All-Russian Congress'; 'this will not weaken, but strengthen the Soviets, by purging them of any admixture of counter-revolution'.

We assembled in the Mensheviks' room, while the futile emergency statements continued in the big hall. Fatigue, nervousness, and chaos kept growing. On our way out we heard a statement in the name of the Bolshevik fraction of the Town Council: 'The Bolshevik Town Hall fraction has come here to conquer or die with the All-Russian Soviet Congress!'

The hall applauded. But it was beginning to be fed up with all this—it was around 1 o'clock in the morning.

* * *

During those same hours when the fractions and the plenum of the Congress were in session at Smolny, the old Provisional Government still languished in a quiet, half-dark room of the Winter Palace. For their part they were far from willing to die. On the contrary, they were hoping for assistance and the preservation of their lives and jobs. Nevertheless they were languishing in torment.

The Cossacks had left the Palace. There were fewer defenders. It was reported on the 'phone that some Town Councillors and others, about 300 men, were coming to the Palace. The military cadets were warned not to shoot at them.

Palchinsky made a report: the mob had pressed forward a few times, but after some shots from the military cadets had retreated. The shots, he said, were in the air. But the clatter of arms and booming of cannon grew more and more frequent. Suddenly there was an uproar and shots in the Palace itself: about thirty or forty armed men had burst in, but were already disarmed and under arrest.

'Great cowards,' reported Palchinsky, and assured his listeners the Palace would hold out till morning.

Again a din, shouts, tramping, and—two explosions one after the other. The Ministers leaped from their seats. Bombs! A few sailors had crept into the Palace and thrown two bombs from a little gallery. The bombs had fallen on the floor near the entrance to Nicholas II's rooms and slightly wounded two military cadets. Dr. Kishkin gave them medical aid. The sailors were arrested; but how had they been able to get in? First forty men had burst in by force, then a few sailors had slipped in secretly. It was obvious that things were proving a bit too much for Palchinsky and his garrison.

It was reported that the women's shock-battalion had gone home. They had felt like it and left, like the Cossacks. It was clear that the besiegers were letting hostile detachments through like water through a sieve.

There was still no real siege at all, but the cross-fire was beginning to take on the character of an out-and-out battle. It was unlikely that they were only shooting in the air, or that there were no casualties. A certain amount of blood was undoubtedly being shed. Why, and what for? *Because* the Military Revolutionary Committee had not thought of arresting the Government before, and had even released those arrested, and the Ministers who had run away from their posts could still console themselves with the thought that they had not run away.

It was reported that cadets from some academy had left. They left as they pleased. The 'Government' didn't hold them back, but gave out telephonic bulletins to the city: 'We are beating them off, we are not surrendering, the attack was beaten off at such and such an hour, we are waiting for reinforcements'. That's the kind of Government we had!

Once again a crowd burst in and was disarmed: once again one of the defence units went off. How many were left now? Which was there more of now in the Palace, defenders or prisoners? But wasn't it all the same? The Ministers were unconcerned. Outside the walls they were shooting as before; it was after 1 o'clock.

Again an uproar. It kept growing, nearer and nearer, up to the very doors. It was clear the Palace was being stormed and taken. A cadet rushed in to the Ministers and, drawing himself up, reported: 'Ready to defend ourselves to the last man. What are the Provisional Government's orders?'

'It's no use. We give up. No bloodshed! We suppose the Palace is already occupied?'

'Yes. Everyone's surrendered. Only this room is being held.'

'Tell them we don't want bloodshed and give up. We yield to force. . .'

'Go, hurry, hurry! We don't want bloodshed!'

You'll say: now the Ministers were beginning to understand something and had come to a sensible decision. On the contrary: it was already too late for a sensible decision; but the Ministers, having finally lost all understanding, did not see how repellent and ridiculous their hypocrisy was.

A cadet on the other side of the door reported the Ministers' decision to the victorious insurgent troops, who were making an impatient racket but didn't take one step further against the will of these single-minded cadets. The noise suddenly took on another character.

'Let's sit down at the table,' said the Ministers, and sat down, in order to look like busy statesmen.

The doors were flung open, and the room filled up at once with armed men, headed by Antonov himself. Palchinsky adroitly hastened forward: 'Gentlemen, we've just come to an agreement with your people on the 'phone. Just wait one moment, you haven't heard the latest!'

The chiefs of the detachment were within a hair's breadth of being disconcerted, but they pulled themselves together at once.

'Members of the Provisional Government!' shouted Antonov, 'I declare you under arrest! I'm a member of the Military Revolutionary Committee!'

'The members of the Provisional Government yield to force and surrender in order to avoid bloodshed,' said Konovalov.

'Bloodshed! And how much blood have you shed yourselves?'

rang out an exclamation sympathetically taken up by the crowd. 'How many of our people have fallen?'

'That's a lie!' shouted the indignant Kishkin. 'We didn't shoot anyone! Our guards simply shot back when they were attacked.'

* * *

If there were any casualties, then our miserable last Ministers were to blame just as much as the organizers of the insurrection. Smolny was to blame for not avoiding bloodshed, in spite of its having been completely possible, but it was justified by a theory that it could not in the nature of things renounce. But what could the statesmen of the last Coalition have said in justification of their criminal senselessness? They preferred not to acknowledge the very fact of the bloodshed they had caused. But this merely makes them either cowards or fools. Louis XVI, on August 10th, set up a strong Swiss guard in the Tuileries, ordered them to defend themselves, and caused bloodshed. He was well aware that he was defending the monarchy and his own throne—an idea, interests, and a person. His crime has a definite meaning, historical and logical. But as for these sage rulers and liberal-humanitarian intellectuals of ours—what did they want?

The temper of the mob that had burst in, armed to the teeth, was extremely high, vengeful, furious, and impetuous. Antonov tried to calm the particularly hot-headed soldiers and sailors, but lacked sufficient authority. They set about drawing up an official report, while the Ministers began to 'agitate' at the victors. Kuzma Gvozdev was especially excited, trying to persuade everyone right and left that he was one of them—a worker. Tempers would rise, then subside. The report that Kerensky was not around had a powerful effect. There were shouts that the others must be slaughtered so that they wouldn't flee after Kerensky.

After rather lengthy proceedings, with interrogations, roll-calls, and the making of lists, the column of prisoners moved out, in the direction of the Peter-Paul Fortress. In the darkness, between 2 and 3 o'clock in the morning, in the midst of a dense, excited mob, the column moved along the Milliony and over Trinity Bridge. More than once the lives of the former Ministers hung by a hair. But it went off without a lynching.

After eight months of revolution the Peter-Paul was receiving within its walls a third variety of prisoner: first, Tsarist functionaries, then Bolsheviks, and now Kerensky's friends, the 'élite' of the Menshevik–SR democracy. What more were these imperturbable walls destined to see?

* * *

In the great hall of Smolny the enormous meeting was clearly becoming disorganized from muddle, crowding, fatigue, and tension. Speakers from the fractions remaining spoke on Trotsky's resolution. Both the Left SRs and the *Novaya Zhizn* people categorically condemned the behaviour of the Right groups, but protested against the harsh resolution. Then 'emergency' speakers appeared again. But the meeting cried for mercy. An interval was announced.

During this time our fraction, extremely tense and nervous, was discussing the situation. Having settled ourselves in any sort of order just inside the door, about thirty of us, some standing up, others sitting on some kind of garden benches, were quarrelling bitterly. I was vigorously attacking, very excited, and not mincing my words. Martov, having yielded to theatricality at the plenary session, defended himself more calmly and patiently. He seemed to feel that he had no firm ground beneath him, but at the same time to be aware that the whole conjunction of circumstances irrevocably compelled him to break with the Congress and go out after Dan—even though only halfway. . .

I gave a good account of myself and did as much as I could. Throughout the revolution I had never defended my position with such conviction and ardour. Not only logic, political sense, and elementary revolutionary truth seemed to be on my side, but also a technical consideration: after all, the question put by Martov had not yet been debated in the Congress, and we still had only Trotsky's speech as the Congress reply. Leaving the Congress now would not only be criminal in general, but also dishonest and frivolous in particular.

Alas! It was clear that Martov was a victim of Menshevik indecisiveness. He was indeed! For the rupture with the bourgeois Compromisers and adherence to Smolny entailed the most decisive struggle in a definite camp. No place was left for neutrality or passivity. This was frightening, and far from natural to us. Martov, like Dan, but not together with him, was 'isolating' the Bolsheviks. In this Dan had a point of support Martov could not accept, while Martov had no point of support at all. But . . . to remain in Smolny with nobody but the Bolsheviks—no, that was beyond our strength.

The fraction divided. About fourteen votes against twelve—Martov had won. I felt that I had suffered a disaster worse than any before in the revolution. I returned to the great hall completely numb.

* * *

There the interval was just over and the meeting had started again. But the deputies had had no rest. There was still the same disorder. People were standing with outstretched necks listening to the statement of the Chairman, Kamenev, who was speaking with special earnestness: 'We have just received the following telephone message. The Winter Palace has been taken by the troops of the Military Revolutionary Committee. The whole Provisional Government was arrested there, except Kerensky, who has fled. . .' etc.

Kamenev read the list of the arrested Ministers. When he mentioned Tereshchenko's name at the end, stormy applause rang out. The broad masses had evidently had time to set a special value on this gentleman's activities.

One of the Left SRs made a statement about the inadmissibility of arresting the Socialist Ministers.

Trotsky answered him at once: First of all, there was no time now for such trifles: secondly, there was no reason to stand on ceremony with these gentlemen who were keeping hundreds of workers and Bolsheviks in the prisons.

Both statements were essentially correct. But what was far more important was the political motive Trotsky didn't touch on: the overturn had not yet been carried to a conclusion, and every Minister left at large, representing the legitimate power, might—in the given circumstances—become a source of civil war. Nevertheless Trotsky's statement—that is, mainly his *tone*—was far from producing, even in Smolny as it was then, a good impression on everyone. This new ruler, on the very first day, was showing his teeth over 'trifles'. An omen for the future.

* * *

So the thing was done. We had left, not knowing where or why, after breaking with the Soviet, getting ourselves mixed up with counter-revolutionary elements, discrediting and debasing ourselves in the eyes of the masses, and ruining the entire future of our organization and our principles. And that was the least of it: in leaving we completely untied the Bolsheviks' hands, making them masters of the entire situation and yielding to them the whole arena of the revolution.

A struggle at the Congress for a united democratic front *might* have had some success. For the Bolsheviks as such, for Lenin and Trotsky, it was more odious than the possible Committees of Public Safety or another Kornilov march on Petersburg. The exit of the 'pure-in-heart' freed the Bolsheviks from this danger. By quitting the Congress and leaving the Bolsheviks with only the Left SR youngsters and the feeble little *Novaya Zhizn* group, we gave the Bolsheviks with our own hands a monopoly of the Soviet, of the masses, and of the revolution. By our own irrational decision we ensured the victory of Lenin's whole 'line'.

I personally committed not a few blunders and errors in the revolution. But I consider my greatest and most indelible crime the fact that I failed to break with the Martov group immediately after our fraction voted to leave, and didn't stay on at the Congress. To this day I have not ceased regretting this October 25th crime of mine.

* * *

Towards the end of the session Lunacharsky read out a proclamation of the Congress to the workers, soldiers, and peasants. It declared: '. . . Basing itself on the will of the enormous majority of workers, soldiers, and peasants, and relying on the achievement in Petersburg of a victorious rising of the workers and garrison, the Congress takes the power into its own hands. The Provisional Government has been overthrown. The powers of the conciliationist Central Ex. Com. have come to an end. . . The Congress decrees that all power throughout the country be transferred to the local Soviets of Workers', Soldiers', and Peasants' Deputies, who must preserve genuine revolutionary order.'

* * *

Thus the October revolution was *politically* consummated and shaped. The 'proclamation' was passed by all the other votes to two, with twelve abstentions. The meeting lasted until after 5 o'clock in the morning.

In a dense throng, delegates swarmed out of Smolny, after the labours, impressions, and events of this world-historical day. The participants in, witnesses and authors of those events swarmed past the cannon and machine-guns standing by the cradle of the 'worldwide Socialist revolution'. But no attendants were visible near them. The Smolny guard were already enjoying their rest: there was no discipline. But there was also no need for a guard. No one had either the strength or the will for an attack. . .

A cold autumn morning was already dawning on Petersburg.

CHAPTER 32

OCTOBER 26TH

Finale

Two or three hours later the capital awoke—without realizing who were now its rulers. From outside, the events had not been at all impressive. Except for the Palace square, there had been order and calm everywhere. The *coup* had begun rather modestly and ended rather swiftly. But *how*?—the man-in-the-street didn't know. The finale in the Winter Palace had come too late at night, and contact with Smolny was weak.

The man-in-the-street rushed to the newspapers. But he couldn't get much light from them. In the 'Latest News' column there were everywhere a few lines reporting the seizure of the Winter Palace and the arrest of the Provisional Government. The accounts of the Soviet Congress consisted solely of 'emergency statements' and testified to the 'isolation' of the Bolsheviks; but they gave no description whatever of the political status that had been created. The leading articles had been written before the final news that night. In general, they were all on one note: patriotic howlings about our unhappy country, accusations of usurpation and violence by the Bolsheviks, predictions of the collapse of their adventure, descriptions of the *coup* of the day before as a military conspiracy.

The Mensheviks and SRs, by the way, later consoled themselves with this military conspiracy for several months, thrusting it in the faces of the Bolsheviks. Incomprehensible! It would have been better if these sharp-witted people had looked and said: was the Petersburg proletariat in sympathy or not with the organizers of the October insurrection? Was it with the Bolsheviks, or were the Bolsheviks acting independently of it? Was it on the side of the overturn, was it neutral, or was it hostile?

Here there can be no two replies. Yes, the Bolsheviks acted with the full backing of the Petersburg workers and soldiers. And they brought about an insurrection, throwing into it as many (very few!) forces as were required for its successful consummation. Guilty as charged: the Bolsheviks threw into it, through negligence and clumsiness, far *more* forces than were necessary. But that has nothing at all to do with grasping the actual conception of the insurrection.

* * *

So on October 26th the man-in-the-street was given into the power of rumours. And of course he was extremely excited. In the streets, in the trams, in public places—nothing but the events was talked of. There was, naturally, a panic at the Stock Exchange, though absolutely no one believed a Bolshevik régime would last. On the contrary, the man-in-the-street had no doubt the crisis would be settled in short order.

Indeed, what sort of power had the Bolsheviks? They had, after all, not yet created a Government. What kind of 'power of the Soviets' was this? All the same, the shops shut tight. The banks did not resume work. In the government offices there were mass-meetings of the employees, and debates about what they should do in case the Bolsheviks sent over their commanders. Almost everywhere it was decided not to recognize their authority, and for the time being stop work. A boycott!

But even without a boycott and without politics nobody could work now. Was everything quiet at home? It was said that plundering and riots would begin at any moment. It was said that there was no bread at all in the city, and what there had been had already been looted. It was said that sailors were making the rounds of the houses and requisitioning fur coats and boots. It was said. . .

But there were also *facts* which powerfully affected the imagination. On the day following the victorious insurrection the Petersburgers found several of the capital's newspapers missing. They had been closed by the Military Revolutionary Committee—for slandering the Soviets and similar crimes. The esteemed Podvoisky, Antonov, and others, acting on Lenin's orders, were not inventive: they borrowed their reasons from the lexicon of the old Tsarist police. But on the strength of their position as revolutionaries and Socialists they allowed themselves the luxury of expressing themselves more crudely and less grammatically. It would have been possible, and better, to give no reasons at all.

Moreover, Podvoisky and Antonov were generally very ham-fisted in carrying out their leaders' directives. For some reason they came down on the second-rate papers and small fry, disregarding the Kornilovite leading semi-official ones. This had to be corrected. That morning some sailors were sent to the distributing centres of *Rech* and *Sovremennoye Slovo* (Contemporary Word). All the numbers they found were confiscated, taken out into the street in an enormous mass, and set fire to then and there. This hitherto unseen *auto-da-fé* collected an enormous crowd.

In the course of that day the *whole* bourgeois press of the capital was shut down. Orders were sent out, and military patrols with them. The type-setters were allowed to stay on in the printing-presses, on condition that they set no type for the closed-down newspapers.

The new Government didn't reveal itself for the time being in any other way. But this *début* made a very powerful impression. Tsarism had never practised any such mass reprisals against the press. Was it necessary? What was the sense of it? References were naturally made to the acute and difficult situation of the new régime in the fire of civil war. But that was nonsense. There was neither civil war nor any particularly difficult situation. Now, in a single day, the insurrection was already actually victorious. Difficulties might begin if Kerensky had some successes at the front, but there was still no news of those. Until now reports on this score had been completely reassuring. Indeed, even if there had been a march on Petersburg, the bourgeois press couldn't have played any rôle. The Socialist press was, if you like, more dangerous, but that wasn't touched.

The destruction of the bourgeois press, completely senseless from a practical point of view, was extremely harmful to the Bolsheviks. It infuriated and alarmed absolutely all the neutral and wavering elements, of which there were many. So this was the start of the new régime! For the time being there was nothing more, but there were already pogroms and senseless violence. The debasement of revolutionary values, the trampling into the mud of elementary democratic principles—were already present.

In the lower strata of the proletariat and soldiery, however, this *début* aroused no protests. For there, after eight months of revolution, these principles had not yet had time to take root. There the matter was substantially simpler—without principles: they used to beat us and we, having seized a club, are going to smash things right and left. That was how the elements reasoned. That was how—without principles—their champions in Smolny reasoned too.

* * *

Meanwhile work went on at Smolny. The Military Revolutionary Committee was taking what steps it could to preserve order and uphold the prestige of the new régime. But it was even busier getting out proclamations. First of all it addressed the Cossacks in the capital and at the front, exhorting them not to oppose the revolution and not to march on Petersburg. This appeal, distributed in great quantities, undoubtedly had its effect on the strongly prejudiced but far from bellicose Cossacks. Then the Military Revolutionary Committee appealed to the railwaymen to pay special attention to the service; it called on the state employees, and especially the military staff employees, not to interrupt their work, for fear of revolutionary justice, etc.

But naturally their principal concern was defence against Kerensky, who was marching on Petersburg. Nothing trustworthy was known about this march, but, to begin with, the fact *a priori* was obvious. Secondly, quite definite *rumours* flowed from the Right *milieux* about it; points were named where Kerensky was to be found, with the number of troops at his disposal. Petty-bourgeois and 'social' strata comforted themselves with this and frightened Smolny. The Military Revolutionary Committee took what steps it could.

Besides written and oral agitation, splendidly organized along the roads to the capital, a few detachments were sent out against Kerensky's supposed hordes. But their strength was very meagre. No volunteers who were at all reliable were found in the garrison. Out of the army of 200,000, *two or three companies* were somehow selected. The workers' militia aroused more confidence, but only, after all, from the point of view of their morale. For the combat fitness of this army, which had never smelt powder or seen a rifle until the last few days, and had no conception of military operations or discipline, was more than dubious. To crown all this there were no officers at all.

It was only the sailors that might prove a serious force. Kronstadt could put out 3,000 or 4,000 reliable fighters. And besides, as we know, 1,800 sailors had come from Helsingfors; they had got to Petersburg when everything was already over, but they could be used at once against Kerensky.

This, as we see, wasn't much. And this 'army' also suffered from an exceptional defect: it had no artillery—only rifles and machine-guns. Close to Petersburg itself it was proposed to use the artillery of the ships anchored in the Neva or off the coast. But it was essential, of course, not to allow matters to get as far as an engagement beneath the very walls of the capital.

How unsatisfactory the position was with artillery, and how crude the steps taken, is evident from this fact. The Putilov Factory 'promised' the Military Revolutionary Committee an armoured platform-car for mounting cannon, but no one knew whether the factory would keep its promise. And this matter, in spite of its triviality, was thought so important in Smolny that Lenin himself, together with Antonov, in the midst of the extravagant labours and chaos of the first days, went off to the Putilov Factory to harangue the workers and spur them on. I don't think it led to anything. . .

In general it was quite impossible to count on any substantial military force. What had to be relied on was Kerensky's weakness, his inability to collect and move a large army, and the inevitable dissolution of such an army while still *en route*. Agitation and the influence of ideas were an incomparably more reliable prop of Smolny than military operations. After all the lessons of the revolution it was possible to set one's hopes on 'spiritual' factors with complete justification. Nicholas II, after all, had moved against Petersburg, and then Kornilov, and both had failed—without a shot fired. During the October Days themselves factors of 'morale' were already paralysing the whole activity of Kerensky and the Staff in Petersburg. Why then not hope that these same methods would liquidate the third march on Petersburg in 1917?

An extremely graphic proclamation on Kerensky's personality, rôle, and campaign was also published and distributed. In any case, in the midst of the primordial confusion of this first day of the Soviet régime all possible measures were taken, as I said, of spiritual as well as of military resistance.

Apart from all this, the Military Revolutionary Committee developed some activity of a purely police character. A great many arrests had been made in the city. They were quite casual and pointless, carried out chiefly as a result of the revolutionary initiative of anyone who had the energy. Whole columns of prisoners trailed into Smolny from all directions. This irritated and repelled the passive part of the population very much. But Smolny had become not only the seat of the new Government, not only the General Staff, but also the supreme police institution, the supreme tribunal, and the gaol.

Finally, that day the Military Revolutionary Committee got out one other special proclamation—an order to the Army Committees to bring General Kornilov and his accomplices to Petersburg for imprisonment in the Peter-Paul Fortress and for trial. . .

Just what did that mean? Why an appeal to the Army Committees, and not a wire to Bykhov gaol to transfer the Kornilovites?

Because on the 26th a perfectly reliable piece of news had been spread through Petersburg—Kornilov had escaped from Bykhov gaol.

Kornilov, having heard about the overturn, had—quite simply—decided to leave. He had not been afraid of a Government of his friends, and had agreed to live for the time being in Bykhov under the protection of his reliable Tekins. But with the Bolsheviks the affair might have turned risky; also it had no point. Kornilov decided to leave. There had been no technical hindrances for him previously either.

* * *

Just about this time I had asked Kamenev in passing: 'Tell me, how are you going to govern? Are you going to set up ministers and ministries, as in a bourgeois society?'

Kamenev explained what was evidently being ventilated in the highest Bolshevik spheres:

'It'll be a Government by Boards, like during the Convention. The chairmen of the Boards will constitute the supreme organ of Government.'

And that is how it was formed on October 26th. But what could this Soviet Cabinet of Ministers be called? Though this of course was not very vital, nevertheless there was a strong desire not to borrow bourgeois terminology. Let everything be quite new and special in the new proletarian State!

They thought and cogitated, and finally Trotsky suggested a name that gratified everyone. It was decided to call the Soviet Cabinet the Council of People's Commissars. Personally I am not very enthusiastic about this great reform. Breaking with bourgeois terminology may have been very agreeable, but philologically the word Minister sounds absolutely correct, while Commissar, on the contrary, definitely smacks of the police. But this, of course, is a matter of taste (and, perhaps, of the new spirit in politics?).

But apart from the name itself, nothing had as yet been changed in the methods of forming a new Government. For the time being the Boards were not and could not be formed. Only the Council of People's Commissars had been constituted, and that had been made up just as cabinets always are.

This is how matters stood politically: The departure of the Mensheviks and SRs had very much simplified and eased the position of Lenin and Trotsky. Now there was no Opposition to get underfoot in forming a proletarian Government. Only the Bolshevik Party could now take power without hindrance and even place all the odium for this on the Mensheviks and SRs themselves. This was what Lenin had been striving for ever since June.

To be sure, there remained at the Congress a rather large group of Left SRs, who had no objection to being the sole representatives of the peasantry. But, to begin with, the Left SRs were in an insignificant minority. Secondly, these Left youngsters were quite harmless as pretenders to power, in view of their lack of anything resembling solidity and of the fact that they could easily be twisted around one's finger. Thirdly, in view of these qualities, bringing the Left SRs into the Soviet Government would even have been useful, for this would have looked like a perfectly popular 'agreement' within the Soviet and a 'broadening of the base' of the new Government—at the expense of the party of the revolutionary peasantry. Fourthly, the Left SRs made absolutely no claim to share power with the Bolsheviks: what they stood for was power for the Soviet bloc, an all-democratic Government.

Consequently the Bolsheviks took power alone. The Council of People's Commissars was expected to act on the directives of the Bolshevik Party Central Committee. This achieved what Lenin had been unsuccessfully striving for—'in a favourable conjunction of circumstances'—on June 10th and July 4th.

It remained to plan the composition of the first Soviet Government. One would have thought that the Bolsheviks must meet with the greatest difficulties. Where could you get people capable of running the State in the given circumstances? I of course wasn't at this meeting of Bolshevik leaders, but I venture to express my conviction that it had no special difficulty in selecting Ministers from its own party people. It produced its best and oldest propagandists, agitators, and organizers. For the difficulties of state administration did not appear in their full scope to the eye of the lofty assemblage.

Lenin was designated Premier without portfolio. Trotsky became the People's Commissar for Foreign Affairs; Lunacharsky for Popular Education. The economist and writer Skvortsov was given Finance. Shlyapnikov, the trade-unionist, whom we know, got the Labour portfolio. Miliutin, author of a brochure on agricultural workers, was appointed Minister of Agriculture, Stalin Minister for Nationalities. A Board consisting of Antonov, the lieutenant Krylenko, and the sailor Dybenko—for Military and Naval affairs. Rykov, whom we haven't met up to now, was given the Interior. Nogin from Moscow was given Industry and Commerce. Lomov, Justice. Teodorovich, Supply. And Glebov, Posts and Telegraphs.

All these were very respected Bolsheviks, with decades of revolutionary work, exile, and imprisonment behind them. But as the supreme power in the Republic, as statesmen entrusted with the fate of the revolution and of the country, this Board as a whole must be acknowledged to be rather unconvincing. We knew most of these new rulers as revolutionaries. Henceforth we were to be acquainted with them as statesmen and learn, by the way, that brilliant work on the platform, underground, and in the emigration, in party circles and as journalists, far from guaranteed their quality as rulers.

We fail to see two stars of the first magnitude amongst the Bolshevik rulers—the 'cronies', Zinoviev and Kamenev. Their absence from the Government might have had a great many valid reasons. First of all, being somewhat in opposition, they might have declined. Secondly, for tactical reasons it was advisable to cut down as much as possible on the number of Ministers of Jewish origin (the sole exception was Trotsky). Thirdly, we must remember that from now on ministerial posts were in fact not the most important in the State: stars of the first magnitude made all high policy in the Party Central Committee. Fourthly, Kamenev was appointed chairman of the Central Ex. Com., which formally was the highest State body, while Zinoviev received a high appointment as editor of the official state newspaper: the *Izvestiya* of the Central Ex. Com.

Such for the time being was the new Government of the new proletarian State.

Martov appeared at this meeting of the Bolshevik Olympus. He came to intercede for the release of the Socialist Ministers. It must be imagined how absurd such a mediator must have felt before these strange new authorities on such a matter.

Martov, their old comrade-in-arms and, for most of them, teacher, was heard out with chilly reserve. But all the same the Socialist Ministers were transferred to house arrest.

* * *

The second session of the Congress opened at 9 o'clock in the evening. Chairman Kamenev, amidst stormy applause, announced the latest measures of the Military Revolutionary Committee: abolition of the death penalty at the front, and consequently in Russia generally; release of all political prisoners; release of the members of the agrarian committees arrested by the Coalition.

Then Lenin was given the floor to report on war and peace. But according to him the question was so clear that he could read without any preamble the draft of an appeal by the Soviet Government to the peoples of all the countries at war. He read a long document, which I shall summarize:

The worker–peasant Government, created by the revolution of October 25th, suggests to all warring nations and their Governments that immediate negotiations be begun for a just and democratic peace, without annexations or indemnities. The Russian Government, for its part, is ready to take all decisive steps without the slightest delay. By annexations it means the absorption by a large or powerful State of a small or weak nationality (?) without its consent; the time of annexation, the cultural-economic level of the absorbed country and its location—are a matter of indifference. Disannexation, in the absence of complete self-determination, is the equivalent of annexation. But the Government doesn't put forward these conditions as an ultimatum; it is willing to consider other conditions as well, insisting only that they be proposed as soon as possible and put clearly, openly, and unequivocally. The worker–peasant Government abolishes secret diplomacy; it is proceeding at once to the publication of secret treaties and declares their contents henceforth invalid. The Russian Government is willing to carry on open negotiations for peace in any way desired: in writing, by telegraph, or at a conference. At the same time the Government proposes to all countries at war the immediate conclusion of a three-month armistice which will be sufficient to conclude peace negotiations and ratify the peace. In addressing the above to the Governments and peoples of the warring countries, the worker–peasant Government appeals especially to the workers of the advanced capitalist countries, Great Britain, Germany, and France; the victorious Russian workers and peasants have no doubt that the proletariat of the West will help them to achieve the cause of peace, and at the same time the cause of the emancipation of the toilers from every form of bondage and exploitation.

He closed with a brief epilogue. 'We address ourselves', he said, 'to the Governments and to the peoples, since an appeal to the peoples alone might involve a postponement of the peace. The conditions of peace as reviewed during the armistice will then be confirmed by the Constituent Assembly. The proposal of peace will meet with opposition from the imperialist Governments—we do not close our eyes to this. But we rely on the imminence of revolution in all the countries at war. The Russian Revolution of October 25th will open an era of Socialist revolution throughout the world. We shall of course defend our peace programme in every way, but we must make it impossible for our enemies to say that their conditions are different and therefore there is no reason to start negotiations with us. We must deprive them of this advantage and therefore must not put our conditions as an ultimatum. We are not afraid of a revolutionary war, but we shall not deliver ultimatums which might facilitate a negative answer to our proposal.'

In general, the proclamation of October 26th was exactly what the revolutionary Government should have done several months earlier. The Bolsheviks, almost before they were in power, had fulfilled this task and met their engagements of March 14th to the proletariat of the West. And they had done it in a correct and worthy form. But it was too late. Several months of revolution had multiplied many times over Russia's collapse and exhaustion. Now, at the end of October, there was no longer even an army in Russia. Now we could no longer fight. Those millions who had until now held back 130 German divisions at the front had begun, from cold and hunger, to run away home. Our peace move of October 26th was objectively no more than a surrender to the mercy of the victor.

I got to Smolny during Lenin's 'epilogue'. The general scene was much the same as the night before. Fewer arms, a smaller crowd. It was easy for me to find an empty seat in the back rows, which I think were for the public. Alas! For the first time in the revolution I came to such a meeting not as one of its fully authorized members, but as one of the public. I found this extremely sad and painful. I felt torn away and separated from everything I had been living by for eight months that were the equivalent of a decade. Such a situation was quite unendurable; I knew I should change it, but didn't know just how.

Lenin finished. Thunderous applause rang out, and didn't die down for a long time. The representatives of the Left SRs and the *Novaya Zhizn* people 'backed' the decree. They merely complained that up to then the text of this document of capital importance hadn't been known to any of those present, and they couldn't make any amendments. They wanted a lot! These requirements of bourgeois parliamentarianism hadn't been complied with by us even in the best of circumstances.

In general, you might say there were no debates. Everyone simply expressed 'support', while the home-spun representatives of the nationalities gave greetings. The 'Peace Decree' was put to the vote without any amendments and passed unanimously. And now there were signs of an unmistakable heightening of mood. Long-drawn-out ovations alternated with singing the *Internationale*. Then Lenin was hailed again, hurrahs were shouted, caps flung into the air. They sang a funeral march in memory of the martyrs of the war. Then they applauded again, shouted, flung up their caps.

The whole Praesidium, headed by Lenin, was standing up and singing, with excited, exalted faces and blazing eyes. But the delegates were more interesting: they were completely revivified. The overturn had gone more smoothly than most of them had expected; it already seemed consummated. Awareness of its success was spreading; the masses were permeated by the faith that all would go well in future too. They were beginning to be persuaded of the imminence of peace, land, and bread, and even beginning to feel some readiness to stand up positively for their newly acquired goods and rights.

Applause, hurrahs, caps flung up in the air. . .

But I didn't believe in the victory, the success, the 'rightfulness', or the historic mission of a Bolshevik régime. Sitting in the back seats, I watched this celebration with a heavy heart. How I longed to join in, and merge with this mass and its leaders in a single feeling! But I couldn't. . .

* * *

Lenin again reported on the next question—land. But once again he didn't make a report, but began directly reading the text of a proposed 'Land Decree'. This time the decree, not having been reproduced or circulated, was not only unfamiliar to everyone: it was so badly written that Lenin stumbled, got confused, and finally stopped altogether. One of the crowd who had squeezed on to the platform came to his rescue. Lenin gladly gave up his place and the illegible piece of paper.

This was what it contained:

Private property in land was abolished immediately without compensation. Estates, whether private, monastic, or ecclesiastical, with all livestock and buildings, were placed at the disposal of rural district agrarian committees and of district Soviets of Peasant Deputies pending the Constituent Assembly. Damage to confiscated property would be considered a serious crime. The peasant 'model decree' written by the editors of the 'Peasant Central Ex. Com. News'[1] on the basis of 242 local

[1] In August. (Ed.)

peasant decrees was to serve as guide in the detailed execution of these measures.

This peasant 'model decree' had been written by SRs, and was nothing but an exposition of the SR agrarian programme. Its basic propositions amounted to the following:

All property in land, not excluding small peasants', was abolished in Russia in perpetuity, and all land within the borders of the State was to become the property of the entire nation.

The right to the use of land belonged to all citizens of the State—provided they worked it themselves. Hired labour was forbidden. The land was to be divided between those working it according to a labour or consumer's norm. The land reserves were subject to periodic reallocation, depending on the growth of the population and changes in agricultural methods, leaving the basic unit untouched.

Then, in conflict with the first point of Lenin's decree itself, the 'model decree' read: the land of ordinary Cossacks and peasants would not be confiscated. Finally, it was twice repeated that the land question could be definitively settled only by the Constituent Assembly.

Personally I had been a partisan of the SR agrarian programme from the very beginning of my political and literary activity. These views of mine were considered a sign of mental confusion, and my SR-mindedness provoked irony and perplexity amongst my fellow-thinkers, the 'consistent Marxists'. However, to this day I persist in them, and maintain that it was precisely in this form that a Socialist agrarian programme in Russia was possible and rational.

This programme laid the foundations of a petty-bourgeois order in the countryside, but in Russia this could not be otherwise, while on the other hand the programme preserves the maximum of Socialist elements possible—in so far as it abolishes private property in land. It gives the proletariat a trump card in its struggle against the reactionary class of petty landlords, and at the same time conforms to the laws of agrarian evolution. Finally, it ensures the conditions for the development of the countryside's productive forces, for (according to Marx) Socialist forms of agricultural production can be realized only by a revolution in the means of production.

However, in order to perceive the rational foundations of the SR agrarian programme, it must be freed of all the utopian and reactionary admixtures, which give it a quite absurd and rather illiterate look. The 'model decree' is full of such admixtures. It attempts to change economic relations by a *decree*. This is vicious nonsense.

Private property in land can be eliminated. Everyone knows this from bourgeois practice. But it cannot be *abolished* by a decree. Every literate person ought to know that too. Hence it is impossible to say that as of a given moment leasehold (between peasants who are neighbours) is prohibited. It is impossible to assert that 'hired labour is prohibited'. This is a futile attack on the fixed principles of economics, which may change organically but cannot be subject to the State's decrees. In addition, it undermines the productive forces of the countryside.

A propos, the first thing I ever published happened to be an exposure of these utopian SR ideas—abolishing leasehold and hired labour by edict. And now Lenin, at the head of his 'Marxist' party, had resurrected and was putting into force this antediluvian piece of SR-ism. But for Lenin in 1917 this was only the flower, the modest beginning; the fruits would come only after the 'Communist Party' began destroying the foundations of capitalist trade by decree, after it began creating a Socialist society by police power, abolitions, prohibitions, and all kinds of violence.

At that time, in October, there was still the press. And the berating Lenin heard from the SRs for this daylight robbery! The SRs cried: A fine Marxist, who for fifteen years baited us from the heights of his grandeur for our petty-bourgeois lack of science, and then executed our programme the moment he took power! And Lenin snapped back: A fine party, that had to be driven out of power for its programme to be realized!

None of this had much point; it was rather like two fishwives in the market-place—cheap, but very agreeable, all the more so since both sides were right.

Now on October 26th, Lenin gave a very interesting commentary—also in an 'epilogue'—on the 'Land Decree':

'Voices can be heard here saying that the decree was drawn up by the SRs. Very well. Isn't it all the same who composed it?

As a democratic Government we could not get round a decision of the rank-and-file, even if we disagreed with it. Life is the best teacher, and it will show who is right. Let the peasants starting from one end and ourselves from the other settle this question. Life will force us to come together in the common stream of revolutionary creativity. We must follow life, and leave the masses of the people complete freedom of creation. . . . We believe the peasantry will be able to settle this question better than ourselves. The point is not whether it's in our spirit or in the spirit of the SRs. The point is for the peasantry to be firmly persuaded that there are no more landlords in the country, and to let the peasants settle all the problems and organize their own lives.'

The 'masses of the people', listening to the head of the 'democratic Government', were in raptures. It took a long time for another ovation to die down. But Lenin's words were really interesting and important. Anyone who wants to understand the spirit of the Soviet régime's policy during the first period of its activity is in duty bound to remember them.

* * *

An interval was announced. I dropped into the buffet from the crowded corridor. There was a crush around the counter. In a secluded corner I ran into Kamenev, hastily gulping down some tea:

'Well, so you're getting ready to govern us alone?'

'But surely you're with us?'

'Depends how, within what limits and ideas. Just now, in a Left SR fraction, I was trying as hard as I could to stop your setting up a dictatorship of your party alone.'

Kamenev lost his temper: 'Well, if that's the case, what's the use of talking to you? You think it right to go around other fractions agitating against us . . .'

'And you think that indecent and inadmissible?' I interrupted. 'So I can't use my right to talk to any audience I like? For after all if it's impossible in Smolny, then it's impossible at a factory too. . .'

Kamenev calmed down at once and started talking about the brilliant progress of the *coup d'état*: it was said that Kerensky had managed to collect only an insignificant and not at all dangerous army.

'So you've definitely decided to govern alone?' I said, returning to the former theme. 'I think that's absolutely scandalous. I'm afraid that when you've made a mess of it it'll be too late to go back. . .'

'Yes, yes', muttered Kamenev irresolutely and vaguely, looking away.

'Although . . . why should we make a mess of it?' he continued, just as irresolutely.

Kamenev was not only a now humiliated opponent of the uprising, but was also against a purely Bolshevik régime, and for an agreement with the Mensheviks and SRs. But he was afraid of being humiliated again. There were quite a few like him. . .

* * *

The session reopened.

Without amendment or discussion the Land Decree was passed. Again the massed crowd applauded, jumped to their feet, and threw their caps into the air. They firmly believed that they had got the land their fathers and grandfathers had yearned for. Spirits were mounting higher and higher. The masses who had hesitated to 'come out' were perhaps ready now to take up arms and defend their new conquests. For the time being this was only in Smolny. But tomorrow the genuine masses in the capital, at the front, and in the heart of Russia, would learn about it.

There was only one question left—that of the Government. Trotsky spoke in defence of a purely Bolshevik régime. He was very clear, trenchant, and largely correct. But he refused to understand the point of his opponents' demands for a united democratic front.

He said: Isolation was a vain threat. It wasn't terrifying. It had been used as a bugbear even before the uprising, but that had ended in a brilliant victory. It was not the Bolsheviks who were isolated, for they were with the masses. Those who were isolated were those who had left the masses. A coalition with the Dans and Liebers would not have strengthened the revolution, but destroyed it. Difficulties and tasks beyond their powers? But Trotsky didn't understand how an alliance with

Lieber and Dan would help the cause of peace and produce bread. . .

The Bolsheviks, however, could not be accused of irreconcilability. 'In spite of the fact that the defensists stopped at nothing in the struggle against us, we did not cast them off. We proposed to the Congress as a whole that it should take power into its own hands. How, after that, is it possible to speak of our irreconcilability? When the party, enveloped in powder smoke, went to them and said, Let's take the power together, they ran to the Town Council and joined up with obvious counter-revolutionaries. They are traitors to the revolution, with whom we shall never ally ourselves. . .'

Here Trotsky, while justly characterizing his enemies, explained his own position in a form that had nothing in common with reality. The Bolsheviks had never taken a single step towards an agreement with the Dans and the Liebers. They had always rejected it. They had carried on a policy that excluded an agreement, and attempted to take power alone. This was quite understandable. Trotsky and the others, after all, couldn't understand why they needed Lieber and Dan, if they had the masses.

Trotsky was always clear and skilful. But you couldn't be seduced by his eloquence: you had to see clearly where he left loose ends, and maintain a critical attitude towards his diplomacy before the masses. He concluded with some characteristic remarks I shall note without comment.

'Don't try to frighten us by talk about a peace at our expense. It's all one—if Europe remains a powerful capitalist society revolutionary Russia must inevitably be crushed. Either the Russian Revolution will lead to a movement in Europe, or else the surviving powerful countries of the West will crush us.'

Such was the outlook of this central figure of the October Revolution.

A rather characteristic episode took place when the representative of the All-Russian Railwaymen's Union spoke. A group of railwaymen had joined the *Novaya Zhizn* people at the Congress and were for an agreement between the Soviet parties. A worker spoke in their name, very excitedly. He began by saying that the railway proletariat had always been 'one of the most revolutionary proletariats', but that didn't mean it was going to back the Bolsheviks' risky ventures. The Railwaymen's Union demanded an agreement and was ready to back this demand with decisive action—including a general railway strike.

'And just take note of this, comrades. Without us you couldn't have coped either with Kornilov or with Kerensky. I know you've just sent some detachments of *saboteurs* to tear up the lines leading to the capital. But without us, you know, you couldn't even do that. We could fix all the damage in twenty minutes. We tell you we're not going to help you, but will fight you if you don't come to an agreement.'

This speech made a great sensation, like a bucket of cold water poured over the head of the meeting. But the Praesidium had ready their own railwayman, who was unleashed at once with the statement that the preceding speaker hadn't represented the views of the masses. But that wasn't so, while as for the claim by the Railway Union's spokesman that the Congress was incompetent, that wasn't true either: even after the exodus of the 'pure-in-heart' the Congress had a full legal quorum.

The 'Council of People's Commissars' was put to the vote and confirmed by an overwhelming majority. I don't recall any great enthusiasm about this. But the Congress was now becoming thoroughly disorganized, from extreme exhaustion and nervous tension.

The concluding act was the election of a new Central Ex. Com. Amidst total disorder, in a rapidly emptying hall, a long list of unknown names was read out. About 100 men in all were elected, of whom seventy were Bolsheviks, then some Left SRs, *Novaya Zhizn* people, and representatives of nationalities.

The meeting closed around 5 o'clock in the morning. Limp and exhausted, in a hurry to get home, the depleted ranks again filled Smolny with the discordant sounds of the *Internationale*, and scrambled for the way out. The Congress was over.

I waited for Lunacharsky, who was to stay with me overnight in the new flat close by. Picking up another delegate we set off together towards the Tauride Garden. It was still quite dark. Lunacharsky was extremely excited, almost in raptures, and rattled along without a stop. Unfortunately I couldn't respond and was a silent, and even rather glum listener.

'At first Lenin didn't want to go into the Government; he said he was going to work in the Party Central Committee. But we said no, we wouldn't agree. We made him take first-hand responsibility; otherwise, everyone likes just criticizing. What? Supplies? They're all quite safe.'

'Ah!' Lunacharsky went on, referring to me, 'he won't work with us! He just won't! But what a Foreign Minister he would make! Come to us! After all, there's no other solution for an honest revolutionary. We're going to work! These events are epoch-making! Our children's children will bow their heads before their grandeur!'

We arrived home. My exhausted mind was incapable of digesting the inexhaustible material of the past days.

* * *

The Second Soviet Congress was the shortest in our history. The local delegates had to hurry home, and the centre had no time for meetings. Toils, troubles and difficulties were making their appearance every hour in ever-increasing numbers, like the heads of the Hydra. Most important was the front, where Kerensky was scraping together mixed detachments to crush the 'rebellion'. Until he had been liquidated it was impossible to have an easy mind. Indeed, the revolution could not be considered complete until the head of the old Government had been reduced to submission and taken prisoner. After all, until this had been achieved, the country could—formally—choose which it would consider the lawful Government and which the rebels.

* * *

On the evening of October 27th, information was given at the first session of the new Central Ex. Com. that columns of Cossack troops with artillery were concentrated round Dno Junction and in Gatchina. Emissaries and agitators had been sent there, but the Cossacks had declared that they would march on Petersburg to smash the Bolsheviks. Then the railwaymen told how they had received a telegram which said Kerensky was in Gatchina with troops and heavy artillery.

During the whole of the 28th very disquieting news of Kerensky's offensive continued to be received. The Military Revolutionary Committee's bulletins read: 'Tsarskoe-Selo is under artillery fire. The garrison has decided to retreat towards Petersburg.' 'There is fighting in Krasnoe Selo; two of our regiments fought heroically but retreated under the pressure of superior forces.' 'Tsarskoe has been taken by Kerensky's troops and we are retreating to Kolpino.'

Smolny took feverish action. On the 28th from morning till night troops, mostly Red Army men, were being moved to the front. A few armoured cars and Red Cross vehicles also passed through the streets leading to the Baltic and Warsaw Stations. Masses of workers were sent outside the town to dig trenches. Petersburg was festooned with barbed-wire entanglements.

In the evening the new Central Ex. Com. met again, and again it was only the news that was interesting. According to Smolny the revolution had taken place painlessly in a whole series of towns: Minsk, Kharkov, Samara, Kazan, Ufa, Yaroslavl, and also Mogilev, the Army Headquarters.

On the 30th it was decided to finish with Kerensky at one blow. The Kronstadt and Helsingfors sailors' detachments were moved *en bloc* to the front. Trotsky himself went too; from now on he was invariably to be present at the most critical points all over the country. . . And by the end of that night Trotsky was already reporting to Petersburg from Pulkov: 'The night of the 30th will go down in history. Kerensky's attempt to move counter-revolutionary troops against the capital has received a decisive setback. KERENSKY IS IN RETREAT—we are advancing. The soldiers, sailors, and workers of Petersburg have shown that arms in hand they can and will assert their will and the power of the democracy. . .'

Kerensky and his counter-revolutionary troops had been broken. If now, after four days of advance and gathering of troops he had been rolled back, he had evidently shot his bolt. It remained only to finish him. . . And the new Government would be the sole lawful Government in Russia.

* * *

The liquidation of Kerensky consummated the October Revolution. Moscow was still an arena of bitter struggle, and the enemies of the Bolsheviks were still far from laying down their arms. Now, however, there was in Smolny a unified and indivisible Government of the Republic, and its armed enemies had become rebels and nothing more.

The revolution that had placed a proletarian party at the head of a first-class world Power was accomplished. A new chapter had opened in the working-class movement of the world and in the history of the Russian State.

June–August 1921.

INDEX

Library of Congress Cataloging in Publication Data

Sukhanov, N. N. (Nikolaĭ Nikolaevich), 1882-1940.
The Russian revolution, 1917.

Translation of: Zapiski o revoli͡ut͡sii.
Reprint. Originally published: London; New York:
Oxford University Press, 1955. With new introd. and map.
1. Sukhanov, N. N. (Nikolaĭ Nikolaevich), 1882-1940.
2. Soviet Union—History—Revolution, 1917-1921—Personal narratives.
3. Journalists—Soviet Union—Biography.
I. Carmichael, Joel. II. Title.
DK265.7.S8813 1984 947.084'1 83-43102
ISBN 0-691-05406-1 (cloth)
ISBN 0-691-00799-3 (pbk.)